MW00390293

FOUR BROTHERS IN BLUE

BY

CAPTAIN ROBERT GOLDTHWAITE CARTER

U. S. Army, Retired

Congressional Medal of Honor Recipient

1913

DISCOVER MORE LOST HISTORY AT BIGBYTEBOOKS.COM

Cover Image

The wonderful photo on the cover is not the Carter brothers but they might as well be. When the Carters were able to get together in the field, much time was spent in leisurely relaxation and conversation.

The image used here has great details. Here are four officers of the 114th Pennsylvania Infantry in camp in front of Petersburg, 1864. With them are two African American camp servants. As United States Colored Troops did not serve with the 114th, these are likely "contraband," or formerly enslaved Americans who escaped to Union lines, being declared contraband of war to prevent having to return them to slavery.

Two of the officers are wearing rings (not wedding rings). Two of the men are wearing ties. Note that everyone is clean, which you'll note from the Carter narrative below, was rare; even the servants are well-dressed. The man on the right with his hat at a jaunty angle is wearing cavalry boots that do not appear to have seen much wear.

The boys are enjoying Hadden Old Tom Cocktail. All three men seated at the table have books.

The 114th at this time in 1864 was often on headquarters guard duty during the siege of Petersburg. The 114th's band was a favorite of General Meade.

Courtesy of the Library of Congress.

Contents

PUBLISHER'S NOTES

Robert Goldthwaite Carter, the author of this work, was thus recalled by a West Point classmate: "Bob was as strong as a bull and as brave as a lion." That classmate was John Gregory Bourke (1846–1896), a close aide to General George Crook for many years and author of one of the seminal works by a participant in the Indian Wars—*On the Border with Crook* (2015, BIG BYTE BOOKS).

Carter and Bourke were close in age, both of them boy soldiers for the Union Army in the Civil War at the age of sixteen. Both graduated West Point after the Civil War and spent years on the frontier in multiple conflicts with Native Americans. Here their careers diverge.

Bourke is widely recognized as a scholar, an ethnographer of Native American culture, and a writer of no mean skills. A posthumous edition of one of Bourke's books included an introduction by none other than Sigmund Freud. Captain Bourke could write a scholarly piece with the narrative of a novelist while inserting his own presence in the action quite modestly. Aside from his signature work, referenced above, his book on *The Snake Dance of the Moquis of Arizona* (2018 BIG BYTE BOOKS) demonstrates his characteristic wry wit, incredible attention to detail, and flowing style. Bourke's books have been read for generations by historians and laypeople alike.

Carter served in the west under the general who was singled out by Ulysses S. Grant as the most promising young officer in the army at the end of the Civil War: Ranald Slidell Mackenzie (1840–1889). Mackenzie came to a sad end after suffering the results of a serious head injury. Not an easy officer to serve, he was described by contemporaries as insane. Nothing was known at the time of traumatic brain injury.

Captain Carter was prone to some exaggeration and romance, inserting himself *without* modesty even into stories ostensibly about others. This is odd, given that his military career was not in need of exaggeration or boasting. He was praised by superiors and was a recipient of the Medal of Honor. And historians consider his work on the campaigns in Texas important contributions to the period written by a participant. As Charles M. Robinson III (editor of Bourke's voluminous campaign diaries) wrote of Carter's book on Mackenzie, "...the basic story rings true." Carter's books were, however, published in tiny print runs and read by few.

Carter was, however, a man of some sympathy and honor, seen by his sincere concern and work on behalf of John Charlton in his waning days, a former sergeant who served with him in Texas. There is something very touching reflected in "The Old Sergeant's" responses to efforts by Carter to see his old non-com rewarded properly for service given a half-century before their correspondence began. That correspondence lasted just over one year but reveals much of both men and the time through which they had lived. (See *The Old Sergeant's Story*, 2019, BIG BYTE BOOKS.)

When it comes to the volume you're reading, Carter left out the self-promotion and relied on family letters.

Frank Vandiver, (Civil War historian, university president) wrote, "Among this select corpus of lasting [Civil War] sources Robert Goldthwaite Carter's *Four Brothers in Blue* ranks right at the top," alongside Joshua Lawrence Chamberlain's *The Passing of the Armies*, Frank Haskell's *The Battle of Gettysburg*, and Ulysses S. Grant's *Memoirs*.

Distinguished historian, John M. Carroll, also lauded *Four Brothers*. Carter's work was originally serialized in *The Maine Bugle* but never completed in that paper. Carter then published the complete work in 1913 in two 100-copy print runs. Despite that, the work garnered both praise by critics and was a best-seller until it ran out.[1]

THE BROTHERS

---

[1] *Four Brothers in Blue*, 1978, University of Texas Press.

The four brothers whose story is told below were sons of Henry Carter (1814–1898) and Elizabeth Jane Caldwell. Henry Carter was a lawyer, State's Attorney in Maine, editor of the *Portland Advertiser*, a judge, and a founding leader of the Maine Republican party.

On the 1860 federal census, the Carters listed all of their children at home (valued at $3,500 in 1860; about $106,000 in 2019). There were two sisters, Catherine Sophia (b. 1840; a "teacher of music") and Amelia Frederika (called Ann, b. 1844).

JOHN H. CARTER

The eldest of the Carter brothers was John Henry (1837–1892), a 24-year-old typesetter when the Civil War broke out. He served as a corporal with Company A of the First Massachusetts Heavy Artillery. He had married Annie Jeffries before the war on December 21, 1858 in Boston.

At his death from pneumonia on January 28, 1892, his occupation was still listed as "printer." His headstone contains his military record.

EUGENE CARTER

Next in line was Eugene (1838–1877), known as Gene, a West Point cadet when the war broke out, assigned to the 8th Illinois Infantry.

In 1866 he was a brevet captain and took a three month leave of absence while serving in the 8th Infantry during Reconstruction in Unionville, SC (today known as Union, SC). He was breveted a major and promoted to captain upon transfer to the 29th Infantry. In 1867 he served in command of Company I, 29th Infantry in Lynchburg, Virginia under Medal of Honor recipient, Colonel Orlando B. Wilcox. By the end of 1867, he was serving in Washington, D.C.

On April 11, 1864, he married Mary E. Ordway in Bradford, Massachusetts. About 3:00 a.m. on December 8, 1866, while a passenger on the new steamer, *Thomas Kelso*, Major Carter was slightly scalded when the boiler exploded, an accident that killed four crew members. On January 6, 1871, the *Boston Daily Advertiser* reported that Major Carter mustered out of the army honorably with one year's pay and allowance.

After his service, Eugene was a partner in the shoe manufacturing firm Carson & Carter and died an early death at 38 on February 10, 1877 of "Lung fever & brain congestion" (pneumonia). Mary filed a widow's pension in 1883.

WALTER CARTER

The third son was Walter, born in 1842, working as a clerk at the time of the 1860 federal census. On May 30, 1868, he married Martha "Mattie" Lee Lovejoy.

Walter and Martha moved to San Francisco, where the 1870 census found them, with a one-year-old son and an Irish servant. Walter was still working as a retail clerk.

Back in Massachusetts in 1880, Walter became employed as a customs inspector. Martha died of "brain disease" in 1881, only 35 years old.

In 1883, Walter married Sarah Southard on New Year's Day.

On Tuesday, March 04, 1890, the *Boston Daily Advertiser* reported that Walter was one of three customs inspectors hoping to replace the outgoing deputy surveyor.

In 1920, again widowed, Walter was still working in customs. He died in 1928.

ROBERT CARTER

The youngest son and youngest child, Robert, was born on October 29, 1845 in Bridgton, Maine.

As stated before, he graduated West Point after the Civil War and was then posted to the 4th Cavalry in Texas in 1870. He was severely wounded in October, 1871 in an action for which he received the Medal of Honor in 1900.

On September 4, 1870, Carter married Mary Maria Dexter, with whom he had four children.

In 1919-1920, Carter wrote several booklets about his life as a young officer of the Fourth U. S. Cavalry on the western frontier of Texas, including the event which led to his early retirement from the service, the *Tragedies of Cañon Blanco*. He was retired from the army in 1876. His most successful work was *On the Border with Mackenzie* (1935).

Carter's post-army life was dominated by activity in the publishing world as a writer and bureau chief.

The author died on January 4, 1936 and is buried in Arlington National Cemetery.

PREFACE

This volume gives a full narrative sketch taken from the letters and diaries of these four brothers, covering the four years of the Civil War from First Bull Run to Appomattox Court House, of what they saw and did, and is replete with reminiscences, stories, etc., of a period of bloody war such as the world had never before witnessed.

It was the boys of the Union Armies who made it possible for the present generation to have a reunited country. "A Government of the people, by the people, and for the people, that it might not perish from the earth, and that our dead shall not have died in vain." And the youth of this great nation should never forget that which is due to those who for the wellbeing of their country pledged and imperiled all that life holds dear, and, in this devotion, gave proof that there are things nobler than mere pleasure and greater than self which both men and women count worthy of bravest endeavor and supreme sacrifice.

This volume deals neither with the strategy or grand tactics of that War.

The writer consulted but few authorities, and such as he did examine were for the purpose of verifying certain data, fixing dates, correcting lines of march, giving conversations with some of the old officers of the Army, etc.

The Author.

Washington, D. C., 1913.

INTRODUCTORY

Journals and letters have been lost and memories have been weakened. Although an urgent appeal went forth some time since for all soldiers of the armies of the Union to preserve their own personal records for future reference, very little if any progress has been made, and the individual cases are very rare where the work has been commenced and finished.

Some ten years after the war, while on a leave of absence from his regiment—the Fourth U. S. Cavalry, then in Texas, the writer was examining a mass of letters written by his brothers and himself during the War of the Rebellion, which had been carefully preserved by a very thoughtful mother. God bless the mothers of the Republic! He found them nearly complete. A strong desire, reinforced by a certain sense of duty, prompted him to copy them entire. He was struck very forcibly with the idea that a connected journal embodying these letters, together with his own personal recollections, then very fresh and distinct, would not only be the means of preserving their subject matter for future historical reference for himself and family, but would present in a connected form, that which hereafter might afford much pleasure to personal friends and relatives.

This has proved true. It was an exceedingly interesting, but extremely difficult and tedious work. Many of these old letters were in lead pencil; mere scraps of paper, yellow with age; the rats had begun to make nests, and all were becoming obliterated and destroyed. These appear chronologically arranged in several record and letter-books. This was but a beginning. The writer has since managed with much patience, and laboring under many difficulties to connect these letters into a continuous narrative, and this has already performed its duty as the basis in part, of a history of the Wilson Regiment—Twenty-second Massachusetts Volunteers,[1] but this included only the impersonal part.

---

[1] The 22nd Massachusetts was organized by Senator Henry Wilson (1812–1875), future Vice-President during the second Grant administration.—2019

These letters were written when we were very young, but they breathe forth but one spirit, that of patriotic devotion to the cause in which we were engaged, under an ever crushing pressure of danger, exposure, hardship, toil, and privation, unequalled or unsurpassed in the history of any country, and certainly worthy of preservation and recital for many generations to come.

Written as they were on the march, upon the battlefield, under fire in the rifle pits, in the sun, rain, snow, and mud—even in the presence of grim death, it is wonderful in our extreme youth, that throughout all there should run such a firm resolve and strict adherence to duty when there was so much to discourage our youthful ardor, depress our spirits, and swerve us from the true course.

They are not the detailed history of campaigns, of grand strategic movements, or tactics on the field, but rather a simple expression of the personality or personal views and every day experiences of *Four Brothers in Blue,* and of the large majority of the rank and file of the Army of the Potomac, and of the best intelligence and pure patriotism of its masses. For it was the true intelligent resolve, patriotic fervor, unflinching courage, and unswerving purpose of the rank and file after all, that won the battles of the War of the Rebellion.

It is a statistical fact, and of record, that the war was fought and the victory won by the boys of this country. A writer has well said that the average age of the men composing the Union armies, was a little over twenty years, and they were the best soldiers on 'God's foot-stool.' With a patriotism that was heroic, and a heroism that was patriotic, they stood by the flag, and in southern prison pens rotted and starved to death, and were buried like dogs, but they never went back on "Old Glory!"

At Shiloh, Stone River, Gettysburg, Vicksburg, in the damp shades of the Wilderness, on countless other fields of strife they fell, and a great nation remembers them, and will, so long as a loyal man or woman remains to strew their graves with flowers.

These four brothers were born in Bridgeton, Cumberland Co., Maine, and were descended in a direct line from families of soldiers. The Carters and Hamlins on the paternal side had done splendid service in both the Colonial and Continental armies. Captain Eleazer Hamlin and three sons, Europe, Africa, and America, served throughout the Revolutionary war, while the Goldthwaite ancestors on the maternal side had been in the Colonial service; three brothers, Colonel Thomas, Colonel Joseph, and Captain Benjamin, and three nephews, Captain Philip, Major Joseph, and Dr. Michael Burrill Goldthwaite; Colonel Joseph G. and Captain Benjamin G. having been present at the Siege of Louisburg, and in January, 1747, the latter commanded the English forces after the death of Colonel Noble in battle with the French at Minas, Nova Scotia.

In 1847, the brothers removed to Portland, Me.; all their young boyhood days therefore were passed in that beautiful, forest city by the sea. Their father was active in politics, and was for ten years or more the editor of the *Portland Advertiser*, then the leading Whig paper in the state; he was also intimately associated at that time with William Pitt Fessenden, Hannibal Hamlin, the Washburns, James G. Blaine, and others in the formation of the Republican party.

In 1857, the family removed to Bradford, Mass., and here the war found the brothers somewhat scattered.

We were living during stirring times and amid stormy scenes, and at a time when boys of our age guided by the superior judgment and wisdom of our parents, and reading the current events in the daily' newspapers, soon became familiar with all the political phrases of that period. Our minds, notwithstanding our extreme youth, soon became familiar with such phrases as the Missouri Compromise, the Dred Scott Decision, the Free Soil Struggle, Border Ruffians, Bleeding Kansas, etc. We had read *Uncle Tom's Cabin.* One of us when but ten years of age, had seen the fugitive slave, Thomas Sims,[2] delivered up to his southern

---

[2] Sims was first captured in 1851 and returned to enslavement in

9

owners, and escorted through the crowded streets of Boston to the vessel which was to bear him back to the doom of servitude.

We had read with much eagerness, the accounts of the first Republican convention at Philadelphia, which nominated John C. Fremont for president in 1856, for our father was a delegate from Maine with James G. Blaine, and occupied the same room with him. We had followed with still greater interest, the Douglas-Lincoln joint debates—those famous sermons, which had at last pricked the consciences, and aroused the sober-minded people of the North, to such a wonderful sense of the wrong of slavery, and what a diabolical and infamous crime it was—this bondage of human beings formed in the image of God.

We had heard the bells tolling their mournful notes when John Brown[3] met his fate so heroically at Charlestown, W. Va., and his soul went marching on. All these events came crowding along in rapid succession to shape our characters and guide our actions for the future. We had not, however, during this exceedingly eventful period, given expression in writing to even our crude ideas of all that was passing, and it was not until the nomination of Abraham Lincoln for president in 1860, that these slumbering thoughts were given vent, and our ideas found free scope on paper. Many very interesting letters now occur.

At this time one of the brothers [Eugene] was about completing his course at the U. S. Military Academy at West Point, having been appointed a cadet from the First Cong[ressional] District of Maine, (Portland.) At no place in the country did feeling run so high or conviction seem so strong that there would be war, as among the cadets at the National academy.

The Southern cadets were purely representative, or mostly from the distinctive classes of their section, were in constant

Georgia under the Fugitive Slave Act. He escaped again to Boston in 1863 and in 1877 was appointed to a position in the Department of Justice.—2019

[3] Brown was hung on December 2, 1859 for attempting to start an insurrection of enslaved people. He'd been taken prisoner by then U.S. Army Colonel Robert E. Lee, soon to be a Confederate general.—2019

communication with their friends, and many a "straw" was flung to the breeze, showing which way the wind blew, long before the slow minds of the Northern masses, deeply engrossed in commercial pursuits, everything but politics, had grasped the situation or were aware that there was any strong movement for secession or the dismemberment of the Union.

The Southerners were carefully instructed what to do, how to deport themselves, when to resign; and as there was no attempt to restrain their ardor, the Northern cadets were, in consequence, kept fully posted as to the strongly growing sentiment. While the conservative politicians at the North were calmly considering the "ways and means" for avoiding war, and grasping at any and all methods for a compromise—whether honorable or otherwise, the Southern cadets knew that their "kin" were eagerly preparing for war, and with no thought of compromise.

Our young cadet's letters are full of the excitement under which he was now laboring. As early as November, 1860, just on the eve of election, Abraham Lincoln was hung in effigy with a Negro wench on a large tree directly in front of the barracks. Several Southern cadets sent in their resignations, and all Southerners were wearing the "cockade." By December 2, six had already resigned, and everyone had his resignation ready, having become convinced that disunion was a sure thing, and only awaited further development to hand them in.

On December 14, Cadet F— of Louisiana received a letter from the governor of that state, informing him that it was certain, and for him, F—, and all other cadets from that state, to regulate their conduct by that of Major Beauregard,[4] the new superintendent "that is to be." On the afternoon of the 20th, Cadets B— and K— left for Alabama. The entire class, and many of the first and third accompanied them to the ferry boat. Both were extremely popular

---

[4] Pierre Gustave Toutant-Beauregard (1818–1893) was a Mexican War Veteran and would soon command the troops that fired on Fort Sumter to open the war. He served the Confederacy throughout the war. See *Generals Johnston and Beauregard at Manassas*, 2014, BIG BYTE BOOKS.

in the corps of cadets, and deservedly so, both expressed much regret at parting, but they knew that Alabama was to secede, and their parents wished them to take this course.

They left the Mess hall amidst cheers and stamping of feet, and as they opened the door both cried out "God bless you, fellows!" and when they left West Point for garrisons across the river, they were borne on the shoulders of their classmates, and both shed tears.

Word then came from this brother, "I believe we are to have civil war, I do not see how it can be avoided; how or where it will end I know not!" January 1, 1861, he says: "Don't you think things begin to look like war? I don't know whether it's our military training, or what it is, but we are all firm believers that the difficulties now existing between the two sections of the country are sure to drag us into a civil war. I don't see how the president can consider their recent acts in any other light than an open declaration of war."

Washington's birthday was celebrated by the hand playing at reveille and tattoo. The Northern cadets heard that it was the intention of the Southerners to hiss Yankee Doodle and the Star Spangled Banner. When the band therefore entered the "arena," every window was filled with heads, some singing out—"Play Dixie," while others shouted—"Star Spangled Banner and Yankee Doodle." The band struck up Yankee Doodle, and such a cheering and clapping of hands was heard as to drown any hisses that may have been made.

On the 13th of April when the news of the [previous day's] bombardment of Fort Sumter was announced, he says: "Nobody can begin to describe the deep feeling which has prevailed among men who have the least spark of patriotism or love of country. We, as young guards of the Republic, feel this terrible state of affairs deeply, and will willingly take our places by the side of older officers, and fight to the death for the flag of our country. This is no idle talk for we are very soon to be called upon to prove our devotion to the flag. If war continues, and I do not see how it can honorably do otherwise, I have no doubt but that my class will graduate in June, and every one of us proceed to join our regiments without even going to our homes.

"We are ready for it, and although young, will do our best, and if Providence wills it that we be cut off early, let it be. We will die honorably, and ask eighteen millions of freemen at the North to avenge us."

He graphically describes an incident which occurred between Cadet R—, who had resigned, and old Professor M—, about whose loyalty there had been some doubtful rumors. The cadet went to the professor to obtain his signature to a voucher, and upon leaving, extended his hand; the old professor straightened himself up and said: "No, Mr. R—, I cannot take your hand, you are going to aid in breaking up one of the best governments the world ever saw, to aid in trampling in the dust the purest and best flag ever cast to the wind, and I cannot even wish you prosperity and happiness. Good morning, sir." After that there was no further doubt of the intense loyalty of Professor M—.[5]

The Southern element had up to the overt act of war, and the wholesale resignation of the Southern cadets, been dominant at the Military academy. The habits, tastes, feelings, and sentiments of the Northern cadets had, for many years, leaned toward their more outspoken, fiery, and impulsive classmates, and if anyone in the corps of cadets had the courage of conviction to speak his sentiments boldly in favor of "a more perfect union," or denied the right of further encroachment of the slave power, he was at once designated as an "abolitionist," and a number of instances could be recorded where this young cadet [the author's brother] from the conservative state of Maine had to maintain his opinions

---

[5] This seems a clear reference to military theorist, Dennis Hart Mahan (1802–1871), a graduate of West Point (1820) and a longtime instructor there. One of Mahan's soldier sons, Frederick August Mahan, noted in a 1917 article that his father had spent much time in the antebellum south, with many friends there, which could have cast suspicion on him. But Mahan had an enormous influence on Civil War tactics, being referenced by many, including his admirer, William Tecumseh Sherman. Mahan was also the father of Admiral Alfred Thayer Mahan.— 2019

in the "fistic arena," and by a display of cool pluck and sheer strength of muscle.

He had, however, tried to reconcile his feelings and opinions to a better state of things in the future, and in his letters had, by a sudden and apparently over-conservatism, incurred the displeasure of a younger brother who had criticised him in the severest manner.

But after the uncalled for attack upon Fort Sumter his sentiments seemed to have suddenly undergone a revulsion, for he says, "I suppose I am like all Northern men at present, but my feelings have undergone a great change within the last month. At first I was for compromising everything but national honor. I was in favor of throwing aside all parties, all platforms, and doing everything to save our beloved country from disunion, rebellion, and anarchy. I even went so far as to believe that the North owed some compromise, and actually had encroached upon Southern rights, and was too grasping. I even went so far that my own brother accused me of being recreant to my early teachings, or, in other words, was a Northern man with Southern principles. God spare the mark! As though they ever had any. But, I take all back now and humbly ask forgiveness for my seeming dough-facedness."

The superintendent of the Military academy at this time was General Richard Delafield; the commandant was Colonel John F. Reynolds, afterwards commanding the First corps, and killed while leading his corps into battle at Gettysburg July 1, 1863. Lieutenants Saxon, Dodge,[6] Williams, and McCook commanded respectively the cadet companies A, D, C, and B, and were all distinguished officers during the war, as were many of the instructors and assistant professors then on duty at the academy. General Fitzhugh Lee[7] and General Charles Field on duty in

---

[6] Richard Irving Dodge (1827–1895) had a long army career, including as aide-de-camp to General Sherman and a prominent role in the Indian Wars. See his *Thirty-Three Years Among the Indians*, 2015, BIG BYTE BOOKS.

[7] Fitzhugh Lee (1835–1905), later the 40th Governor of Virginia, a

cavalry were both distinguished major-generals in the Confederate army.

At length after stating in one of his letters that—"It is hard to study here under such intense excitement," chafing under the restraints that kept him there after one class had already graduated in May, and commenting upon the Battle of Big Bethel, and the death of his beloved instructor, Lieutenant John Grebble of the artillery, killed in that battle; after wading through what he thought were many trials and tribulations about uniform, equipments, etc., and passing a successful examination, he announced the fact that "This is the last time I shall sign my name Eugene Carter, U. S. C. C." With his tin case containing his academic diploma he emerged from the military academy a full-fledged brevet second lieutenant, and started for Washington, June 29, 1861. He was assigned to the Eighth U. S. Infantry, but as his regiment was then held in Texas as prisoners of war he was ordered to report to Brigadier-General Joseph K. F. Mansfield for duty in drilling newly arrived volunteer regiments, and was detached to drill the Sixteenth New York, Colonel [Thomas A.] Davis [commanding].

At 4 a. m. he went daily to East Capitol street where the regiment was encamped, and with another officer, a classmate, gave them a drill of two hours, and again in the evening at 4 p. m., each drilling a battalion of about four hundred and fifty men.

General [Irwin] McDowell's troops were crossing the river daily, however, and the young officer chafed at the monotony of the drill, especially as a "big fight" was expected, and eight of his classmates had already left their quarters at the Ebbitt house and accompanied General McDowell as aids, or had been attached to Sherman's and the West Point Light Battery (Griffin's.)

But at last on the evening of July 10, he received orders to report to General McDowell, and the same night started, taking one suit of clothes, two flannel shirts, four under shirts, five white

---

diplomat, and a United States Army general in the Spanish–American War. He was the nephew of General Robert E. Lee.—2019

shirts, (without bosoms), one pair of thick boots, one pair of blankets, one Colt's revolver, handkerchiefs, socks, brush, comb, note paper, some Seidlitz powders, cholera pills, etc.

THE BATTLE OF BULL RUN

By Captain Robert Goldthwaite Carter, U. S. Army

In dim lead pencil, on the two sides of four small visiting-cards, now in the possession of the writer, written from Arlington by our brother [Eugene], but recently graduated from West Point, occurs the following brief description of his experience in this, his first battle:

> Thank God! I am alive! I commanded a company alone at Bull Run from eleven until five. We were the last to leave the field, and were very near being cut off. Kent—acting captain of my company—was wounded in the leg and foot when we first came on the field. I sent him to the rear, and took command myself. I lost one corporal and nine men; the former was shot through the heart, and fell by my side. We had marched twelve miles without food and scarcely any water. Don't believe anything you hear! We were whipped, and it ended in a total rout. Our battalion of regulars could only be kept together by the most superhuman efforts of our officers. We had to keep out of the road, so that our retreat could not be observed. We marched twelve miles, resting half an hour, and started for our old encampment, which we reached about 8 o'clock the next morning. Our march in all was forty-eight miles—besides fighting from eleven until five—in forty-eight hours. The West Point Battery, suffered terribly, losing forty men, most of their horses, and five pieces—no officers. We had two officers wounded, and would have lost all, had we not taken the precaution to lie flat on our bellies while we were supporting the Rhode Island battery. The large rifle balls struck a few inches above us. You will hear great stories about the bravery of this and that regiment of volunteers, but believe me, most of them acted like cowards in my division. I was on a hill and saw them, and had it not been for our Regular batteries, the whole army would have been taken prisoners or killed.

> When we first went into action, our men—who are mostly recruits—seemed inclined to back out, but we stationed ourselves behind them and threatened to shoot the first man that turned. We then talked to them, told them they were considered the mainstay of the brigade, and finally, after having rested a little (although still under fire), we moved up in very good style.

17

I am completely worn out; my bedding all lost on the road, but my baggage all up. I wore the same underclothes for one week, and they were perfectly filthy when I changed. I was perfectly cool throughout the action, and never thought of myself a moment. I saw the dead and wounded lying about me, without the slightest feeling, and saw my corporal shot dead by my side without a single tear. I knew I had great responsibility resting upon me, and I knew if I flinched the least my command was ruined. I feel quite well this morning, and after a good dinner, which is being prepared, I will be all right again.

Affec. your son,

E. C.

U. S. A.

Although he had been regularly assigned to the Eighth U. S. Infantry upon graduation, he had, on account of the Eighth being then held prisoners of war in Texas, been temporarily attached to Company B, Third U. S. Infantry (Lieutenant J. F. Kent), in the little Battalion of Regulars, under the command of that gallant soldier, Major George Sykes,[1] Fourteenth Infantry, afterward a major-general, commanding the Fifth Army Corps. It was composed of Companies C and G of the Second,—B, D. G, H, of the Third, and G of the Eighth U. S. Infantry, Captain Nelson H. Davis, Second Infantry, acting major. Few of the officers had had but little experience in the field, being for the most part either fresh from West Point or civil life. This battalion, which General Beauregard has since the war characterized—"a small but incomparable body of Regular Infantry," formed a part of the First Brigade (Andrew Porter), Second Division (David Hunter). The troops comprising the remainder of this brigade, were a battalion of seven companies of regular cavalry belonging to the First and Second regiments, and Second Dragoons, under the command of Major Innis Palmer; a battalion of marines under Major [John] Reynolds; the Eighth, Fourteenth, and Twenty-

---

[1] George Sykes (1822–1880) was a career officer and Mexican War veteran. After Bull Run, he was promoted to brigadier general of volunteers on September 28.—2019

seventh N. Y. state militia, and Captain Charles Griffin's Battery of the Fifth U. S. Artillery (West Point Battery).

The regulars, militia, and volunteers preserved their distinctive names, and to a certain extent their uniforms. The Fourteenth Brooklyn wore a semi-Zouave uniform; the Twelfth New York wore the full dress hat of the regulars, while some of the Wisconsin and Minnesota troops were uniformed in grey. In a letter, dated July 16, our young officer says,—

> We march at 3 p. m., with three days' rations and nothing but our arms and blankets; our destination is Fairfax; the whole line moves. We will march about six miles today, five miles tomorrow, and then fight. Fairfax has been reinforced by about 12,000 rebels, and we expect to have a good time. The Fourteenth N. Y. Zouaves will deploy as skirmishers, and we have the 'post of honor'—the right. I am second in command of my company. I hope all will turn out well. It will be some time before you hear from me again, and perhaps never.

G. O. No. 17, Headquarters Department of N. E. Virginia, Arlington, July 16, 1861, read as follows:

> The Second Division (Hunter's) will leave their camps in light marching order, and go on the Columbia turnpike as far as the Little River turnpike, but not to cross it, the Second Brigade (Burnside's) leading. The Second Division (Hunter's) will, after the road shall be cleared of the Fifth Division, move on the direct road to Fairfax Court House by the Little River Turnpike.

The account of what follows is in his own language, written from [Eugene's] journal after the battle.

"As you wish very much to have me give you some of my experiences in the campaign of Bull Run I will strike out this evening. I will begin from the time we left Arlington. Major Sykes received orders to hold himself in readiness to march at 3 o'clock on the 16th. We brought up the rear of Colonel [Andrew] Porter's brigade. We were considerably harassed by the haltings made by the volunteers in front of us, and slept in a field by the roadside. Up bright and early the next morning; got my servant to bring me some water in a canteen; washed;

19

cleaned my teeth; brushed my hair; looked at my pocket looking-glass; and ate a sumptuous breakfast, composed of hard bread and half-boiled tongue. We started on our march at 8 o'clock. Did not make much headway on account of continued stops; reached Fairfax about 12 o'clock; found it occupied by [Colonel Dixon] Miles's brigade and a portion of Heintzelman's. Volunteers conducted themselves in a most shocking manner; broke open stores and scattered the contents in the streets; killed all the pigs and poultry they could find; robbed the bee-hives; dug all the new potatoes they could get from the gardens; broke open houses; stole the sweet meats, etc.

"Regular officers went to McDowell and complained, telling him they would tender their resignations if it was not stopped. Had a stampede the first night. All under arms except our regiment. We told our men to lie low or they would get shot by the volunteers. Started the next morning towards Centerville; had a long, tedious march in the hot sun; reached our camping-place about 7 o'clock; took a bite, and went to bed on our oil cloths and blankets (and I had an India rubber pillow); slept soundly until 12 o'clock, when we were stampeded. Our men received the customary command to lie down and go to sleep, as it was a false alarm. Some of the volunteers actually formed a line of battle, and marched to the woods and fired three rounds at the trees, and then deployed skirmishers.

"Somebody fired a gun, and the fusillade commenced. One of the officer's 'strikers,'[2] who was leisurely crossing the camp-ground at this moment, apparently oblivious that anything unusual was going on, suddenly had his march arrested by Captain Dodge, who shouted: 'Lie down, you d—d fool!' which he proceeded to obey 'instantly.' He had been taught to obey orders, but not to avoid friendly bullets in an enemy's country.

"Our mess chests arrived the next day (and we had taken good care to fill them well before starting). We had flour, tea, coffee, sugar, pickles, sardines, boiled ham, nice loaf bread,

---

[2] An orderly or body servant.—2019

molasses, butter, and all our mess furniture, consisting of a table, plenty of crockery, and pots to cook in. Of course we lived well now, and besides we bought cake on the road. The next day was extremely warm, and our men built booths of bushes for us, which were very comfortable. We heard of Tyler's foolish and headstrong movement[3] with much chagrin, inasmuch as he had been defeated and had not gained a single point, and had ventured the move in spite of all the written protests of Major Barnard and others, who were chief engineers of the Army of the Potomac.

"Went and took a bath in the afternoon; had no clean clothes to put on; old ones perfectly filthy. Band played in the evening 'Home, Sweet Home,' and many other airs.

"Next morning, the regiment was formed into a hollow square to witness the flogging of two deserters, who had been sentenced by a general court martial. Fifty lashes were well laid on with a rawhide; a letter 'D' one and a half inches long branded on one, and the same on the other, with the addition of a large 'W' on his hip. They stood it well. Volunteers were shocked at such a spectacle. One inquired of an officer of the Third Infantry,—'If I should desert, would I receive such punishment?' The reply was,—'No; you would be shot!'[4]

"Our camp was nearly the same until we received orders to hold ourselves in readiness to march at 2 o'clock on the morning of the 21st. We then knew there was a fight ahead. I forgot one thing: The first night we were in camp a volunteer captain came to Major Sykes, and said our supply train had been cut off by the enemy's cavalry. Major Sykes immediately detailed three companies, and Colonel Porter sent one company of cavalry to retake them. My company was one of the number.

---

[3] Daniel P. Tyler IV (1799–1882) was an industrialist. He was assigned much blame for the Bull Run disaster and was mustered out in August. However, he was then appointed a brigadier-general in March, 1862 and served, with more criticism, until 1864. His granddaughter was later First Lady alongside Teddy Roosevelt.—2019
[4] This was the last flogging ever witnessed in the regular army, but not the last branding.—note in original

I looked at my pistol, bid Ferris good-bye, and started, ready for anything that might turn up. We marched about a mile, and met our train safe and sound. If we had caught 'Mr. Voluntario' we would have pulled his nose."

An officer, who was with the battalion on this day's march—a hot and dusty one—relates that "A private belonging to some militia or volunteer organization ahead, passed the regulars at a 'double quick' on his way to the front. Like many others commencing this campaign, he had literally packed himself, and appeared—besides his rifle, equipments, etc.—to carry an assorted cargo of 'a little of everything.' As he passed, with pots, dippers, etc., rattling, he turned a jolly red face towards the column, and exclaimed, 'Lord, Jee! but I wish't I was a mule!' The roars of laughter that followed seemed greatly to refresh and speed him on his way."

[journal con't]

"We had coffee made for us before we started, for it was a bitter cold morning. We drank sundry cups full and started on the march, or, as I thought, some secret expedition. But all the volunteer bands commenced to play patriotic airs, and they would cheer like wild demons. We marched quite fast until we got to Centerville, and there made quite a long halt. Tyler's division moved on in advance, and then came Heintzelman's and Hunter's divisions, we bringing up the rear of the whole. Our march was long and hot, but we knew that we were going to have a fight, and the excitement kept us in good cheer.

"We passed Cub Creek bridge, and left Tyler. He went straight ahead, and we took a direction to our right, something like this (sketch). As we turned off, we heard firing ahead, and concluded that Tyler was engaged. As soon as we got about a mile from where we branched off, Major Sykes halted our regiment, and caused them to load their muskets. He then made them a short speech, cautioning them to keep from getting excited, and to fire low. He told them that they were regulars, and were regarded as the mainstay of the brigade. He called his officers about him, and told them that he had every confidence in us, although most of us had never been in action. He told us to keep our companies well in hand and make them 'fire low.' We then started, and had a long march through the woods, on the Sudley and Newmarket road, over a very good road. When we arrived within two miles of Bull Run, we were marched into a large field, and the men took off their blankets and laid them in a pile, and the bands were left to guard them. We then forded a creek (Young's branch, near the intersection of the Warrenton turnpike with the Sudley road), and marched very rapidly until we came in sight of the field. The first thing I saw was a man stretched out dead, with his head shot nearly away.

"We could see the Rhode Island battery firing and see the return shots from the rebel battery. We marched in this direction by fours, and came behind the two Rhode Island regiments. We met [Ambrose] Burnside and he ran towards us, saying, 'Good God! Major Sykes, you regulars are just what we want: form on my left and give aid to my men who are being cut to pieces!' We formed on the right by file into line on the run, the Rhode Islanders cheering and exciting our men.

"As soon as we were formed, we commenced firing, and the rebels did not like the taste of our long range rifles. Our men fired badly; they were excited, and some of the recruits fired at the stars. There was some confusion, but we immediately formed line of battle and marched across the field in splendid order for about forty rods. We were then wheeled by company to the right, to gain a wood on our right, but immediately took our men out of column of companies by the command, 'Right flank, by file left!' As we got to the edge of the wood we observed a white flag upon a sword, held by someone lying down. We went to the spot and found Colonel Jones[5] of one of the Alabama regiments mortally

---

[5]This was Colonel Egbert Jones of the Fourth Alabama. Just previous to the battle he had been requested to resign by his regiment on account of some trifling misunderstanding. He declined to do so, but told his men that if they would wait until after the battle he would then resign if they still demanded it. During the battle he sat on his horse and gave his orders with great coolness and deliberation, exciting the admiration and enthusiasm of his men. While in this position, a ball struck him in the

wounded. He asked for a drink of water, which we gave him. He asked what we intended to do, and we told him to whip them. He said, 'Gentlemen, you have got me, but a hundred thousand more await you!'

"We went through the woods, which were about twenty rods long and full of dead bodies, and then turned to our left and formed line again. We were here fired upon by two regiments, and many of our men fell. Kent was wounded here. We fell back into the woods, and the men all laid down for fifteen minutes. We then received orders to support the Rhode Island battery, which was brought up to where we had fallen back from a few moments before.

"We formed upon their left flank, and immediately received a shower of shell, grape, and canister from the rebel batteries. The crest of the hill protected us in a great degree, but we were obliged to lie flat upon our faces for one hour, and all the time hearing the rifle balls, etc., flying in close proximity to our heads, and not infrequently seeing a few rolling about among the men.

"The Rhode Island battery had as brave men to manage it as I would wish to see, but they did no execution. I did not see the elevating screw touched; neither did I see a pendulum hausse [sight], nor a tangent scale. They would fire, allow the guns to recoil, load again, push them up to the crest of the hill, and pull away in the direction of the battery which was firing upon us. After they had ceased firing, we rose up and stood still for a few moments, watching the Sixty-ninth and Fourteenth New York Volunteers. The Sixty-ninth had got into a battery, and our flag was waving from its parapet; the Fourteenth was marching to support them. Presently we saw four or five regiments deploy in front of the woods, where they had been held in reserve, and march to attack our men; terrific firing then commenced, and lasted five or ten minutes.

thigh near the hip: it ranged down the marrow of his bone to the knee. He survived several weeks, and died at Orange Court House, Va. He was an immensely large man, being 6 ft. 3 in. in height.—Brewer's *History of Alabama*—note in original

"We then saw the American flag waver, and its supporters turned and fled, apparently 'all cut up.' No two men went the same way, but covered the field with flying fugitives. We then marched over towards the hill on our right (the plateau where the Henry and Robinson houses were), where these regiments were retreating to, and tried to form them, or at least to cover their retreat. One company formed, and joined our little regiment and did good service, but the rest were panic stricken and nothing could save them. We formed line of battle, and then deployed them as skirmishers. We fired into a regiment about five hundred yards from us, but stopped immediately as they carried the American flag. We saw our mistake very quickly when they joined three other regiments carrying the rebel flag, and gave them a dose of lead they will long remember. We are very certain that a private in Company G killed General Barnard E. Bee,[6] who, by the way, was a very dear friend of Major Sykes.

"We found that our troops were all leaving the field, and that we were being surrounded. One or two squadrons of cavalry were trying to get on our flank, but we formed square so quickly that they became convinced who we were, and kept out of range of our rifles."

"By that time one of their batteries had got our range, and was plying us with round shot and rifle. We now saw that every regiment had left the field, and our chances for safety were very slim. We formed line of battle, and faced by the rear rank, and then pushed for 'Sawyer s.'

"We were followed for three miles by a battery of rifled cannon, and the music the shots made about our ears was anything but amusing. We kept together admirably, but we were surrounded by fugitives. We kept away from the road, so that our trail could not be followed by our dust.

---

[6] Confederate general Barnard Elliott Bee Jr. (1824–1861) was a career officer and Mexican War veteran. It is Bee who is said to have uttered the phrase that gave Stonewall Jackson his nickname: "There is Jackson standing like a stone wall." Bee died from a wound caused by an artillery shell.—2019

"We were threatened by cavalry twice, but we were put into the woods, and cavalry are good for nothing there. Well, we reached Centerville, and went into a little field or garden and rested for twenty minutes. We held a council of war, and told the major we would surely be cut off at Fairfax if we did not get back there soon. We immediately called our men to attention and started on the march, and continued until we arrived at our old camping place, one mile and a half from Centerville. We were bound to stay there for a little while, for we could not go on: our feet and legs refused to do duty, 'fairly mutinied,' and charges have been preferred against them since. You remember I had given my rations to a drummer boy in the morning. He returned with my haversack, and Captains Averill, Griffin, Dodge, Douglass, with the assistance of several lieutenants of Griffin's and Sykes's command, gallantly devoured the contents. We discussed the late battle, congratulated each other on his safety, and then turned in for the night. We found all our baggage that had been left at Arlington, and I indulged in some clean clothes and dry shoes, and besides I had a blanket tied to my carpet bag.

"We were called up at twelve, and started again, we bringing up the rear as usual. We marched without halting until we were within ten miles of Arlington. We then halted in a little lane by the roadside. About five o'clock we were again roused up, and started in a drizzling rain, which soon came down in torrents. We reached Arlington about nine, and after my tent was pitched I knew nothing for the next twenty-four hours.

On the 2d of August our young officer was ordered, with his company, to report to General Andrew Porter, provost marshal, for duty in Washington. On that day he crossed Long Bridge in a drenching rain, arriving at three o'clock. At eight p. m., with twenty men, he was sent to patrol the city. He was quartered in Franklin Square. Wooden barracks were built for the men, while the officers were placed in furnished houses, for which the government paid $165 per month. Our young officer was quartered in a house formerly occupied by John B. Floyd, ex-secretary of war. Here his duties—hard, constant, and disagreeable—of attempting to preserve order in the city of Washington after the Battle of Bull Run, commenced.

After the Battle of Bull Run, the streets of the city fairly swarmed with troops, either mustered out and going home, or coming to the front, all militia or partially-organized volunteers, not yet leavened or disciplined. The music of the bands of the incoming regiments filled the air. Many officers and men were absent without leave from their commands. The hotel corridors were filled with embryo brigadiers, and all was excitement, bustle, and seeming confusion. In fact, it was a small bedlam. The provost marshal had charge of a class of duties which had not before, in our service, been defined and grouped under the management of a special department. The following subjects indicate its sphere:

"Suppression of marauding and depredations, and of all brawls and disturbances." "Preservation of good order, and suppression of drunkenness beyond the limits of the camps." "Prevention of straggling on the march." "Suppression of gambling-houses, drinking houses, or bar-rooms, and brothels." "Regulations of hotels, taverns, markets, and places of public amusement." "Searches, services, and arrests." "Execution of sentences of general court martial, involving imprisonment or capital punishment." "Enforcement of orders prohibiting the sale of intoxicating liquors (liquor houses were not allowed to keep open after 9:30 p. m., whether by tradesmen or sutlers, and of orders respecting passes; desertions from the army, prisoners of war taken from the enemy, countersigning safeguards, passes to citizens, within the lines and for purposes of trade." "Complaints of citizens as to the conduct of soldiers."

There was a limited censorship of the press. With these multifarious duties, the reader can imagine of what importance this command was in the city, directly after the Battle of Bull Run, and the commencement of four years of horrible war.

It was the office of duty then for this small band of disciplined Regulars to restore order from chaos, sift out the good from the bad, and keep the wheels in motion. Washington bore no resemblance to the beautiful city of today. The streets were wretchedly paved, or not paved at all; they were worse lighted, and when it rained they became almost impassable. An air of shabby, dirty neglect everywhere prevailed. The guard-house was constantly besieged with visitors, and crowded with people brought in for examination. Officers of every grade, from brigadier-general down, were arrested, and if unable to give an account of themselves, were placed in the guard-house until their cases could be investigated. The officers of the guard acted in the capacity of magistrates. Saloons, houses of ill fame, and dens and dives of all descriptions, had sprung up like mushrooms; but one of the most prolific sources of trouble to the City Guard was "Canterbury Hall," the old variety theatre. What old soldier who visited Washington about this period does not remember this marvelous dispenser of amusement and good cheer to the volunteer soldier, from his dull and monotonous camp-life on the other side of the river, and what a temptation it was to take a "French leave," just for a few hours of boisterous entertainment within those festive walls? It was on the south side of Louisiana avenue, between Four-and-a half and Sixth streets, now occupied by lawyers' offices. All had to be visited, day and night, and cleaned out and purged. But soon system and good order reigned at the national capital.

General McClellan assumed command of the Army of the Potomac and the defenses about Washington, July 27, 1861. He says of that period: "Many soldiers had deserted, and the streets of Washington were crowded with straggling officers and men absent from their stations without authority, whose behavior indicated the general want of discipline and organization. The restoration of order in the City of Washington was effected through the appointment of a provost marshal, whose authority was supported by the few regular troops within my command."

Extracts from our brothers' letters will give the reader a partial idea of the life and duties performed in those days in and about the city of Washington: "Camp Trumbull, Arlington, Va., July 31, 1861. Our battalion is now very small; the Second and Eighth have left us and gone into the city to act as guard. Colonel Porter is appointed military commander, and he wants the Third also; we will know this evening."

Ebbitt House, August 2, 1861.

Colonel P. has been made provost marshal, and ordered us over immediately.

Although I am almost dead with fatigue, I will answer your letters. We are in Washington as a military guard of the city. My company is quartered in a splendid house, directly opposite my room at the Ebbitt, and all the others are very near."

(Some were around the corner on the south side of Thirteenth street.)

We marched over from Arlington in one of the most terrific rain storms I ever witnessed. We got drenched through and through.

I have been patrolling the city all day, and oh, how warm! But I was relieved at parade. I do not know how long we will remain here, but should judge the time will be quite long." "Mr. Goodwin, M. C., has a room opposite mine, on the other side of the street. I go to see him very often, and like him very much. Mr. Fessenden invited me to call on him, but I have not had time to do so." "I met Mr. Washburn, of Illinois, on the morning of the Battle at Centreville. He introduced himself, and we had quite a talk. He knew you when you were at Bridgton.

Have just learned that two lieutenant-colonels and three captains of volunteers have been lodged in the guard-house for want of proper passes.

Central Guard-House, August 4.

Have just returned from Mrs. King's, wife of Horatio King;[1] passed a very pleasant evening with herself and son, and received an invitation to tea for tomorrow evening. I spent the evening with Mr. Goodwin, M. C. He seems very kind, and very anxious to do something for me."

August 18, 1861.

---

[1] Horatio King (1811–1897) was Postmaster General of the United States under Buchanan and then under Lincoln from February 12 until March 7, 1861.—2019

I am on duty as officer of the patrol, and have just brought them in for the men to get their suppers. I go out again about half past eight, and remain out until eleven or twelve. I made a seizure this afternoon of five soldiers in a low den, and carried them to the guard-house; but as a general thing the streets are pretty clear of volunteer officers and soldiers, and the city is now very quiet. We move our quarters tomorrow, two streets above the present one. Booths have been constructed in a large open place, and our soldiers are to occupy them. The officers are to have two furnished houses very near, but we will not get into them for a week, as the furniture has not all arrived. I think each officer will have two rooms, and we will all mess together; as we are now situated, we draw no commutation, and have to pay very largely to live.

I suppose you have heard all about the mutiny of the Seventy-ninth N. Y. Volunteers. We were ordered to march to their camp and quell it, and remained from 11 a. m. until 1 p. m. When I arrived home, I found a note from John, saying he had enlisted and was then at the depot. I immediately jumped into a carriage and drove down, but found that he had left. I found where the regiment he had enlisted in was encamped, and started for it; after wandering about until 11 p. m., I found it, and learned that the recruits had not arrived. I could not go up the next day, as I was on duty, but the following day I drove up; found him, got permission to bring him home with me; dressed him up in citizens' clothes, and had him one day and a half with me; got him sworn in, gave him a blanket and a few necessaries, and started him back again.

I was very much pleased with the colonel, and his regiment generally.

I gave John all the good advice I could, and promised to come and see him as often as I could. This afternoon I saw his regiment march over Long Bridge, and do not know where it is bound for. Will find out, and see him again.

The alleged causes for discontent [of the 79th NY] were the refusal to allow them to go home on furlough to visit their families, and to reorganize by filling vacancies among their officers, etc. But the true cause arose from discontent in relation to their term of service. Having enlisted during the first excitement, for two or three years, or for the war, when they saw

31

the three months' regiments returning home after the disastrous Battle of Bull Run, their dissatisfaction broke out in open mutiny among the men of the Second Maine, and Seventy-ninth New York. In the case of the former, sixty-three men were sent to the Dry Tortugas, there to serve out the rest of the war as prisoners at hard labor.

One very comical incident connected with this event, is related by Captain Edward Lynch, U. S. Army, retired, who was then at General Sykes's headquarters. When the battery had been posted, and the infantry and cavalry had surrounded the camp, and it looked as though the wretched mutineers were about to be blown from the face of the earth by this formidable array of regular troops; the Adjutant had ceased reading the order commanding them to surrender when a very tall, thin sergeant of the culprit Highlanders marched out, holding a very long pole, and waving from the end of it was an empty, striped bed tick, which, after a few moments of grotesque pause, mingled with some surprise and amusement, was recognized as the flag of truce by which the stubborn members of the Seventy-ninth, now driven to this last resort, wished to convey to Sykes's regulars that they had unconditionally surrendered.

Although he had strongly advised against another brother's enlistment, when [Eugene] returned from this unpleasant duty it was to find the note awaiting him (already referred to) stating that this brother had enlisted in the Fourteenth Massachusetts Volunteers, and was then at the depot. Our eldest brother, John H. Carter, who had enlisted under the president's first call in Company E, Fourteenth Massachusetts Volunteers, was mustered into the service August 16, 1861. The regiment was mustered into the service July 5, 1861, at Fort Warren, Boston Harbor. It left the state July 7, 1861, and was immediately placed upon garrison duty in the various forts about Washington, garrisoning principally Forts Albany, Runyan, Tillinghast, Craig, and Scott, most of which it built. On the first of January, 1862, in accordance with orders from the war department, it was changed into the First Regiment of Heavy Artillery, and consequently

32

received fifty new recruits for each company, and two additional companies of one hundred and fifty men each to fill it to its maximum standard and complete its organization. In addition to their duties of garrisoning the forts, they were, with the exception of one short period, employed in throwing up new works and connecting all with infantry parapets and covered ways, and building bomb proofs.

It was laborious; they were unused to it, and they chafed under such work. Our brother was not a very frequent writer; many of his letters have been lost. Although his life in the forts was comparatively monotonous and his service devoid of severe hardships until 1864, his journal of events have a smack of humor to them, and a decided interest in connection with those more important movements of which the defenses of Washington seemed at times to be the central point.

On Sunday, August 18, 1861, it marched across Long Bridge and took up its quarters in Virginia. In Company E, Fourteenth Massachusetts was also a cousin, Lewis Powell Caldwell from Amesbury, Mass., but born in Readfield, Me., who as a first lieutenant and battalion adjutant of the First Massachusetts Heavy Artillery, was mortally wounded by a shell in the charge upon the enemy's works at Petersburg, Va., June 16, 1864, dying on the 17th. His father, William Powell Caldwell, also from Redfield, Me., was a private in the Third Maine Volunteers, was detached for duty with the Mississippi River flotilla in February, 1862, and had charge of Mortar Boat No. 38, in the operations about Memphis, Island No. 10, and Vicksburg, and died from the effects of a congestive chill on the ordnance gunboat *Judge Torrence*, July 14, 1863, and was buried on the Louisiana shore August 20, 1861.

August 28, the young regular writes as follows:

We are on duty every day, and the duties are not very pleasant. Since I commenced this letter, I have had no less than twenty persons to see me, and have had to talk with them all.

I enjoy army life very much. John is now encamped on the Virginia side. I will try to make him comfortable and will go to see him as soon as possible. We were under orders to be ready at a moment's notice last night, but did not have to move. General McClellan keeps everything to himself and none of us know anything of the movements, but rest assured that Washington will never be attacked, and if they do they will get most woefully whipped.

Our brother of the Fourteenth writes his first letter from the John B. Floyd[2] house September 5, 1861.

Through Gene's influence I have been granted a furlough until tonight. There are better writing facilities here than at Fort Albany, which is about five miles distant. I got up early, answered to my name at 'roll-call,' and immediately started for the city, furnished with a pass by Brigadier-General Richardson who commands our brigade. I am very much pleased with a soldier s life, taken as a whole, but sometimes our duties are severe, for instance: We had to be up at five o'clock for roll-call; breakfast at six; guard mounting at seven; and such as are not on guard have to go on 'fatigue duty,' which consists as follows: Chopping down the woods and digging trenches around different forts with pickaxes and shovels, and I feel about as lame and stiff as a man can feel who is unused to such work. Monday I was on guard, Tuesday I was detailed for 'fatigue,' but when we had worked during the forenoon and started for 'dinner,' I with two or three of my comrades 'fell in the rear' in the bushes, and started for Blenker's brigade, about two miles distant, and we had a good time.

We got any quantity of melons, tomatoes, and peaches on the road, for the white population have nearly all left, and there are nothing but niggers left. Gene has, now gone to General Porter's office to prefer charges against his orderly sergeant, whom he left in charge of some government prisoners while he was at dinner. The sergeant got very drunk and G. says he will 'break' him for it, as it was a very important duty. G. is quartered in the traitor Floyd's former residence, and a splendid house it is, too. Our camp is in a constant state of alarm, and we sleep on our arms every night in case anything should happen. Twelve men from each company in

---

[2] John Floyd (1806–1863) was the 31st Governor of Virginia, U.S. Secretary of War under Buchanan, and he was accused in the press of having sent large stores of government arms to Federal arsenals in the South in the anticipation of the Civil War.—2019

our regiment, joined by an equal number from the Michigan and New York regiments attached to the brigade, went out last night to attack a rebel work on Munson's Hill, about three miles distant, and were successful, driving the devils from the fortification and taking a number of prisoners, who are now in our little guard-house, including one captain. The country here is literally swarming with troops, and you may expect to hear some good news soon. Everything is kept secret from the soldiers, and we all move in the night. All you see in the papers is 'gammon.' Banks with his whole army is within five miles of us, he having moved very secretly under orders from McClellan (who is a general whom our country will be proud of soon), and you will soon hear of a great Northern victory, for our army is now thoroughly organized, and if we do not beat them now we never can.

Our lieutenant-colonel had a narrow escape the other day, while out scouting with several other officers from other regiments, one of whom was wounded quite severely in the leg and hip, and it is doubtful if he recovers; but they gave shot for shot and some were seen to fall, and they had their flag at half-mast all day; our men had telescopic rifles. It is believed here that Jeff Davis is dead.

Our brother of the Eighth Infantry writes now as follows:

Sept. 21, 1861.

This is the only paper to be found in the vicinity of Long Bridge, where I am stationed today. John's regiment guards one end of Long Bridge, and we guard the other.

I have been second in command of Company B since the fight at Bull Run. Last night, Lieutenant Bell, commanding Company D, was relieved from duty with this regiment and ordered to turn over the property belonging to the company to Lieutenant Carter. The Major has put me in command of a company. Nothing new has come to light; troops arriving constantly. We have artillery and cavalry in abundance. Jeff Davis and his angels cannot lake Washington now. I think we shall advance about the middle of next month.

Our recently enlisted brother writes from Fort Albany:

I stood guard[3] yesterday and last night, and so have today to do as I like. This forenoon I went over to Mason's Hill, recently occupied by rebel forces. I should think they lived pretty much on green corn by the piles of corn cobs piled up around their works. I then went about a mile beyond, and came to a little one-story school-house, and you would have laughed to see the caricatures written "on the walls with charcoal, pencils, and chalk, making game of the 'd—n Yankees,' as they term our soldiers. Here are some of the inscriptions: 'Yankee race-course to Bull Run.' 'Lafayette Guards, Mobile, Alabama, a terror to the Yankees.' 'D—n the Yankees!' The walls are covered with just such stuff as this.

Some of our men went out the other day and captured an orderly sergeant, and when they brought him into camp we had quite a lively time. They put him in the guard-house, where an Irishman was confined who bears the sobriquet of 'Happy Jack.' He is a great favorite with the whole regiment, but has got just about enough of the devil in him to keep in the guard-house about all the time. No sooner is he out, than in he goes again. When they put Secesh in he seemed very much pleased and welcomed him with a speech, shook hands, asked after the health of Jeff, and then took out his knife and asked for a loan of the few remaining buttons he had on his clothes.

We expect to have a new uniform in a few days, of the artillery pattern, as we are an artillery regiment. We are making great progress in our drill on the guns, and can now fire them very rapidly. I have a fine chance to see all the leading men of the nation here, and scarcely a day passes that we are not honored by a visit from 'Old Abe,' or a member of his cabinet. I was on guard at the gate of Fort Runyon, the other day, and along come two officers and simply said, 'The President,' and pretty soon along came 'Old Abe,' in a splendid carriage, accompanied by a young lady, followed by Secretaries Cameron and Seward,[4] also accompanied by ladies. We are quite alone here now, for all the troops have moved, God knows where. At night they are with us; in the morning they are gone. Mrs. Greene, the colonel's wife, arrived here the other evening, and the next day after her arrival she presented each company with three bushels of sweet potatoes. In the evening we turned out and

---

[3] It is a well-authenticated fact that on several occasions one brother was at the north end of the bridge, in command of the guard, examining passes, while the other brother was a sentinel at the south end, performing the same duty.—note in original

[4] Secretary of War Simon Cameron (soon to be replaced by Edwin Stanton) and Secretary of State William Seward.—2019

proceeded to his quarters and gave her cheer after cheer, and sung 'John Brown's Chorus.' Colonel Greene is very popular with his men, and is a very kind man.

Our brother in Washington now writes:

Oct. 2, 1861.

I have not got command of my company yet, but expect to have it in a few days. Lieutenant Noble, now in command, was ordered away, but owing to some informality, the provost marshal (under whose command we all are) refused to relieve him. He has been to the War Department twice, and expects to get away soon. I am now acting adjutant, and have to form all guard mountings and all parades, but am not relieved from any other duty.

I am officer of the guard this morning, and am rather glad that I am, for otherwise I would have to attend the funeral of General Gibson, in full uniform. The Second, Third, and Eighth, joined in one regiment, and under command of Major Sykes, act as escort, and it is raining like guns.

Oct. 13, 1861.

I thought I had written you that I had left Major Sykes's immediate command, and had joined the Eighth, where I have command of my own company, G. The captain, Dodge, who was my instructor at West Point, has a leave of absence for one year. The first lieutenant is on parole, and I, being the next in rank, take command of the company. I am the only graduate with the Eighth, and Captain Willard,[5] who commands the Post, makes me his right-hand man. I am acting adjutant, and have to form all parades and guards; all my duties together keep me pretty busy most of the time. I ask Captain Willard's advice in everything, for Major Sykes told me he was a model captain, and I find him very attentive to his duties, and he has a splendidly equipped company. I mean to be a good officer or none at all. You shall never hear anything of me that shall wound your pride. If you should, however, doubt of the performance of my duties heretofore, or my conduct as an officer and gentleman, I refer you to Colonel Davies, whose regiment (Sixteenth N. Y. Vols.) I drilled when I first came to Washington; to

---

[5] George Lamb Willard (1827–July 2, 1863), a Mexican War veteran, later of the 19th and 29th Infantry regiments. He was killed by an artillery round in battle on July 2, 1863 at Gettysburg.—2019

General Sykes, who commanded us at Bull Run; or Captain Willard, who commands the two companies of the Eighth stationed at Washington. We have been under orders since last night to be ready at a minute's notice with two days' rations. I went to see General Sykes last evening about the movement, and he said that the rebels had advanced to make a reconnaissance of our position, but a second report was that they were retreating. I thought then it was only a feint to cover the retreat of their main army, and my supposition has been confirmed this morning. McClellan is following them slowly but surely. O'Rorke[6] goes with the expedition which—" *[The remainder of letter cannot be found.]*

Our brother in Virginia writes:

Four-Mile Run, Oct. 15, 1861.

I am out on picket duty, about one mile and a half from the fort. The whole army has advanced, and we are now alone. There are three of us out here under charge of a corporal, and will remain during the week, when we will be relieved. We got some boards and have made us quite a shanty, covered with our rubber blankets to make it waterproof. Our duty is to examine passes, and is not very dangerous, but we have to be up night and day; two hours on and four hours off. I don't believe there will be any fighting for some time yet, unless the rebels attack us, and that seems to be the general opinion here. McClellan's plan seems to be to feel his way, and to keep near the enemy, so that when they make a final stand his troops will be fresh. He now has an immense army around him. I think there could not have been less than 200,000 men around here before they advanced, and all day Sunday the roads were crowded with army wagons and troops. If he does not beat them now, we had better all come-home. I am almost homesick, now the troops have left, for everything is so quiet. I hope something will turn up, so that we can have a share in some of the fighting, but it does not look much like it now. There is really nothing to write about, for we are kept entirely in ignorance of any movements. When you see a regiment moving, and you ask them where they are going, they do not know, not even their officers. We get most of our news from papers we receive from home.

---

[6] Colonel Patrick O'Rorke, 140th N. Y. Vols., killed [in the battle for Little Roundtop] at Gettysburg, July 2, 1863.—note in original

Our brother of the provost guard writes,

Oct. 22, 1861

I am officer of the day, and have to remain in my quarters, or near them, during the day and night of my tour. It is raining very hard, and I shall not take my patrol out unless it ceases. I have been discussing army matters with Captain Willard, commandant of the post, most of the evening, and he has just left my room to go down town to hear the news, if any, of the Leesburg fight, in which Colonel Baker[7] (U. S. senator from Oregon) was killed. I think he was a very brave man, but he knew very little about army affairs. Never mind; we will not speak ill of the dead. He died in a good cause, while gallantly leading his men, so the papers say. But why feel sad and discouraged at the loss of one man? Before this war is ended, the soil of Virginia will be soaked with as good blood as ever flowed in the veins of Colonel Baker. I now command a company of eighty men. When I took them the company books were very much behindhand; the returns, muster-rolls, descriptive rolls, and all papers were made out wrong, and I have had to correct them. The company had no clothing; many were in the guardhouse; they were not properly fed, and they had no company fund. Now my books are correct: so are my papers; the company has plenty of clothing; I have very few in the guard-house; they have plenty to eat, and their quarters are kept clean. I have a company fund amounting to seventy dollars. Captain Willard congratulated me this very morning on the marked improvement of my company since I took command of .it. I received a short note from John today; he is coming over to spend the day with me sometime this week.

On the 26th of October, he was promoted to be a First Lieutenant, Eighth U. S. Infantry.

On the 28th of October, there occurred a tragic incident which cast a gloom over the entire provost guard. Sergeant Joseph Brennan, Company A, Second U. S. Infantry, was shot dead by Private Michael Lennahan, Company D, of the same regiment in Georgetown. He was tried by a court, found guilty and sentenced

---

[7] Edward Dickinson Baker (1811–October 21, 1861) was a Mexican War veteran, politician, and a close friend of Abraham Lincoln, who named one of his sons after Baker. The Colonel was killed at the Battle of Ball's Bluff.—2019

to be hanged. He was kept confined in Georgetown until the night before the execution, when he was brought in a closed carriage to the guardhouse in Franklin Square. On the morning of January 6, 1862, he was taken to an open lot just north of where the Lutheran church now stands (on Thomas Circle), between Thirteenth and Fourteenth streets. All the details of the execution were arranged and carried out by the provost marshal, Lieutenant Frederick Devoe, acting adjutant of the battalion, read the death warrant to the prisoner at the scaffold, and the law was then and there carried into effect. His spiritual advisor was Father Walter of St. Patrick's church. He met his doom with firmness. Several detachments of infantry from the provost guard were detailed to proceed to the place of execution, whither they marched without music.

Our brother in Virginia, says,

October 28, 1861

I spent Sunday with Gene. Our encampment is about four miles from the city in Fairfax County, Virginia, on a high bill overlooking the town, the Potomac running between. I got a pass Friday night and started early in the morning for the promised land. After walking about half a mile, I got into a sutler's wagon and rode the remainder of the way. I found G—, who was officer of the day.

I shaved off the extensive beard which I have cultivated during my residence on the 'sacred soil [of Virginia]'; changed my dilapidated uniform for a nice suit of black; went to Brown's hotel and got my hair cut, and I think I made quite a decent appearance for a volunteer. I had a splendid breakfast and then went out with G— with the patrol under his charge, and he took me through most of the principal parts of the city, and after arresting about half a dozen officers and soldiers, without proper passes, and taking them to the guardhouse, returned to his quarters, and then we had a splendid dinner. I think he (G—) has more authority here than any mayor or police judge at home. Here are some of his doings: While we were going around he spied three soldiers going into a rum-shop, the proprietors of which he had before warned; he followed them with his men, and entered just as they were taking a 'smile' he arrested the soldiers for having no papers, searched the shop, and poured all the liquor into the gutter, and marched the proprietors (a man and a woman) to the guardhouse, where they will have to come down with twenty-five dollars for the offense. The guard also brought in three men detected in smuggling liquor across the river. He (G—) ordered the liquor (four barrels of whiskey) poured out and the three poor devils to be discharged.

I spent the afternoon very pleasantly; about six o'clock I resumed my garb of a 'sodger,' and soon after invaded the 'sacred soil,' and reached my quarters about eight, after spending one of the most pleasant days within my recollection.

There is nothing new to write about with the exception that six regiments just passed here, going over to the navy yard, where they are going to embark down river, to clean out the rebel batteries on the river. Don't come out here to fight, Bob, if you do you will be sorry; mind what I tell you. Today is pleasant for a wonder. Last night I like to have frozen, it was so cold, and the rats and the mice are as thick as mosquitoes in warm weather. I found a nest in my knapsack this morning, and you ought to see one of my best shirts; it is a beautiful looking garment now.

November 3, 1861.

We usually have a grand review and inspection on Sunday, but for the last forty-eight hours it has been blowing a perfect gale, and I began to think the Lord was about to deluge the land again, for such 'tall raining,' I never yet witnessed. About ten o'clock last night, just for a change, our tent took a notion to come down, and you never saw such a time!! Down came guns, cartridge boxes, crossbelts and all, and such a scene! We were all wet through, and therefore could not get much more moist, so we formed around our 'fallen house,' and sang 'Glory Hallelujah' about ten minutes, the men as happy as ducks in the mud. It took us about half an hour to put our tent up, and you can judge how luxuriously we spent the night. We turned out at daybreak; picked up our things from the heap and they are now out drying on the bushes. I got out my old clothes from my knapsack; changed my socks; cleaned my gun; went after the bread with two or three others; had my breakfast, which consisted of baked beans, bread, and coffee, and here I am writing you. Most of the time we live very well, but whatever we have I never grumble, for I think as you do, that it does no good, and I gain by it, for the other day seven men were detailed for guard duty at the canal, and they have to sleep in the open air. However, it was soon found out

41

that but six were required and each one was anxious to be let off. The captain came out and said, 'Carter, you need not go, for I never hear you grumble about anything.' So much for not grumbling. It was a sad day here when we learned of the Battle of Ball's Bluff, but it did not dispirit the men, and only makes them more anxious to fight. A fellow in our tent lost a father in that battle, and God help the 'Secesh' who crosses his path. There seems to be but one sentiment among our men—that of revenge for the barbarities of the rebels, and when we win a victory they will be as cruel and relentless as were our enemies. There have been great fears for the safety of the fleet during the storm, but there is a report in camp this morning that it is safe. If that should fail, it would almost be a death-blow to our hopes and we should fee] that there would be but one thing left for us to do—to give them battle at Manassas; and we are bound to whip them when we do at whatever cost of life. All we need is officers. The men are full of fight, and if the officers do their duty the men will know no defeat."

Nov. 7, 1861.

I have to write evenings as I have to drill most of the day with pick-axe and shovel. I have been wanting to go out to Falls church for some time to visit N—, but I had not the face to ask the captain for a pass, as I have had so many recently, but yesterday two of my comrades got passes to go there, and one of them named Harris did not feel well, so I went on his pass. There is a provost guard that goes out every day, composed of two from each company, who pick up all who are caught one mile from camp, without a pass from the captain, countersigned by the colonel, and they are court-martialed and have to go through the 'knapsack drill," in the ditch around the fort. I knew two men, and if we were overhauled *my name was Harris*. When we came back the provost halted us, and examined our passes; the two boys from our company said, 'How are you, Harris?' and everything was lovely; I had a splendid time; saw N— and another fellow who used to work with me, and while I was walking about the camp, who should I meet but Mose N., formerly of Portland. He is homesick and 'wants to go home,' but I think the young man will pass the remainder of the season here. I went with him over to the Second Maine, and there I met Horatio S—, also of Portland. He is a second lieutenant; was with his regiment as a private at the Battle of Bull Run, and has had a pretty hard time generally. The regiment lost about one hundred men in that

42

disgraceful fight. Vice-President Hamlin was out there on a visit. There are any quantity of rumors every day in our camp, but they all end in smoke. Just for the fun of the thing, when we returned last night we started a story that the Twenty-second Massachusetts had had a bloody fight, beating the rebels at all points, and in less than five minutes, all through the camp it was, 'Bully for the Twenty-second! they are the boys!! Three cheers for the Wilson boys!! etc.'

Nov. 9, 1861

I have only time to acknowledge receipt of the generous box. It is nearly 'taps,' and I expect to go out on picket again tomorrow night. The blanket and quilt will be very comfortable while I am out, as it is very cool nights and we have no tents, and are allowed no fire. Yesterday, I went into the fort and who should be there but John A. Poor of Portland, accompanied by his wife, wife's niece (Mrs. Dr. Gilman), also Ex-Governor Williams[8] of Maine? John A. recognized me in a moment, so did Mrs. Gilman, and I had quite a talk with them. Mrs. Poor met Gene in Washington. The past week has been a very uncomfortable one for us in our tents, and we have suffered considerably from wet and cold, but have plenty of 'salt horse,' and good bread to eat.

Nov. 27, 1861

A grand review of all the regular troops took place. The infantry was commanded by General George Sykes; cavalry by Lieutenant-Colonel W. H. Emory,[9] and the artillery by Colonel Henry J. Hunt;[10] the entire command under General Andrew Porter.

December 2, the young lieutenant says,

I gave my company a small dinner on Thanksgiving day. I feel very proud of my company, and I know they would fight to the death for me. They keep their quarters very clean, and always look splendidly in all parades. Captain Willard (the commanding officer)

---

[8] Joseph Hartwell Williams (1814–1896) was a Harvard-educated lawyer, politician, and the 27th Governor of Maine from 1857 to 1858.—2019

[9] William Hemsley Emory (1811–1887) was a prominent civil engineer and Mexican War veteran who played a prominent role in the Shenandoah Valley in 1864, especially at the Battle of Cedar Creek.

[10] Henry Jackson Hunt (1819–1889) was later Chief of Artillery in the Army of the Potomac.—2019

says the company has improved vastly under my command. I received an invitation from Mrs. Ex-Governor Anderson to dine with her on Thanksgiving day, which I accepted. She says she was acquainted with Mother before she was Mrs. Carter. If we should have another officer join us, I think of applying for a leave of seven days, and I know General Sykes will endorse it, but at present I am alone with my company, and the army regulations expressly state that when there is only one officer to a company, he shall not be granted a leave of absence. I shall call upon Senator Fessenden and Morrill as soon as possible. I am on duty, as usual, and feel very tired, for I have patrolled all day with a vengeance. I think I am known in the city of Washington better than Abraham Lincoln, and I have the reputation of being a mighty military man when on duty. I would make a mighty good detective, for patrolling makes a man keep his eyes and ears open, and quick on his feet.[11]

Dec. 24.

Christmas Eve, and I am on duty as officer of the day, but I am not on duty tomorrow. As much as I desire to see you all, I would not leave my company alone. I know that my company loves me, and I have been made sure of the fact by receiving a very large, ornamental fruit cake, with a very respectful note signed by men whom I have had occasion to punish very severely, but they know I did it justly, and out of no ill will towards them. My company funds and papers are all in admirable condition, and as soon as another officer joins the command, I shall apply for a leave. I applied in person to General Porter, yesterday, to send more officers to us, and I think we shall be reinforced very soon. I shall expect J— over to see me tomorrow. I give my company a Christmas dinner tomorrow, consisting of turkey, oysters, pies, apples, etc.; no liquors. I am called to quell a disturbance and must close this short note.

Our brother in Virginia says, Jan. 9, 1862,

It is pleasant today, for a wonder; it has rained continually for about six weeks, and it really makes me feel in good spirits to see

---

[11] On Nov. 12, 1861, the abstract from the consolidated morning report of the Army of the Potomac shows that the "City Guard" had an "aggregate present for duty equipped,"—1,078, infantry, 123 cavalry, and six guns. Aggregate present, 1,418.—note in original

the sun again, together with the glorious news of the continued success of our arms in all quarters. The picture you spoke of, in Harper's Weekly, is an exact copy of our quarters, only they look much better on paper than they really are. They are made of pine logs, the crevices being 'chucked up' with mud and chips. The roofs were first covered with straw, then with mud, and finally with tarred paper, which makes them waterproof. Our battery (E) occupies the first two tents from the telegraph wires. I am an inmate of the first tent. The buildings at the left are an old barn, belonging to an old 'Secesh,' named Roach, and out-buildings belonging to his house; also some tents used by the tent and picket guard. The officers' quarters are not in view, nor the fort. We still keep up our infantry drill, which, to me, is far preferable to the very hard work of handling heavy cannon. It has already given me the asthma and pleurisy badly, and today I can hardly 'wheeze,' but I suppose it will be all the same in the end. There is not much mercy shown down here to a sick man. I never was better in my life than when I commenced to work on heavy guns. The men, as a general thing, are dissatisfied with the change; many have deserted, and doubtless many more will do so.[12]

Our brother of the regulars now went home on a seven days' leave, and returning Jan. 14, 1862, writes:

I saw Captain Pitcher, acting commander of the regiment, Noble, Worth, and Ferris at Fort Hamilton in New York. They all received me very cordially, and invited me to dine. The regiment is picking up fast, and I think before many months the gallant old Eighth will shine with its usual lustre. I found Captain Willard and all very well, and very glad to see me. My company has suffered under green hands, but I will shortly bring them into the beaten path. The inspector-general was about this morning and went away, saying. 'Everything is lovely and the goose hangs high!' I am officer of the day, tomorrow, and shall meet my old friends once more.

On the 28th of January, 1862, the following order was issued:

War Department,

Washington City, D. C.,

---

[12] See *Desertion in the Civil War* by Dr. Ella Lonn, the only full-length treatment of this important topic.—2019

Jan. 28, 1862.

Order No.

Ordered—That the commanding general be and is hereby directed to relieve Brigadier-General C. P. Stone from command of his division in the Army of the Potomac forthwith, and that he be placed in arrest and kept in close confinement until further orders.

Edwin M. Stanton, Secretary of War

And now occurred an incident that caused the provost guard no little excitement, although all the details were kept very secret. This was occasioned by the following letter:

Headquarters of the Army,

Washington, Feb. 8, 1862.

General: You will please at once arrest Brigadier-General Charles P. Stone,[13] United States Volunteers, and retain him in close custody, sending him under suitable escort by the first train to Fort Lafayette, where he will be placed in charge of the commanding officer. See that he has no communication with anyone from the time of his arrest.

Very respectfully yours, (Signed)

Geo. B. McClellan,

Major-General.

Brig.-Gen. Andrew Porter,

Provost Marshal.

---

[13] Charlie Pomeroy Stone (1824–1887) had served with honor in the Mexican War. He was charged with security for Abraham Lincoln's first inaugural. He was reputed to be the first volunteer officer mustered into service in the Civil War. He incurred the wrath of Massachusetts Governor Andrews by returning escaped slaves to their owners. He was arrested for the disaster at Ball's Bluff, accused of disloyalty. Neither General Winfield Scott nor McClellan blamed him. He was released without apology or explanation in August and later exonerated He served 13 years in the Egyptian Army after the war. Stone supervised the planning and construction of the pedestal of the Statue of Liberty.— 2019

Two lieutenants, Dangerfield Parker and J. A. Snyder, with Sergeant C.B. Heitman of Company B, Third United States Infantry (our brother's old company), and about fifteen men were sent, between eleven and twelve o'clock on Saturday night, Feb. 8,1862, to make the arrest. General George Sykes accompanied the guard. They halted in front of Lord Lyons's (British minister) house on H street (now known as the Admiral Porter house). General Sykes went in; there seemed to be a reception or ball; he soon reappeared. The guard was then marched to a house on the west side of Seventeenth street, between H street and the north side of Pennsylvania avenue. General Sykes disappeared again. Soon he returned with a gentleman whom none of the officers or the guard knew, and proceeding to the "chain building" already referred to, on H street between Thirteenth and Fourteenth streets, occupied by some of the officers of the guard, he was placed in a room on the upper floor, and Lieutenant James A. Snyder and a sentinel placed outside the door. He was taken to Fort Lafayette on the 9th, by Lieutenant Dangerfield Parker. Sergeant Heitman was offered the detail of sergeant of the guard to accompany him, but declined.

Our brother at Fort Albany says, Feb. 23,

It is all talk about the soldiers not having sufficient to wear. I don't believe half of them were ever so well clothed in their lives. If we were called upon to advance upon the enemy tomorrow, we should be compelled to throw a large portion of our clothing away. I am pretty well now. Don't write to any of the doctors, tor it won't do the least particle of good. Our lieutenant is a doctor, and he has done me more good than they could do at the hospital. Our regiment has been placed in the division of General McDowell, but we are not brigaded. Washington's birthday was celebrated by the 'Grand Army' in fine style. There was nothing to be heard all day but the roar of artillery, and such a roar I never before heard. It must have been fine music to our friends (?) at Manassas, who, by the way, are making tracks for Richmond, or some other sacred spot. The Army of the Potomac will soon give them a trial of their steel. It is impossible to move an army now, for the roads are in a wretched condition, the mud being two or three feet deep in many places.

I have not seen Gene for a fortnight; we can get no papers since we have been in McDowell's division, so I don't expect to see him very often.

Our brother of the provost guard writes February 24,

We have only two officers for duty; Lieutenant Martin and Fisher have joined their own regiments (companies), and I am alone with my company. I am officer of the day now, but I have just come back from patrolling; very wet (got caught in a rain storm), and not being fond of travelling about in the rain and mud I will take the liberty— 'being commanding officer of the Post pro tem,'—to remain at home during the morning. The streets of Washington are perfect rivers, and unless a person can swim, it is very dangerous for short persons to attempt to navigate them. I have a pair of very large boots and do not have very much trouble. I suppose you received the news of the capture of Forts Henry and Donelson with as much joy as we did. I hardly believe you felt as glad as I did, for I felt, father, for the past two or three months that our country was in a bad way. I feared that England would interfere and I knew if she did we were ruined, for our blockade would be raised; Sherman (T. W.),[14] would be cut off; our forces at Ship Island and Pickens would have to surrender, and we were totally unprepared for a war with such a power; and rivers, lakes and large cities were not defended as they should be and we had no navy, compared with that of England.[15]

When the news came that France intended to aid the South, I thought indeed our cup was full. I felt so badly about it that I would frequently find myself almost in tears, and Capt. Willard felt as I did. I told him one day that I thought if they would allow us to attend to our own affairs and remain away, we would crush out this rebellion very soon, and in six months after we would whip France and England both together if they did not keep quiet. I have no doubt that they think or have thought, that the South was more powerful than we, but Forts Donelson and Henry and Roanoke will

[14] Thomas West Sherman (1813–1879), a Mexican War veteran who lost a leg at Port Hudson in 1863.—2019

[15] Until 1863, the worry that France or England would recognize the Confederacy—or worse, support it—was intense. The famed Confederate raider, *Alabama*, was built in English shipyards, an event of very serious contention. For a fascinating examination of U.S.-English relations of the time, see *The Adams Letters in the Civil War*, 2016, BIG BYTE BOOKS.

convince them to the contrary. I only wish I had been at Donelson. I see almost every day the capture or death of some of my old friends; Capt. Dixon, the chief engineer and builder of Fort D., was killed in his own work. I know General Buckner[16] quite well. He married a sister of Kingsbury, who was in the class above me, and who was adjutant of the Corps. You have heard me speak of him as being a very fine fellow. Buckner was here when I reported, and was going to take a position in our army. ...

We are only waiting for good travelling and the grand advance; we will have bloody work, for we are bound for Richmond, and by the aid of God we will be there before long. Frank[17] is here; I was with him all day on the 22d. He was taken in Texas, and refused to give the parole that many did, and was consequently detained a prisoner since March. He has just been exchanged; he was well treated (being a regular). He says the troops are half clothed, half fed, and not paid at all. Richmond and New Orleans are under martial law, and there is no business anywhere. Everything is very high. General McClellan told him that his course was very praiseworthy. Frank don't know what to do; he will remain about here a week and make up his mind. Our uniform is to be changed, and in my next letter I will describe it to you.

Fort Albany, Feb. 26, 1862

I will write you just a word or two, as perhaps I may never have another opportunity. We have just received marching orders and don't know at what moment we go. The orders arc that we go with only four wagons and two days' rations. The officers are to take nothing but a carpet bag. I shall take nothing but my blankets, rubber and woolen. If I escape uninjured I shall then send for the rest of my valuable wardrobe. The Colonel has just been talking to us about our canteens, haversacks, etc., 1 but be sure, boys,' he said, 'and have plenty of powder and shot.' He has got fight in him. I have got fifty pounds and I shall try and shoot. Give love to Mother, and tell her not to worry. I have not heard from Gene.

---

[16] Simon Bolivar Buckner (1823–1914), later governor of Kentucky.—2019

[17] First Lieutenant Royal T. Frank graduated from the Military Academy in the class of 1858. He was from Maine. He is now Colonel First United States Artillery, and commandant of the Artillery School at Fort Monroe, Va.—note in original

49

Our brother of the regulars now writes:

I write in great haste. We are under orders to hold ourselves in readiness at a moment's notice to have two days' rations cooked, and to have all company property stored. I am all picked up and ready to start anywhere at any time. If anything happens to me send to John Golden, Massachusetts Avenue, between First and Seventh streets for my effects, and you will receive them instanter. Good-by to all.

February 28

I have been in my room since yesterday evening with my knapsack packed and all ready to move. I believe that [Union General Nathaniel] Banks attempted to take Williamsport, and got defeated, and this is the cause of all the getting ready, etc. Yesterday morning the Fourth United States Cavalry went off somewhere, and returned this morning covered with mud. I did not see any of them, consequently do not know where they went. Captain Willard has been promoted to be Major in the Nineteenth Infantry. He just left my room, after telling me privately some good news. The provost marshal-general of the Grand Army, General Andrew Porter, has applied for Major Willard to command a battalion which is to move with him. Major asked me how I would like to be adjutant. He says I am not sure of commanding a company, and now that Frank is here, he may be ordered to take command at any moment. If I act as adjutant I will have a horse to ride, which is a very fine thing to have in the field, 'a la Sparrowgrass.' Major wishes to have me very much. I rather think I shall like it. It is very cold and windy here, and I hope if we move, we will wait until it is a little pleasant. I am busy with my muster and pay-rolls, and have to see that my monthly return is made out properly.

Our brother at Fort Albany writes, March 5th.

We still continue here, but do not know at what moment the 'long roll' will summon us to march on the enemy. It has been understood by us till recently that we were to be stationed here permanently, but such is not the fact; we advance with the Grand Army. By accident I met with a late H. paper, and in it I saw a 'Call' for a meeting to drum up recruits for the "Web-footed Fourteenth," giving these individuals to understand that this regiment would see none of Jeff's friends. It is too bad for them to be so deceived. I suppose Major Wright has been to H.to recruit. He thought when he left that we should not advance, but we have received different orders since he left, and I am glad of it.

Our brother of the provost guard writes, March 10, 1862.

We move this morning at twelve noon. We are on the provost marshal-general's guard. The entire army moves, good-by. God bless you all!

On the 28th of February, 1862, it had become known that General Andrew Porter was appointed provost marshal general of the Army of the Potomac, and having applied for a battalion of regulars as provost guard, with Major George L. Willard, Nineteenth United States Infantry in command, and the order having been received to move on the 10th of March, it crossed the river and went into camp the same day, near Fairfax seminary.

The following officers composed the staff of General Porter: Major, W. H. Wood, Seventeenth United States Infantry; chief of staff, Captain James McMillan, Seventeenth United States Infantry; acting assistant adjutant-general, Captain J. W. Forsythe, Eighteenth; lieutenants, J. W. Jones, Twelfth, C. F. Trowbridge, Sixteenth, and C. D. Mchaffey, First United States Infantry; aide-de-camp, General Andrew Porter; provost marshal, General Army of the Potomac.

The provost guard was now composed as follows: a battalion of infantry under Major G. L. Willard, the latter being Companies F" and G, Eighth Infantry, under Captain Royal T. Frank and First Lieutenant Eugene Carter, with two Companies, B and D, of the Seventeenth. At general headquarters, two companies.

A and E, Fourth United States Cavalry; Lieutenants J. B. McIntire and William O'Connell, one company, Oneida Cavalry (New York Volunteers), one company, Sturges Rifles (Illinois Volunteers).

The Sturges Rifles was a single, unattached company of eighty-three men, organized at Chicago in April, 1861, mustered May 6. It was equipped and subsisted for nearly two months by the munificence of Mr. Solomon Sturges. The commissioned officers were Captain James Steele, First Lieutenant N. W. Sheldon, Second Lieutenant Foster. It was armed with Sharpes rifles. It served as body guard to General McClellan in West Virginia, and accompanied him to Washington, reaching there July 26, 1861. From that time it was a part of the headquarters guard. It left the army at Falmouth, Virginia, and was mustered out November 27, 1862.

Our brother at Fort Albany writes March 11:

Last night the long roll beat in all the encampments for miles around, and the 'Web-footed Fourteenth' sallied forth to see what was up. We soon learned that this regiment was not to move at present. Soon we saw General McDowell with his division approaching, followed by Blenker and his division. The whole army was moved. About 12 o'clock we discovered that Long Bridge was covered with troops, and in about half an hour they approached, and it. was rumored that they were regulars; so of course I was interested, and I waited patiently for nearly three hours for the thousands of cavalry, and over one hundred gun pieces of artillery to pass us. Then came the regular infantry; Gene's company was the first, he in command. He is in fine spirits, and looking as healthy as a buck. His two companies, with two companies of cavalry were selected for a body guard to General Porter, the provost marshal, but would not accept until they were assured by General McClellan that they would have the same privileges of promotion as if they were to be in the thickest of the fight. In all probability, unless we have a reverse, which we shall not, Gene or myself will be in no very great danger of losing our valuable lives.

It is very hard marching, as the mud is very deep. He will probably sleep on the ground tonight. I walked by his side nearly to Munson's Hill, and then bade him adieu, and I felt almost like cursing my fortune, that we were not permitted to advance with him.

Our brother of McClellan's headquarters writes from Fairfax Seminary, March 19:

I have been on the jump for the past two weeks. One week ago last Sunday night, at 1 o'clock, we were ordered to march at 12 the next day. The Major succeeded in getting plenty of transportation, and we started very well provided for.

I have one large tent for the rations of my company. I took a wall tent for myself, and a small one for my servant, my carpet-bag and camp bed, three blankets, and a pillow.

We marched about three miles the first day and bivouacked. In Long Bridge, Washington, D. C. passing Fort Albany, I found John on the lookout, and he walked along with me for three miles, and then started back, looking as forlorn as possible. The first night was some cold, but we managed to make ourselves comfortable. Reveille was beaten at 4 o'clock, and we started towards Fairfax court-house at 6; arrived there at 2 p. m., and went into camp very near General McClellan's quarters. We remained there until last Sunday (16th) morning, and then received orders to report at headquarters at Fairfax Seminary.

The Friday and Saturday before, it rained very hard; my blankets, boots, and everything I had got wet. My throat troubled me considerably. We marched on Sunday to within two miles of the Seminary, and there found an overflowed river, which we could not ford with our wagons; we remained here for an hour, not knowing what to do, but we were informed that we could go back a mile and find a cross-road which would bring us into the main road to Washington, and then we could take the main road to Alexandria, which is very near our present camp.

We started, and such a road I never saw before; mud knee-deep. We finally arrived at our destination, after having marched about twenty-five miles. Our wagons had been stalled, and we had nothing to cook or eat with. We remained totally inactive for two hours, and just at dusk our wagons came up, our tents were pitched, our fires were lighted, and supper cooked.

Of course we felt like new men. The next morning we arranged our camp, and now we have everything comfortable. General Porter and staff are with us; General McClellan and staff are very near, and the medical director and chief of ordnance directly behind us. We are to be changed from provost guard duty to the guard of the commander-in-chief. I think I shall decline the staff appointment offered to me and keep my company. I have seen enough of 'mounted orderlies' duties.

Frank commands one company of the Eighth, I command the other. Two companies of the Seventeenth are with us, and the officers and men are worse than those of any volunteer regiment in the service. I went over to Washington this morning, saw John on my return. I think we shall embark in two or three days, but where we go to, I know not. I wish we could have a chance to fight, for I want a brevet captaincy. General McClellan says that we may have a chance.

Our brother of the artillery [John] now writes:

March 19.

Today I saw Gene; since they marched a week ago Monday, I have heard nothing from him; but today as I came from the provost guard, the boys told me that my brother had been to see me, and that he was out by the roadside, feeding his horse; so I went and found him. He is pretty well tired out, having marched from Fairfax last night, and is now camped about a mile from Alexandria. McClellan with his whole army has returned. Banks has about 45,000 men beyond Manassas, and McClellan, with nearly 200,000 men, are embarking on board steamers for God only knows where. There is 'some game up.'

Two companies of the Eighth are now a part of the body guard of 'Little Mac.'

Camp Porter, Alexandria, March 25, 1862.

Your letter reached me this morning, and found me, as usual, officer of the day but no patrol duty to perform. The duties now are comparatively light, there being six officers to divide with. I am alone with my company, but I have applied for my second lieutenant. I think I told you that Frank commands one company of the Eighth and I the other. We are very good friends. I have been to W. twice since we came back from Fairfax, and obtained all I needed for a long campaign. As we go with General McClellan, it becomes us to look as well as possible, so I got my uniform coat and pants, woolen shirts without collars, and one hundred paper collars. Now I can have a clean collar every day, and shall not be put to the trouble of having them washed. All the regular infantry have embarked. I rode down to Alexandria yesterday and saw General Sykes and all the officers. The General said he wished I was going along with him; and I really wish I was, for I know they will see enough fighting, and God knows I had rather fight under General Sykes as my immediate commander than any man living. I feel now as though we were isolated, mere tent raisers; but I will content myself with General Porter's promise to give us a chance, and he is a good man and a brave soldier. I hear nothing of our moving, but I know when we do go, we go on board the *Commodore* with General McClellan.

Our brother of the artillery now writes;

March 19.

I have been drilling my company as skirmishers for the past week, and firing with blank cartridges; it is the best practice we can give them, for it teaches them to be cool under fire. This morning Frank was sick, and Major Willard took command of the company, and challenged me to have a sham battle with him. Friday night, March 28, General McClellan was serenaded by the band and glee club of the Ninety-fifth Pennsylvania Volunteers, and they were cordially welcomed by him, who made them a brief but spirited address.

General McClellan, with headquarters of the army, embarked April 2, 1862, from Alexandria on the Steamer *Commodore*; Companies F and G of the Eighth, on the Steamer *Wilson Small* for Fortress Monroe. They arrived on the 3d, and went into camp one mile from Hampton. Leaving Hampton on the morning of April 4, the march was resumed slowly across Newmarket Bridge, and through Little Bethel, and headquarters were located in a house at Big Bethel very near where Lieutenant John Greble[1] of the Artillery, and our brother's instructor at West Point, had been killed ten months before. On Saturday, April 5, three miles beyond Big Bethel, the Halfway House was reached, once a roadside hotel; there had been a store connected with it, the windows to which had iron bars; it was now deserted. About one-half mile from it "Rosedown" was passed, a plantation house three stories in height, of some pretensions. It was painted white, and had large chimneys and many outbuildings. W. Russell, the owner of this place, stood outside, and answered the numerous questions put to him. He claimed to be a Union man, complained that the Confederates had burnt up his fences; his slaves, many of them, were nearly white.[2]

---

[1] John Trout Greble (1834–June 10, 1861), West Point class of 1854. Fort Greble, part of the capital defenses, was named for him.—2019

[2] Confederate diarist, Mary Chesnut (a close friend of Varina Davis) noted with disgust in her diary the prevalence of enslaved African Americans who were the spitting image of their masters due to rape and

This was about twelve miles from Yorktown. Camp and headquarters were at Chesapeake Church at night. On the 6th, after a long, tedious, and slow march across Howard's bridge and through Cockletown, during which cannonading could be heard in the advance, camp was made near Yorktown. General McClellan was in a hut in a deserted Rebel camp. On the 7th, the camp of the general headquarters and provost guard was five miles from Yorktown, near Dr. Powers's. It rained all night, the 7th, and all day of the 8th. Remained in this camp until the 11th, reconnaissances, skirmishes, and cannonading going on most of the time. The roads were horrible from the recent rains, and the baggage, most of the time, was far in the rear.

On the 11th, camp was moved further to the front, and nearer to Yorktown. This camp they occupied until the siege was raised. It was between two small branches of the southeasterly arm of Wormley Creek. It was situated on a magnificent plateau in the midst of about 30,000 men, and was about one mile from York river. A little to the right of camp one could obtain a good view of the river, and a walk of about half a mile around the woods, Yorktown, Gloucester Point, and a long line of the enemy's works could be seen. To the south of camp was a ravine through which ran a small creek, along which were some fine springs. It was about two miles from the enemy's line. A short distance to the rear was a large swamp, reeking with malaria, along which ran the camp of the One Hundred Fifth New York volunteers.

A very thick wood of pine, elm, and sassafras almost surrounded the camp, but it was soon all cut away. Facing camp, and but one fourth of a mile to the front, Prof. Low[3] had his apparatus for filling his balloons, which, during the siege of Yorktown, could frequently be seen almost daily above the trees for short reconnaissances of the enemy's works.

A detail of the Fifth New York Volunteers (Duryea's Zouaves), which had been attached to Skyes's Regular brigade, pitched the

---

concubinage.—2019

[3] Thaddeus Lowe (1832–1913). George Armstrong Custer was briefly one of Lowe's aeronauts.—2019

headquarter camp, and laid out the ground about them, and a detail was made daily for guard duty over General McClellan's quarters, which were very near regimental headquarters of the Fifth New York.

The camp was laid out in the form of a great parallelogram or rectangle, with the staff tents on the long sides, and the commander-in-chief on one of the shorter sides, the guard tents being upon the other. On the side occupied by General McClellan, a space, 100 feet square, was marked out, around which sentinels walked day and night, and upon which no one was allowed to approach without a pass or unless they had urgent business with the general. In the centre of this square two large tents were pitched alongside with a small space between them. One of them was occupied by General McClellan, and the other by General Marcy,[4] his father-in-law, and chief-of-staff. Both were furnished alike, with stove, table, lounge, camp bed, camp stools, desk, and toilet articles. In front of these a street 100 feet wide (width of the rectangle) ran to the guard tents on the other side of the camp.

Upon each side of this street the staff tents were pitched, all arranged according to rank from General McClellan's tent. In these were the provost marshal, adjutant-general, inspector-general, quartermaster-general, the heads of departments, aides to the commanding general, etc.

A line back of the staff tents were devoted to subalterns, servants, etc. Outside of all, the horses were picketed; and further away was the headquarter train in park. It was an immensely imposing affair, and nothing like it was ever seen in the Army of the Potomac again.

The provost guard extended all through the camps; picked up stragglers and contrabands, and if they had passes they were released, if not, they were sent to the nearest guardhouse, from which the soldiers were sent to their respective regiments, and

---

[4] Randolph Barnes Marcy (1812–1887) was a career officer, chiefly noted for his frontier guidebook, the Prairie Traveler (1859). See his *Thirty Years of Army Life on the Border*, 2014, BIG BYTE BOOKS.

the contrabands to the nearest subsistence department, if they were wanted there for labor, or, if not, they were kept by the guard until otherwise disposed of. All stray horses and mules were picked up and returned to the herds to which they belonged. It took charge of all rebel spies; all prisoners of war, who were turned over to them by their captors. Stolen property of every description was traced up, and a thousand and one duties were performed by this headquarter and provost guard that would fill columns to enumerate. It was a terror to all evil-doers. A writer has well said: "Better order never was kept anywhere on the continent than in the Army of the Potomac."

The entire camp was named "Camp Winfield Scott" by G. O. No. 115, dated April 12, 1862. On the same day, in the forenoon, the enemy sent up a balloon, but it remained up only a few minutes, and it was surmised that it was a failure. One of the most exciting incidents that happened near headquarters was the ascent of General Fitz-john Porter in one of Prof. Low's balloons, early on the morning of April 11. The rope broke a few hundred feet from the ground, and away he went, rising higher and higher over the enemy's works. There was great excitement for a time, and cavalry were ordered to saddle up and capture it. General Porter did not consider it wise to pull the valve when he saw he was going towards the enemy's lines, although many shouted for him to do so; but soon, at a high altitude, a fortunate counter-current set him back, and opening the valve, he descended within a few rods of headquarters, landing directly on top of a soldier's shelter tent.

Batteries sprang up in every direction, and the army sat down before Yorktown for a long siege. One of the most remarkable of these batteries, and one with quite a history, was Battery No. 1, which was the first to open on the enemy's works, on April 30, only a few days before the evacuation. It was located at the mouth of Wormley creek on the banks of York River. It was built by details from the Fifth New York, and the First Conn. H. A. directly in front of Farinholt's house in his peach orchard. Its guns were 1-

200 and 5-100 Pdr. parrots, and it was garrisoned by one battery, First Conn. H. A., Captain Burke.

The plantation had been apparently abandoned by the whites, and Farinholt was said to be a lieutenant in the Confederate army; but on May 5th, during the advance of the army through and beyond Yorktown, a great many stragglers came into headquarters and were sent to the provost guard from the rear guard of the fleeing Johnnies and among them was Farinholt and a neighbor by the name of Davis. Farinholt stated that he had been impressed into the Confederate service. He narrowly escaped being shot and arrested several times during his hazardous escape. He sent in a note to headquarters saying he wished to "take the oath of allegation," and the "oath of allegiance" was at once administered.

On the night of the 18th, the camp was alarmed by heavy and continuous firing of artillery and musketry. General McClellan sent some of his staff officers to ascertain the cause. On the 2ist of April Companies A, F, H, and K of the Ninety-third New York Volunteers were attached to the headquarter guard, and Major Granville O. Haller was assigned as commandant of headquarters.

On the 25th of April our brother in Fort Tillinghast wrote as follows:

I can, with full confidence assure you that I am freed at last from that interesting species of vermin called 'lice.' After a long and desperate siege, they have evacuated, leaving many of their dead behind. We are anxiously awaiting to hear the result of the battle of Yorktown, and feel sorry that our regiment was not permitted to participate in it; yet I know that the army must suffer much, as they have had nothing to shelter themselves with, since they have been there, with the exception of little booths, formed of rubber tents.

I fear we shall have a desperate fight there, and I worry for Gene's safety; yet I trust he will be spared.

I see by the papers that Frank Fessenden was badly wounded at the battle of Pittsburg Landing. I sometimes think that this will be a long and bloody war, though 'Jeff's' seeing bad times now. I thought when I 'enlisted for a soldier,' that I should have returned ere this, or have become 'food for powder;' but God only can see the end.

There is nothing here to keep up one's spirits, for we are away from everybody and everything, with the exception of the Arlington House, the residence of the traitor Lee, and formerly of Washington, the Father of his Country. It has been a splendid place, but now everything has been destroyed, the magnificent forest around it having been cut down, and the flower gardens neglected. The pictures have nearly all been taken away, and the house much injured. The rooms are very large, and there is a long entry running the entire length of the house, adorned with stags' heads, and a few splendid paintings still remain. Lee's 'niggers,' about fifty in number, still occupy their quarters, and make themselves useful by washing for the soldiers, etc. Arlington has been until recently the headquarters of General McDowell.

Last week I was confined to my bunk two or three days, having got wet through while on guard, and taking cold.

I witnessed the battle between the forces of Gene and Willard. It was a desperate engagement. Nobody killed on our side; the loss of the enemy unknown.   .

Camp Winfield Scott,

May 4, 1862.

I may not have a chance to write again for some time. The enemy have evacuated Yorktown, and we are pressing hard upon their rear guard. They commenced last Friday night, and have left a large amount of munitions of war behind. Our bands, which for two weeks have been as silent as the grave, are now playing with all their might, and we hear nothing but 'Yankee Doodle,' 'Hail Columbia,' 'Star Spangled Fanner,' and 'Dixie.' We can hear the cannonading going on very distinctly, and it cannot be very far from us. I wish I were with the advance. I expect we will all move tomorrow, and follow up the retreating army of Secession so fast that we will give them a general battle before many days. The reason for evacuating seems to be their fear of our gunboats. We will whip them in a fair, open field fight, and they will find a vast difference between fighting three months' Volunteers, and our present army.

We have had a very lively time for the last three days; solid shot and shell whistling over our heads, and falling about us in every direction. You cannot imagine the noise made by a hundred-pound rifle shell whizzing through the air, even at the distance of half a mile from you. It seems like three or four engines going at the top of their speed, and when it bursts—thunder and zounds; what a noise!! But I have heard their music so often, that I scarcely notice them now. I wish John was with this army, I know he would be better contented than he is now. He used to take so much pleasure in coming to see me when I was at the seminary. He would walk miles to see and spend the day with me.

I have just been talking to the major; he has just come from headquarters, and of course has heard all the news. This morning we sent out a strong reconnoissance composed of horse artillery and cavalry. We met the rear guard of the enemy, and a brisk skirmish took place; full particulars not received. The Sixth Regular Cavalry lost about thirty men, and captured fifty prisoners (privates), and one captain. I think that Johnston intends to throw about sixty thousand men upon McDowell, and keep forty thousand behind entrenchments for our benefit.

The Rebels have erected batteries again at Acquia Creek. Our officers are almost satisfied that we would have had to fight at Yorktown for months before we could reduce it, and it was owing to the over-caution of General Robert E. Lee of the Confederate army that it was evacuated.

We will follow them very closely. Our advance is at Williamsburg tonight. Many have been killed by the explosion of torpedoes, which the Rebels placed in the ground all about their fortifications. Our gunboats have gone to West Point, and all our supplies are being carried there as rapidly as possible. Prisoners are being brought to us very fast; many, deserters. Signals are flying in every direction, and rockets of all kinds and sizes.

I must get some rest, for I think we will move tomorrow. I have been kept awake for some nights past by heavy cannonading.

France will recognize the Southern Confederacy in less than a month, for the purpose of dividing us on Mexican affairs. If she does, I hope every man and boy in the great North will shoulder his musket and give himself to his country.

We do nothing but drill from morning until night.

During this terrific cannonading, one of the youngsters attached headquarters thought he would play a practical joke upon General —, so he asked him to come over and see one of the great shells the enemy had pitched into the headquarter camp. When he arrived the young fledgling showed him an immense oyster shell obtained from the York River, much to the disgust of the dignified general.

General McClellan, leaving everything behind, taking only his immediate staff, went to the front to conduct the pursuit. His temporary headquarters in Yorktown were at the Anderson house. On that day he had no dinner or supper, and on the morning of the 6th he had no breakfast but a biscuit, nor dinner; all his baggage was back in camp. He was out in a heavy rain until late at night. He slept in his clothes and boots, and his bed was a buffalo robe and horse blanket; he was without even a hair-brush or tooth-brush; his headquarters during that night on the field of Williamsburg were in the Whittaker house, but, on the night of the 6th, were in a fine house which General Joe Johnston had been occupying, in Williamsburg.

The provost guard had been kept busy, guarding prisoners, deserters, and attending to the many duties incident to the excitement and bustle of breaking up Camp Winfield Scott.

At 12:30 p. m. on the night of the 7th, General McClellan sent a despatch to General Marcy to bring up headquarters at once to Williamsburg. It moved at early daylight, and passing through Yorktown, overtook the general by 2 p. m. on the 9th, at Williamsburg, and moving out late in the afternoon of the same day, camp was pitched at Ewell's Farm, three miles from Williamsburg.

Starting at 5 a. m. on the 10th, at 11:45 a. m. headquarters had moved through James City, Burnt Ordinary, by many churches and chapels, to Barhamsville, where camp was pitched near an old church, Roper's meeting-house, in a pine grove. Here they remained until the morning of the 13th. On the night of the 12th, the army was up and gathered for miles about this place. It was a beautiful, bright moonlight night. The band of the Second Dragoons was serenading headquarters, and fifty other bands nearby were sounding off "tattoo." It was a grand and inspiriting scene.

On the 13th, moved at 6 a. m. from Roper's church to Cumberland Landing on the Pamunkey River, where a temporary depot was established. This place sprang into importance almost in a single night. From a little landing with an occasional oyster boat tied up to the wharf, it had become an immense seaport with a forest of masts, government transports, and trading vessels crowding each other, and every indication of busy life and commercial importance.

The army was visited here by Secretaries[5] Seward, Bates, and Welles, Frederick Seward and wife, Admiral and Mrs. Goldsborough, Admiral Dahlgren, who were guests at General McClellan's headquarters. They were taken about camp in ambulances; a number of ladies were in the party. On the 14th, the army had a grand review in their honor. It was a most magnificent spectacle. When Secretary Seward rode around one of the regiments from Massachusetts, he remarked to General McClellan, "This is 'old Massachusetts,' God bless her!" "Yes," replied General McClellan, with a smile, pointing to the line which was nearly double that of any other, "it will take the Rebels a long time to get around this regiment." It rained on the 14th and 15th, and on the 16th, headquarters left camp in a heavy rain and marched to White House, the home of the Lees. Here a very singular incident came near depriving the commander-in-chief of his wagon train with all headquarter baggage, etc. The roads, from heavy rains, were horrible. In coming to White House, it had missed the road where it forked; had taken one leading directly into the enemy's lines, and was only rescued and turned back by

[5] Secretary of State William Seward and his son Fred (later grievously injured in the attack on his father the night Lincoln was assassinated), Attorney General Edward Bates, Secretary of the Navy Gideon Welles, Admiral Louis M. Goldborough, and Admiral John A. Dahlgren, whose son Ulric was killed during an 1864 raid on Richmond.—2019

some of our cavalry, and then only after a skirmish with the enemy's scouts and pickets.

General McClellan was, therefore, compelled to take up temporary headquarters in the house. As soon as the wagons arrived, he moved to about one-half mile in rear of the Landing, and pitched his camp as usual. This was about one mile from Dr. Macon's. He neither occupied the house himself nor allowed others to do so, but placed a strong guard about the entire grounds and property.

On the 17th of May it had been determined by General McClellan to break up, if possible, the enemy's depot of supplies on the Pamunkey River above White House. He designated a portion of the headquarter guard to accomplish this important task. Under verbal orders from Genera] Andrew Porter, the command started at 9 o'clock on the morning of the 17th, under Major George L. Willard. It was composed of Companies F and G, Eighth United States Infantry, under Captain Royal T. Frank and First Lieutenant Eugene Carter, and Lieutenants A. T. Smith of the Eighth, and F. A. Field, Eleventh Infantry; ten men of Company B, and fifteen men of Company D, Seventeenth Infantry, with Assistant-surgeon J. H. Frantz, and thirty-four men of the Sturges Rifles, Captain James Steele; a total of one hundred and forty enlisted men.

They embarked on the light draft tug boat *Seth Lowe*, where Captain Murray, United States Navy, was found, who commanded the United States steamship *Sebago*, with whom Major Willard had been directed to cooperate; Captain R. B. Ayres's Battery F, Fifth United States Artillery, came aboard with two 10-pounder Parrott guns of his battery.

Steaming slowly up the river, about 10 o'clock the gunboat *Currituck*, Captain Nicholson, was overtaken. The Pamunkey was a beautiful river, with high bluffs and a most picturesque scenery. It was so narrow, however, that at times the boats were brushing the treetops along its banks, and one could almost leap ashore. The bluffs were thickly wooded, and it was expected that the enemy might have a concealed force along the shore.

Frequently the *Currituck* got aground. White flags were flying from nearly every house that could be seen. Few whites were discovered. But at Putney's mill or ferry, the Negroes came down by couples and families to make grimaces and gestures of welcome. Captain Ayres said they reminded him of the Mojave Indians when he made his exploration of the Colorado River. They reported that at Smith's store, ten miles from White House, the enemy had a strong picket of thirty. At 2 o'clock the "Thoroughfare" was reached, the narrowest part of the river, where the boats could not turn around. The stream widened into pools, however, and at times one could see stretches of country, covered with waving grain, gently sloping meadows, farmhouses, large plantation mansions and picturesque Negro quarters, which Captain Ayres said "made a man weep for very admiration."

The stream was found to be obstructed at several points by timber felled from opposite sides, so that the tops met and the branches were interlaced in the middle of the narrow channel.

It was decided that the quickest way to get rid of the barricades was to run them down. Putting on a full head of steam, a run was made at them and they were run down with the greatest ease; the boughs were crushed to splinters, while the piles that had been at these points were so bent over that they could no longer impede navigation.

Shortly after 2 o'clock, dense smoke was discovered ahead. At 3 o'clock a point was reached, about twenty miles from White House, where a boom of two or more sunken schooners or canal-boats effectually barred the way. In the distance a number of Rebel steamers and schooners could be seen, with a line of the enemy drawn up on the high bluffs.

These boats were filled with stone, and it was found impossible to raise or remove them. This was at a place called Bassett's Landing, fifteen miles from Richmond. The command, with the exception of a small picket-guard left with the boats, was now landed on the left bank (North side), and the little force set out on its hazardous march. It proceeded two or more miles in the direction of Richmond, pushing its way through a thick undergrowth for nearly a mile. The mounted pickets of the enemy retired. Things were beginning to look very interesting, and like a fight, with the possible chance of being cut off from a retreat to the boats, when, suddenly, with a flash of blue smoke, a hollow explosion, and a burst of flame, the Rebel craft were ignited, and soon were completely enveloped in flame; at the same time the enemy ran away without firing a shot.

One propeller and one large sound steamer, the *Logan*, and a number of schooners, variously estimated at from ten to twenty, were counted, all of which were totally destroyed. The command was so close that the noise and the crackling of the burning timbers could be distinctly heard. The object of the expedition having now been accomplished, the command at 4 o'clock returned to the steamers.

During its absence, a sailor from the *Currituck* reported a body of troops on the south side of the river, drawn up in line of battle, at a point nearly opposite the burning vessels. The sergeant of the picket that had been left behind, sent a Negro to ascertain if this was correct. He returned in a few minutes after the command had re-embarked, and reported a large force of the enemy drawn up in the road leading from the burning fleet to the Chickahominy River, and just within a line of woods some distance from the Pamunkey. The return was at once made, the steamers having to back some distance before they could turn. About half way down, a small force of the enemy's cavalry was seen, but they were not molested. It was learned from the Negroes that these vessels had contained about 20,000 bushels of corn, besides coal and other stores, one Negro stating that he had been engaged in hauling the corn to the Chickahominy Swamp.

All along the banks of the river were collected herds of cattle and flocks of sheep, driven thus far in the retreat of the enemy from Yorktown. The little battalion reached White House between Sand 9 p. m., creating much excitement and no little enthusiasm about the headquarter camp. General McClellan said of this expedition: "It was admirably managed, and all concerned deserve great credit."

While at White House, an artist of one of the illustrated newspapers started to walk from Yorktown to Williamsburg, but was stopped by a company of cavalry some little distance from Yorktown and told it was dangerous to proceed. Two Massachusetts soldiers had been found hanging to trees, shot, and with their throats cut. Two had been shot the day before, and they had been scouting between the two places.

The steamers brought many persons who came provided with coffins to remove the friends killed in battle. These mournful processions were the first thing that struck one oddly while at White House. These visitors soon became so numerous and persistent that the authorities at headquarters began to seriously consider a return to the old Roman method of burning the dead.

Millions of dollars' worth of supplies were shipped to this point, and until it was destroyed it assumed the proportions of an immense city.

On Monday, May 19th, headquarters moved from White House at 7 a. m., to Tunstall's Station on the York railroad. This was the most beautiful camp of the entire campaign. It was at G. Bosher's plantation, on the summit of a high hill overlooking the entire country, and commanding a superb view in all directions.

The country was highly cultivated, being covered with fine plantations. Towards Richmond, about seventeen miles distant, the bivouacs of almost the entire army could be seen, stretching out in every direction, and at night the countless fires made it almost a fairy scene, grand and brilliant beyond description. It was about six miles from White House, three quarters of a mile from the Pamunkey, two miles from Lipscomb's. On the 20th, General Fitz John Porter's entire corps was reviewed, a magnificent spectacle as seen by all the officers on duty at headquarters. Rained heavily also on 24th. Cool nights and fires necessary.

May 22d, moved to near Cold Harbor, two miles from New Bridge and seven or eight from Richmond, and on the 26th moved at 2 p. m. nearer to the Bridge, at Dr. E. Curtis's farm. This was about three quarters of a mile northwest of Gaines's grist-mill and about a mile from the Chickahominy river, five miles from Richmond. It rained hard at 3 p. m.

Our brother in the artillery writes from Fort Tillinghast:

May 25, 1862.

We are now having some excitement in camp, as we received marching orders tonight, to be ready to march at a moment's notice, and the cooks are busily engaged cooking 'salt horse' for a march.

When I write again, I shall probably be out of this place. If we do not move from here for a day or two, I will get one taken (photo), so that you can see how your hopeful son looks since he 'went for a soldier.' I have not heard from Gene since he left, and think it strange. It is of no use to try to write, for there is such a 'hubbub' it is impossible. The boys are dancing, bellowing, and having a good time generally; they feel so good that there is a chance of at least getting sight of a 'Secesh.'

May 27, an important event occurred at headquarters, in the capture by some of General F. J. Porter's troops, of the mail bags en route from Richmond to Fredericksburg. There were about 500 papers in the bags, among them the *Richmond Dispatch* of that date. General Porter gave it in charge of our brother who took it immediately to General McClellan at headquarters. It doubtless furnished good material for post-prandial reading.

On the night of May 31, General McClellan made his headquarters on the field at Fair Oaks, at the Tyler house. It is related that about ten o'clock on this night he ordered all camp followers, including newspaper correspondents, without exception, to turn out on fatigue duty, and assist the details of soldiers in their work repairing the roads, and getting the artillery out of the mud.

Our brother of the regulars writes from Camp at New Bridge, Va , near Richmond, June 2, 1862:

I feel it my duty to write to you this evening, or I would be asleep at this moment. I have written so much of late that I am heartily sick of the sight of pen and ink. I was a recorder of a garrison court martial and I had to write up the proceedings, and it all amounted to nearly fifty pages. I will now endeavor to write you often, and keep you posted as well as my position will allow.

You have heard by telegraph that the Army of the Potomac has had a bloody and desperate fight. Our left and centre are on the other side of the Chickahominy; the left advanced some. We had one bridge across the river. The recent rains and the cutting away of the dams by the Rebels above, induced them to send about sixty thousand men down to attempt to clean out Heintzelman's entire corps, consisting of thirty thousand men, on Saturday.

They were determined to drive him into the river, which had risen fearfully, and drown as many as escaped them. They attacked our extreme left (General Casey's division) and drove us back, Casey's division behaving shamefully, skedaddling in all directions before a charge made by South Carolinians; but Henry Ward Beecher's pet lambs started it—the First Long Islanders. Old Heintzelman was up and dressed, and before night he had gained all that had been lost except twelve guns, which are now in the hands of the enemy. Very little artillery was used, as the position was unfavorable.

Night closed the scene. Report circulated that Generals Palmer, Casey, and Negley were killed; afterwards contradicted. Generals Franklin's and Fitz John Porter's corps, which occupy the right, were under arms, and old "Bull" Sumner's,[6] the centre corps, prepared for action. The attack commenced on Sumner's corps very early Sunday morning, but he had prepared two lines, covered by skirmishers, and it was evident that he intended to retrieve himself from his temporary disgrace at Williamsburg.

He led his corps in person, assisted by General McClellan, who rode in front of our skirmishers. 'Old Bull' was grand! His face as smooth as a mirror, and burning with enthusiasm. We had three corps engaged during the two days. Finally we gave them a polishing touch with our cold steel, and they skedaddled. Three thousand men will cover our losses. I know nothing of theirs, only two thousand went into Richmond wounded, and they now lie as thick as leaves about the battle ground.

---

[6] Edwin Vose Sumner (1797–1863) was the oldest field commander on either side in the war. He died of illness, not in combat.—2019

70

Our men fight splendidly. They would let the Rebels fire, and then give three cheers for the 'rat killers,' and sing out 'Bully for you—you fight pretty well!'

General McClellan regards it as a complete victory, and we know from deserters and contrabands just from Richmond that they have no hope of whipping us.

Wait until Generals Fitz John and Franklin touch them up with our regular brigade under General Sykes and our one hundred and four pieces of reserve artillery; and if everything else fails the provost guard will arrest the entire army. We took two of their brigadiers. I am very healthy, but suffer some from the heat. I weigh ten pounds more than when in Washington. I have received letters from K., B., and W., and will answer them when I get to Richmond. Don't be alarmed about Washington. If General McDowell cannot take care of 'Stonewall' Jackson, 'Little Mac' will send Fitz John up with a small portion of the Army of the Potomac. This army never yet met with a reverse, and it never will. I had charge of five hundred and fifty-nine rebels taken at Hanover Court-house for one day and night. None escaped me.

For the next week the floods descended, overflowing the river, flooding the roads and fields, and making movements of any kind almost impossible. The bridges were carried away, and there was a constant fire from the enemy upon the working parties. On the 6th, Colonel Sweitzer, one of General McClellan's aides, was fired upon while carrying a flag of truce into the enemy's lines. June 8th General Prim[7] and staff of the Spanish army arrived, stirring up headquarters to its depths. He came to White House Landing on the mail boat *Nellie Baker*. Accompanying him were Brigadier-General Milans del Bosch, chief of staff, Señor Justo San Miguel, Colonel Deutenre. Colonel Cortazar, Señor de Sales, and Señor Peres Calvo, the latter one of the most talented and widely-known writers of Spain.

Captain Joseph Keller, First New York Excelsior Cavalry, escorted them. They were received at the White House Landing by General Van Vliet, Lieutenant-colonel Rufus Ingalls, Captain

---

[7] Juan Prim, 1st Count of Reus (1814–1870), briefly Prime Minister of Spain until his assassination.—2019

C. Sawtelle and Captain Rankin, who escorted the party to Forest Station on the railroad; here they were met by the Prince de Joinville, and Count de Paris,[8] the French princes attached to General McClellan's staff. The ride from here to headquarters could be likened to the "Slough of Despond" in Bunyan. They rode through Generals Heintzelman's and Sumner's to General Hooker's camp, where they lunched; then to General W. F. Smith's camp, where a brigade was reviewed in the mud; thence to General Keyes's, and over the late battle-field of Fair Oaks, and finally brought up in the headquarter camp near New Bridge, much the worse for wear, being met by Generals Marcy, Andrew Porter, Seth Williams, and others.

General Prim was informally introduced to all the other officers at headquarters. He was a dark-faced, black-haired, bright, young looking man of about forty-five. He spoke only French and Spanish. General Milans, his chief of staff, spoke English and was the source of much amusement among all the officers. He seemed like the man in the play; he had iron grey hair and beard, with long, fierce mustachios of the Spanish cavalier type, and wore a loose, green coat well covered with silver embroidery; red pants tucked into his boots, and a funny little monkey cap perched on his head; a riding whip or stick was suspended from his buttonhole.

On the 9th, a grand review was given in their honor, the corps reviewed being Fitz John Porter's, and lasting from 2 to 3 p. m. It was witnessed by all at headquarters, and was considered a grand success, making a great impression upon the Spanish general, but not quite as brilliant as that given to Secretary Seward at Cumberland Landing.

It took place in a large open field on the right of the road from Gaines Mill to Mechanicsville.

---

[8] Prince Philippe, Count of Paris (1838–1894) and his brother served as Union officers. An historian, the Compte de Paris was later a respected scholar of the American Civil War.—2019

After the review, the party went with General F. J. Porter to the new bridge, upon which a large party was at work, and while there they were fired upon by the enemy. General Porter, taking charge of a battery near at hand, returned the fire with so much vigor that the enemy's guns were silenced, much to the delight of General Milans. On the 10th it rained in torrents; a programe had been laid out, but General Prim decided to hasten his departure. He was escorted to the station by Lieutenant T. B. Dewees of the Second Cavalry, and upon the arrival of the train at White House Landing he was again escorted to the boat by Colonels Van Vliet and Ingalls, and Captains Sawtelle and Rankin.

On the 12th, camp of the provost guard was moved to the south side of the Chickahominy at Dr. Trent's house. This was named by General Orders the same day, "Camp Lincoln," and was about one-half mile from the river, beautifully located on a high hill. General McClellan had his tent under two large walnut trees near the house, while the others were massed in a large field back of the house. While here the heat was intolerable. On this day there was heavy artillery firing, and on the 14th several arrests were made of citizens for giving information to the enemy.

On the 15th, a large party of ladies arrived in camp with Senator—. A heavy rain came up while they were at lunch in General McClellan's tent. About every evening camp was enlivened by a skirmish going on at some part of the line, and hearing the report of officers whose duties had called them to different points along the front.

On the 17th, the weather was again clear and bright, the mud commenced to dry up, and the river was falling rapidly; the bridges were nearly finished.

Our brother writes, June 18, 1862 as follows:

' Camp Lincoln. For the first time since the campaign commenced, I am a little unwell. I have a slight cold, and am inclined to be feverish, but it will all pass away, and I shall be the same lively, fat, jolly fellow as ever. I have not written to John, because I imagined that his regiment was with the standing joke, McDowell's army, and I did not know how to direct, nor do I now; but I will send to you when I write. It will be a long day before I get a leave of absence, and I may take an insane notion to get killed in front of Richmond.

Our brother of the artillery also writes, June 22, 1862:

I received a letter from Gene last night dated Camp Lincoln, across the Chickahominy, and he was momentarily expecting a fight. It was a short letter; he did not say anything about receiving any of my letters, so I suppose he did not get them. I directed to General Andrew Porter, Provost Marshal General, Headquarters Army of the Potomac, with his direction inside. I have entirely recovered from the asthma, but still have the grass cold, and suppose I shall have until fall, as the natives all skedaddled, and there is no one to do the haying.

They do not pay much attention here to haying, building no barns to store it as at home, but stacking it in the open field. They can keep their stock out to pasture nearly all the year round, as there is no snow to amount to anything. Mother, I wish you were out here for a short time to have some of the strawberries and cherries. The former have about gone. The 'Secesh' strawberries beat anything I ever saw at home, both for quality and quantity, wild and cultivated.

I have foresworn 'salt horse' and army rations, and intend to live on fruit during the summer, as the owners have cleared out, and the soldiers have it all their own way. As I write now, there is a bushel basket setting in my barrack, nearly filled with splendid cherries, and the boys gather about it, eating and talking over the war, when they shall get home, etc. After cherries come blackberries and blueberries; the bushes are full, and the peach-trees already begin to hang low with their weight of peaches. This is no country for apples, there being very few; but peaches even grow in the woods. I cannot live on such stuff as we get to eat, and the sutlers are robbers; yet we must trade with them or go without. I have already eaten so much salt meat that I am covered with humor. The boys now 'tap their shoes with salt horse.'

Lewis heard from his father last week; he was at Memphis, in good health, and enjoying himself generally. Lewis has been promoted to a second lieutenant. I am glad of it. The choice lay between himself and another sergeant. The colonel came up, and submitted it to a vote of the company, and he was voted down; but the colonel changed his mind, and they tossed up a cent, "best in

74

three," and Lewis won. He now acts as lieutenant, and the colonel has recommended him to the governor.

On the 23d of June, Camp Lincoln was visited by a terrible storm-thunder and lightning—and almost a hurricane, blowing down tents and trees in all directions.

On the 26th and 27th the attack was made upon the right flank of the army, which finally terminated with the change of base to the James river. The cannonading all day long was incessant on the 26th, and on the 27th, as it grew nearer, and the tide of battle surged towards the river, it became evident that a change was to be made at once.

About 2 p.m. headquarters commenced to move over to Savage's Station, and by dusk the camp at Dr. Trent's was practically abandoned. At 11 p. m., General McClellan called a council of war in front of his tent at Dr. Trent's, at which all corps commanders, personal aides, chief of engineers, the Prince de Joinville, Count de Paris, and the most trusted of his staff were present.

A large fire was built in front of, and they sat under, the arbor that had formed a pavilion to one of the tents, only one of which was now standing. General McClellan here informed all of his intended change of base, his reasons, choice of route, and method of execution. Our brother had charge of the guard around the bivouac fire. It did not adjourn until 2 a. m. of the 28th. Before daylight he went to Savage's Station, and there remained all that day and night, directing the withdrawal of trains, destruction of supplies, etc. Headquarters left Savage's between 2 and 3 a. m., on the 29th, and moved across White Oak Swamp to a large clearing. It drizzled, and there was a dense fog, which did not lift. The day and night at Savage's, and the intense strain and excitement of trying to stem the almost irresistible tide of fugitives and stragglers streaming to the rear, had almost exhausted the little provost guard, and now occurred a little incident which strongly demonstrates the necessity of having such a well-organized force for use in such an emergency.

75

The object of the enemy was to gain possession of the Quaker road in rear of White Oak Swamp, and thus cut off the retreat; a result which would have been most disastrous, if not absolutely fatal to General McClellan's plans. Early on the 29th, it was seen that the position of affairs was critical, owing to the fact that our line of movement had become known to the enemy. General McClellan was busy in examining the ground, keeping the trains in motion, and posting troops in such position as to cover their passage from attacks by way of New Market and Richmond roads. The columns were debouching from the swamp to the south side, and had reached a point near Willis Church, when an attempt was made by the enemy's cavalry to cut the lines. There was a sharp fight. Had Stuart's cavalry at that moment not all been on the north side of the Chickahominy, this attempt to check the retreat might have proved successful. As it was, it came near being so and creating a general panic. The provost guard, almost exhausted from their forty-eight hours of unremitting toil and vigilant watch, was deployed across the road in line of battle, and standing like a stone wall, it held all the would-be skedaddlers to their work.

Everything seemed on the point of going to pieces. All realized it, and the gallant little command, led by tired officers, who stemmed the rout at Bull Run, never did better service to the country than when it checked the threatened panic on the Quaker road. It is just such little acts of firmness on the part of a handful of men that have in times past saved great armies from defeat and total annihilation.

It is said that on this occasion, a well-known New York regiment fled to the rear in a perfect panic, and were not only checked by the provost guard, but were arrested and sent as prisoners to headquarters. On June 28th, Whitehouse was in charge of the Ninety-third New York, four companies of which were now attached to the provost guard. A signal station, about thirty or forty feet high, had been built on top of the house. At a given signal on this day, which was one gun fired for this purpose, the immense stores which had been accumulated all about the

76

house were fired by Lieutenant Swain, Company B, of that regiment, and they were totally destroyed, including the mansion itself.

At 5 a. m., on the 30th, headquarters were at a house about three miles south of White Oak Swamp, but as soon as all the troops had crossed, and the bridge was destroyed, it moved via Quaker road, across Turkey Creek bridge to Haxall's Landing, arriving soon after noon. From here our brother writes a hasty note,—

Bivouac near James river,

July 1, 1862.

> We have been fighting for three days. Communications cut off. Regular brigade covered itself with glory. Loss very heavy. I am well, and have to work very hard.

During the night of July 1, or early on the morning of the 2d, headquarters moved to Harrison's Landing, six miles from Haxall's, and camp was located at the Harrison House, where William Henry Harrison, President of the United States, was born.

For fully five miles up and down the James River, and for three miles back, the country was covered with the camps of the Army of the Potomac. It was about twenty-five miles in a direct line from Richmond, and eight or ten miles from City Point. On Monday, June 30, the French princes left headquarters for Fortress Monroe, on the gunboat *Jacob Bell*.

On the third of July, before camp could be made comfortable, our brother was detailed with his company to escort 480 prisoners of war to Fort Columbus, New York harbor. Lieut. J. A. Mchaffey accompanied him. They were placed on the United States transport *Hero*, Captain Hancox, and arrived at Fort Monroe about noon on the fourth.

Reaching New York on the sixth, they were turned over to Colonel Loomis, commanding, and Lieutenant Casey, provost marshal of the post, and the return was made immediately.

Among the prisoners was Lieut.-Col. Edward Pendleton,[9] Third Louisiana Artillery (see list of prisoners in the *New York Herald*, July 7, 1862), and 53 officers, two colonels, three lieutenant-colonels, and three majors.

He arrived back from this arduous trip July 9th. On the same day President Lincoln arrived on the steamer *Ariel*, with Assistant Secretary of War Watson, Frank P. Blair, Jr., and General Negley. On the way up the James River, the steamer grounded on Kettle Shoals, and while the crew were getting her off, the president and his party improved the opportunity to go in bathing. He reviewed the army, commencing in the afternoon and continuing into the evening, which although bright moonlight, was too dark to distinguish his features, thus proving a source of disappointment to the thousands of men who had never seen him. While at Harrison's Landing he visited the *Galena*, the *Monitor*, and *Maratanza*, and left the next morning at 10 a. m., on the *Ariel* for Fort Monroe.

On the 18th our brother wrote:

Camp near Harrison's Landing,

James River, Va.,

July 18, 1862.

"It is so warm here that writing seems almost out of the question, but I know you will expect a letter. If you would like to see the location of our camp, get a *Herald* of the 16th, but don't pay fifteen cents for it as I do every night. Our camp is directly opposite Jordan's Point. The line of officers' tents is situated on a high bluff, so near its edge that we can jump into the James River.

Our camp is in a thick wood we have cleared up until we have a large place for parade and drill, and upon the whole, I think we have the best camp in the Army of the Potomac. I was a little sick for two days after I returned, but now I am as well as ever. I did not have time while on my Northern trip to eat. The change of climate, diet, water, and living generally, made me almost sick, and honestly I felt like a new man when I arrived back at camp. I was very uneasy

---

[9] Third Brigade, A. P. Hill's Light Division.—2019

while on my way from Fortress Monroe to Fort Columbus, for I knew that one company was a very-small escort for the number of prisoners I had with me, and I knew they were a determined and bloodthirsty set.

The steamer was a miserable old hulk to go so far in. I kept my eyes open, and if they had attempted any outbreak, many of them would never have lived to see the 'sunny South' again. I kept the leading spirit, Colonel Pendleton, under my eye constantly, and although our intercourse was very friendly, he knew his life was not worth a copper if any movement was made. I am trying for the adjutancy of the Eighth. If I do not get it, I am thinking very strongly of taking a lieutenant-colonelcy of a Maine regiment, with Frank as colonel.

Maine men fight well, and I would rather be with them than any other volunteers. I can command my company for a very long time yet it I wish it, but regular officers are thought so little of now . that almost anything is preferable to remaining in the regular service.

Our paymasters 'skedaddled' so fast on the famous 'flank movement,' that they have not yet made their appearance and consequently we are all short of cash. John will now see all the activeness he wishes; I hope and trust he will come out safe. Impress him with the necessity of keeping clean, and being careful about his eating. Tell him never to throw away his knapsack, and always to have three days' rations on hand.

July 24,

Provost Guard Camp,

near Harrison's Landing, Va.

I have been upon a court martial for several days, and have been pretty busy. I suppose we will adjourn tomorrow unless General Williams sends us another batch of cases, and I sincerely hope he will not, for I am tired of 'banging.' Dr. Frantz, our surgeon, left us this morning, and with him as faithful a Negro as ever breathed. The doctor has been with us since we left Washington, and has always messed with me. We took Jerry from the guard-house (he was a contraband) at Yorktown, and he has been faithful and true, while others 'skedaddled.'

Poor Jerry allowed two or three large drops to fall from his eyes when he bade me good-by, and I acknowledge I felt badly. The doctor goes to Fort Monroe as medical purveyor. We were fast friends, and I felt sorry to have him go. Our new medico is a very fine fellow; he messes with me, and we bid fair to be as fast friends as Frantz and myself. Major Willard has recommended me for a brevet, and I reckon I will get it. General Porter promised when we started out on this duty, to give us all a fair chance, and those who attended to their duties well would be remembered. I think the General recommended Major Willard, Captain Frank, Lieutenant Smith, and myself for the Pamunkey expedition.

Major W. received an order a few days since to send in a list of officers in his command, whom he considered worthy of brevets, and he wrote a long letter to the General, recommending Frank, Smith, and myself. He showed the letter to me. I do not care for the brevet so much, but it pleases me to be mentioned as highly as I have been. A soldier's life is very uncertain, especially in battle, for we cannot tell when or where, as 'Old Bull' Sumner says, 'the hell the balls will strike.'

This is a bloody war, and 'doubtful things are mighty uncertain.' The Army of the Potomac is flourishing, and the provost guard is on the top wave. We have a boat to ourselves, and we row, fish, and sail, waiting for reinforcements. The health of the army is rapidly increasing, and if you will only send the loafing, cowardly devils that got home under the plea of sickness, and had their certificates signed by rascally surgeons, we will do something as we are. The entire Southern Confederacy cannot move us one pin, unless they, by some means, cut off our communications with Fortress Monroe, Our gunboats are the little fellows that play the deuce with them. I have never said much about the 'flank movement' for many reasons, but I will now tell you the truth about the matter.[10]

We had to keep what force we had across the Chickahominy; it weakened our right flank and line of communication, and we could not strengthen it, because we had not the means. McCall was

---

[10] While at White House, G. O. No. 125 was published, strictly prohibiting all officers of the army from communicating in private letters the strength, position, or movement, etc., of the army, under penalty of punishment for giving information to the enemy.—note in original

attacked; he was supported by Fitz John Porter. and together they drove the Rebels back; in the meanwhile, 1 Stonewall' Jackson was at Hanover Junction, twenty-five miles from Mechanicsville. In spite of the gallant trio in front of Washington, he made a forced march to outflank Porter and succeeded. They were rapidly reinforced from Richmond by rail, and Porter could not get away as it was intended.

The intention was to have him come off during the night, cross the swamp, and leave the Rebels in the dark, and go into Richmond the next morning, or else to the James river. Porter had to fight desperately to get away at all; he had not 30,000 men under him, and he had to fight three times that number. The regular division alone fought 20,000 al] day long at the Gaines house.

John Edwards[11] lost two guns through the confounded willfulness of a brigadier-general. John acted splendidly, and is one of the best artillery officers in the service.

Well, Porter retreated. Headquarters moved to Savage's Station. On Friday evening, all the generals commanding corps had a council of war. I commanded the guard around the bivouac fire. I saw them adjourn. The next morning the movement commenced. We left Savage's Sunday. I saw General McClellan at White Oak Swamp, and he was very cool. I saw him the morning of the Battle of Malvern Hill, and he was a little excited. I was very near him and heard him give his orders, and anyone who says he is not a competent general lies. His retreat was conducted with most consummate skill; the turning moment was when he arrived at the river.

It was the letter dated March 4, 1862, from Camp Winfield Scott, in which he prophesied that France would recognize the Confederacy within a month, and he hoped every man and boy in the great North would shoulder his musket and give themselves to their country, that hastened the enlistment of the other two brothers of this quartette, and called forth the following letters:

---

[11] Brevet Lieutenant-Colonel John Edwards, captain Third U. S. Artillery, was born in Portland, Me.; graduated from the military academy, July 1, 1851.—note in original. It was Lt. Horace Hayden's guns that were captured by the 20th North Carolina regiments. (Ward, 2018).

Aug. 2, 1862.

I feel very sad, more so than I ever did before, for I feel as though I should never see all my brothers again. I believe as you do that two better boys were never born, and to lose either by sickness or wounds, I know it would be a crushing blow to me, but I feared it, and now that it is done, my experience enables me to give them some good advice, and you must see that they follow it. They are coming from a Northern climate into a much warmer and unhealthy one; the heat and water will affect them, I know. Give them some Jamaica ginger; it is the best thing in the world. Tell them to be careful what they eat, and never under any circumstances whatever to eat fried meat. They can eat fried pork when fried upon a stick.

This one thing, together with what is called 'fried hardtack' (hard bread fried in fat), has caused more sickness than anything else; I know it! Tell them never to throw away their knapsacks, haversacks or canteens, and shelter tents, if they have them.

Tell them to always keep their clothes in as good order as possible. Get them commissions if you can, commissioned officers if possible, if not non-commissioned, and get them into an old regiment by all means.

Your idea of sending them here into Captain Thompson's regiment is an admirable one, and you must do it. All depends upon the commanding officer of a company. My company has not averaged three sick men per day, and during the entire month of July, I did not have more than three sick. I allow no frying, but give them plenty of bean soup and hard bread. I draw onions, cabbages, and potatoes often, and fresh beef once or twice a week.

Frank's company is like mine, and we pride ourselves upon having the two model companies in this army. I think the two other companies of the Eighth will be ordered here, and the provost guard will then be the Eighth Infantry under the command of Captain Pitcher. Major Willard is going to take command of a volunteer regiment (One Hundred and Twenty-fifth New York), and wants me to be major.

I expect Mother will feel terribly sad at parting with Walter and Bob. Tell her to keep up, for she is a noble mother. You also, my dear Father, must not allow it to depress you. Look upon the bright side; but I write you with a heart overflowing with sadness, that you

82

will be extremely fortunate if you ever see all of your four sons again.

If any of us should fall, you must think that you are not alone in your sadness; that there are many homes more miserable and desolated by the loss of sons and brothers as dear to them as yours are to you. Everything is quiet. The Rebels attempted to shell our camp the other night, from across the river, but we soon made them skedaddle.

Aug. 4, 1862.

I feel this evening as if I would be unworthy to be your boy, if I did not write to you. I know that your hour of trial and bereavement is at hand, for you are to part with your last and youngest boy [Robert, our author]; but, Mother, do not allow it to affect you. If they are with the Army of the Potomac, they shall never know what it is to want for anything as long as I have enough; and if they should be wounded, they should be cared for and taken to my own tent.

But do not think of such things. It will be a godsend if they both get into the same company. Send them to Captain Thompson's company. I will see him tomorrow, and my word for it, they will receive a hearty welcome.

I wish the government would draft; there are a few people in this world I would like to see driven to the battle-field; and it must be done sooner or later, for we are in need of men very much. The Rebels are straining every nerve and filling this state with troops, and I really would not be surprised to hear at any moment that they had forced their way to Washington; but Richmond falls at the same moment, and then their supplies are cut off, and if we have reinforcements, they are all lagged.

Important movements are on foot, but it is a secret. We have crossed the river in large force, and whipped their cavalry in a fair fight. General Hooker advanced and seized Malvern Hill this evening. General Burnside is coming up the river, and Fort Darling will be taken in a short while.

Major Willard leaves us shortly to take a volunteer regiment. He has offered me a majority, and I shall accept, provided I can obtain a leave. My health is excellent; I weigh twenty pounds more than when in Washington. My duties are now light, and I have an easy time.

Our camp is the envy of the army, and our position as provost guard sought after by all the regulars; but the Eighth Infantry was noted while in Washington for the prompt discharge of all duties (and they always have been), and we will be kept here against all aspirants. It is extremely warm, and the flies are very troublesome. Good-night! God bless you, my dear Mother, is the prayer of your loving son. All was "quiet on the James."

On August 13, our brother went home on a short leave of absence, while the army was remaining inactive at Harrison's Landing. He joined headquarters again about September 1, at or near Washington, and marching with General McClellan again in command of the army, through Rockville, Clarksville, Urbana, and Frederick, we met him on the battlefield of South Mountain.

Alas! how near we came to following his sage advice, the advice of a regular officer to two volunteer privates, in an old regiment from Antietam to the siege of Petersburg, during the next two years of bloody struggle, will be most amusing to note, and a gentle retrospect at this period always reminds the writer of a non-combatant friend who visited us at Fredericksburg about the time of the Burnside "Mud March." He was attached to some state commission. He distributed some of *Dr. Hall's Laws on Health*, gave us all sound advice, a most learned and valuable lecture as to how to take care of our health, and hastened home himself the next day, having caught a most violent cold while sleeping on our rough pole bunk in the damp, although we had nearly stripped the tent that night for blankets to keep him warm.

From this time on, the fates of the "Four Brothers in Blue" were joined together, and the anxiety which each displayed for the other was never relieved night or day until news from the battlefield denied or confirmed the many rumors that were ever flying about in camp or on the march.

When nearby, miles would be traversed to gain each other's camp, and on more than one occasion, he—the regular— whenever in a position where he could do so, rode over the battlefields to gain news of us, .or satisfy himself that we were not among the wounded or the silent dead.

What Northern man, or he who was a boy at the outbreak of the war, can look back upon those stormy days, and not remember the flushed face, the eager glance, the heavy, anxious hearts of all? Who does not recall when that fateful spring of 1861 opened, fraught with wild rumors of political troubles and national disasters, the thrill that darted through his heart like an electric shock, and the swelling, choking sensations in his throat, when the amazing, almost stupefying announcement came flashing along the wires of the attack upon Fort Sumter?

The flag, "Old Glory," our "Stars and Stripes," had been mocked, spit upon, torn down, and trampled underfoot. This certainly meant war, and if the great and powerful North had been blind or asleep before, and had turned a deaf ear to those who had for a long time seen the storm coming, she could no longer resist this practical appeal to the patriotism of her sons.

The resolve came instantly—that come what may, the insult must be atoned, and "wiped out."

Men and women, girls and boys, became as it were one power. Business—except with the more avaricious and sordid—was almost entirely neglected; rosettes of tricolored ribbons, tiny flags, and medallion pictures of the President, were worn upon the breast or in the hair of everybody. The warlike and inspiring sound of drum and fife was heard all over the land. Men of brains and means hurried forth with their cool heads and ready pockets to direct and bring dire confusion and chaos to a standstill, and to stay the tide of excitement until order could reign and system regulate.

The writer was too young to go, but his heart was continually fired, and many a day in the cornfield, his hand grasped the hoe with a firmer grip, and he almost imagined each blade of corn a rebel of the deepest dye, and until he awoke from his warlike thoughts, there was danger of total destruction to the innocent crop of his imaginary foes.

86

During these troublous times there was no spirit for work. Amidst this inspiration of war, throbbing and wildly surging through his veins, he had obtained consent of his parents, and following the bent of his own inclinations, although but fifteen years of age, on April 20. 1861, had started in a perfect deluge of rain for Boston, and attempted to enlist in Company G, (Hale Guards) Fifth Massachusetts Volunteers, from Haverhill, Massachusetts. It was already filled to overflowing; this, and his age caused him to be peremptorily rejected.

He was, therefore, doomed amidst the vibration and clamor of war to wait, and sigh and wish. What a year of expectancy and wistful waiting that was! How many nights did we toss on our pillow, too excited to sleep; and how busy were our restless brains! Bull Run came like a thunderbolt upon our confused senses. At last, 1862 came along, crowded with fast thickening events. A special call for 300,000 more troops had been made: our army had met with repulse on the Peninsula, and our brother's letter of May 4th from General McClellan's headquarters seemed to inspire anew the patriotic ardor which we had attempted to suppress and stifle during that long year of waiting, hoping; of anxiety and fears.

We watched the companies drill, saw them depart one by one for the "Front," first our eldest brother, then an uncle, and many cousins and kin. How we did chafe! Many an aircastle did we build, only to have it rudely torn down, by an awakening to a stern realization of our duties. The constant cackling of loud-voiced politicians, and the "stay-at-home" warriors, with their ever-ready cry of "On to Richmond!" was daily heard.

Things looked gloomy, indeed. The writer had grown in a year, and was large for his age. Why could he not pass for eighteen years of age? He determined to try again. He went to the nearest rendezvous at "Camp Stanton," Lynnfield, Massachusetts, where the Thirty-third Massachusetts was then being organized, but his conscience began to prick. Like the "Immortal George" he felt that he could not stifle it for so trifling a cause. Upon announcing to the recruiting officer that he was sixteen, he was immediately rejected; resulting in a decidedly cold bath to our zeal and patriotic ardor, now at the boiling-point.

There was not then that eagerness displayed for such young volunteers as was afterwards shown in the war.

There was no other way than to gain the necessary stretch of two years in our age. We felt then, and have always felt since, that the Lord would forgive us, and in a few days, that gain was announced at the same rendezvous, and to the same officer, and we were greedily examined, accepted, and upon reporting in Boston, our enlistment papers were made out by Lieutenant W. H. White, Twenty-second Massachusetts, August 5, 1862, who was recruiting for that regiment.

His office was on the west side of Sudbury Street, about half way down to Haymarket square. Our brother Walter, three years older, here joined us for the same regiment, and on the same day our little squad was transferred to Camp Cameron, North Cambridge, and was on that day mustered into the United States service by Captain J. B. Collins, United States Army, and we were now full-fledged recruits for Company H, Twenty-second Massachusetts Volunteers.

The writer was now the youngest of four brothers in the Union army. Our informal or unofficial enlistment was made at a large and enthusiastic war meeting held on the village common in front of the First Congregational church, at Bradford, Massachusetts, July 23, 1862, at which our father presided. An interesting account is given in full in the Haverhill *Tri-Weekly Publisher* of July 24. Our father explained his reasons for consenting that such youthful sons should thus be given to the cause; he might urge as a plea against their going into the service, that two were already in the army; but at the conclusions of his remarks "he brought them forward and gave them to his country, and with them some eight or ten more, youthful and strong—the very flower of the community. The scene was indeed a thrilling one, and will form a brilliant record in the history of the war."

Many letters were written from Camp Cameron during our brief stay, giving a description of our plain barracks, with the hard, board bunks; the cold nights in which we tried to sleep; the many friends coming to see us, and filling us so full of the good things of this life that the writer had a serious attack of cholera morbus, etc., etc. We were all happy and jolly in this camp, but, oh, my! weren't we raw? All was hurry and scurry; sergeants, who had been sent from their regiments for this purpose, were organizing and assigning the recruits, now pouring in under this second call, to squads in barracks. They were supervising the issue of clothing, rations, etc.

There was no time for drill. We lay upon the hard bunks first without mattresses or blankets, and then with a straw tick and only a few old quilts, sent to us from home.

We marched on guard with one set of old muskets for all the reliefs; many were minus locks, bayonet, gun slings, etc. How strange it all seemed to our young imaginations! How proud we felt as we grasped that worthless old weapon—harmless as a club—and paced up and down that peaceful beat, as we had been diligently instructed to do, in the dark hours of the night!

The 12 o'clock, and "A-a-a-l-l-s w-e-e-e-l!" rang out in the still, clear air, as it went forth from No. 1, at the guard-house, and happy boys were we when our turns came, although we were afraid our voices trembled just a little, as we reflected upon the fearful responsibilities that seemed to be resting upon us with such a crushing weight.

How we peered forth into the night, that no object should escape our vision, or sound our ear, and oh, how mean and guilty we fell when we heard the threatening voice of some old soldier, who was returning from a "French leave," say "Sentinel, turn your back and walk the other way," and a large watermelon shot over our beat, followed by the precipitate rush of its several owners! But they were no enemy! And this was not the "Front," but only "Old Camp Cameron," and, as soon as our consciences cleared up a little, we felt better.

At last, all was ready for our departure, and on Friday, August 15, 1862, we left via the Fall River Line steamer *Metropolis* for New York. Our dear father and mother followed us into Boston, with eyes full of tears. We marched to the tap of the drum, and were, in our ill-fitting, grotesque uniforms, the proudest boys in the world.

Four of us had sung as a quartette, and our "John Brown's Body," "Marching Along," and "We Belong to Gideon's Band," rang out at intervals, the outpouring of happy hearts. The parting from our parents was a sad one, the first in our young lives, and had it not been for the excitement of the occasion, and the jolly companionship of our comrades, it would have proved too much for us. We left them sorrowing over the last boys they could send to war.

We slept on the floor of the cabin on the boat, for we were now soldiers, and enjoyed our sleep. Upon arriving in New York the next morning, we were marched to the barracks on Franklin Street. Here we met with our first experience of filth and wretchedness. The hard side of our plank was coming uppermost.

Sour, greasy, loathsome food, and cold slop coffee were issued, at which our stomachs revolted, and we cast it aside; and the mouldy, vermin-laden floors made our bodies rebellious. Our letters say, "We had some string beans for dinner that would have puzzled mortal man to dissect. I don't believe the like of them was ever seen before. I don't see how anyone could have gone to work to get up such a unique mess. It was an insult to a soldier to offer such a mess to him."

Late in the afternoon we left New York by boat, via South Amboy and Camden, for Philadelphia. Arriving at Camden, we crossed the ferry at the foot of Washington avenue, and were glad to find ourselves in good old Philadelphia. A walk of a few yards along the avenue, and around the corner to Otsego street, brought us to the Cooper Shop Volunteer Refreshment saloon, which was fifty yards south on the latter street. A few moments later, after a refreshing wash, we were waited upon by a bevy of Christian ladies, overflowing with sympathy and kindness, who served to us

90

the first good, wholesome, clean food since our enlistment, and which we relished exceedingly-

The little, low, narrow cars on the Camden and Amboy road were dimly lighted with candles a part of the night, which cast a sickly glimmer over all. They were redolent with the stifling odor of bad pipes, worse whiskey, strong onions, and the villainous exhalations of many perspiring bodies. The air in the famous "Black Hole" of Calcutta could not have been more foul.

We were tired out, sleepy, and non-combatant. We tried to be cheerful—for recruits—by singing our old songs, and attempting a feeble sort of a joke now and then, but occasionally a regular old-fashioned growl escaped us. The candles went out, leaving us in impenetrable darkness and gloom. The road was rough, and most of the night a burly, drunken Irishman, over flowing with bad whiskey and pugilistic ambition, amused himself, but nobody else, by passing along the narrow aisle, bumping our drowsy heads against the seats, snatching our caps off and throwing them away into the darkest portions of the car.

If we mildly demurred in our desire for peace, he threatened to thrash us, "knock a lung" out of us, etc., and as we did not want that to happen so soon after we had enlisted, and before we had actually seen the "front," we patiently bore it for a while. Then two of us, our stalwart brother and myself, got near to where a light from one of the small windows glimmered in, and watching our opportunity when the bully was passing, energetically "knocked him out in one round," into a corner, extracted the "benzine" from his pocket, poured it out, and as the result, enjoyed peace, if not comfort, the remainder of the night.

He never knew who or what hurt him, and the next morning, wore upon a smiling face, somewhat disfigured by a mourning eye, the happiness he felt that the whiskey had "let go."

At six o'clock we were again about to move, and taking a train from the corner of Broad street and Washington avenue, over the Philadelphia, Wilmington & Baltimore railroad, were soon speeding on our way to Baltimore, which we reached about 12, and after taking a light lunch of crackers, cheese, and coffee, kindly furnished by some good Samaritans at the depot, we were placed in a cattle freight train, and after jolting slowly on, seeing for the first time in our lives the tobacco fields, the Negroes working, the large plantation houses and quarters far removed from the road, etc., we arrived in Washington, completely exhausted by our travels on land and sea, and overcome mentally and physically by this continual round of excitement to our youthful senses.

We were sent to the "Soldiers' Retreat,"—an excellent name for a very vile place. Oh, such a retreat! So soothing and quieting!(?) Where leather pies at exorbitant prices, and chicory slop for coffee, boiled in the same kettles with greasy pork, prevailed, causing our cake-and-pie-nurtured stomachs to revolt and the filthy floors made our bodies shrink away and shiver.

At night, to our New England ears Pandemonium seemed to be turned loose. It was, we believe, sometimes called the "Soldiers' Rest." Oh, what a Rest! If we rested there during those exciting nights and days of our embryonic soldierhood, we have never been able to realize or appreciate it after the lapse of more than thirty-five years. It now stands (1897) just north of the B. & O. depot, on New Jersey Avenue, and is used as a freight office.

"Nineteen thousand eight hundred and sixty volunteers arrived in Washington from the 15th to five o'clock on the evening of the 22d. All had to be fed one meal, and too much credit cannot be awarded the commissariats at the 'Retreat,' Messrs. Donahoe and Searles, who are at work night and day, personally superintending this vast boarding and sleeping saloon."—*National Intelligencer*, August 23, 1862.

Rations For Recruits.

War Department, Adjutant-General's Office, Washington, D. C., Aug. 20, 1862.

Orders No. 113.

Detachments of recruits will be furnished with at least two days' cooked rations before starting from the depot for their regiment. If delayed in any city en route, a detachment will be marched to the 'Soldiers' Rest,' where additional cooked rations will be issued to the men to last until their arrival at the next 'Rest,' or at the destination of the detachment, according to circumstances.

By order of the Secretary of War.

E. D. Townsend,[1]

Assistant Adjutant-General.

Our first letter is dated:

Washington, D. C.,

Sunday, August 17, 1862, five o'clock p. m.

We have been in Washington just one-half hour, having come through Baltimore today. We have eaten our rations at the volunteer receiving room, consisting of the most horrid coffee and bread, so George Ball says (I did not eat any). We are now in the recruiting barracks for the night.

We go early in the morning to our various regiments; when, where, or how we know not. It is expected that we are to march to Fort Albany. I have sent word to John to that effect. Probably it will never reach him. There are over 1,000 men in the room where I am writing. Some are playing cards for money; some cursing; some playing games, and in general singing, and doing things contrary to our New England Sabbath rules. Edgar, George, and myself are in the middle of the room, stretched out full length, and are the only ones that are writing home, and it was only to relieve your anxiety that I know you at this present moment feel, that I endure the disagreeable position in which I am now placed.

We stopped in New York all day Saturday, after coming in the *Metropolis* from Fall River. We marched about two miles up Broadway to Franklin street barracks. At night we started for South Amboy, about forty miles, in a ferry steamer; we got there about eight; traveled all night in cars that were about six by ten; stopped about three or four hours on the road near peach orchards. The boys got out and got all they wanted; that was about twelve o'clock

---

[1] No military man met more often with Abraham Lincoln and Edwin Stanton than Major-General Edward Davis Townsend. See his memoir, *Saving the Union*, 2014, BIG BYTE BOOKS

at night; we didn't have lights in the cars, neither did we have places to sleep in, but we were crowded in like sheep.

Arrived at Camden about four o'clock; crossed the river to Philadelphia, where we were splendidly treated; went into the far-famed Cooper establishment, and had a nice breakfast at five o'clock; the only good meal that we have had since we left home. 'God bless the Quaker city!' Why, Mother, the truth is, soldiers are of no account, and are treated like dogs wherever they go; but I am bound to stick by, and do my best. I never experienced such a passage as I have on my way thither. We have ridden day and night, and suffered all the hardships of common cattle. I have not slept but once, and that was on the Fall River steamer. We all slept on the floor. Bob is now well and sends his ambrotype.[2]

We had an awful night's passage to Philadelphia on the Camden & Amboy R. R. We were awake all night, surrounded by roughs and drunken soldiers. We had a small fight, and I left the mark of my fist on a drunken rowdy's eye. I cut it and blacked it, and no sooner had I got through with him, than Bob gave him a pelter that knocked him down.

The bully insulted us, and squared off to hit one of our Twenty-second boys, and Bob and I pitched in. We are disgusted with our journey, and now only long to reach our regiment, even if the battlefield is open before us immediately, so long as we are in the midst of discipline. We marched through Philadelphia, started for Baltimore at six, got into Baltimore about twelve; marched up West Pratt Street, the famous place where they had the riot [April 19, 1861]. Everything was quiet, it being the Sabbath.

On the Susquehanna we crossed at Havre de Grace on a boat; the cars ran right on it, and then we crossed. We remained at Baltimore Depot until 1:30 o'clock, then they put us aboard the train for Washington The cars were baggage cars with boards nailed in for seats. Well, now for the route. It beat everything I ever saw. 'Niggers' everywhere. The meeting-houses are different; the grass, the soil, the fences (what there were of them, for there are plaguey few). There are immense plantations of this great Southern corn and tobacco, growing in red soil, with no fences up in front, and the houses way up in the middle of the field.

---

[2] This was taken on Broadway, Saturday, Aug. 16, 1862.—note in original

The train went about as fast as I could run all the way, forty miles. We had a good time on top, looking around. They stopped at the famous Relay House. I saw the viaduct where the First Massachusetts Battery guarded. We stopped again on the route to water up. I went up in a field to a plastered nigger hut. What a sight! About ten little 'nigs,' about of a size all going to see the 'sojers' Massa.'[3]

She (the woman) gave me some native tobacco as a curiosity. We arrived at Washington about o'clock; went into this coop where we are all writing. I told the boys a little while ago that I was bound to go around and see the sights; they were afraid, because there were guards stationed at the doors, but I got out a good way, and went to see the elephant. I first walked to the capitol and went up into the dome, wrote my name, saw all the beautiful pictures that you have heard so much about, and all around the different rooms.

From the top of the dome I saw Long Bridge, Arlington Heights, General Lee's house, and Fort Albany; I went down Pennsylvania avenue, and saw all the business part of the city: Willard's [Hotel], the Treasury, the famous White House, the War Department, the Smithsonian institute, and Washington monument, patent office, etc. I walked through the gardens where portly senators and the high gentry of the land have trod. In fact, I looked at everything of importance in the city, and saw sights I never expected to see, and which I may never see again. I never saw such quiet in a city where military movements are carried on in such a grand scale. There is no life, no excitement; I never should know from its outward appearance that it was threatened by a rebel army, nor should I in the least dream that it was our national capital, except by its public buildings.

It lacks all the supposed grandeur of a presidential city, a royal abiding place.

I have just come back. I cannot write to you now as I would if I were in a nice place. This is full of men hollering, fiddling, etc., so I cannot write well. I had my picture taken in New York just for the

---

[3] One is tempted to believe the offensive epithet was common among all Northern boys but some soldiers made note of their disdain especially for officers who "could not correctly pronounce 'Negro.'" See also, Hallowell and Sherman, 2019, BIG BYTE BOOKS.

fun of it; it isn't very good, but I thought, dear Mother, that you would like to see me as I am in uniform.

Alexandria was our next objective point. Our letters of August 19, say:

We started from Washington at 5:30 o'clock this morning, and after marching two miles, went aboard of a river steamer, and came down here to Alexandria. It is six miles from Washington, and the ride is fine. We are in an old 'secesh' house, quartered until further orders. We are to stay here in Alexandria today, and I am going to try and see John four miles from here. I couldn't help thinking of you at five o'clock this morning (only think of it!), when I got up and took my housewife to put on a button. I have put a side pocket into my coat, and am really an adept in needle and thread yet. I spent a most horrid night in our barracks on the outskirts of the city. There were over 1,000 men, raw recruits, on the floor, and such a noise I never heard.

I never slept a wink all night. It did seem like a hell upon earth; most barbarous profanity and hideous screaming were heard all night, and it was cold as Greenland, and I slept (?) cold.

We have not been furnished with woolen blankets, and a hard, board floor, covered with filth, is not very pleasant. However, I do not complain, although I do wish the upper sides of the planks were a little softer.

My resolves before I left Boston have been sorely tempted out here, but all my good principles still remain firm. We have to write any way, on our knees or on the floor. We don't know where we shall go to from this hole, for McClellan is moving, and therefore they don't know where to send us; but I do hope, for Heaven's sake they will get us off soon, as I think this is the worst we shall see— this knocking around in Camp Cameron, and barracks in different cities. While I was out in the city (yesterday) George Ball was taken with a violent colic, and suffered everything for about an hour. When I got to the 'Rest' I found him bent up double in an empty barrack, with Frank Kimball over him, rubbing his stomach with whiskey. I stayed and helped Frank, and soon he was himself again. Ed Holt was sick all day, but Virginia air is improving him. Leroy Kimball is most miserable, and looks a fit subject for a hospital. We are tenderly nursing him. Bob is now well, and I was never better in

96

my life. Loss of sleep and hard usage have thinned me a good deal in flesh, but my eye is bright in health. There is a certain something in my system that defies disease.

We are all wondering why F. Kimball stands it so well. He is in first-rate spirits. Morrison, the one who lived at Nat. Carleton's, and threw down his scythe when his country called, has been well also, although he has eaten every kind of fruit and vegetable. He has already received the sobriquet of 'Gingerbread.' He eats all the time, and after four of our recruits had died in the barracks in Washington, from eating poisoned fruits sold by the peddlers, and he was warned of his danger, he said he had made up his mind not to starve, even if he was poisoned.

He wrote home that he was never coming back from the 'sacred soil.' He is a quaint specimen of the genus homo, and keeps us roaring at his remarks.

I sent word over to John yesterday by Ed Walton (who took advantage of his Fourteenth-regiment dress), when he went to Fort Albany, that Bob and I were in the city, and wanted him if possible, to come over and see us, as it was impossible for us to get over to see him. He sent word by Ed that it was just as impossible for him to get over to Washington. We couldn't get a pass over Long Bridge, so we have missed seeing him. When I found out that this was our route, I had 'lotted [*sic*] upon seeing him, and was very much disappointed.

I have been all over the city; seen the Marshall House, where Ellsworth was killed,[4] and the slave pen. It is a dirty place, this hotbed of secession, but the people seem kind and pleasant. They are obliged to, for the streets are full of Union soldiers. At night they place small American flags over 'secesh' residences, and if they are removed the occupants suffer well. They clean them out. It is amusing to see the 'nigs' in Washington. They are the most aristocratic personages I ever beheld. Here they are the most abject,

---

[4] Elmer Ephraim Ellsworth (1837–May 24, 1861) was a law clerk to Abraham Lincoln and the first Union officer to die in the war. He went to the Marshall House to remove a Confederate flag that was visible from Washington and was killed by a shotgun blast as he was coming down from the roof with the flag. Lincoln called him "the greatest little man I ever knew." Ellsworth's body lay in state in the White House.—2019

and cringe at a white man. The teams and carriages have the most grotesque appearance. We shall probably stay here in Alexandria until we find out where McClellan has moved to, and then shall join our regiment. Stirring events are soon to happen in Virginia, and I know that in less than two weeks the 'raw recruits' are to go into the ranks to meet the foe.

God help me to nerve myself manfully for the fight. I am hopeful, and full of bright anticipation. May I always be as happy as I am now! The streets are full of rumors—Pope retreating; then he is victoriously engaged; again, he is advancing. All our troops are leaving Culpepper, and the sick and wounded of the Cedar Mountain fight are arriving in town, and it is a sickening sight to see them, without either arm or leg, and a gash here and there over their poor, languishing bodies. I have already seen enough among the wounded to lead me to hope that my lot may not fall among them.

Quite a number of men for the Twenty-second from the hospitals, where they have been for the last few months, came along with us, to join our regiment. They gave me some heart-rending accounts. I was talking yesterday on King street with a young lieutenant of an Ohio regiment, who has a ball in his shoulder, and he says there is work ahead, and in our immediate vicinity. I shall soon be in the fight, I know. I went in swimming this morning with some of the boys, in the Potomac River.

I send you my ambrotype." (It cannot be found.)

The weather was oppressively hot. Although under the control of a provost marshal, the results of the war were seen in the dilapidated buildings and filthy streets. The house we occupied, on the corner of King and Fairfax(?) streets, was alive with vermin, and what we first thought was the ground itch, prickly rash, or some other kindred disease incident to our new experience and change of climate, habits of life, food, etc., soon proved to our uninitiated recruits to be the genuine and unmistakable "grey-back [lice]."

Owing to the non-energetic nature of the officer in charge of us, Captain H. P. Williams, Twenty-second Massachusetts, and some imperative duty, or mysterious business, that always kept him in

Washington, we were left to shift for ourselves. Our resources were few, but we were compelled to rely mainly upon the little money we had, and so far as rations, clothing, or any of the ordinary allowances provided by the government for organized or unorganized bodies are concerned, we endured, and unnecessarily, while here, more than for the next two years, except on several occasions of extreme exigency.

We marched through the streets of Alexandria, singing, and as martyrs to the slaughter, our knapsacks on our backs, the perspiration flowing like water, to this old, deserted house. Our letters continue:

Alexandria, Va., Aug. 20, 1862.

We don't know when we shall leave here. It may be this day, or tomorrow, or a week, but I hope we shall leave soon, as I am sick of this place already. The guard has just come up and says we may go at any moment, so I must hurry. What will Leroy do? He is sick with a fever upstairs. But we must go, and if he can't keep up, he will have to go into the Alexandria hospital. Poor fellow! I am writing on a board on my knee. I send you this card as a curiosity. The boys are having their pictures taken, and I got this to send to you.

It is awful writing, but I can't help it, as I am tired holding this board. The order has come for us to go, and I must defer this letter till another time, when I know not. We go to camp about one and three-fourths miles from here, there to remain a few days.

From Alexandria we moved on the 20th of August to the heights in the rear of the south of the city. It was near Fort Ellsworth, and the camp, which was designated as "Camp Excelsior," was commanded by Colonel J. S. Belknap, Eighty-fifth New York Volunteers. It was on the summit of Shuter's hill, overlooking Alexandria, and between the Little River and Leesburg turnpikes.

On the crest of the hill, and but a few yards from our tents, was a small family burial lot, enclosed, which contained several gravestones, bearing the following inscriptions:

Elizabeth L. Carter, died April 17, 1846
Mary B. Carter
Fanny A. C. Dulany, died May 3, 1835

This camp was also designated as "Excelsior Hospital," which afterwards became "Camp Convalescent." Our little squad of recruits, so eager to join our regiments, the exact whereabouts of which could not then be ascertained, formed the nucleus of what subsequently assumed huge proportions, and proved a burning disgrace to the country.

It was here that the sick and wounded men who had recovered from their wounds, were sent, until, in the following year, they had accumulated to many thousands.

It was here that a show of greenbacks procured a man's discharge from the service as easy as tumbling off a log; here, in the early morning, the bummers and beats took a little gentle exercise up and down the steep hills in the vicinity, just before surgeon's call, and then religiously attending it, with hearts thumping from a hard run, and a generous display of the filthy lucre, were pronounced badly affected with heart disease, and booked for what they had long desired—a journey to "Home, Sweet Home."

It was here that red ink, or some other substitute, was skillfully used to simulate blood from the mouth and lungs, or the last stages of a consumptive, and the greenback "prolapses" dodge was so successfully worked.

The camp was investigated by a committee of congress, and matters were, after a while, somewhat remedied, but for the greater portion of its existence it remained a perfect scourge to the army. There were many old soldiers sprinkled in among us, returning to their regiments.

Our letters describe it as "within a stone's throw of Fort Ellsworth, within plain view of Fairfax Seminary, and over across the valley, about one and one-half miles, is Fort Lyon, garrisoned by the Sixty-ninth New York, who go home today, their time, three months, being up."

"There are forts in all directions. Below lies the dirty, nasty city of Alexandria. Oh, what a place! Full of 'niggers' and soldiers, and it looks as though the hand of God were upon it; it is under the guns of three or four forts, all of which can blow it to pieces. It is under army control, and the sick and wounded fill every house that has been confiscated. The result of war is seen in its dilapidated buildings, and miserable, filthy streets. All the slops of soldiers, fragrant with loathsome diseases, run foul in the gutters, and it is a sickening sight to walk through the streets of Alexandria. Verily, 'Old Virginia' will be but a vestige of her former self, when we have marched through her stricken domains."

Saturday, August 24, 1862,

Alexandria Heights,

Fort Ellsworth, in Camp.

After closing this letter the other day, we moved from Alexandria, and are now about two miles from there, towards Fort Scott. Our camp is situated splendidly; it commands a view of Alexandria, Fairfax Seminary, Washington city, and the Potomac river.

We are now in better quarters, and begin to feel settled. Our camp is under control of a York colonel; I do not yet know his name. We are in small wedge tents, and five of us occupy one of them,—Ed Holt, William Webster, Asa Fletcher, Bob, and your humble servant. We have hay on the dusty floor, and at night, rubber and woolen blankets answer every purpose of beds. Fletcher found a nice mattress, filled with shavings, on the road to Fairfax Seminary, so we are all right there. But, oh, the dirt and filth of all our surroundings! It is perfectly awful. It is only the hope of future fight, and victory, that keeps us bright and jolly. If we could only have the rations the government provides for us, we should be well satisfied; but we are deprived of them in some way. If we could only cook our own coffee, and draw our own sugar, I should be contented, for then I could use it as I pleased; but now one fellow pretends to cook for our mess or squad of Twenty-second boys, and most certainly he doesn't put in my quantity of sugar in the coffee, and he throws in more grease than government allows; but I do not complain with a mean tone; I *lump it all*, and *don't care a snap*.

It isn't half what we have got to endure, for, as I see the war-worn veterans of McClellan's army wend their weary way along the turnpikes that pass our camp, and hear the horrid stories of Hooker's brigade, my heart grows sick within me, and I consider that I am now in a blissful state, only patiently waiting transportation to purgatory.

From this camp the turnpikes are seen full of soldiers, moving forward to join the army. Regiment after regiment from Pennsylvania and New York pass us daily, and at night their camp-fires light up the surrounding country with thousands of beacon-fires, bidding the anxious hearts of our Northern people to rejoice in their coming strength.

It would do your heart good to hear the welcoming cheers of the troops as they pass the encampments of their brethren in arms. It is a glorious sight to us in our embryo state of soldierhood.

We expect to hear from our regiment every minute. A report is going the rounds that they are to come to Alexandria, and go from there to join with Pope and Burnside. Kearney's division came up night before last, and have gone today; no one knows where, but if they did, they probably would not tell.

There are about 3,000 raw recruits with us for the various regiments of all the states. I tell you if things don't work at odds and ends. You will excuse the blots and general looks of this, won't you, Mother? I am away from the rest of the boys, and down in the woods, beside the hill, writing to you, and my poor contrivances, with the help of Virginia flies and mosquitoes, prevent a great display of writing faculties. I have been writing on a tin plate; it don't go very well. My handwriting is just about spoiled, but I can't help it. Good-night!

Sunday morning.—I wish you would tell Mrs. M., with my kind remembrance, that her little Testament has not been laid aside, and that when we were in the cars from Philadelphia to Baltimore last Sunday, I read two chapters in it, while gambling and every kind of wickedness, was being practised in the car.

It is a most beautiful day, but no one would ever know it was the Sabbath. Some of the Irish Ninth are drunk, gambling, howling, and every vice is going the rounds of the camp. Itis monstrous! I have already seen sights that I never dreamed I should, and at Alexandria, I believe the fiends of hell are let loose while the Army of Potomac is passing through, for such noises and horrid scenes I never heard nor beheld before. People are killed there every day, and I saw there today two Negroes dead on stretchers, on King street. Our young men from Bradford are very quiet; some are reading their Testaments, while others are writing. We have been singing psalm tunes, and it was a strange contrast to the rest of the camp; yet many gathered around, and seemed interested. We are going to have baked beans and roast pork for dinner today. Four of our fellows (old soldiers) borrowed my knife, and went to a 'secesh' house and stuck a pig, a little while ago, and we are to have a feast in consequence.

I 'drew' (term for foraging from the plantations) some green corn and apples today, and I mean to have roast corn and apple sauce for supper.

Last night we had some boiled rice; it tasted like salve, with lard for seasoning; you know I am very particular about that dish. But no more about the stomach now, although, talk as you may, it is a sadly-neglected function out here if you rely upon the government. That is 'honest' as Ball says.

The first morning I 'drew' some hard bread and coffee, and cooked my own coffee; it was the first cup of that article that I ever cooked myself, but it tasted better than any I have yet had from Uncle Sam. I wish you would send me your method of making pure Mocha, as far as process is concerned, for you cannot expect it pure, when the raw material is two-thirds adulterated.

Edgar, Bob, a New York Cavalry boy, and myself made the acquaintance of a Virginia planter (at the foot of the hill, across the road), where we bought milk of him, and he was very good indeed to us. We fell into the good graces of the 'nigs,' and they gave us peach pies, and flapjacks, etc. At night we patronized the 'nigs' again, and had a good treat; since then we have bought milk occasionally of them, and they generally throw in something extra. The first night we had no tents, and no supper; Bob and myself put up together on the ground, and about 12 o'clock it rained like guns; our rubber blankets saved us a soaking, but as it was, I got no sleep, and kicked it off and got wet. It was a perfect paradise, however, to the mean, lousy apartments at Alexandria, where the bedbugs, cockroaches, and filth were knee-deep. Bob got bitten all over one night there. We didn't get half enough to eat there either, for we had no plates or large dippers, and rations were not regular at all. One day we only had one small ration of bread and salt pork. I bought my grub, as did most of the others, even old soldiers returning to their regiments.

The second night, we went into a tent where an old soldier of the Pennsylvania Bucktail Rifles,[5] two boys of the Seventh Maine, from Cape Elizabeth, and several New Yorkers were, and they cooked us a good supper. We sung all our good songs, and they were much pleased. The next day we were transferred to a new camping ground (us Massachusetts boys), and a mighty mean place it is; right upon a dusty plat of ground, with nothing green around us, and water most a mile.

We have not had a single thing furnished to us yet; I have bought a dipper and two plates.

I don't expect to get anything when I get to my regiment, for in the present move, the quartermaster's department cannot be attended to; so I shall buy as I need, as fast as I want, and draw commutation hereafter for articles I don't get from the government. Even the old regiments can't get clothes, and when they encamp they can't get enough to eat, and I am sure if provisions are not plenty, how can clothes be? I am all covered over with prickly heat, and my sufferings from it are almost unbearable; but I apprehend when I get through with this cruise, I shall be able to endure almost anything with reasonable patience.

My neck is all burned to a crisp. The heat of the sun is severe. It penetrates away through. We are waiting to hear from our regiment. They are now at Acquia creek. While I am in my tent, the boys keep coming in, and it don't take many to fill it up. They talk and laugh, and of course it is impossible to write, but wait a while and I will close this.

From this camp we made many visits to Alexandria, to Forts Albany, Scott, Craig, and Tillinghast, where we saw our brother, John, some cousins, and many friends whom we knew in the First Massachusetts Heavy Artillery; also the Thirty-third and Thirty-fifth Massachusetts, the latter near Hunter's chapel, in which we had many friends. Our letters describe these visits, with numerous amusing incidents, etc., but they are, while interesting, too voluminous for introduction within the limits of these papers.

---

[5] Thirteenth Pennsylvania Reserve Regiment.—2019

On one of these visits we had learned that the First Massachusetts Heavy Artillery was then under orders to join General Pope's army, and when the latter was wrestling with Longstreet and Jackson on the 25th of August, the "First Heavies" were ordered out, and that same day we learned that they were out beyond Fort Ellsworth, on the Fairfax C. H. road, near Cloud's Mill.

Our letters say:

Saturday night, about six o'clock, we heard that the Fourteenth (First Massachusetts Heavy Artillery), was encamped about one and one-half miles up the road, near Cloud's Mill. Hardly believing it, we started with nothing but our canteens. We traveled about two miles, falling in with drunken soldiers of the First, Eleventh, and Sixteenth Massachusetts regiments, who, as soon as they found out that we were Massachusetts boys for the Twenty-second, were completely crazy to have us shake hands and have a drink with them. We shook hands with more than fifty, but nary a drink. Night was fast settling down upon us, and the encampments of Hooker's and Kearney's brigades looked splendid.

We soon got on the track, and got in the camp of the Fourteenth, and such a splendid sight I never saw. The camp-fires lit up the tents and fields for miles around. Some were roasting sweet potatoes, making coffee, etc. We found Lewis's tent, and found that John was on picket at Cloud's Mill, about three fourths of a mile from there, and wouldn't be in till morning; so, after seeing lots of boys that we used to know, we 'turned in' on four cents' worth of hay that Lewis bought, making one and one-third cents a-piece— enough to keep our bones from getting sore.

In the morning, I went down to the Mill, and found John asleep on the soft side of a plank. We woke him, and he was delighted to see us. He said after we left the fort the other day, he never expected to see us again. I tell you, Father, he is almost tickled to death to see us. It cheers him up; and to think that we should travel fifteen miles at one time (seven and one half out and back), and six miles at another time, it makes him feel glad.

When he woke up, he said that rats as large as mules had been running over his body all night, and practicing battalion drill. Cloud's Mill, if you remember, was the scene of a sharp skirmish at one time. It is an old wooden and brick mill, used once for grinding corn; now occupied by 'contrabands.'[6] They invited us in, and gave us hoe cake, coffee, and fish— the best food I have had since leaving home. After staying with John about two hours, we again bade him good-by, and left him there, as he could not be relieved from guard duty. If it (the regiment) is not gone, I shall go again tomorrow.

The visit was repeated the following day, and our brother, having "foraged" a lot of cabbages and other vegetables, gave us a royal boiled dinner, which he cooked himself.

He writes:

Cloud's Mill, August 26, 1862.

I go in about ten minutes on my way to Warrenton. Can't write but a word. Have to destroy everything. Bob took dinner with me this afternoon. They are at Fort Ellsworth, and will probably follow shortly. Do not write until you hear from me. We shall now see fighting.

It was the last campaign of this regiment until the spring of 1864, when the movement across the Rapidan took place. It then joined Grant's army, and distinguished itself in nearly all of the bloody battles of the Second army corps, until the surrender at Appomattox, and we shall have occasion to refer to it often in following up the fortunes of our eldest "brother in blue."

But while in the fortifications, their restlessness and anxiety to join General Pope and engage in the second Battle of Bull Run[7] became so great that when this, their first opportunity, and its inglorious result, became known in the Army of the Potomac, the "Heavies" were for a long time chafed most unmercifully by their veteran comrades, and they never manifested the same impatience for an advance from their fortified position.

Our brother thus describes his share in the "forward movement:"

Fort Tillinghast, Sept. 7, 1862.

---

[6] Enslaved people who escaped to Union lines were declared contraband of war to legally prevent having them returned to their owners.—2019
[7] See *Second Battle of Bull Run*, Cox, 2016.

106

We have just been inspected by General Fitz John Porter, who complimented us highly. We were very foolishly ordered away from here some two weeks ago, but we are back again by order of General McClellan.

We had a pretty tough time during our absence, having to lie in the woods for over two days, in line of battle, with two pieces of artillery, which we found abandoned by a New York battery. We lost about eight or ten men, who were taken prisoners, and took about the same number in return. We saved a large amount of property to the government. Our colonel is a 'brick.' He was some distance in advance, when he discovered a regiment of cavalry approaching to overtake the wagon trains. He rode back 'double quick,' and immediately gave the order: 'Head of column to the right (into the woods)! Cannon to the front!' This checked the 'rebs.' There are four roads leading into Fairfax, but we only had men to cover three, so the next day they got to our rear by the fourth road, and made a dash at our hospital, which was half a mile or so to the rear, capturing all the hospital stores, the two surgeons, a wounded soldier, the hospital steward (J. Riley of Haverhill), one ambulance, and one or two other teams, and teamsters.

The surgeons were immediately paroled, and General Lee (W. H. F.?)[8] sent his compliments to Colonel Green, saying that if he (Green) had camped in an open field the previous night, he would have captured and dispersed his entire command.

The Colonel was slightly mad, the General being an old acquaintance of his. We afterwards captured two of his scouts, being taken in trees, watching our movements. Before all this happened, we heard heavy cannonading ahead, and knew that a battle was in progress; so the Colonel ordered us to unsling knapsacks in the woods, and we were hurrying on to join in the battle, when old Lee came down on us.

On our return, we found the knapsacks were ransacked by fugitive 'niggers,' who were running away, and by the poor soldiers of McClellan's army, who are hurrying forward; so we lost everything except what we wore.

It would almost make you weep to look at the remnant of the beautiful army that left here but a few months since, so full of hope.

---

[8] William Henry Fitzhugh Lee, second son of Robert E. Lee.—2019

Some of the regiments are not so large as our company, which numbers one hundred and fifty. There is now a large army of troops here, and there is some active movement on foot which, I hope, will soon wipe out our recent severe reverses. The men are all anxious to fight, except those in the corps of McDowell, who swear they will run at the first fire, if he leads them; for they know that he leads them to certain death and defeat. One and all denounce him as a traitor.

The Army of the Potomac, as our letters indicate, moved directly by our camp on Shuter's Hill, on the turnpike leading from Alexandria to Fairfax Court-House, to join Pope. Hooker's and Kearney's veterans were among them, and, going to their camps just beyond ours, we took from these well-versed "patriots," some of our first lessons of what was to come, especially in "drawing" articles not on the list of commissary rations, "chickenraising," etc., etc.

Our letters say:

O Father, we are having exciting times! At the bottom of the hill is the main road to Manassas, and as you know, McClellan's army, a great part of it, has landed at Alexandria, and are reinforcing Pope at Culpepper and vicinity, which is about sixty miles from here.

They all have to go on this road, and we go down and sit on a rock and watch them as they file along, regiment after regiment, brigade after brigade. Such looking fellows I never saw! Some of them with straw and felt hats, look blacker than their hats; are dusty and dirty; beards all tangled, and, with their ponchos slung on their shoulders, they present a worn appearance.

They all seem to feel discouraged to think that they have seen their brothers and friends shot down by their side, and then have had to turn right back and go way round up the Potomac again, and are now one hundred miles from Richmond. They all blow for 'Little Mac,' although they can't understand all their movements. Pope is fighting every day, and reinforcements are rushing along the roads by thousands. New regiments are camping all around us, and the night is made noisy by their continual cheering. We have about 2,000 men waiting to join their regiments, in camp here. Yesterday some went down on the road, and, as Hooker's and Kearney's war-scarred veterans filed along, they joined their respective commands, cheering and shouting.

It seemed to give them confidence to think that the North was pouring in recruits, but they have suffered so much, Father, in the Chickahominy swamps, that when we talk with them, they discourage us a little, but only a little.

I am writing on my knee, with poor ink and pen, and of course it looks awfully; I can only just write so you can read it, and that is all. I am covered with great heat blotches from head to foot, and they itch fearfully, which, together with mosquitoes and flies, is awful.

When John told us the other day that Gene was in Washington the same day I was, and that he was on a leave of twenty days to go home, and I couldn't see him, I could hardly restrain my feelings. Now, I suppose, he is at home enjoying himself, and I may never see him again. Oh, that we four boys could have met in Washington on that day! Wouldn't we have had a breakdown?

The Twenty-second stopped at Acquia Creek, and went to join Pope in that direction. As soon as they get settled somewhere, then we shall move; but my opinion is that we shall remain here for a week or two. I hear the continual booming of guns. Last night they shot two or three 'niggers' in Alexandria: I suppose the soldiers were drunk. Edgar saw one 'nig' shot through the head.

On the 28th, being informed that General McClellan's headquarters were only about one and three-quarter miles from our camp, we struck out to gratify our desire to see him and make a personal inspection of his camp.

As we approached the headquarter tents, we saw the General come out of one of them, and immediately recognized him by his photographs, although we had mentally pictured him as somewhat nearer the heroic size—at least six feet.

Not content with absorbing all we could of the commander-in-chief, we strolled towards the rude, brush-covered stables, where we were soon pointed out the celebrated war-horse of the General's—Dan Webster. We blush now to record the fact that, becoming suddenly possessed of the devil, or the twin spirit of vandalism—not alone confined to us during that period of the war—we watched our chance, and, when the sentinel's back was turned, we deliberately cut off a lock of hair from Dan Webster's mane, and, secreting it in my pocket, coolly walked away.

We have always thought we were richly punished for that act, for we had scarcely started to retrace our steps, when a terrific thunderstorm burst upon us, blew down a part of the headquarter tents, and, before we got back to Fort Ellsworth, completely drenched us; and, besides, upon sending the trophy home, our parents, not fully appreciating our efforts as a relic hunter, carelessly placed it in a drawer with a lot of old scraps, where it became lost or destroyed.

Dan Webster was a magnificent dark chestnut, and under the saddle, with a numerous mounted staff about him, was easily conspicuous by his glossy coat and fine action.

Our letters say:

'Little Mac' is about two miles from us in camp. Bob, Fletcher, and myself went down to see him last Thursday, and were fortunate enough to catch a glimpse of him. He is not half so handsome as his photographs at the North would seem to indicate. His moustache is brown, and he wears an imperial. He is short and quite broad-shouldered. He wore a dirty military coat and regulation pants, with high boots and an old Kossuth hat. Altogether, he was a very modest man in appearance. I wasn't much struck.

While there, a heavy shower fell upon us, and the tents of his staff were all blown down; we got wet through. I saw his horse, Dan Webster, and he is a noble horse. I never saw a better-looking or more powerfully built one for speed and everything else requisite for his station:—a general's horse in every particular. Bob has some hair that he cut from his mane, which he is going to send home.[9]

On that night, after our return from General McClellan's headquarters, we saw a young man brought into camp in the

---

[9] The Baltimore *South* of October 25, 1861 states that Dan Webster was purchased in St. Louis by a "group of gentlemen" and presented to McClellan. The article went into great detail about the horse's appearance and that he was 16-hands high, sired by General Jackson, dam of Sir Archy and Messenger.—2019

agonies of death. He was the son of wealthy parents, and was in the last stages of delirium tremens; he gasped his last at 9 p. m., and we saw him pass into another world. The following day, another man, older, was brought in. He seemed to have on the uniform of a Confederate artilleryman. He had been found wandering through our lines in a half-crazed state, and he died without having made known his identity.

It was our first experience with death in any form, and it made a lasting impression on our young minds, which the after horrors of many bloody battles hardly effaced.

On the 29th of August we moved through the fields and over very rough ground, to a point a little more than one mile directly west of Camp Excelsior, and just north of Fairfax Seminary, on a small branch of Cameron Run.

Our letter, dated in Camp near Fairfax Seminary, Sunday, Aug. 31, 1862, says:

We have moved to this place, about one fourth of a mile from Fairfax Seminary, perhaps the very spot where Gene encamped when he returned from his grand advance in the spring. We came here last Friday morning, and the first night slept with no tents; they were promised for last night, but when I got back from a long tour to the camp of the Thirty-fifth regiment and Fort Tillinghast, nary a tent did I find, and this morning I woke up to find it raining finely.

I spread my rubber blanket, and stood it until I got up. We cooked our breakfast in the rain, consisting of drawn rations from the fields on our route; applesauce, roast corn, some bread, and mean coffee (although the latter I cooked myself).

It is still raining, and the boys have put their duds in a heap, put their rubber blankets over them, and gone into some tents put up by some old settlers, while I have wandered over here to the Seminary, and under an old shed, free from the noise and bustle of the camp, am spending my Sabbath in writing to you.

It is raining quite hard out, and once in a while it spatters through on my paper (letter badly stained), but the place is much better than a shelter in a tent where all the boys are talking and laughing, especially on such a wet day as this, when the cloth of the tents is just like a sieve. Fairfax Seminary is a fine building, and is now used as a hospital. It was the greatest seat of learning in the South before the war broke out; 'so they say.' It is certainly a beautiful situation, and the grounds give indications of former beauty. I should judge the buildings were all fine; everything is going to ruin here. 'It -was, and is not,' may truly be said of every building in Fairfax County, Va. We have orders to go today, but very likely they will be countermanded, as it is almost impossible to join them (the regiment) while they are fighting as they are now.

All day yesterday the cannons' roar was incessant, and the rumors among the various camps we passed through were very exciting. At the forts they were digging rifle-pits, and new guns were being mounted; the magazines were open, and ammunition was being carried to the many places of convenience inside the battlements. You could hear very distinctly the boom of the guns towards Centreville, and I saw Sumner's Corps as it passed Fort Tillinghast, as also Meagher's Irish Brigade of Peninsular veterans, as they marched to reinforce our army, then and now in conflict with 'Stonewall' Jackson.

I saw a straggler of the Twenty-second, Thomas Branigan, Co. G, when we were coming back. He said there were about two hundred and fifty in the regiment, able for duty, and they were then fighting at Manassas. He got out of cartridges, and being liable to capture in the rear, 'skedaddled' to Alexandria, and was making tracks for Fort Albany when we saw him, where he had a brother whom he had not seen for twelve months.

He told me some pretty hard stories of his Peninsular campaign, and said as soon as he got rested, he should travel for the Twenty-second again.

He hailed from Lawrence, (Mass.), and had lost his knapsack at Gaines Mill, and nothing covered him but a coat (ragged blouse) and pair of pants. He had his two blankets coiled about him, but his overcoat and sick were among the missing; a hard-looking boy and no mistake. We started for Hunter's Chapel early yesterday morning, and when we got there we found that the Thirty-fifth had changed their camp, and gone down towards Fort Craig, near Fort Tillinghast, and we found them all there.

We saw John; he looked pretty well, considering what he has been through lately: he has lost everything; I suppose you have heard of their march to Centreville, and of their narrow escape from capture by Colonel Lee of the rebel army ... After some tall tramping, and the loss of all their baggage and duds, they have returned to their forts, satisfied, they all say, to remain there until the war is over.

They are now putting the forts in a good state of defense. That is a smashing regiment, Colonel Green's, of 1800 strong. The Peninsular soldiers, as the Fourteenth passed, asked if it was not a division. Their own brigades scarcely vie with it in point of numbers.

While we were there (before their advance), about five hundred recruits arrived, and they were received with shouts of joy. Many of them were taken in, I reckon, for they didn't expect an advance quite yet.

Before I left Hospital Camp (Shuter's Hill), I went to see the Thirty-third regiment, Colonel Maggi, and stayed until dress parade was over at 6 o'clock p. m. I saw those two lieutenants we conversed with at Camp Stanton, if you remember, on the possibility of Bob's being accepted at 17 years of age, and whether or not there were any regulations to the effect that all under 18 were to be refused.

They were glad to see us; it is a fine regiment; I almost wish I were in it. We have been kicked about so since we started! If McClellan had stayed at Harrison's Landing, we should have been with our regiment in good drill, and all right; but his moving away makes a heap of trouble for us, the government scarcely knowing what to do with us.

I am afraid now that the Thirty-fifth will get drilled before us, and be off for the field before we are. They twitted us to that effect yesterday, and it was a little mortifying to me, when I remember what I said about old regiments before leaving home.

Three days' rations were dealt out to us last night, and we were to have gone today. Upon someone asking the commanding officer what we raw recruits could do before the enemy, he replied, 'they can fight like the devil so in all probability, as soon as we get arms, according to reports and orders, we shall go to meet the foe with our regiment without even knowing how to handle a musket or come into line of battle. I can only say, 'Bully for that!' The sooner the better for me. This climate is making me terribly lazy. I lose all my strength here, and feel dumpish continually; I want to lie down constantly; there seems to be something in the atmosphere that absorbs all my vitality. The heat has been tremendous, and we have suffered terribly from it. All the recruits for Porter's Corps are in camp with us; about a thousand men. It is not quite as pretty as the old place, but much better. I do not see a paper very often, but I hear that McClellan is commander-in-chief over the Army of Virginia, and that Halleck now is merely military adviser.

One night I was troubled a good deal by something running about on my neck all night long; I suspected that it was an army of lice, and in the morning, I found outside my tent, by my corner (and I sleep close, for there were five in the tent) an old dirty shirt, all covered over with body lice, and they had been marching at close quarters all night.

I found four large ones on my shirt, and three 'slimmers' inside, on the seams; and in the seams under my arms, and on my neck, any quantity of little eggs, or young divils, hardly formed. I cleaned them all off, but have scarcely gotten rid of them yet.

It is perfectly horrid, and I lose flesh in thinking of it; who under heavens could have been fiendish enough to have put that shirt under my head? I know not! If the Irishman I whipped on board the Camden & Amboy R. R. had been in camp I should have thought him the guilty one; but he had joined his regiment. I have never found out the villain yet. We have all got to come to it, however, for all soldiers have lice; you can keep from it a short time, but when you are on the march, and maybe have thrown away soap and towels to lighten your load, and bivouac on some old camping ground alive with these animals, it is certain that a lousy carcass is your lot for some time to come. It is impossible to keep clean in the days of adversity, but now, while we are stationary, and have everything pretty handy, we delight in our morning bath.

There are a lot of green recruits who keep firing their revolvers around camp, and bullets are constantly flying about us; it isn't very agreeable. I have been near enough to being shot. I have just got back to camp. It is still raining, and we are without tents; I am most wet through, things and all.

Monday afternoon, September 1, 1862.

114

We move tonight with two days' rations. The enemy are at Fairfax Court-House, ten miles from here. The battle Saturday was 'nip and tuck,' I could hear the cannonading all day long. Today, the wounded are coming by the road; some shot through the arm, leg, or hand. I have talked with them, and they all say that McDowell is a traitor, and should be shot as one. I thought I would write to let you know that we go tonight, for tomorrow we§ may be in battle; but if we do, God be with the right, and protect them from the bullets of the enemy. "Mac" went out by us last Saturday night, to take charge of the troops. The boys are in good spirits, notwithstanding our hard treatment, and are ready for the march.

The *New York Herald* of September 1, 1862, says: "The bustle and confusion of Alexandria exceeds that of any previous occasion, not excepting even the tumult of McClellan's departure for the Peninsula; the army wagons, regiments and stragglers block up the streets from daylight till the small hours of the morning, so that pedestrianism becomes almost impossible.

"The river is obstructed with shipping; the wharves groan beneath the weight of army paraphernalia; long trains of cars creep through the mass of humanity, and artillery now and then, with its deafening rumble, adds to the din, while a dense cloud of dust hangs above all the town, blinding the eyes and choking up the respiratory organs of every visitor of this modern Babel.

"All the restaurants have been closed by the authorities, and infantry patrol every street. All the hotels and boarding-houses were crowded beyond comfort, and hundreds of officers go about the street disconsolate, vainly seeking for a place to lay their heads.

"Of course the 'secesh' element is jubilant. Delight upon the countenances of rebel sympathizers too plainly marks their long-nurtured hopes of deliverance from the 'Yankees,' and the bitter experience of former delinquents only checks the full expression of disloyalty.

"There has been continual anxiety all the morning relative to the engagement now going on in the vicinity of Centreville. It is 12 o'clock, and there is a lull in the cannonading, which has been very severe up to this hour. On every hill from Fort Ellsworth to the city, and on many of the roofs of the houses, crowds were observed listening to the distant cannonading. The 'secesh ' families kept their houses closed, and occasionally would partially open their doors, and with dark and scowling features peer up the street, as if anxiously expecting Jackson."

The following morning we moved to the foot of Arlington Heights, and camped in the meadow near the spring on the north of the mansion. A letter dated September 3, 1862, in camp on Arlington Heights, near Fort Albany, Virginia, says:

Night before last Bob just enclosed a few words to some of you at home, stating the fact that we were then under orders to march at a moment's notice with three days' rations ....

That same night we stood in our tent during a violent thunder-storm, until 8 o'clock, expecting every moment to leave. At that time the order came, and we packed our knapsacks and started. We marched about one quarter of a mile through the rain and Virginia mud, and then halted for equipments.

I wet my feet all through, and only having one pair of stockings, they are in a bad condition. We had to wade across streams from our camping ground, and it was over our shoes. We stayed in this (that) place until 11 o'clock, raining all the time, and then after being partly equipped with poor arms (second-hand), we were ordered back to our camp, with instructions to be back with the rising of the sun, to renew the process of arming.

There were about 4,000 men in all, mostly recruits, and on that muddy, rainy night, it was a scene I shall never forget; those men all mixed up, trying to get arms; everything was helter-skelter, and order and method were beyond looking for. It was a regular mob, and when you consider that the commanding officer gave us to understand that we were going to aid our regiments and that they were retreating, you can conceive of the whole arrangement somewhat; and remember, too, that not one of us had ever put on a belt, buckle, cartridge-box or cap pouch.

What a picture we did present! Most of us boys went back to camp, but Edgar being sick, I got him a box and made him a bed, put my knapsack under him for a pillow, and he was provided for as

116

comfortably as circumstances would permit. I slept next to him; I put eight or ten muddy muskets under me, and a box on one side, and got in between it and Edgar; my well-filled haversack was my pillow, but all I had to cover me was my overcoat; everything was in my knapsack under Ed's head, and I hated to disturb him.

I threw away the quilt that John gave me, just before leaving camp, to ease my load, so that now I have only my rubber blanket, which, as I said before, was under his head.

It rained all night long, I got wet through, I was very cold, and it did seem as though my feet would freeze. Early in the morning we were up, and Ed., after vomiting, was much better.

The boys came over from camp, and about 10 o'clock, having been all armed and equipped, we started, we know not where. Some of our boys got Austrian rifles, some Enfield, and others the Springfield. I got the Enfield, and Bob got the finest arm of the whole lot, a fine United States Springfield rifle.

This letter does not give full justice to the scene on that night. We were marched across these streams in the darkness of a terrific thunder storm to an octagonal building, or as we always termed it the 'Round House,' which must have been on or near the Leesburg turnpike.

Our recruits represented every Massachusetts regiment in the field.

We were all mixed up, there was no organization, no discipline, no system in issuing anything. All was helter-skelter. Every kind of an old, rusty, worthless gun was handed out to us in the darkness, and we did not know one from the other. Ammunition for a Belgian was given to a man with a Springfield rifle; "buck and ball" was passed out for the Enfield, etc.

We were told that our regiments were retreating upon the fortifications; we were to join in the fight with them at once.

Not a man had ever put on a cartridge box or a buckle on a belt, and there was nobody to show us: besides, the rain was beating down in torrents; it was dark as Erebus, and the only light we had this wild night, was the flashes of lightning, reinforced (?) by one or two dim candles that frequently went out in the deluge of rain that struck them.

All was dire confusion. Belts, boxes, etc., were put on upside down, often without cap-boxes or bayonet scabbards, and, during our momentary excitement, through constant rumors of the near approach of the enemy, the appalling darkness of the night, the incessant flashes of lightning and the rattling and continuous booming of the thunder, could "Johnny Reb" have struck us just then, "John Gilpin's race" would have been as nothing compared with the "skedaddle" on that fearful night.

The average intelligence of those recruits marveled and chafed under such a needless and disgraceful state of incompetency.

We stalked about awhile in the ever increasing depth of mud, and then taking some pieces of ammunition boxes and some old guns, filled with mud and water, we made a raised bed on the mire-trodden ground, and, in all the utter wretchedness and gloom, we recruits of but three weeks, just from our comfortable New England homes, wore out the night, while in our fevered imagination we were momentarily expecting the enemy upon us.

All day long, Sept. 2, the startling boom! boom! of cannon was heard, and to our yet uninitiated ears it sounded ominously, indeed. With our heavy loads, soaked bed-quilts, with which we had been so kindly supplied by our friends in the forts, we were marched here and there and everywhere; first to Fort Tillinghast, then to Fort Albany, with nobody, apparently, in charge of us, who seemed to know where to go, or what to do with this huge recruit, "White Elephant," until we finally arrived at the foot of the slopes of Arlington, near the "Springs," just below the house.

Our letter continues:

We marched to this place, about seven miles, and it came pretty tough on some of us. I assure you we were pretty well loaded. I had everything but a U. S. blanket; but my rubber blanket is heavier than regulation, and we had twenty rounds extra of cartridges, and our knapsacks were pretty well filled. I came near throwing mine away several times; I should, had it not been for a very acceptable

118

halt at the time being. ... I hate to do it, but I tell you they pull on a fellow's back dreadfully; the kind of knapsacks that Father bought us have very narrow straps, and that, with no other straps, makes a very severe bind across the lungs; so much so, that it is painful to breathe.

We had sixty rounds of ammunition, weighing six or seven pounds; our haversacks were filled with dry, sour bread, (melted) coffee, and sugar (sickening), and plenty of 'hard tack.'

Here we are this fine morning, all well and hungry, after a night's sleep on the cold ground. I slept well, but was cold. We are directly opposite the Capitol and a short distance from Fort Albany. Tillinghast must be back of us on the same road, only higher up.

I think they intend to keep us here for drill, until our regiment comes up, for our captain in charge says that they will get to us before we get to them.

What kind of drilling it will be I know not, but I think it will be poor, if I take our sergeant for a specimen of drill master. I am heartily sick of the way things are carried on.

Oh, for a West Pointer to teach me the way I should go, before I reach or see my regiment! I am hoping for the best, however. That night we were out in the rain, I expected we should march to our regiments, and see fighting the next day, and we were disappointed enough to be toted way over here............I should rejoice in the privilege of sleeping on our banking at home, if I could have the rest of the comforts in close proximity daytime...............I won't complain, though, for I knew it must be so, before I started. Last night, Fletcher, Webster, Ed and myself separated from the rest, and slept in the woods. The mosquitoes troubled us somewhat, and the ants filled our haversacks, but with these exceptions, we were very comfortable.

O my dear Mother, you can scarcely imagine the feelings I have towards you now, when I remember how far away from you I am, and how long I may be separated from you; and think, too, of your health and how often you are sick—when, I know not.

Here, while enjoying this bewildered state, and momentarily expecting to move out and join our regiment, now on the march, where we knew not, the writer "drew" some beans, and, squatted over a green wood fire, was industriously trying to stew them and to flank the smoke on the arc of a circle, when his brother of the "Heavies" found him.

There were nearly enough beans before boiling, to fill a quart tin; they now commenced to swell and I dipped out a few. They swelled more, and kept increasing—dropping over the sides—until, in my spirit of agony, and with eyes full of smoke, I was about to pitch them into the fire, when a loud "fall in!" was given, and suddenly changing my mind—recruit-like—angry at being disturbed at my first culinary efforts, I dumped the mess of swelled and partially stewed beans into my haversack, nearly filling it. I inwardly resolved and outwardly shouted that I "would have stewed beans out of that mess anyway," when I got to the regiment, much to the amusement of the brothers standing by.

Finally, on the 4th of September, after many trials and tribulations, we proceeded to join the regiment at Hall's Hill, accompanied part of the way by our brother of the "Heavies," to help carry the "plunder" and assist in "veteranizing" us. A new era now began to dawn upon our uneducated, undisciplined minds.

BATTLE OF ANTIETAM

The Twenty-second Massachusetts Volunteers was then a part of the Fifth Corps (Fitz John Porter), First Division (Morell), First Brigade (Martindale), now commanded by Colonel James Barnes, of the Eighteenth Massachusetts Volunteers, and was composed of the Second Maine, First Michigan, Eighteenth Massachusetts, Twenty-second Massachusetts, Twenty-fifth New York, Thirteenth New York, and First Berdan Sharpshooters.[1]

It was merely bivouacked a few hundred yards southwest of the told camp it had occupied the previous winter, and the remains of its old stockaded Sibley tents were distinctly visible across the little run. It bore evidence of its disastrous campaign on the Peninsula, and its march from Acquia Creek, via Bull Run, to this place. To the uninitiated eyes of our recruits what a looking regiment it was! At the Battle of Gaines Mills [June 27, 1862] they had "'piled their knapsacks,'" had been nearly surrounded by "Stonewall" Jackson; had fought an unequal contest with great gallantry; had "skipped out" and lost everything, and were now without even shelter tents, blankets, overcoats, etc.; many were barefooted, and their clothes were ragged and torn. Some wore straw hats of every shape and color, others a black or white slouch, while many sported a vizorless cap of that unique pattern so well remembered by all old soldiers, almost impossible to describe, which had increased the brown on their faces to a rich mahogany.

How mean we recruits did feel in our good clothes, spick-and-span-new. We felt like jerking them off as we had seen the drunken sailor (?) in the circus, and letting them go as far as they would.

Shortly after our arrival in this camp, the pickets of the Second Maine and First Michigan were driven in from the direction of Fairfax Court-House. The bugles sounded the assembly, across the hills, and the brigade with a battery was soon in motion. This

---

[1] See *Berdan's United States Sharpshooters in the Army of the Potomac*, Stevens, 2014.

was our first experience of actual war, and our boyish enthusiasm and eagerness to get into battle as soon as possible, was nowhere so prominently displayed as in the letters we wrote home after this event, and our disappointment at not being allowed to go with the regiment to the point of danger was keen and genuine. What did we come out for—simply to draw and eat rations? And when were we going to have a chance at a "Johnny "?

It was but an alarm, and they soon returned. The scenes about the bivouac fires that night as we gathered in groups and listened to the stories of our newly-found veteran companions of the Peninsular campaign, were vivid and soul-inspiring, and our fevered imaginations pictured with unrestrained eagerness the coming years and glory of service to our country.

Our letters say:

In Camp, Hall's Hill,

September 5, 1862.

I am at my new home, and my joy is full. The way stations on the journey have been too disagreeable for a pleasant remembrance, and I consider the experience of them the forgotten things of the past, and am happy and contented in the present. Our little family of brave men were delighted to see us last night (only twenty-six in Captain Thompson's company), and at night the campfires were crowded with scarred and war-worn veterans' faces, anxious to hear from home. They have now been on the march for three weeks from Harrison's Landing, and arrived here night before last at the same company ground they left so full of hope and big in numbers last spring, now a small band of noble men, only numbering one hundred and fifty men fit for duty when we got here. I am now *e pluribus unum* and am glad I am in an old regiment. Henry Wilson was here to see them as soon as they arrived, and they say he cried like a child when he saw how devoid of everything they were. The regiment idolizes him as their benefactor, and as the one who is ever having an eye single to their well-being. He is the man above all others who has done so much for the poor soldier, and I say all honor to the kind-hearted Natick shoemaker, a man worthy of high position in the senate chamber.

Some of these poor chaps have had nothing to cover their poor bodies these cold September nights but a thin blouse and tattered breeches; their shirts gone, and their shoes and stockings; they lost everything at Gaines Mills. We are going to have new muskets and light blue pants; already does the regiment begin to assume order in everything after all the confusion and chaos of the last month.

I am glad that I am here, for everything bids fair to be as gay as can be. We begin to draw rations as a company now, and it is cooked well. This morning I drew the first ration of coffee, and it was as good as it could be without milk and sugar. I drank it down with a relish, and I have not tasted it before for a week, not even of my own making, it was so sickening to my stomach.

When we got here last night we met Captain Thompson, who was glad enough to see us; he is a man of few words, and very unassuming, but looks like a brave man, and every inch a soldier when on duty; at other times he mingles freely with his soldiers and eats with them, and has now an old hut made of leaves for his quarters, while the rest of the 'shoulder straps' have their fine tents, etc.

Our lieutenants are both gone, the second lieutenant, Shute, being still at home. ... Our other lieutenant (Salter) was killed before Richmond, but our drill-master, Billy Salter, brother to Tom Salter (first lieutenant), is alive, and we have commenced to like him very much; he is a genuine favorite, and the best-drilled fellow in the company; he is the best sergeant in the regiment, so Captain T. says.

We have been drilled for the first time this morning, and I never felt better in my life. We were drilled in a squad without muskets, and went through the various steps and facings common to company drill: we were complimented by the sergeant, who said we should be able to take our muskets in hand in a day or two. It is even so, for our boys are all smart and intelligent; we learn quick, and have a good teacher, both worthy of each other.

John is now here; he came up with a fellow named West, and I will stop this letter writing in the hot sun until he leaves.

John has gone now; he is going to the camps of the Twelfth and Thirteenth (Mass.) Regiments; when he gets back to Tillinghast (Fort), he will have to come a spread eagle on a cannon wheel for leaving without permission, so Captain Sargent told them if they went away. John received Gene's note asking him to be at the National Hotel, Washington, last Saturday, but he couldn't get over. ... I am sorry he has been so sick, and it is a great surprise to me to learn of the bare possibility of his being a Massachusetts colonel. It has been spoken of in several of the letters the boys received last night. We are all going up to Fort Tillinghast to get some beans Sunday, if we get a pass: John invited us. I mean to obey all rules and regulations now, but while in the chrysalis state I mean to hook, run guards, etc., etc.

It meant nothing but red tape, so we didn't care; now we are in the regiment, and I am bound to be straight, as an example to others.

When we got here last night the pickets of the First Michigan and Second Maine were driven in (they belong to our brigade) by a brigade of rebels, near Fairfax Court-House. The bugle's call to arms sounded across the fields, and they were soon on the move with Martin's Battery (formerly Follet's, which went out with the Twenty-second). They marched about a mile and were ordered back. The recruits were denied the privilege of going with them. Our pickets told some great stories. Tell Mother that we are soon to have some woolen blankets and some small tents. We slept on the ground last night; there was a heavy dew. I spread my rubber blanket and Edgar and I slept on it, with his woolen blanket over us.. .. I hear that letter writing has been prohibited in the Army of the Potomac; I hope this will be allowed to go safely. The rebels are shelling the woods five miles distant, while I am writing; I can hear the cannon boom as plainly as though they were right here.

There is a tremendous army about here, everywhere, in camps, and at night it is a sight to behold. I have to write with pencil now, for a few days ago I spilt my ink. Depend upon it, my dear sister, we are happy now and in good spirits.

Hall's Hill, Sept. 5, 1862.

You can never know how I felt, after four weeks of jolting round, lying out in all sorts of weather, no tents, no blankets, nothing to eat but raw pork and 'hardtack' (so hard that it is almost impossible to break them), after all our hardships and privations, and after our hard, hot, dusty march of yesterday, to get that letter. It was like a bright light, dispelling the gloom; like a shining star in the black, cloudy night. You need not think that I am suffering so much; this lying on the ground and eating this food is tough at first, and so is drinking bad, muddy water, but you soon get used to it, and it does not seem as bad as you imagine. I have seen the time when I would not honestly give the food that I have eaten to the swine, but now, when I am hungry, salt pork tastes as good as chicken and the hardtack as good as biscuits. So you see that it is all in getting used to these things.

Now it was awful hard at first to put on my coat and lie down on the ground with a knapsack for a pillow, but now I can lie down with perfect composure and sleep; not as sweetly as at home, to be sure, for it is so awful cold nights here that you can't do it. Sometimes we make up a hot fire, and all lie with our feet to it, and even then in the morning we are wet and shivering. The dew is like rain; the days are hot, though, and so it goes—hot days and cold nights.

Probably you have seen pictures of soldiers lying about a campfire, have you not? If not, I must describe it. You will see some in their shirt-sleeves, some cooking, some smoking, some sleeping, some telling stories of their terrible campaign on the Peninsula—all this, with the bright glare of the fires all around, goes to make up one of the most beautiful pictures that can be imagined.

We are now near Ball's Cross Roads, where the sharp skirmish was. Fall's Church is about a mile from here, where another fight was. General McClellan is in command of the whole Army of Virginia: Pope's, Banks's, McDowell's, and Sigel's armies are all around us in a circuit of eight or ten miles; the rebels are about four miles from here. They do not think the fight will be here, but at Edward's Ferry, about twenty miles from here, near the famous Ball's Bluff battle-ground. We may stop here some time, and if I go on picket, which I shall probably do in a day or two, I will write you more exciting news; as it is now, it is quite dull, with the exception of the great masses of troops that are continually passing near us.

I have changed very much since I left; as I sit now you would hardly know me. I am under a tree in shirt-sleeves, writing on an old barrel head, and my black face and hands, shaved head, etc., make a rough-looking youth of me. You ought to see the other fellows, some that left home a year ago. I hardly knew them. They have been on the march twenty-one days, and are all exhausted and beaten out.

125

This morning I went foraging, and got corn, potatoes, cabbages, beets, etc., to make a grand boiled dinner. It was a great treat, after living so long on nothing; it tasted like home. It is fun to see the boys roasting corn and potatoes, frying meat, and making coffee. I can cook most anything now in a rude way. Excuse this penciling, as it is almost impossible to write with pen and ink; also excuse the general looks and writing. It has blown away twice and has got soiled. I am very tired, as I am sitting with my back against a small tree. I have been on drill once since I commenced this letter, and as I expect to have to drill again in a few minutes, I will close.

We wrote many letters from here, describing little matters and incidents about camp, and our first impressions, etc., but although interesting, they would prove altogether too voluminous for the limits of these articles.

At dark on the night of the 6th, we were suddenly ordered to move. This was to be our first march beside the veterans from the Peninsula, and our pride was touched. It came hard; every strap cut at every step. The "bureau" was full of good things, and hung off like a camel's hump enlarged. Every movement was painful. Nothing could be heard but the tramp, tramp, the clink, clink, of the tin dippers or coffee cups against the bayonets, and the low murmuring of voices as we moved rapidly along in the darkness.

The laugh and jest had long ago died out, and each individual in that hurrying column was a busy thinker, a machine, which, once set in motion, goes to the utmost of its endurance. The knapsacks we wore had been purchased for us by our father in Boston. They were "patent," were small, with narrow breast straps, and were ill-suited for packing or carrying loads under any circumstance, and especially now that we had no instruction in arranging the same. It was a hard march, but all did well, and morning found us on Arlington Heights with an immense army all about us. Our bivouac was at Fort Worth, near Fairfax seminary, not far from Fort Ellsworth, which we had left but a few days before, and which the regiment had helped to build. But after making coffee, we again took up the march, passed the seminary towards Fairfax Court-House, and after winding about in various directions, finally pitched upon a spot, as an old soldier remarked, "especially adapted to the regiment," the ground being covered with stumps, stones, underbrush, and briars.

We had scarcely cleared a space large enough to spread our blankets and lie down upon, before we were ordered to "Fall in" under arms immediately. We got into line and awaited the next order, which did not come. We lay upon our arms all night, and in the morning drew rations. We remained all day in this place, and on the 9th, at 8 a. m., moved again.

After marching a few miles in rather a perplexing manner, we turned off to the left, passed by Fort Albany on the Alexandria road, and up over Arlington Heights, and finally halted near Fort Corcoran. Here the command was mustered for pay, received many visitors and boxes, whose contents were nearly or quite spoiled, and some knapsacks, out of which a few men extracted some desirable articles and flung the knapsacks away.

Morell's division had been left in the fortifications, while the balance of the Fifth Corps was already on the march into Maryland to intercept the advance of the enemy, now overrunning the state.

The camp of our regiment was on the slope of a very steep hill. No sooner did we go to sleep than we woke up to find ourselves down at the foot of the slope, where we had gradually slipped. The camp was thoroughly "policed," rations of "soft bread" were drawn, and on the 11th some clothing. Three days' rations were issued towards night, which was equivalent to an order to move, and, on the morning of the 12th, when it did come, at 8 a. m., the cooks, not having time to cook the meat, left it on the ground, to be brought along in the wagons, if there was room, if not, to be thrown away as usual.

A soldier will not carry more than his haversack will hold. The turnpikes were full of soldiers moving forward to join this great force, and at night their camp-fires lighted up the surrounding hillside with innumerable fires. Their glorious and genuine cheers resounded in every valley. It was an inspiring sight to us in our embryo state of soldierhood. We lay behind the fortifications looking expectantly for the conflict to begin.

Pope had been defeated; McClellan deposed; petty jealousies and internal dissensions had taken the place of what ought to have been a united army under the leadership of a general in whom it could have implicit confidence. Even the recruits felt this and knew the situation, although we fully realized that we could not all be generals.

General McClellan was still looked up to by the masses and the troops, as the only man then competent to command the army which he had been instrumental in creating, organizing, and molding into shape. It was a very critical period; there was apparent, even to our verdant selves, much disgraceful confusion and disorganization. He assumed command. In the hurried reorganization, many things so essential to the comfort and morale of the rank and file, were overlooked, which afterwards resulted in unnecessary suffering, beyond our power to relieve, causing much growling and grumbling among the men in the ranks, no more so than among the recruits just joined, but especially among the Peninsular veterans, who had, many of them, by this time, got their stomachs more than full, and their appetites thoroughly appeased.

It had rained on the night of the nth, just enough to soak our blankets and clothing, without laying the dust or cooling the atmosphere. On the morning of the 12th, soon after reveille and before our breakfast was finished, pack up was sounded, and we were soon moving across the old aqueduct bridge, through Georgetown to Capitol Hill, where we were expected to take cars for Frederick; but upon reaching the high ground south of the capitol, the orders were countermanded, and, countermarching, we took the Rockville road. Our colonel, Jesse A. Gove, formerly captain of the Tenth United States Infantry, had been killed at Gaines Mill. We were now commanded by Lieutenant-Colonel William Stowell Tilton,[2] of Boston, who, having been wounded

---

[2] William Stowell Tilton (1828–1889), a businessman before and after

and captured at Gaines Mill, and exchanged, had joined us on the 10th, near Fort Ellsworth, the regiment giving him three cheers.

A new regiment, the One Hundred and Eighteenth Pennsylvania, had been assigned to our brigade, the famous "corn exchange" of Philadelphia. It was brand new, gay, and gaudy in its complete outfit, and what baggage it carried! It held over even us recruits. The wet, heavy loads soon began to tell upon the men, especially upon our new-found friends from Pennsylvania. The beat was intolerable, the dust almost suffocating, blinding our eyes and filling our noses and mouths to overflowing; fine and penetrating, it sifted into our faces, which, wet with perspiration, soon changed the appearance of the moving column. The expressions of the countenances were certainly irresistibly comical, and one could have hardly refrained from laughing at the dust and sweat-be-streaked face of some individual who, with rueful glance, looked with such a pleading, beseeching expression, seemingly asking for sympathies, which, under the circumstances, could not be given, had not the condition of all been so nearly alike. Every step was a weary and painful effort, and there was need for great pluck and powers of endurance.

Our bivouac for the night was just beyond Silver Spring on the Rockville road. Soon after we made camp, orders were given to leave all unnecessary things behind to be taken back to Washington. By the light of the fire, all superfluous things were packed, and many now reduced themselves to the clothes they stood in, rations, cartridges, rifle, and canteen.

The straggling had been terrible. Everywhere along the route were to be seen the stragglers of the One Hundred and Eighteenth Pennsylvania, always to be recognized by the huge, brass regulation letters and numbers on their caps. They literally strewed the road. In many a convenient fence corner could be seen a council of war; deliberating, while overhauling their loads, as to whether the Jamaica ginger, soap, writing (patent) desks, blacking, tactics, emery powder, cholera powder, pills, paper collars, extra shirts, etc., should be dropped from their "bureaus," now discovered to be a "little heavy," much to the delight of the Peninsular "vets," who, while unmercifully chaffing us, now regaled themselves and their light-loaded bodies with many a long-denied article at our expense.

Stragglers were coming in all night, and ludicrous were the sights and comical the questions asked by some of these patriots of Uncle Sam, as they wandered about in the darkness after their commands.

The march to Frederick City, via Rockville, Seneca Mills, Clarksburg, Hyattstown, and Urbana, was a terrible one upon those who had just joined, and on the 14th of September, when our march kept step with the booming of the cannon from the South Mountain battle-field, after a twenty-four mile march and without rations, we camped on the banks of the Monocacy river. We, chafed, sorefooted, and empty recruits, reckoned we had struck a "crusher" for our initiation, and—well, we wished ourselves snugly and safely at home in the good old state of Massachusetts.

At this bivouac, on the edge of Frederick, the writer thought he would be safer and secure better sleep, perhaps avoid a wetting, by getting under one of the wagons. A mule is not particular whether he eats a wagon pole, the harnesses or the canvas cover, chews his mate's tail or—regales himself on a recruit. They were very hungry, had been pushed all day, and gave vent to their uneasiness and weariness by the longest drawn-out brays, groans, and wee-bawings.

Finally, one of them, after vainly endeavoring to masticate his iron-bound feed-box, smelled the writer, this fresh recruit, and seizing him by the blouse, dragged him forth for a better chance at him.

The writer had been in dreamland, and when he discovered where he was and what had him, he almost shrieked aloud. He never slept under a wagon after that; he didn't like that kind of a nightmare.

As we passed through Frederick on the morning of the 15th, we halted for a short time in one of the main streets. The good Samaritans of the loyal old town vied with each other in contributions of water. Bread in loaves as large as a milk pan, and often fruit were pressed upon our unwilling (?), but grateful, victims (?).

On the sidewalks were many prisoners who had just been sent in from the field of South Mountain. Among them were some North Carolinians, as slim as a lath and as tall as a church spire. They were gathered in groups. Pretty soon, two of their number, who seemed to be pointing out and gesticulating towards our colonel, drawled out in the usual "Tar-heel" vernacular, "I say, Bill, thar's the 'old cock' we uns had a prisoner at Richmond." The other looked again, and nodding assent, replied loudly, "I reckon you uns is right." The colonel pricked up his ears. Before the war, it was said, he had been in the tobacco business in Richmond, and after being wounded and captured, he was confined, it seems, through some singular freak of fortune, in his old warehouse. His old acquaintances, upon learning that he was there, placed the following placard upon the door: "If the friends of Col. W. S. Tilton wish to see him, they will find him at his former place of business." Colonel Tilton had but just rejoined, was scarcely recovered from his wound, and this, with the remark of the prisoners, intended for his ears, nettled him. He turned his angry face towards the elongated "Tar-heelers," and with a strong, nasal twang, for which he was noted, said, "Yes, you d—d scoundrels!

I'm the same 'old cock,' but blank! blank!! you'll never get him there again! "

Our bivouac that night in the valley of Middletown was near where a long bridge had been burned by the rebels. It was Frederick's loveliest surroundings, and lives yet in our memories. It was a picture of unparalleled beauty. Innumerable camp-fires sprung up as if by magic; groups of men were about them; a moon lent its enchantment to the scene. As far as the eye could reach in that extensive valley, it was a grand, illuminated panoramic view.

Wagons were parked, their long rows of white canvas tops reflected in the moonlight; horses were at the picket ropes; mules at the wagon tongues. The former were neighing their shrillest notes; the latter weehawing their loudest brays; men were bringing in forage and armfuls of rails, and soon the expectant sounds gave way to munching, and with coffee-cup in hand all were happy, man and beast, regardless of tomorrow's dangers and duties.

As we wound along the hilly road leading to South Mountain on the morning of the 16th, we met more prisoners on the road and the wounded being conveyed to the hospitals at Frederick. Here we observed the camp of the regulars on the left of the road, and a moment later, much to our joy and surprise, saw our brother coming down the slope to the side of the road, and were soon walking with him towards the gap in the mountains.

Camp near Boonsborough,

September 17, 1862

Thank God, I have seen the boys! We were encamped near the battle-field of Middletown with a crowd of prisoners, awaiting to be relieved by a regiment of General Morell's division. I knew that he belonged to General Porter's corps, and thought the Twenty-second might be with him. After waiting two days, General Morell arrived. I had just got up and washed my face, when I saw the division pass. I rushed down and inquired for the Twenty-second; it was just passing. Bob rushed at me; Walter soon followed. I walked along with them two miles and then returned. They both looked hearty and well. I asked them if they wanted money, and they said "No." Walter had enough; Bob had lost his all—somewhere. I shall look for them again, but, Father, one or both may now be sleeping his last sleep. We are having a terrible battle; it commenced at daylight this morning and has been raging furiously all day. All other battles in this country are merely skirmishes compared to it.[3]

[Stonewall] Jackson took Harper's Ferry with the entire garrison. Franklin has probably retaken it. Jackson crossed the river to

---

[3] September 17, 1862 still stands as the bloodiest day of fighting in U.S. history. It was a Union victory.—2019

Virginia, and recrossed above with a part of his corps to assist Lee, etc., against McClellan. Burnside has the left, forcing them up from Harper's Ferry; Sumner and Fitz John Porter have the centre.

The rebels have only two fords. Franklin is trying to cut them off from one, and Hooker the other. We have taken many prisoners, but the fighting has been bloody and obstinate. General Mansfield is killed, and Generals Hartsuff and Meagher -wounded. The fighting has ceased for the night. What will the morrow bring forth? I understood that General Morell's division would be held in reserve with the regulars; if so, I think they have not been engaged. Do not be too anxious. I will do all I possibly can to find out about them. I think "Little Mac' has taken them this time. We have slaughtered them fearfully, and driven them some. Our artillery has a greater range than theirs. I saw the fight at Middletown (South Mountain), and will tell you about it as soon as possible.

Our brother of the artillery writes a letter dated,

Fort Tillinghast,

September 7, 1862

Walt and Bob I have seen quite often. Frank Kimball stopped with me Thursday night, he being too sick to go to his regiment. Friday he felt much better, and I took his gun and knapsack, and went with him to Hall's hill, where the Twenty-second lay. I spent about two hours with the boys, read your letters, etc. Poor boys! You little know what they will have to suffer; yet they seem contented, and I hope they will be so. I was going to see them today, but I hear they have all gone, and do not know where. Hall's hill is about five miles from our camp."

Hospital, Fort Albany,

September 17, 1862

You will perceive that I am now in the hospital; I have been quite sick for the past week, having had a severe attack of jaundice, and am not much better now, excepting that I am not so sick at my stomach as I have been.

My skin is about as yellow as it well can be. I do not have any bed to lie on, and the rats have a 'battalion drill' over my body about every night. Last night a poor devil (as a soldier is called here) died next to me, and I did not know it until morning, he died so' easily. The doctor had not been to see him for twenty-four hours.

I am now sitting on the floor, writing on a box, having made a penholder with a knife, borrowed paper and envelope, and have got a stamp that Kate enclosed for me to forward a letter to Bob, but as I some time ago delivered that letter in person, I have decided to 'freeze' to the stamp.

They (Bob and Walt) encamped a short distance from Tillinghast for a day or two, but I woke up one morning and found they had departed but do not know where they have gone. I hear that they are with McClellan's victorious army, and hope they are safe.

If I do not soon get relieved of this 'yellow fever,' I shall not be fit for anything. You must miss Bob and Walt greatly, and I do not see how you made up your mind to part with them both. I should think you and Mother would feel about lost without them. God grant they may be safely returned to you! They will have to endure hardships that people little dream of at home. It would almost make you weep to see the soldiers that returned from the Peninsula, after they arrived here. To tell the truth, it was the worst sight I ever saw, the men being completely dirty, and most of them covered with vermin, as they had no change of clothing; and what made them feel worse was taking McClellan away from them.

The men almost worship him, and all agree in saying that if he had had twenty thousand fresh men after the Battle of Fair Oaks, his headquarters would now be at the 'Spottswood Hotel' in Richmond. Is there anything sure of Gene's being colonel of a regiment, and what one is it? Where is Gene now? I wish you would answer me as soon as you can. If I knew he was in Washington, I would go to see him. I have walked five or six miles to see him, yet failed to meet him. I suppose it is nothing but 'war' at home. The old soldiers here feel rather hard to think that they had come out here with nothing to hope for but to be 'wrapped up in an American flag' and die a 'glorious death,' while these new ones come on to serve half time, and get a bounty of from two to three hundred dollars. It is rather rough on the old ones, don't you think so?

There are a great many who come out here now who have been in the service before, and have got their discharge on various pretexts from old regiments. They come out here merely for the money, and commence 'playing sick' soon after they get here. If a new soldier is sick, he gets but very little sympathy from the old ones; they commence, 'Another two hundred dollars gone to the devil" 'There's a two hundred dollar chap!' 'Government is two hundred dollars out on him! etc., etc. There was a fellow, the other day, who belonged to a Pennsylvania regiment, had been out before, got discharged, gone home, got a large bounty, and returned. He was playing the 'rheumatism dodge' a second time, and was boasting how much money he had made by the operation, and that he would soon have his second discharge, to an old Michigan regiment that had been with McClellan. These men could not stand it; they 'dipped into' that fellow and beat him shockingly so that I hardly think he will recover. When I saw him, he was completely covered with blood, and senseless.

We passed through Turner's Gap. The Confederate dead were still lying by the roadside, awaiting the arrival of the burial party. Unkempt and unwashed, their ashy faces and ragged, bloody, bloated bodies presented a ghastly and repulsive spectacle to us recruits, as yet uneducated or unhardened to the dreadful horrors of war. Many of our number began to surmise, if not to fully realize, that there was no romance about that spectacle.

The debris of the fight lay scattered all about; knapsacks, guns, canteens, blankets, hats, etc. As we descended into the lovely valley of Boonesboro' and passed through the little town of the same name, all seemed to be hurry and excitement.

Cavalry and infantry were going hurriedly to the front, and frequently we were moved to the side of the road as a staff officer hastily galloped along and ordered the passage of a battery, a column of cavalry, or sent the wagon trains into the fields to park. Occasionally the boom of cannon could be heard ahead. The town was full of prisoners, stragglers, squads of mounted men, wagons, mules, etc., and for a time this busy and significant preparation and these bustling scenes about us diverted cur attention as we hurried along. Just beyond the town we halted to make coffee. Later in the afternoon of the 16th, the column passed through Keedysville, making many tiresome halts at the edge of the town, while passing through the masses of artillery, cavalry, and wagon trains. At times the road seemed entirely blocked.

Upon gaining the westerly edge of the town, towards the Antietam, we filed to the left, near a small chapel (now replaced by a new brick church), and inclining, or obliquing to our right, passing over a small knoll, halted in what we supposed was our fighting position. It was on the south side of the Keedysville and Sharpsburg road, and about 300 yards from where there is now a new brick schoolhouse. This chapel was packed with wounded after the battle.

On the right of the road could be seen the lines of battle; the slopes seemed black with them, as far as the eye could reach. Batteries were in position, and columns were moving. Everything clearly indicated extensive preparations for the coming fight. Just before dark, while we were gathered about our fires, making coffee and eating our supper, the enemy commenced shelling our position and was promptly responded to by our guns. A lively artillery duel ensued, continuing long into the night.

From our bivouac on the knoll we had a fine view; the fuses looked like fireflies, as they swiftly darted through the sky, and the harsh grating of the pieces as the shells burst and filled the air, were ominous sounds to our inexperienced ears. It was, however, quite a pyrotechnic treat for us, especially when we felt that we were far enough removed to feel a certain degree of safety.

We little realized, as yet, the danger and terrible destruction attending these awful missiles of war. As we lay upon the ground for the night, it commenced raining. There was no sleep, and late into the midnight hours, groups of "owls," who never sleep, it would seem, were gathered about the small, low fires, listening to the far-off cheering on the right, and gravely discussing the probabilities of the coming morrow.

As soon as it was light, the firing was renewed, and by sunrise it had increased to a loud, incessant, bellowing cannonade. The black lines of battle which we had seen the night before on the slopes to our right, had now all disappeared. The Battle of Antietam was on.

Between 7 and 8 o'clock we were ordered to "fall in," and moving slowly to our front in column, parallel to the road, we proceeded to a point where the Keedysville and Sharpsburg road meets the Rohrersville road at Porterstown, and crossing the former, halted under an abrupt line of hills, just a few yards to the north of the road. We filled a gap, which had been made by the withdrawal just before our arrival, of Richardson's division of Sumner's corps. The Pry house,[4] General McClellan's headquarters, was in full view, about 1,000 yards northeast, and the nearest house was that of Eckers, 350 yards directly in our rear, occupied at this time by Straub, or Staub. It was a square brick, with a peaked roof facing the Keedysville and Sharpsburg pike, and at that time had a large garden filled with old-fashioned flowers and shrubbery, fruit trees, etc.

Our position was in reserve, near the centre, supporting several heavy batteries, among which were Kusserow's, Taft's, and Weed's (Battery D, Fifth U. S. Artillery). Here we lay on our arms all day, ready to move at a moment's notice. Several times we were ordered to "fall in," and move to the support of Hooker, on the right, and started to do so, but in a few moments were told to lie down again. We were at no time actively engaged, and lost but one man, wounded, in the regiment. We were, however, witnesses of the entire battle from one of the most commanding positions on the field. It was a grand spectacle. Occasionally a shell would sail, shrieking and rasping over our heads. Once or twice they burst accurately over us, and a horse or mule, tied into Straub's fences, was killed. We often went up and watched the great battle, now at its height. Once or twice, when several shells came uncomfortably near, we dodged so conspicuously, that the old cannoneers, standing by their unlimbered pieces, laughed at us; but, in a few moments we had the laugh on them, for suddenly a shell came right for and into the battery. They very discreetly and hastily sought cover, while we, somewhat mortified by their derisive laughs, and failing to fully appreciate the real danger, remained in our places. The shell failed to explode, and

---

[4] Now the Pry House Hospital Museum.—2019

fortunately, for had it done so, some of us might not be alive to write of it.

We could see the lines of battle go up on the right—an indistinct, irregular mass—almost hidden in the dense smoke, the battle-flags floating out from their staffs and showing the different regiments and brigades. Fresh and rapid rolls of musketry would break out—then puff! puff!! a boom, boom, boom, in one, two, three order, told us of the light batteries.

Sometimes we could see the line waver and break, the fire from the guns would slacken; a pause, and through the smoke we could see the confused and shattered fragments come staggering, flying back, and now came the "yi-yih's," the screeches, or yells of the "Johnnies," followed by the sturdy, ringing cheers of our boys. The renewed cracking of the Parrots followed, as battery after battery came up to check the onward rush; but the confusion was only temporary; a reinforcement from some other portion of the line, and the same ground was again and again passed over in fearful struggle. We saw the Irish Brigade (Meagher's) make its famous charge, its green flag, with the harp of Erin, outlined clearly against the sky.

On the left was Burnside. Once or twice his lines had advanced towards a great cornfield, which was alive with the blaze of the Confederate rifles, but as often had he been driven back. Sometimes we could see his line go through this cornfield, nearly to the edge of the fringe of timber that skirted Antietam creek. It was a magnificent exhibition of pluck and bravery. The Thirty-fifth Massachusetts was a new regiment; we had many friends in it. It had joined Burnside's corps just before starting from Washington. It was composed of splendid material. It was said that while near the edge of the cornfield, with its flank resting on nothing, or "in the air," in line of battle, a staff officer of Burnside's was sent to inquire what brigade that was, and to withdraw it from such an exposed position. "It is the Thirty-ninth Massachusetts," was the reply. It had uselessly sacrificed 50 per cent, of its strength to satisfy a false pride, and fulfil certain conditions of bravery, which was never afterwards attempted.

Later in the afternoon, after severe fighting on both sides, Burnside was ordered to carry the bridge across the creek, at all hazards. He obeyed the order, but the attacking column met with a fearful loss. Colonel Henry W. Kingsbury[5] of the Eleventh Connecticut was killed at the head of his column; he was adjutant of the Corps of Cadets before our brother's graduation; was frequently mentioned in his letters, and was greatly beloved by all who knew him.

Shortly after two o'clock, General McClellan rode down the road from the Pry house, with his staff, passing by our line. As we rose up and every man cheered to the echo, we were greeted with the same kindly smile, and removal of the hat, with a courteous bow, which bespoke the true gentleman and appreciative soldier.

Before leaving Washington, many boxes had reached the regiment, and most of their contents had been hurriedly distributed among the men. Much had to be thrown away. One man had received a can of honey, had distributed the sweet morsel, which he could not carry, and a recruit having begged the can, it was given to him. No one could imagine what use he was going to make of it. While lying behind this hill in line of battle, whenever there was a lull in the firing, the men indulged in what had now become a chronic pastime-cooking. Soon there was a rousing fire, and having "flipped up" to see who would fill the canteens at Straub's house, the choice places along the line of flaming rails were, in a few minutes, covered with black coffee cups—among them the new, bright honey can, with the lid screwed down. The recruit was chuckling to himself, while watching the pot, that he would have his coffee first, when, alas! through his lack of knowledge of the expansive force of steam, this innocent man came near blowing his own head off, and scalding the whole company.

He stooped over his patent coffeepot to see how near done his coffee was when, whi-z-z-z! bang!! and up went the can like a rocket into the air, tearing the fire to pieces, scattering the rails

---

5 Henry Walter Kingsbury (1836–1862), West Point class of 1861.

and cups in every direction, and making a cloud of steam which, fortunately without scalding anybody, must have deluded the "Johnnies" with the hope that a caisson had exploded. How that recruit did get roundly cursed for his thick-headed stupidity, nor were the old grumblers satisfied, or their anger cooled off, until the bugler had filled all of the canteens again, and once more started the coffee cups on their bubbling rounds.

Among the number in our little tent at "Camp Excelsior," near Fort Ellsworth, was a man, somewhat past middle-age, who had joined us at Camp Cameron. He was full-bearded and bronzed; was possessed of much native good sense and shrewdness, and had enlisted for Andrew's First Company of Massachusetts Sharpshooters, then attached to the Fifteenth Massachusetts.

His name was Asa Fletcher,[6] and his home was Winchester, Mass, According to his own story, related in the most modest manner, and afterwards fully substantiated, he was an expert gunner, and a "crack rifle shot." Not of the "wind-gauge-don't-talk-above-a-whisper" order of today, but one who could step out with a rifle at from two to five hundred yards, at arm's length, and put the lead into a bull's-eye, with an old-fashioned target rifle.

He was cool, perfectly self-possessed, and gave as his reason for enlisting in the sharpshooters, that he was "determined to place himself where he could do the most good." He had gunned a great deal along the North Carolina coast and about Chesapeake Bay, and many a juicy canvas-back of his shooting had found its way into the Baltimore market. We boys all looked up to Asa Fletcher, and regarded his advice and opinions, although sometimes rather gruffly expressed, as worth following.

His long-shore campaigns had taught him much that we now derived the benefit of. He had a kind heart, and was always trying to contribute to our comfort, and regulating the affairs of the tent.

---

[6] Asa Fletcher (1820–1880) was a 41-year-old carpenter when he enlisted as a private. He returned to that profession after the war. A ball through the lung at Antietam and days spent without proper care ended his military career (census and pension records, 2019).

The blankets must be shaken mornings, left to air a few minutes in the sun, then folded up; the tent brushed out and things righted—those essentials which volunteer recruits so little regarded at the beginning of the war. Some "kicked" at all this "nonsense," but Fletcher good-naturedly insisted, and soon all acquiesced.

One day, Fletcher, in his eagerness to make us more comfortable, brought in a hospital bed-tick which he had found thrown away on the road to Fairfax seminary, and had filled with hay to keep us off the damp ground. He generously offered to share it with the "tent's crew." In a few nights we were all itching and scratching. We called it "prickly heat," but a closer examination revealed to our horrified gaze genuine "gray-backs" of huge proportions, and upon a rigid inspection of the mattress, which we insisted upon but Fletcher poo-hoohed at, we found "'em thick," and he never heard the last of that bed-tick. When arms were issued during that violent storm and dreadful night, at the "Round House," Fletcher was given a Remington rifle of small calibre, such as were issued to many of the New York regiments at the beginning of the war. He was furnished with but twenty rounds of ammunition. His quick marksman's eye at once discovered the deficiencies of such a weapon for a sharpshooter. In his strong, high-keyed, nasal voice, with Yankee-like readiness for a trade, he suggested a "swap" for my new Springfield rifle, the envy of our little squad; but, boy-like, I refused, confident that I "knew a good thing when I saw it." He joined our regiment with us, at Hall's Hill, as he could get no trace of his company, and he was the only man for Andrew's Sharpshooters; but there was no provision made for him, nor could rations be issued to him, and he determined to push on in search of his command, which, he was informed from a reliable source, was already on its way through Maryland, and alone he set out.

He died some years ago, but he thus related this story to the writer, years after the war;

"The second or third day out from Washington, the rations you boys so generously furnished me, gave out. I knew that I must not waste my cartridges, and having fallen in with some stragglers of the chronic stamp, knowing what strict orders there were against straggling and foraging, I was continually in fear that I might be arrested. But hunger knows no law. I used one of my precious cartridges in killing a hog, which I tumbled over at the first shot as he was running two hundred yards distant.

"This supplied us with fresh meat. I begged some hard bread, and with plenty of peaches and green corn, I got along all right. I joined my company at Antietam, the evening of the 16th, as they were lying in line of battle. I did not know right face from left. Their rifles were not like mine, so Captain A. said, 'Go in! Get under cover and do all the harm you can to the Johnnies; the first man killed in the company, if within your reach, take his rifle and cartridges.' This was good advice, but not at all reassuring to a new recruit just going into battle; how did I know that I should not be the first to be killed myself?

"On the morning of the 17th, when going in with the company, and I saw the frightful slaughter all about me, I found myself trying to dodge every shot and shell that came in our direction. My nerves were all unstrung under this altogether new and novel excitement; it was different kind of gunning from what I was used to; my hands shook and I was mad with myself that I acted so like a coward, and found it so hard to control my feelings.

"The moment we halted in line, however, and the captain said, 'Lie down! every man on his own hook!' I was all right, and was just as cool as though shooting at a target, or watching behind a 'blind' for shot at a duck on the rise. I got behind a tree, and kneeling, watched my chances. I had but nineteen cartridges, and that worried me some; but I determined, upon the captain's suggestion, to change my rifle and ammunition at the first opportunity, for then I should have plenty.

"The 'Johnnies' were behind haystacks. I shot five times deliberately, and dropped a man every time. How do I know it? Well, I did not shoot until I saw a body, and a good, fair mark; then I sighted to kill, and saw the man drop after I had fired.

"Just as I expected, though, the Remington rifle heated right up, and fouled. I rammed down a ball; it stuck. I partially rose up, either to draw it, or to force it home, when I saw a rebel steadily aim at me from the haystack where I had dropped the others. I dodged down, but wasn't quick enough; he fired; the ball took me here, through the body, going through a portion of my lung. I fell, with a dull numbness all over me.

"All daylong I lay, unable to move hand or foot. The battle raged over and around me. Once a horse almost trampled on my prostrate body; again, a party of rebels came up to me, and were deliberating whether to pin their bayonets through me. I told them that I was virtually their prisoner, although on the battle field, and after roundly cursing me they left me.

"I saw near me many of our own men struck a second time when attempting to move, and whenever I lifted my head or moved my arm, I was shot at. I finally determined to play dead, which I did, until the rebel wounded were picked up, when, seeing that they were going to leave me, and knowing I would die on the field that night without assistance, I begged to be taken off. After robbing me of everything about my person, we were taken to a barn and placed on some straw. My wound had not been dressed. After suffering many torments for want of water, I finally was given some, and immediately felt better.

"When I asked how soon I was to be attended to, I got nothing but curses, and 'when we uns are taken care of,' for a reply.

"Stonewall Jackson's brigade went by, and he was pointed out to me. When the rebels retreated across the river, I was paroled, and carried with other prisoners, wounded and paroled, to Frederick City, where I lay for many weeks before I could be sent home and discharged."

Such was the experience of a sharpshooter, after four weeks' service. He subsequently died from the effects of this wound.

Night had closed in upon the scenes and incidents of the day. A bloody battle had been fought. The worst features were to come afterwards. It seemed like Sunday in a quiet New England village, when we moved out early on the morning of the 18th, a bright, beautiful, sunshiny day. Such a hush! Such a still calm had succeeded the incessant uproar of the previous day.

Our progress was necessarily slow; through fields, and barnyards filled with hundreds of wounded; everywhere in and out, amidst a vast out-of-door hospital.

The direction of our march was southwest along a high ridge, towards H. B. Rohrbach's[7] (now Wyand's) house, where Colonel Kingsbury died, a few hundred yards from the Antietam [Creek]. We halted for some time at the Burnside Bridge, on the east side of the creek. It bore evidence of having been the scene of a desperate fight; bullet holes were to be seen in every direction, and the trees and fences were scarred and splintered. The dead and dying strewed the ground, and all about was the wreckage of battle. On the steep hillside, completely overlooking and commanding the bridge and its approaches, were the rebel rifle-pits, which, with large rocks and trunks of trees, had served as a shelter for the enemy when our column advanced on the charge across the bridge.

Late in the afternoon, in the midst of a drenching shower, and after some marching and countermarching, we relieved a division of the Ninth Corps (Sturgis's),[8] on the west side, having crossed the bridge for this purpose, our regiment relieving the Forty-fifth Pennsylvania, and were placed on picket for the night, about 500 yards above the bridge, under an abrupt bank that extended along the Antietam.

It drizzled during the entire night. Our beds were upon some wet, split-out shingles. Some fresh beef, issued to us just before starting, and which we had no opportunity to cook, was eaten

---

[7] The Rohrbach farm with the original house now restored is east of Burnside Bridge. In recent years it was listed for sale for $ 1,349,000 (Historic Homes Network).—2019

[8] Samuel Davis Sturgis (1822–1889) was a career officer most famous for being colonel of the 7th Cavalry (on detached service) when it met its disaster at the Little Bighorn in 1876. Sturgis' son was killed along with General Custer.—2019

raw, and, without coffee, relished in the gloom and silence. About midnight, a squadron of cavalry came galloping up the road from the direction of the bridge and attacked a house (Sherrick's)[9] on the north side of the road. It was occupied by the enemy's sharpshooters, and was just outside our line. They gave a wild cheer, half yell. The bullets flew pretty thickly for a while, as they went clattering and chattering over the slope. The noise and uproar had aroused us from a sort of drowse, and after that nobody thought of sleep. We could hear the cracking of carbines, the intermingled cheers and yells, and soon they came back, reporting that the "Johnnies" had gone out of the house like "rats." The dead were all about us, and many wounded. It was our first night upon a battle-field. The sights were terrifying; sounds horrible and startling. A kind of hardness crept over us during the long, wakeful night we passed in that blood-stained, death-strewn spot by the Burnside Bridge, and we grew older in thought and feeling by having come in contact with such misery and suffering, which we never so fully realized afterwards.

On the following morning, the 19th, the sun came out bright and beautiful; the blackened faces and bloated bodies were beyond recognition, and were disgusting to look upon for a moment. Some wore the air of despair, while others had a calm and peaceful face, as though in dream land, and had not known prolonged pain.

The enemy had now, it was soon discovered, left our front, and while awaiting the command to move forward, we went over that portion of the field. There was a certain fascination in it to my young mind, although exceedingly sad and impressive; horrible to contemplate even at this distance of time, and which has never faded from my recollection during all these succeeding years.

Volumes could be filled with personal incidents and reminiscences of this field of Antietam alone, Upon visiting Sherrick's house this morning, we found it quite a sumptuous

---

[9] The Sherrick farm and buildings are today owned by the National Park Service within the Antietam National Battlefield.—2019

affair. It had been hastily evacuated, as it was between the lines. The foragers ahead of us had pulled out what edibles it contained, and among them a splendid assortment of jellies, preserves, etc., the pride of every Maryland woman's heart, but now scattered all about. The orchard was filled with the choicest fruit. What a feast! Our stomachs just beginning to become accustomed to "salt horse" and "hard tack," earnestly opened and yearned for this line of good things. No crowd of schoolboys, let loose from the confinement of a recitation room, ever acted so absurdly, as did these rough, bronzed soldiers and recruit allies, on that death-strewn ground about Sherrick's yard and orchard. They would seize a pot of jam, grape jelly, huckleberry stew, or pineapple preserve, and after capering about a while, with the most extravagant exhibitions of joy, would sit upon the ground, and with one piece of hard bread for a plate, and another for a scoop, would shovel out great heaps of the delectable stuff, which rapidly disappeared into their capacious mouths. This went on for some time while waiting for the order to move; when some wag, "not wisely but too well," started one of those famous camp rumors, which gathers as it rolls, that the rebel pickets who had occupied the house, had, out of revenge, poisoned every pot and jar we had eaten from; had carefully left them in full sight as a bait, and sure death was now our near future.

Such looks of consternation; such elongated faces, were never seen before. Numerous inquiries were made for emetics; others rushed for the surgeon, many imagining upon the spur of the moment, and feeling nauseated from over-gorging, that they could distinctly feel the pain of the poison now working, while the wiser ones relieved their stomachs, and with them—their fears— by nature's process. Nor did the panic subside, and confidence become fully restored, until hours afterwards, when it was discovered that nobody had died from the effects.

Opposite to Sherrick's is Stern's, in which Otto[10] lived during the battle, and near it the old stone grist-mill.[11]

---

[10] The Otto farm and original house still stand on Antietam National Battlefield.—2019

It was a lively scene that morning of the 19th as we hurried through the streets of Sharpsburg and out on the main pike beyond, through the fields, to a position near one of the fords on the Potomac, where it had been found by a hasty reconnoissance that the whole Rebel army had crossed into Virginia.

We led the advance. The men trudged through the mud, and joked and chatted with the regiments of other brigades and divisions. The signal flags on top of the church tower were wig-wagging like mad, conveying rapid messages. Orderlies and staff officers, bespattered from head to foot, were galloping here and there, exciting the ire of our grumblers, by the coat of slime and mud they splashed on them in their hasty ride. The streets were filled with wreckage. Here and there a wagon, a wheel, a dead mule, or a defunct caisson were keeled up as though in their death agonies. Artillery and cavalry were hurrying forward, and long columns of infantry were being directed along the main streets to different positions along the new front.

Many of the houses and front yards were filled with the wounded of both armies, whom the enemy in their hurried retreat could not take with them. Hundreds out in the open air were lying on clean straw that had been provided by our men, together with such other acts of kindness and attention as they had never received before.

We moved about four miles, halting once or twice, where the rebels had camped, especially at General Lee's headquarters on the north side of the road in the grove near the outskirts of

---

[11] Michael Tenant, who occupies the house next east of Sherrick's, told the writer three years ago, while standing at the spring, and near the mill, many incidents. His house, he said, was built out of the squared logs that came out of the old Lutheran church when it was torn down, one year after the battle. This church tower was used as a signal tower by General McClellan, and it was converted into a hospital after the battle. He showed the writer where he saw a soldier fall dead at his gate, shot by a Confederate sharpshooter in the mill; he buried him, after much difficulty, in the hard limestone soil, and later identified the spot for his disinterment and conveyal [sic] to the National Cemetery when it was located at Sharpsburg.—note in original

Sharpsburg. They were scattered with plunder of all kinds, and many old letters, which we amused ourselves with reading as we marched, and would prove rich literature in these pages had they been preserved, but we cared not for such trifles then, and soon threw them back into the debris and filth that cumbered the ground.

We left the road near J. D. Groves's[12] house (used as General Fitz John Porter's headquarters), opposite Captain D. Smith's (which was used as an immense hospital for the wounded of both sides), and turning south through the fields, soon struck the river near Blackford's Ford, below Shepardstown. We halted to reconnoitre. The enemy were all across. Several old caissons with their wheels chopped, and much wreckage, lay about on the banks. The pickets of the enemy were seen on the opposite bank. A few shots were fired by some guns planted on the bluff over our heads; the sharpshooters of our regiment were sent under cover and to remain there that night, while the balance were withdrawn to about one mile back towards Groves's house where we went into bivouac for the night, furnishing ourselves liberally with straw from the stacks nearby.

---

[12] Jacob Grove house still stands in Sharpsburg.—2019

ENGAGEMENT WITH THE REAR GUARD

On the night of September 19, a lively scouting column under the command of General Griffen, crossed the river and succeeded in capturing two guns, one of which was a gun of his old West Point battery (afterwards Battery D, Fifth United States Artillery) captured from him at the first battle of Bull Run, when attached to the battalion of regulars in which was our brother. The other was of English make, having the Tower stamp on it. The party came through our camp some time before morning making a great clatter, shouting, and giving the awakened men in their bivouac the joyful news.

Early on the morning of the 20th we were ordered to make a reconnoissance in force across the Potomac, at Blackford's Ford. This had been used by Lee, both in coming into and retreating from Maryland. It was, where we forded it, some distance below the dam, quite shallow, a little over the knees, with a somewhat pebbly bottom, but not many large rocks. We were to ascertain the whereabouts of Lee's rear guard. We had no trouble in finding it. Innocent of the diversion which was in store for us, we splashed and pad-died our way along. Some of the men had taken off both shoes and stockings; others, perhaps the majority, had kept them on; these were the wise ones, for we had use for them on our return.

The cavalry were met returning. The splashing of their horses sent the water flying into the faces of some of our grumblers, who out of spite, shouted out, "Are there any dead cavalrymen ahead? What guerillas do you belong to?" etc., etc., to which the answer comes back promptly, "Yes, you bummers, we do the fighting and leave the dead cavalrymen for the 'dough boys' to pick up. Go to the rear you 'worm crushers'!"

The chaffing continued until the river was crossed. We were then hurriedly, and with sharp commands, formed into the line of battle, ordered to "load at will," and by the flank were directed to move by a narrow cart path up a rather sheltered ravine, on one

149

side of which was a protecting bank, and on the other, a rather abrupt bluff that formed the bank of the Potomac.

We again hastily formed line of battle. A crack, a crash, followed by another and another, in quick succession, directly over our heads, came from our batteries on the Maryland shore, and was the first intimation we had that a rebel line of battle was rapidly moving down upon us.

"Fix bayonets!" came the command, followed by "Lie down!" and, although from our sheltered position we could not then see the enemy's line, a moment later the roll of musketry from the right of our brigade told us that the. engagement had begun.

It was a sharp fight. One man in our regiment. Corporal George Davis of Co. B, had the right side of his face knocked off by one of our own shells. Another, Private Chauncey C. Knowlton of Co. I, was terribly wounded in the leg, probably by a shot from our own guns; it was amputated. Both died.

As the firing surged along the line towards us, and the men commenced firing at the grey line now beginning to show up over the bank, we were ordered to withdraw. As we fell back, the One Hundred and Eighteenth Pennsylvania, which had received the full force of the blow thus far, did not follow us, and being overwhelmed by superior numbers, were driven from their position on the extreme right to the crest of the bluff, where many were killed, wounded, or captured, and driven pell-mell over its precipitous slopes.

Our passage back to the Maryland shore was a hard one, higher up and nearer the dam; the river was full of snares and pitfalls, and up to our necks in many places, besides being very rocky.

As we emerged from the stream and passed through Berdan's Sharpshooters, in the dry bed of the Canal, we halted for a moment to gain our breath. While resting here, a little officer of the 118th Pennsylvania (Captain Henry O'Neill [?]) came in behind us. He was dripping with water. In his enthusiastic energy to move across and get to the rear, he had not stopped to see how many of the regiment had followed. Waving his sword, he shouted in a high and squeaky voice—"Follow me, all that are left of the gallant 'Corn Exchange.'" He turned as he did so, and there behind him stood one half drowned little corporal, smaller than himself, beside a very tall private. Both the officer and corporal pieced together could hardly have equaled his size. We broke out into uncontrollable laughter at the absurdity of the group. It seems that the order for the brigade to withdraw across the river had not reached this regiment on the right, for some still unexplained reason, or they attempted to retire when too late, but, either on account of the chaffing they received, or the sensitiveness which they naturally felt at this, their first battle, from that time on there was a lack of cordiality between the rest of the brigade and our brethren from the Keystone State, who stoutly asserted that we ran away and left them to their fate, and whenever on picket, scrambling for water at a small spring, gathering rails, or "reaching" for straw, there were numerous collisions, although no bloodshed, between the two commands. A conversation on picket occurred shortly after, between one of our sharp-witted Irishmen and a member of the "Corn Exchange" regiment. The latter was upholding their cause and its gallant conduct in staying, while our fellow was very strongly arguing that "any regiment after being ordered to retreat, that did not do so, deserved all they got," etc. The other angrily rejoined, "If you had behaved as well as the 'gallant Corn Exchange' the Johnnies would have been whipped." "Oh! be gorra! 'Corn Exchange!' 'Corn Exchange!'" said Pat, "there is no such regiment as that now. It is the 'Cob Exchange,' for didn't the 'rebs' shell all the corn off yez the other day?"

We returned to our camp, dried ourselves out by large, roaring fires, related our adventures, and soon grappled with our featherless beds.

Nine or ten rebel brigades took part in this affair. "Stonewall" Jackson's report states that "it ended in an appalling scene of the destruction of human life." General A. P. Hill, who commanded, reports: "Then commenced the most terrible slaughter that this war has yet witnessed. The broad surface of the Potomac was blue with the floating bodies of our foe. But few escaped to tell the tale. By their own account they lost three thousand men, killed and drowned, from one brigade alone."

On the following day, Sunday, we opened with skirmishing, but it soon closed as our dead were brought across for burial.

Newspapers were exchanged, etc.

The truce closed at 5 p. m., when our batteries promptly opened to show that we were all alive.

We picketed near the river, sleeping at night in the dry canal, our bodies at an angle of nearly 45 degrees, and here we suffered all the ills of violent colds and malaria, from the low bottoms and foggy atmosphere about us, and diarrhea from drinking the limestone water to which we were unaccustomed, and for want of proper shelter, clothes, shoes and blankets. On the 21st of September, headquarters of the Army of the Potomac were at Captain Smith's farm, nearly opposite General Fitz John Porter's headquarters at the Grove house. Smith's house and barns were filled with wounded.

While on picket, September 24th, a large squad—some five hundred prisoners—went splashing across the river, overjoyed to get back to their native Southland.

The President reviewed the army, and here we saw for the first time, Abraham Lincoln. How long and gaunt he looked, but with what a kindly smile did he greet the Boys in Blue as he hastily rode with the General along line after line.

How the smile from a careworn and anxious face touched the hearts of those bronzed, rough looking men. It was like an electric shock. It flew from elbow to elbow, and with a loud cheer, every soldier gave vent to his suppressed feeling, making the welkin ring, and conveyed to him the fact that his smile had gone home and found a response.

September 27. Headquarters moved two miles in the direction of Harper's Ferry and camped.

October 8. General M. Patrick was assigned as provost marshal of the army, and headquarters moved to Knoxville, Md.

October 13. Headquarters moved to Brownsville, in Pleasant Valley, Md.

October 19. A provisional brigade was formed from the Ninety-third New York, Twentieth New York, Eighth United States Infantry and Sturgis Guard. The first was designated as Headquarter Guard, the second and third as Provost Guard, and the last as Body Guard.

October 23. Bishop McIlvaine preached at headquarters. One lady only attended. She had a very sweet voice, and led in singing the hymns.

The first night on picket we lay on the slope of the canal between two rails, with head over the peaked side for a pillow, and woke up with our necks most broken, and with threatened strangulation. The next relief, we tried a bed "without," and woke up to find ourselves in the fire, with our breeches scorched in several places, and our legs well warmed.

We had slid down the inclined plane of moist clay. Our hips were black and blue from too much hard ground in our beds. While on picket, we contrived a way to make meal, and enjoy that delicacy so longed for by a New England boy, "fried hasty pudding."

This pieced out our rations of "hard tack" and "salt horse," the latter so ropy and glistening with briny preservative, as to give our pie-loving, Yankee-recruit-stomachs an ache, to even look at its long drawn-out saltness.

We reached the corn, made graters of our cartridge-box tins by patiently punching holes with our bayonets.

We then grated the corn from the cob, boiled the coarse meal, cooled, sliced, and fried it on tin plates, eating it with sugar, or, we poured the boiled meal upon clean flat stones, and baked it in the hot ashes.

Our division was camped on two sides of a small valley, down which ran a small road through Blackford's (W. M.) woods to the river.

It was located about three fourths of a mile southwest from S. P. Grove's house, where Fitz John Porter had his headquarters, and about half a mile nearly south from where Crow now lives. It was the practice of sutlers and traders of all kinds to come down that road to our camp. They mostly came from Pennsylvania, and asked exorbitant prices for everything. One dollar a pound for butter, six small cakes for fifty cents, etc., was a fair sample of the outrageous advantage and monopoly which these non-combatant sharks seized upon.

We remonstrated, but in vain, and the consequences soon followed. A vigilance committee was organized, with spies to go ahead and sound the traders. If the prices were too high, according to our tariff, a moderate one, a signal was given, and the cry immediately went up "Rally! Rally 1!"

In a moment clouds of soldiers were seen issuing like magic from the ground. They closed in on both sides and rear, and "rounded up" the traders. There was no escape from this kind of a .spider's web. The cart was overturned, everything taken from it; apples, leather pies, gingercakes, etc., and every soldier skurried back with pockets, hats, and arms full of plunder.

In five minutes not a soul was visible, and the dazed peddler gathered up his traps, appealed to the officers, was asked to point out the guilty man, which he could not, and he departed a sadder but wiser man for a new load.

One of our recruits, Milton M. Ingalls, suddenly died, October 24, after a few days' illness. We performed our first burial service, stood guard over his remains at the hospital tent, made his rude coffin of cracker boxes, and late one afternoon marched to the hillside to bury him, the chaplain of the Second Maine officiating.

While making his coffin, another recruit, a large Norwegian sailor, very weak from chronic diarrhea, sat upon the other end of it, and when the last nail was driven, mournfully said, "I shall be next."

The nights grew bitter cold; the sick grew numerous. Many were sick with typhoid fever, and our condition at all times in this camp was mentally, morally, and physically bad. We remained near Sharpsburg until October 30th, and besides doing picket duty opposite Shepardstown, we performed guard and fatigue duty, drilled, and became more and more seasoned for the long two years before us, sheltering ourselves from the heat by day, and shivering through the long, frosty nights.

Not infrequently we got up before dawn to find many running up and down the hard ground to thaw out their congealed blood, or sitting by the smouldering embers of the fire, making "scouse" at the "cook house."

The ground was covered thick with frost, yet we slept in our thin, unlined blouses upon it, with no "ponchos," blankets, or overcoats. The spread or two that we had left by order back near Rockville, had been stored at Washington, never again to see the light of day.

During our gloomy and desponding hours, before getting seasoned and hardened, and while in this chrysalis state, many bright sunbeams crept in; many laughable adventures and ludicrous incidents took place. Frequent visits to the camps of other regiments, and to prisoners under treatment nearby, varied the monotony. The usual camp rumors were rife. "We were going to build log huts, and guard the river for the winter." "Provost duty in Frederick City," etc.

Our letters say:

Sunday, Sept. 21, 1862,

In Camp Near Potomac,

Near Sharpsburg.

I commenced a letter to you at Fort Corcoran, just after we had left Fort Worth, where Bob wrote to you, and just before we left on our long march of six days. I had just written one sheet when we were ordered to march. ***

When passing through Washington, I looked in vain for Gene. We had a long march, and I suffered; especially for food. I never knew what it was to want for bread before. I had to beg, for I was actually weak from total abstinence. *** Bob, Edgar, G. B., and myself were the only ones of the whole company (old fellows and all), who kept up and never straggled. The road was lined with these latter individuals, and even now (though we started a week ago Friday), seven of our company have not yet come up. Frank and LeRoy are thirty miles back, used up. Captain Thompson is back on the supply train, sick. We have only one corporal; our two sergeants are sick, and the company is nowhere. We are not yet drilled; we have not been taught to fire a gun. We were in reserve on Wednesday, and I saw all the tight, except on our left, where Burnside carried the bridge. Thursday we passed that spot on the advance, and were on picket all night in that terrible place, where dead men were piled up in heaps beside us. Such horrid sights I never saw before. Two of our company were on the outpost, skirmishing all night. George Lovejoy and Ed Walton were detailed from us to fill vacancies. We slept on our arms all night.

During the night, a squadron of cavalry attacked a brick mansion occupied by rebel sharpshooters. *** The next morning I visited the place, and got any quantity of jellies, preserves, etc.; but was obliged to leave it all when we marched. It was so before we left our camp near Fort Corcoran; there were four or live boxes came to the company filled with nice things, and we could have lived like princes if we could have stayed, but orders came to march, and we had to leave it all. I left four cans of honey given me, for I could not take it. ***

Well, about the march. We didn't commence marching until two or three days after the account you read. That was the advance of Porter's corps (Syke's division); we were the rear guard and marched Friday, September 12, on a different route, not touching Darnestown. *** When we started, I had no idea where we were going; instead of going directly from Georgetown to Maryland, after we crossed the Aqueduct, we kept on to Washington, and I thought we were going to Baltimore, but, after resting for grub, near the Capitol, we marched way back to Georgetown, and from there started on our march to Rockville. *** You at home can never realize the intense suffering we endured on those five days of marching. The first day we went fifteen miles with our wet stuff on our backs, and hot and dusty enough to suffocate a person. * * * Of course they took the longest way to exercise us. The next morning, seeing that we would never hold out with our loads, the order was to leave everything except what we actually needed. I (R. G. C.) only took my rubber coat.

We marched through Hyattstown and Urbana, and then stopped. They routed us out early the next morning, which was Sunday, and marched us twenty-four miles to Frederick City. My 'fod' (food) had given out in the morning, as had most of them, and when we bivouacked on the banks of the Monocacy river I had nothing to eat but one hardtack about three inches square. What do you think of that, after twenty-four miles of marching on the road, and loaded up at that? We had nothing to eat all night, our rations being gone, and our teams to the rear, on horrid roads. Nothing but hills, hills, and mountains. We suffered as much as the advance, I reckon; those long, hot days of marching, the din of battle in the distance, ever in our ears, and we hurrying forward to be in at the death. That Sunday night we camped at 8 o'clock, and it was as dark as Erebus. These were hard times for the raw recruits, but we did well.***The next morning rations were served out, the teams having come up in the night. ***

We rested at Keediesville that night, and I could see that they were preparing for a great battle the next morning, as I thought, for they had commenced shelling then.***

Say to father that knapsacks are no go any way in the army; a man can't carry one on the march. At the least estimate of weight, and of the best pattern, it is clumsy, and ten to one if you leave it anywhere during a battle, it is lost. I don't want to lug another of the articles while I have my other luggage. I would carry a rubber blanket and poncho coiled up over my back, and perhaps I might add my woolen blanket; but an overcoat is altogether too heavy for light marching order. I should not have thrown away the last two articles in W., if they had not been wet, and I almost dead from sheer exhaustion.

I should not have lived to tell the tale if I had carried them ten miles further, and during even then I should have straggled, and I hated to do that; a thing I didn't do the entire distance, though only four recruits came in on the home-stretch. Many a night I flung myself on the ground supperless and too tired to eat. In the daytime I ate dust, and drank the perspiration that rolled down my face. It was a bitter experience.

Monday, we passed through it (Frederick City), amid the shouts and cheers of the people. We passed through Rockville, Hyattstown, Urbana, Boonesboro, Keediesville [*sic*], and Sharpsburg. Near Middletown heights, between M. and Boonesboro, where Reno[1] was killed and where Hooker stormed the battery of the rebels (I saw any quantity of dead rebels there), we passed by a camp of regulars, with prisoners in charge. I was on guard behind the regimental ambulances, and upon casting my eyes about, I saw Eugene standing in the middle of the road with Bob. I left the guard I tell you, and we walked over a mile together, when we parted. *** He showed us the battle-ground. ***

Gene said he would see us (again) in a day or two, but we have not seen him yet. We talked about everything while we were together, and oh! I was so delighted to see him. He was going back to Frederick City with his prisoners, and expected to return.

Bob lost his wallet before he marched with seven dollars in it. When we were on the march from Hall's Hill to Alexandria, and from there to Fort Worth, as Bob told you in his last letter, I threw my knapsack away at the first stopping place; it almost cut the life out of me. I could carry the load well enough, though much heavier than Bob's, for I had extra books, medicine, and writing-desk, but the mode of carrying it was not so easy. I kept all of my things, but did them up in a rubber blanket, and slung them over my shoulders by straps. I carried them in this way very well. Just before we started from Fort Corcoran, we saw John; and we also saw Lewis, and were going over to see them the next day, but were ordered off. We had extra shirts, stockings, blankets, etc., given us before we started, and that added to our heavy loads. I was barefooted when my stockings came to hand; my shoes hurt my bare feet, covered with sore, uncut corns* and my stockings were too full of holes for a second mending, so I threw them away.

The night before we started, it rained all night, and as I slept on the ground, I got wet, and ditto my things, so that when I started

---

[1] Jesse Lee Reno (1823–September 14, 1862), career officer, not to be confused with Marcus Reno of Little Bighorn infamy.—2019

next morning I had a very heavy load. I carried it six miles until I was almost gone, and I just fell out of ranks and disposed of all the articles I could. I threw away my medicine, books, checkers, towels, and lots of little things, and gave my heavy wet overcoat and blanket to a Union family on the road. My bundle was still heavy, but smaller, and I carried it to our first night's resting-place, twelve or more miles from Washington. Let Gene talk about clinging to your knapsacks, things, etc.; it's all "bosh!" I reckon he never carried either on a long march. No one hated to throw away things as I did, but I couldn't help it. I had over seventy-five pounds on my back, besides eighty rounds of cartridges, gun, etc.

The road was full of stragglers all the way back to Washington, and during the night they came in. One new regiment in our brigade, 118th Pennsylvania, twelve hundred strong, only numbered two hundred at our first stopping-place; they all had knapsacks.

The second morning we were all ordered to move in light marching order, and to leave our luggage. I thought it was only temporary and that our duds would be brought forward in the teams, so I took only my poncho, leaving my rubber blanket over my other things, it being the only covering I had for them, so you see that I must have suffered from cold the next day (night) on the ground with nothing but my poncho over me.

I got some milk once on the road, and with some hard-tack crumbled into it, I enjoyed a splendid meal. I have now my cotton shirt on (others behind), breeches, coat, one pair of dirty stockings, wet through yesterday (in what manner I will tell you presently), and my shoes and cap, all my wardrobe in this part of the country available. I lost my poncho yesterday on the other side of the Potomac.

Two brigades crossed this classic stream in the morning (Martindale's and Griffin's) while Butterfield's (the three composing Morell's division), remained on this side. As soon as we got there we were attacked by a superior rebel force, and, after fighting a short time, were recalled, and forded the Potomac (up to my breast in some places), in good order. I wet myself through, cartridges and all. *** On reaching the Virginia shore, I fired my gun off, loaded up, and the first thing I knew I saw all of our officers dismount hurriedly, and order us into line of battle up the hill. By this time twenty pieces of our artillery on the Maryland shore were shelling

159

over us, and such a racket! Shells bursting over our heads, officers ordering, balls whizzing! It was gay!*** Our own shells burst in among us, within six feet of me all around. I never heard such a terrific noise in my life.

Two of them struck into our own regiment, bursting in Company I, and knocked a man's face off, mortally wounding him. Another of our men was struck in the leg by a shrapnel shell fired by the enemy, and his leg had to be amputated. The bullets flew about me, but I minded them not. I was only watching for a shot *** we were in a queer position, on the side of an ascending ridge from a ravine, close to the river's bank. When the order came to cross the river, I was so mad that I forgot my poncho, which I threw off by my side to aid me in firing better. * * *

One time while lying down on our bellies, we heard the cry on our right from the Second Maine boys: 'They're coming!' The order was given to 'Fix bayonets!' and prepare for a volley when the enemy appeared in sight. I thought we were going to see some fun then. * * * I hadn't got warmed into it hardly, and I retreated backwards so as to get a pop at them when they came over the hill. *** We had then to leave *** our crossing the river was no joke; all I could think of was Ball's Bluff, for certainly, had it not been for our batteries and two regiments of Berdan's sharpshooters in a dry canal on the Maryland side, we would none of us have reached the shore alive. ***

We went (came back) across above where we went over (under the dam), and it was up to my armpits, with the current running like mad and the bullets buzzing like bees. The river was full of slippery ledges, and in the crevices it was very deep.

I did not fall once. *** I was so exhausted that I could hardly stand, for I had to keep my powder dry, and had to keep up a man who was most strangled, having fallen three times in coming across. * * * While fording, the 'rebs' appeared on the banks, and the bullets whistled into us good. *** I helped one short captain (H. P. Williams) across; he fell twice, and I picked him up, wetting my gun and ammunition in the act.

You ought to have seen them tumble down. Our acting colonel (W. S. Tilton), went down flat into the river, and wet himself all over, so did Bob, and got soaked. ***

I did not fall once. I did not dry myself, but slept under some straw, and this morning am all right and .steaming. *** The 'rebs' had about ten or twenty thousand troops pouring down upon us; it seems they crossed the night before, and set a trap to cut us all up when we crossed, but thank Heaven! our sharpshooters and cannon saved us. * * * We had no hard fight; we only discovered the enemy in force, and caused him, perhaps, to take too much notice for his own good.

McClellan rode by us on his return to camp, and he looked pleased as if everything had worked to his satisfaction. You will probably see the details of this affair in the papers. Oh! if I could only see a Bouton *Journal*. We have not had a mail for a week and a half, and have not been permitted to write home during these battles. * * * When I read the accounts of the fight in which we were engaged across the river, I am only thankful that we escaped so well; it was a pretty bout after all. *** Of course, in retreating down the precipice (as it were), we could not go in perfect line of battle, neither in going across the river, as the current was so swift. * ** I read 'Carleton's' account again, and also 'why the fight was not renewed,' and the report that Martindale's brigade got into an ambuscade when they crossed the river, and was roughly handled, the latter a miserable hoax.

Most of the boys have given out on shoe leather, but Bob and I still hold on; God bless those shoes! If it had not been for them, what should we have done? They have not even commenced to wear out. The maker of them—Williams—is now in a better land, and will peg and sew no more. He was shot on Wednesday, as were many more of the Thirty-fifth. Ed Morrill was shot through the foot. Haven't heard about Haze (Goodrich), but hope he is safe. I hear that Fred Brooks, Flanders, Cram and Nichols all are wounded, and thus it is with war. Horrid! and how my whole soul is troubled when I think of these associations severed, these hearts crushed; may you all be spared the sorrow of some, but O Father, you can scarcely know the dangers to which your affectionate boys are subjected, both on the field of battle and the low-minded camp. My mind is turning fondly to you all at home this beautiful Sabbath morning, and how I wish I were with you, but my work must be done before I ever see you again, and that it may be done in earnest, quickly, and I be an humble instrument in the grand resulting victory, is the hopeful prayer of your affectionate son. It is hard to write in this army. Love to all, and kiss them all for Bob and myself.

"In Camp, near Sharpsburg, on the Potomac side,

Sept. 23, 1862.

The letters of our brothers, Walter and Bob, now say:

As soon as I finished my letter to father on Sunday, I went down from the woods to the camp, and there found Gene waiting for me. He had been relieved from his prisoner guarding by a regiment of our brigade (Martindale's now commanded by Colonel [James] Barnes of Massachusetts, senior colonel of the brigade, and until recently, in the Bull Run fight, and sometime since by Colonel [Charles W.] Roberts of the Second Maine, a brave officer and better liked than Barnes), and is now on the provost guard, and acts with Frank's company as a part of 'Mac's' bodyguard. I was glad enough to see him, I can assure you. He is in camp about three miles from us. I cannot get down so far to see him, but he can come and see us daily if he chooses. *** He told us if we were wounded, to ask to be carried to McClellan's headquarters, and he would see to it that we were well taken care of by a good surgeon. *** I know that is what dear mother fears, that we will get wounded, and either die on the field, or get into some saw-bone hospital, and to tell the truth that is what I fear most myself, f don't fear to go into battle, for last week I was as cool all through it as could be; neither do I fear the wounds, or even death itself, for that is what I came out for, if need be to give up my life in defense of my country, but it is the thought that I shall he uncared for, that I shall be buried where no loving hand can strew flowers and shed tears of love over my grave. Oh! I have seen too much of that already. After a big battle, they tumble them in without mark or sign ***

He showed me your letter of September 3th to him, and I was overjoyed to see it. It was so much in the same loving, motherly strain, and so full of tender anxiety for her boys. How is it that we can ever forget such an interest, and fail to repay such with kindness, when we are at home, when opportunities are so frequently offered?

Gene left us, promising to call again. He spoke of the possibility of his getting a Massachusetts regiment; he said it was easy enough, if someone would influence Governor Andrew to ask his release from (the) regular service, he thinks they would grant it readily.

Since Sunday I have been on picket on the banks of the Potomac. Our whole corps occupy the position in front where the rebels appeared in force, and compelled our small force to retreat across the river on Saturday. Three regiments go on at night, alternately, and stay until the next night. We all sleep on the bank of a canal, and on the tow path post our sentinels during the night. Our object is to look out for the 'rebs,' and give the alarm. Their sharpshooters are stationed on the opposite bank, 500 yards, and we pop away at each other well. All day long matters of interest were continually taking place. I only suffered at night in the canal, I couldn't sleep I was so cold; we were relieved last night, and are in camp today. Our stragglers are fast coming up, thanks to the provost guard; Frank and LeRoy are still missing though. *** Quite a number of ambulances were over yesterday, under a flag of truce, to get the wounded and bury dead. Fifty men went over with them for the latter purpose. If man can't stand a cold on the lungs he must die, that's all. There are poor fellows now in our regiment who are sick and past recovery, yet they linger on, in hopes, perhaps, that a welcome bullet may bring peace to their weary bodies; if they ever do get home it will be to die. ***

I know not what they mean by not drilling us; we do not understand anything as yet of field movements, and what a poor show we shall make on the battle-field; all confusion and disorder.

I saw something of it last Saturday while recrossing the river; it was an orderly retreat, yet everything was out of place. I was excited somewhat when I came back, for I heard nothing but our Parrot shells screaming over our heads into the ranks of the enemy, and their minie balls whizzing past our ears. On Wednesday, while being held in reserve, I went up on the hill several times, back of where our brigade was drawn up, and I saw our 20-pound Parrots drop their shells into the enemy's ranks, and saw Meagher's Irish brigade charge on the 'rebs' and wavering once, charge again, with victory as their bloody purchase. I could hear Burnside on the left, as he fought to take the Stone Bridge at all hazards, flanked by woody hills, filled with rebel riflemen, and the next day I saw the result of that hard fought ground where so many were lying around me. I saw one poor fellow who had lain all night with a bullet in his brain, wholly unconscious, yet breathing still in perfect spasms, as

163

his life blood ebbed away; it was a gone case, and, ere this, he has gone forever from earthly battle-fields. ***

We had to lie to all day and night under a hill, in reserve, supporting some 20-pound Parrot guns. The shells came over that day just enough for me to get used to them; one burst within five rods of me. General McClellan went by us to cheer up the men about two or three o'clock; he took off his hat to us when we hurrahed, * ** You ought to see a great battle as I have seen one; * * * You at home can never realize the horrors: the continual roar of cannon; the bursting of shells around you; the rattling of musketry; the dense smoke, etc., make it a grand, sight; but marching over it the next day, was what would make your heart bleed, dear mother. The brave and lion-hearted patriots lay dead and dying all around; the blackened corpses that had not been buried, lay out in a heavy shower, that we had to march through.

When the sun came out, oh, heavens, what a smell. I have done picket duty within a few yards of a dead horse for thirty-six hours, and gone by any quantity of them, but the decaying bodies of men beat anything I ever smelt, and to think, too, that they had to die without a mother's tear, or a friendly care; and not to be recognized, but to be shoved in a little hole, that is just what I don't relish. I don't fear the fight at all, but it is getting wounded and having to suffer and die on the battle-field. ***

Weren't they excited in Haverhill when they heard of the Thirty-fifth being so cut up? Company G got into a cross-fire which killed eight, and wounded thirty more: among the killed was Clarence Woodman. Poor fellow! he lay with his head down hill, the blood settled in his neck, and he was an awful looking object. A cannon-ball killed him.

We whipped them awfully that day, as you will see by the papers, but with a heavy loss on our side of officers and men.

I send you a Baltimore *Clipper*, with a detailed account of the great Battle of Antietam. *** Mother may bless the day that Fitz John Porter's corps was in reserve, for had we gone into that fight, we should have been all cut up, and perhaps my body would have been this day lying under the sod on the banks of Antietam creek, and sure I am that many of our boys would be low in the dust now. *** Oh! if you could have seen the sights that I have seen: the poor fellows strewn around * * * just as they were charging across the bridge, full of savage fight; but, alas, the unerring bullet through the brain ended their brief resolve 'to do, or die!'

Thursday, we went through the rain over the celebrated bridge where the terrible fighting was. We were on picket that night, and exchanged shots with the 'rebs.' The next morning we started after them. ***

Why in the name of heaven McClellan did not let our corps finish up the 'rebs,' and why he did not renew the battle on Thursday, and follow speedily across the river, I can't understand. It looks to me as though it would have been better to have crushed them with fresh troops on Thursday, than to have them skedaddle off under the pretext of burying their dead in plain sight of our general. I am provoked, perhaps, without cause, but I cannot help feeling that it prolongs this horrid war. *** Why we are not ordered to whip the enemy *** is more than I know. ***

Carleton's account of it in the *Journal* that Father sent me was superb: it was just as I witnessed the fight, where Hooker, brave and gallant, fought and fell. I agree with Carleton, and wonder when the fight was waning and well-nigh lost on the left that Porter or Sykes was not ordered to the support, and win the day, and not let the sun go down on an undecided fight, to be opened on the morrow by an agreement to bury the dead, under which plea the whole rebel army prepared to retreat, and which they carried out on Friday morning (when we were ordered forward to Sharpsburg), to our shame, without much loss to their rear guard. Now, why not whip them on Wednesday with fresh men, and on Thursday beat them with Pennsylvania reserves at Hagerstown, and on Friday cut them up on the retreat, with our cavalry and light batteries, while they were being pushed into the river at the point of the bayonet, and amid our Parrot shells? We could have done it! Why not? Time will tell! Now the papers are freighted with the welcome (?) intelligence that the rebels are in force across the river, advantageously posted, etc., and peace is proposed tons in haughty terms, they claiming the victories of South Mountain and Antietam. ***

Now follows a letter from our brother in the artillery:

Fort Tillinghast, Sept. 26, 1862.

I am now out of the hospital, but am not quite able to do duty. **

165

I was quite sick for a time, but now my skin is getting bleached out once more, by the use of pills, castor oil, turpentine, and rhubarb. Mother asked me some questions about the loss of things: I have not had a thing made up to me, and what I get I have to pay for. I have drawn a blanket, but the nights are very cold here now, and I need a quilt or something of that sort. We are not in barracks, but have had to go into our tents; but I ought not to complain, for we are leading a life of luxury to some of the poor soldiers on the march. Poor Walt and Bob! I think of them often, for I do not doubt they have had to throw away everything. It cannot be helped while soldiers are on a march, loaded down with a heavy cartridge-box, with forty rounds, cross belt, haversack with two or three days' rations, and a heavy gun and bayonet. When the old troops left, I found a good knapsack and overcoat; the coat was full of vermin, so I had to leave it, but I will not have to draw a knapsack.

A regular imposition is practised upon the soldiers, for instance, the poor fellows from the peninsula were compelled, by their officers, to throw away everything they possessed two or three times, and then to draw everything new. Yesterday, the Eleventh Massachusetts, which now number scarcely one hundred and fifty men, and have received no pay for over four months, were paid off, and most of them didn't get more than five or six dollars, as all of these things which they were ordered to throw away, and which they could not possibly carry, were charged to them; thus these poor fellows, after undergoing everything but death itself, were robbed of even the small pay which they had so nobly earned.

If they treat soldiers in this way, they will fight no more. *** Two of our companies, 'I' and LH,' went to Harper's Ferry last night, where they are to garrison some of the fortifications, but we have probably got a steady situation now. This regiment is the envy of the other regiments, for we have a comparatively easy time to them, yet we have seen some rather hard times, and may see more. * * * I suppose you know that Barnes commands the brigade in which our brothers are. It seems as though God protected them, for part of that brigade went over the river, and were nearly all massacred. * * * The Pennsylvania regiment lay near us before the advance, and it was a very fine regiment, with full ranks, but today they are, nearly all of them, in their graves.

General Martindale is sick. It is foolishness to send anything to a regimental hospital, for a sick soldier seldom gets the benefit. The cooks, hospital steward, doctors, waiters, and 'hangers on' devour everything they can lay their hands on, and if a soldier is very sick, and has no money, God help him! In a general hospital there is more system, and they get more benefit from contributions. In the .hospitals, the attendants witness such scenes of want and misery that their hearts become hardened, and only when a man is nearly dead do they begin to notice him, and then it is often too late. Write soon, for you don't know how much better it makes me feel to get a letter from home.

Our brothers, Walter and Bob, now say in their letters dated:

Opposite Shepardstown,

Sept. 26-29, 1862.

We are now having comparative rest after our long march, but at best camp life, and duties with it, is hard, and it is only in periods that the lazy days come, and then it takes all the time to rest. I am tired enough, for we few boys had to do all the guard duty for our regiment on the march, and it takes hold to march all day, and stand guard all night; and now what makes it most aggravating, our sergeant puts it on just the same, although many of the old men are with us now. Besides, we have put up officers' tents and dig sinks and other fatigue duty. It is altogether worse than I could possibly have imagined before I left home. Verily our beloved country is worth a vast deal to have its integrity maintained at such a cost of suffering and hardship, as is endured in the army.

We recruits are getting kicked round pretty well now; we do all the duty in our company, and they call us d—d recruits, etc., etc. * * *

I put up with things from minor officers, petty officers, and even privates without a murmur, which I would have resented with a blow if I had been at home. But it is no go here, I have to submit or else be arrested. *** Captain Thompson is sick now, and attends to no duty, and we have run behind in drill. Our drill-master (Sergeant William Salter), has gone to a hospital sick, and common privates. grown old in sin and musty in discipline, are detailed to go through the movements with us. They are sick of soldiering, and have no ambition to teach others, and we are, consequently, minus in that department. I only hope that it will be remedied. *** Captain T. is one of those kinds of men not at all genial, or easy to get acquainted with. He is not in the least upper crust, for he messes with his men, and hates salutations and red tape, but he is a stern man, hard to get on the right side of, and difficult to understand; and now, while sick, is grouty and cross. He is a brave man, and a good officer, I guess, but, as a man, with all the feelings natural to us, I don't think much of him.

Our second lieutenant is a young man (Edwin C. Bennett) I used to know when in S. B. Pierce's. * * * We shall be on the march in a few days for Virginia, and then for the danger. Don't make my unworthy letters too public, mother; my writing is necessarily bad; my paper dirty, etc. I have to beg paper and envelopes, my writing-desk being left behind; I am used up for everything. *** A box might be sent directed to the care of 'Captain J. J. Thompson, Twenty-second regiment, Hamden's Express,' and it might reach me sooner or later, depending greatly on our moving. A fellow had a box come Saturday, and was obliged to leave all his 'fod' (food) behind for a trip across the river; when he had returned it had disappeared; wasn't it too bad? I must close now for a day or two, for we are going on picket now down to the river.

Sunday, Sept. 29, 1862.

We have changed camp to a neater, cleaner place, only a few rods from our old place. I was down to the Potomac this morning, and washed myself, shirt, and stockings, and while they were drying, swam into the middle of the river. The rebel pickets do not fire at us now; we made an agreement to that effect. * * * It was pretty lonely guard duty for me. I was sick with my cold, and had a headache and symptoms of dyspepsia (the latter most nauseating). While I lay sick, during my time of relief, Bob, who, was two or three posts above me, was writing to you, and I got him to excuse me in it for not finishing this sooner. I am much better today, though my cold is still bad, and I sleep on the ground at night, and have perfect horrors in the choking, coughing line. I thought I could stand this cursed climate, but I give in. Shall be dead if I stay here much longer, and if I ever do get home, it will be hard to recruit, if I don't get this cough off me. I am going to try our doctor once more, and present claims for his highest skill. I hope to be better soon, at least before we march into Dixie, never to return until we have swept the originators of this wicked rebellion into purgatory.

Last night we gathered around a camp-fire for the first time in Maryland, and we had a jolly time: we sung all our songs, and a lot of boys joined in with *** of sacred hymns. We talked of home and spent a very pleasant evening. Bob went to bed slightly sick; he had a toothache and a headache; he is better this morning after tending to the wants of his inner tabernacle. We have not been allowed to build regular camp-fires before. I am afraid our little general is letting the 'rebs' have too much time to recruit their wasted energies; he ought to follow up a retreat more promptly in my great military opine. Captain T. has gone to Washington, for how long I know not. Gene hasn't been here since last time. Bob and I intend going over to see him tomorrow if we can get a pass from headquarters. We shall manage to be in at dinner time.

September 30

Since I stopped last, I have been on picket again. We are there all the time, and when I do commence this letter, I have to keep stopping to do duty. They can talk about the Army of the Potomac resting from their labors, but I say we have to work as hard as ever. I would rather be on the march after the 'rebs,' who, I fear, are now resting and recruiting.

They say we are stopping to have the quartermaster clothe and fix us up, but most of us have signed for blankets, etc., sometime since, and have, as yet, not seen them. I see indications, by papers and otherwise, of Gene's being appointed to the colonelcy of the Forty-eighth Massachusetts regiment, nine months volunteers. It will be a good thing for him. *** While on picket this time (only since yesterday morning until this noon), we have had a splendid time bathing, eating, etc. At night, General Sykes' band played, and it did sound beautifully beside the Potomac. Some of our familiar tunes made me *kinder* [sic] home-sick. They played: 'Wood Up,' 'Annie Laurie,' 'Silvery Shower,' and 'Dixie.' It was a rich treat. I wish we had a band. We couldn't go to see Gene yesterday, as we intended, on account of picket duty. It is too late today to try. My ears are burned raw, my cap having no rim; I can't even wash them.* * * all you hear about our receiving vegetables, or anything but 'hard-tack,' 'salt-horse,' sugar and coffee (in small quantities), with beans, rice, and fresh beef occasionally, is humbug. We are much obliged to father for list of nine months Bradford recruits.

October 3

You must have been so anxious during our long, unavoidable silence, since we left Virginia's shore; but, after many tribulations, we have reached the River Jordan, and now are on our oars. Today most of our regiment have gone on picket again, but Bob and myself were detailed to lug water all day; no easy job. We have only two pails for coffee to bring up tonight, and, in the meantime, being relieved from all other duty, Bob is writing to father, and I am trying to do your letter all the justice it deserves. We are within three miles of Sharpsburg, and about a mile from the river. * * * We have decent food in camp now; have to go on picket, fatigue duty, etc.,*** which keeps us pretty well to work. * * * We have to go almost to the river, through a beautiful piece of woods to get it (water); when on picket we don't have anything to do, as the 'rebs' don't shoot at us, and we don't at them. We were on picket when those 400 prisoners were paroled, and had to cross the river. They were a motley looking crew; but, nevertheless, the officers were smart looking fellows, some of them. Shepardstown is about a mile across the river, above Blackburn's (Blackford's) ford, where we went across. McClellan's headquarters have been within two miles of us. ***

Gene looks rather thin, but pretty well. *** It rained last night, and for once I had the shelter of a tent, and a borrowed overcoat and rubber blanket for my portion. I slept well. I went to see the doctor this morning, and he gave me licorice to chew for my cold, and a big pill. He said I must take the latter at night and be covered warm. The latter is a *leetle difficult*, for all the boys are away, and all their rags are with them. A poor fellow in the Michigan regiment (First), fell down dead while digging a trench around his tent, prior to the approaching shower. He gave someone his address in the morning and told them to 'send him home tomorrow,' as he should 'be dead before night.' They laughed at him, and now his lifeless body is on its way to a Western home of sadness. Today, in the same regiment, a fellow threw an old shell (as he supposed), into the fire, and it burst, killing one man and wounding three. Isn't it dreadful? All this in plain sight of camp. My cold is some better, but I hack dreadfully.

Abraham Lincoln is expected to pay the army a visit tomorrow. We are under orders to turn out at a moment's notice 'well rigged.' *** I have been on review, and have seen Father Abraham.' He reviewed the whole army: it was a splendid sight. He looks the same as his pictures, though much more careworn; one of his feet is in the grave. *** The president was attended by 'Little Mac,' on his right hand and F. J. Porter on his left, with their staffs and body-guards. *** He rode by and between each regiment, so that he came within a rod of me, as also did 'Little Mac.' We stayed about five hours in the hot sun, and while most of them were growling, I stood it like a 'major,' being used to the heat. Our brother, Walter, says: 'It gave me the headache dreadfully.' ***

I am suffering with diarrhea, and have been for three weeks; they say it is lying on the ground that causes it. Our doctor says it is owing to the hard, limy water we drink. One thing is certain, 'Camp Baker Cordial' doesn't affect it in the least; it weakens me dreadfully. ***Asa Fletcher, our friend from Winchester, who was with us so long, was terribly wounded in the late battle; he left us on the march to join the Andrew's sharpshooters, for which company he enlisted, and was wounded the time the captain was killed. He is a first-rate man, and a friend of Uncle John's. Our regiment is back, and I have to go on dress parade. I am also on guard tonight.

For our seeming lack of prudence in leaving behind and throwing away so many things so essential to our comfort, we were accused by our father with a lack of 'good generalship,' etc., etc., and were criticised rather severely for the same.

To this we responded with much spirit in two very long letters, which, although written in the midst of sickness and distress,1 are characterized by a vein of good humor and apt illustrations. But beyond detailing all the harassing incidents of our first long march to Sharpsburg, the weight, piece by piece, of our wet loads, the dreadful heat, which was g8°; and stating as our belief that these things, which we were told to leave back near Rockville, were to be sent forward to us very soon in the teams; their contents would be but a repetition of the other letters. They are, however, very amusing as an unanswerable argument from a soldier's standpoint to our non-combatant, lawyer father, who was viewing matters, as were many others, through glasses at a secure and comfortable home station.

Our brother in the forts now writes:

Fort Tillinghast,

October 3, 1862.

I suppose you have, ere this, received long and interesting letters from Walt and Bob, giving you a graphic account of the horrid battles of Antietam. It was a dear bought victory, and will cause many a bitter tear at the North. As Gene or my other brothers never write to me, I shall expect to hear from them through you at home. Night before last I was on guard for the first time since I returned from the hospital, and it was quite an exciting night, for nearly 25,000 troops took their departure to join the army of McClellan, and another large force went in the direction of Centreville. Regiments continually come over the bridge, but they are very green, and they have to keep them here for two or three weeks before they are fit to take the field, and even then, they are not what they should be; but something has got to be done within the coming eight weeks, for by that time we shall be again wallowing in the mud, and another winter of inactivity would stare us in the face; but I think McClellan will be at them before long, and God grant that he may be victorious, and that this unhappy war may be brought to a speedy close, for it is fast ruining the country.

I lately found out that I had a relative in this regiment, Austin Carter, a son of Uncle Henry's; he made me a call today. About half of our company are sick with the same complaint I was troubled with, but in a lighter form; yet they are not fit for duty. The doctor says it is owing to the manner in which we live. We have not been paid for four months; we have a company fund of $200, but the officer who has it in charge, spends it, as he has no money from the government, and when we try to get him to buy something to eat for us, he makes all sorts of excuses, but we don't see the grub. It is salt horse, bread and oak leaf gruel every day except Sundays,; when we have a luxury, baked beans. I wish I had some of your gingerbread and doughnuts; I do really hanker for something of that sort. We have got our tents stockaded for the winter, but we will not be allowed any fire in them, as we are in the fort, and it will not do to have fire near the magazines. We are. having six additional guns placed in the fort, and a whole regiment of engineers are digging rifle-pits and breastworks between the forts. Secesh would stand a poor sight if they advanced on the capital in this direction. I saw a Salem paper the other day, which said that the Forty-eighth Regiment would be commanded by Colonel Carter, with E. P. Stone as lieutenant-colonel. Has it been decided upon, and can Gene get his leave? I hope so. I am now pretty well, but I do not feel as I did

172

before, and am quite thin. Since I have been here, I have weighed nearly one hundred and fifty; today I weighed one hundred and fifteen.

I regret to tell you that Uncle William has been missing for a long time; Lewis has not heard from him since June, and he is reported as missing. He thinks him either dead or a prisoner, as he promised to write soon............Something has surely befallen him, yet Lewis still has hopes of hearing from him; he used to write quite often to him............What horrible work the rebels made in that Haverhill company. I am so thankful that Robert and Walter escaped; but the poor boys have yet to meet the enemy; but I have a sort of feeling that they are not destined to die by a butternut bullet.

The two brothers in the Twenty-second Massachusetts now write:

October 5, 1862.

We didn't have baked beans today, for the reason that we couldn't draw the pork; but instead of that luxury, we had a most acceptable mail brought in, of which Bob and myself received a good share, letters and papers. For them, accept our best thanks, for they serve to while many of our weary hours away, as we pass in our weary pilgrimage. Within three nights I have enjoyed an overcoat, a tent, and a woolen blanket. Today I drew a blouse, and tomorrow the ponchos are coming, 'so they say,' and with this let me say that the doctor has taken me in hand, and under his treatment I am almost well of my cough and cold, thanks to pills, etc. I have done duty always, never so used up but what I could do my share of work, and I never shirk under the plea of temporary ailment; my diarrhea is getting to be much better and I feel like my old self again. Today I am on fatigue, and this holy forenoon has been alternately employed, the first half in digging a trench for slops, and the other in attending divine service in front of Colonel Barnes's headquarters. I listened to a most eloquent and interesting address from the chaplain of the One Hundred and Eighteenth Pennsylvania. The opposite extremes met there surely.

I hope we shall soon see a fight. I am anxious to show a little of my essence, for I believe I would never leave a good field and a fair show for victory, until death was my only alternative, and then I should hesitate.

173

I think of poor J's death, and her sleeping in the quiet graveyard, but such is life; we are all destined sooner or later to pass from this world to another. It must be considered a great blessing to be buried at home, and if I am killed in battle, I should wish to be brought home, and buried according to the laws of civilization, not as I have seen them here, like dogs.

Our brother at McClellan's headquarters now writes:

Camp near Sharpsburg,

October 5, 1862.

Enclosed, please find a group [photo] of Captain Frank, Lieutenant Worth, and your humble servant; although not very good, you can form some idea how we look. I wish Lieutenants Andrews and Cooper were here, we then would have a group of the Light Infantry; they went out riding this morning, and have not returned. I have just commenced my twenty-fifth year. Why don't I hear from some of you? It is very strange; I receive no letters at all. I shall try to see Walt and Bob tomorrow.

October 9.

The regiment was ordered out without arms, and was marched a few rods to the left of the camp to clear up a piece of ground, for the purpose of shifting camp. We had the rocks well gathered up in heaps, when further progress was stopped by the major of Berdan's Sharpshooters (1st), who came out, and claimed the ground; so we went back to quarters to await further orders, Had our usual squad and company drill. Battalion drill was had in the afternoon, and dress parade. Just at sunset one of the batteries fired a few shots over the river, but received no reply.

We were inspected October 7 by Colonel A. S. Webb, inspector-general on General Porter's staff. Line was formed in four and one half minutes.

October 10.

Drilled in the forenoon. Commenced to rain towards night. No dress parade. In the afternoon a sutler came into camp with bread to sell. Not being able to deal it out fast enough, and charging exorbitant rates, Colonel Barnes confiscated the entire lot. October 11 and 12. Cold and rainy.

·The brothers, Walter and, Bob now say:

Sunday, October 12, 1862.

Today has been a day of rest for me, and I cannot let it close without writing for once a short letter home. I have had a good quality of food today, and that has seemed to content me, for my stomach has been at ease, and not continually yearning for a fullness scarcely ever satisfied in this barren land. I have had a plate of baked beans for breakfast, and some soup made of the water in which our meat was boiled, and rice, beef, pepper, etc., boiled in with the mess for dinner. Very rich living that! The surgeon came to our company, and said that we must have food of that kind, or else we would all die, so our cook (Hazen Clements), ... pitched in and got up this savory dish. I have been to meeting twice in the open air, and heard very fine addresses delivered by Pennsylvania and Michigan chaplains; it was a rich treat. You ought to have seen these old veterans weep when the preacher alluded to the dear ones at home, whom they had not seen for years; and it affected me, I assure you, to hear the many tender allusions these two good men made about our relations with the dear home circles left so far behind. How I wish we had a chaplain; but all sich [sic], sutlers included, are denied us. Bob is on guard, and during the time of his relief, he has been popping this old yellow corn in an old iron pan; it tasted good, and most of it reminded me of the leavings at home — the 'old maids'[2] in the bottom of the dish. They tasted even better than those at home, for Bob cooked them in pork fat and let them do brown and crispy. 1 got hold of some fresh bread and gingerbread that some of our boys cleaned out of a transient sutler, who had no license, and that went good between us. They do the same with everyone who comes along, and declare they will continue to do so, until Uncle Sam comes along with his iron box. The boys are expecting him daily; we recruits will not get a cent, as they left us out when the regiment was mustered.

We still continue in our daily duties of picket and camp guard, some drilling, fatigue duty for shoulder straps, company police duty, cleaning up street, inspections, dress parade, etc. Still there are many idle hours, and I try to improve them by writing to you at home, reading books, and other avocations. I often am ambitious

---

[2] Even in the 21st century, the unpopped kernels of popcorn are called "old maids" in American culture.—2019

enough to take my 'tactics,' and study it, but I find the finer senses of understanding are dulled by the influences around me, and it affects the mental powers, I do verily believe, as it does the physical. ... Bob and I got a pass Saturday, and started for McClellan's headquarters to see Gene. We started in high glee, in bright anticipations of a pleasant visit and a good time, for we had worked hard for the pass, and three officers' names had to be affixed before we could start.

When we got there we found no headquarters, and "Little Mac' had flown to Harper's Ferry with the provost guard, Gene and all. Wasn't that a disappointment? We had to come back without seeing him. There are rumors in camp today that we leave for Washington in less than a week to take up our winter quarters. There are many other reports, but I never give credence to them, and scarcely ever repeat them. The 'secesh' prisoners near us say that if it was not for the last proclamation the trouble would have been settled this winter. A pretty dodge that! How artful in them! I have slept well the last two nights under a blanket. Do not be too anxious. I shall soon manage to be all right. It is growing terribly cold, and the leaves are falling.

Thursday morning, October 16, 1862, my birthday. On reserve picket above Shepardstown, Md.? (Va.)

On the 13th of October it was cold and dreary, raining at intervals, but on the 14th it cleared, but it grew very cold. Men suffered much for clothing. About two hundred shelter-tents were issued to the command. Had battalion drill. It was a very busy day on the 15th, pitching tents and trying to make ourselves comfortable. Received first mail for a week.

Our brother Walter writes:

Today I am twenty years old, and I confess I am astonished; it has come upon me unawares, and really it does seem as though time had stolen a march on me. I celebrated this morn by getting a breakfast with another young man of H. at a farm-house. I paid fifty cents for the two of us, and it was a decent meal. We had bread and poor butter, *middling* coffee, stewed mutton, cold ham, and some Stewart's syrup; the first time I have sat down to a morning repast for a month and a half. I have not even sat down in a chair, the ground being the resting place for my sore limbs and racked hips. I saw something of the mode of living in this heathen country by this

176

transitory repast. The old woman sat at the head of the table in a high-backed chair, cane seat, and the legs were up from the floor, and she leaning towards the table, and when eating, one of her elbows was continually on; when she replenished the bread plate (the loaf lying beside her), she would seize her knife and gouge out half the loaf, and then turning it around would repeat the operation. Such half slices you never saw: thick, thin, and hacked from every side, and she with head down, leaning forward and pulling away at it. I thought ... how long it would take you to teach her to cut some of your neat, even slices of bread.

Every one of the family used their own knife for butter and syrup, and it made no difference whether it came from the mouth or not; into the plates of butter and syrup it would go. Down came the children, one by one, hair uncombed, faces dirty, and they pitched in 'lemons,' their noses receiving the application of their fingers for want of rags, though there were plenty of them on the poor urchins. My hair was uncombed, but it was because I couldn't comb it, it being too short as yet. This is the way they live; isn't it horrid? While I write our cavalry are crossing the river, and the head of the column is at Shepardstown. The rebel pickets are firing, skedaddling as they run. All the brigades are under arms tonight, except ours (which is on picket), and the whole army was crossing last night. I can hear the booming of cannon, and everything betokens a fight; what our army does must be done now, for in a month the roads will be impassable, and the winter season will usher in winter quarters for the men. We may now cross as soon as we are relieved.

Griffin's and Butterfield's brigades of our division have gone over, and Martindale's will follow, very likely. Bob is back at camp, and I only hope he will get a mail. I wish Father would send me a paper with a detailed account of the 'review,' by President Lincoln, if he can get it. I saw a paper for the first time during the week, and I was surprised to learn of the two Union victories at Corinth and Perryville,[3] and how I hope the latter was followed up. The cavalry raid by the rebel [J.E.B.] Stuart is a disgrace to our army, and I hope it will teach us a lesson. Captain (Thompson) has resigned, but

---

[3] The Union victory at the 2nd Battle of Corinth was October 3–4, 1862. The strategic Union victory at Perryville was October 8, 1862.

177

it will not be accepted, and he is expected back from W. He has been there long enough, his furlough having long since run out.

... We have an inspection of ourselves every day in camp, to prevent our bodily enemies coming the flank movement on us; you may start at the word lice, in the peaceful, cleanly cottage in Bradford; so did I, at first, but now it is our family conversation here, while armies of them invade our borders. I am not troubled much, but some of the boys are. It is perfectly horrid, and too disgusting to us, but we have to come to it on account of others. I have to be plain on such a subject, but I shall not broach it often. I am quite well now, except a hoarseness in my throat. My voice for singing has been gone for some time. I don't know when I shall get over it. It is a cold, raw day, and the wind blows just as it does at home these fall days. I hear the rustling of the corn, and the leaves falling from the trees. I long to get back to camp; we have been out two days, and tonight sees us through. I have got to stand extra tonight, one of our number being sick; there are fewer on post; one sick, and one a corporal, leaving myself and Craig (a lad from Boston), to stand guard the twelve hours of the night. I guess I can stand it. How often do I think of you all, and many things besides, during the long hours of the night guard, especially when on picket.

By Camp-fire, 8 p. m.

Since I finished my letter to Mother this afternoon, I have had to take Newman up to camp, three miles distant, a sick man. They have orders to move with two days' rations. (Midnight). My two hours on post are just out, and I will say a few words more. It is hard to write by the fire, but my last hour has been spent in reading Charles Sumner's[4] splendid speech, and if I can read, I can write. Did you read Dickinson's[5] great speech in New York a few days since? It was a magnificent harangue. We shall march today, probably, and already I begin to smell fight. We go as reinforcements to the contending parties on the other side; the battle will probably be renewed in the morning. It has been raining

---

[4] Massachusetts senator and Radical Republican, Charles Sumner (1811–1874).

[5] New York Senator Daniel Stevens Dickinson (1800–1866). Although a War Democrat, he was supported by Republicans and appointed by Lincoln as United States attorney for the southern district of New York 1865-1866.

like guns all the first part of the night, but it is now starlight. (Heavy thunder-storm). I was pretty wet; we had to stand and take it. I don't know when I shall write again.

When shivering with cold, without shelter, and awaiting the tardy issuing of blankets, shoes, shelter tents, etc., at Sharpsburg, we had first tried to sec, then had written, our brother, who was in camp in the beautiful Pleasant Valley, at Knoxville, near Harper's Ferry, and on the fourteenth, we received the following reply.

But upon going over to get them, found he had gone on furlough, and before another letter could reach the camp of the Eighth, it had vanished, we knew not where, and we were doomed to shiver the long nights out in patient waiting and suffering.

Camp near Norfolk (?) (Knoxville), beyond Harper's Ferry, and in Pleasant Valley, October 14, 1862.

Dear Brothers: I received your letter this morning, and answer immediately. I think you are a little hard on me. ... God knows I would see you every day if I could, but you must know I am nearly twenty miles from you by the road, and besides, my duties are many. I am quartermaster and commissary for the five companies of the Eighth Infantry, besides commanding my own company. Why, in God's name, did you not tell me that you were wanting blankets when I saw you?... If you want anything that I can give you, always ask for it; do not forget that I am your brother, and that, whatever I have, I shall always gladly share with you, even to my last shirt. . Kate told me of Julia J.'s death. I wish my pen could do my thoughts justice, for I always liked her so much. But soldiers have no time to think of the dead; a sudden pang, a tear, and all is forgotten for the time.

As to your blankets, what kind of a quartermaster have you? I would give you money, and would give you blankets from my own bed, if I could get them to you, but that seems impossible. The only way I know of is to go to the quartermaster of the Third United States Infantry, which is encamped somewhere near you, with the enclosed note. I do not know about the Forty-eighth regiment. I may be colonel of it, and I may not; I do not care much either way. You would never believe me when I told you how volunteer soldiers had to suffer, notwithstanding all my experience. I wish I could see you; write to me again shortly, and I may see you again soon.

179

The enclosed note was as follows:

Lieutenant J. H. McCool, Quartermaster Third U. S. Infantry, Colonel Buchanan's Brigade (First), Sykes' Division:

Dear Mac: The bearer of this is my brother, of the Twenty-second Massachusetts Volunteers. During all these cold nights, he and another brother have been sleeping without a rag to cover them. They are privates, Mac, but they have hearts as big as elephants; they cannot get blankets for love or money; if you can furnish them with the articles, do so for God's sake, for I cannot be easy while they suffer that which they never dreamed of doing. Please write me the cost of the blankets. I will send you the money immediately. Yours truly,

Carter,

Eighth Infantry

Our brother of the artillery now writes as follows:

Fort Tillinghast,

October 16th. 1862.

The box came this morning, everything in good order. I have not time to write, but I thought I would let you know that the box was all right. This noon I scoured my knife and fork, gave my plate a good cleaning, washed my face, combed my hair, drew out the box from under my bunk (we have two bunks in our tent), and took dinner. I tried to imagine myself at home. It was the best dinner I have had since I have been in the army. You know, Mother, better than I can tell you, how thankful I was for all the articles you sent. They taste so good to me. The stockings I needed, as I have worn the pair I have on about a month. ... The quilt is what I want, but I am most sorry you sent so good a one, for if we should be ordered on a long march, I fear it would follow the fate of my other things, but I will try to cling to it. ... I can't help thinking how much you and father must miss 'the boys,' as you used to call them. I knew they would have to throw away their things, as it is impossible for a soldier to carry all they require.

Colonel Greene[6] has resigned, and the men feel very badly about it, as he has done a great deal for the regiment, and we owe our

---

[6] William Batchelder Greene (1819–1878).—2019

good fortune to being here to his efforts. He is a good soldier, kind and indulgent to the men, and a terror to the officers. He shows no partiality to them, and if they wrong any of the men, he is after them with a sharp stick. Our old captain don't dare to look him in the eye, for he is not much of a military man, and the colonel knows it and rubs him occasionally. I do not know the cause of his resignation.

Please excuse this short note, but I have to drill most of the time, and have to go out in about ten minutes. I am writing out of doors, as I cannot write in the tent, for the boys are always skylarking and making such a noise that it is almost impossible for me to do so. ...

On October 19th, some of our officers were arrested and ordered to Harper's Ferry to report to the provost marshal-general, for having been in Sharpsburg without a pass. Our major reported by letter, but that would not do, and he was directed to report in person. On the 20th, it was again very cold,—not much sleep after midnight—but it came out warm enough at 4 p. m. to have battalion drill. On the 21st, there was a sharp frost, ground white, and very cold. On the 22d, a heavy gale set in, threatening to destroy our frail tents. Blew all day, but we drilled; almost impossible to hear orders given. On the 24th, there was an inspection in the afternoon.

Our brothers in the Twenty-second now say:

Near Sharpsburg,

October 24, 1862.

I did think we should be on the march before this, but the order to march was countermanded after we got in from picket. .. Since that time, I have expected to leave this place several times, but now can scarcely tell; the order at dress parade, and the general appearance of things indicated a movement, but at headquarters they are building log huts and seem as contented and happy as possible. I am in a quandary. Our requisitions for overcoats and blankets have been sent in, and we are eagerly, patiently awaiting the arrival of the brigade teams.

Gene has answered my letter, and has sent an order to a brother quartermaster of his in the Third Regulars near at hand, for two blankets. I went over a day or two since, but found he had gone on a furlough of thirty days, so we are dished unless we get them from our quartermaster and the acting quartermaster did not know

181

Gene, so we did not get them. Our ponchos are but slight shelter these cold nights, and if we do not get them soon, I shall not attempt to sleep, but go up to the cook-house and stay by the fire nights. The cook-house is composed of half a dozen cracker boxes, two or three barrels, kettles, pans, etc., in a heap.

Bob, Edgar, Webster, and myself are in a small tent, composed of four ponchos (about six feet square, with buttons and buttonholes on every side, made of cotton cloth tightly woven), with boards at the top, bottom, and both sides, and we manage to keep pretty warm by 'spooning in' until 12 o'clock, and then we turn out to warm up, and generally hang about the fire until morning. We hope soon to be more comfortable; we are trying as hard as possible.

I thought I should have the pleasure of informing you that we were the possessors of everything needful in this note, but 1 am disappointed. ... I hope we may be classed with the wise, and learn from all that experience. ... It is very hard, I assure you, now for us to write at all, for it is so cold nights that we can sleep but little, and in the daytime we are so sleepy, and having a great deal of duty to do, we find it very hard to undertake the composition of a letter. ...We have a regular feast over them; we exchange papers, and ask 'What is the news from home?' ...

I send you a piece of poetry which I cut from a paper, describing the scene very well. ... Pepper is always useful now that we are in camp; sometimes we have a sort of rice soup, and if we do not have pepper it tastes tame, and it also makes our 'salt horse' very palatable, so that we can eat it; when you write again, and if it is convenient, chuck in some more, whether father laughs or hot. If he were in our situation, he would think pepper a huge thing.

We have had two frosts this week, and a great deal of cold wind. . . . They are cutting down everything here in the shape of trees; we burn black walnut sticks to make coffee, as if it didn't cost anything.

Things look as if we were going to stop here sometime; then again it is rumored that we march this day and that; all sorts of rumors about us now. I think myself that we shall leave here soon. ... The way we cook our coffee, meat, etc., we have two crotched sticks, with a long pole to string them (the kettles) on, with a big fire under it. ...

Last Sunday we had baked beans for breakfast. Went to hear the chaplain of the Fourth Michigan preach in the afternoon, and in the evening went down in the woods, built a fire, rolled up some logs to sit on, and had a prayer-meeting. That day seemed more like Sunday to me than any other day yet.

Yesterday was a sad day, the saddest of my experience in the army. I had, dear mother, to perform the last sad offices to the departed dead; one of our Bradford boys is no more. He sleeps the sleep that knows no waking, and as I write, and cast my eyes out of the tent, his grave is before me, under a tree upon the hill. Milton Ingalls brother of Oliver I., who has been in the company since it started, both of whom I used to go to school with. Oliver was wounded at Gaines' Mills; Milton came out just after we did, and joined the regiment at Hall's Hill the same night we marched from there. We had been here but a short time, during which they seemed to enjoy each other's company very much, for they had not seen each other for more than a year.

Two weeks ago, Milton was taken sick, and one cold, blustering day, after Oliver and I had taken him to the hospital, the poor fellow (he had typhoid fever) died before his brother could reach him. Walt and I stood guard over his body all the afternoon till six o'clock, when we marched without arms to bury him. He was buried very well, considering the circumstances. Two of our men made a box, and we got the chaplain of the Second Maine to officiate. I helped lower him to his last resting-place. ... Newman is in the hospital, and when we were making his box, he sat on one end of it and watched them, and said: 'I shall be there next.' He has changed wonderfully, although I think he will live. George Ball is used up, having been sick two weeks or more ... you would never know him. I never saw such a change. The Lord knows we have all changed enough, but he is completely metamorphosed ... he is all faded out, his hair, eyes, etc., and his quick step is changed to a slow, dragging step, and he moves around with a careworn, beseeching look that is really ... pitiful. . . . Yes! that strong fellow, the one they thought would stand everything, is reduced down, and looks like some careworn old man; he is not in the hospital. ... You have no idea what a life this is; none but the strongest, the iron constitution, can stand it. It is the roughest, toughest life that I ever experienced. ...

The sights I have seen, death in every form; the cutting of limbs; the suffering I have endured, besides seeing others suffer; the discouragement I have met with, together with other things, have taken some of the spirit out of me. ... If I am ever sick, and you are written to come, don't hesitate a moment. You don't know how a poor soldier suffers in the hospitals, when they are in the field; I won't attempt to describe it, for it will make you feel badly. ... Now I must make an inspection of my clothes.

Crawling lice, diarrhea, and cold are the curses of the soldier. What if I should tell you that every soldier in this army has them, and that you even have to throw away your shirt, they swarm so in the night; they form hollow squares, and deploy skirmishers, have dress parades, etc.

I send you a piece of thread that I took from a dead man, on the battlefield of Antietam. I send it because it may be a curiosity to you, I could have picked up a lot of stuff, but could not lug it. It is hard work to get it, as we have to hurry along. ... I will write on the 29th, my birthday (17), to some of you.

Our brother of the Regulars now writes:

Camp near Weverton,

October 25, 1862.

My excuse for not writing before is a good one; I have so much to do since I have been quartermaster, that I write very few letters. In the first place, we have had such a miserable quartermaster and poor train that I was disgusted, and have been trying to mend the entire concern, to get rid of broken teams, worn-out horses, to get into shape the rolling stock of the battalion of the Eighth Infantry. I have had to furnish wood and forage, and have had to send long distances for them both. I was at Harper's Ferry from last Monday until yesterday morning, with my train, after clothing; the entire train of the army seemed to be there, and my time was among the last. I rode to camp every night, and left my train so that I could keep my place. I got up at daylight, and started usually without my breakfast. It is very cold there, and I dread a winter campaign unless I am in Washington, and that town has lost its charm for me. ... I received a letter from John yesterday; he is well, but a little low-spirited, I thought. Walt and Bob are too far away for me to get time to see them. I received a letter from them some time since, asking for blankets. I gave them money, and an order on a quartermaster for blankets. I have got to make out duplicate inspection reports, to get an ambulance and a horse condemned, and if I do not commence them soon, my hands will be so stiff that I will not be able to finish them.

A very heavy picket guard was furnished on the 25th; it was cold and raw, with a northeast storm. Inspection was ordered for the 26th, but the storm prevented. Artillery firing was heard in the direction of the river. Martin's battery opened on a party of rebels who came to the river to get stray cattle, and drove them back. One of the sharpshooters had his jaw broken in two places by the kick of a horse. We were ordered at night to have three days' rations ready in haversacks to move at any moment. There was a rumor that McClellan had been superseded, and Hooker placed in command.[7] On the 27th there was a cold and piercing gale of wind all day.

Our brother Walter now writes:

October 29, 1862.

Mr. Ingalls is going home today; he felt dreadfully when he found his son was dead and buried. When he inquired after his boys, especially the one who was sick, he was told the sad news by our sergeant, 'We buried him yesterday.' We had an awful cold night last night: the frost was very heavy. We slept very comfortably during the night, Ed having drawn a rubber blanket, which he stretched over us all. Bob and I didn't sign for one, he having a coat, and I a blanket in my bundle. If I get my coat and woolen blanket I shall be satisfied. But it is just our luck to have them come the very last. If I had thought of the long delay, and of rubber blankets coming first, I should have ordered one; and there's the great trouble out here; no one can see a day ahead, and cannot calculate on anything that is certain. I have a nice rubber blanket, and hate to buy another one of (the) government. They have already swindled us on our clothing at Camp Cameron. Two horses froze to death last night, or rather perished from exposure, and you ought to see the poor horses and mules tremble and shake in the morning; they suffer everything. Some are out in the open air, others (officers') have stables made out of green boughs. We have a nice bed of cedar, which tends towards comfort, and manage pretty well, though pretty close for convenience, but none too much so for warmth. We

---

[7] Hooker took command of the Army of the Potomac on January 26, 1863.

'spoon in' lively, and sleep like hogs, until we are tired out, having but one position, and then turn out.

We have drill enough lately; out lieutenant-colonel gives a battalion drill every afternoon. I am getting to be quite proficient in the manual, and study tactics a good deal, for some of our boys, sergeants and corporals, are leaving to join the regulars, and I am looking out for a position. I do some writing up to the lieutenant's tent, and that helps me; he noticed my writing today, and I stepped in. I might have got a clerkship for the adjutant if I only had the influence a short time ago; but no matter, I am on the lookout; might as well be somebody while in this great arrangement. We are on the 'ready' still, to move, and if they do before Bob and 1 get our coverings, we are dished, and will be subjects for the box. T think we go towards the enemy; if not, then we go towards Washington, and then there will be a chance to send us something.

Wednesday Eve, October 29th.

Bob's birthday, seventeen years old

Bob and I have just finished our celebration supper, eaten by candle-light, while Ed and Webster have gone down to the woods to the prayer-meeting, at which we are all attendants. It consisted of flap jacks fried by Bob, ingredients furnished by myself, and soft bread and butter. We ate sugar and butter on 'slabs," and had a good apple to wind up with. 'We hail this day so full of joy, and greet it with a song!' and we have been singing, 'For this night we'll merry, merry be!' and many other songs. We are really happy, so much so that I cannot help sitting down to our first candle light for four nights (sometimes they give us candles, and sometimes they purposely forget it), and express to you the joy of our hearts, even though it be feebly expressed, and that, too, with a lead pencil, a hard writing material in the night time, simply because we both have blankets to sleep under, and shall be comfortable this night. Bob was sick last night, and was threatened with a severe turn. He had felt a cold coming on, and had said to me several times, 'If I have to lie on that tent floor of cedar without any covering two or three nights more, I shall be sick.' It was very cold last night, and his head ached and burned, yet he had no covering, and we both determined to do wonders in the blanket line today, in view of our expected move. Poor prospects of our requisitions being furnished today, and future suffering from cold, and a shelter tent only to go into, and that scarcely ever relieved by the gladdening warmth of a candle, which, in its dim rays, gives joy to the soldier at night.

Well, we got them! One we bought of a young man, Dawson (Frank) of Haverhill, who went to the regulars today, and the other our lieutenant let me have, it being one he receipted for to cover George Ball while he was sick, and which he now transfers to me subject to my responsibility, and liable to be returned when mine arrives. George Ball, Newman, and five of our company have gone to a hospital back of Sharpsburg or Keediesville. Orders were read at dress parade to be ready to march in six hours, and all our sick are sent to the rear. Two of the hours are now past and gone, and I am not at all alarmed. These orders are getting -played out with us, although it does look all about like an advance into Virginia and a winter campaign. Of course, just because we are now comfortable, we shall be routed out; but I say, go! We ought to light and whip the rebels, and I say 'go in!' To be sure we are now having things decent here; we can buy articles that we need, and can change our diet slightly, and everything is lovely in the camp, especially at night.

Our whole brigade, with Griffin's, is right between two hills. The Michigan and Pennsylvania regiments are getting things from home, and these moonlight nights the camps are echoing with joyful voices, and musical instruments are abundant. I believe ours is the stillest of them all. It is charming here at night. We had potatoes and fresh meat for dinner, the former for the first time. It is really too bad to move just now. We ought to have gone long ago, but I am ready for anything. We were very fortunate in getting our blankets: it was all by chance, and was one of those lucky things that will happen to a Carter in a lifetime. We paid $2.50[8] for the blanket. If we had not got it, I was determined for Bob's sake to buy an officer's blanket (white and soft) that was priced to me at $6. As it was, we had to almost beg a sale of Dawson, and we should have had to fight almost for the above. ... You ought to see Bob. ... He is all wound up in one of them. ... It is really amusing. He is well tonight. ... I never would have come out here without him and our boys for the world, knowing now what I do: it is the only thing that keeps us leavened. We should never be happy without each other. How I have risen up within myself and cursed the very name of England since I read Gladstone's speech,[9] and the general tone of

---

[8] About $62 in 2019.

187

the governmental reception of 'Honest Old Abe's' [Emancipation] proclamation. How I despise their criticisms, slurs, and jests, and their making fun of us. Their turn will come next, and then her whole course of infamy will be summed up total, and just will be her reward. Whip the 'rebs,' and then up Yankees and at John Bull! I am in then again for three years or the war. It is queer about the intentions of the government to place McClellan where Halleck is, and put Hooker at the head of the Army of the Potomac; what can be the meaning of it? The army thinks everything of 'Little Mac,' and think he is the best planner in the world, but I think 'Fighting Joe' will do more in the field, if he keeps out of the way of the bullets.

I have mended my pants and am now whole, although my general appearance in the clothing department might fall short of your standard at home. My shirt hasn't come yet.

I have made out our company muster roll, and we recruits are on the list, so we shall be paid on next pay day, if we do not move on the enemy. . . . the boys have come back and our small tent is too full for comfort in writing. We retire to a warm bed; and I know the intelligence will make you glad, for your words indicate a warm, fatherly anxiety for the comfort of his boys. Our backs and limbs are sore from the effect of sleeping on our tent floor the way we have, and now I hope to get them straightened out; we shall spread one blanket and cover over with the other. ... If we move soon, and I be denied the pleasure of writing to you at home for a while, then here's good luck in the interim, and if I live, I shall constantly think of you all; if I am shot by Johnny Reb, be sure I drop with face to the foe, fighting like a tiger, yet with thoughts of home in my mind.

Thursday night,

October 30, 1862.

We are packing up to leave; where we go to, God only knows, but probably towards the foe, and I hope we may never come back until

---

[9] The Union blockade of southern ports meant England was only getting what American cotton they could from blockade runners. One of Lincoln's greatest worries was that the Confederacy would be recognized by England. Chancellor of the Exchequer, William Gladstone, strongly supported British recognition and gave a speech at Newcastle upon Tyne on October 7, 1862 to that effect.2019

we have made our election sure, and everything Secesh is gone for, and they be numbered with the past. On every hilltop may be heard preparations for breaking camp, and the bugles are sounding, the men singing, and altogether it is a gala, novel scene; you can hardly imagine it. I am as calm as can be, and I feel hopeful for the future. I know not what is before me, but if it is the danger of the battle, depend upon it I am in for some tall lighting. Bob says he has looked out for 'fod' this time, and I can vouch for it, by the looks of his well-filled haversack; mine is ditto. Tell father we are 'living and learning,' and try to follow his good advice. I have got more than three days' rations, and have got to lug a blanket and a poncho, with my other soldier load. Tell mother that we have two stakes stuck into the ground with crotches at the top of each, and a long pole is put across them, and upon it we hang our kettles, and under it we build our fires. We have a cook for the company, who cooks coffee, boils beef, salt horse, rice, etc., and we can cook extra dishes ourselves; he has a cook-house (a tent), with all his ingredients, kettles, spiders, etc. He draws our rations from the quartermaster's tent in our regiment, and the quartermaster of each regiment of a brigade, draws from the brigade commissary. My love to you all at home, and I rejoice that I am contented and happy, as I think of you all tonight, so happy in the little 'straw cottage.' That a wish might bring you every blessing, is but an expression of my sincere feeling.

NARROW ESCAPE FROM CAPTURE

Building fires of our now deserted huts, the straw, dried cedar boughs, shelter tent poles, etc., we gathered in knots, around the crackling blaze, to discuss pro and con the objective point, the probabilities of when we would reach it, how, what object was in view, etc.

The grumblers and growlers threw in a few opinions well interlarded with "cuss words," about the government, the war, niggers, etc. At 9 p. m., were off, and marching via the Antietam Iron Works, Harper's Ferry, and the Loudon Valley, through Middleburg and Warrenton, soon knew that we were enroute for Fredericksburg.

Our march continued until after midnight, along a very good road, and with the usual amount of joking, hard talk, and amusing incidents. We bivouacked four miles from Harper's Ferry in a large field. The next day we marched leisurely, and with many halts to the river, crossed the pontoons, and stopping just long enough for us to see the "John Brown celebrities," and to admire the beautiful scenery about Maryland and Loudon Heights, at the junction of the Shenandoah river with the Potomac, we crossed the former, also, on pontoons, and bivouacked near Hillsboro, about six miles beyond, and in the open valley of Loudon.

Our brother Walter says:

Bivouacked in a field about six miles from Harper's Ferry, in what direction, or towards what place, I know not, Nov. 1, 1862.

Dear Ones at Home: We are on the march, and report says we are to reinforce Sigel and Burnside, and while I write, the cannon are booming about ten miles off, towards Leesburg some persons say. We have been in this field all day, and have been mustered for pay; when it will come, we do not know. We started night before last about 9 o'clock (just after I wrote Kate), and marched until 1:30 a. m., and bivouacked about four miles from Harper's Ferry; yesterday morning we started again, and marched with ease about ten miles to this place, from which we expect to move in the advance on the rebs every moment. My feet are somewhat blistered, but I guess I can go it. Bob had a hard time with a sore chest, but is now in for it, being a little better. We halted for three hours before Harper's

Ferry, it took so long for the teams to cross the pontoon bridge there.

Some of our boys saw Bill Mills of Bradford, of Company H, 14th Mass., which is stationed on Maryland Heights. We are now in full view of a most beautiful valley, extending for miles. I thought it was the Shenandoah, but have found out different; it is on the other side of hills near us ... the way the rails owned by the rebs disappear is a caution. Imagine an army moving through Bradford; in the morning, after one night's rest, all our fields would be converted into one general, common property; every fence would be gone for miles around. We draw rations every three days on the march, and if a battle is expected, they give us all we can lug, and we trust to Providence for supplies after it, for a week the trains being nowhere. Our beans are never soaked at night, our cook not knowing enough; they are very good though without; we can't go through the whole programe. Scarfs would be grand, so would woolen caps, for we freeze our pates nightly; we try to wear our caps, but they drop off, and the dew wets our skulls through. Last night we turned in to this place from our march at 8 o'clock; it was a beautiful evening, and the frogs were singing as lustily as they do in May at home. ... As this accommodation mail leaves at 5 o'clock for Harper's Ferry, I must be closing. We heard from Gene; he has moved from Knoxville to Berlin, and I doubt if we shall see him.

Our brother Bob now adds:

I thought I would add a few lines. ... I am O. K. meaning that I am in good spirits and health. ... Last night we spooned in, sleeping on a rubber blanket, and covering us with both blankets; slept quite warm. I caught an awful cold on my lungs, owing to sleeping without covering, but am better. We have had quite a rest today. ... I shall write as soon as we reach our stopping place.

Here we drew some blankets, and by "doubling up" and sleeping on our rubbers, were once more comfortable. Our march on the following day, Sunday, up the valley, was enlivened by the booming of guns nearly all day, and after a march of fifteen miles, we camped at Snicker's Gap. The marching was easier, our blankets were in rolls, our equipments seemed to fit better, and we took things in a more philosophical light. We were becoming soldiers. A fight had occurred at the Gap. Once or twice we packed up to move. The Rebels were crowding along on the other side of the Blue Ridge, and it was necessary for us to guard the pass.

Snicker's Gap,

Near Snickersville, Va.,

Nov. 5, 1862.

We arrived here Sunday afternoon, after a tedious ride of fifteen miles; before leaving our camping ground, five miles this side of Harper's Ferry, where we stayed all day Saturday, and from which place I wrote a short letter home, we drew a blanket apiece, swelling our blankets to three in number (of course just as we were on the march), and I drew a shirt, white (cotton and wool shoddy, no shape or make), canteen, haversack and a pair of stockings; also went in for an overcoat. Our packs are rather heavy, but somehow they don't hang so heavy as formerly. I have got to be a soldier now, and my rig fits better, and I can march like a trooper; there's no falling out now, like unto our Washington march, and we have to keep to the front and bear up well.

Our lieutenant commanding, Joseph H. Baxter of Cambridge, an orderly sergeant of another company formerly, now second lieutenant of ours, gave me an old rubber blanket before I started, which answers very well for Bob and myself, as protection from the ground, and we spread two blankets over us, Bob having loaned our blanket that we bought, just to have it carried. Weren't we lucky in that? We have our old dress coats for pillows, and wear them in the cold weather for overcoats, but we sweat under them on these marches in the warm valley.

We have to wear them, our packs are so large, besides it is the easiest way to carry them, with the one exception of being too warm. We have our tent full of straw, and Ed, Bob and myself spoon in together so comfortably, ever remembering our mutual suffering in camp near Sharpsburg, Maryland. We have let Webster slide, for four are too many in our tent on a march; it answers very well in camp, for we put down boards, and widen things to suit, but here we pull our ponchos as close to the ground as possible, two inches.

Our old doctor is at Brigade headquarters, and we can have all the hay and straw we want to lie upon; he thought they were unhealthy, and fried hard bread healthy, the old reprobate! I wish he had had my black and blue hips. We are real comfortable here, and only need an overcoat for guard duty, and mittens during night picket. We shall probably move in a day or two from here. It is likely to come in order form every day, every hour, every moment; we packed up yesterday, and were under orders to move all day. We got here too late to participate in the Snicker's Gap[1] fight, but we shall be reckoned in in a day or two I guess, for on the other side of the Ridge the Rebs are crowding the left bank of the Shenandoah. We may stay here to protect the Gap, and tonight the Second Maine go on picket. General Butterfield has command of our division now, and probably Colonel Barnes of the Massachusetts Eighteenth (right flank regiment of the brigade) will command Martindale's brigade, in consequence of the wind up of the Martindale court martial[2] in Washington; I am glad he got clear. Bob is on guard tonight, and he will wear his dress coat over his shoulders, and wrap his blanket about himself. . . .

.... There will be a great battle soon, and then may Heaven protect your boys as they fight for the country, and in the language of C.W., "Stick to their flag." At every opportunity I shall write and relieve you of your anxiety, and living or dying, be assured my thoughts are centered on home, and if you do not hear from me when you most wish or expect to, be sure it is because it is impossible.

Bob has just come into the tent, and says we move tomorrow morning for Ashby's Gap, eight miles below; our teams are being loaded, and I guess it is so. We keep three days' rations with us all the time, and our hard bread is very nice at present; real good crackers . . . keep them all cheerful in the house by assurances of our present comparative comfort, and do not allow them to give way so readily to their feelings.

---

[1] Since it is a major thoroughfare between the Piedmont and the Shenandoah Valley, the gap was the scene of many small American Civil War skirmishes.—2019

[2] This was not a court martial but a court of inquiry requested by General John Henry Martindale to clear himself of charges made by Fitz John Porter related to actions at Malvern Hill. Insufficient evidence was presented to bring him to court martial and Martindale returned to the field.—2019

Wells were dug, company books were over-hauled, all sorts of rumors were started, and then we knew we would move. It was a cold, raw, bitter day as we filed out of camp, and wound through the one dirty street of Snickersville.

A cold drizzle set in. The snow commenced to spit occasionally. The halts were few and far between. The men had become too cold and numb to hold a musket, and resort was had to old stockings and haversack bags, to make up the deficiency of mittens. Our route was through Philomont, Mountville P. O., and Middleburg. As we were in rear of the brigade, when we arrived in camp at 7 o'clock, the ground was occupied, and our bivouac was upon a bald knoll, where the wind blew hard all night. We were on the farm of J. W. Patterson, five miles beyond Middleburg.

There was little sleep. The fires were crowded; many pant legs suffered; water froze hard in canteens at our heads, and we wished for and heartily welcomed daylight. But, after starting upon the road in the morning and encountering a dense snow storm which soon drove us into the woods for a camp, we wished again, like Napoleon, "for night."

Our little shelter tents were pitched by tying the front and rear cords to trees the proper distance apart, and staking down the sides as usual in the deep snow and placing our guns with fixed bayonets as uprights at the front and rear; some hay was obtained with much difficulty from a long distance, and soon, with the aid of large, blazing fires we partially forgot our transient misery.

At night we received a large mail which we read, partly by the aid of pieces of candles which we had saved and carried for the purpose, and when they went out, by the dim light of the fires.

A ration of whiskey and quinine was issued. We were temperance to the backbone, yet freezing outwardly and being dry inwardly, with wet feet and chattering teeth, we hesitated but a brief moment, and then with a feeling akin to desperation, worried it down.

The following morning the sun came out. The snow melted, the roads grew sloppy, and after starting from our feathery white bivouac, we slipped and waded along the stony, wretched turnpike until thoroughly tired out we camped beyond and near New Baltimore. Passing through Georgetown, a march of nearly eighteen miles, long to be remembered, during which the wet, cold, and thoroughly worn out men gave vent to their feelings in curses loud and deep.

We again moved about four miles to a better camp in a piece of thin woods, where we filled our pouches with cedar tips and leaves, and "crowding it" at night, using our blankets to best advantage, tried in the midst of haversacks, canteens, dippers, guns, boxes, and the equipments of the men to imagine ourselves surrounded by luxuries. Our camp was on the left side of the Warrenton road near the Cattail branch of Cedar Run.

The nights were bitter. Ice formed on the streams and in our canteens. Men and animals suffered intensely from the cold, and it was said some died. Here our corps commander, General Fitz John Porter, was relieved, and the general commanding the army, George B. McClellan. Then came the leave-taking. It was a magnificent sight, and as regiment after regiment cheered, waved their tattered flags, and saluted the departing commanders it was enough to move a heart of stone.

Our letters say:

In Camp Near Warrenton,

November 10, 1862.

We expect to move tomorrow, so I will avail myself of all the intervening time to satisfy the thoughts that are always running in the stiller waters of my mind, viz.: the desire to ever have home before me, and to talk and converse with you all by writing and thereby keep the influence pure and fresh, unsullied by the scenes and daily occurrences of the camp; for truly I fall in with father's kind words of advice, and care most for how much I am thought of in B,, and all about the dear old home.

I closed my last letter at Snicker's Gap with this 'Bob has just come into the tent and said we were to move the next morning.' He was right, and that Thursday morning at daylight, before we had any time to get breakfast, we started. It was a bitter cold day and we footed it until 7 o'clock at night, not at all minding the usual stop of 8 minutes to the hour; for sometimes we would march two hours steady without a particle of rest, and that would convert the regiment into a cursing, swearing body of men who, tired out, would give vent to their feelings in curses and imprecations about the army, officers, and the whole concern anyway. . . . Oh, my Lord! wasn't it cold? No overcoat, no gloves, hands benumbed, so that I could hardly handle my gun. I remembered that I had an old pair of holey stockings in the bottom of my haversack, and I pulled them on, after which ... I was more comfortable. . . . We camped on the top of a bleak hill in the dead grass, and being rear guard to our division, we arrived in camp later than the rest of the brigade, and consequently had the worst pick of ground, as we had the poorest place during the day, being jolted about in the rear of the teams, ambulances, etc. It was a fit ending to a day of hard usage. ... The wind blew bitter cold ... I suffered the whole night. ...

I couldn't stand it ... 'turned out' two or three times to warm my feet by the fire. ... It was so cold that the water in our canteens froze by our sides, so that we had to shake them to break the ice so that we could drink. ... Bob and I slept under two blankets upon my rubber blanket; we had no time to pitch ponchos. We were off early; routed out at 4 o'clock, and started without anything to eat; no coffee or anything ... went about a mile, the wind blowing right through us, when, Heavens and Earth! If you will believe it, it commenced to snow, and we had to march in a driving snow storm ... two hours, it being colder than any November day I ever remember at home. ...

They marched us until about 12 o'clock, when the officers flushed out, and could not stand it themselves. We filed into the woods by regiments, and cold, wet, and hungry we had to button our ponchos and pitch them. ... Stayed until the next morning. We had an awful time getting up our tents in the snow. Of course we had to go for rails, etc., to make a fire, so that we would not actually freeze. ... I went a mile and a half to get some hay. I filled the tent well up. Ed put his rubber up in front to keep the driving snow out, and we all spooned in together, and managed quite well. My feet were sopping wet and cold, and that night they served out whiskey (and quinine) rations to the men.

Imagine the scene! Every one of us temperance to the backbone, yet freezing inwardly, and there the relieving article before us. Bob

and I had never tasted it, and Ed but once. We could not hesitate. ..
I actually thought it would do me good, cold, wet, and chilled as I
was.

I worried down one spoonful of it; it almost made me sick for a
moment, but the after sensation was very agreeable. Bob and Ed
drank the rest, saving some for the next day, which came in very
opportunely, as it was cold. Ed was on guard, and it was rather
severe on him, as he had been ordered on arrival to help put up
headquarter tents, and do general fatigue. We experienced some
inconvenience too, for his duties compelled him to leave the tent at
stated times, and the clothes, etc., had to be disturbed. When in the
tent, before roll-call the unexpected and welcome call of 'mail' was
heard. We fell in lively I assure you. ... We started again the next
morn, and in the forenoon the sun came out, and the roads were
perfectly awful; such muddy, stony turnpikes I, hope never to see
again. We marched 18 miles, through Philemont and Middleburg to
within a few miles of New Baltimore—seven without a rest or halt,
and camped back here 4 miles. I went again for hay, and a second
nice bed was the result, although we suffered from the cold blow
that had lasted during the latter part of the afternoon.

The next morning we marched to our present camping ground,
and after a hard time at tent raising in the cold, and a poor
experience of a Sabbath day, we came into possession of a pretty
good night's quarters, our bed being composed of forest leaves, and
our covering as usual.

.. We are now encamped in the woods. At night we were subjected
to a long dress parade, at which over thirty ridiculous orders were
read; we like to have frozen to death. ... "Now, if that is not rough ...
marching in snow storms, cold, freezing days, lying on the ground
nights ... for ten days; routing out, packing up before light; and yet,
there are some devilish fools at home who will go home and sit by
their comfortable fires, with paper in hand, and swear about
McClellan and the army, their not moving, etc. Oh! wouldn't I like
to have some of those loafers out here and march them at the point
of the bayonet, with nothing but their salt pork and crackers to eat,
twenty miles a day for a fortnight? Well! I guess so! They would
soon know whether the army moves or not.

Sunday, November 9.

Here we are still, and two inches deep in snow, with the weather, oh! so bitter cold. As cold as I ever knew it to be at home; running water frozen two inches thick this morning, and we are slowly freezing to death in our slight poncho tents. I wish you might have looked in upon us last night after we had rolled ourselves in our blankets, and prepared to sleep; if you could have peeked in, and by the aid of a candle light, gazed upon the 'sleeping beauties.' It did seem as if we would freeze up solid last night; the wind was most keen, and the snow being damp, froze as it fell, I guess, for in the first of the evening, it was most raining, and this morning our tent is covered with icy snow, and within there is a frost equal to any I ever saw on the window of our little chamber.

Two men of the Massachusetts Ninth died from exposure last night, and I apprehend there will be many more of other regiments who will follow them, when we go on picket duty and do extra marching. We got up early, for we couldn't sleep, and had the meanest breakfast I ever ate; wormy hard-tack, and black coffee; the bread was so hard I could scarcely chew it. ... I have worn my back teeth all down, and the fillings of two are ground to powder, so that they ache often. ... We have to go most a mile for wood twice a day, and wading in snow and mud with only shoes on is rather tough; besides I am barefoot now, my stockings having caved in, being of most miserable quality, and having been subjected to extra hard usage—mud, snow, and rain travelling.

We no sooner get one comfort, before we are out in another, and we cannot draw when we please. .. When I stick these feet of mine, so poorly clad with woolen yarn, into cold shoes in the morning, you can imagine my *phelinks*; my pedal extremities are generally cold all day. But, such is my manifest destiny, and I will grin and bear it. If I am only allowed to get my revenge out of the true originators of this war, the rebels, I will be content; but I wish for the opportunity very soon before my Northern Union blood congeals in too great quantities from the severity of the weather. ... Just stopped for a moment to see Gene; he and Lieutenant Worth rode up on their way to General Sykes; he only stopped long enough to ask me how I liked the 'winter campaign,' and that he was almost frozen, and wanted something warming. He has just dashed off; he rides elegantly.

I ate some bread (hard) this morning that wasn't fit for hogs, and some rice that was splendid. Mother, I shall never be dainty when I get home, for I can eat rice that *runs salvy*, which you know I detested when at home. I love it now. I saw a sutler yesterday and bought paper, envelopes, and ink; I can't write with the latter, it is so cold to hold a pen; I only use it to direct envelopes. .. The lint, bandages, needles, and item, are all carefully reserved safely for future use, if not for us, for others. They are only additional mementoes of your love for us. It does seem as if there never was such a mother ... so supremely good, so regardless of self, so full of loving kindness to all mankind, so sympathetic, so, .so, so—I could go on almost indefinitely. *You are such a patriotic woman— hurrah! for you, I say. You are a fit subject for every beatitude in the Bible, and I do not enlarge, either.*

Monday Morning.

Slept very comfortably, though it was cold. Water froze solid in our canteens; we had four in a tent, Le Roy still being without necessary comforts; it crowds us dreadfully. Think of four sleeping in the front bedroom with all of our blankets and accoutrements thrown over us. We had baked beans for breakfast, and really, mother, they were, nice; it is the only good dish we have. We are expecting a review by General Burnside this afternoon. I wish we could be reviewed before the enemy. Gene says we shall move in a day or two. Some officers are exceptions, but the general run of them I despise. It seems as if it were impossible to find a noble-hearted man among them. If I were one, I believe I could make my men like me; there is a way to do it. You don't know how nice we keep our tent; every morning, after we have eaten our rations. I fix up our blankets, and put them at our heads, and we look as nice as you please; others keep them like pigpens.

We suffer dreadfully from the smoke of the campfires; our whole camp is full of it, and our eyes are severely affected; we can't close them at night, they ache so, and when they are open, they are filled continually with smoke.

Later,

November 10, 1862.

Today we have been on review. We took leave of McClellan, and the whole army is discouraged and sad. I will not complain. I have learned not to do it; neither will I hope for evil to befall the

199

government, but just as sure as George B. McClellan leaves, the courage, enthusiasm, and pluck of the army go with him.

It is all the talk in camp .... It would amuse you to hear the soldiers talk about the government and Abolitionists; 'hope they will be murdered, and the army defeated,' etc. They can't understand it; it is a problem to them; they see no papers, and know not the sequel. Some say that General McClellan is entirely relieved, and some say that it is only to give him the (position of) commander-in-chief of the army instead of General Halleck. I am inclined to believe the latter, for it has been hinted at in the papers for some time, and why should he be superseded?

We also hear that he has been ordered to report at his home in New Jersey. If you could only hear the soldiers talk about it, you wouldn't give much for the patriotism of the Army of the Potomac, and as for their being in good spirits and eager to advance, as the papers say, it is all bosh! For many of them are discouraged, and swear they won't fight under any other general than 'Little Mac'; besides the cold weather is killing the men. In our company three are down with fever; they go to bed well, and in the night wake up shivering, and sore across the chest; then commences their death march unless speedily seen to. It is almost impossible to cure on the march. Bob has had a headache for a day or two past, and his face looks swollen; he is very fat, and that may account for it. I am doing everything to cheer him up and keep him lively, but he says he knows he will not escape a sick time. I say he shall! ... Eugene was over to see us this afternoon; he is an enraged individual about McClellan's removal; he only stayed five minutes, having made arrangements to be back to General McClellan's reception to officers. ... Just long enough to swear and damn about their removing 'Mac.' Oh! isn't he mad? Aren't all of them mad? We shall try to go over and see him tomorrow. You don't know what a commotion the change in the army has made. Officers threaten to resign, and men refuse to fight. In heaven's name why make the transfer now, when all plans are made, and McClellan is our leader, the idol of the army? Why give the enemy the victory?[3]... They are cannonading out ahead this morning, showing the rebs are near.

---

[3] The troops loved him but McClellan was not only slow to act and overly cautious, he placed little stock in the authority of the Commander-in-Chief and the Secretary of War.—2019

There is a large army around us, consisting of Sigel's, Burnside's, and Porter's corps. Burnside was with 'Mac' this morning; he succeeds him in command. I fear for the result of our grand advance, for it is almost suicidal removing McClellan now, and although I am willing to do my part, God knows I have so far, yet ...

I think what we do is no good. This winter is to see more suffering than America has seen before for some time, that is if we do not winter somewhere. ... I feel as if my constitution and health will be ruined, for who can stand it to lay out all winter, fight, march, etc.?

When your photograph turned up we were too full for utterance. ... How we did laugh at father's pepper. ... We use it a great deal in scouse, made of hardtack, salt horse, pork, and water, all stewed together, which makes a very palatable mess. You would laugh, I know, to see me this noon, eat raw pork and hard bread, with a dipper of coffee, just from necessity. I could but just get it down, but it was so heavy it stayed after I swallowed it.

On the 28th of October, the provost guard left their camp in Pleasant Valley and marched to Berlin, Md., camping a short distance back from the Potomac river. October 31, Company G, Ninth New York (Hawkins's Zouaves), Captain Childs, marched back from Wheatland and reported on headquarter guard. November 2, it crossed the river and marched to Wheatland, Va. November 3, it marched to Bloomfield, via Philemont, a distance of eighteen miles. November 4, marched to William Hall's place at Middleburg, Va. November 5, moved to Rectortown, and on the 8th to Warrenton.

Our brother, now of the Eighth Infantry, writes from Warrenton as follows:

Camp at Warrenton,

Nov. 10, 1862.

The pride of headquarters and of the army left us this morning. I would have given a month's pay to have had Abraham Lincoln present to witness the ovation given to General George B. McClellan yesterday morning by the troops of this army. He leaves us the proudest man in America. Night before last he received all his staff, and all connected with headquarters. The Eighth Infantry and Second Cavalry went with General Patrick, provost marshal general;

when the tent was crowded, and all had shaken hands with the General, the champagne was opened, and the General proposed 'The old Army of the Potomac,' and 'Bless the day when he was with it again.' Yesterday he reviewed the provost guard, and it was the finest sight ever witnessed. The old Eighth Infantry and the old Second Cavalry, and his body guard. The Eighth and Second never before cheered for mortal man, but on this occasion such yells as we gave when he passed, were never heard before. After he had passed in review, and was returning to the front, General Patrick, who was riding by his side, suddenly put spurs to his horse and rushed away from him; uncovering his old gray head, he cried out: 'Once more and all together!' They then shook hands, both in tears. Yesterday evening the General received at Fitz John Porter's headquarters. I was there, and it was a melancholy sight to see old men, major-generals, and brigadiers, shed tears when they parted from him.

General Burnside is one of his best friends, and regrets this thing as much as any of us. When General McClellan received the order, relieving him, we were pursuing the rebels, and would have forced them to fight the next day; now the rebels are ahead of us, and I expect we shall be skedaddling back to Washington very soon. I saw Walter and Bob yesterday; I never saw them so fat before; they appear to be comfortably situated; I shall see them again soon. Our command has just been ordered to turn out and receive General Burnside, who will occupy the old headquarters tonight. I suppose we must transfer our affections to him now.[4]

On the 16th the provost guard left Warrenton, marched to Weaversville, crossing Cedar run, bivouacking near Catlett's Station. On the 17th it bivouacked at Spotted Tavern, and on the 18th at Hartwood Church. On the 19th it reached Falmouth, Va., about 11 o'clock A. M., and went into camp."

Our brother in the forts now writes:

---

[4] U.S. Grant was later magnanimous towards McClellan, stating that everyone early in the war was trying to figure out how to fight it. That argument falls apart a bit when you consider Grant's own early victories in the west. But he also correctly gave McClellan great credit for having built the Army of the Potomac. Little Mac was Lincoln's Democratic opponent in 1864 and later served as the Governor of New Jersey. See *McClellan's Own Story*, 2014, BIG BYTE BOOKS.

Fort Tillinghast,

Nov. 13, 1862.

I do not feel like writing tonight, as I am very tired, having had to work hard all day on a 'bomb-proof' which we are digging in the fort for protection in case of an attack, but am obliged to communicate to you some unwelcome intelligence. Lewis tonight received a letter from the commander of the gunboat *Judge*—(I could not make out the name), informing him of the death of his father; he died (or was killed) at the bombardment of Vicksburg. He had written before, but Lewis did not get the letter. . . . Lewis feels very badly, but I try to cheer him all I can. I received mother's letter . . . please tell her she had better not send them (the little things she mentions), for I should have to throw them away if we should move. One pair of stockings, one shirt, and a blanket, with ammunition and equipments, are all I can possibly stagger under. It is 'the last hair that breaks the camel's back,' you know. ... We have had a big snow storm here, and it has been pretty rough in these tents, but when I think of how poor Walt and Bob must suffer, I do not complain. Do you hear from them, and how are they? ... The Twenty-fifth Maine is encamped near us; it is mostly made up of my old schoolmates, and it seems like old times. Frank Fessenden is colonel. Luther Dana, Ham. Ilisley, Freeman Clark, and a host of others are among the privates. ... Tell father that that little George Goss who used to do up the mail with Gene ... is sergeant-major, and was local editor of the *Argus* before he came to the war.

He is the present correspondent of that sheet. One of our company died the other day, and they had him embalmed and sent to Amesbury. We borrowed the money to be paid 'pay day.' The removal of McClellan does not cause much talk here, and if Burnside will only fight and do something towards closing the war, it will be all right. The men would rather do a month's steady fighting, and then go home, than to remain here a year doing nothing.

Our brothers of the Twenty-second now say;

Warrenton, Nov. 15 and 16, 1862.

Last night after our return from a visit to Gene, we received your last letter accompanied with the package containing the caps, gloves, one needle, and some thread, tokens of your fond interest,

203

and continual efforts for our best comfort and pleasure at home. If you only knew how overjoyed we were to receive them. ... The caps are the envy of the company, and the gloves are the best we could desire. ...

The day your letter came, Eugene was over in the afternoon, towards night; Bob was down sick at the time, but has since recovered; Gene stayed with us until late in the evening, and when he went away, it was with the understanding that if Bob was better, we would be over to see him the next day; his visit was very pleasant to us. He seems just as he used to, and talked with us about everything; he was cross and snappish though about the removal of 'Little Mac' and Fitz John Porter.

The next day Bob was no better, and we couldn't go over to the Eighth Infantry; we were called out on review (our corps), to take leave of General Porter, and welcome 'Fighting Joe' as our new commander. It was a sad parting, and many an officer shed tears, while Porter was very much overcome; it was a magnificent sight, and as the various regiments cheered, waved their tattered banners, and saluted their departing commander, it was enough to move a heart of stone. It has had a great effect upon this part of the army, the supersedure of McClellan, and his favorite general, Porter.[5]

Gene came over at noon, and stopped most of the afternoon; Bob was much better, and we had a gay time. We saw General Howard and Governor Washburne of Maine, at the camp of the Maine Second (in our brigade, next regiment.) ...

The next day, Friday, Bob and myself went over to see Gene; we got a pass from headquarters of the brigade, and started early in the forenoon. We found Gene glad to see us, and he introduced us to Frank Worth (son of General Worth of Mexican war fame); a young fellow, Captain McKee, (formerly captain of Gene's company at West Point), now of the First Cavalry; also Lieutenant (J. N.) Andrews, adjutant of the battalion, and ever so many more officers (of his class) who called to see him, that I can't recollect.

---

[5] Fitz John Porter (1822–1901) was arrested on November 25, 1862, and court-martialed for his actions at Second Bull Run. He was under a cloud until exonerated in 1878. Eight years later, President Cleveland commuted Porter's sentence and his rank was restored to colonel. He retired two days later. Of interest is *Grant's Letters in the Case of Fitz John Porter*, 2015, BIG BYTE BOOKS.

We were treated splendidly by them all, just the same as though we were one of their number, and particular friends at that. ... We sat in a little arm (camp) chair, the first one since leaving home. He has got a nice wall tent all to himself. We had a long, nice chat with him, and talked and joked. He showed us one or two of his camp pictures, gave us one, grew quite confidential, discussed the war, removal of his idol, 'Little Mac,' etc. etc., till dinner time.

We had a royal meal, composed of roast beef, pickled tongue, sweet and Irish potatoes (the latter mashed in butter and milk, bread and butter, and sherry wine. ... We enjoyed that kind of 'fod' until our stomachs were not big enough for our eyes. ... We had a gay dinner, and a gay time ... After waiting for the mess (of which Gene is the worthy caterer this month) to get through their smoke, Gene, Bob, and myself adjourned to the tent (where he lives in style), and had a long confab on politics, the army, regulars and volunteers, his company, home, the letter you sent to him, John Andrew and his niggers, and many more topics worthy of mention, but forgotten just now. We found him a queer genius in his ideas, and in politics he beats the Dutch. We felt perfectly at home, and talked freely. We stayed there until four o'clock, when we went to see guard mounting; and oh, father, how splendidly the regulars drill; it is perfectly sickening and disgusting to get back here and see our regiment and officers manoeuver, after seeing those West Pointers and those veterans of eighteen years' service go through guard mounting. I need not go into detail, nor mention any of the differences; you know it all. I am only glad I saw, for now I know I am a better soldier after seeing them perform. Gene sent for a lot of apples, and took us to the sutler's tent and gave us some cheese, a can of strawberries to carry to our camp. While there we saw Colonel (Adelbert) Ames[6] of the Twentieth Maine, and John (Marshall) Brown, his adjutant ... and Tom Edwards, the latter in government employ. ...

Gene walked half way back with us; on the road he introduced us to Fuller, a former classmate of his from Maine, and another classmate whom I cannot recollect. They seemed as glad to see us as if we were their own brothers, and shook our hands cordially; they

---

[6] Beside his Civil War record, Adelbert Ames(1835–1933) played an important role during Reconstruction as Governor of Mississippi. He married the strikingly beautiful Blanche Butler, daughter of the strikingly un-beautiful General Benjamin F. Butler.—2019

are such a genial set of fellows, these West Pointers, and yet such perfect soldiers. Gene seems to be a great favorite too with them all. Gene left us at camp. We had a real nice visit, and he treated us splendidly.

That morning we drew overcoats, and upon our arrival in camp, found a letter from father. We could not imagine what the bundle was, but upon opening it and seeing the contents, we actually jumped up and down. .. We found Henry Wilson (Senator) in camp; he walked around to every camp fire, and sat down and talked to the men ... he was out to inspection; Hooker told him yesterday that we made a fine appearance. .. We are very busy preparing for a march. I am finishing this Sunday, and tomorrow we move ... rumor has it that we go to Fredericksburg. Yesterday General Hooker reviewed the whole corps; our division was in one field, and it was a splendid sight; he rode round at a trot by every regiment, when he posted himself on a hill, and the whole division marched by, by companies. He took off his hat to the flags, all of them.

Gene was to have been here today but I guess he has moved; the whole army is on the move but us 'Reserves.' Hooker has now command of the Center Grand Division, composed of the Third and Fifth army corps, the latter being ours, under temporary command of the ranking brigadier, General Sykes. So I am under Gene's old commander; may I be true to him, as was Gene, and the remembrances of the gallant major (at home) cause me to fight well, and whistle and sing after the victory is won. We march on the morrow, dear father; where we go I know not, but I trust all will be well with us; you shall hear from us as soon as possible. Trusting that the last words of your letter may be verified in the future. ... Things look blue out here in respect to McClellan's removal; its tendencies are bad for the army, yet I do not despond. If all will do their duty, as I hope to do mine, we shall beat the fleeing enemy.

Our brother Bob adds on the 16th

Of course you have read ere this of the removal of 'Little Mack' and his right hand man, Fitz John Porter; that together with Hooker's review is the chief talk now in camp. At night the boys will huddle around the fire, and will blow and talk, until there is no end of opinions ... you have no idea of the feeling expressed in the army on this subject.

This is the third review I have been in since I came out here; one by the president, farewell review by 'Mack,' and this one. Fitz John Porter's I did not go to, as I was sick in my tent. Since I wrote my last letters I have been threatened with a fever; I laid in my tent for three or four days without scarcely moving out; two or three of our boys were sick after this march. I suppose I caught cold during that last snow storm, in which we suffered severely, being without overcoats or gloves, and our feet soaked. ... I wish ... that you who have never seen a large army, and its movements, could see it, and also the celebrated generals, 'Mac,' Burnside, Sumner, Hooker, Franklin, Richardson (dead), Griffin, Wilcox, and half a score of others, for I know it must be a great sight to you. ... Gene has been to see us twice, stopping a long time each visit ... he laid in our little coop, and talked with us ever so long; shook hands with us at leaving, told us to be sure and come to see him. That was when I was sick, but was getting better.

The next day he came again, making us another pleasant visit.

Tell father I will try and profit by his advice; let him never fear of my lowering myself in any way, for I am resolved that I will come back as good as when I went out. ... We have to rout out mornings at five o'clock, reveille.

Won't the gloves be gay tomorrow? My holy stocking will be at a discount. ... I am writing on my knee, so don't laugh at the writing; with an old blunt, lead pencil, and my knee pan ain't just the thing. .. I will write just as soon as we stop long enough if we move tomorrow. ...

Our brother of the artillery now writes;

Fort Tillinghast,

Nov. 18, 1862.

About the box; we expect to go to Harper's Ferry soon, but cannot tell when, and it would be much easier for me to get it here, so if you can make it convenient, you had better send it as soon as you can. ... Two or three of the Portland [Maine] boys were over to see me yesterday, and we went down to old Lee's place, and drew some persimmons, and afterwards sat down to salt horse. I believe you asked me for a piece of my 'wool.' You have it enclosed; it's sure death to rats, but has no visible effect on lice. They do not trouble my head, but are very partial to woolen goods. Isn't it awful? They will get into the tents in spite of all we can do, but I have not had any about me for some time. I got some mercurial ointment, which fixed them, and came pretty near fixing me, for it took the skin nearly off my body. ... I suppose you feel very badly about Uncle William's death ... He was killed on board the gunboat *Judge Torrence* at the storming of Vicksburg.

In the rain and gloom of the morning of November 17, we filed out again for the march, and moving through Warrenton, Warrenton Junction, and other small hamlets (Elkton and Spotted Tavern) found ourselves on the 22d, near Hartwood church, a soaked, bedraggled lot of patriots.

It was called the "Mud Camp." It was a low, marshy piece of ground. The rain pouring in torrents, had overflowed it; the tent pegs, although two feet or more in length, would not hold. A gust of wind at night swept it down upon our faces, and drenched to the skin, about midnight, after several unsuccessful efforts to disentangle cords, pegs, poles, etc., we abandoned it, and in the inky blackness, steered for a fire, where we found about half of the company "sitting around," and here we wore out the night, crouching, nodding, and vainly endeavoring to sit upon a log, sleep bolt upright, keep from getting any wetter and colder, and at the same time, avoid tumbling into the fire.

Upon the 23d, we slowly paddled along the awful roads, through bog, mire, and liquid mud, about ten miles, and at night, bivouacked in our fighting position, about four miles from Falmouth, near Stoneman's Switch on the Acquia creek and Fredericksburg railroad. We had reached our base.

When our small band of patriots was gathered at old Camp Cameron, in Cambridge, impatiently awaiting the seemingly slow movements of the powers that be, and transportation to our regiment; engaged and absorbed in the many novelties of the occasion, and in eager anticipation of events, we had given but little time or thought to individuals, or their characteristic traits.

Among our number, however, we had noticed a tall, slim boy, straight as an arrow. His face was a perfect oval, his hair was as black as a raven's wing, and his eyes were large and of that peculiar soft, melting blackness, which excites pity when one is in distress. His skin was a clear, dark olive, bordering on the swarthy, and this, with his high cheek bones, would have led us to suppose that his nationality was different from our own, had we not known that his name was plain Henry P—. There was an air of good breeding and refinement about him, that, with his small hands and feet, would have set us to thinking, had it not been that in our youth and intensely enthusiastic natures, we gave no thought to our comrades' personal appearance.

We can look back now and see the shy, reserved nature of the boy, the dark, melancholy eyes, the sad smile, the sensitive twitching of the lips. We had more time to observe our comrades. Hardships, privations, danger, with death often staring us in the face, was beginning to draw us nearer. Strong sympathies were aroused. The tall, slim, dark haired boy began to yearn for companionship.

On the Maryland campaign to Antietam, sometimes the burden had been greater than he could bear, and the rough, hard jokes of the Peninsula veterans, accompanied with a— "You d—d two hundred dollar recruit," had closed the portals of his heart. His quiet, uncomplaining ways attracted the writer's attention. I was drawn to him, and while around Sharpsburg, we had become warm, fast friends. His face grew brighter. His sad eyes looked happier. An occasional smile crept about his lips, lingered for a moment, and was gone.

There was a burden upon his mind which I felt anxious to know, yet hesitatingly shrank from intruding myself upon his sensitive, reticent nature. One day, however, Henry felt communicative. A letter from his sister had cheered him up, and in a sudden fit of confidence, he told me his long buried secret.

This boy was the son of a Sandwich Island princess near relative of the royal king, Kamehameha. His father, a native of Boston, became a merchant in Honolulu. He had, while living at the island, become enamoured of this princess, and after a short courtship, married her. He brought her to Boston where Henry was born.

209

It is the old story—the beautiful princess died; the father married again. Henry was educated in the public schools of Roxbury. In the midst of the clamor of war, when the very air vibrated with excitement, the wild enthusiasm of the crowds, and the inspiring sound of the drum, his Indian nature rose within him. His resolve was made. He would enlist. It was a beautiful face that Henry showed me that bright October day, as we sat in the shadows of the huge black walnuts and white oaks, that formed the grove by our camp near Shepardstown, on the banks of the Potomac. It was an ambrotype of the native princess, his mother, taken in Boston, after her marriage. With the exception of a slight fullness of the lips, and the prominent cheek bones, it was a perfect face. The blue-black hair, waving over a high forehead; those large, mellow, black eyes, like a gazelle's, and the sweet smile that lighted the whole face, would have made anyone proud of such a lovely mother.

But even as he replaced it in its sacred spot near his heart, the tears trembled upon his long, dark lashes, and rolled down the swarthy cheeks of the boy soldier. As we hastened along the hard Warrenton turnpike, on this 18th day of November, on our march to the "Spotted Tavern," every step seemed accompanied by a groan of fatigue or exhaustion, from the worn and weary men.

It was long, hard, and uncompromising. Henry had kept up; was cheerful in his newfound friendships. But the unfortunate boy had, in his want of experience, purchased somewhere, a pair of thin, high-heeled and narrow soled boots.

The poor fellow's feet became blistered. His pain-contorted face, as he hobbled along, mile after mile, showed plainly the agony he endured. His swollen feet became a torture, which even his Indian nature could no longer endure. He announced that he would be compelled to fall out. We tried to persuade him. It was useless. It became a law of stern necessity. A sudden impulse seized me. I resolved to fall out too, and take care of him, for, although younger than he even, I was stronger, more robust, and had now become hardened into good soldier trim. We started a fire and prepared our coffee. Henry had removed his boots, and was enjoying a partial relief from his aching feet, when it suddenly occurred to me that this friendly act of pity and sympathy was contrary to the then existing orders, now so strictly enforced, and to every soldierly principle, and besides we might be picked up by the provost guard in rear, and punished for straggling.

This I made known to him, and urged him to make another effort to rejoin the command, as it was late in the afternoon, and it would soon go into camp. But without avail. He raised his tin cup of coffee to his lips, and replied,—"I will be in camp by night, good bye." The rear of the corps was about passing. I joined it, and an hour later was in bivouac with the regiment. It was the last we ever saw of poor Henry P—. Week after week rolled by, Fredericksburg's murderous battle had been fought, yet no trace of the absent soldier. He had not been arrested by the provost guard. He was reported as "missing." We can hear the words now, as the roll was called in the gray of those fateful mornings, and gone over and over again in the chilly, frosty air of approaching night,—"Henry P—, missing."

Time wore on. The spring of 1863 approached. A paper was received one day in the company, and this item caught our eyes,— "At the Parole Camp, Annapolis, Henry P—, late Twenty-second Regiment Massachusetts Volunteers. Funeral at Roxbury on — at—o'clock.'

A letter was received some time afterwards, and the mystery was solved. He had been brought to the Parole Camp at Annapolis, a paroled prisoner of war. His emaciated frame, far gone with disease and suffering, had succumbed, and his spirit was at rest.

Five minutes after I had left him, near Warrenton Junction, and joined the rear of the Fifth Corps, as it passed, a band of Mosby's guerillas came out of the oaks, where they had been watching our movements, and without a struggle, had surrounded and made a prisoner of the worn-out, shoeless boy, and marched him to Richmond.

Libby prison and Belle Isle soon wore out the brave spirit, and at last, when by apparent good fortune, he was exchanged, it was only to linger feebly a few weeks, like the flickering of an expiring flame, then quietly pass away to an eternal life. The princess's son was dead.

Our letters now continue, describing the march to Fredericksburg.

Near Falmouth, Nov. 22, 1862.

Just after finishing my letter to father, (which I sent yesterday and wrote at Warrenton), we received positive orders to be ready to march next morning, last Monday, and before I could get a chance to get it into the mail bag, the headquarter tent was struck, and in the midst of a drizzling rain we started, both of us being compelled to take our letters with us, and wait for a chance to send them; yesterday was our first opportunity, and I hope they will be received in due time. ... We are now within ten miles of Falmouth, camped in a most desolate place, and expecting to move hourly; the sun is out for the first time since we started, and such a specimen of the rainy season as we have had, I never wish to witness again.

We have struck tents twice today, and both times had our orders countermanded; and now we have pitched them again for the night, with hopes of a comfortable night's rest, the first we shall have had since Sunday night. We have boughs on the ground, and side sticks in the tent to keep out the wind; our shelters are very frail, and are made by buttoning three square pieces of drilling together, and pinning them to the ground with stakes, the two side pieces being thrown over a pole, which rests in the crotches of two end stakes, and ropes from the ponchos drawn tight to pins in the ground, keep these two ends firm, while side pins keep the rest in place, and one poncho at the back end completes a tent for three, unless you wish to be more comfortable, and put a poncho over at the foot, and I have drawn a poncho for the latter purpose, or at least signed for it; I expect to get it soon.

I send you a rough sketch of a poncho tent, at the same time endeavoring to explain it. It has been one continual rain since we left Warrenton, and when we got here man and beast suffered alike. We have been here two nights, and last night I was a perfectly soaked man. Sometimes we exaggerate when we say we are wet

212

through, but I solemnly declare I was truly soaked; here's the way of it: yesterday our tent blew down in a squall of rain and wind, while I was in the woods after boughs for a bed, and before Bob and Ed could get it up, our kit, blankets and all, got wet through, and our tent ground filled with water; we did the best possible, and all day long it poured, so that our personal bodies were wet when we retired to a wet bed. I spread my rubber blanket, and then put my woollen on that (I could wring the water from it in sufficient quantities to fill a water, pail), and until midnight I lay awake suffering from the cold, our tents filling every minute with puddles. I got up at two o'clock, and was so sore I could hardly stir. I went to the fires (kept burning by the guards, who were wallowing in mud and water); I stood there in the rain until the sun rose and dispelled the clouds, the first light for five days, and today we have fixed the tent and dried ourselves somewhat. Bob and Ed were troubled too, but had a better part of the tent and saved their blankets dry; Bob was up in the night several times, not well. He is plumb today. Must close now, as it is dark; we leave tomorrow, and I know not for what spot, Fredericksburg I guess. I shall finish this as soon as we stop; I have two letters by me now, which I wrote at Warrenton and couldn't send them.

I am on fatigue, and have got to lug wood. I do it cheerfully, for I am strong tonight, while many poor fellows are sick in the regiment. I am acting corporal of the squad detailed, but always do my share of the work: we have to do it tonight for we are in late, and we are cold; it is moonlight, and we can see I guess. I may add more as soon as I get paper.

Wednesday, Nov. 26, 1862.

This whole letter I consider as a sort of diary, and as soon as I get it sufficiently long I will send it. Since Sunday we have been here, and we have all been wondering at the delay in our operations upon Fredericksburg; there are many rumors about Burnside, intervention, etc., etc., but as I have seen no paper yet, I am at a loss to understand why we are here at a standstill, idle, and allowing the. rebs to fortify and gain strength. We have lots of work to do, and the fatigue labor of forming a camp of even four days' duration, is enormous. We have to cut and lug from the woods all our wood, while many regiments have theirs brought by their quartermaster's teams. We are out of grub also; I have had two hard bread today, and yet there is great quantity at the commissary waiting for the head boss to deliver them out, and while I am hungry, the officers at headquarters are having roast beef, hot bread, potatoes, and pudding. The government isn't to blame, neither is our worthy chief, Abraham (although misled, ignorant soldiers swear at 'Abe' for it), but it is all owing to miserable, petty officers, who forget all their ideas of right and wrong under the shoulder straps. ... We shall draw rations tonight they say. ... We draw no beans, rice, or candles yet. While in the mud hole, Bob saw Brainard Blanchard;[7] I was away; he passed by in the Thirteenth (Mas?.) on the skedaddle from Rappahannock Station; the Rebs drove them away. He wanted to see me dreadfully, so Bob said.

Our brother Bob, of the same date, says:

Walt has been writing this forenoon with his overcoat and blanket on him, it is so cold. Now having finished my humble meal of boiled crackers, I will try and see if I can manage to write a short letter, for it is too cold to write long. Remember when we write, we have to be out of doors as it were, and no fire to sit by. Tomorrow is Thanksgiving, and I know you would like to hear from us. The last letter that I wrote was at Warrenton, Sunday afternoon. That night it rained; reveille at three o'clock, and we packed up our wet stuff and started. It rained for five days, in which we suffered extremely; the third day we pitched ponchos in the rain and mud up to our ankles; wet feet, cold and wet blankets, we laid that night, the rain pouring in torrents. I had the diarrhea, and of course, miserable, cold, wet, and lying in the mud and water, had to turn out several times, because of that curse to the soldier: you can't cure it. But rain was not to be our worst; we left the next morning with about eight or nine hard tack and a hunk of salt pork. The Second Maine were out and hollering for hard tack. We lived that day, and arrived at this place Sunday night (which is within five miles of Fredericksburg, which is across the river, Falmouth being just on this side). The next day we did not get a cracker, although our rations were up; the boys looked blue enough; some hadn't even a crumb. ...

The next day came, and not a cracker. I thought we should all starve; we were hungry enough to eat a nail. I picked up pieces of

---

[7] Brainard P. Blanchard enlisted in the 13th Massachusetts on August 15, 1862 at the age of 18 and was later in the 39th MA infantry. He survived the war and died in 1878.—2019

cracker in the mud, under the mules' feet; some picked up bones, and ate the marrow; this with cold, frosty weather, and diarrhea from eating raw pork, took us down a peg. Yesterday we got three days' rations of cracker and pork, and the boys set up a howl; I thought there would be a mutiny; they were yelling 'hard tack!' even in the night; some of the regiments haven't any now; good prospect for Thanksgiving, isn't there? It is getting to be rainy; last night it rained good, and I had to 'turn out,' of course on account of diarrhea. ... You have no idea what it is, this winter campaign, with nothing for Shelter but thin, open cotton tents, in these extremely rainy, frosty, cold nights with nothing but coffee, pork, and hard bread, when we get into camp after a hard march.

We have to go sometimes a mile for rails, then pitch our tents with numb fingers, after which, in the dark and smoke, we cook our coffee in our little black pails, toast our hard tack, eat, and 'turn in,' provided we are so fortunate as not to be on guard. Oh! what a blessing those caps and gloves are, and now our overcoats that we drew at Warrenton are quite comfortable. Only think of 'Carleton,' the *Journal* (Boston) correspondent, saying that in that cold, driving snowstorm at White Plains, had it not been for the stoves in our tents, we would have suffered terribly. ... I would liked to have warmed his fingers by those stoves in our tents nary a stove did we see. ... If his back had been in two inches of snow that night, he would have wished himself out of the warm tents. ... I think it is almost suicidal keeping men out this winter, in water and rain, mud and snow, with nothing to cover us, and no shoes on our feet. ... I have got the rheumatism, and a cold which has hung over me for six weeks, owing to getting wet, sleeping in water and snow with wet feet, etc.

A great many of the boys have it. It is true ... half the time we don't know so much about the army movements as you do, although when we are on the march, we generally have some idea of where we are going, and that is all we know for a day or two, except by rumor, which is sometimes that we are surrounded, and everything else impossible. ... You must have had cold weather, and that storm you had, must have been 'the same one we had at White Plains.

Our brother of the regulars now makes an elaborate defense of General McClellan, in answer to a long letter written him by our father, who was a strong anti-McClellan man:

215

Camp Opposite Fredericksburg,

November 22, 1862.

I was very glad to receive your long letter this morning, and will give it to Walter and Bob as soon as I see them. While near Warrenton I saw them quite often, but since we left there, the Eighth Infantry has been in advance of everything except Sumner's Corps. Our quartermaster's department is becoming noted; I always bring my train into camp with the battalion. Before we reached Falmouth, headquarters train did not get in, and General Burnside was obliged to go back seven miles to reach it. General Patrick and staff remained with the Eighth Infantry, and the general occupied my tent and bed for the night, and said he had never slept better in his life.

The next morning General Burnside and staff honored us with a call, drank all our water and whiskey up, ate all of our apples, and started us off for Fredericksburg; 'but we are not there yet.' The article,— 'McClellan at Antietam,' I have read before; it came from the *New York Tribune*. Now, I know more about that battle, and McClellan generally, than these lively newspaper correspondents who infest this army, and the provost guard. Two of these individuals came to our camp in Pleasant Valley; we treated them very politely, and asked them to dine with us, which invitation they greedily accepted. What was the result? We never eat but what they are about; they follow us night and day, and I was compelled a day or two since, to 'jerk' one, a '*Times* reporter,' from one of my teams.

You have doubtless learned before this that Burnside's advance was in Fredericksburg; we are not there, and what is more, we shall have to fight hard before we get there. Now to commence with, I know that General Burnside is not the equal, or does not compare with General McClellan in military strategy; of his patriotism I have not a doubt; but if a man should assert that General McClellan was not a patriot, I would tell him he lied, if I forfeited my life for it. I am not an idolizer; if you remember, I told you that General McDowell was not the cause of our first Bull Run disaster; I firmly believed it then, and I as firmly believe it now. I do not think that general was to blame for the disasters on the peninsula; I only ask you to read De Joinville's account of that campaign, and as I hope to live through tomorrow, his account is a correct one.

216

General Patrick 'who knows you well,' (he was in a class above you, and told me you used to come and see Plummer), commanded a division in McDowell's Corps.

When McDowell was at Fredericksburg, his advance was within seven miles of Fitz John Porter when he fought the battle of Hanover Court House; why did he not join him? Was it McDowell's fault? No, it was owing entirely to General Wardsworth [sic],[8] who was his junior, but who, possessed with more influence than McDowell, succeeded in making President Lincoln and the secretary of war believe that it was all for the best. McDowell protested to General Wardsworth that he (McDowell) was a ruined man. General Patrick told me of this.

After the battle of Fair Oaks, every available man was sent across the swamp; Fitz John Porter's corps, 'originally (he reserve,' now formed our right wing, and protected our communications; should he withdraw, where would our supplies come from? Would it have been policy to have withdrawn him and plunged into Richmond, or, rather 'risked a battle,' with our communications abandoned? What would have been the result if we had been defeated? Surrender! Our right flank was turned; McClellan expected it, and did the best in his power, changed his line of communications to James River. We arrived at Harrison's Landing after hard fighting, and our army thinned by disease and the bullet, but they had confidence in McClellan still.

Newspapers and political gentlemen generally, commenced to get frightened, and cry out, 'Down with McClellan.' Harrison's Landing was evacuated and McClellan was deposed by an order from the war department, assigning him to the command of all troops not under the command of Pope.

His own body guard and orderlies were taken from him; Pope's army was routed; McDowell lost his reputation unjustly; all came rushing madly upon Washington, and terror was depicted upon every countenance. McClellan was begged to take command again. He had to protect Washington, organize a routed army, plan a campaign into Maryland, get ammunition and supplies generally, and then find the enemy, which is no easy matter when you do not

---

[8] James Samuel Wadsworth (1807–May 8, 1864) was a philanthropist and politician, without military experience, who served without pay. He was killed at the Battle of the Wilderness.—2019

know whom to trust for information. General Pleasanton's advance fought the enemy almost every day; the battle of South Mountain was fought, and General Reno killed; his place had to be supplied. We followed close on the heels of the enemy; fought them through Boonesboro. General Franklin's corps had gone to the relief of Harper's Ferry, but arrived too late. Old Miles's inefficiency had done its work. We found General Lee in a very strong natural position, offering us battle with a force superior to our own, and having all the means in the world. The battle was fought; General Burnside called for aid, and it could not be sent for very good reasons; the regular division was supporting batteries, and the remainder of Porter's corps were needed somewhere else than with Burnside.

The battle was won, and we occupied the field. We were out of ammunition, out of supplies, shoeless, and twelve or thirteen brigade generals hors-du-combat; regiments, brigades, divisions and corps partially disorganized; no forage for animals, none for men, the enemy retreating upon their line of supplies (you ask what supplies; I answer those taken from Pope at Manassas, and those captured at Harper's Ferry). They retreated across the river. Why did not McClellan follow them? For the very same reason that Burnside now lies at Falmouth, and does not cross the river to Fredericksburg.

Crossing a river in the face of the enemy is, you know, the most dangerous undertaking in warfare, and if once across without supplies, and then beaten, what would become of the army? General Sumner's advance wished to cross the river and occupy Fredericksburg; General Burnside would not allow it. One or two Rebel regiments then occupied the other side; now they have an army. We are within four miles of our supplies, and get all the forage and rations we want; we have been reinforced by General Sigel, and have now a large army. General McClellan did not have 80,000 man; was almost a hundred miles from supplies, and the communication was not established. One word about quartermasters' stores; General Meigs[9] said we had plenty, or at least he sent plenty. I went with my train for three weeks to

Harper's Ferry, with one requisition for clothing. I never had it filled; I never got a single shirt for my command, and I was told that only six thousand had been sent by the quartermaster's department for the entire army. I saw whole division trains go away with not a tenth part of the articles required, and I will take my oath that I heard General (Rufus) Ingalls, 'chief quartermaster of this army,' give orders to Captain Bliss (issuing quartermaster at Harper's Ferry), to 'cut down the requisitions,' and as regards clothing being drawn and kept without issuing, the only case of the kind that could occur, is when we were ordered to move and had no time to issue.

If division quartermasters should issue to regimental quartermasters, how much clothing do you suppose three wagons would carry, besides regimental and company property, rations, etc.? That story is simply foolish, and no one who knows anything about a quartermaster's duties would circulate.it.

When McClellan was removed, he was advancing rapidly, and had gained two or three days on Lee's calculations; we would have been in Culpepper or Gordonsville tonight if it had not occurred. There is not a military man in this army who does not regard McClellan as the best man for commander-in-chief of this army. Old Hooker, who won all under McClellan's directions, sneaked away from Manassas Junction in an ambulance, while the up train was waiting for the down train containing McClellan; be was ashamed of the part he had taken, and sooner or later his conduct on several battle fields will get a sifting.

General Burnside I regard as a good man, a brave man, and a good soldier, but (I know what I say) he cannot be compared to George B. McClellan for an instant; he has not got the brains, the energy, the coolness of 'Little Mac.' General Burnside will be supported by all officers and men. You never saw a more disgusted man in your life than this same patriot at the news of the removal of McClellan; he actually shed tears when McClellan turned over the command to him. He said he was not capable, and begged McClellan to remain until he had learned more about affairs; McClellan said he would remain as long as possible, but he must obey his orders. Your story about Burnside's saying that he 'loved his friend, but his country better,' must have originated in the fertile brain of the 'Tribune reporter.' Perhaps the enclosed order will spread a little light upon why he accepted the command.

As to McClellan's politics, I do not know or care what they are; I don't believe they ever influenced him a particle in the discharge of his duty. He has borne 'insult upon injury' with a patience like Job; he has been sacrificed for political capital, and sooner or later he will triumph. If I thought for a moment his removal would benefit the cause for which we are fighting, I would submit without a murmur, but more cogent reasons than those already given for his removal must be explained to me before I will ever believe that he has been sacrificed for his country's good.

You may teach me politics, but you cannot strategy or tactics. I am in a position where I see, hear, and learn something about such matters. I hope I shall see the day when you will be convinced that what I have told you about McClellan is true. I never expect you to believe what I tell you about the imbecility, rascality, and cowardice displayed by some of our precious jewels, until some of your sons are numbered among the many victims of their incapacity and worthlessness. How many officers do you suppose are appointed out of merit? ... My fingers are cold, and it is late. The pontoon train will be here in the morning, and the ball will open.

November 24

Pontoon train arrived early this morning; the bridges were to have been built tonight, but some blundering fool did not send anchors and oars for boats, and did not send enough by fourteen. Sumner crosses first; how the blood will flow.

Our brother Walter now writes:

In camp near Falmouth,

November 27, 1862.

After a long march from Warrenton taking eleven days, we are at last in our position with the Third army corps, as the center division under General Hooker, on the banks of the Rappahannock, and are no longer considered a reserve corps, for 'Fighting Joe' is our leader, and we shall have to buckle down to pure pugilistic qualities. We suffered terribly on the road, the rain being our greatest cause for complaint. I have a long letter which I commenced to mother in a mud hole back on the march which I shall finish and send as soon as possible; in it I tell you all, and am now only writing a short note to relieve any anxiety as to our whereabouts in this blissful community; it is almost too cold to write, and my fingers are as cold

220

as can be; the weather is our greatest drawback now; it rained all night, and I am damp all through, but still I am well, so is Bob.

We received our first mail last night, and such a flow of good things never was received from a happier couple. ... Oh, our joy this festive day, over this Thanksgiving treat! How it tends to center all our love and affection around that table, which today shall be set in our dining room, and be occupied by those most dear to us; our allowance of salt pork, coffee, sugar and hard bread, (all we get on the march), will be seasoned to a delicate taste by those fond remembrances. ... Your letters, so full of love and tender sympathy, are enough to make the day pleasant for us, and that we are thought of as you sit down to the feast, and are remembered all over old Massachusetts by its noble and patriotic Governor Andrew, as well as its generous-hearted, noble people, shall be our satisfying meditation, and shall we not have occasion to be thankful for it, even though we be far away from you all, and the horrid thought of war displaying itself in fearful reality at every step?

How I wish I could be with you, but I know I cannot; it is my first absence, but in spirit I am already in the 'straw cottage,' and I can seem to think that I am speaking to you all, and everything is as of old. ... We had Governor Andrew's proclamation and his address to Massachusetts soldiers read to us last night on dress parade, and I think them most beautiful, in every respect so touching, and so well designed to awaken our better feelings; they are the best productions of the time I have yet read from any governor.

Eugene is encamped about four miles from us, so I hear; he will probably be over soon with your letter. I believe every word you say in your short letter, and I know that it is only the pro-slavery, ignorant, at home loafer soldiers that cling to McClellan now. There was a sort of something about 'Little Mac' that deprived him of a fruitful victory; I think him a great general, and I think they removed him at the wrong time, just in the midst of a campaign, thus occasioning a delay hurtful to the cause. McClellan and [John C.] Fremont are of little consequence only as they affect the cause of our country, and I do think the former's removal at such a critical time, when the whole army adored him (*Tribune* correspondents to the contrary notwithstanding), has affected to some extent a good, loyal feeling in the army, and there is not so much fight in our ranks now, as there was before, for we feel as if the fighting at home, the constant removal of generals, the elections in New York,

Philadelphia, and Ohio, and the probable quarrels in the approaching session of congress, all tend as a drawback to the doings of the army.

I only hope his removal will set things right; time will show. I think my opinion of 'McClellan at Antietam' is exactly set forth in a piece of that heading in the *New York Tribune* of a few weeks since; I expressed myself to the same effect in letters home just after the fight. The talk about there not being much enthusiasm at McClellan's last review, is all bosh; such a reception by the different regiments I never saw given to any man, and it is no more than true, that in no man will the army place that implicit confidence that it did in George B. McClellan. I cannot account for it, but his presence was magical. ...

We may be ordered to move at almost any moment; the 'rebs' are over across the river, and we are over 100,000 strong 'en masse ' to the river on this side; we have a commanding position, and Fredericksburg is at our mercy. There are many reports as to an order for its surrender, and an armistice granted for thirty days just afterwards; also about the relative strength of the batteries planted on either side, and our being ordered forward with twelve days' rations toward Richmond, and the commencement of our laying our pontoons, etc., etc., but not knowing anything about them, I shall say nothing.

We had an awful disagreeable march, commencing Sunday night before we started, (Gene started Sunday morn), the day he was to come and see us.

We were wet through night and day, and slept in mud and water; we suffered also from cold and want of food, teams not coming up until after' our rations had expired; the weather was so cold that we ate more, and indeed, what we get on the march isn't enough for us, twelve crackers a day, salt pork, (most of the time with us), and two spoonfuls of sugar and coffee each. Why, I ate twelve hardtack yesterday at dinner I was so hungry; it takes a good deal of such stuff to keep the blood warm enough to engender sufficient bodily heat for existence, and you would laugh to see me eat raw pork, hard-tack, and drink black, pot coffee now, I have had to come to it, for I cannot get different in this, the enemy's country; as for forage, we are not allowed even that; they guard all secesh property, rather than run the risk of having one Union Southern man (I have not seen them yet), lose a single chicken; as for the weather being delightful, and stoves being in our tents, and the army being urgent to move forward, and everything being lovely, as the 'army correspondents' make it out, it is a base lie.

When we first got here we were all out of grub, and the teams being in the rear, we couldn't draw our rations, and for a day and a half I only had a cup of coffee, two hardtack (which I bought), and some crumbs in the bottom of my haversack; now I am flush again with our peculiar line of provisions, and shall celebrate today with a hearty dinner.

We may have some fresh meat, for they are killing over in the butcher's department; Ed Morrill fell out of the ranks of his company with a sore foot (wounded at Antietam), and our regiment overtook him on the march, much to the pleasure of us all. He stayed with us two days, riding in an ambulance belonging to our corps. His foot is inflamed by a severe cold in it, and he will be obliged to go to the hospital again.

November 28, 1862.

Bob was sick last night suffering from headache and pain in his stomach; while returning this morning from the brook, he was seized with a violent cramp in his stomach and while crawling into his tent, his breath was almost taken away from him; I turned around and saw him gasping, and by signs he told me what was the matter; we got him out of the tent, and I rubbed his stomach with hot cloths until he recovered, during which process he suffered excruciating pain. Afterwards his stomach was sore, and he has had a dull headache until now, but at this time seems quite well, up and walking about as usual. ...

Captain T. is dismissed from the service; dishonorably discharged.

After finishing my letter to father yesterday, Bob and I thought of going to see Gene; we procured a pass and started. After walking five miles on the railroad to Falmouth, (now completed, and in running order, insuring a speedier delivery of both rations and mail), we passed to the left towards Sumner's headquarters and obtained a grand sight of Fredericksburg; could see their wagons and military works. After inquiry, got to Burnside's headquarters,, a mile from Sumner's, and soon reached the provost guard, Eighth

223

Infantry; Gene was gone, and Frank with him; it was almost one o'clock, and our pass expired at four with provosts all about us to arrest just *sich*; we waited until two o'clock, in the meantime being politely treated by Gene's officers (and I notice this in the regulars, they are always very courteous to their friend's friends; invite them to drink, etc., etc., a sort of etiquette with them), and was about to start for home, when Gene rode in; he seemed so glad to see us; got us bread and apples to eat, and gave me a shave, and made everything comfortable for a short visit; he had been over to General Sykes'. We read father's long letter over (on General McClellan, etc.), and discussed it, I side with father, Gene obstinately hanging to his whims, Bob neutral.

Gene urgently invited us to stay to dinner (at 5 o'clock, for Gene and Frank mess together, and have two meals, one at morn and at night), a Thanksgiving one too, but Bob and I dared not, think of the self-denial just to obey orders, and at 3 o'clock, after a pleasant visit, started for camp. Gene gave Bob some smoking tobacco and promised to come and see us tomorrow, with sutler's stores with him. We were afraid to stay mainly for this, that we might get lost returning at night, having in our minds a new way to get to camp.

We came away loaded with hardtack, which with our rations drawn now, makes us well off; we hated to leave but had to. On our way home we struck the Thirty-fifth (Mass.), and I saw W. N. and others; I ate supper with Haze Goodrich. It was my Thanksgiving feast; very unexpectedly I assure you; it consisted of sardines, chicken soup, flapjacks, hard bread and coffee. Well! we got home late, and everything is lovely now; we expect Gene tomorrow .... Sunday.

November 30, 1862.

It is bitter cold today. Bob and myself were on guard last night, and being on the first relief, had to stand our relief altogether in the night; all the while I was on the first relief in front of the colonel's tent, I had many things to look upon that kept my mind in constant occupation.

There were big fires in all the tents and candles in abundance, while the poor privates were without either. That furnished material for one hour's thoughts, and then I saw their supper carried into the tents for them, and smelt the savory odor of good things therein; that was another comparison to the poor fellows who lay near me in their camp streets, eating their salt pork and hard bread, and on Thanksgiving day; while Acting-Brigadier 'Betty' Barnes and his staff were eating their dinners of geese, turkey and fixings, the privates of the Thirty-second Massachusetts were trying to buy hard bread at the brigade commissaries, within ten feet of their mess tent; that is abominable, yet I do not mean to say our food is not suitable, for it is the best the government can give us, and of the best material and kind, when you remember the transportation and everything concerned; they can't possibly give us any other kind of grub, although I never lose an opportunity to better it, when a chance presents itself.

But it is hard to cut us short, and keep us without hard-tack, when it is in abundance at the commissary to sell, while officers are faring like princes.

We are drawing beans, rice and molasses today, and candles are coming. It would make your heart bleed almost to see our poor fellows digging in the dirt, and getting wood for chimneys to officers' fireplaces, and today, Sunday, (the president's request to the contrary notwithstanding), a fatigue party is making a fireplace and chimney for the colonel's tent, and against their will too, for many of them, I observe, are Christian men, who attend regularly the prayer meetings and live a good life, and besides all the everyday fatigue.

We are liable at a moment's notice to be called by the colonel and staff to cut wood for their comfort. I imagine they have no right to do the latter, for they draw their full pay .... and are expected to hire servants; nevertheless, we suffer by it, and contribute wholly to their pleasure. Even in bringing wood for them, we have to bring it up from the woods, while other regiments have it brought by their teams. In the Thirty-fifth, company wood is drawn by horses. I am my own horse and many a time have made an ox of myself in carrying prodigious loads on my shoulders ....

Many there are in this regiment who, if they follow out their McClellan ideas of right, and after talking as they do, play the white feather on the field, will find my bayonet in them as quick as a rebel private's. They must be patriotic, or else the day is lost, and one man playing false to his country is death to many a patriot's endeavor on the day of battle; there are many such in our army, and it is almost a crime for an honest, freedom-loving spirit to speak itself forth at the camp-fire urging on for the cause, and for war to the knife.

He is then beset by men in authority, who are his inferiors in most every kind of knowledge and together, they try to bear him down, and many are the epithets given to him as he strives for the maintenance of his doctrine; he is called an abolitionist, Charles Sumner-ite, and even Massachusetts democrats seek to insult him by saying he is a John Andrew-ite. Wait until the day of the fight .... I will remember the foe in camp who hates his country, and thinks her not worth fighting for, and says that nigger freedom is the object of this war. ... I will remember him, and if he falters from deliberate cowardice, I will make him step up, or into him I go, bayonet first and bullet afterward.

I am for Judge Holt[10] and his views as expressed to Collector Varney in a recent letter, and you can't imagine how such letters from home serve to cheer us up; how often would I despond were it not for kind words and ceaseless endeavors for our comfort. Every letter is so full of love, and mother's pen seems to speak in every line of such inexpressible affection for us. It is enough to make a stout heart melt, and I can never read a message from you without emotion. If it requires nothing but the elements to remind you of us, so steady and unceasing is your thought of us. ...

If every soldier could see at home a friend like you. how their hearts would rejoice, and yet Governor Andrew is of the same kind. I know full well that the senate has a soldier's friend in its seats when you make your debut; would they were all as patriotic as you.

We were on guard from 5 to 7, 11 to 1, 5 to 7, and today, 11 to 1; now we are at the guard house (the open air), and I am writing on a cracker box, sitting on a log; tomorrow we go on fatigue, the usual custom.

Oh! if it wasn't freezing between the hours of 11 and 1; I believe I walked fifteen miles in my three tours of two hours each; I streaked it lively back and forth on my beat, and this morning the ground was white with frost. Don't be alarmed about Bob, from my last letter to mother, of Friday's date; he is quite well now, his attack

---

[10] Lincoln appointed Joseph Holt (1807–1894) as Judge Advocate General in 1862. He was later Chief Prosecutor at the trial of the Lincoln-assassination conspirators.—2019

being only temporary; when I first began to rub him, the pit of his stomach was sunken in, making a large cavity, while just above there was a hard bunch, just like rock, as big as my head; it seemed as if his intestines were all bound up in a bunch; however, he is cured now, and seems well.

I do pity anyone sick here without friends; I have weighed your words well; that is the way it is, father, there is no sympathy for a poor sick man. At the hospital it is worse for him than it is in his tent, for there they use him shamefully. LeRoy Kimball arrived today, and although he is looking finely, I think he says he has the diarrhea; we were glad to see him I assure you. I shall never forget the night we enlisted, and the speech you made; that speech will live with me forever, as it showed your regard for us, and every letter brings fresh proof of your anxiety for us. I hope we may live to return; what a happy greeting it will be. I think your letter to Gene, Bob, and myself simply perfect. ... I never read such a good letter from you before.

As soon as McClellan gets cleaned out, why this stuff comes from their lips, and it leaks away in streams, and is swallowed by the humblest private who spits it out again. Just as soon as 'Mac' is removed, all this talk about there being no fight in the army, abolitionists, etc., leaks out; it must certainly have emanated from the fountain head. Your letter is most splendid; it ought to be read all over the land. ... Rumor of a move. ...

Good-by.

Our brother Bob now says:

Dec. 3, 1862.

It is a cold, dismal afternoon. ... Of course ere this reaches you, Walt will have communicated the news, rumors, etc., etc., as we get them. Of our Thanksgiving visit to Gene, and the Thirty-fifth, and our march to this camp, lack of food, etc., so that I will not repeat. Gene seems to think more and more of us ... and seems to take pride in introducing us to his West Point chums, and in various ways shows his kindness and brotherly love for us; yet he is sharp and quick in his manner, having changed greatly from the time when we were brothers and sisters in the good old city of Portland. .. If you could see him in the army, and the way he lives as a regular officer, you would not wonder. ... I passed my first Thanksgiving from home in a profitable and pleasant manner; we could look into the streets of Fredericksburg and see the rebel wagons. Captain Frank was up to Sumner's headquarters, and with the aid of a glass, could see them at work upon the redoubts; I think we must move soon, and then for a bloody fight. We are making every preparation, and for my part, I am willing to risk my life in the encounter just to please the croakers at home, who insist upon our making a 1winter campaign.' I want this thing closed up, and if it cannot be done without fighting, I say fight! till the quarreling, wrangling politicians are satisfied that we can't fight any longer. ... One thing is certain, it can never be settled so long as they conduct things as they have been doing for the past year.

There have been too many traitors at home, too much fighting among ourselves, too much cheating, too much shoving out of generals, etc. to ever hope to succeed. There never was a more intelligent, self-sacrificing army in the world, but how can it hope to succeed when it is held back by an unseen agency, as it were? But I must hold my wind, for I am cold and must finish Monday morning.

On the morning of December 1st, when a movement of any kind was furthest from our minds, the call suddenly rang out. Pack up. Down went our shelter tents, and we were on the march in short notice. Our destination, as usual, we did not know, but supposed we were going on picket. The entire brigade and a battery went. After marching about five miles, at a very rapid gait, we knew it was no picket detail. Still we went on, going back to near our 'Mud Camp' at Hartwood Church. We moved into the woods. No noise was allowed, neither bugle calls nor fires, and we 'munched' our crackers in moody silence.

We lay at night, in a wet, marshy piece of woods, through which ran a ravine. Pickets were sent out, and our Cavalry brought in a prisoner. On the following morning, we had just got breakfast, when orders came to pack up with all possible despatch.

Some of the boys remarked that 'Old Betty B.' had got frightened and was going back to camp, and so it proved, and such marching, mile after mile through woods and underbrush, across mud-holes, almost at a double quick, before a halt was made.

Then we swung out again, and at a terrific pace, kept on until we reached camp, the entire command much exhausted. Many were the curses loud and deep, that trailed through the air that day. It was called a reconnoisance, and we let it go at that, but we have never understood to this day, what the home movement was, nor the necessity for such barbarous, up and down hill 'double quicking,' with but one halt in a march of nearly ten miles.

This movement was in support of a reconnoisance which Gen. W. W. Averell, commanding cavalry brigade, had been directed to make with two regiments of his command to Grove Church, Deep Run, and that vicinity, to reestablish the picket line which Captain Johnson of the Third Pennsylvania cavalry is said to have permitted to be surprised, and a part of them to be captured near there on November 28th, and to attack and destroy any force of the enemy's cavalry found there, supposed to belong to [Confederate] Gen. [Wade] Hampton's command.

The man captured was an old Mexican war veteran, who belonged to a company of confidential scouts; be stated that there was a system of signals established by men on horseback so that information could be conveyed very rapidly from point to point.

The enemy had, however, by this method, or, perhaps, by the fires which some of our men had made in the woods, been frightened off, and were beyond reach.

Our letters say:

While on fatigue, the call came, 'pack up.' Down went tents, and we were on the march in a short time. Our destination we did not know as usual, but supposed we were going on picket; the whole brigade went. After marching five miles, we thought picketing teas played out, and still we went, going way back 10 or n miles to the place where it rained so and was so muddy; went into the woods; no bugling, no fires, and nothing to eat but crackers; lay that night in a wet, marshy piece of woods. Our cavalry brought in a rebel scout, captured about three miles from our position. The next morning, (yesterday), we went 11 miles through woods, across mud holes and brush, back to camp; and such marching! We never halted but once, a short stop of ten minutes. It seemed as if they could not make us go fast enough; up hill and down as fast as we could. The boys swore dreadfully, I never heard such oaths. It was a shameful, cruel, and barbarous trick to march men so; worse than a drove of cattle; but what does a Brigadier care for a private? We got back tired, sweaty, dusty and used up; just pitched our tents when Gene came riding up. He noticed my dirty face instantly; told him to come

229

(today) tomorrow, and I would shine as much as he. He asked after our wants, kindly told us there was a prospect of moving across soon, and after a short, but pleasant visit, left for headquarters.

I was on guard Saturday night; it was awful cold, and as I paced my lonely beat in the midnight hours, oh! how I did think and think of home. ... I thought of mother, who, although pale, care-worn and anxious for her soldier boys, now is bowed down with a new grief, that of the death of a brother. ... Poor Mother! I sympathize with her in her loss, and as I tramped up and down that night, it seemed as if I could see her sitting up and waiting for us to come. ... Walt wants to write a few lines, and I will close.

December 3, 1862.

It is evening, and we have finished our supper, coffee, hard bread and boiled tongue that I bought from the butcher and cooked; are seated for the first time in this camp, in our tent, with a candle light, and a poncho covering in front, drawn today, and an extra occupant, LeRoy, who, as yet, has no tent, and we crowd him in with us. ... Rest assured, in the tent tonight, we are all fondly thinking of you at home.

Baked beans in the morning; good times are coming at last, and we are living well after much tribulation.

December 4, 1862.

Verily, it needs not the rain, or the sunshine, the storm or the calm, to speak to you in words concerning us, for it seems one continual thought with you, to have an unceasing regard for our welfare, and always 'Walt and Bob' are subjects of your own voluntary goodness. We could not feel it in our hearts to ask that which you do for us both in word and deed, we can scarcely acknowledge in fitting words; we can only thank you, dear father, assuring you that although we sometimes forget to mention it, we are susceptible to all its kind intent, showing as it does your love for your soldier boys, which we can never repay. ... Your few words in mother's letter have been read, and meaning noted.

Our situation is still the same, in camp before Fredericksburg; the Lord knows when we shall advance, yet the greater part of the army, who are sick of strife, are satisfied to remain inactive, even in winter quarters, which are not yet officially announced. I am not; I want to go ahead, or else stop for winter; we have poor shelter for the present cold weather, and I hate to live in expectation; if we are going to stop. I want to build a winter shanty; if not, I wish to see the enemy, and force from him his right (as he thinks) to secede, and thereby give freedom to the slave,[11] and hereafter have a true land of liberty. What a lack of interest in the cause the privates in the array have. To their shame be it said, two thirds would leave for home today, if they were allowed, and leave things as they are, and give the rebel government the victory, and a place among the nations of the earth, an established revolutionary nation, in the face of the mighty north, and that, too, by force of arms.

It is disgraceful and unworthy a civilized power, and yet I believe it to be a fact, from what I have seen. How I wish every man was like Thomas Francis Meagher[12] in the army, and led by the skill of McClellan (for I believe he was competent, only his politics and feelings made him go in for a do-nothing policy, or rather soft patriotism, in the compromising line), and influenced by the fighting spirit of Joe Hooker. I don't want 'Mac' at the head, but a man with his ability to do (if he chose), but different feelings. I am waiting for better things soon. ... Our quartermaster has gone to Washington to look after all regimental and company boxes. The result of his labors is already at Acquia Creek Landing: all the boys are sending for boxes. I hardly think it will pay, for Gene says we shall move soon surely. Yesterday two mince pies came by mail; they looked so tempting.

Mother, be cheerful, and derive comfort from the assurance that your boys, a gallant quota from the family, a quartette of heroes perhaps still live, and loving her of old are fighting for the flag.

Bob's shoes are out, and he has drawn a pair of government brogans (gun-boats). Mine are like adamant. ... I have lost all my

---

[11] It is interesting to note that one brother wants to convince us the war is not about emancipation and this one fervently desires it. A great many soldiers expressed their disgust for slavery and desire for freedom for all. In contrast to 21st century statements that the war was not about slavery, Confederate guerilla leader, John Singleton Mosby, argued to the end of his life that it absolutely was about slavery. The argument that it was about "states' rights" falls to pieces when you consider that the only right being fought over was that of the institution of slavery.
[12] Thomas Francis Meagher (1823–1867), Irish nationalist and immigrant to America. He drown in the Missouri River after the war.— 2019

Sharpsburg feeling of laziness, and languor, and can work with a will; cold weather agrees with me.

LeRoy is back; has been making a bridge; there is to be a grand review tomorrow by General Burnside. We are all in our tent now with our new poncho up in front; we have eaten a dinner of beef soup and hard bread; and how often we have spoken of home during our frugal meal. LeRoy talks continually of Bradford .. longing to get home. Webster has been detailed to go in a pioneer corps of the regiment, to form with details of other regiments in the brigade, a brigade pioneer corps, who carry with their other duds, axes, shovels, and picks, to clear the way, make bridges, etc., etc.; he doesn't like the idea of it. ... It has commenced to snow now, and it bids fair to be a long storm; we are pretty comfortable though, for we are prepared in having our tents pitched before it came along.

December 6, 1862.

We had a hard day's march to our old mud-hole, and a tough one back; I suppose it was deemed necessary that we should have one more look at the place, or else it was thought advisable that we have exercise with a load on our backs; we went ten miles in three and one fourth hours.

Our brother in the artillery now writes a short letter;

Fort Tillinghast,

December 8, 1862.

Captain Sargent just received your letter, and as I am not sick, but very well indeed, I hasten to answer, but can only write a note, as I am on guard, and have to go on my beat shortly. I received the splendid box which you sent, and I have had a feast I can tell you. ... I invited several Portland boys to dine with me Thanksgiving day, among whom was the sergeant-major of the Twenty-fifth Maine, and he gave me quite a puff in the Portland Argus. Do you hear from the boys now? I have thought of them about all the time for a day or two, as it has been very cold, the snow being quite deep; I have suffered considerably in my tent from cold, and don't know what I should have done if it had not been for the quilt which you sent me; how must it be with them? Lewis sends his love, and is very much obliged for his stockings.

Our brother Walter now says:

In Camp Near Falmouth,

December 10, 1862.

Tomorrow we cross the Rappahannock at daybreak, and you know what awaits us there; I have only time left to write once more. Your messages were so good, and you were so thoughtful of your soldier brothers, that I cannot let this last opportunity pass unimproved, without acknowledging it all; besides I want to let you all know at home that we start for the field with high hopes and anticipations, both for the cause and ourselves; I cannot believe that I shall never see you again, and yet I am counting the cost; I wish to write once more before I go, and this is a good chance. Your letters were in every way calculated to cheer us. ... That's the kind of letter that does us good, and we do thank you for them so much. ... .

I hope I may in some way repay in the same coin by writing this letter, short though it may be, at this time, on the eve of starting on a great tour of great results, and of great concern both to ourselves and to those at those at home. ... I have no news to write, for I know of no great events. ... Eugene rode up today to bid us good-by; he is under orders to move, and General Patrick said that the Eighth had got to make a dash, and if so, Gene will go in; he said that he was under orders to move so soon that he might not see us for some time, and so he rode over to give us a parting word; I hope no evil will befall him, or either of us, but that we may meet again as full of regard for each other as ever.

I was on guard last night at brigade headquarters, and as I stood on my beat at three o'clock this morning, freezing with the cold, I couldn't help thinking of how comfortable you .are at home, and yet it is better that you should never know or see all that happens in this army, for if you did, you couldn't rest a single night, it would work upon, your feelings so. Better be happy at home, not knowing the miseries of this vast concourse of men, than to be miserable constantly over all the horrors of this life.

I saw things last night that would have made your hearts freeze if you had been witnesses; such sufferings I never beheld. Nightly the camp showeth forth the wickedness of men, and the treatment of horses and mules; the condition of some of these animals (I saw a mule with his right fore leg kicked all to pieces by another horse, and as the joint-water oozed out, he groaned with pain most hideously; he was dead this morning,—no one to help, and I could not leave my post); the cattle-pen full of poor oxen, cold and hungry, walking about in the midst of offal and leavings of their dead comrades, soon to be shot in the morn, before the rest, and dressed in the same pen of butchery; it is perfectly horrible; and the sick and care-forsaken men who have no one to look after them as they near their end; oh, how many they lie in their poor tents, and have to rise and walk, when at home they would be considered crazy to do it.

But enough of this! I am not following your example. I will close the melancholy story, rendered so much more awful by actual sight, by hoping that you will never see the like of it, that a land of peace may be yours, and that war may be far away from your immediate vicinity, so that its horrors may be heard of but not seen.

We have days of severe trial to go through now, for how can we pitch our tents these cold nights, after a long march and hard battle? The ground freezes as solid as it does at home in Bradford. We have perfect spring days, thaws in the morning, mud at noon, and winter at night.

The snow has all melted, and we had just commenced to get ready our winter quarters when this order reached us; you ought to see the forests disappear by the soldier's axe; Virginia will be cleared by the strong arms of Northern laborers if we continue much longer on its 'sacred soil'; we will hope for the best on this active campaign. I am thankful that I enter upon it in perfect health, and I pity the man who does not, for he is certain to (have) acute sufferings. You will find many blunders in my letters; I am getting uncivilized, and forgetting all I ever knew; what wonder is it, in the midst of such scenes as we are? If we are perfect brutes, I shall not wonder. ... And now good-bye, father, mother, sisters; to advance is necessary, and why delay? It is sudden to us at this time, for we have been deluded with vain hopes of staying; I know not when you will hear from me again, but rest assured that every opportunity shall be improved to inform you all of my health and good spirits, and you well know that my face will be to the foe, and as I march along to Richmond, my thoughts shall be with you all, and I shall always be as ever your loving son and brother, Walt.

THE BATTLE OF FREDERICKSBURG

Much has been said, sketched, and written about the great Battle of Fredericksburg, by war correspondents, who were in the streets of the city, or on the north side of the Rappahannock river; by historians who were in neither place; by "our artists on the spot," who were not on the spot, and by officers of nearly every' grade, from the commanding general down to junior subalterns, in print and out, covering every possible point, from the first inception of the campaign, with subsequent plan of battle, to the minutest tactical manoeuvre; giving the dispositions of corps, divisions, brigades and battalions' all valuable, and contributing in no small degree to the future historian's labors, who is yet to sift this mass of material, so that it shall be a truthful and accurate account, embodying all that shall be useful to the military student, and rejecting whatever may smack of misrepresentation, high coloring, or exaggeration. It is the purpose of the writer, however, to give some personal incidents of the Battle of Fredericksburg, with no embellishments; not as coming from the commanding general, the war correspondent, the artist, or historical critic; nor even covering the plan of battle, the tactical or strategical points, but a plain, unvarnished statement of facts, given from the standpoint of a private soldier.

General McClellan had been relieved: General Burnside had assumed command; the "nine days' wonder," that had come upon everybody, even General McClellan himself, like a thunderbolt, had been freely discussed pro and con around the camp fires during those cold, frosty, or drizzling November nights of 1862. The president never knew what a strain was put upon the loyal Army of the Potomac; commanding officers of corps, divisions and brigades, and officers of high rank, never knew, perhaps the country will never know.

It was certainly a most dangerous move, as many who were in the ranks can even today testify, *and no act of the government tested the loyalty and devoted patriotism of the majority of our noble army to the last notch as the relieving of George B. McClellan at White Plains, Va., on November 7, 1862.*

He himself says: "The order depriving me of the command created a deep feeling in the army, so much so that many were in favor of my refusing to obey the order, and of marching upon Washington to take possession of the government."

The half has never been told! Night after night about the bivouac fires, the bitter debates and rancorous discussions ran high. It was not understood in the ranks, and the sequel could not be foreseen.

The advent of extreme cold weather now upon us, and the prospects of a winter campaign ahead, failure to secure the fruits of Antietam, with its negative results, and the jealousies and heart burnings of the Pope campaign, all had combined to contribute their demoralizing effects to the rank and file, and were among the chief causes of dissatisfaction, discontent, and ominous growling which occurred then and later.

Much bad blood had been engendered, not infrequently resulting in personal encounters, in a general scattering of coffee dippers, and ends of rails, the fire being put out, and the men going to their cheerless bivouacs in the mud sullen and almost disheartened. Volumes could be filled with the hard words, grumbling, growling, the heat and passion of arguments, and useless bickerings at the bivouac fires about Warrenton, but at last, discipline, loyalty, and a better feeling prevailed.

All these active forces had now set the private soldiers in ranks to thinking for themselves, and there was a strong division of opinion as to whether McClellan could longer be set up as the idol of the army, which from that time on, induced a more healthy reaction from the old Peninsula days.

General McClellan says: "My chief purpose in remaining with the army as long as I did after being relieved was to calm this feeling, in which I succeeded."

The writer desires to diverge for a brief moment, and state that while General McClellan's personal influence may have stayed the insubordinate feeling that was prevalent about headquarters, it was, nevertheless, the intelligent action of the college and school

236

boys, the rank and file of the volunteer regiments about those bivouac fires, that quelled the mutinous sentiment in the ranks, and not all of that army would have moved on Washington at the command of any military dictator. The republic was safe in the hands of such intelligent patriotism. A careful reading of our letters, will, he thinks, bear him out in this assertion. The early and violent snow storm had benumbed our bodies; the march through the mud and rain of that ever memorable stormy season had taken out some of the fire and spirit of the rank and file, and the Army of the Potomac had floundered out on comparatively dry land and gone into its camps about Falmouth, Va. Ours, near Stone-man's Switch on the west side of the railroad. It was known as "Smoky Camp." The almost countless camp fires made of green oak and cedar, caused great volumes of acrid smoke to constantly hang over us, and so near the ground that it made one's eyes smart night and day.

There was no air stirring, and the smoke shifted without rising, from point to point, and drove us about on the arc of a circle, until daylight welcomed us with a returning warmth of the sun and the busy duties of camp made us partly forget our miseries.

We were still in our little "dog" tents, pitched on the hard frozen ground. They are airy without being spacious. They hold three men; ours held four by expansion out of charity to a poor fellow just from the hospital who was sick and had no tent. There were no telephones and, if in the night one forgot his promise and turned over, a nudge or thump, started from the outside man, indicated that all were to accept the inevitable and "lop over."

The shelters were filled with cedar boughs; a log was rolled to each side, pegged in place, and banked with earth; the blankets were spread, the rubber on cedar boughs, the woollen on top, as far as they would go, the outside men getting little indeed, especially in the haste and scramble of a "turn over."

If a man was too cold during the night, he quietly arose, left his bed, and unbuttoning the front poncho, hastened to the cook-house by the fire, where he was sure to find several midnight ghouls, as boon companions who, like himself, had lost overcoat or blanket, and were attempting to down their misery at the fire, and gain a little comfort by smoking, growling, and casting reflections upon the government, the commanding general, the "contraband," or somebody, they cared little whom, who had placed them in such a "d—d miserable fix as this."

These midnight grumblings generally wound up by one or two burning their well-worn blue pants to a rich brown, as a puff of wind blew a stray flame their way, and they crawled back to bed more miserable than ever, for their tent mates had generally managed to appropriate the absentees' share of the blankets, leaving them to the tender mercies of the outside of the tent, with no cover.

Drills, guard and picket duty, with an occasional reconnoissance to the river fords, filled up the time during our three weeks' sojourn in this camp.

November 27th was Thanksgiving Day in the Army of the Potomac. It had rained, snowed, sleeted, frozen and thawed alternately, nearly every day since our departure from Sharpsburg on the night of October 3Ist.

We were daily expecting to hear the welcome order to build log huts and make ourselves comfortable in winter quarters. The mud, which covered the plain, froze hard and stiff at night, only to be thawed by the next day's sun into a vast skating-rink, over which we skated, slipped, and slid, in our efforts to move from one camp to another, collecting as we went, much valuable Virginia soil, which we did not scruple to deposit wherever and whenever convenient.

Many were suffering from chronic diarrhea, caused by eating so much raw pork on the march, and drinking water from the hard limestone springs about Sharpsburg, adding greatly to the burden of discomforts which would naturally unfit us mentally and physically for a Thanksgiving feast, or the great campaign about to open.

The weather was still raw, cold, gloomy, and disagreeable. The nights spent in our thin, inadequate shelter, now filled with the almost unendurable smoke referred to, were keenly and most bitterly uncompromising.

The new base of supplies was Acquia Creek. The Richmond and Fredericksburg railroad had been torn up, and while it was being repaired, and for a few days after we had arrived, our rations were *non est*.

Tired out with long marching, pinched with cold, tortured with smoke night and day, and almost famished with hunger, we were in no mood to enjoy this glorious anniversary day of our New England forefathers—of turkeys, geese, mince-pies, etc., and of stomach stuffing and general good cheer.

The hungry men were collected on their parades, shouting "Hard tack! hard tack?" or fishing about in the mud, among the mules' feet, and under the wagons, for the few' crumbs that might have jarred from the empty wagons through the cracks.

A well picked and polished pork bone, boiled with some of these muddy crumbs, comprised the sum total of the writer's luxurious (?) dinner, followed by no dessert, nuts, or raisins.

Life at this period for the private soldier was indeed a burden, and a great strain upon our youthful and patriotic ardor.

Such was the status, moral and physical, of the gallant old Army of the Potomac a few days preceding the Battle of Fredericksburg; yet extracts from our letters, even under this pressure of cold, hunger, sickness, and adversity, have the true ring.

November 23d,

Sunday eve, by camp-fire

We are near to Falmouth and Fredericksburg, and have our fighting position. Our tent is pitched, and for want of candle light I am beside a flickering fire, with my thoughts on two grand extremes,—my home, and my country and her enemies. We marched this morning from our last mudhole, and have paddled along the awful roads slowly, only eight miles today; yet we have reached our base, and the enemy is on the other side; I long to grapple with him in deadly conflict, so that God may give us the victory and the blessed influences of it, or a masterstroke of Burnside's may ease the North; I want a battle-cry and a waking up, an enthusiastic survey of the whole field; a rush, a triumph, as shall gladden you all who love the flag, even though it cut the heart-strings of many fond mothers as you, and break as dear a circle as ours.

It is a fact, father, that if half the energy and go-ahead that is put to the wheels of the officers' pleasure and comfort-coach were directed to the great end for which we are here, victory to our flag and dismay to our enemies would be the glorious result.

The mud is deep, and it is most uncomfortable both inside and outside our tent; still we are patriotic, and I am disgusted with the poor dupes in our army, rank and file, who curse the army, damn the Abolitionists, and who think the fight has been won by the enemy when our little George B. McClellan left us. I am for the cause, and unless the army is for it we shall never be victorious. The whole miserable twaddle comes from officers first, and is sifted down to the privates; it may come direct from headquarters; I know it is abroad as soon as 'Mac' leaves.

I only wish for victory; and to gain it we must have a principle to fight for.

I am for pushing this matter ahead, and never faltering until, if necessary, every rebel hearthstone is desolate, to secure our former prosperity and bring about peace; and my bones may moulder in Virginia if thereby one 'jot or one tittle' is added to the good of the Federal army; and in view of all these, my ideas, I say it is discouraging to see things go on as they do.

Taking every difficulty into consideration (and I am no enthusiast on the subject of a fight; I hate the sound of bullets as much as any other man, and I dislike strife of this kind as much as anyone; and besides all this, I have had stories of suffering and anguish poured into my ears, such as is hardly possible for the imagination to picture, much less to be actually true; I have also seen sights most sickening, and have heard prisoners relate their Richmond trials, and stories of horror), yet, with all these ills, as likely to be my lot in the train of earthly circumstances as anyone's, I am for war and an immediate advance on the enemy's works! Oh, for a Bonaparte to lead us on, that thunder-bolts might fall upon the stricken enemy'! Oh, for a campaign like his memorable one of six days on his first

Italian campaign! Oh, that it were just as much an honor to belong to the 'Army of the Potomac 'as to the proud 'Army of Italy!' and yet I have confidence in General Burnside, if the morale of the army is improved.

I believe I am patriotic; else why did I come out here? Surely, money could have been no object compared to the treasures I left behind. And again, money is a small compensation for one's sufferings.

I hate the life, and who does not among the private soldiers? And who of us ever dreamed we should like it? Not one! On the contrary, it was well represented to us before we left our dear homes, how we might be compelled to undergo all that we have now, and much more besides; and while I would much rather be at home, with peace all over the land, and attending to my studies, yet now I am out here, such is our cause that I want to fight it through to a victorious, righteous ending.

So far, I believe, I am a true patriot, and I have taken my life in my hands to meet the foe, and for Freedom and the Old Constitution I will battle on.

If an arm off or a leg shattered increases one's value to that of 'a Bank of England,' then indeed are we four boys, with such a father and mother, a patriotic family, and it is enough to spur anyone to high aims and noble deeds.

Such was the youthful spirit of enthusiasm, yet truly patriotic sentiments of a boy' in blue, a private soldier, one of four brothers in the Army of the Potomac. It breathes fourth a spirit of high resolve and lofty purpose, in the midst of the depressing gloom which had settled upon the army, most wonderful by contrast.

The pontoons arrived at last, so had the enemy, and our pickets in full sight of each other, were in daily conversation, exchanging hard bread, coffee, and sugar for tobacco, sent across the river on boats made of boards, propelled by paper sails.

They told us the army was all there, and invited us to come over, which we politely declined until we were ready. Several times had we been notified to be ready to move at a moment's notice; but they were camp rumors, and a blissful ignorance of movements with which every private of that army was at all times endowed, deluded us with the vain hope that we would not have a fight after all. False delusion!

On Wednesday night, December 10th, we received positive orders to hold ourselves in readiness to move in the morning. We had now been told this so many times, that we turned in, taking perhaps, a little more precaution that our cartridges (one hundred rounds per man) were all right, and our haversacks, canteens, etc., were placed where we could readily reach them in the dark, if chance should this time decree that we were to break camp.

Peaceful slumber reigned in our midst. There was about three inches of light snow on the ground. At 3 a. m., on the nth, the long drawn out and dismal "general" or "pack up" call was sounded, and as the shivering men gathered about the innumerable fires in the keen, frosty air, to draw their coffee, sugar, hard bread and pork, the boom! boom! of the guns at Falmouth and along Stafford Heights announced that the bombardment of Fredericksburg had begun.

The column was soon moving in silence and darkness, over the hard, frozen ground, and two hours later, we were on the large plain, overlooking the river and city, near General Burnside's headquarters, where we lay under arms, the cannonading becoming more and more terrific as the day advanced.

The sun came out, thawing the mud as usual, and soon the plain was a huge, pasty quagmire, trampled and kneaded by the thousands of troops moving hither and thither. About 4 p. m. we moved back nearly a mile, into some woods, where we bivouacked for the night, and being within a few hundred yards of headquarters, we started for our brother's tent.

A bright log fire blazed in the stone fireplace, a good hot supper, with plenty of hot biscuits and coffee, cheered us up. The tent, after coming from the gloom, brightly lighted with candles, was cosy and comfortable, and added much to our general morale and good spirit.

Our brother Walter says:

In Gene's Tent,

Thursday Evening, "December 11, 1862.

We started from our old camping ground at 3 o'clock this morn, and have been under arms all day long before Fredericksburg; the cannonading has been perfectly awful. ... Some of our troops are across; we shall go in the morn. We have been all day in the mud, and tonight have come to a piece of woods near Gene's quarters, and Bob and myself are here.

We have had a good supper, and have been sitting beside a fire and talking about home.

Gene has got your letter, and we got three last night, with a ration of whiskey. We are trained, father, and I have the animus to take me through. It is tough on the march, but we are bound to put it through, best foot forward. If our general hard times were only enlivened by such pleasant intervals as the present, oftener, with what a stout heart I should go forward. But we are well, and at this time full of good 'fod.' Bob is better of his diarrhea, and is as happy as a clam tonight; we are in for whatever is before us tomorrow, and I bid you a last good night, assuring you of our good cheer and wellbeing, so good-by, father and mother! All will be well with us, I feel confident. Gene sends love, and so do we all; I wish John was with us tonight; wouldn't we have a jolly quartette? .... Captain Frank is now in the tent; he is capital; I don't wonder Gene likes him.

Our brother at headquarters adds the following note:

December 12.

We occupy Fredericksburg; Walt was over this morning before I was up, but he woke me; he crosses the river this forenoon.

Some think a great fight will take place today.

Eugene.

Shortly after midnight, we wended our way in the darkness through the lines of sleeping forms, stepping softly as possible, that the crackling sticks might not awaken the wearied men, and took our places among them in the silent bivouac. But not to sleep.

Our thoughts dwelt upon the morrow, with its fateful future. On the following morning, the 12th, we moved a little nearer the river, where we remained inactive all day. We had witnessed at a distance, all the preliminaries of the day before; heard the deafening cannonading, could see the smoke, and hear the cheers and yells, and were told of the call for volunteers to lay the bridges in the face of a terrific fire from the sharpshooters. Our bivouac while waiting for the order to move, was on the farm of Mary, the mother of George Washington.

At dark the last round of musketry had died away, and only the occasional shot of some picket was heard, and when we learned that the gallant Nineteenth Massachusetts, and Seventh Michigan, had crossed in the pontoon boats, and were even now in the streets of the city, our enthusiasm broke forth in ringing cheers.

Saturday the 13th came, misty and foggy, but at 9 or 10 a. m., it broke, the sun came forth, and it proved a beautiful day. Soon we heard General Franklin's guns down the river, then skirmishing across at the city, followed by the roar of our heavy guns on Stafford Heights in their endeavor to reach the enemy's batteries, in rear of Fredericksburg.

The battle had commenced. Sumner's Corps was all across, being the first to gain a foothold. While lying on this muddy flat, and listening to the turmoil of battle, expectant and ready for our turn at any moment, our attention was attracted to men passing our command in regular procession, loaded to the chin with large plugs of tobacco.

The eyes of our chewers grew large, their faces wistful, and soon men might be seen stealing off in the direction of the coveted treasure. A short time before the bombardment, some of the large tobacco dealers in Fredericksburg, fearing that they could have no facilities for transporting their stock to Richmond, in case of the occupation of the city, broke open large boxes of the precious weed, and tumbled them off the wharves into the river, determined to so bury it that the "Yanks" should not have the benefit of it, at all events.

Many thousand dollars' worth thus found a watery grave. Our pickets had noticed this, and marked that watery grave in their mind's eye. No sooner was Sumner's advance across, than the Yankee spirit and natural love for gain, asserted itself. Box after box was fished out, some pretty wet on top, but the middle layers were still undamaged, and the stream of men seen during the entire day with arms full of "Army and Navy Plug," was thus accounted for.

They were at once subjected to a running cross fire of criticism and "chaffing" which invariably included the following category of questions: "I say, partner, where did you get that?" "How much did you give for it?" "Where's the sutler?" "How much will you take for the whole lot?" etc., and occasionally some individual bolder than his companions, and his mouth watering for that luxury of luxuries to an old chewer, would shout, "Oh, don't be mean partner, give us a plug:" some was generously given away, some was sold, and eventually many hearts and mouths made happy.

About two o'clock the order rang out "fall in;" we knew what it meant. It took some time to reach the pontoon bridge. The enemy turned their guns on our relieving column, but somewhat sheltered by the houses, we suffered no loss. Our heavy batteries played over our heads. When crossing the river a man rushed by us, just coming out of the fight. He was bareheaded, his face ghastly white, both hands clutched his throat, and through his fingers the blood could be seen fairly spurting. He grew paler, weaker; he staggered and fell upon the edge of the bridge, almost into the water, and by the side of our hurrying, anxious column. Not one dared lend him the assistance which he needed and beseechingly implored. He must have run nearly a mile from where he was shot, a strong illustration of man's tenacious hold upon life.

We had crossed at the lower bridge, after passing down a deep-cut road that skirts the Washington farm. It is where the old ferry used to run, and a short distance above the steamboat wharf, at the lower end of the town. To the west of the end of the pontoon bridge was a rocky street leading up through two stone-faced walls. It is very narrow, and is called "Rocky Hill." Taking the street next to the north, we soon reached Caroline (now Main) street. Filing right, we then moved to Princess Elizabeth Street.

As we turned this corner, filing left, we were immediately brought under a sharp fire from the enemy's guns controlling the cross streets. The first spherical case burst accurately in Company "F," but ten feet ahead of us. Three men went down as though by a lightning stroke, one shot through the lungs. An officer's servant, so black that charcoal would make a white streak on his shiny face, was carrying a basket on the sidewalk. This shell to him was a genuine surprise, for he was partly loping or shambling along, with no thought of danger. Instantly he dropped the basket, his sable countenance became a dirty, ashen hue, his eyes rolled in his head, and he shot back again around the corner at full speed. At any other time this would have called for the shouts of our men. We crossed the canal on a bridge without knowing it, as we could not see the water. After a number of halts, we found ourselves in a large brickyard, called then and now Knight's brickyard.

The mud was thick, glutinous, and churned into the usual shape and consistency. Many piles of burnt brick were all about. General Charles Griffin,[1] that gallant and accomplished soldier, the original commander of the "West Point" Battery at the first battle of Bull Run, the skillful artillerist who commanded a brigade at Malvern Hill, now commanded our division.

He was omnipresent, cool, quick, magnetic, and inspiring. The enemy had our range; the bricks flew; the mud spirted; the missiles came thick and fast. There was no room for deployment.

---

[1] Charles Griffin (1825–1867) was a career officer and Mexican War veteran. He commanded Battery D, 5th U.S. Artillery at Bull Run.—2019

A solid shot passed between our ranks; a man next on our left (Stephen Fitts) sank like a log into the mud, with a groan, and the writer fell as if struck by the flat side of a board.

Looking at him for a brief moment, it flashed across me that he was shot through the body, while I got the effect of the wind. Taking a long breath, and satisfying myself I was not hurt, I sprang to my feet and pressed on. Now the knapsacks and roils began to be cast off, sometimes a haversack heavy with precious food. We scrambled out of the yard, crossed the railroad and then the railroad cut, now a narrow-gauge road running to Orange Court House, through scores of wounded and dying men, bummers and stragglers, who had taken refuge there from the terrible fire, which now swept everything, and scrambling up the gravel embankment, debouched upon the plain. We were immediately subjected, for the first time, to the full effects of the most murderous fire the enemy could concentrate. It seemed to have been especially renewed for us.

The crest of the gravel bank was swept, and half blinded by dust and gravel thrown directly in our faces by the tempest of iron, we swept forward. Now the men commenced to fall.

We were next to the left of a brigade of seven regiments, The command was given: "Fix bayonets! Left front into line!! Double quick!!!" The right flank regiment was the pivot, and under this terrific fire we were called upon to describe nearly the arc of a circle. We gained a slight rise, and as if by a common impulse, every man on the left sank to the ground exhausted.

We hugged Mother Earth closely for a brief period, to gain our wind. From here we could see Marye's Heights, crowned with smoke and flame, could hear the constant swish and screaming, grating sound of the projectiles, as they burst accurately in front and over our line, knocking the dirt and sand into our very eyes. The writer was perfectly rigid and cool from nervous excitement; he turned to the next man, who said, "This is awful; we better go forward!" We started up, expecting to receive some response, or at least to see him follow us, for the whole left of our line was now up and advancing with ringing cheers. The writer glanced at him.

He had sprung up, but a thud, and his brains covered his face and were spattered about us. In that short interval (a brief second) a ball had penetrated his brain. He was gasping in that peculiar, almost indescribable way, that a mortally wounded man has. I shall never forget the pleading expression, speechless, yet imploring.

We reached the next slight rise (now marked by a white board fence), the line half crouching as it ran, and moving sideways, as though breasting a "blizzard" or a wind and hail-storm in bluff old New England.

This slope was black with lines of battle lying flat on the ground, over which hung the dense smoke of battle. We moved quickly through these masses, until we met such a withering fire directly in our faces, from the stonewall on the lower slope of the heights, just below the Marye house, as to cause the line to recoil, then to break, and finally, after one or two more efforts, to fall back to the front line, where we were soon employed loading, firing, and cheering.

There was hardly a thought for the dead and dying lying everywhere thickly about us. Some rebels had got into the houses overlooking our position, just to our front, and from the second-story windows their sharpshooters were now' dealing death to our ranks. We directed nearly all of our shots towards those windows.

As the smoke lifted, the flashes came thick and fast, and the heads popped in and out. The writer's rifle soon became hot and foul from rapid firing, and the rammer stuck. I could get it neither up nor down, and without thinking whether the rifle would burst, as soon as I saw some heads I fired, rammer and all, into the open window. The idea struck me at the time, while waiting for another rifle, as supremely ridiculous, this long rammer whizzing through the opening, perchance impaling some astonished "Johnny " to the wall, and I laughed aloud a nervous laugh. Once I looked over my shoulder. I saw the Twentieth Maine,[2] which was in our

[2] Led by Colonel Joshua Lawrence Chamberlain, months later the hero of Little Round Top at Gettysburg.—2019

248

division, coming across the held in line of battle, as upon parade, easily recognized by their new state colors, the great gaps plainly visible as the shot and shell tore through the now tremulous line. It was a grand sight, and a striking example of what discipline will do for such material in such a battle.

Shortly after, a tall, slim colonel coolly walked over our bodies. "Who commands this regiment?" he asked. Our colonel responded. "I will move over your line and relieve your men," he quietly rejoined. It was Colonel Adelbert Ames, who afterwards commanded a division, and subsequently became governor of, and United States senator from, Mississippi. He was in the class at West Point next preceding our brother's. We fell back through the lines a few yards. The Twentieth Maine swept forward, and as it was its first engagement the rattle and roar instantly grew furious.

Our position was now' along a board fence, skirting a sunken road. This road cut our line of battle, and steep gravel banks sloped down on either side. Our officers had crossed the road to attend to a wounded brother officer, and we were without a company commander. The filing had lulled somewhat, when suddenly a most terrific fire opened, with a blaze which dispelled the now fast approaching darkness. This was followed by loud cheering and yelling.

We were in a very exposed position, subjected to a terrible crossfire. The shells, shot, and canister tore through the fence and into the gravel bank directly in front of us. One shell burst in the road, directly on or near a mess-kettle. The pieces of shell and kettle came tearing up the bank and into our ranks, carrying gravel and splinters enough to almost cover our little band, now spread out in a vile spot, which had been used frequently by distressed men attending calls of nature.

Many of our men were shot through the clothing. Our brother's haversack was cut away, his canteen was bored through and flung upon mv body; the water poured out over me, and in the blaze of the explosion, terrific noise and confusion, I suspected it was blood. For a moment my heart choked in my mouth, my hand

249

stole quietly down, I felt the water gurgling from the perforated canteen, and I again devoted all my energies to my making myself thinner.

"Who commands the company?" came in precise, but sepulchral tones from the midst of the filth, debris, splinters, gravel, etc. The owner of the voice was Webster, frequently mentioned in this story; he had been a schoolmaster (afterwards killed at Mobile, while gallantly charging with his command, a colored regiment). "I motion the ranking non-commissioned officer take us out of here, or we will all be killed," slowly added the well-modulated, but half smothered voice. "Blank! blankety blank!! lay down!!! you d—d fool!" said our first sergeant. A fresh bursting of shrieking missiles, another shower of gravel, and a perfect roar of cheers drowned the schoolmaster's voice, and as nobody responded, we still "held the fort." We had been under a perfect blizzard of fire for three hours. As darkness came on, we settled down quietly to rest in the midst of this awful field of blood and suffering. Except an occasional heavy gun from the Heights, a spluttering of musketry, or the occasional crack of a sharpshooter's rifle, the hitherto incessant roar had ceased.

Those who had thrown away their haversacks in the charge now proposed to go out "foraging," which meant a search for blankets, food, etc. We started, stumbling over dead bodies and the wounded, every few steps. A haversack belonging to an officer of the Twelfth Rhode Island, its former possessor now stiff and ghastly beside it, was the first trophy. We drew out pieces of hard bread, some silver spoons, and then in the bottom, a handful or two of hard bread crumbs, closely mixed with granulated sugar, which we thought a surprise. We commenced to eat for the first time since early morning. The first mouthful was enough to satisfy the most ardent admirer of all saccharine sweets. We sneezed, coughed, choked, spluttered and spit, until it seemed as though our tongues were on fire, and our throats burned out. Red pepper had been a part of that officer's rations. The package had broken, and freely mingled with the sugar. I went to where I had seen a lot of bodies lying by a well-curb near a small house, in and behind which many skulkers from the fight had met with terrible slaughter. It was literally torn to pieces with shell, and bodies, blood, hair, brains, and flesh strewed the floors and walls.*

I found a full haversack, its owner's body upon it. In the darkness I rolled the cold, stiff corpse away, thrust my hand in eagerly, and to my horror, encountered—not hard bread, but a paste of hard, clotted blood, mingled with flour. My hand had plunged into the wrist. A large wound in the man's side had been over the opening, and the blood pouring in had soon congealed-. A chill almost froze the marrow in my bones; my teeth came together with a snap, my hair slowly rose on end. I was all alone with the dead, in utter darkness, upon the battle-field, and my hand dripping with cold, clotted lifeblood. Hastily dropping my treasure (?), I fled from the spot; I foraged no more, for I was not hungry again that night. We lay down among the dead, upon the cold, mire-trodden, death-strewn, and anguish-laden field that bitter, black December night, but not to sleep.

The scenes of horror, of dark despair, and gradual death, in the piercing cold and darkness, can never be described. Imagination shrinks even from such a picture. The actual, bare reality as we saw it, can never be known or described, and scarcely approached. A low murmur was at all times heard about us, and along the irregular lines ambulances were rumbling; men were groaning, imploring, screaming out for assistance, as they slowly chilled and stiffened to death. Hundreds of dead and wounded lay thickly about us. No help for them as they lay in the cold, clammy mud fast freezing about them. Not for them affection's soothing hand, or the many nameless attentions of loving hands. Several nearest us were in the last agonies of death, their harsh, distressed death-rattles, sounding strangely on the midnight air. Drearily, with faint hope for the morrow; exhausted, bleeding, dying by inches, they must lie, their heroic efforts wasted in a useless sacrifice.

In a little shed doorway, not ten feet from us, propped against the side, sat a man, his leg barely hanging by the skin, the blood fast flowing from the untied arteries. Life and hope were strong within him. He begged as I never knew mortal man, for someone to take him into the city. He said he knew he could be saved if we would only carry him in. "Do for Heaven s sake carry me in, and not leave me to die by inches! I am freezing to death! I will give fifty dollars, yes, one hundred dollars to any man." The long, cold night of waiting, wishing, of hope and despair, wore his life away, for in the gray morning, his body, stiff and lifeless, still occupied the little doorway, a look of almost savage hopelessness about the eyes and half-closed mouth, in which his teeth were clinched, for a final struggle with the Great Unknown. Our bivouac was among the dead of the Twelfth Rhode Island (Nagle's Brigade). The first sergeant, Charles F. Knowles (afterwards killed at Gettysburg), went about distributing cartridges for a renewal of the fight. Those most sleepy, he moved with his foot, and a "get up for your cartridges." His foot came against one obstinate fellow, who seemed deaf to his command. He was completely covered up with a blanket, and in the midst of our company. "Get up!" he did not stir. A repetition of the foot movement, and still no motion.

Cold and shivering, the sergeant stooped, a little out of patience, pulled off the blanket, and at great risk, struck a match and held to his face. The glassy eyes, fixed and stony in death, the rigid, ashy face, told him the truth. He had attempted to issue cartridges to the dead, and compel him to answer to the roll-call.

He had answered hours before, his duty to his country in the ranks of the army was done! Who shall know who that stranger comrade in our company was? How he died? or what were his last thoughts and wishes, on that bitter cold night?

Our brother of the regulars writes:

Camp Near Falmouth,

December 13, 1862.

I have just returned from the battlefield, where I have been acting as aid to General Patrick all day; we commenced this morning about 11 o'clock to storm their batteries, and have made no headway as yet. I feel terribly, for I saw Walter and Bob's division go gayly into action, and I know the carnage has been awful; I could not see them, as I was riding with the general, but tears came to my eyes as I saw Hooker's Grand Division pass me. I pray God to save them, for they are brave good boys; I shall never live a happy moment if they are killed.

I gave them both instructions to come to me immediately if they were wounded. How gaily I could go into action myself, if it were not for these boys. I think of them all the time; but, dear father, do not worry; I will let you know the worst as soon as possible. General Griffin is wounded slightly; General Bayard mortally; General Wilcox reported killed. General Meagher's brigade has one hundred men left. A report has just come in that General Franklin has whipped 'Stonewall' Jackson, and now bolds their railroad communication. Old Hooker is as sour as he can be; Sumner smiles as usual; Burnside is in consultation with Sigel who has just arrived with his corps; a report that Slocum has arrived with his corps from Harper's Ferry.

This is the battle of the rebellion, and might have been stopped (prevented) if Burnside had crossed the river at first. Regular infantry were sent forward, but did not get in: will go in tomorrow.

As day began to dawn, Sunday the 14th, we pushed noiselessly forward on the line. Soon the sun rose, and the shots which had, in the earlier hours, been only occasional, now came thick and fast. The cold, misty fog drifted slowly away. Shadowy forms now became distinct, in the quickening light, and the deadly contest was renewed.

We had absolutely no shelter. To the front, lay extended the Heights with its tiers of batteries frowning down upon us. The low, grey stone wall, was clearly visible, from which we received such a murderous fire the day before.

By raising ourselves slightly on our elbows, we saw the rebels stirring, and busily moving to and fro like angry bees. The houses but a few hundred yards distant, were alive with sharpshooters, overlooking our prostrate bodies, which stretched in a blue, irregular line, to conform to the ground.

The dead lay in full view all about us, and many a poor, wounded fellow, who, too weak to call out, had been passed by the ambulances for dead. The sharpshooters were now at work picking off any man who dared stir an inch. To do so was almost certain death. Behind lay the city, every avenue under fire, and controlled by the rebel light batteries. We could clearly trace the weary and dangerous course of the day before, across the plain, but now it was deserted.

Not a living thing could pass over it unnoticed. Many attempted to regain the line, by dodging, crawling, feigning dead, etc., but few succeeded, and many fell victims to their zeal. For some time our minds were diverted by watching their futile efforts.

Just to our right, a little in advance of where we lay, were two dead bodies, one disemboweled by a solid shot, the other with a leg shot off, and dangling, the mangled flesh in shreds, and the bones and sinews exposed to view. We were in a direct line with the small shed already referred to. Men constantly darted from the line and ran behind it. The bullets tore and sung all about us and our position was a deadly one. Something must be done.

We, our brother and the writer, crawled up, seized the bodies, piled one on top of the other, placed our rolls against them, and tucking our heads under the rolls, and against these human bodies, now rapidly undergoing decomposition, we wore out the livelong day of fourteen hours, under a constantly destructive fire, during which we never moved but once from a prostrate position.

The fixed and glassy eyes stared us in the face, and the stench from our comrades of clay, became repulsive to the last degree. We dragged ourselves painfully on our stomachs to the rear, not daring to raise our heads, got some loose ponchos and rubbers, and soon covered them from view. This breast work of the dead saved outlives more than once during the day, as they were struck several times at least, as denoted by that peculiar dull thud in the dead flesh; and a shiver ran through our spinal column at every fresh clip.

Our colonel wore glasses; he was industriously hugging the ground. His curiosity, like ours, prompted him occasionally to lift his head, a z-i-p—pi-i-i-n-g, instantly warned us, and the men dropped or hastily scrambled like crabs to their places. "Boys, don't dodge so," said the colonel, with a nasal twang; his head came up to emphasize it. Wh-i-i-iz-z-z, pi-i-i-ng and a bullet by his ear caused his head to go down with a spasmodic, and rather comical, ungraceful jerk, throwing his glasses off, and he was at once greeted with a hearty shout for his kind advisory speech. There were many laughable incidents and adventures during the day.

Night began to approach. Still we lay. The fire slackened. The mud again began to stiffen. Our bodies, cramped by the long position in the one place, in the very jaws of death, were stiff and sore.

We roused ourselves, and eagerly looked for our relief, or darkness to come, and had almost resigned ourselves to another wretched night on the field, a cold chill creeping over our hearts and bodies, when a low hum, steadily increasing as it neared us, indicated the unmistakable tramp and murmur of a column, and a division of the Ninth Corps (Sturgis') crept up and relieved us.

Gladly, impatiently, we fell in, and swiftly moved towards the city, the memory of our ghastly comrades haunting us at every step. We passed through the streets. What a relief from our painful and prolonged suspense, and to the severe tension upon the overwrought nerves. The houses were lighted to the brightness of day. The groups of men upon the sidewalks, in the gutters, inside the houses, and on the galleries, or balconies, were indulging in a huge picnic or carnival. Fires were built on the pavement, illuminating the streets as if a torchlight procession were in motion.

Groups of men were mixing bread or flapjacks, frying pork or making coffee. The ruddy light shone upon their faces, and showed the eagerness and delight with which, even in the midst of danger and death, they were carrying on their culinary designs.

Kitchen stoves were in full blast; lighted candles were extravagantly-placed upon the tables. All kinds of music sounded upon the air. Cracked fiddles, with sonorous notes, under the hands of most un-skillful performers. Flutes, fifes, and untuned pianos, accompanied by most melodious voices, added to the uproar.

Some were dancing, while others played cards, or vainly endeavored to write, or laughing, told their eventful experiences of the past fateful hours. All were engaged in some kind of occupation, which to us, just from the darkness, gloom, and dreadful ordeal, almost despair, of that Sunday line of battle at the front, presented the strangest, most novel mixture of grim-visaged war and his strange satellites, that it had yet been our fortune to observe.

But there was a warm cheerfulness that had its effect. It smoothed the hard lines of anxiety and suspense from our faces. It thawed the chill from our sorrow-stricken, hardened hearts, and compelled many a half-suppressed smile to break forth into ripples of hearty laughter.

We halted in a vacant lot; a sigh of relief went up. Before resuming our bivouac on the hard, frozen ground, some of us went to a deserted house nearby, and finding a piano within, one of our number, an accomplished musician, volunteered to cheer us up by playing some of his most lively selections. It proved to be a most delightful diversion to our tired minds and bodies.

Our brother at headquarters now writes:

Camp near Falmouth,

December 14, 1862.

Nothing has been done today, although it was planned to storm the enemies' works again at 2 o'clock, and in case of a failure, General Burnside was to lead an attacking column in person, and General Sumner another; the whole long and short of the matter is this: We have bulled our heads against a stump, and men have been murdered in cold blood to the amount of twenty thousand; we have not accomplished a single thing, and the enemy's loss, here in the center, is comparatively nothing. If you can understand the following you will know something about it (Encloses a pencil sketch.).

The enemy had an enfilading fire upon us with very heavy guns. Under hill number one, was a very high stone wall, behind which was rebel infantry, and their own guns playing over their heads at us. Franklin was some few miles down the river with fifty thousand men fighting Jackson, Hill, and Long-street, he had some advantage, but lost it again; he, however, holds his own.

All of Hooker's grand division would have gone in, but darkness came to our relief. From all that I can learn, Walter and Bob were not engaged, although under fire; I may be mistaken about their division. Humphreys's division of Butterfield's corps was engaged, but I think Sykes and Griffin were not. Two divisions of Hooker's grand division were sent to Franklin, and old Joe acted like a child about it.

Humphreys's division acted badly, but all of Sumner's corps acted very bravely; they were under fire for ten long, mortal hours, and General Couch lost nearly two thirds of his corps. You may call this generalship, but I call it murder; as to our troops fighting, they fight like devils, but no human being can stand in front of such fortifications, 1 not a rebel to be seen but ours did stand and get slaughtered like sheep. We have got to abandon our attack on the center, and aid Franklin. General Sigel was at Dumfries, twenty miles from here, at two o'clock this morning, and I understand General Slocum is thirty miles from here. The gallant Bayard is now probably breathing his last; he was with General Franklin standing by a tree, when a round shot glanced and mashed his thigh. I have been busy all day paroling prisoners, and could not go over to the battlefield, but tomorrow I shall go over and look up the Twenty-second, if I have to go into action to find it; I cannot eat or sleep without thinking of them; we cannot get at our dead to bury them.

The next morning, the 15th, after a short march, we reached the bank of the river, where we washed off the powder, sweat, and accumulated dirt of forty-eight hours.

While thus engaged, and before we had hardly completed our ablutions, we heard a shout, and our brother, mounted, appeared before us.

He says:

Camp Near Falmouth,

December 15, 1862.

Walter and Bob are safe; I went over to town this morning, and after a three hours' search, I found their regiment; but, as I knew positively that it had been in action, I rode up to it with a trembling heart; Walt soon appeared, followed by Bob. They are both in good spirits, and looked very clean. I understand that the rebels have given us a certain number of hours to remove our wounded from the town, for they intend shelling it. Sumner's and Hooker's grand divisions are in the streets; Sigel and Slocum will be here tonight. Don't believe newspaper reports; we have not gained a single inch; the enemy still hold their fortifications, and we have lost fifteen thousand men.

Our brother Walter writes a short pencil scrap as follows:

December 15, 1862.

I sent in a short note a moment ago, as the doctor came round for the letters, and this wasn't finished. I must close now.

Note, Monday Morning

We still live both of us, though having passed through a storm of lead and iron; we have done our duty, and fought bravely, for Bob was a noble, fearless boy throughout, and I know I never flinched. I had a bullet put through my canteen and another cut ray haversack strap, spoiling both. LeRoy says: 'Tell them I am safe; not one of our gallant band from B. are injured. I will write as soon as possible.

During the almost unaccountable cessation of hostilities we took ourselves to the streets of the city, and to find our wounded at the hospitals. No one could better understand what actual war was, than by traversing the alleys and by-ways of this almost destroyed city. Had there been a wind during the bombardment, nothing could have saved it from total destruction. Whatever now remained, was in the hands of the men, who for a time, held a high carnival, and paraded the streets in the cast-off apparel of past ages, and the old bell-crowned, long-haired beaver hats, poke bonnets, hoop skirts, huge umbrellas, etc., convulsed all with laughter, until checked by the provost guard. We found our division hospital located in a shell-shattered, bullet-ridden mansion, whose frescoed walls, and adornments indicated that it had been the abode of some wealthy person, who had hastily vacated it before the bombardment.

The first man I saw among the dead and dying scattered about on the floor, was our comrade, who, when next to me in John P. Knight's brickyard, had been knocked over by a solid shot, the wind from which had also sent me sprawling upon my back. He was propped up against the wall, and was stripped to the waist while the surgeon examined him. Strange to say, the skin was not broken. He had been picked up unconscious, but the extent of his injuries was a large contusion, which was black, blue, and yellow, and stood out from his breast like a hard lump, and about the size of a canteen.

He could talk with difficulty. He never recovered, and was discharged on account of this singular wound. The next man to him was from Company "F" (W. H. Mudgett), who had a spherical case shot through his lung, but afterwards recovered. We did not stay long. At night, we were moved cautiously into Caroline, now called Main, street, and after much marching and countermarching, to avoid halting across streets in line of the enemy's fire, formed line of battle; it was rumored that the division was to compose an assaulting column to be led by General Burnside in person.

It was dark and cloudy. We stacked arms, and while some sought the sidewalks for a little rest, others entered the shops and houses for shelter from the raw wind, which now rose to a gale. Fires were ordered to be put out by the provost guard. No matches could be lighted. We entered a lamp and jewelry store, the show cases having been stripped of the latter, but with all the shelves lined with the former, and amused ourselves, by the aid of a fire which we had started in a fireplace, for a brief period, by throwing lamps at a target we had set up on the mantel. It was on the north side of the street, not far from where the Exchange Hotel now stands at the corner of Princess Anne and Main streets.

There was no sleep for anybody; the loose windows loudly rattled, the signs creaked, the blinds slammed. Mounted aids and orderlies continually galloped over the pavement, and the rain, which until midnight came in occasional drops, now increased to fitful gusts, that chilled all to the bone. We steadily looked forward for the command, which we felt quite certain was to send us to our doom.

At three a. m. loud raps on the doors were heard, and word was passed along, "Make no noise; get up; get up; fall in! fall in-n-n!" and we were instantly in line with our arms. These were moments for quick and sad reflection. In a few moments, we would be moving towards those murderous heights again. The morning approached. The dark clouds scudded. The strong wind, laden with rain now soaking us to the skin, drove down the streets. It was anxious suspense for the word—forward. The order came, but the aid said aloud—"Which bridge, General?" and the agony was over. We knew then we were the rear guard of the Army of the Potomac which, as soon as the pickets were whisperingly withdrawn, crossed the upper pontoon (which had been strewn with hay to muffle the sound), in a drenching, pouring rain, the storm now at its height. General Burnside rode by us. The stillness of death reigned over the column; not a murmur from the ranks of disapprobation; not a cheer or shout of joy or relief.

His hat was slouched over his face, which bore a saddened and disappointed look. Our vast thinking machine, each man intent upon, and industriously chewing the cud of bitter reflection, floundered, plodded, limped, and dragged itself into the old "Smoky Camp," and wearily sought the soaked ground for rest and relief, from the dangers, fatigues, and privations of these long, bitter nights and days during the campaign and battle of Fredericksburg.

AFTER THE BATTLE

After the battle of Fredericksburg we naturally indulged in many allusions to the campaign, comments, reflections, and criticisms, and while some references to, and extracts from, these letters may seem like repetition, it will be seen by the reader that the principal object in their introduction is, as was stated in the first paper, to closely connect them with the incidents and details of these campaigns-in such a way as they shall be our statement alone, and reflect our opinions and no others.

Our brother Bob now says:

Camp Near Falmouth,

December 18, 1862.

It is now some time since we occupied our present camp again, and I wrote you, but knowing that Walt was writing so often, I thought he would do as well as myself, and for a week I have had no chance to write owing to a grand forward movement, which, ere this, you have read about.

I suppose you have seen by the papers that we have had terrible weather, two inches of snow and ice, and so cold that we could scarcely keep from freezing, yet, as you say, it is now 'a question of endurance,' and as the old sailor said, so say we 'I'll be plagued if I'll freeze!'

I would not tell half the sufferings we went through, for it would only make Mother feel worse, and increase your anxiety, but any man of sense can see that we suffered beyond description, for wood and water was to be got, and the company is so small it all comes on us few recruits; and this we have to do without axes, picking up small stuff, and pieces of brush off the snow, and then great iron pails of water; this we have to do constantly.

Gene came over, and seemed very anxious to make us comfortable and in good condition.

Wednesday night we knew we had got to start at midnight; we heard the heavy guns, and at reveille, three o'clock, it was quite brisk. We started at five for the river and after marching we reached the plain that overlooks Fredericksburg, where we halted. The sun came out quite warm, and soon the snow and ice was a nasty mess of mud, which stuck like wax; we stayed here all day; at night we moved back about a mile into some woods, and were very near Gene. We crossed the field into the woods, where he was encamped, and as Walt has told you, enjoyed ourselves hugely, having a good chair, fireplace, floor to the tent, etc. Gene lay on his bed, with his grey sleeping cap on, while we ate biscuits, the first I have tasted since I came out here; we left about twelve o'clock, much pleased at our good time; slept in the woods until morning, when we started for the river again, this time much nearer than before. Burnside had succeeded in laying his bridges the day before, raising the 'Old Harry' with the city, and Sumner's corps crossed that night; we didn't move that day. Hooker crossed most of his men but us; that night we slept without shelter, as it was not a decent place to pitch (tents) on, being hubbly [sic] and muddy.

Saturday morning came along, and with it the usual shelling, but we dreamed not of the work in store for us. I thought I could write, but about nine o'clock, we began to hear skirmishing, and then quite a volley, and soon the guns began to roar, and then I knew the battle had commenced; after that it was one incessant roar.

Franklin began first, and his firing was very heavy, but did not begin with the firing on the right. We saw two or three charges, and could hear them cheer (remember we had not crossed the river, but could look over across, and see them back of the city). About two o'clock we 'fell in' and started for the battle; I felt as cool as a cucumber, and marched as if on review. After crossing the river we stopped to breathe a moment, then loaded and marched out a side street, under a heavy shelling, which knocked out two ahead of me, and one at the side of our company. We crossed the railroad under a tough fire, and as we scrambled up the embankment I heard the order 'charge!' given, and saw the whole brigade 'into line' charging; the Eighteenth on the right, the New York regiments next.

One hundred and Eighteenth Pennsylvania, First Michigan, then ours: being the next one to the left we had the hardest chance to keep up, and then our company is the left flank company, and of course we had to run like the 'Old Nick' to come into line. I fixed my bayonet on the run, and we went across that field under the most murderous fire of the day; it was nothing but one roar; the bursting of the shells; the swishing of the canister; and the singing, buzzing

262

sound of the bullets, was all that could be heard; even the cheering we gave seemed to be drowned in the terrible noise.

I kept my bundle on all the time, and it did seem as if I should die, I was so exhausted carrying such a load; yet I remembered what you said about throwing away my things, and I stuck to them. They got an enfilade fire on us as we went, and the way the dirt did fly was a caution, and I naturally went sideways, with my head curled into my collar, the same as I would go through a storm of hail and wind.

When we got to a small hill we stopped for a moment, and then I thought I was gone through with. The shells burst right over, in front, behind, in fact all over us, throwing the dirt into my face and eyes; at the same time, the bullets sounded like a huge swarm of bees, going between my legs, brushing my clothes, and everywhere but into me, killing and wounding at the side of me, and yet 'your Uncle Dudley' was not hurt.

Give us credit then, father, for keeping our rolls on, for the boys slung them off, and came back without a thing, and have suffered, some of them, considerably. Walt kept his on all the time, so did I mine, and now I thank God that I kept mine, for I should have suffered awfully these cold nights without them; but I don't see now how I ever charged with it on. Well! to continue. We thought it a 'leetle' too hot behind the rise in the ground, so we rose up and cut for the next rise which was larger and came in good style on the left of the regiment. Thought it was about time to commence firing. .. My gun missing, drew the charge, got daylight through my rifle, loaded, and the way I pitched in then was a caution.

Walt and I stood side by side, the sweat rolling off our faces in great streams, and the powder, dirt, and smoke all over them, and we loaded and fired, cheering and yelling, *'Here's for B! give it to them! put the — into them!!!'*

Our regiment behaved splendidly. The Second Maine, which was on the extreme left, tried three times to cross over the ground, and could not come until dark, such was the fire. When such a regiment as the Second Maine falters, then you may think there was hard work. The Twentieth Maine, Colonel Ames, came in gallant style, and after we were exhausted, both in body and cartridges, the Twelfth Rhode Island relieved us, and they behaved so cowardly that their officers went to Ames, and requested him to relieve them, which he did at dark.

We had fallen back by the fence, and had just laid low when the Twentieth Maine and Ninth Massachusetts opened a terrible fire on the rebels, who were creeping up for a charge.

By Jingo! didn't the balls fly? We were in an exposed position; our company and the lieutenant got cut off just as we fell back, and could not get to us for some time; Walt got his haversack carried away, and his canteen had a bullet put through it, which knocked him over on to me; three shells exploded so near my head that I was all covered with mud: soon darkness came on, and all firing ceased except an occasional shot, when we fell back from the hill and were relieved.

Walt grasped me by the hand, and the tears almost came into his eyes, as he said, 'Bob, we are safe and sound, aren't we?' That night seemed worse to me than the battle, for we had to lie down among the dead and dying. The groanings and moans of the wounded were awful; sometimes they would almost shriek for someone to take them off the field; most of them were taken off before morning.

Sunday, all day we lay exposed to the fire of their sharpshooters. Walt and I lay in range of a shed, about twelve feet wide, and some of the boys kept passing by for water, and they (the enemy) put . . . many bullet-holes through the side, ... all of them only a few inches over our heads, and we flat on our backs in the mud. . . . We never so much as put up our hands for fourteen hours. Walt and I had two dead men for a shelter of work, one with his whole back up to his neck scooped out with a solid shot, the other with his leg shot away.

Sunday night we were relieved, and marched noiselessly back to the city, where we bivouacked all day Monday on the wharves, eating flapjacks and raising the "Old Nick." . . . Fredericksburg is a mere wreck; you never saw such a sight; we completely gutted the whole concern. Some houses beautifully frescoed and furnished inside, were literally stove into kindling wood, and the boys got hold of rocking-chairs, looking-glasses, sofas, even to dresses and bonnets, beaver hats, pans, kettles, clocks, and in fact everything. . . . We were all powder from head to foot, and after scrubbing up, had quite a rest.

Gene came riding along the lines in the afternoon, and when he saw us his eyes watered and he grasped us by the hand. He had been looking . . . hours for us; . . . he thought one of us must have been killed. Monday night we were started up into the main street again, and manoeuvred around in a strange manner until ten o'clock, marching backwards and forwards . . . until we were tired almost to death. We then stacked arms, and slept on the sidewalk, with the exception of a few of us, who went into a store, and slept on the floor until two or three o'clock, when we were ordered into Hue and no noise to be made.

We started back to the wharf, crossed the pontoon, and the rearguard of Burnside's army was across the Rappahannock, for we did not know until then that our brigade covered the evacuation.

The bridge was taken up as soon as we had crossed, and the wind blew, the rain descended in torrents, and we marched back to our old encampment, with the mud half way up to our knees, in a raging cold rain-storm, where we arrived wet, cold, and hungry, and where we are now pretty well used up,—I only wonder not dead, for tonight is a week since we started, and we have laid without shelter in the rain and mud, through the battle, with nothing to eat but crackers and pork, and yet I am still kicking, and hoping you wall accept this letter as a rough account of myself. I am forever your loving son.

Our brother Walter adds:

December 20, 1862.

I am not well, so I shall not write a letter now; I shall as soon as I feel better, and it will.be a rich one. I shall tell you all in it. . . . I could not sit in my tent and fail to acknowledge in some way your continued thoughtfulness of us.

As soon as we got back here, cold, wet, hungry, and used up (for we had nothing but hard bread to eat the whole time—live days, no fires for coffee being allowed, and it made me sick to eat in view of such sickening sights as were before me), we found the things awaiting us. My feelings of gratitude for all these blessings that have been shown me during the perils of battle, bursts the bands of sickness, and I speak forth feebly my heartfelt thanks

I am not cast down. I want another chance, then 'up guards' and at 'em. It is awful cold; I can hardly write. I have not been well for the last thirty-six hours, in consequence of our excitement, fatigue, and exposure; I was wet through with rain and mud on our march to this place on that memorable morning that we, as rear-guard to our retreating forces, marched across the pontoon bridge. It was a time I never shall forget, for the wind howled and the rain poured; the roads were awful, and I visited Mother Earth enough to make impressions more lasting upon my mind than upon my clothes and body. We waded in Virginia mud way back to this, our old camping ground, and yet, when we were routed from our soft (?) beds in the houses of Fredericksburg (they were all cosy, even if it was a hard floor, for we had been on the cold ground too long), where we were ordered after I wrote mother, from the banks of the river, we all thought it was to meet the foe. We were not greatly mistaken.

What can I say, father, about the battle and its results? When I consider the stupendousness of the issue, and the great cause at stake, I could exclaim, almost in agony: 'Oh, how have the mighty fallen!' How disastrous are the ways of man! God plows deep furrows in the homes of Northern freemen, but the great sheaves still grow in the Southern rebel's husbandry.

The worth of liberty is shown in the gallant fighting of our men; the price is seen in the ghastly corpses we have left behind. The fault is in our generals and head officials. We fought well, except in a few instances. Our division had over a thousand men straggling in the streets of Fredericksburg when we went into the fight. Our colonel has fined all those in our regiment $13, and reduced all non-commissioned officers to the ranks. Our company numbers six in disgrace—all old fellows; those who have doubted our pluck, and I rejoice to see the cowards humbled.

I went so far ahead when I fired, that I was ordered back by our major and lieutenant. I was mad, yet calm; how I itched for a hand-to-hand struggle. If I wouldn't have been some in that case. I believe I could have whipped my weight.

Our brother of the regulars now writes:

December 21, 1862.

You keep remarkably quiet about our late disaster in front of this place; why is it? Can you inform me why the Army of the Potomac does not advance, or seek a new scene for its operations? We have had a terrible battle, and yet it does not compare with Antietam, for at the latter place it was fought by both parties, face to face.

The rebels had the superiority in numbers and position of ground. Almost all of our troops were engaged; here not half, yet our loss exceeds that at Antietam. It amounts to this: The recent battle was only a murder, for which the commander-in-chief and A. E. Burnside are responsible. 'Little Mac' will have to be called upon again, even if he comes at Secretary Stanton's and General Halleck's expense. When George was commander-in-chief, everything went as merry as we would wish to have it, but from the moment they commenced to interfere with him, we have had nothing but disaster.

McDowell is coming out all straight, and I wish they would send him down here to command a corps; if George B. McClellan should come here again in command of this army, I believe the soldiers would go crazy with joy. I tell you he has more military talent than any other man in this country.

The secretary of war's approval of Captain Frank's nomination of First Lieutenant Eugene Carter as regimental quartermaster,[1] came last night, so I am now a full blooded quartermaster. I was detailed yesterday to inspect the First brigade of regular infantry; General Sykes and Colonel Buchanan were there, and after I got through, I was invited to dine with the colonel who commands the brigade. I considered it quite an honor to inspect a brigade of regular troops, and I only a first lieutenant.

I have not seen Walter and Bob since the army recrossed the river; I should have gone over this morning but we were expecting orders to move camp, and I did not like to be absent."

The weather continued bitterly cold, and there was much suffering among the men. About the 22d of December we moved across the railroad from "Stoneman's Switch" about a mile, and here laid out and built our winter quarters. It was but a short half mile from where the bridge (railroad) crossed. Potomac creek, and was located upon a steep side hill, in the midst of a growth of small timber and underbrush, which we had to clear away. There was but one ax in the company, and at night, with a borrowed shovel, and a candle stuck on a log, we worked, with "the candle dimly burning," until nearly midnight, digging our cellar.

Every soldier had his own ideas and tastes to display in the erection of these edifices, and as none of us had been educated for

---

[1]: First Lieutenant Eugene Carter, Eighth United States Infantry, was appointed regimental quartermaster, December 10, 1862; relieved February 2, 1864.—note in original

architects or builders, many were crude indeed. Each seemed to vie with the other, however, as to who should get up the best "coop," and perhaps it was this generous spirit of rivalry that enabled us to succeed as well as we finally did.

We dug into the side hill, about six feet for width, and ten or twelve in length, by about four in depth on the upper side. We then logged up with spruce and cedar, notching the logs at the ends, so that they would fit into each other, leaving a doorway.

A fireplace was dug out of the hard clay, which was merely a hole with another smaller one leading to the surface, about which we (those who were fortunate enough) placed a pork barrel, or if not, sticks, built up cob-house fashion, and profusely plastered with the red clay mud. Slim cedar poles were tacked on the top logs for rafters, with as steep a pitch as possible. A ridgepole completed the superstructure. Six ponchos, buttoned together, and thrown over the frame, two more at the back and front, all closely cleated down, completed this curious "dug-out."

A bunk of cedar poles was made by driving upright stakes with crotches, and laying stout horizontal poles in them, then covering closely with springy poles first, and cedar tips (laboriously gathered in rubber blankets) afterwards, and over all our rubber and woolen blankets.

It proved a bed not to be despised, and surprisingly comfortable to one who had slept upon boards, in furrows, on rocks, etc. Here we lived and performed the ordinary routine of camp life, and extra work of all kinds, hardly to be expected or required of a soldier, such as ornamental board fences leading to officers' quarters, fancy arbors, etc.

The camp was named "Camp Gove"—after Capt. Jesse A. Gove,[2] formerly Captain Tenth United States Infantry, appointed to succeed Senator Henry Wilson as colonel of the Twenty-second, and killed at the battle of Gaines' Mills.

---

[2] Jesse Augustus Gove (1824–June 27, 1862) was a career officer, Mexican War veteran, and a lawyer killed during the Seven Days Battles.—2019

We debated as to whether we should work on Sunday, and looked on with dismal faces to see the houses of the wicked undergoing rapid completion, while ours were yet in the incipient stages. We had already learned to make coffee, fry and broil meat, boil "scouse," which consisted of pork and cracker boiled together to the consistency of a thick soup and seasoned with pepper, and go through with the coarser kinds of cooking, but it was here in this camp that we mastered the intricate modes of making puddings, biscuits, "flippers," etc.

Our brother Walter writes as follows:

In Camp, Christmas Eve,

By Candle Light,

December 24, 1862.

Since I wrote you last we have moved camp, and are nearer Burnside's headquarters than before; we have orders to build log huts for winter quarters, and have commenced operations already. I hadn't time to get sick, for the word was 'up and go!' Weak as I was, I kept up, and after a few days at a new business, I feel as if I must rouse myself and be perfectly well, else things will work bad in my tent; but, father, I haven't been well since I came back from Fredericksburg; I am all unstrung, and have a cold all through me; I have no appetite for the common ration, and scarcely eat three hard bread a day; I did not while I was gone either.

The whole tote gave me a severe shaking both outwardly and inwardly, and then to be defeated[3] is enough to make one sorely grieved, and all on account of inability of high officials, who still ride the waves of ease, while we suffer, and have been made to see death at our very footsteps. We poor recruits do not see much to encourage us: we have seen defeat every time so far; we have met the jibes and sneers of the old soldiers, doubting our ability to go through a battle, and now we hear those very ones talk infinitely worse than ever before about the war, and especially do the fined stragglers swear and curse against the cause.

I know that it is all empty, spent wind, for the cause will yet be triumphant; but it troubles me to see the spirit worse than it was

---

[3] The Confederate victory at Fredericksburg cost the Union 12,653 casualties to 5,377 on the opposing side.—2019

before, particularly among the ardent admirers of 'Little Mac,' and it certainly does not inspire us to hear men say they will never fight when they can 'skedaddle.' I never want to myself again, when my life hangs by a thread, and the prospect of success is so poor; although rely upon me when duty calls, for my sense of right, and love of country and its glorious cause would impel me forward to death, even if my poor, weak nature hung back, and human feelings gained control over me. ... I never lose self-control; I care not for myself, I only shuddered for Bob (the boy hero). I can only thank God that my body does not lie on Virginia soil on the banks of the Rappahannock. When I had my canteen pierced I was thrown over on my side, but kept cooler still and hugged Mother Earth all the closer. While we were firing, I advanced ... every time ... presenting a splendid mark for the 'rebs,' and Bob would sing out: 'Did you hit 'em, Walt?' I would retreat back and answer, 'Guess so, that time!' How the bullets whistled by my head; it was one of my careless, forward movements, reckless, yet full of the right pluck, and I gloried in it. I was ordered back by our Lieutenant Baxter;[4] he has been so good to us ever since; he seems to be proud of us, and says so. We like him better than ever, and he is a brave man; he is with us constantly on company grounds, and when he buys a paper, sits by our fire and reads to us the general news of the day and items of interest.

He said he was going to write to the *Triweekly* about the fight; whether he has or not, I do not know. Bob and myself are going over to see Gene tomorrow. Many thanks for all; every day brings fresh memorials of your goodness to us. If we could only repay, but oh, father,—if love of home, constant heed of all your good advice, and good motives for the future will suffice at present, I desire to assure you of it all, and may He who knows all distant, future time, keep us safe, so that we may be able to balance all when we meet again, happy and joyous in our own dear home, with peace as the heritage of our tributary endeavors out here in the wilderness.

When we went into the battle, the fire on Griffin's division was terrible, and when I remember how the bullets flew, and the shells exploded right among us, I wonder more and more how we escaped. Griffin was in a brickyard, trying to get one of his batteries into

---

[4] Joseph H. Baxter (1837–June 4, 1864) was mortally wounded at Cold Harbor.—2019

play, when ours, his first brigade, passed, and he said: 'There goes one of my brigades to hell, and the other two will soon follow!'

Even that 'old war horse,' proof against bullets, saw our position, and spoke as he did: he couldn't get his battery to work the fire was so severe; unusual for him, the best artilleryman in the service.

How can we measure the damage done to the cause? Instead of being victorious, and in pursuit toward Richmond, we are now inactive, and have received a check. No matter whether it could have been otherwise or not, it is as it is now, and the deed cannot be altered. If the pontoons had arrived sooner, and a position for batteries gained, we might have succeeded; we surely would have stood a better chance.

I think if more men had been given to Franklin, and operations in front had been confined merely to holding position and keeping the enemy occupied there, we might have done better, for Franklin gained the earthworks on the left, but was forced to relinquish them, on account of his meeting fresh bodies of rebel infantry, and his force being fatigued and inadequate; and yet old Joe Hooker raved because he had one of his divisions detached to help Sumner and Franklin. He is reported to have said when his two corps went in, 'Now I'll fix this thing!'

It is idle to speculate; the battle was gained and thousands of brave men fell, while the rebs suffered but little, and we have not the wherewith to show for the bravery of our troops. It is a cruel, a sad result: Why can the Almighty permit it? Henry Wilson was here for a day; has gone to Washington. I guess this will do for war matters.

Sunday, December 28, 1862.

It is a magnificent day.

We are situated in such a way that if a rain should descend we would be totally submerged and washed down into the valley. We are now building winter quarters on the woody side of a hill, and while our log structures are in process of building, we are living any way as regards shelter, and how fortunate we have been in having good weather. It seems as if Heaven had smiled on us in this particular.

All our fond hopes, however, to escape safely until our shanties were built, seemed ready to go down deep last night, the clouds were so fierce in their exteriors, and I expected nothing else but a rich bath, clothes, poncho, household furniture generally reckoned in, before this morning. Contrary to expectations, we still swim dry, and have been led to suspend operations on our houses on this Holy Day.

We had quite a discussion last evening about the propriety of working on our huts today, provided it rained during the night; all our Bradford boys, with one or two from Haverhill, declared that we would not, and the old follows said they should. It is a most lovely day, and they are at work, while we still cling to the good advice of Mr. McCollum (Congregational minister), and in every way possible, 'strive to be men.' But you little know the difficulties we meet with, and how often we are tried both in mind and body; the army is the greatest place for human nature to display itself, and we all display our several faults immediately upon entering its enclosure, subject until discharge therefrom to all its vile influences.

We shall yet weather the storm, and won't it be a blessed day when we return to you all, as pure and honorable as when we bade you a long farewell at the Bradford depot. God grant that it may be so in his own good future.

We have hard work to get up our huts, only having one ax in the company to cut down trees with, and a borrowed shovel at night. Ed, Walton, LeRoy Kimball, Bob, Edgar Holt, and myself are going to keep house together; we worked night before last until 11 o'clock, digging in our cellar; it was an odd sight to see us there at dead of night with 'candle dimly burning.'

You ought to see the different kinds of houses that we soldiers put up; every kind of taste is displayed, and all sorts of original inventions practised, each one seeming to vie with the other to see who gets up the best coop. We are now living much better than formerly, and are in a warmer place. We draw fresh meat regularly, and have soups, rice, and good hard bread: we go into a little private cooking on our own expense. Sam Apple-ton and myself made a pudding yesterday, as good as any I ever ate at home; if we had had raisins and eggs, it would have been a perfect plum pudding. I bought crackers (good home kind), condensed milk and butter, while Sam had clove, nutmeg, and cinnamon; we mixed pounded cracker (pounded on a stump) with all these ingredients, sweetened with sugar, and put the sum total into a greased dish, and baked it in hot ashes, covered over with a plate, coals on top. It was baked splendidly, and we all agreed upon its being the pudding of the season. I have got so that I can cook quite decently.

Of course you have heard all about the battle of Fredericksburg, and know by our letters home how your brothers went through it all; how we were baptized in lead and iron; how they fought with noble men against odds, and how we were all defeated and cast down.

I need not repeat it, that campaign of six days, the horrid sights we saw, how we suffered for food, how we lay the whole of one day upon the ground with the bullets whistling through our ranks, and we were wet, cold and tired, covered with mud from head to foot, etc., etc.

We could not even spread our blankets nights, for fear of a forward movement. It was an awful experience, and I don t care to see another of-the same kind, although I am always ready to fight; if I could only meet 'Johnny Reb' at the point of the bayonet at close quarters, I would be satisfied, even if I were used up in the scrape. I want just one good show, one hack at them, where I can reach them; when our army can be victorious; and that's what we want—a victory!! Oh! what a shout would go up from the United North, over one grand triumph; it would hush forever these vile home croakers, who 'knew it would be so,' and who ought to be crushed. I am still patriotic, and full of hope; I have never faltered yet, and I know I fought the best I could in the late battle, so did Bob, the young hero. Midst a perfect storm of shot and shell, he kept at my side 'double quick,' for more than a half mile, his blankets on him, and scores falling around him, mangled terribly. ... You can scarcely realize the horrors of the field, and all that Saturday night, as I went about giving water to the wounded; everything testified that 'man was made to mourn.' I shall never forget the scenes of that night.

The army don't seem to be in very good spirits; as Sumner said, 'I can't explain it, but there is a lack of confidence, and the old fellows who talked bad before the fight, now talk worse.' I am acting corporal in the place of one of the old veterans in our company who skedaddled at Fredericksburg. ... Bob went to see Gene a day or two since; he is all down at the heel and dreadfully blue over Burnside's defeat.

December 29, 1862.

It is quite warm here today, and Walt is writing. I feel it my duty to add a few lines, which opportunity I have not had since the battle, as we have been changing camp, cold weather, etc., but now the weather is delightful, and you would be surprised to see the ground with no snow and the warm sun, so different from home, where there is sleighing, skating, etc.; it does not seem like winter at all.

Of course, ere this reaches you, you will have been apprised of our safety in the recent battle. We (First brigade) went in under the most terrible fire of the day. They got a cross fire upon us, and the way the shot, shell, grape, and canister and bullets flew was a caution; yet I never thought of fear during the whole of it. My face was all covered with powder and sweat, and shoulder to shoulder Walt and I stood and fired, the shells bursting over our heads, striking and throwing the dirt into our eyes and mouths, the bullets brushing our clothes. Three shells exploded so near me that I was almost stunned, and my mouth was plugged with dirt; yet I never thought of but two things—home and the rebels.

Yes, even in the terrible fire I thought of home, and father, mother, and my dear sisters came up before me as distinctly as if they were there in the smoke and noise. You may thank God that we ever lived to come out of it safely. I always thought that the dying and wounded would be the worst of it, and as I lay on the battle-field that night it proved to be so. ... I hope I shall not witness it again. I dread it worse than the fight. It is all humbug about their being so comfortably taken care of; that cold night I went around and talked with them, and the poor fellows begged and begged to be carried off.

Our cousin in the defences of Washington now writes:

Fort Tillinghast, Va.,

New Year's Eve, 1863.

I was glad to receive a letter from you, also to learn that Walter and Bob were safe, also Eugene. In regard to father's death, the first communication, which was dated November 9th, in answer to one previously written by me, gave me to understand that he was killed in front of Vicksburg. This was from James F. Richardson, commanding the United States gunboat *Judge Torrence*. The next one I received was written previous to this (but for some unknown reason I did not get it) by the paymaster's clerk of same steamer, dated above Vicksburg, on the Mississippi river, July 17th. He says: 'Your father died quite suddenly on the night of July 14th.' Also his account at the auditor's office in Washington corroborates this statement. He had no connection with the Third Maine regiment, as he was transferred from that regiment into the navy sometime in February last.

If you should wish to communicate with the commander of the boat you can do so by directing to Cairo, Ill., as it may become necessary to use those letters in Washington. ... I am at present very comfortably situated: also same with the men. I have a room 12x12: I have a fireplace, and my room is papered all over, top and all, with little birds; I have a good kerosene lamp, also a bedroom, and taking everything into consideration, live quite easily. John comes in occasionally and sits with me; can do so whenever he chooses. ... I have got me a pretty little mule at my command. I gave $25 for him; today was offered $80. This afternoon I rode out into the country, and called upon some young ladies who reside in the vicinity, who were not foolish enough to go off with the secesh. They brought on the cider and egg-nog in true Virginia style. I will send my 'phiz' [photo of his face] in this.

It was from this camp that we emerged on the 30th of December, to go upon a reconnoissance, connected with a forward movement of the army, to Richard's ford, on the Rappahannock river, and when we packed up it was with the thought that we would never see the old camp again.

Upon the first night out, a drunken aid, who had directed us on the wrong road, caused us much hard running after dark, to catch up with the rest of the command, which was miles ahead; while we were halted an hour or two by his stupidity, bringing down much hard language from "the boys." After this impromptu and chilly bivouac, about 8 a. m. the next morning we moved slowly and with painful steps down a road badly blockaded with fallen trees, which was cleared by our pioneers, to the ford.

The water was skimmed over with ice, and wading, slipping upon wet stones, and shivering with cold, we crossed, breaking the ice as we forded. Berdan's Sharpshooters, with the advance as skirmishers, soon cleared the way for the cavalry, and during this brief skirmish a woman, Mrs. Richards, was accidentally wounded in the thigh, while hastening into her house near the ford. A cavalry vidette, belonging to the First South Carolina, and whose horse had been wounded, was captured. When passing through our lines in the woods, with a kind of oil-skin tarpaulin hat on his head, and two greasy cloth haversacks upon his hips, he was asked by one of our wags: "What have you got in there, Johnny?" at the same time lifting the flap of the haversack.

The Confederate smiled grimly, then scowled, and replied: "Confederate hard-tack, by God;" while our bummer extracted a hard, sour, indigestible flour pone, which seemed to our astonished eyes as large as a cart wheel.

A very rapid march of about six or eight miles, on the arc of a circle and through a strange country, brought us to Ellis ford. We were now reeking with perspiration.

There was one small, flat boat, which accommodated about ten or twelve of those who did not care to get any wetter. The rest of us plunged into the cold, black, icy waters up to our breasts, and pushing up to the slope on the other side, near a house and some large out-buildings owned by Mr. Ellis, were informed that without fires (which, of course, meant without coffee), we would "picket the river at night." There was a large garden filled with half-frozen turnips and cabbages; some of the latter we ate raw.

Our clothes froze stiff on our backs that cold, bitter night (it was reported that some men died), and back from the river's bank we saw the bright reflections of the huge fires of our brethren in the woods, at the top of the hill. January 1st (New Year's), it was said that some officers had made a private bet, that the brigade would arrive in camp at a certain hour. We always thought it must be true, for at early daylight we started at a rapid gait, and without halts of any consequence, marched nearly thirty miles in about ten hours back to our old camp, where the men (those who did not "fall out" inside the picket lines near Hartwood church) arrived chafed, sore, and blistered, and cursing everything and everybody, from the commanding general down, for such inhuman methods.

The brigade afterwards enjoyed the title of "Betty Barnes Cavalry."

The plan of General Burnside was to cross the river six miles below Fredericksburg, at a point opposite the Seddon House a short distance below Hayfield, and to make a feint above the town; this latter to be converted into an assault, if discovered below, and if not, to throw the entire army across at the point opposite the Seddon House, or points nearby, where bridges could be built. Positions for artillery to protect the crossings were selected, roads surveyed, and corduroy necessary to prepare the road cut. In connection with this, a cavalry expedition, under General Averell, was organized of picked men who were to cross the river at Kelly's and Raccoon Fords, cut the Virginia Central railroad, cross the James, and then cutting the Lynchburg also the Weldon roads, destroying all bridges, canal locks, etc., was to join General Peck at Suffolk. To insure the success of this expedition, Griffin's division of the Fifth Corps with a battery were detailed to accompany it and secure the passage of the Rapidan River. An extra brigade was to go with it and cross the river, then, turning to the right with five hundred additional cavalry, it was to attack any and all forces in the direction of Culpeper Court House, returning by crossing further up the Rappahannock. The expedition was organized the Monday before New Year's and was completed the next day, and Tuesday the 30th we were on the road as narrated. Here jealousy, or something worse, again thwarted General Burnside's plans. Two well-known officers of the army notified the president of this contemplated move and General Burnside was directed to suspend operations.

Letters now describe this reconnoissance as follows:

We waited and watched in vain for a word from home in answer to our battle letter, and a word of comfort and good cheer, after doing our whole duty, and I must say for the first time since we have been on this perilous mission, I felt as if I was neglected. Every night after taps we sat up for the mail, yet no word; at work hard at night and during the day on our log cabin, and not a single word from the 1 clearing;' all a wilderness, and for our lives we could not assure ourselves of the facts of the case. ... Close upon this, an order came last Tuesday to move; where we knew not.

We started in a cold rainstorm, and marched until midnight, and such marching, almost a run, in this slippery clay and mud. All this was the mistake of a drunken aid to Butterfield. We were allowed no fires, and we were squatted on the ground and mud, wet, cold and sleepy, expecting to move every minute.

If that giant evil (whiskey) could be removed from the officers' grasp, how little we should suffer comparatively, and how soon would rebellion be 'non est.' I say we suffered; aye! we agonized, for just that order given without authority from the lips of a man who was sweltering under the effects of strong drink. We remained there about an hour before the true situation of things was discovered, and then our brigade was miles behind; our colonel did not know what road they had taken, and it was dark. Things looked dubious, but he started us and we double-quicked it for about two miles and then streaked it at a fast walk until we caught up, about n o'clock; only fifty men in in the regiment then; they had all fallen out from sheer exhaustion. It was the hardest march I ever experienced. I was all perspiration, my shoulders were cut with straps, and I was nearly gone up, when we caught the rear guard of our brigade. Bob hung to it, and only nine or ten more of the company got up in time. ... I went to bed with dry feet; I was determined to do that, for well I remembered my last experience at Sharpsburg; I shall never be likely to do that thing over again if I know myself.

We were allowed no fires. We started again about 2 a. m. and marched seven miles further and waited for the morning; marched about 7 without anything to eat but crackers and pork (no coffee), and then, cold as we were, that raw, windy morning, we forded the river half way up to our waists. The water struck like an icicle to our very vitals. Cold! how cold!!

We skirmished with their cavalry, took three prisoners, marched eight miles further, crossed the river again—this time up above our waists—almost swimming, then had to picket the ford all night (our

278

regiment), and wet and cold, and my legs full of rheumatism, I waited for the New Year to dawn upon us, fearing, for the worst was to come. In the morning, we started for camp, twenty-four miles, and marched, and I believe such marching the brigade never had.

I believe your eyes would have filled with tears to see the poor boys limp along, for we actually dragged ourselves along, groaning at every step. We actually got into camp, loaded as we were, at 4 o'clock, then human endurance gave in, and we lay down, and some could scarcely stir. ... We dropped right down on the muddy ground, equipments still on, and many of our boys fell asleep.

Bob was all jaded out; had the rheumatism in his left leg terribly. Le R. had his feet blistered in five different places, and suffered much. Edgar was perfectly gone, and Webster, Day, Morrison, and six of the old fellows we left way back on the road.

I determined to fall out several times, and come in easy, for it seemed a shame to march men so hard when they were most home. I guess old Barnes tried to win a name for his brigade on the walking part of that famous reconnoissance.

It was far into the night when I awoke, and it seemed as if I slept the sleep of death. I could not move; a coffin in the grave could not have bound me down closer. I was sore, stiff, and lame, and the frost was thick upon me. I dreamed of home while I was sleeping, and I shall never forget all of your faces as I rushed into the house that night, with all the horrors of that march upon me, my face dirty, hair uncombed, clothes muddy, gun rusty, and equipments soiled; tired, hungry, and utterly used up. I found you in the sitting-room, and when I walked in you all raised your hands, and as if amazed and thunderstruck at such a strange appearance, said not a word; you did not know me, your own son, and before I could announce myself I awoke, and to my surprise found myself still on the ground where I had laid myself when I got into camp.

January 7, 1863.

I am very busy now. I have been doing all the company writing, making muster and pay rolls, and yesterday the quartermaster sent for me to do some writing. I have been doing some of his quarterly return writing today; I maybe his clerk. The adjutant also sent for me, and wanted me to help him our house is not finished yet, and we can't find time to complete it; we have moved in, and have a fire every night; quite comfortable.

I have a corporal's warrant; my name was read out at dress parade last night; one step on the ladder, but my ambition is higher yet. I consider it an honor though, for I am the first recruit advanced, and there is many an old veteran who is yet a private.

January 13, 1863.

I, too, am in hopes that ere this you have received some of my letters since the reconnoissance across the R.; that awful march did not delay my writing; never so long as I can move a finger, shall my hardships keep me from sending you word as to our health and general condition, for too well now am I aware with what anxiety and increasing watchfulness do you think of us. Your last letter written in the senate chamber is amply significant of the place we hold in your best affections. To be 'first in one's thoughts' while sitting in halls of honor, with your mind overburdened with business, is enough for us; we need no better manifestations than the every-day, practical showings forth of your goodness for us, and what can we do? Filled with a sense of unworthiness, I can only write and tell you how we thank and assure you that we are true to every home teaching, and turn anxiously to the future time when all these troubles will cease, and we shall be returned to you all, ever to remain in peace until our earthly pilgrimage is over. Bob hasn't written, for he has had no chance.

I think I told you in my last that Gene was over to see me, Bob being out on picket; he said that he and Frank were to have a leave of fifteen days, and were going home, and to Maine. He wanted Bob and myself to be sure and get over to see him before he went, and I promised him that we would come over in a few days, intending then to go over last Saturday, but Bob didn't get in from picket, so I deferred it until Sunday, so that he could go too; again I was disappointed in Bob's not coming, and started off alone. I wrote a short letter to Bob telling him where I had gone, and left him your letter, and also yours to Gene.

I visited the Thirty-fifth on my way to Burnside's headquarters, and saw Ed M., Haze G., and many other friends. When I got to the Eighth Infantry, I found Quartermaster Gene gone to Washington; I felt badly enough, I can assure you. I wrote him a letter, and his man, Barrett, showed me every attention (he thinks the world of

280

Gene) possible; I saw Captain Frank, who invited me to a magnificent supper, and I spent the evening with him, enjoying every second of the time, listening to his details of Mexican curiosities, and of his experiences when in command of Fort Fillmore, near Santa Fe, New Mexico.

It was very instructive and amusing, and he is such capital company; he treated me so politely that I can never cease to remember him for a future return if it lies in my power. I stayed all night, and slept in Gene's nice bed, and ordered one of the same dimensions immediately upon rising; I appreciated that night's rest, I can assure you. In the morning I made a fire; got up early, and started for home, having lived an officer's life for half a day, just long enough to know its pleasures. They know how to live better than these volunteers; besides, they have a better chance. A man who caters for headquarters also sells to them chickens, turkeys, oysters on half shell, game, and every kind of high 'fod' with all the common etceteras [*sic*], such as pies, cake, bread, butter, cheese, ham, eggs, and all kinds of meat and preserves.

However, this will do for such things. When I got home I found Bob; he had had a hard time on picket, got out of rations, been in the rain two nights, and had seen rough usage generally: his duties in the company are more severe than ever before; he has fatigue, guard, picket, and provost duty constantly, and gets no chance to write. I only get what I steal. Our house isn't finished yet, and I don't know when it will be. .. We thought we were going to the front when we started on our tramp, and I never expected to see this camp again; I felt bad enough I can tell you, for our houses had just begun to assume a degree of comfort that was too inviting to leave for a campaign. We were reviewed by our new corps commander and General Burnside the other day. I admire General Meade's appearance, but Burnside looked as though he had just crawled out of bed; he is a splendid looking man, but dresses rather slouchy. We had to march five miles and back to the review ground; that is always the way when we are reviewed. I am still writing for the quartermaster, and am looking for a permanent job; if so, I shall mess with the non-commissioned staff, and may ride a pony. Adjutant has gone to Washington, and Lieutenant Steele is acting; pretty good for him; quartermaster sergeant gone to Acquia Creek, and I am lord of this realm.

Our brother, the regular, now says:

I returned from Washington last night; I was ordered there on duty just for one day; I had no time for anything. I saw Colonel Willard, Frank Fessenden (the first time since I entered West Point), and several of my young friends. Lieutenants Andrews and Cooper are away on a fifteen days' leave. Captain Read is now in command of the regiment, and I have a second lieutenant with my company, but he does not know much about military matters. Captain Read asked me if I would still command my company, and I could not refuse. As soon as Andrews and Cooper get back we will have nine officers with us, and Frank and I are to have a leave if we can get it. ... I do not want one until I can be spared, and can ask for one with a clear conscience; then it must come.* I shall go over to see Walter tomorrow, but I may not see him or Bob, for I understand that Hooker is under marching orders; we are to have a big fight here soon.

What do you think of the recent fight, the Banks expedition,[5] etc.? Poor Gwynn, who was killed at Vicksburg, I knew very well, and a greater loss we could not have sustained. I buried a man of my company this morning.

Our brother Bob now says:

January 17, 1863.

I have tried in vain to write for the past two weeks. ... We now have to keep stirring continually; reveille at six o'clock, and drill at seven; company drill at 9.30, battalion at 2.30, dress parade and guard mounting; then between, lugging water, wood, fatigue, etc., so that it gives one no chance at all.

When you think you have a chance then comes two or three days' reconnoissance, or four days' picket ... the company is so small that it takes what few there are left to do guard duty and nigger work. I am as well as usual except the rheumatism. Ever since that reconnoissance I have had repeated attacks of it. I suppose that you, upon reading that little paragraph, thought you had some idea of it,

---

[5] It's unclear which battle he's referring to. Politician and general, Nathaniel Prentice Banks (1816–1894) was appointed by Lincoln to be commander of the Department of the Gulf in December, 1863.

but I tell you, father, you can never form any idea of the awful suffering endured during those two days. If I should attempt it, I should fail.

Since then I have been on picket for four days, and was out in a tremendous rainstorm, which drenched me through, and again brought on the *rheumatiz.*

We received two letters last night from you. ... in our hard situation, no matter how cold or how tired, a letter or a bundle from home makes us happy, and fatigue and exhaustion are forgotten in the pleasure they afford us.

Old R— was a character in camp, who went to make up the sum total of our many and varied phases of human nature. He had been enlisted for our regiment when nearly sixty years of age, by some recruiting officer who ought to have been hung or dismissed from service for such an inhuman act, for it was manifest the poor old man was totally unfit for the service. On the Fredericksburg campaign he had slipped and stumbled along, and unable to keep up had been left behind, and was consequently out of the fight. On every reconnoissance, tour of picket duty, and, in fact, every march, or military service of any nature whatsoever, except ordinary camp guard, he had been found unable to perform.

Every morning at surgeon's call, he crept out of his miserable dug-out, and repaired to the hospital to get excused from duty. He spent his days in the dark, gloomy, smoky hole, never leaving it except to "fall in for soup," etc., in which he failed not. The army was a cruel place for a sick man, and worse for a man who, by reason of age, incapacity, or disability, still remained about camp, without performing his share of duty.

There was little pity, true sympathy, or commiseration, therefore, for the misfortunes of this "non-hewer of wood." The company got "down on him," and from certain men he got nothing but curses and abuse, and by them was dubbed, the "Biled Owl" "Old Hell pestle," etc.

He became thoroughly discouraged at the slow process that promised, at some future date, to release him from this dreadful life. He neglected himself, and sitting over the smoke and ashes of the small fire, which he scarcely manifested enough energy to replenish, his face became pinched, smoke-begrimed, dirty and repulsive; his hair long, tangled, and matted. Soon it was discovered that he was alive with vermin, and as the spring approached it became evident that old R— would die from nostalgia (homesickness) or lice unless something was speedily done to set him upon his feet again. A detail was made. He was carried to the creek. His head and face were "lathered and shaved," his clothes stripped from him and burnt, and he was then scrubbed from head to foot with a blacking brush, and a new, clean change of clothes placed upon him. The metamorphosis was complete, and for a week or so he was quite spruce; but he soon began to relapse into his old ways again, which so disgusted the men, that whatever pity they had entertained before was now changed into positive dislike, which soon found vent in mischief and numberless jokes. Among these was smoking him out, by dropping a blanket over the low chimney to his ranch, which always brought him out in the most hasty yet comical manner, crawling on all fours .like a crab. His favorite expression was: "Oh! thunder boys,— take k-e-e-er; " when his tormentors would set up a roar of laughter.

Another favorite trick on the poor fellow was dropping cartridges down the chimney into his fire. A puff, a dull explosion, and the agility which the old man displayed when he darted out of the low mud doorway of the shack, was remarkable. Again, watching when he was frying his pork, some deviltry-loving wag would steal up quietly and shake a lot of red pepper down the chimney, part of which going into the fire, and the rest into his fry-pan, down his neck and into his nose, would cause him to splutter, sneeze, and cough, when his tormentors would shout down, "Oh, thunder, you old dead beat, take k-e-e-er!"

The rumor at last came that his discharge papers were at brigade headquarters, and when we moved out, one bright sunny morning, for a tour of picket duty, "Old R—" had scarcely got half a. mile from camp, before he stabbed his toe, went down on his knees with his immense bureau and load of rations, was ordered back to camp, got his discharge, and we never saw him more.

Our brother Walter now writes:

January 18, 1863.

We were to move yesterday, but now it is delayed until tomorrow. We are having a real day of rest today, and we are enjoying it hugely; a fire is in the fireplace; Bob and LeRoy are frying 'flippers' (flap-jacks); Edgar is writing on the bunk; and Ed W. is quietly sleeping; our house looks quite clean, too. We are very nice for soldiers, but we don't live up to some of John R's advice, a la *Hall's Health*; it can't be done in the army; no time, no conveniences, liable to interruption, and as a whole, utterly impossible. It is wholly played out. If we move I do not know whether I shall have to shoulder a gun and 'frog it' with the company or not. The quartermaster said he wanted to keep me with him, and thought he could get me a horse, etc., but still I shall be out of my element to be thinking of Bob as under fire, and I not at his side. Rely upon it, though, all of you, that wherever I am, I shall do my whole duty, never flinching. If I go into battle again, I am in for a better chance and taller fighting than at F. If I remain behind, I shall look out for Bob most faithfully. We are certainly going to move for a fight, and Heaven only knows what will be the result.

I wish there was more confidence in Burnside among our officers; he does not seem to inspire the army like McClellan. I hope it will be a grand, successful move, and that Richmond will be the prize. Our successes are about divided elsewhere, and it seems as though we ought to give the preponderating stroke, one that shall give us the victory, amid the applause of the word.

Our brother Walter says:

January 19, 1863.

This is our last night in our winter quarters, and it may be the last chance I shall have of writing home for some time. I therefore, avail myself of this evening's leisure to speak a word or two concerning our prospects in the move now' pending. We are going for a fight, and I am reckoned in; we have bitter cold nights, and our march is to be a long one, for Hooker and Siegel are going up the river and come down upon the enemy's left flank. I have been thinking of what we shall have to endure, and lest we 'cave in' on this campaign I write just before starting. If it continues as cold as tonight, some of us will freeze while asleep, and in the approaching battle I fear some of us must fall. ... I wrote for the colonel today, and the adjutant got me to pen a paper for him. Colonel Tilton told me I would have to march with my company, as the regiment is so small; quartermaster does not like it; he says I shall have extra pay for what I have done, and when I stop at a camp he shall want me again, and will try to have me detailed; we will see about that.

Now I am in for a fight, and the Lord protect and defend any poor, miserable rebel who may happen to cross my path; if I don't settle Fredericksburg's account with him.

Good-by, dear mother; I hope it may be my lot to write again soon; sweet thoughts of Bradford days spent at home serve to cheer our lonelier hours, and make us wish more and more for the wished-for day of welcome return.

On the 20th of January, 1863, at one p. m. we again emerged from Camp Gove, and traversing the old road across the railroad at the "Switch," and by Sykes's division of regulars, made that famous "mud march " of General Burnside, winch shall go down to history, as one of the most remarkable movements ever made by the Army of the Potomac; when the bottom literally dropped out of the whole immediate country, and men floundered up to their knees in the liquid filth, and mud-puddles, which had been churned by the artillery, cavalry, and infantry of the entire command.

Rain descended by day and night. Wagons were stalled, never to be resurrected. Mules stuck fast, only to lie down and die, and were completely submerged, with ears only faintly visible over the sea of mud. Guns and caissons became inextricably confused and mixed up in their oozing beds, where they lay with the mud in the muzzles of the pieces, until the road could be corduroyed for their relief, and conveyance to a place of safety. Pontoon boats might as well have been unloaded and floated to their positions on the river's bank, where the "Johnnies," with kind invitations "to come over," tacked to the trees, were exultantly waiting for the picnic to commence.

We marched a mile or more, halted three hours, started again, marched two miles and went into camp rather disgusted at our slow progress. The plan General Burnside had in view was much the same as before described—a flanking movement, both up and down the river, one a feint; the other proved a faint before we got through. Our route was the same as in the reconnoissance, toward the fords. On the 21st, General Griffin in person roused Colonel Tilton and ordered him to get the regiment ready to march immediately. We were soon in line: and without coffee, remained for four long hours until Humphreys's and Sykes's divisions had tiled past us. The rain, which had poured in torrents during the entire night, had not ceased, but, accompanied by an east wind, penetrated and sought our bones. We marched about half a mile further, then halted in a bleak field where we made coffee and felt better. In an hour or more we again moved, going two miles further toward Hartwood church. We bivouacked in a fine old forest of oak, and got ready for the night. The way was blocked ahead. The floods descended; all was a sea above and beneath. January 20th, the provost guard struck camp and started on the "mud march," but returned on the 21st.

On the 22d, Thursday, we lay still. The one incident worth relating as occurring on this day, was the unfortunate whiskey riot. The rain was still descending in torrents. The men were chilled through and through. Under these conditions it was deemed advisable to issue the usual whiskey ration. Some of our men procured more than one ration of the ardent fluid; in fact, one or more canteens, on orders from the officers, in some cases raising the orders from one to ten until there were several canteens to each company, enough to start the noisy and quarrelsome ones. A fight commenced in one of our best companies, C, by one Murray. In attempting to quell what was at first a slight matter, the officers from other regiments came over and fanned the flames, and soon the One Hundred and Eighteenth Pennsylvania (our old friends), the Twenty-second, Second Maine and First Michigan were inextricably mingled.

It now became a Donnybrook Fair. Hit wherever a head could be seen, as it came up smiling from the depths of the clayey mire. The major of the One Hundred and Eighteenth (O'Neil) was threatening our boys with instant death if the fighting did not cease at once. He was backing up his threat with the display of two cocked six-shooters, one in each hand. This was too great a temptation for some of our whiskey-laden pugilists, one of whom stole up behind him, and sent him sprawling in the mud by a dexterous blow behind the ear. The only wonder is that the pistols did not go off and kill somebody. The giants of the Second Maine soon cleared the field, and the whiskey having given out, and the effects somewhat worn off, quiet soon reigned over the battle-ground, no more sanguinary than a few bloody noses and black eyes.

Friday, the 23d, we turned out at daybreak to corduroy the roads back to camp, under the impression that it was to enable supplies to be pushed out to us.

The sun came out on the morning of the 24th, and the commands were set in motion for their old camps, wallowing, sliding, and slipping at every step; the artillery being gathered in the next day. To describe this movement with its gloom, rain, cold, mud, and dispiriting, demoralizing, and humiliating scenes, would be beyond our power; we are content that it was a part of the history of that army in which we suffered, and that we did our entire duty there as upon the more bloody battle-fields.

Whole volumes might be written upon it, the exposure and sufferings of the men, whereby many a poor fellow laid down his life; the sea of mud; the ropes bent to the pontoon trains, artillery, caissons and limbers, in vain efforts to move them from their oozy beds; the dead mules and horses by the roadsides, more than half buried where they fell; the deluge of cold, penetrating rain that constantly soaked us to the skin.

It is beyond description; all things have their end, and, we were glad when this had its end, as we floundered and waded back again, partly over the corduroys, which we were compelled to build for our relief, especially the writer, who for not being drunk,

288

was rewarded (?) by being detailed to go into our old camp, and bring out axes to cut logs for corduroying.

It would be hard to tell which was the meanest, or, as the Western boys express it, the most ornery time the Army of the Potomac ever had, but for mud, rain, cold, whiskey drowned-out men, horses, mules, and abandoned wagons and batteries, for pure unadulterated demoralization, Kilkenny fighting and downright cussedness, this took the cake.

All these scenes have been described, drawn, and vividly painted for the new generation of military readers and students; and yet it would be hard for the boy reader of today to fully realize those scenes, or what suffering and sacrifices were endured by our brave boys, and what treasure was poured out by our country to redeem it from the curse of human slavery, and to establish the supremacy of the Union.

On the 24th, at eleven a. m., upon our return, somebody too drunk to know a road from a hole in a blanket, led us at right angles from our proper course, and we were marched by a short cut, which proved in the end a very long one, over hill and valley, through briers and brambles, and a very dense growth of saplings and scrub trees, after which we halted; but once more in motion, we kept on until about noon, when we found ourselves just one eighth of a mile from the spot we had left. After Sykes's and Humphreys's divisions had passed us, our march was resumed again on a short cut through every muddy corn-field that could be found, and within two miles of our old camp, we struck off into a cow path, exactly in the wrong direction, and again we ascended and descended. Oh! such hills as we explored; and what brooks and small streams we waded, with our wet luggage upon our broken backs, only to find ourselves about one half mile nearer our old camp than when we left the main road.

The whiskey having finally lost its grip we arrived in Camp Gove, about four p. m., and again pitched our ponchos upon the rain-soaked ground we had left five days before.

Our brother Bob says:

January 25, 1863.

I have just read your letter.

If you could only know how such letters serve to raise the drooping spirit, of your soldier brothers, you would never hesitate a moment between pleasure and writing a letter to them; and to have them come at this time of all others, when the Army of the Potomac is most despondent and discouraged, just come in from the last grand forward movement, wallowing in the mud and water, sleeping in mud, eating and drinking it; in fact for four days we have been wet through, and had to sleep so, for there has not been a dry day since we started; cannon, teams, ambulances, pontoons, everything stuck fast, and to crown all the 'rebs' are in position across the river at the ford, where we were to cross with cannon planted, etc., all ready to give us Hail Columbia when we were crossing.

Oh! the misery of this move. The men were wet, tired, hungry,- and desponding. They gave out whiskey, and the whole brigade got drunk, and got into a regular riot, or nearly that, and when a detail came for four men from our company to go into camp for axes,

I being about the only one sober, had to go. Wet and tired as I was, I waded seven miles into camp, got axes and started back, but had to stop on the way and corduroy the roads. We worked hard the next day, and then were ordered ahead to the regiment, where we arrived all used up; the next day we came into our camp, as usual on the run, and had just got our ponchos up, a fire built, and had sat down to rest, when who should come in but Sam Hopkinson.[6]

I am glad mother saw Fletcher, and enjoyed his description of our journey together; he was a first-rate man, full of life and good humor, always willing to take hold and work at anything, and I felt badly when I heard he was wounded.

If we had crossed the river you would have had a good prospect of seeing me at home, for we would have .had a great battle, and I would have been wounded, or worse, killed;....I am spared perhaps to be the victim of the next engagement; but know this one thing, that wherever my body is, there is one who never shirked from the

---

[6] Sam Hopkinson was a Bradford resident, 32 years old at the outbreak of war. Apparently he did not serve (census records, 2019).

fight, and if Walt is not with me by my side, I will do my best, and fight alone, although it is hard for me to have him away. He has been for the second time promoted, this time to be sergeant-major of the regiment. Tell mother I suffered badly from the rheumatism on the last march, and as to being careful about getting cold, it is out of the question; you can't wade through mud and water in a cold rain storm, sleep in woods, raining all night and the next day; sleep in wet blankets the next night, then sweat under a load that a good sized jackass can't begin to carry; have to wade into camp 'double quick,' and yet be careful about getting cold; neither will all the medicines that ever were given cure one, for as soon as he is well of it, he has to go right through the same performance, and the most discouraging thing about it is, that it never seems to be of any good.

This army Seems to be fated: if I could only sit right down with father, and talk to him, I could soon-convince him, and let him into the reasons of the failure of the Army of the Potomac, but paper will not suffice ... I don't think we shall move from here for some time; the army is demoralized to a great extent, and something will have to be done to restore order in it before it moves again; they have no confidence in Burnside.

Burnside was relieved. Hooker assumed command. We were better fed, better clothed, desertions grew less frequent, furloughs were granted in homeopathic doses; grumbling was reduced to a minimum.

The president wrote his famous letter[7] to General Hooker, and visited the army. Inspections, reviews, and discipline were the

---

[7] Executive Mansion
Washington, January 26, 1863

Major General Hooker:
General.

I have placed you at the head of the Army of the Potomac. Of course I have done this upon what appear to me to be sufficient reasons. And yet I think it best for you to know that there are some things in regard to which, I am not quite satisfied with you. I believe you to be a brave and a skilful soldier, which, of course, I like. I also believe you do not mix politics with your profession, in which you are right. You have confidence in yourself, which is a valuable, if not an indispensable quality. You are ambitious, which, within reasonable bounds, does good

order of the day. The army picketed nearly forty miles of line on its front, it is said. We thought sometimes it must have been eighty. Our brigade line was between Hartwood Church, and Stafford Court House, near "Stafford Corner." Several times we marched nearly seven miles in cold, wet snow storms, which soon soaked us through, and with slush and mud half up to our knees, and after wading several deep brooks, with our papery flimsy shoes, we arrived4 at the picket posts, in anything but an enviable condition of body, or cheerful frame of mind, to perform such important duties. We wore out the nights about the huge, sparkling, white oak log tires, at the picket reserve, with our backs arched up, to shed the fast falling snow, roasting our faces and freezing our backs. Lost in a protracted deliberation, whether we

---

rather than harm. But I think that during Gen. Burnside's command of the Army, you have taken counsel of your ambition, and thwarted him as much as you could, in which you did a great wrong to the country, and to a most meritorious and honorable brother officer. I have heard, in such way as to believe it, of your recently saying that both the Army and the Government needed a Dictator. Of course it was not for this, but in spite of it, that I have given you the command. Only those generals who gain successes, can set up dictators. What I now ask of you is military success, and I will risk the dictatorship. The government will support you to the utmost of its ability, which is neither more nor less than it has done and will do for all commanders. I much fear that the spirit which you have aided to infuse into the Army, of criticising their Commander, and withholding confidence from him, will now turn upon you. I shall assist you as far as I can, to put it down. Neither you, nor Napoleon, if he were alive again, could get any good out of an army, while such a spirit prevails in it.

And now, beware of rashness. Beware of rashness, but with energy, and sleepless vigilance, go forward, and give us victories.

Yours very truly
Abraham. Lincoln

(*Collected Works of Abraham Lincoln*, Basler et al.)

Hooker told reporter Noah Brooks "That is just such a letter as a father might write to his son. It is a beautiful letter, and, although I think he was harder on me than I deserved, I will say that I love the man who wrote it."

would take our chances on the slushy, sloppy, mire-trodden ground, with the rest of the curiously hunched-up, blanketed forms in that picket-circle, or "take it out," in "pinning down the log" until time to go on post again.

Or, after being conducted by the corporal along the dark, gloomy forest path to the edge of the timber, we were posted for two or four hours. We strove to chew the cud of bitter reflection, nurse up our patriotism and, after trying the red-pepper scheme in our stockings, to keep us awake, briskly moved up and down the beat, pinching ourselves to establish our identity. Vainly did we try to throw off our imaginative minds, during the cold, gray hours of the early morning, the groups of stumps in the open space between the lines, that had so often assumed the shapes of men, and bug-a-boos to our bewildered eyes. Such was the dark side of our picket duties, during the winter of 1862-3.

Our brother Walter writes:

Sunday Evening,

January 26, 1863.

I am just back from Gene's headquarters. ... I learned upon my arrival in camp that I am promoted to the berth of sergeant-major of the Twenty-second Massachusetts regiment. I wrote to Gene from his camp today, and he will probably get it before you get this, and will hear from that about our last move. In getting my pass signed at headquarters, I was somewhat surprised to see Horatio Staples' name signed A. A. A. General; I inquired and was shown the individual, and behold it was the old Portland boy a first-lieutenant in the Second Maine regiment. I am writing with no candle light.

January 30.

When I got back to camp I was accosted with many congratulations and salutations of our noble little tent's crew, in regard to my promotion, which was read on dress parade during my absence.

I was ordered to report that very evening to the adjutant, with no instructions as to my duties, etc.

Our quartermaster said to me when congratulating me upon my good luck 'brains are wanted besides.' Our surgeon said to me yesterday: 'I am glad you got promoted. When I first saw you I thought you would be higher than a private soon. I can tell a man at first sight,' said he. I have an easy berth as soon as I know my business; I assist the adjutant at all times, guard mounting, dress parade, etc.; do all the detailing, and do writing in the office. I rank all the non-commissioned officers, and live with the non-commissioned staff; we live pretty well. I have been out on guard mounting several times; the first time I made several blunders and was a little nervous; the regiment en masse almost, turned out to see the new sergeant-major perform. .. I found it a little hard to use a sword gracefully, but I improve daily.

The regiment is out on picket, and the snow is eight inches deep; they will doubtless have a hard time of it, not taking their ponchos, which are fast to the log huts. I pity poor Bob, and think of him continually; trust to it, his lot shall be easier in the future; good cheer awaits him on his return; I will have a warm fire in his tent, and will contrive to have bread, butter and doughnuts on hand. .. I am so glad that Gene is at home.

I send a paragraph in regard to our late move; I have no time to describe our hardships in that stick in the mud. .. Hooker is now in command; now for a move: I only wish he was a great general; his fighting qualities would do great things for us. I fear he will be rash.

January 31

Bob is just in from picket, and he with the rest of the boys reports a hard time; they have been out in all the storm, and the mud mixed with snow has been almost unendurable. They took no Tents with them, and the first night were awake, sitting beside fires up to their knees in snow and mud. The second night they were on post, and third (last) night, was passed very comfortably by them.

Yesterday they sent in word for some rations, being all out of grub. I sent Bob some coffee, sugar, hard and soft bread, butter, cheese, doughnuts and pork, with two boiled potatoes; he seemed so thankful for it upon coming in. I had a nice fire for them, plenty of wood cut, and we are going to be happy tonight.

You want to know about the forward movement, and how we are on account of it; I have already written about it briefly, perhaps as extended as it deserves. We suffered from mud and wet and as usual were defeated in our plans; it is so discouraging to us raw recruits. Still I have faith in the ultimate success of the Army of the Potomac, and when I consider your words of truth in regard to the outside pressure brought to bear upon this army, I must say that the army is terribly deceived; the men do not understand; they do not look ahead. They are discouraged, and forget to reason in love of self. I am still confident; I can seem to see a light beaming way ahead through this deep darkness; I am sure we will yet win.

General Hooker is now in command, and truly, father, I have more faith in him than in Burnside, for he doesn't acknowledge himself incompetent, but asserts that he can whip them all out and out. He doesn't wish the people to think of him as 'Fighting Joe Hooker,' a dashing, *harum scarum*, foolhardy fighter, but would have them trust in him as a wise and able general. Hurrah for him, I say, and on to victory!

If he can make the grand division plan work better than Burnside did, then I am in for it; but, after all, the true Napoleonic plan of thorough detail ill the commander's knowledge is the best.

Poor Burnside! what a pity it is that he couldn't have retired upon his Newbern and Antietam laurels, instead of being permitted to spoil his good name for a general in the late disaster; but history will accord to him his rightful due, that lie was a noble man, and did the best he could, and only went down when he was overwhelmed by a position lie could not fill.

We all wait now for future events, and the horizon casts its shadow before. May everything be full of glory for our country. I only hope this army may be fortunate in the future. .. Tonight we are to be paid off, and the camp is in a jubilee.

Saturday night.—We have just been paid off for almost three months, up to the first of November, and your letter to Bob, with enclosed letter from Senator Sumner, has been handed him.

'In view of all things,' we are 'gay and happy still.' 'Now let the wide world wag as it will.'

... Tell Gene we still prosper.

Our brother of the artillery now writes:

Fort Tillinghast,

February 1, 1863.

I have neglected writing you for some time. . If I had been sick and unable to write, Lewis would have informed you, so I knew you would not worry on that account. I have had a very bad cold for the past two or three weeks, and I cough myself almost to death, but I hope to be better soon if this mud dries up. I have not had dry feet for three weeks, for when you step out of a tent the mud and water is knee deep, so you can judge what beautiful times we are having; but I suppose it is nothing to what poor Wall and Bob have to endure. I am so glad that Walter is so much liked in the regiment, and that there is a prospect of his being promoted; he is, and always was a good boy, and deserves it. We have recently received our pay for four months, where they owed us seven; this is the way we have been served. We lost everything we had when we advanced, and on our return had to draw everything over again, even to knapsacks. It is a custom to settle our clothing account every year, and we settled last July; but this year an order came out for us to settle every quarter, and all this extra clothing was deducted from our pay. Soldiering is a gay life! I suppose I have to draw a new dress coat, as the rats with which our tents are swarming, gnawed the collar off mine a night or two since. I have had such a cold that I have not been on duty lately, and consequently have not needed it, but it will not do to come out without any collar on my coat.

I had rather a thousand times be in the field (I have changed my mind), than where we are now, for the officers have nothing to do, are continually fighting among themselves and 'issuing orders' to the men.

There have been about a dozen resignations of officers in the regiment during the past month, all on account of our new colonel, who is very unpopular with both officers and men. Have you heard from Gene lately, and when do you expect him home? When I last heard from him he thought of starting soon, but letters I received, said that he had not yet arrived; he promised to call on me.

You should see the jackass that Lewis got; he is a fine animal. Do you think there is any prospect of the war closing within a year?

It has commenced to rain again, and I have to pass another night in a wet bunk, for our tents are old and leak badly. It is not now as it was last winter, for then we had good quarters. There are two companies at the fort commanded by a major, and the officers need a good deal of room, consequently we have to suffer.

Our brother Bob now says:

February 2, 1863.

Since Walt has been promoted, I miss him. .. We have always been together on marches and on picket, doubling-blankets, etc. .. he is up to headquarters about all the time, so I see little of him compared to what I did. I had just returned from four days' picket duty in a tough snow storm when your first letter, enclosing mother's, came, and sweaty, and plastered with mud, I sat down to read them. We had a hard time on picket, as you must imagine; we marched seven miles in a cold, wet snow storm, which soon wet us through, and the mud was awful; the only way I can describe it was that we waded in running, sloshy mud up to our knees, and also waded one or two brooks, and then to make ourselves comfortable for the night, went into the woods and chopped wood, started a fire, and cold and wet, and snowing like the 'Old Nick.' We sat up all night with the snow on our backs two inches thick; we would get up and shake, then resume our seats: quite a picture. The next day we got quite decently dry, after which a soldier can keep quite comfortable with a rousing fire.

You were quite right in supposing us in the last 'forward movement;' mud and rain were predominant, but as I have described it pretty well in K's letter, and the papers also give a pretty good account of it, I will not attempt it again; we had a rough time. I send a good description of a soldier on the march; it is pretty good. you were mistaken in my meaning when you thought that I said the papers bragged about our defeat at Fredericksburg; I was speaking with reference to our reconnoissance, and said that the papers bragged about our regiment performing it so well and so quickly, etc. We hate to have them do so as it reminds us too forcibly of the sufferings we had to undergo to accomplish it. .. I get into discussions very often at the guard house and elsewhere. .. Such a demoralized set they, the old ones, were after the battle you never saw, and they would talk about laying down their arms, and were disloyal; I would do all I could to discourage it, and even get them '*huffy*'; they would say: 'You d—d two hundred dollar men can well afford to talk patriotism to us; you have not seen as much as we have.' Yet, mind you, they all say they have not suffered so much as they have in the past three months, all owing to the winter campaign.

When I write home to you, I don't mean it in a grumbling way, but to describe to the best of my ability, our marches, movements, etc. It is as you say, the new ones have, to a great extent, caught the spirit, and it is awful discouraging to see the undercurrent at work, if you were only here to see it all; cheating by the quartermaster, the drunken officers, removal of the generals, etc. .. We have had more to discourage us than, most of them; I have crossed two rivers to fight, and had to leave in a hurry.

Yet I am willing to try 'Johnny' again. .. If they would only stop this quarreling among the cabinet and politicians at home, hang off a few traitors like Wood, Seymour, Van Buren & Co., and take hold with a will to help the president and army, then the boys would feel encouraged; but they know that is what is pulling back the Army of the Potomac, therefore they do feel despondent, and some of them grumble considerably. . I hear that Burnside has been removed; also Franklin and Sumner; Hooker takes command, Meade the (grand) division, and Griffin the corps; they better stop such fooling. .. We were paid three months' pay night before last at midnight, (by Paymaster Holman). .. with the paymaster comes the sutler, who is in camp as large as can be. I have just been out on dress parade; Joe Hooker is in command of the Army of the Potomac; look out for great things. As it is getting gun time and wood time I will close.

Our brother Walter says:

February 5, 1863.

Bob went to Acquia Creek yesterday on a detail, and on the cars he met a Mrs. Eaton[8] of Portland (nurse in the army hospital), accompanied by a Mr. Hayes of Portland, agent for a soldiers' society. They both knew you, and her son, Frank E., and Bob and myself went to school together. .. The adjutant's clerk has gone to Boston for twelve days, and I am acting with my other duties; I am busy from morning till late at night, and my only time now is to write after all are abed and asleep, a custom I got pretty well used to last winter. It is now after twelve at night and I have written in great haste.

---

[8] This may have been Elizabeth Eaton of Bath and her son Frank E. Eaton the writer is referring to.—2019

298

Let me assure you that Bob is well, and the storm did not totally use him up. He went to bed last night with a headache, but this morning is all right. Edgar H. is somewhat sick, and off duty, excused by the surgeon. Calvin S. Mixter,[9] adjutant's clerk, whose place I am now filling, will probably call upon you at the senate chamber; I asked him to, and he partly promised to. .. He is a very nice man and was formerly engaged on some Boston newspaper. .. You can't imagine how pleased we were to get your picture.

Volumes could be filled with reminiscences of this, that and other duties, during that long, trying winter of picket guard, and fatigue; of the debating society, pleasant sings, either in our own tent, or serenading the officers, visiting our friends in the regiments of other corps, etc.

Many boxes were received, and also the barrel, which, after three months of trials and tribulations on the road, looked when opened, as though there had been a free fight, everything turned loose, and the package of red pepper, which had unfortunately been packed with turkey, pies, and other good things, had come out first-best, for it was liberally sprinkled over all.

Our brother has been appointed quartermaster of the Eighth Infantry, but he still retained command of "G" company, February 8th, 1863, and during the temporary absence of Captain R— he commanded the regiment, and received news that his name had been sent into the senate, for confirmation as a brevet captain, for distinguished services on the Peninsula campaign.

His company was about the 25th of March selected as General Hooker's body guard, and the following order published to the regiment:

"This company was selected by the commanding general, because of its fine appearance and the soldierly bearing of the men, when last inspected, and the commanding officer accepts the selection, as a compliment to the company, and sincerely

---

[9] Lieutenant Calvin Symmes Mixter (1832–1911) worked in the census office in Boston after the war.—2019

hopes that the reputation earned may be retained, and that by a strict performance of every duty, this company will prove itself second to no other in the army, not only in point of appearance, but in every respect that constitutes a good company.

By order of

Captain E. W. H. Read, (Signed) John N. Andrews, First-Lieutenant Eighth Infantry Adjutant

He applied to be relieved from the command, as his duties were really more than he could perform, but the commanding general would not listen to it, and gave him the highly personal compliment of saying that he "wanted him with his company."

We visited our brother often, and whenever possible he dashed up to our little hillside camp, on his dapple gray horse, and after a short stop, again disappeared like a flash over the hills towards Falmouth. On one of our visits we witnessed the parade of the regulars, which we had never seen before, and watched with envious eye the sharp, simultaneous click of their guns, as they executed the manual of arms, and wondered if our regiment would ever approach such perfection of dress, equipment, drill and absolute discipline, or if we would ever command a company of regulars.

Although in our soldier blouses, and oftentimes hard up for money and good clothes, the courtesy of the officers was as marked, their treatment was as kind and considerate, as though we belonged to their own immediate military family, and we never wanted for a decided increase in our rations, or change in diet, from the sow belly and hard tack of our volunteer camp.

April 4th President Lincoln, Mrs. Lincoln and "Tad" were at General Hooker's headquarters. Monday, April 6th, at ten o'clock, all officers at headquarters were invited to a reception for the president. About forty attended. The president was very sociable and agreeable to all, and with some he joked a little.

Again on April 14th, General Fogliardi, a Swedish general, reviewed our division; was at headquarters April 27th and sauntering over to where the band was playing its sweetest airs, he conversed with all, and upon finishing a cigar, our youthful minds intent upon securing relics, we obtained that cigar stub for future historical reference and pleasure.

Our letters of the 22d'of April, in describing a visit to our brother, speak of General Fogliardi's coming over to his (our brother's) tent, and that "Halleck, Stanton, and the president were at General Hooker's headquarters."

Our brother's letters say:

April 27th.

They (the boys) were over to spend the day with me a week ago; saw parade, heard the band of the Eighth Infantry play in front of the line of officers' tents, and saw General Fogliardi (who strolled over from headquarters to hear the music). The general seemed to be very much pleased with everything he saw and heard. He spoke German with Captain Kimball of General Patrick's staff, and French with someone else. He gave me a very fine Swiss cigar, the stub of which I gave to Bob as a relic. Secretary Seward and ladies, the Swiss and Prussian ministers are here: our band serenaded them last night; they review the Third Corps tomorrow; Dan Sickles commands it.

On the 7th of April we fell in about twelve o'clock, for review by the president. We stacked arms on the parade, and waited until two p. m., when he rode by accompanied by General Hooker and bodyguard, and a large staff of officers. We gave him three cheers. He looked careworn and anxious, and we thought there must be a heap of trouble on the old man's mind.

On this day the Fifth corps was reviewed by the president. Whether intentionally or inadvertently, Mr. Lincoln had been furnished with a small, pony built horse about fourteen hands high. The president's legs looked longer than ever, and his toes seemed almost to touch the ground. He wore the same solemn suit of black that he always assumed, a tall, silk hat, a little the worse for wear, with a long, full-skirted black coat.

He had neglected to strap down his pant legs while riding, and, as most of the time he was kept at a jog trot, his pants began to draw up until finally, first one white drawers leg, then the other, began to be conspicuous, with strings dangling. The hard trot had settled his tall beaver hat on the back of his head, until it had rested upon his ears, which were large and somewhat projecting, and it looked as though it had been purposely jammed down into that position. Altogether he presented a very comical picture, calculated to provoke laughter along the entire length of the lines, had it not been for that sad, anxious face, so full of melancholy foreboding, that peered forth from his shaggy eyebrows. He rode remarkably well, i. e., with a wonderfully good seat, but with a loose, swaying, undulating movement, peculiar to the Western circuit rider, whom one might see riding from town to town about that period.

The next day it was pleasant but cold. We were ordered into line at eight a. m., and after marching about four miles from camp, reached the plain opposite Fredericksburg, in plain sight of the rebel camps, where we were to be reviewed by General Hooker, prior to the opening spring campaign.

After General Hooker took command, we were in a semi-state of moving for some time. Reviews and inspections were very frequent, of a division, a brigade, perhaps a corps, and finally on the 8th of April, the grand review of the Army of the Potomac, at which the president and little "Tad" Lincoln were present.

The army had been looking forward to this for some time, and great preparations had been made for a fine display. For several days large parties had been busy with spade, pick and shovel, levelling, filling ditches, removing stumps and stones, cutting down ridges and draining puddles, until the country was more level than the inhabitants had ever seen it before. Stakes, with the corps badges to designate the positions of the various corps, were planted. The moving masses gathered, the flags grew more numerous, and the sounds of bands and drum-corps were mixed up.

The men impatiently waited in the bitter, stinging cold, .until their fingers grew numb. The wind swept across the open space. The horses grew restless but finally a salute from the guns of a battery announced the approach of the president, and he soon appeared, mounted upon a horse, which seemed to us, several sizes too small for his long, gaunt figure.

He was followed by a large and brilliant staff, all the regular officers about headquarters helping swell the number. Our brother was there, and in vain did we strain our eyes, as much as we dared to in ranks, to catch a glimpse of his dapple-gray.

As the president rode along the lines, the flags were dipped, the bands played "Hail to the Chief," and the bugle and drum corps sounded off. The corps were then reviewed separately, the men in the meantime stamping their feet, and thrashing their hands to keep warm. The batteries passed first, then the infantry in column of divisions. It was a beautiful sight, this military pageant of over a hundred thousand veteran soldiers passing by in a steady stream. Hours went by. The sunlight and shadow chased each other over the plain. In the distance were the camps, mile upon mile of log huts, the spires of Fredericksburg, the batteries beyond and the shining river.

When the light caught upon the bayonet tips, and flashed over flags and numerous equipments, as regiment after regiment, and brigade after brigade, swept by in endless procession, one could hardly refrain from dwelling with wondering eye, upon such a beautiful fairy-like scene. The uniforms were clean, rifles bright, and everything indicated the pride which that perfectly organized army felt in presenting to the president, especially after the discouragements it had been subjected to, only the best side of the thoroughly disciplined soldier.

The drums and bands kept up their ceaseless music, and the light still danced among the moving columns. But at last, the rearmost regiment came, dipped its flag and disappeared. The immense cavalcade of officers and orderlies, rode slowly back to camp.

The magnificent spectacle was over. It was full of bright visions, splendid groupings, wonderful effects, rarely seen in a man's lifetime, never forgotten by the Army of the Potomac. What must have been the thoughts of the president, as he glanced along the almost interminable lines of bronzed faces, and knew that in a few days they were to go forth to the blood and carnage of Chancellorsville.

Our letters say:

We have been reviewed by President Lincoln today; the whole infantry force of the Army of the Potomac was drawn up on the plain before Fredericksburg and a magnificent sight it was; over one hundred thousand men on review. Abraham looks poorly;... thin and in bad health ... he is to all outward appearances much careworn, and anxiety is fast wearing him out, poor man, I could but pity as I looked at him, and remembered the weight of responsibility resting upon his burdened mind; what an ordeal he has passed through, and what is yet before him! All I can say is, Poor Abe! with faith still good in the honest man.

Our brother at headquarters says:

President Lincoln and wife are here, and there is no end of reviews for him; day before yesterday he reviewed about 15,000 cavalry; today he reviewed 75,000 infantry, and the reserve artillery. I rode around with his escort both times, and I got pretty tired of it today for it was bitter cold.

Many letters were written from this camp, all of them are full of patriotic ring, but the limits of these papers will only admit of brief extracts.

When we do move, bones will crack like hailstones. Your letter to Bob made the dimples come upon his cheeks. .. you make him a special subject of exhortation in this letter. I don't know but what he needs it. Stouter hearts than his quail, and firmer lips tremble when hardships have to be borne. .. No one in the family is second to our noble Bob in true patriotic principle. . . I know your words will do him good and that you will yet have reason to be prouder still of your youngest boy. .. Where has George B. seen enough of duty; where has his coward blood been made to boil at the sight of blood, and dead comrades butchered, when no revenge or redress could be had? What one of his companions would crawl in the dishonored path to get his discharge? I answer for all of our heroic little band, not one! and thereby nail the lie to his foolish declaration. We shall

all hail our nation's deliverance, and ours in the day of our triumph, and in your words and your meaning, would crawl home on our hands and knees for the result, viz.: our country's freedom, and our discharge as a consequence. But we would not accept our discharge today, and thereby escape our duty, and belie our oath, and loyal endeavors towards the chief end of the war, a restoration of the Union; we think the pleasures of home would scarcely repay us for the dishonor we should get for our choice, and the sting of our consciences at abandoning outposts. We know our way is hard, though we do not transgress, and all long to get home. But, I say, never will I leave the field while I can stand, until all be fulfilled.

We stand on our honor still, and plighted our vows are to our nation's defense, and you may never doubt that our courage is firm, and our faith in the final success is perfect: we will do our noble duty.

Our brother Eugene says:

I think of riding over to see Walter and Bob tomorrow; they are noble boys, and I hope and trust that the God of battles will spare their lives. The roads are drying up rapidly, and we will soon be on the move. I send you a photograph of my tentmate, Lieutenant Andrews, adjutant of the regiment.

I was out Friday for the first time, and the day before our division was reviewed by Generals Meade and Griffin, and General Hooker happened around as a spectator. We have been ordered to be ready at a moment's notice to move, and the commands have been deprived of the usual system of passes and furloughs at present; all our ladies in the army have been ordered away from the army, and they leave by special boat tomorrow (March 30) from Acquia Creek to Washington; everything betokens a move.

Our letters continue:—

Last night (April 1st), we had a terrible snow and rain storm. I woke up early in the morning, long before reveille, and found my blanket wet through, and myself in a puddle of water, where the weight of snow had caused the ponchos to sink, and the water to sink through instead of running off; I had to sit up in the cold for four hours. .. We have some idea that the Fifth Corps will be left here to guard this railroad, for our transportation wagons have been turned in to division headquarters.

When will this mad handed demon of war cease its rage? Will the tearful showers upon the home altars never quench his bloody appetite? Shall we ever see the sacred walls of home again; when will time answer?

You can't imagine how beautifully they have fixed up brigade headquarters; everyone says it is the most tasty camp in the army. In front it is one wall of evergreens, with arches and small entrances; back of it a large, open space of ground, laid out in gravel walks, lined with evergreen borders, and all sorts of devices are represented by evergreen on the ground, then another fence of evergreen, with openings to every officer's tent behind, Colonel Barnes, (now brigadier general) in front.... Bob is on division guard (April 5th) for three days.

Our brother at headquarters writes:

April 9th

Why is it that the country permits old Joe to remain here so long? McClellan started out of Washington one month before this, and then they accused him of being too slow; if McClellan had command of this army now, he could not rest; the politicians would meddle and overthrow all of his plans. The army is now in very fine condition, and I believe there is no army in the world that can stand against it in an open field: but what can we do? The rebels will retreat to Richmond; we will follow, and when we get to their fortifications, we will be all broken down with fatigue, and disorganized generally. We can never do anything until there is sure cooperation; we should make several attacks at the same time. Charleston, Mobile, Savannah, Vicksburg, and Richmond should all be attacked at the same time; we are bound to win somewhere, and we must follow up our victory. My opinion is that when Hooker does move, he will go very rapidly, and if the rebels will only stand a fight, he will cut their entire army to pieces. I went over to see the boys a few days ago; I dined with their lieutenant colonel, major, and adjutant. I was in W. last week for a few days; returned Sunday night.

Letters from our brother Eugene on the 12th of April, and our own on the 14th, say:

The entire cavalry move tomorrow; we will follow soon. We move very light: I may have to take all I possess on my horse.

306

April 14th

Just got orders to move with eight days rations, and 60 rounds of ammunition; we have got to pack our eatables, hard bread, pork, coffee, and sugar (farewell to good living now), and are limited to clothing in our knapsacks; we are surely off now. .. I don't know when I shall write again, but for Bob and myself, let me say in closing words, that although we shall not expose ourselves needlessly, yet we shall do our duty. Love to dear mother, and tell her not to be so sorrowful over our coming hardships, but say to her to be firm in the faith that her sons are safe, and never harbor a thought that a bullet may crush many hopes; think of us always, as in health, and flushed with victory; think of us as full of love for home, and always endeavoring to be happy on the march how often I think of you all on the tramp, and in the bivouac . and now with firm resolves to do our duty, let me assure you that every means possible shall be used for our comfort, and all the generalship I possess shall be displayed; we will show you now our enduring powers, and I want you to think always that we are doing well. Good-by, and may we all meet again before many days.

Our brother in the defences of Washington says:

April 15th, 1863

The Twenty-fifth Maine have left us, and I think they will have to meet the 'greybacks' before their term of enlistment expires, the latter part of June. This morning a large force of infantry left our vicinity to join Hooker, I suppose to take the place of the Ninth Corps which has gone to the Southwest. Poor Walt and Bob will soon have to be under fire again; and God grant they may escape unharmed; yet, I feel that it would be almost a miracle if they escape.

The defences of Washington are growing stronger every day; thousands of workmen being employed in digging rifle pits, and throwing up intrenchments. I really wish the 'rebs' would give us a call some day; they would *find slaughter pens* to their hearts' content. Our men can strike a target at 1,200 yards, with a thirty-two pounder more than half the time. You can imagine the execution we could do if a body of men should approach us.

Our letters of April 18th say:

307

I hardly thought I should have time to write you again from this camp, but it seems that 'Joe' Hooker has got stuck in the mud. We have had rain continually, while the orders to move have been pending, and the state of the roads, even now while pleasant, is shocking; we shall probably move in a day or two; everything is packed up for a start.

He says again April 27th:

Patience is a great virtue, and 'Uncle Joe' has had his tried to the utmost. Sometimes he is a little cross, but the greater portion, of the time he is very serene.

For the last two days the weather has been perfectly beautiful, and the roads are drying up very rapidly; but it has been raining night and day for the past two weeks; we have been ready to move three or four times, but have been prevented by the elements. .. We have been here so long that camp life seems a little stale to me; I want to be on the road; the excitement of marching, bivouacking, and battles I like, and would be perfectly contented to always live in this way, were it not for the anxiety I feel for Walter and Bob. The possession of Richmond, Vicksburg, and all their seaport towns, would not atone for the death of one of them; my patriotism is not that great. I would willingly give my own life to save my country, but not the life of one of my brothers. April 27th Secretaries Seward, Stanton, and Montgomery Blair[10] visited General Hooker and had a long conference with him.

Effort after effort had been made to start on the new campaign, but the elements had as often objected, and we remained in our camps putting on the finishing touches. The Army of the Potomac was never in a finer condition mentally, physically, or morally, than when about to start upon the campaign of Chancellorsville. The weather was now beautiful.

The mud had dried, the roads were now passable. The *esprit de corps* of the whole army, excellent.

---

[10] Montgomery Blair (1813–1883), Postmaster General. The Blairs were an influential family and friends of Lincoln. Francis Preston Blair (1791–1876) was portrayed by Hal Holbrook in Spielberg's 2012 movie, *Lincoln*. The Blair's home on Lafayette Square by the White House still stands and is used as a presidential guest house.—2019

As the dreaded "Pack up" call sounded in our ears, and we stripped the ponchos from the roofs of our old huts, we moved out of our winter quarters on the 27th of April, never expecting to behold them again, but with a certain sense of relief from the winter's inaction, of joy to be making some movement for what we fully believed was to be the crushing blow of the Rebellion. Our confidence in "Joe" Hooker was strong. Our hopes of victory were stronger.

Even the most doubtful skeptic would have pronounced that bronzed-faced, well-disciplined, well-fed and well-clothed column of men a model army, and our steps towards the old familiar roads on that day were elastic and buoyant, and our frame of mind cheerful. The Army of the Potomac was at its high-water mark. But who can tell what a day may bring forth?

At a moment's notice, loaded with our blankets, ammunition, etc., we moved towards the fords of the Rappahannock. Wagons had been cut down to a minimum; officers were required to carry their blankets and baggage on pack mules, led by the buglers and drummers, and all had to carry three-day rations in haversacks, and five in knapsacks. This was a new wrinkle in the many strange experiments that had been tried to test our patience and powers of endurance.

We bivouacked near Hartwood Church the first night, and on the 28th about two miles from Kelly's Ford, near Morrisville. It came hard. We were soft from our long rest in camp, the day was hot, and the march was about eighteen miles.

The roads were lined with stragglers and the ground was covered with the cast-off clothing of the overloaded men. We crossed at Kelly's Ford about 8 A. M. on the 29th; then shortly afterwards Mountain Run, after a rapid march, the latter part forced, which caused much straggling, with the usual expressive language. Our division (Griffin's) had the advance, and our brigade (Barnes') led the corps.

309

General Meade, commanding the corps, was instructed to "exercise all your accustomed zeal and devotion in hastening the passage of the troops across the Rappahannock; he feels assured you will. It is a great object to effect the passage of the Rapidan tomorrow, as you well know, and in so doing, the United States ford will be uncovered, and our communications established with the left wing of the army. *** Use your cavalry, and send them well out to bring you timely information. *** Would it not be well to detach a division to seize the fords?"

After crossing Mountain Run our clothes were wet, heavy, and bedraggled; the roads were heavy and the mud pasty and slippery; each step loaded our shoes, and, as the pace increased and the march was now made without halts, it soon began to tell upon the column with exhausting effect. Word was sent ahead to General Barnes that the men were falling out in squads, entirely unable to keep up with the rapid gait, now almost a double quick. Barnes sent word back that celerity was necessary, his object being to seize the bluffs on the opposite bank before the enemy, as it would save us a battle.

We reached the Rapidan, at Ely's Ford,[1] just before dark, in a light rain, but just in time to hastily seize the opposite bank. Slight skirmishing ensued between our advance and the rebel skirmishers. Some prisoners were captured, and while halted in the sunken road, stripping and preparing to ford the river, they passed through our open ranks, not, however, without a slight sprinkling of chaff between the downcast, sulky looking Johnnies and our principal wags.

It was an ugly place for a fight, and even the most thickheaded constitutional grumblers in our ranks soon saw the necessity for the rapid and exhausting march of that afternoon. It saved a battle for possession of the ford.

Having cleared the ford, the majority stripped, made a small, compact bundle of their clothes, cartridge boxes, etc., and

---

[1] Ely's Ford on the Rapidan River is only four miles from the Chancellorsville battlefield.—2019

running their rifles under the knot, and holding all above or upon their heads, just as it was fairly dark we forded the Rapidan, the water being, nearly to our arm-pits, with a swift current.

Cavalry was deployed below the ford, to catch any that might be swept from their feet. A few drummer boys only had to be rescued, and by midnight all were across. We bivouacked, without tents, upon the slopes of the abrupt banks or bluff. We had scarcely resumed our clothes, made all snug for the night by the fires, and were comfortably rolled up in our blankets asleep, when it commenced raining again, and by daybreak of the 30th we were soaked.

Early on the morning of the 30th we were astir, and at 7 A. M., floundering out in column, were at once inextricably mixed with the red sea of sacred soil. Many who had thus far clung to their knapsacks now began to chafe and curse in their distress and exhaustion incident to wet clothes and soaked blankets, and had scarcely proceeded a mile before, notwithstanding repeated warnings, they began to throw off their loads, many pitching their knapsacks with their loads of precious food into the mud, and the hurrying column stumbling over them soon sank them deep in the liquid wallow holes.

A mile or two farther on we moved into the right of the road, loaded, recapped our pieces, and shortly after, slowly feeling our way along with our sharpshooters in the advance, came to the clearing at the "Bullock" or "White House," where the enemy had some earthworks thrown up. Our cavalry advance skirmished lightly; we formed lines of battle in the dense thickets, and about 11 o'clock swept up the slope at the Chancellor House,[2] and halted in the open space on the left of the Ely's Ford Road. We were the first troops in the clearing. Our position was just across the

---

[2] Chancellorsville was not a town, but an intersection where the Chancellor family lived. A house was constructed about 1816 and occasionally functioned as an Inn for travelers on the busy Orange Turnpike. The building burned during the battle. The family rebuilt the house, but it burned in 1927. Archaeologists found and marked the outline of the original house (National Park Service website, 2019).

turnpike, and 100 yards southeast of the house. Our halt was brief. Some of the men made coffee. No other troops were to be seen.

We pushed out on the old Fredericksburg turnpike, crossed the branches of Golin Run, and further on met the enemy in earthworks (part of Anderson's division, "Stonewall" Jackson's corps) near the Zoan Church, preparing to give us battle. We were soon counter-marched and, moving back over the same road, went through a part of Sykes Division and the 12th Corps, just arrived.

We passed the Chancellor House again, and toward dark took our position on the left of the line in a piece of dense woods near the Bank's Ford Road. Friday morning, May 1, the famous order, "bagging the enemy," etc., was read to us by the Adjutant.

The bright sun beamed down upon us through the trees. The trilling of thousands of songsters made the woods ring, and the leaves, already burst from the buds, completed a charming picture in nature. We all thought, however, that the bag would prove to have a rubber string, and so expressed ourselves.

But as we moved out to the inspiring sound of Sykes' guns, now heard on the old turnpike on our right and front, we felt cheerful and ready for the worst. We soon passed a deserted camp, the huts still standing. A man of the Second Maine picked up in this camp a small rubber portfolio, and finding several photographs inside, one with the name of Walter Carter, some man nearby recognized the name. It was reported to the Major of his regiment, and then to our Colonel, and soon my brother was in possession of seven photographs, lost on Sunday, December 14, from his blouse pocket at Fredericksburg.

There were about twenty-five in the case when lost, but his joy and gratitude at the almost miraculous recovery of even these were very great. It was one of the singular incidents in our war experience.[3] Our brother at headquarters says: Camp Near Falmouth, Va.,

April 29, 1863.

The campaign has opened with the Army of the Potomac; we have five bridges across the river, where Franklin crossed before, and portions of the First (General [John] Reynolds) and Sixth Corps (General [John] Sedgwick) are on the rebel side; they captured one hundred prisoners, which we have just sent to Washington. The Second and Third Corps are on our bank ready to cross; the Fifth, Eleventh, and Twelfth made an attempt to cross at Kelly's Ford this morning, but met with slight resistance at first; they very soon forded the river, and everything goes on finely so far.

The Fifth Corps will be fought very desperately, and I feel very bad, for Walter and Bob are so far away from me that I can render them no assistance should they be wounded. The rebels will make a desperate fight, but I feel it in my bones that they will be whipped; our troops look finely.

Our movement on Friday, May 1, at 9 a. m., was to Bank's Ford by the river road, crossing Mott and Golin Runs. We saw the balloons up at Fredericksburg, heard the firing receding to our right and rear, and late in the afternoon, when near Decker's House, the order to countermarch was given. On our return we met many of Duryea's red-legged Zouaves (5th New York) coming out of the timber, who said Sykes had fallen back.

Soon we met some prisoners being sent to the ford (I remember one smooth-faced boy, about fifteen years of age, and mentally compared him with my own youthful self), and a moment later we were put in rapid motion, and by a double quick barely escaped being cut off by a force of the enemy coming over from the old turnpike by the old mine road which, leading to United States ford, intersects the river road at this point. We were quickly placed in position in dense timber, where the roads make this angle.

The enemy now made himself known in this effort, by pushing his line so closely that we could hear in the reverberating forest all commands as distinctly as in our own regiment, and running

---

3 The event of the photos was recounted in the *Washington Chronicle* of May 14, 1863.—note in original

his guns, probably up the main road, shelled us vigorously. Lying closely and pushing out our skirmishers, we remained in this desperate position. The pioneers were set to work with their axes making barricades and soon their strokes, followed by those of the rebels, each striving to outdo the other, resounded and echoed in the dense forest. Our skirmishers, in the meantime, kept up a sharp fire. Fortunately, the enemy, as much at sea as ourselves, ventured to advance no farther.

The woods were now alive with shells, which glared, shrieked, and burst against the trunks of the huge pines and oaks, or sharply screamed through the thickets in our rear, making the forest roar with the noise and confusion and lighting our prostrate line to the brightness of day. It was appalling even to the stoutest hearts; and still we hugged the ground.

The moon rose high in the heavens, but our spirits were still below the horizon. All night we heard the rumble of batteries on our front, and the tramp, tramp of the rebel infantry, and could only surmise what our fate was to be. Our intense nervous strain increased. Not a man dared to close his eyes in slumber, for when our safety seemed to be assured by a temporary lull in the storm, the guns would again open and drive us to closer cover.

We made ourselves very thin; still the uproar and din went on. A very singular incident occurred here. Our surgeon or assistant surgeon[4] had left camp with his little boy (about ten years of age), and not thinking we would get under fire, he was with us on the line of battle. As most of the shells went over us, it was more dangerous to go to the rear than stay.

The child became frightened by the noise of the exploding shells and shrapnel and the terrifying glare in the forest, and high above the terrible din and tumult, the roar of the guns and explosion of shells, arose the shrieks and hysterical sobs of the thoroughly panic-stricken boy, and it was not until complete exhaustion came to his relief that they ceased.

---

[4] This may have been surgeon Major Isaac H. Stearns (1825–1897), although Stearns' son was in his teens at the time.—2019

One of our sharpshooters, Private Cyrus M. Osgood, was chopping on one side of a huge pine, not more than ten or fifteen yards in front of the center of our regimental line. By the strong moonlight we could almost see the chips fly. Private William Webster of our own company was at work on the other side, toward our line. All eyes were upon their big forms, for they were very large, and had been detailed as pioneers. Both men were exposed to the full view of the enemy's gunners, not more than a hundred yards away. We were watching for the tree to fall—our minds diverted, for the moment, from the agonizing cries and shrieks of the little boy and the terrors of this night battle—when a shell struck and burst directly on the tree at which they were working, and a fragment broke both of Osgood's hips. We saw him carried out on a blanket. He died of his wounds May 27.

In the early morning the word was whispered along the line, and every man holding on to his coffee cup and bayonet that they might not clink, crouching and creeping, we painfully and without daring to draw a long breath dragged ourselves out upon some by-path, and in the bright moonlight passed through the parked trains, reserve artillery, and sleeping forms of thousands of wearied men in the clearing of the Chancellor House, and moved along some interminable forest road to a position on the extreme left of the army, near Mine Creek, and covering United States ford. It was a narrow escape. We had seemed to be isolated from the rest of the army.

We spent all day Saturday in throwing up barricades. General Hooker passed along the line, everywhere receiving the loyal cheers of the worn but heroic men.

Our brother Walter now writes:

Camp 'Nowhere,' May 2, 1863.

Chancellorsville Campaign.

Your letter was received yesterday, very fortunately on the march** * a word from home now is like a 'sweet morsel to a hungry man.'*** the scenes we have been through with since I last wrote, I could write a week about them, and then the description would not be exhausted.

We started last Monday forenoon (April 27th), at a moment's notice, heavily loaded with knapsacks and eight days' rations; after long tiresome marches, we crossed the Rappahannock river at Kelly's Ford, about thirty miles from camp; on Wednesday morning it rained, and we got wet through, and at night we forded the swift Rapidan and gained the heights just in season to prevent a battle, for the rebels hove in sight just as our advance guard gained the hills on the other side. It rained all night, and Bob and myself were wet to the skin, blanket, ponchos and all; Bob suffered terribly with blistered feet and rheumatism. We started Thursday morning and marched all day, until we came in sight of the enemy on the Fredericksburg side of the Rappahannock, and then our brigade went on a reconnaissance (Bob calls it the 'flying brigade,' 'Barnes' cavalry,' etc.). You ought to have seen the roads, lined as they were with knapsacks, blankets, and rations that the men could not carry on such a hard march.

We are all short on grub, and we do not get anything until next Tuesday; I haven't got a single ration, nor Bob either, and the regiment is in a like predicament, officers and all.

We went forward to the front four miles, threw out skirmishers, fired, and received a volley, and seeing that the enemy were bringing up guns to shell us out of the woods, we retraced our steps, having accomplished our design. We had a good night's rest, and yesterday (May 1) went out on another reconnaissance; we went two miles and back; saw Falmouth on the other side of the river, two balloons in the air, and accomplished all we desired; we got back just in time to save being cut off by the rebs, who got wind of our doings. We went into the woods, formed line of battle, joining our right with Hancock's left, and at 9 o'clock at night the 'rebs' commenced shelling the woods; if there is anything terrible in war it is lying flat on the ground and having the messengers of death dropping in among you, screaming through the air, and exploding like volcanoes all about you. We lay there until 2 o'clock this morning, when we were relieved, having lost 1 man killed and 2 wounded; the man that was killed had a hole cut through both his two legs, just below the hip, by a piece of shell, breaking all the bones; wasn't it horrible? He was in the pioneer corps, and was chopping down trees for a barricade at the time; I had been talking

316

with him often during the day. We came to our present place during the day; slept till daylight; cooked coffee, fresh meat, and are now in line of battle awaiting orders. The cannon are booming not far off and the skirmishers are busy.

We shall probably have a big battle in a few days. Hooker says he has got them 'bagged,' and, of course, all that remains is to pull the string; but I fear it will prove a rubber string, easy of stretching, and they will escape.

We have done some tall marching, and now we are going to wind up by some big fighting. Bob is disgusted; says he wishes 'he was in the backyard chained,' 'never would leave his mother's apron strings,' is an 'old man before he is twenty,' etc., and keeps us all laughing, telling about his sore joints, etc. If he isn't a queer genius, then I am mistaken. ***

Let me tell you of the queerest coincidence that I ever heard of in regard to myself; while on the march yesterday, we passed a rebel camp, lately deserted apparently, and a Second Maine corporal picked up a rubber portfolio for note paper, and opening it, discovered some photographs, and read on the bottom ones aloud, 'Walter Carter, Bradford, Mass.' Emerson, the cook, happening to be near, recognized it, told the fellow that he knew a man in his regiment by that name, and it was reported to the Second Maine major. He went to our colonel, I was called, and went forward to the Second Maine, and there recovered seven of the photographs lost at the battle of Fredericksburg; three of myself, one of Emeline J., one of Brainard Blanchard, one of Al Carlton, and the best and dearest of all, one of mother which I shall so much prize now.

About 6 P. M., when just about completing our formidable log breastworks, a rattle, then a perfect roar of musketry suddenly burst upon our ears, followed by the startling boom! boom! of the batteries.

It was "Stonewall" Jackson's flank attack. It came no nearer; it did not recede. We were in blissful ignorance of its portentous nature, and as it was on the extreme right flank, gave no special attention to it, except to remark "They're at it!" The bands of the regular divisions struck up the national airs, "Hail Columbia" and "The Star-Spangled Banner," which contrasted strangely with the clamor of rolling musketry and bursting shells. It inspired the boys, however, and quieted any apprehension that may have been felt that there was any disaster on our right, besides demonstrating the true value of music under every condition of fatigue, despondency or battle panic to all classes of men. We had not heard it before, we never heard it again during a battle.

Night came. We were pushed out on the picket line. Springing over the logs, we made our way a few hundred yards to the front, and being posted behind the huge trees, we watched our front all night. The soft light of a full moon glittered and glimmered through the trees. Hundreds of whip-poor-wills kept up their melancholy notes, the chattering katy did [*sic*] its incessant monotony. A crackling! A sharp—"Who comes there?" and a voice in broken English, shouted some unintelligible jargon for a reply. Again the challenge rang out, and then a shot, and the picket line opened.

"Cease firing!" came sharply from the rear. A sergeant went forward. He found three stragglers from the 11th Corps[5] who had wandered miles from where Jackson had "skedaddled" their command. Neither could speak English, and were sent to the rear. Midnight approached, and we were again startled into wakefulness by the dreadful attack on the plank road. The incessant booming of guns and roaring of the conflict echoed again and again along our wooded front.

It was the 3d Corps fighting its way in. Shortly before daybreak, again there broke forth a startling volley, then a roll as of thunder followed by one of the most deafening and incessant musketry fire that we had yet heard. For hours it surged but came no nearer. Soon we saw the forms of the relieving line of the nth Corps.

---

[5] Fought from April 30 to May 6, 1863, Chancellorsville is considered Lee's "perfect battle." He audaciously divided his outnumbered force *twice*. The 11th Corps on the Union right, under the one-armed General Oliver Otis Howard, were surprised by Jackson's 2nd Corps of about 28,000 men. The stragglers above were probably some of the many German immigrants in 11th Corps.—2019

It was with the greatest difficulty that they could be prodded and driven to the shelter of our huge trees. "Fall in!" We reached the breastworks. The corps had gone! Our little regiment followed swiftly towards the sound of the terrible conflict.

We now met the wounded of the Jersey Brigade of the 3d Corps, and several captured battle flags, coming through the woods. Upon a stump sat the form of a woman. We rubbed our eyes; there was no mistake. Her long black hair had fallen from its coil; no covering was upon her head. A rubber blanket was about her form. It was Annie Etheridge,[6] the heroine of Birney's division. She had been out all night on the plank road, had been hit through the clothing several times, and now, pale and exhausted, but resolute, she was cheering on the poor fellows, whose life-blood dripped from the stretchers as the carriers sped in rapid procession by her position. Her dark, expressive eyes, clear-cut face, and a firm mouth betokened the courageous, daring woman who won the respect of all alike during those dark and perilous days.

We reached the center and joined the brigade. Closed en masse, we moved by the flank, and found ourselves near a large field hospital which was under an immense oak, the yellow flag flying from its top. The enemy shelled us most unmercifully. The missiles tore through the hospital. The wounded, some of whom had been operated on, or were just about to undergo amputation, were removed to a place of safety in the midst of the uproar, many being knocked to pieces as they went

We were ordered to "lie down." A piece of shrieking shell seemed to come for my head. I gathered myself for the blow. It rasped over my neck, struck a man in the First Michigan in the back, and literally split him in two. A groan. I turned. He was an unrecognizable mass of flesh.

---

[6] Lorinda Anna Blair Etheridge ("Gentle Annie;" 1839–1913) was a Union nurse famed for serving on the front lines and under fire. She later received the Kearny Cross. She was inducted into the Michigan Women's Hall of Fame in 2010 (michiganwomen.org). Etheridge was buried with veteran's honors in Arlington National Cemetery.—2019

We moved upon the line and for an interminable hour or two supported the batteries. The Chancellor House was smoking; the woods in which were our wounded were on fire and the smoke grew stifling. Dimmick's regular battery (Battery "H," 1st Artillery), completely disabled, was hauled with the prolonge ropes by the Eleventh Massachusetts, by our prostrate forms. Two horses were limping; each had a leg dangling. Nearly all the rest had been killed, and a noncommissioned officer commanded the battery. Justin Dimmick was a classmate of our brother.

We lay under a shell fire all the afternoon, luckily with no loss. At dark, jumping over the logs, we moved down the slight slope to the edge of the woods, and went on picket. About midnight while the clear, bright moon illuminated the open space to the brightness of day, a shot on our right, a one—two—three, a startling rattle, and the whole line rose up and blazed away.

"Steady, men!" came hoarsely the commands. It was a reconnaissance by the enemy. The left fell back. "Lie down for your lives!" and from forty guns swept the double canister, swishing over our heads into the thickets, cutting the trees as though they were but straw's.

It was a hot place. The "Johnnies" vanished. All night the spluttering of the pickets was heard, breaking out occasionally into a roar.

Just here occurred a very singular incident. A division or more of the enemy was attempting to feel of and force our picket line. Through the thicket we could hear the heavy tramping and crashing of a line of battle. The left of our line flushed and gave way. Our Major (Mason W. Burt[7]), in command of the pickets at this point, shouted out—"Sergeant-major, drive all of those men back to the line!" Our brother drew his sword and started; in the bright moonlight several of our men could be seen making across the open space for the breastworks. It was a sprinting match; he reached and turned back all except one of the fleeing men. Yelling

---

[7] Massachusetts native, Mason W. Burt (1839–1913), was a clerk, farmer, and mining superintendent (census records, 2019).

at him to "go back!" and finding that he did not obey, he laid the flat of his sword over his back; the man had on an overcoat. As he turned in the strong light, our brother recognized in him a well-known officer in the regiment. Not a word was said by either. The recreant officer went back and nothing further was known about it in the regiment.

Our brother at headquarters now writes:

In Camp at Falmouth,

May.3, 1863.

Lieutenant Cooper will mail this for me in Washington, as no mails go from here at present. The Heights of Fredericksburg are ours; we took them by several brilliant charges of the Sixth Corps; I saw the whole affair. We first charged the heights where Sumner's Corps was so fearfully slaughtered, and captured their works in grand style; we took seven hundred prisoners and ten guns; our loss will probably amount to about three or four hundred killed and wounded.

The fighting on our right, where Hooker commands, has been terrible; it seems to be a hand-to-hand conflict. Yesterday we were doing finely when the Eleventh Corps (General Howard), were thrown into disorder, and our right forced back, but the timely arrival of the First Corps, which had been withdrawn from our left, immediately put things to rights again.

Hooker telegraphs tonight that he has driven the enemy at every point, and he now only wishes to finish them. Our loss has been very heavy on the right, and when I think that the boys have been in it all, my heart sinks within me, but I will hope for the best. Hooker swears that he will whip them. The report is tonight that Sickles with the Third Corps, has got their baggage trains and our cavalry have destroyed 15 miles of railroad near the Hanover Junction, and have cut off their supplies.

If Walter and Bob are only alive and well, it is all that I wish for. Sedgwick will probably attack in the enemy's rear tomorrow, and Sickles will join in the attack; then good-bye, rebels.

On the 4th, at daybreak, we were relieved, and clambering again over the breastworks, occupied the front line of rifle-pits, with the 3d Corps just in rear. We were within a few yards of the little white house (Bullocks).

The sharpshooters overlooked our position. The bullets spit, sung, and glanced in among the caissons of the batteries. All day long we lay flat, covered as much as possible, but a groan would often convince us that one more of nature's noblemen had met his doom. General Whipple was mortally wounded. We could see his tent from where we were lying. Beeves had been driven across the river. The meat was issued warm to the hungry men, many of whom had thrown away their knapsacks with rations, in their distress. While cooking it over our small fires, General Sickles[8] sauntered up. "Well, boys, this is cooking under difficulties!" Hardly had he uttered these words, when a z-i-p!—zi-i-i-p!! and the bullets began to buzz about his head.

"I am too tall for this place!" said he, and walked quietly away. A shriek from a man who, under cover of the caissons, was dodging along the line, hurried some of us to his side. His groans convinced us that he was mortally wounded; he evidently thought so too. We stripped off his shirt. A large black and blue spot on the small of the back showed that the ball had glanced somewhere, and, somewhat spent, had struck hard, but failed to penetrate. Somebody said: "Shut up, you d—d fool; you are only hit by a spent ball!"

His courage rose as we announced it, and his groans gave place to—"Oh! if I don't have sweet revenge for that. If I do-o-o-n-n-n't have sw-e-e-t revenge!!" In the early afternoon, a part of our division swept out from the right, found the enemy, and again our batteries rung out in deafening discharges. Then came a lull. An officer of Berdan's sharpshooters sprang nimbly over the logs directly in front of our position, and creeping to the edge of the

---

[8] Daniel Edgar Sickles (1819–1914) was a controversial public figure before, during, and after the war until the end of his long life. A political general, he engendered intense feelings pro and con. He murdered the son of the composer of the Star Spangled Banner across the street from the White House, was an inveterate womanizer, and made a career out of defending his actions at Gettysburg, usually at the expense of George Meade.—2019

woods with a telescopic rifle, watched carefully for a death-dealing sharpshooter who had persistently picked off our gunners.

We were silent and breathless spectators for a long time, but soon a puff and a sharp crack rewarded the officer's patience, and a moment later he came in. The story was short. He had swept the horizon with the telescope for a long time, had seen the puffs from a leafy tree. Soon the wily sharpshooter, becoming tired, shifted his position across the field and the cross hairs of the telescope. A pull, and the bullet sped to the "Johnny's" heart.

While lying here on this day many of the Seventeenth Maine, which was directly in our rear, in the second line, came to see us; among them Charles Roberts, Adjutant of that regiment; Fred Bosworth, Fontaine Sparrow, Herman Mason, and Lute Bartels, all old schoolmates in the good city of Portland, when we were young boys together. The latter "was in Louisiana when the war broke out, and was taken prisoner by our troops at the first capture of Baton Rouge; he was tried as a spy, got clear, and coming north, after travelling about New York City awhile with Herman Mason, they were both overcome with a fit of patriotism, and went to Portland and enlisted."

In the afternoon, the 3d brigade was pushed out from our right, across the field, and met and repulsed a reconnaissance sent to ascertain if our position was too strong to attack. The fight was short and sharp. All our batteries opened with shrapnel, then canister; the roar was deafening as we hugged the ground. Heavy cannonading could be distinctly heard in the direction of Fredericksburg, and then cheering, followed by the sharp, high-keyed Yi! yis!! of the Johnnies. There was no sleep; all were on the alert. About 11 o'clock on the 5th, a flag of truce went out from the right of our line, said to be for the recovery of the body of some officer. When going to the rear for water we saw "Gentle Annie" Etheridge again, sitting down behind the rifle pits in the second line, across the road.

On this same day, while lying in this spot, we heard a call, and looking up, saw our brother ride up on his dapple-grey, a shining mark for the enemy's sharpshooters. A dozen voices shouted, "You will be killed; dismount!" He quickly threw himself from the saddle, and placing the animal behind a caisson, he was soon lying under cover.

A saddle pocket full of tongue sandwiches, and a smell of his private restorative, was distributed as far as it would go, and toward dark he started on his dangerous return trip.

Our brother Walter says:

May 4, 1863.

We yet live, although we have been in some pretty tight places; we have done more marching, more picketing in front of the enemy, more lying under the enemy's shells, etc., than any other brigade of the army. We are now lying behind the entrenchments in the center, supported by the Third Corps (General Sickles), which has done some terrible fighting for the last two days. Birney's division came near being cut to pieces night before last, having followed up the enemy on the Plank Road for four miles, and getting surrounded, they had to cut their way through the enemy during the night; Lieutenant Houghton had his horse shot from under him, and was so badly stunned that they, left him for dead on the field. He recovered, however, and is safe; was over to see Noyes and myself today.

Annie Etheridge, a female heroine of Birney's division, accompanied them on their perilous journey on horseback, and was under fire the whole time; she was perfectly cool, and often dismounted to help the poor wounded soldiers.

We have made some splendid barricades, and our whole line, seven miles, is one continuous breastwork, defended by rifle pits, men in the ditches, and cannon overlooking them all. I saw General Whipple this morning washing himself, apparently very happy and cheerful; a few moments ago a ball went through him, and he cannot live.

May 5th

I was obliged to stop yesterday, on account of a grand splurge on both sides' first picket, then skirmishing, and lastly artillery; such a roar of many noises I never heard; the shells flew about dreadfully

324

numerous, and our canister went through the woods at a terrible rate. We had 72 pieces of cannon all playing at a time; it was nothing but a deafening roar for an hour. The Eleventh Corps hold the plank road to Gordonsville, directly in front of us through the woods, and the brick house too (you will know where it is when you see the account). We are in a line of breastworks at the rear, and the Third Corps behind; they have done terrific fighting, and we have relieved them. I haven't slept for four nights now; Bob is well, though much fatigued. The battle has opened again, and the shells are flying; one man near me was just hit, in the First Michigan. I am behind the entrenchments, and close, for safety's sake. Good-bye! I am full of fight, and am calm enough to express myself amid the din of battle; I fear not.

Our brother at headquarters writes:

Camp of the Eighth Infantry,

May 4, 1863, near Falmouth.

I start tomorrow morning for the right, for the express purpose of hearing something of the boys. Captain Marsh of the Second U. S. Infantry was killed; I dined with him a week ago yesterday, and lived on the same floor, and opposite to him for three years at West Point. Lieutenant-Colonel (Jacob Ford) Kent, Inspector-General of the Sixth Corps, and a first lieutenant of the Third Infantry, is in my tent wounded."

He was in the same company with me at the first battle of Bull Run, was wounded and taken prisoner there. General Berry[9] of Sickles Corps is killed. Sedgwick has been fighting hard this evening; the enemy fight desperately, and it is 'nip and tuck.' The grand attack is to be made tomorrow.

---

[9] Hiram Gregory Berry (1824–May 3, 1863). Berry was a self-made man, politician, and one of the promising generals of the war. Berry's decisive action at the Battle of Williamsburg was essential to General Hooker. Reportedly at Chancellorsville, Hooker rode up, and asked officers gathered around, "Whom have you got there, gentlemen?" When told it was Major-General Berry, he got off his horse, knelt, kissed the young general's forehead, and wept bitterly. Berry immediately knew how bad he was hit and merely said, "My wife and child." See *Major-General Hiram G. Berry: Bull Run to Chancellorsville*, Gould, 2014.

The rain commenced. Darkness came on. The batteries were limbered up, the gun platforms abandoned. All night the columns moved by us in the gloom, clink! clank! The rain poured in torrents. We were drowned out of the trenches, and half crouching, with a sea of mud fast gathering about us, the cold rain-laden wind piercing us to the bone, we wore out that long bitter night.

At daybreak we started, gained a line of barricades on the wooded road to the United States ford, faced about, formed line of battle, threw out skirmishers, and then we knew that Barnes' Brigade of the 5th Corps was to cover the retreat.

Among the characters of the, regiment was one Dennis Coghlin of Company K, who was known by the officers and men only as "Dinny." He was a short, sawed-off little Irishman, not much over 5 feet 5 inches, who had been in this country only long enough to learn a little English.

Frequently, in asking or giving orders when on guard and his stock of our language gave out, he would use the first word of his native tongue that came into his head to express his meaning. It was with the greatest difficulty at all times that he could be understood by anybody.

If some of the wags pressed him too closely, and he got incensed, his one laconic expression was "Bocklish," whatever that may mean, translated. His hair was the color of a dirty unbleached flax, and about as fine; his complexion was of that muddy mixture of brunette and blond, which, when tanned, covered with sweat, and liberally sprinkled with Virginia dust on the march, was simply indescribable.

A small, rough pug nose, little, greyish-blue eyes and a typical Irish mouth, with large ears standing out at the side of his head, gave a most comical expression to this son of Erin. Add to this, pants two sizes too small for him and a loose blouse two sizes too large, one of those fall-down-in-front-recruit caps with the vizor turned up, and a short dudheen [pipe] stuck between his lips, and one has the tout ensemble of the queerest character we had ever, under any circumstances, seen in the uniform of Uncle Sam.

One rainy day, "Dinny" was on guard at No. 3, in front of camp, which skirted the parade. The company sinks were across a small stream, on the other side of the parade, which had to be crossed to reach them. On rainy nights some of the men were accustomed to stop this side of the stream, instead of using the sinks.

On this dark night "Dinny," industriously and patiently pressing mud, was given special orders to prevent any nuisances from being committed on the parade ground, and if he could not stop it, to call the corporal of the guard.

He had a hard night. One after another slipped by him in the darkness, and refused to obey him; he could only partially locate them by sound. Becoming enraged, and forgetting his orders, instead of calling the corporal, he broke out into several loud "Bocklishes," and then, laying down his gun in the mud, and collecting a pile of stones, he commenced pelting them in true Hibernian style. This soon cleared the ground, but subjected "Dinny" to a severe reprimand from the officer of the guard as soon as it became known.

While waiting here in this terrific storm, and expecting the enemy's skirmishers to show up at any moment, orders were given for the guns to be inspected, charges to be drawn, caps snapped on the nipples to dry them out, and then to load and recap.

"Dinny," our quondam Irish friend, with a bland smile upon his worn, wan face, pinched from loss of sleep and the hardships we had been through, asked one of the duty sergeants to draw the charge from his piece, as they were always, as file closers, furnished with ball screws for that purpose.

The sergeant, to his surprise, found the muzzle completely filled with soft mud and then following came one charge after another, to the bottom of the bore. "Dinny" had in the excitement of battle loaded his rifle with cartridges to the muzzle, and with an old, wet cap on the nipple, it would have proved, in the expected attack, as harmless as an old club.

Another quaint character of the same company was William Mulhearn, otherwise known as "Daddy."[10] There are few men in the regiment who knew then or even now his real name, so closely had this sobriquet stuck to him throughout his entire term of enlistment.

Like "Dinny," old "Daddy" was a son of Erin, but of a more rollicking, fun-loving nature. There was nothing of the melancholy expression about his face, but on the contrary it was always wreathed in a homely smile, and his brogue could be heard rolling all over camp; when on picket, his challenge always gave him away and was sure to provoke the laughter of all along the line. Unlike "Dinny," he enjoyed a joke, and could always hold his own; was more voluble; had a better knowledge and use of pure English than his confrere; was more intelligent, and being much larger and stronger, was a much better and more useful soldier.

The enemy did not press us, and in column of companies, with colors flying, and at a "Support" or "Shoulder arms," we slipped, wallowed and waded over the greasy track to the river, and crossed the pontoons. We were the last troops to cross the river and, resting a few minutes, commenced the task of stripping the bridges and loading the boats, etc., upon the wagons. The mules stalled. The teamsters cursed. Whiskey circulated. Rope cables were bent on the teams, and the wearied, exhausted men strained to get them over the bluff where several batteries were planted to cover this movement. But by dark the regiments, as independent commands, commenced the march for the old winter camps; whether by order or not was never known.

---

[10] It's no wonder the boys called him daddy. Mulhearn was born in 1820 and was 42 at enlistment. He served until October, 1864. He died in 1901 and is buried beneath a rather impressive monument in Mount Calvary Cemetery, Roslindale, MA (census records and Find a Grave website, 2019).

Darkness came on. The rain poured in torrents. The country was a wilderness of mud and forest. Men fell out by scores, became exhausted and separated among the trees; officers became chilled and benumbed. Men lighted matches in order to regain the roads, but it was not until the next afternoon that the regiment was gathered, and then just in time to receive orders from General Hooker to return to the pontoon train and conduct it safely inside the picket line. How many times could we record that whiskey was the cause of too much of the suffering and distress in the ranks of the Army of the Potomac!

Our brother, when he left us at the Bullock House, rode till darkness and the storm overtook him, when his horse wandered into a picket post. They challenged, he shouted, and believing he was outside our line, and that they were rebel pickets, put spurs to his horse, and attempted to escape.

The pickets opened fire. He soon ran into the picket line, and a blaze of fire disclosed him to view. He was taken prisoner, but to his joy by our own men. It was a narrow escape. The speed of his horse and the intense darkness alone saved him from instant death.

He passed the night at a hut full of wounded men and gladly mounted in the morning and recrossed the river. Some men from our company were arrested by the Provost Guard on the 5th, but upon writing our brother a note explaining that they became lost at night in the rain, he remembered his own experience of the night before. The magic word "Open Sesame" was given and they returned to us, richer by a pound of cheese and plenty of hard bread, through his generosity.

We bailed out our cellars, now full of water, replaced our poncho coverings, built huge fires, and in our wet clothes and muddy boots threw ourselves upon the wet bunks for sleep, which we had gone without, and upon scanty rations, for nearly a week.

Our brother Bob now gives a detailed account of the movement in four long letters dated May 9, 10, 13, and 20, 1863, short extracts from which are given:

329

I have not yet sufficiently recovered from Joe Hooker's forward movement, but still I will muster up courage today. *** I cannot conceal my feelings if I tried to. I saw when we started from here, that if we did not succeed this time, I would have no hope. In the first place, the army has never been in a better condition for a move; we had comparatively good quarters and food this winter, and had been better treated every way than before; we were clothed well for the army, and April 27th started in good spirits.

Walt, I think, wrote you on the march, therefore I will not give you a full account of our start. ***

It being a hot day we marched slowly and went about ten miles. We were loaded heavily. The eight days' ration business did not exactly suit us, but still we were willing to try it, if it could in any way be of advantage, so as to accomplish our purpose and secure us victory. *** It went hard, and the boys commenced throwing away blankets, overcoats, etc., so that the road was lined. The next day it rained, and the going was harder as it was slippery, and my feet began to blister. We went twelve miles, and there was a great deal of straggling; we went into camp at 10 o'clock at night. The next day we reached Kelly's Ford, crossed the pontoons, the going muddy; we then forded the North Fork of the Rappahannock (Mountain Run), up over our knees; after that we marched faster and faster, and the boys, being tired and wet, began to lag; still on we went, faster and faster, the going worse; something evidently was up. We reached the Rapidan and forded it, that rapid, rushing current up to our armpits, the current running like mad, so that it foamed. It was dark, and there we were in the water, and tired as we were it almost swept us away.

Our brother Walter adds May 10:

Sam Appleton had charge of a pack mule in crossing; he led him, and all the way Sam's feet never touched bottom scarcely; he had to catch hold of the Doctor (Stearns), bridle, and be drawn along by the horse and mule.

Thus in one day we forded three rivers. The Colonel sent word to General Barnes that the men were falling out in squads and that if he did not stop and rest there would be none left. My feet by this time were covered with blisters as large as quarter dollars. Barnes sent word that it was his great object to gain the hills on the other side of the Rapidan before the enemy, which, if we did, would save us a battle; as you saw by the papers, the movement of our corps was very rapid, so much so that the rebels knew nothing scarcely of our destination. They forced us to our utmost. You have no idea of a soldier's load until you try it. That night it poured and we started the next morning through the sticky Virginia mud, ankle deep, many with wet blankets. The boys threw them away by the score and everything else that was heavy. Soon we came to a halt, threw out skirmishers and advanced slowly, and continued so all day, which made it awful tedious for us to keep on our wet loads and go so slowly. We came across their breastworks deserted. We worked slowly out a few miles beyond the Chancellor House, which is a very large, old-fashioned brick house, with a portico, and is about three rods in from the plank road. We soon found the 'Johnnies;' we gave them a volley and got one in return; they ran out a battery and we fell back into the woods. Griffin reconnoitered them awhile, thought it better to withdraw, and we went back; passed through Sykes (division) who was encamped, past the brick house into camp.

This was Thursday, four days from camp, and we had smelt the 'Johnnies,' forded three rivers, been wet through and through, no chance to get dry, and our feet in bad condition. Friday was a beautiful day; we had fresh meat given out—for who could carry eight days' rations?—the line officers had none scarcely, and 'bummed' on the boys. Sykes advanced one road, and we went another (Banks' Ford road). All this was feeling them; our whole army had, by this time, got pretty well used up. Sykes commenced firing pretty soon, and we kept on without seeing anything; they still kept firing, and we went out four miles. Sykes fought all day. We went to the ford to keep that clear. When we came back, the firing was fast getting to the rear of us. We soon commenced to go like the 'Old Boy;' we met a squad of Sykes' (Duryea's) Zouaves; they said that they were falling back. We came near being cut off, for Sykes had fallen back so as to bring them (the rebs), between Sykes and us. We soon went into line of battle in the woods, our right touching Hancock's division. That night our pioneers commenced felling trees for an abattis; that drew fire, and they shelled -us awfully. The moon was rising, and the fuses seemed like stars as they came howling at us.

One pioneer ahead .of me was killed by a shell going through both legs. I saw the blaze coming, dodged, and heard the groans of the dying man, and the pieces flew by my ear. That night, sometime after midnight, we went through the woods, away down on the left; marched all night; had an awful march. The next day (Saturday), we made breastworks all day; felled trees, and although tired almost to death, we worked until four—until the battle commenced—when boom! boom!! and the fight commenced on the right of us ('Stonewall' Jackson's attack on the Eleventh Corps). Our company went out skirmishing; it was a tough fight. The Eleventh Corps broke, and the rebs drove them to the brick house. General Howard must feel badly. We were on picket all night; fired at some 'skedaddlers' of the Eleventh Corps, and in the morning my eyes ached awfully; watching behind a tree all night ain't very beneficial.

The fight on the plank road commenced about midnight. Sunday was a beautiful morning. About 7 o'clock, we were deployed as skirmishers, and were about being relieved by the aforesaid Germans, who were frightened out of their wits, when there commenced the most awful firing that I ever heard on the right of us. I will venture to say that it was never equaled on this continent.[11] It was truly terrible; the musketry was a continual roar, no slackening whatever for hours, and the artillery I cannot describe; it was a continual boom! boom!! We expected every moment to be driven in. Our divisions had moved, and there we were, down in the woods, the battle raging awfully; it was one continual roar for hours. We were soon relieved by the devilish Dutchmen of the Eleventh Corps; they were shaking with fear—and we started down to the center to rejoin our regiment. Oh! the horrors of war!! Every few steps we came across some wounded man, some of them discouraged. We met the 'skedaddlers,' of whom there are always a great many in a fight, coming with doleful tales, which I did not fully credit, as they are generally exhausted and discouraged. Some of the regiments had captured the rebel colors. We soon joined the regiment, and got into line, when the rebs got range of us, and soon the shells raked us in every direction; the bloody, groaning, disfigured wretches came straggling in, or were borne to the rear; the caissons were bursting; the roar of artillery was awful. Yet I felt encouraged Sunday and in good spirits, even if the Dutchmen did run.

We had the strongest place (on Ely's Ford road, near a small, white house with a portico, near which was a sloping field, which

---

[11] It would be surpassed within weeks at Gettysburg.—2019

ran down to the edge of the woods near General Sykes' headquarters. Perhaps you may see the position described). We were in the center and right where the fiercest attack was made, and where all the generals were centered; Hooker, Meade, Couch, Sickles, and Griffin were all there, Hooker shaking his fist, and Griffin putting his batteries into action, and saying—'I'll fix them!' I saw Hooker all day; I stood right beside him at dark, and heard him talking with Sickles. I saw the Chancellor House when it was burned. General Sickles' headquarters were not ten rods[12] from me.

We moved into the woods and were shelled, and under fire all day; we had some narrow escapes; a piece of shell passed through my blouse. At night we went on picket again and lay there all night. We could hear the rebels talking, hear their artillery moving, etc. We were driven in once, but we lay there without undoing our bundles; we shook almost out of our clothes with ague. We came in about 4 o'clock A. M. the next day (Monday) and lay still until 5 p. m., when we then threw out two regiments to feel them. They opened on us with shell and we with canister, and we had a lively time for about an hour. The sharpshooters flanked us on Monday.

General Whipple was killed within ten rods of me. I saw him just before he was wounded and the night before stood right beside him. I had some narrow escapes that day, as they were popping someone every little while. The next day (Tuesday) we lay behind the barricades till afternoon, when Gene made his appearance with some sandwiches, etc. We were glad to see him, I tell you; he told us about Sedgwick being beaten, etc. We heard him fighting all night. He (Gene) could not stay long, and started back. Just think how kind he was to ride all the way from Falmouth just to look after us. I can never forget his self-sacrifice, for he put his own life in danger. He said he would write you immediately upon his return to camp, informing you of having seen us. He lost his way while going back, was shot at by the pickets, slept in a nigger shanty, and lost his way the next day returning to his quarters.

From what I heard the generals say, and by what I could see and hear, I thought we should give them "Hail Columbia," and I was never more surprised in my life than when I heard Tuesday night that we were to retreat.

---

[12] 1 rod = 16 1⁄2 feet; 5.02 meters.—2019

Our brother Walter adds, May 10:

I need not recount all the events of the past week or two. *** Bob has written (poor boy), and given you a description of the whole movement, as far as his experience went, and it would be useless for me to repeat*** I will, however, indulge in a few general descriptions which may be of interest.

At the end of five days I gave out on grub and for two days I ate only the crumbs of hard bread found on the battlefield, well baked by the sun. On the seventh day Colonel T. took account of our provisions, and my report was 'nary ration!' He called me to him, and asked me how it happened. I explained it to him *** that it was an impossibility with me as well as some others to carry eight days' rations, and he very coolly remarked that I 'would have to starve.' 'Very well!' said I. 'I shall, before I carry eight days' rations on my back!' I was fortunate enough to get some provisions that night, and on the next day, the 5th, while supporting Reynolds on the right, where the Eleventh Corps ran, Colonel T. came to me and asked if I 'had a hard bread to spare;' I told him 'no,' but gave him a boiled potato, and others gave him hard bread. He, with two horses and a servant, could not bring eight days' rations. How could he expect a soldier on foot to carry such a load?

Our brother Bob's letters continue:

Wednesday morning we retreated. That afternoon (Tuesday), and night it poured down awfully. It was a most wretched night, the most miserable night I ever passed; for three nights we had not had a wink of sleep; it poured in torrents from 3 o'clock in the afternoon until morning; the thunder rattled, and the mud and water were so deep that we could neither lie down nor sit down, but slept on our guns standing, the rain driving through us at every sweep. After being drowned out of the pits and darkness came on, it was rumored that we were going to retreat; soon the guns were run back and hitched to the limbers; then my heart sank within me; still it rained; troops were moving, and wet and despondent, we sat and took it, all worn out, no sleep for four nights, drenched to the skin, the cold wind sweeping through us.

Our brother adds, May 10:

Some of our boys fell down in the mud, and slept soundly, even while it poured the hardest. I would walk about the entrenchments, stop, and before I knew myself would fall asleep and drop on one knee; as soon as I touched the ground I would wake up, but soon I would be on the other. I at last lay down and slept, and only awoke when I was benumbed with wet and cold.

Our brother Bob continues:

We were in this condition until about 4 o'clock in the morning (Wednesday), when we started, and heavens, what a retreat! The mud was up to our waists (now this is no exaggeration); our brigade was the last, the rear guard of the army; our corps was the last to cross the pontoons; we stayed behind three hours until they had crossed, expecting every moment to have a bloody fight; our hands were so numb that we could scarcely draw our ramrods, and had to make little fires for the purpose of warming them. We then retreated in good order, column by companies, expecting an attack, but it did not come. We wallowed through the mud up to our middles, the rain pouring and wetting us to the bone. *** On the retreat, I tumbled down, fell on the hammer of my gun, cut my ear and knuckle very badly, and with the blood streaming down my neck, and my fingers so benumbed from cold, I could hardly grasp my gun. We crossed the pontoons with colors flying, at the 'shoulder arms,' in splendid order, but a more exhausted brigade never handled a gun. As soon as we crossed, we stacked arms, and, do you believe it, had to take in two pontoon bridges? *** I had the rheumatism so I could hardly move. *** I almost fell asleep while marching. The officers all got drunk (with a few worthy exceptions) from General B. down to the line officers.

The teams got stuck in the mud; we had to bend on cables and haul those great heavy boats up the bluff. The drunken, miserable fiends drew their swords and pistols, and fell off their horses in the mud, cursing. What a scene that was! It was a miserable, disgraceful affair. We worked till dark, and got them over the hill after staving up some of them, and upsetting others over the bluff. We expected all the time to have the rebels plant their batteries on the other side. Some of the men started in squads for camp, all demoralized and half dead. Old B. got lost going into camp. T. got benumbed. It was fifteen miles into camp, and our Lieutenant-Colonel started with about half of the regiment and got into the woods; darkness came on; it poured in torrents. I was up to my knees; everything was mud. Each step I took 1 stumbled over stumps, and cold and exhausted I came near getting discouraged and 'going up a spout.' I soon saw a light, which proved to be a fire; I stayed there all night; went into camp the next morning 'at 9 o'clock. A more desperate, demoralized, discouraged, blistered and exhausted soldier there never was. I found Walt, who had started ahead of me about an hour, and thus got out of the woods, and got into camp about midnight, which he never could have done had it not been for some Second Maine boys. Yesterday morning came orders for our brigade to go back to the pontoons, and come in with them. That was the order before—to stay there; but drunkenness was the cause of our going into camp.

Barnes ordered the regiment into camp while drunk. The remnant started back. I went five miles and dumped. I rested all day out at the picket line, and hobbled back last night, my feet all swollen up. Officers refused duty, and damned the army in a heap; they say the Peninsula campaign and retreat was nothing compared to this; they suffered nearly as much as we. The Colonel begged food from Walt. They went without a thing (to eat) for nearly two days. I never threw away a thing; I have my blankets, so has Walt. I suffered from want of food; was used up with rheumatism. *** It seems a dream; that I could have stood so much without dying seems a mystery to me.

Our brother Walter adds, May 10:

Our general and staff all got drunk, and instead of obeying orders and resting the men where the pontoon wagons were fast in the mud, they left them, and hurried into camp. Most of our company fell out on the road, utterly exhausted, and when we reached Hartwood Church, the brigade halted to make coffee and obtain a few moments' rest. I rode a horse for about two miles, and as a Captain in our regiment was all 'gone up' at this point, 1 volunteered to give up my chance to ride, to him, and instead of stopping to rest, and get my limbs all sore and stiff, I kept on through the mud to camp. I sank to my knees at every step, except when 1 cut across fields and through woods, then very often I would have to wade streams and swamps up to my waist, and clear mud and water, mixed half and half.

I kept on until it was so dark that I lost the road, and was about to give it up, when some Second Maine boys came along, bound for camp. I joined them and soon found out the points of the compass;

all that night I plodded along, so dark that I couldn't see where to place my feet, and in we would go, into every mud hole, sometimes ankle deep, then knee and waist alternately, a varying depth continually, but an average of two feet dear mud.

Still it rained and we kept on, until midnight saw us in camp, and I was soon asleep in an old tent that had been left standing. One of our men who started the same time did not arrive until the next night. The regiment started an hour after I did and arrived in camp the next morning. Bob and Edgar stayed at Hartwood Church and got in the next day. *** Such a tired set of men as they were I never saw.

While at the ford, the officers behaved shamefully; got drunk and used the men like brutes; drew their swords upon the privates to compel them to work upon the wagons, getting them up over the winding hill road that ascends over the bluffs that skirt the Rappahannock, on the Falmouth side.

They used switches, and I saw them strike unarmed men, who could not lift because of their weakness. They detailed the whole brigade to go into the work and hurry it up to prevent pursuit and shelling, and the men got mixed up, and couldn't work to advantage.

Instead of dividing us up into squads to relieve one another, they adopted the most miserable plan for a successful result, and then damned and threatened to exterminate, because things didn't work right. *** I saw a lieutenant-colonel of the One Hundred and Eighteenth Pennsylvania whip our Major's servant into some work, and I was disgusted with the drunken brute. (He, the servant, was not an enlisted man). *** the brother of the young man, Lieutenant R. of our regiment, resented the insult, when General B. rode up, reeling in his saddle, and informed him (R.), with a swing of his stick, that if he didn't go to work too, he would put it over him also. I saw R.'s hand steal quietly to his sword hilt several times, but he overcame himself, for the better perhaps. I saw Colonel J. of the Twenty-fifth New York ride up to a group of officers and soldiers, waiting for a chance to work to advantage, and rising in his stirrups he said: 'Hie! you are a disgrace to your country, go to work! hie!!' And straightway rolled off his saddle, a beastly sot. *** I was mud clear up to my shoulders where I had worked on the teams, *** my face was black with smoke and powder, and I felt like a perfect

337

fiend. I would have been tempted at the least provocation to have run any drunken shoulder strap [officer] through the body. I cared not for rebel shells then; I courted the sight of a rebel battery on the heights across the river *** for the probability of some of the scoundrels getting their quietus. This is what they feared, and what we longed for.

I had seen horrid sights enough for two weeks, and to think they were all in vain, was enough to crush the hopes of the strongest.

On our march back, LeRoy Kimball, Ed Walton and several of our boys fell out and were taken by the Fifth U. S. Cavalry to the Provost Guard, Army of the Potomac, Eighth Infantry. LeRoy sent a note to Gene, was sent for, and after it was all explained, Gene went to General Patrick and got them all released.

After we got back to camp, we were ordered to move again to recover the pontoons, and the next day we started; Bob and Edgar fell out six miles from camp, rested and returned. I had to keep on, and when our regiment halted for the night, we only had 100 men for duty. We got the pontoons in safe, and in the evening were serenaded by the band attached to the pontoon train. (Fiftieth N. Y. Engineer regiment.) The next day we started for camp, and after marching ten miles, arrived safe, and we are now having some rest.

Our brother Bob continues:

I have no time for comment on Hooker or his plans, or even the fight now * * * some time I will tell you more. * * * This is no exaggerated statement; if anything, I have held back many things. *** Why we did not succeed is a mystery to me. *** I do believe we are fated. It is nine months since we left (home), and yet of all these awful marches, battles, and everything that I have been through, what have we accomplished? Not one single iota! It does really seem a cruel shame and sin to be out here in this heathenish wilderness and throw one's life away to glorify and gratify the swarms of envious generals in this army. It is well enough for the rich merchant to sit down and read that such a body of troops have marched so far, or fought such a battle; does it ever enter his mind how much the private soldiers suffered in doing it? Does he ever see the soldier by the bivouac fire with the bright canopy above him for a roof, or the rain pouring down and drenching him as he sleeps? No! not he. As long as everything goes well, so that he can make money out of it, what does he care? *** Never refuse a soldier anything that lies in your power! Think of your brothers and act accordingly.

May 10

Today is Sunday, and a lovely one it is to a partially demoralized soldier, who has a good home. *** To think of you all, either going to church, or otherwise enjoying the privileges of a sweet New England Sabbath! Here, we have been engaged in scraping the immense amount of mud, which covered us from head to foot, cleaning our rusty rifles, washing or otherwise removing traces of our last grand movement, and marks of the dreadful retreat. *** I have had my hair cut, washed and cleaned up, and my mind is a little clearer; but still 1 am 'a perfect used up man,' both in mind and body and who under Heavens would not be;*** you cannot realize how much suffering, danger, and horrors we passed through. *** You know that I am naturally strong and tough, and would never give in till the last, but when they go beyond the powers of human endurance, then it is time for me to give in. *** We thought of you during the fighting, and spoke of you a great many times. I have thought of you all day.

Oh, how sad it is to look forward to the many dreary, oh, how many dreary months that I have got to be a lousy prisoner, and a tortured dog in this fated army!! But I am in for it, and have got to make myself contented for a year and a half at least. ***

*** We tried to go and see Gene today, but they would not let us go, as it is rumored that we move right away.

May 13

Gene came over this morning and stopped a little while; he is blue and discouraged; he lost two classmates in the battle. We are losing thousands of men whose times are up. Our whole Corps will dwindle down to nothing. 'Stonewall' Jackson is at last gone; he was wounded in the arm; in amputating it he lost his life.

There will always be much mystery surrounding the death of "Stonewall" Jackson, during the terrible night attack on the plank road, May 2. On that night he rode out in front of his lines to reconnoitre. It was dark, and only a small escort accompanied him. No directions were given by Jackson or his staff to the pickets. It is said, however, that they had been previously instructed to fire upon any party approaching from the Union lines.

It has always been emphatically urged by the Confederates, and supported by what might appear to be incontrovertible proof, that he was mortally wounded by these pickets as he was returning. The writer gives a version of this affair, obtained only two months after it took place from a most reliable man, Corp. Moses H. Gale,[13] of the Twentieth Massachusetts Volunteers, then in the 2d Corps.

This man had been wounded on that afternoon and taken prisoner. There was no time in the darkness and confusion in the Confederate lines just then to take him very far to the rear, especially as he was wounded. He was, therefore, held just in front of our line, and barely inside theirs, near the plank road. While under guard and keenly observing all that was going on about him, not being dangerously wounded, he saw a mounted party ride out by him on this road. Knowing by the escort that the officer must be of high rank, he asked his guard who he was, and was told that it was "Stonewall" Jackson.

Jackson rode to the front, and soon after Gale heard a heavy volley of musketry, followed by sharp firing, with some cannonading. In a short time General Jackson was borne by on a litter to the Confederate rear and near our wounded prisoner on the same road; in fact the litter was set down at that spot.

The escort with and carrying him, said: "The general almost rode into the Federal lines, they were so near, before he knew it, and was fired upon before he could turn back." In the confusion and darkness Gale seized the opportunity to escape. He crawled straight out on that road, and kept its general direction into our lines. The regiment he first struck in line of battle across this road, was the First Massachusetts, which had maintained this position before he was wounded, and while he was a prisoner.

---

[13] Moses H. Gale (1827–?) was 35 years old at enlistment, a shoemaker. He survived the war and was still living in 1900, though I could not determine his death date (enlistment and census records, 2019)

When he told his story, the regiment confirmed it by stating that they fired upon this mounted party after discovering them to be Confederates. It has since been substantiated by others and by the colonel commanding this regiment, Brevet-Brig. Napoleon B. McLaughlin, who makes this statement in his report of the battle.

General McLaughlin (now dead), was a captain in the 4th U. S. Cavalry, the writer's regiment, and he often related this circumstance to him while serving with McLaughlin in Texas after the war.

He stated that his regiment occupied this position, that he saw the mounted party ride up the road almost into the lines of the First Massachusetts; that his men without orders from him opened a terrific fire upon them, and there never was any doubt in his own mind that this was the fire that killed "Stonewall" Jackson; and he so reported it to the Adjutant General of Massachusetts.

Corporal Gale was a very intelligent man from the writer's own town; he was a member of the church there, and there was never any reason in the writer's mind for questioning in the least the veracity of his statement.[14]

Now came discouraging words. Our brother Walter writes, May 10:

> I have spent the most lonesome day of my army life. Every breath of air has seemed a moan over our great misfortune. Every bird song has been a wail for the unburied dead at Chancellorsville, and all things have spoken to us in disheartening whispers, until, at the close of the day, we sit in the weather-beaten camp tent, well-nigh demoralized soldiers.
>
> No rebel shells or bullets have caused this reaction in a loyal heart. No rebel bayonet has gleamed with terror, causing us to shudder with a coward's frightened spirit. Love of country and cause have not been wanting. Patriotism is not on the wane, but we feel as if we had wasted our strength on long, weary marches, kept tedious watch by night and day, passed sleepless nights, been wet,

---

[14] The consensus today is that Jackson was killed by friendly fire.—2019

341

cold and hungry, and fought all in vain. Nothing seems to have been gained but everything lost, and that too before we were whipped or half of the army seen the 'Grey backs.'

If all had been in the battle and got whipped we would be satisfied, but to think when all was bright in the prospectus, everyone so full of victory or death, and we, holding our second line secure, to think we should lose all and march way back to camp in that terrible storm, is enough to quench all hopes of victory in the mind of a poor recruit, the hero of continual defeats.

Call it what you please, demoralization or discouragement, we care not to ford rivers, sleep standing and fight running, when sure defeat always awaits such a doomed army."

Joe Hooker, we think his withdrawal of us somewhat mysterious. * ** It is such a catastrophe that his * * * plan apparently failed on the eve of victory. Now what's up? Three regiments of our brigade go home next month, and all the nine months' troops; our army will be materially diminished; and what are we going to do to fill up these large gaps? It will take time to make conscripts answer; you cannot make soldiers of citizens in a day. I don't see but what the Army of the Potomac is 'up a spout' although we are now under orders to move and our rations are ready; when, or where we go, I don't know and don't care. I shall not have much enthusiasm in any present move, but still shall always do my duty whenever or wherever I go.

I only hope that we may be allowed to regain our former good spirits before we move again; then go in 'Joe' Hooker! I say, and get another thrashing. We were much worn out while lying on the battlefield; it was so tiresome to lie close to the ground. During the awful carnage of Sunday, while you were writing we were in danger of losing our lives at any moment. The shells and bullets were ploughing through our ranks; no wonder you were anxious, while you were thinking of us then. How our thoughts were going forth to you all the time; but it is all over now and we are safe, and it is a mystery to me that we Bradford boys are still an unbroken band. Everyone is a brave lad among them, and showed himself a hero.

Last night as I wrote, Bob, while sleeping, talked in his sleep, saying: 'Oh, my leg! how can I march?' and the poor fellow, dreaming, would groan in his sleep. He suffered on that march.

Our brother was now ordered to Acquia Creek, the Eighth Infantry having been detached from headquarters for the purpose of regulating the departure of regiments whose term of enlistments had expired and were homeward bound.

Our brother writes as follows:

Camp at Acquia Creek,

May 27, 1863.

Since I last wrote you, we have been detached from headquarters, and sent to this point, for the purpose of regulating the departure of regiments whose terms of enlistment have expired and are homeward bound; also to keep affairs generally straight. It was reported to General Hooker that many deserters got away with these outgoing regiments, and that there was no system in regulating the workings of the various departments here; as far as desertions went he would stop it if he 'took his entire army to do it,' but he 'must have a regiment whose officers were to be depended upon,' to send down to this important post.

General Seth Williams (his adjutant general), proposed the Eighth, and we were taken away from General Patrick, much to his disgust. The order came while the old fellow was away; when he got home (back), we serenaded him, and all the officers called to pay their respects. The general did not know anything about the arrangements and thought it was a permanent thing; he felt very badly and said that he 'could not get along without us.' We then called on Generals Hooker, Hunt, Williams, and Ingalls; Hooker and Williams assured us that it was only temporary, and intended it as a compliment to the regiment.

I was at headquarters yesterday, and General Williams said that we would be ordered back tomorrow. I applied for a leave of absence some time since, and the General told me I had better wait until I returned to headquarters. I think we (the army) will remain in this position for some time, for the outgoing regiments and our losses will decrease the Army of the Potomac at least 40,000 men. I will wait until I see you before expressing any opinion relative to the late movement. If we take Vicksburg,[15] I have a very strong hope

---

[15] Grant's forces had Vicksburg under siege since May 18 and would accept its surrender the day after Gettysburg ended.—2019

that this war will end soon, and favorably to us; but if we fail there, after getting so near, I am fearful that neither you nor I will live to see what we are hoping for, the reestablishment of the Old Union.

I suppose Walt has written his views pretty freely; he can do it without any risk, but I intend to be discreet in expressing mine; I shall either say nothing about the affairs of this army, or else swear that 'Old Joe' is the greatest man living.

I think that Burnside stands above them all in patriotism and manhood; he will be relieved in six months and be put away in some pigeon hole. I really would like to see Charles Sumner President, for I believe he has some will of his own, and we know he has plenty of sense. *** My health is excellent; I have not been unwell scarcely an hour since I was last home. *** Write to General Headquarters, Army of the Potomac.

Our brother Bob says:

Camp Gove,

Near Potomac Creek, Va.,

May 20, 1863.

Words cannot express the Joy it gave me at receiving your excellent letter of the 14th inst., so full of good parental advice and sympathy for your soldier boys. I feared, or rather expected that I should receive a severe reprimand for the demoralizing tone of my letter, and yet I knew you would take into consideration the awful state of mind and body I was in, and as it proved, you did, like a good father as you are.

Who could realize the terrible scenes we passed through, both on the march and on the battlefield, without participating in them? *** I would never have believed, even if an angel from Heaven had said so, that I could pass through so much exposure and fatigue, and yet come out safe and well. *** It is curious, and yet a fact, that no matter how much a soldier passes through, a few days, rest in camp makes a different being of him, and no person, to see them after a long, tedious march, would ever suppose but what they had always been in camp. Let him get his 'bureau' and other numerous straps, etc., off, lie down a little while, or pitch a poncho, if he has time, and he is 'O.K.'

Citizens never share the private's hard tack and pork, or his bed. In battle they are always 'to the rear' thus they never see any more of a soldier's real life than though they had never come out, and are not reliable informants.

I am now in good health; rather fleshy for warm weather; the rheumatism has disappeared *** and when 'Joe' Hooker's caravan is ready to move, and 'Barnes' Flying Brigade' is ordered forward, *** I will gird on my armor, sling my extensive wardrobe on my back, and go as far as I can, try the 'Johnnies' another hack, and, if need be, retreat as usual in good order. I have drilled in those tactics under Hooker, Burnside and Co., so that I am pretty perfect, and can retreat in good style. *** When a soldier gets into camp or bivouac, he is generally so tired and hungry that he first cooks his supper, clears a place for a bed, rolls himself up in his blankets, and loses himself in sleep, for he knows not how soon he may be called upon, sometimes at midnight, and sometimes before dawn, and sleep is necessary to him. Yet, many a time have I, when we camped, struck off for a brook, and cooled my burning, blistered feet in the cool, running water. A soldier knows how to take care of his feet if he has time. *** I knew, before, the recipe for keeping the feet in good order by rubbing the stockings with bar soap; have tried it a great many times; it is a great thing. I tried it on our late march, and it helped me a great deal. How often have I wished that you could follow us along on a march, see us cook our coffee in our old black dippers, eat our common 'army pies,' clear away the brush, sticks and stones, and then have Walt, you and I, lie down together, roll up in our army blankets, and sleep until the bugler blows reveille; not that I wish you the fatigue attending said march, but that you could be with us, and see us as soldiers. *** I am pretty tired today, having been on guard three times within six days. Thursday eve we guarded the Twenty-fifth New York, who refused to do duty, their time being out as they supposed. I stood twelve hours, four on, and four off. Saturday I was on provost. Last night (Monday), at 9 o'clock, I had to go to guard the recruits of the Thirteenth, Seventeenth, and Twelfth New York, and was not relieved till 12 last night.

This morning we had a hard skirmish drill; I was very hot, and I am now rather used up. Gene I hear has moved to Acquia Creek, his regiment having been ordered to some other duty. I may get a chance someday to go down and see him. There are rumors that we are to do guard duty in Washington or Baltimore; it has been the rumor all the time that we are to go somewhere, but Meade would rather keep the field.

We escorted the Second Maine to the station this morning, and cheered the brave boys, wishing them a safe return; they have been in almost every battle since the First Bull Run, which they were in. They are a tough, hardy set of fellows, and deserve a hearty welcome wherever they go. ***

It will soon be time for parade, and I have my gun to clean. *** We ought to be truly thankful that we escaped death or wounds, for when I look back and see the bleeding disfigured and mangled bodies borne to the rear, I shudder and thank the Lord.

There is to be a presentation at General Barnes' tomorrow.

Our brother Walter writes, May 25:

As to army matters, and the late movement, I think General Hooker ought to have considered Stoneman's raid a success until it proved a failure, even if he had not heard from him. Because one corps ran, it was no sign that the rest of us would have done likewise, and 'Old Joe' ought to have run the risk of an attack upon the enemy; we can fight as well as they, if we only have a chance given us, and I long for the day when we can be allowed to fight them successfully and not be hampered. We are too near Washington to ever win a victory.

Thus ended the campaign of Chancellorsville[16] with its incidents which, for brilliancy of conception, rapidity of concentration, but for blundering stupidity of execution, and hard, demoralizing influence upon the rank and file of the Army of the Potomac, never had a parallel in history.

We have briefly stated the facts, the incidents that came under our observance, and have so far attempted no descriptive analysis of the movements, objects or results; that belongs to a history of the battle of Chancellorsville. But every private soldier had his opinion. We had ours.

---

[16] The defeat was a terrible shock to the north. Lincoln was quoted as saying, "My God! My God! What will the country say?"—2019

It may not be well known but nevertheless it is a fact, susceptible of proof, that the inception and plan of the campaign of Chancellorsville never had a lodgment in the brain of General Hooker until it had been suggested and fully explained to him by others. It was the sole product of Gen. G. K. Warren, who, after submitting it to Hooker and Gen. H. J. Hunt, chief of artillery of the Army of the Potomac, at a conference of these three officers, carefully elaborated the plan, and it was adopted in full by the commanding general.

General Hunt stated this shortly before his death. Its failure, and the death, after a long illness, of General Warren, of chagrin and a broken heart at his failure to exonerate himself from the stigma cast upon him by General Sheridan, was probably the reason why Warren never claimed this plan as his own.

It was to be an offensive campaign from the start, and after the fords had been cleared, and the march of concentration safely accomplished, an offensive battle was to have been fought in open country, in conjunction with General Sedgwick operating from the rear, after capturing the heights of Fredericksburg. There was to be no backward movement. It was no part of this well-conceived and partially successful plan that the Army of the Potomac should be locked up in the forests about the Chancellor House and its esprit de corps and fighting capacity paralyzed by less than 30,000 men under bee on its front.

This well-matured and well-considered plan did not miss fire from any failure in the march of concentration on Thursday, April 30, for that was well-timed, and proved the most perfect success of any move in the history of the Army of the Potomac. The heads of columns of the 5th, 11th, and 12th Corps arrived at the clearing about the Chancellor House within a surprisingly short time of each other, and the fords were uncovered with slight losses.

It did not arise from the failure of Sykes to promptly attack on Friday, May 1, for after he had succeeded in securing all the salient points in the advance upon the Fredericksburg turnpike on that morning, he was recalled; but when it was too late, the order was countermanded by Hooker-through Warren, both of whom well knew that this movement was one of the vital points in the original offensive plan; to advance into sufficiently open ground to give battle beyond the debouches of the forest roads, of which so much has been said by Hooker's friends. Sykes had cleared the way and the connections planned for this move were about to be made, when he was directed to abandon his positions. Both Couch and Slocum protested against this retrograde movement, and Hancock was opposed to such a step.

The failure of this plan was not due to the disaster to the 11th Corps on the evening of Saturday, May 2, for that was but a mere incident, a bungling mistake of Jackson which should never have succeeded, and ought to, and doubtless would have proved a decided advantage in our favor under the leadership of a bold general of Sheridan's type, and Jackson's Corps, in its disorganized condition after the death of its erratic leader, could have been scattered or captured and bee's main army placed in great jeopardy if not totally defeated.

The failure of this great plan cannot be laid to the seizure of the plateau about the Chancellor House by Stuart, then in command of Jackson's Corps, on Sunday morning, May 3, and the subsequent contraction of Hookers lines, although there can be but little doubt that this lent courage to the Confederates in the belief that Hooker was now becoming timid, and had had enough.

It was not due to General Sedgwick's withdrawal across the river at Banks' Ford on the night of Tuesday, May 4, for that was a logical sequence of Hooker's failure to connect with Sedgwick, and to his change of the original plan of campaign, which Warren was striving with almost superhuman energy, nearly to the point of exhaustion, to carry out to the letter; nor to the rain and subsequent rise in the river, as some writers in their ignorance of the facts have asserted, compelling Hooker to recross to reestablish his base of supplies; for the storm did not commence until 3 P. M. on May 3, and it had already become known along the lines that Hooker had given the order for withdrawal long before a drop of rain had fallen. Our brother, who had ridden from Falmouth, told us this when lying behind the rifle pits, shortly after noon on that day. Besides, his line of communications and bridges were secure, and were not then even threatened. If not due to any of these causes, some of which historians and the near friends of General Hooker have at all times been so ready to ascribe the failure to secure a victory at Chancellorsville; what then?

We must look to some other cause for this sudden letting down in the aggressive, offensive campaign of General Hooker; some cause for this lack of boldness, indecision, timidity, vacillation, or whatever it may be termed, of this general, who had so long enjoyed the high-sounding title of "Fighting Joe."

To tell the solemn truth at any time about the campaigns of that war, especially to impugn the motives or courage, and to assail the character of a man who possessed so many solid traits and attractive qualities of heart and mind as General Hooker; to tell the truth about the battle of Chancellorsville, was to bring down a storm of criticism from the friends of General Hooker, and he who dares to do so at this late day may invite the same fate.

But that Hooker was so much under the influence of liquor as to be totally unable to command the Army of the Potomac, from Sunday noon, or shortly after he was injured at the Chancellor House, until it was decided to recross the river, no one will deny who was near the little white house at the junction of the Ely's ford and United States' ford roads, from that time until the army retired from its contracted position at that point.

It is not maligning, or desecration of the memory of the dead to do justice to the living patriots of today, who, though alive, suffered untold agony for the misdeeds of others; those superior officers who owed it to themselves, their oaths and to their country to keep sober when the lives of thousands and the safety of the Republic rested in the hollow of their hands.

The friends of General Hooker have strenuously exerted themselves, and strained every point consistent with honor, to cover this defect in his character, but without avail; but no one who was with us on the right flank of the Twenty-second

Massachusetts, within less than one hundred and fifty yards of the white house, where Hooker lay during the period mentioned, can deny the fact of this fatal error on his part; in fact, there are plenty of men living who saw this exhibition, and can solemnly testify to the truth of this statement.

These friends who have endeavored, almost to the limit of ridicule, to shield their chief all these years, have admitted and urged, for the sake of covering up the real cause of failure, that he was disabled by the shock received at the Chancellor House on the morning of Sunday, May 3, and was not himself after that day.

This can no longer be pleaded in extenuation. If General Hooker was disabled or rendered *hors de combat* by the concussion at the Chancellor House, and his friends plead that as the only ground for his inaction, that in itself was the very best reason in the world why he should have turned over the command to the next in rank, General Couch, thus relieving himself from what followed. By not doing so he became fully responsible for all subsequent disaster, and the old soldiers of the Army of the Potomac will, in the future, never accept this or any other such flimsy excuses as have been given why this was not done.

What we wanted at the supreme moment was not a disabled or inert commander, but a bold, aggressive man, capable of carrying put the offensive plan of battle with which the campaign had been initiated.

If he was not disabled by his wound or the shock of whiskey, why did he not get into the saddle and lead nearly 80,000 men, over 30,000 of whom had not snapped a cap and were eager for battle and say: "Boys, there are but 30,000 men in through the forest; we will advance, join Sedgwick, and crush Bee's army." Who doubts the result?

Is it possible that "Fighting" Joe Hooker misunderstood the fiber and temper of the Army of the Potomac, and believed that it was willing to be thus inert, to lie as supinely on its back as its leader then was? A writer has well said: "When Hooker commanded a division or corps, he planned badly and fought well; when he commanded the army, he planned well (?) and fought badly."

The failure at Chancellorsville was due to the incompetency which comes from a besotted brain. There are men living today, belonging to the writer's company, who were on guard during the winter at General Hooker's headquarters, in front of his tent, who can testify to his habits; in fact it was well known among us that General Hooker was drinking heavily all that season.

To the Committee on the Conduct of the War, it had been "loosely reported" that General Hooker was under the influence of drink at the battle of Chancellorsville, and when they summoned the corps commanders to testify, the question was put to them. Was it to be expected that they would affirm these reports, and state that their chief was drunk, and thus spread broadcast such a scandal over the entire country, to the demoralization of the army and of irreparable damage to the cause?

Why did not the committee send for some of the rank and file of the army, especially the men of those regiments who were near to the white house (Bullocks?) As at Antietam and Fredericksburg, there were thousands of men .who, although under fire, had not been engaged or come in contact with the enemy. Standing or lying with arms in their hands as spectators, they could at an opportune moment, led by a Sheridan or any other bold commander willing to take such a safe responsibility, have advanced all along the lines and swept Lee's army out of existence.

It is said that so cautious a man as Meade asked Hooker's permission to let the 1st and 5th Corps push in. The former had not been engaged and was fresh; but indecision had succeeded Hooker's boldness of conception, and division after division, and driblet after driblet had been sent in, only to be rolled away by Lee's constant watchfulness, and confidence that "Fighting Joe" was inert and paralyzed.

No historian can gloss over Fredericksburg and Chancellorsville so long as an intelligent soldier of the Army of the Potomac is alive and on deck to testify to the wretched incompetency of its commanding generals; and it is full time now that they speak out boldly what they know and believe.

The Army of the Potomac had marched, fought and endured, and was there at Chancellorsville, as it always had been, superior to the genius of any commander yet appointed.

For most of the time during two days and a half nobody but a drunken general was in command of the Army of the Potomac, and Chancellorsville was the most lamentable and unnecessary failure in the history of the War of the Rebellion.

The Official Records, many of them, have been found to be absolutely worthless by the military students of the Civil War. The so-called "Apocrypha," autobiographies, memoirs and papers, including magazine articles, have been found much more reliable, but the zeal of some army, corps, division and brigade commanders have carried them away beyond the limits of reliability—even when padding their diaries—in an effort to enlarge upon the importance of the doings of their respective commanders, and in attempts to belittle others, but especially in trying to whitewash or gloss over the defects, bad habits, failures and shortcomings of those who, although now dead, caused by their jealousies innumerable disasters and defeats. The old Latin adage "Speak only good of the dead" is a truth which few seek to disregard, but something is due to the living, and so I turn to the last literature of that war—the so-called "Profane Literature"—the accounts of humble participants and obscure observers and commentators.

The boys who served in the ranks during the Civil War, although perhaps obscure, in the sense that while carrying a rifle they wore no stars, bars nor eagles, were, nevertheless, the flower of the land. Bright, intelligent and right from the schools, colleges, stores, workshops and offices, they were very close observers, and what they saw and heard they jotted down in diaries and letters home. Many of these memorandums form today the basis of many a regimental history—the most valuable of all data upon which to found the future historians' account of that war. They looked with a critical eye upon the initiation and progress of every campaign, and can now give their judgment as to the causes for their failure, especially for the failure at Chancellorsville. Many of these boys have been back to these battlefields and made a careful study of them. This is the conclusion which one of them now makes of the failure of General Hooker at this battle of Chancellorsville.

He had been drinking heavily all winter. Shortly after Mr. Lincoln's visit to him (General Hooker), near Falmouth, Va., his friends urged General Hooker to stop. He did so—and completely. He went to Chancellorsville to fight an offensive battle. Official Records and all subsequent histories show this. He met with the accident while leaning against the pillar at the Chancellor House. It was a mere contused wound or bruise, and was not sufficient to disable him; he himself said so, and he also says he was not drunk. But he was, and there were plenty of men there, and who are living now, who saw him. Their testimony could have been had before the Committee on the Conduct of the War. It was not "abstinence from his customary draughts that left him not at his best, when his faculties should have been most alert." It was at just this time when he was carried back to the Chandler House near the intersection of the Ely's ford and the United States ford roads, that his staff officers, seeing that he needed and must have stimulants—after he had had it all the winter, and had now himself lost confidence in Hooker (as he told General Doubleday) gave them to him. The consequence was that he was inert and stupid, or more or less drunk from 12 o'clock Sunday, May 3, until he left his tent on the night of May 5, at the Chandler House.

Barnes' Brigade, 1st Brigade, 1st Division, '5th Army Corps, lay with its right within a few yards of General Hooker's tent at the Chandler House. We had occasion to pass it frequently during lulls in the battle, Monday and Tuesday, for water and for other purposes. His tent flap was thrown back for air. We saw him lying there inactive, inert, in a stupor most of the time. While we did not go in and smell his breath, we smelt the odor coming from his tent, and saw the bottles lying about in great numbers. This regiment was in Barnes' Brigade of the 5th Corps. What this historian saw, we all saw. So much for "Profane Literature."

To use the rather coarse observation of an humble participant and obscure observer and commentator (fifty years after the battle), General Hooker was not injured by any shot that was supposed to have disabled him after Sunday, May 3, but he was "shot in the neck" with brandy for nearly three days, during which his drunken adjutant-general, one Col. Joseph Dickinson, and his other staff officers, for fear of exposure, and to cover up Hooker's condition, either did not dare to issue an order delegating the command of the Army of the Potomac to General Couch, the senior corps commander present—or did not have sense enough. Result, nobody in command, except an incompetent drunken general; consequently withdrawal without defeat, a shameful disaster, for which General Hooker should have been cashiered.

THE CAMPAIGN OF GETTYSBURG

On the 29th of May, 1863, after nearly a month of uninteresting drill fatigue, picket, etc.—following the battle of Chancellorsville— the 5th Corps as a corps of observation, preceding the great campaign so soon to follow, moved out of its winter cantonment for the fourth time, and as it proved for the last, for we never saw our old huts and shacks again. Its duty was to cover the fords of the Rappahannock River, to prevent the enemy from crossing in force or attempting any movement on our flanks, without due notice being given by our scouts and pickets.

Our brother Walter writes:

Camp Gove, May 28th, 1863.

We have just received orders to pack up and move; the regiment is still out on picket, but the order of General Meade is that it will join us on the march. Everything is hurley burley, the boys having left everything in camp. No one knows where we are going, but I hope to 'Dixie' and to a glorious victory. Shells and bullets are but as music, if the result shall only be a song of triumph. With love to all, and a prayer that Heaven will bless us, I am your loving son.

It was a beautiful, bright, sunny day and our march of fifteen miles from our old camp at Potomac Creek led us by Stoneman's Switch, through Sykes' camp of regulars, by Hartwood Church, over the old familiar roads— never to be traversed again; to Wykoff's Gold Mine [near Morrisville, VA], where we encamped. On the 30th we moved to Morrisville, four miles, and on the 31st the brigade moved back about two miles to Gove Church.

Our brother Walter again says:

Camp Near Morrisville, Va.,

Sunday, May 31, 1863.

We started day before yesterday morning, and marched about twenty miles, on one of the warmest days of the season; we were much fatigued when we halted for the night. It came hard upon us, for we had just begun to get 'fat and lazy' in camp again. We started yesterday morning and after marching five miles, camped in our present place; we are beautifully situated in a grove, and an opening in front, with a house in the center (a 'ville' I suppose). Where we are going, and how soon, I know not; all sorts of rumors are rife— the rebs have crossed the river, taken Warrenton, we are cut off,' etc., etc. But I do not derive much uneasiness from the stories that are spread abroad by the boys. I only want to see 'Johnny Reb' in a hand to hand fight, where we can be allowed to do a share in winding up this rebellion in a hurry.

I am somewhat disappointed in hearing that Vicksburg is not taken yet; I wasted my breath in cheering too soon, and the Colonel made a rich speech for nothing, over the report of its fall, in a despatch to General Hooker. Our teams are all hitched up, and we may move at any moment today; no one knows a thing about it. I reckon that the Brigadier is at a loss to know what to do; he is waiting orders from General Meade. In the meantime we are in the cool shade, and are making ourselves as comfortable as possible this glorious day. It is magnificent over head and under foot; *** Bob is very well; stood the march tip-top; so did all the boys.

Here our camp was pitched in a most delightful locality—a vast stretch of open fields, sloping to the river, surrounded by groves of fragrant spruce, cedar and other evergreens. We were a few miles only from Kelly's Ford. Here we remained until June 13. Our duties were many and arduous, consisting of numerous details for picket, scout, guard, fatigue, building earthworks, etc. Our camp was ornamented with shades over our shelter tents; company streets were laid out and springy bunks made, the whole enclosed by leafy arbors, and during our leisure moments we enjoyed during these five almost perfect Virginia days the *dolce far niente* [sweet doing nothing] of our army life.

The writer was dreamily engaged in reflections upon his past year's army life, when a sharp voice rang out—"You are detailed to go with the forage train to 'Stoneman's Switch,'" and all his air castles were shattered.

Only the night before, our favorite little chaplain of the Fourth Michigan had been ruthlessly murdered by the guerillas and freebooters of Stuart's and Mosby's Cavalry, that infested all the wood paths and trails leading to the fords of the river. Our route led us by this spot over the rough corduroy road. Seated in the

356

bottom of a springless wagon, a six-mule team strung out on the trot or run nearly the entire distance of eighteen miles, and with guns firmly braced between our knees we made a mad race for the station.

Having loaded, we started by dark on our return. The moon rose full and bright. Hartwood Church was reached, that black ogre that stood in our path, where so many prisoners had been "gobbled," when smash! crash!! and the wagon was a wreck upon the corduroy, a few rods only from the spot where the chaplain's throat had been cut. [1]

The forest and road were as light as day, though it was midnight. The mules gave vent to their hunger, fatigue and impatience in the most dismal and unearthly brays. The whips cracked like pistols. The teamsters cursed in their unique way, and in the still quiet of the night the suspense was more terrible than the lull preceding a battle. Every sound, voice and movement seemed like the crash of an explosion, reverberating through the woods for miles. The ghastly corpse of the chaplain loomed up before us in every conceivable position. At every moment we expected to hear the dread cry "Surrender!" Our little squad of six unloaded and righted the wagon, lashed the wheel, reloaded, and after about an hour's delay, which seemed an interminable age, we again started, breathing freer as we left the ghostly shape behind us.

Our brother Walter now says:

Camp near Grove Church,

June 2, 1863.

We have come back from our position of last Sunday, and we now occupy a camp two miles from Morrisville, and about six miles from Kelly's Ford, where we crossed the Rappahannock on our advance

---

[1] There was a chaplain named John Seage (1817–) of the 4th Michigan who was wounded in action on June 8, 1863, shot in the shoulder, while carrying the mail and payroll to Washington. He returned to service after his recovery; mustered out in 1865. I found no other records for the 4th Michigan listing the death of a chaplain (military and pension records, 2019).

357

to Chancellorsville. *** We came back Sabbath evening, about an hour after I had finished my letter. *** The whole brigade is here, and we are the reserve to our two other brigades of the division which guard and occupy the fords on this side. We are in one large field, the greenest and most like New England's early grass plats that I have yet seen. We are upon the level surface of a roomy hill summit; curving the whole length of the field, to our rear, is a splendid grove of pines extending a mile back; in the foreground, an easy sloping descent to a convenient brook; then an ascent of a few hundred yards, a dividing fence, and another field to a crowning awn of woods. Three houses are in the open space to add variety and lend enchantment to the scene.

On our left are deep forests; on our right the road to Morrisville, Kelly's Ford, Warrenton, and back to Camp Grove, twenty-five miles to the rear.

Our whole open ground, I should judge, contained 400 acres. It affords a magnificent view, is airy, and pleasant in every way *** the whole regiment say it is the finest, most beautiful ground they have yet had, including that at Gaines' Mills. ***

How long we stop I do not dare even to imagine; I only know we are fixing up the best we know how for warm weather; everything green and shady about us is being used to decorate the camp, and already our headquarters are assuming a very genteel and even gaudy appearance. *** Our duty has been continuous and unceasing; detail after detail, for fatigue, guard, picket and sundries, have kept the regiment busy. Bob had to go way back to camp, with a guard of ten men for the wagons. Before he went, Monday, he said—'Good-bye, Walt, you may never see me again; danger of being gobbled by gorrils [sic; guerillas], you know they have a way of paroling 'em by running a knife across the wind pipe.' *** Bob got back this morning, and while he was gone, the Colonel knocked all our plans askew by telling me that I must tent with the non-commissioned staff or nearer headquarters; so I had to leave the company, and Bob found me gone, house and baggage, and now he and I must be separated for the first time as bedfellows. I shall miss him so much; I am homesick already. I could not sleep last night, everything seemed so strange to me and it is hard for him too; while he was gone, all the boys mated, and there is no one left to go in with him; and besides, Bob has only one piece of shelter tent; and then the poor fellow, just off duty this morning, is on picket tonight, and does not come in from post until relieved tomorrow night. The whole company has been detailed to work for officers since he has been gone, and it is his turn again. ***

I tent with Emerson, the headquarters cook, who was at Camp Cameron with us; he is a nice man, and having been all over the world, makes a nice tent companion; *** we have got a pretty tent made of five ponchos, and have bunks made of poles and boughs; we have set out trees in all directions, so that we are in a shady wood lot all by ourselves, within call of headquarters;

The old Sibley tent is within a few paces, and the mess tent of the Colonel and staff. Emerson cooks nearby, the non-commissioned staff are a few rods in the woods, and the commissary department, hospital, etc. etc. The whole camp is perfectly beautiful both in design and carrying out. ***

I see by the papers that the Eighteenth Massachusetts was the escort to the Second Maine to the depot; they forgot to mention the Twenty-second; we formed an important part to the whole display, being on the left, with the Maine boys between us. I am glad they have at last got safely back to the old Pine Tree State; wasn't it a good plan to transport them by steamer instead of by rail?

Good-night! May I see you at no distant day, and always live in your smiles and approbations.

Our brother Bob now adds:

Camp near Morrisville,

21 miles from old camp,

June 5, 1863.

Since I last wrote we have moved, and of course it has been attended with much fatigue and tiresome duty, having to go on guard nearly every day or on picket. We are ten miles from Hartwood Church, three miles from Morrisville—a small village of two or three old shanties—on the turnpike road to Warrenton. * * * I have been on guard or on picket for the last four or five days, besides going way back to our old camp, traveling all day and all night to get back; the wagon tipped over four times, once at midnight, when we expected the 'Johnnies to gobble us.' *** When I got back, I found myself houseless, Walt having to pitch his near headquarters, and I have no one to pitch with.

When I got back from that hard tramp I thought I should have a little rest, but no! that night I went on picket; came off last night; will have to go on guard tomorrow morning. *** Our division is guarding the fords, from Bank's to Kelly's Fords. Of course it is the brigade's luck to have to go the farthest. We are between Ellis' and Kelly's Fords; they marched us to within a mile of here the first day. It was a terribly hot, dusty, tough march. The next morning we went to Morrisville, three miles ahead, stayed there a little over a day, and came back to this place. Three batteries just came here; I went down and found out that one was Dimmick's battery, First Regulars, a classmate of Gene's and who was killed at Chancellorsville, near the brick house; Gene thought a great deal of him. We are thirty miles from Gene; I have not seen him for some time.

Our brother Walter writes again:

June 6, 1863.

We are now under marching orders to be ready to move at five minutes' notice *** all sorts of rumors are being constantly circulated, and as we have had no daily papers *** we know nothing scarcely of the present state of affairs and things in the Army of the Potomac; we only know that we are going to vacate our present beautiful camp, and that very quickly.

Guards were placed on all rebel property, the owners of which were rebel spies—generally in the butternut or light grey that millers wear. On June 5, while on picket, an officer and nine men of the regiment scouted around near the river until they approached a house. Supposing they might find concealed some guerillas with which that section of the country was filled, they advanced cautiously, surrounded it and then, making a dash through a wheat field, entered it. Upon searching it they found only an old couple; but the Negroes soon gave information which led to securing four horses, secreted in the brush nearby, but the birds had flown.

Field works had been thrown up by a detail of about 100 men from the brigade to cover our two positions at the two fords. Two batteries of Napoleon guns were placed in them, but though finished June 7, they were of no use.

On the 8th, while picketing in the Morrisville road, we saw the corps flags of all the corps in the army approaching through a thick dust. It proved to be two brigades of infantry under Generals Ames and Russell going to the support of the cavalry in their reconnaissance to Beverly Ford. They carried the corps flags to deceive the enemy into the belief that the entire Army of the Potomac was there.

On the 9th there was a heavy booming of guns all day, indicating a sharp cavalry fight. On the 10th we were ordered to "fall in" about 11 a. m., and we moved to Kelly's Ford as a support to the cavalry, but not being needed soon returned to our camps. On the 11th we again received orders to move.

Our brother Walter's letter says:

June 11th, 1863.

Orders have just come for us to move either today or tomorrow morning, and away we go at that time I suppose. Yesterday we went to Kelly's Ford to act as an aid to the cavalry force, which fought such a glorious fight the day before; the greatest cavalry combat of the war, they say;[2] we had a long, dusty march, and not being needed, returned at night. We cannot imagine where we are bound for now. Perhaps the rebs are on their way to Washington; I seem to dread continually now a third 'Bull Run,' and yet I think it will not be realized; everything breathes of approaching fight, and I say 'let it come!' We can fight now as well as ever, and men can die as gloriously as they did at Chancellorsville, with all the radiance of ancient chivalry. Nothing so inspiring as to see a dauntless, brave man rush into battle fearlessly, and I am proud of the risk a soldier runs of at least dying in a worthy cause.

It would have pained you, mother, to have seen the scattered graves of soldiers all along our march yesterday; as I thought of the poor fellows who lay beneath the mound and head board, there seemed to be a tear ready for everyone; each told of a saddened home, and really, are not these names, humble though they may be, worthy of being remembered as household treasures? Heaven bless the poor mourning families that this war occasions, and would that

---

[2] The Battle of Brandy Station, June 9th, was a victory for Union morale.—2019

I could shout to them the grand future day, which shall be sanctified to them by the blood of their loved ones, and the tears they may shed over their memory.

When I shall write again, no one knows; but wherever I am, I am thinking of you all, and constantly write my love and affection in the spirit. Good-bye! my love to all, and with ever increasing affection for you whom I long to see, I am your loving son. * * * Bob is out on picket; has been out two days; will join us tomorrow at the outposts, and then we will go side by side to anything that awaits us.

Our brother of the regulars, who had been on a short leave of absence, now writes:

Camp of the Eighth U.S. Infantry,

At General Headquarters,

June 11, 1863.

I am back once more, and find everything about camp the same as when I left it. *** I am pained to record the death of two most dear friends; you have often heard me speak of Cross of the Engineers; his father lived at Lawrence and died a few years since. Captain Cross was shot through the head while laying a pontoon bridge at Franklin's crossing. His men wept and kissed his face as they passed him; his body was embalmed and sent to Lawrence.

During the cavalry fight a few days since, Col. Grimes Davis,[3] Eighth New York Cavalry Volunteers, and Captain of the First U. S. Cavalry, was shot through his heart. He saw his regiment wavering and rushed to the head of it, when a rebel lieutenant drew his pistol and ordered him to surrender, shooting him at the same instant. The Adjutant of the Eighth New York Cavalry caught Davis with his left hand and killed his murderer with his sabre. Grimes Davis is the man who cut his way out of Harper's Ferry, and was regarded as the very best cavalry officer in the service; he was brave even to rashness, but that you know is an essential qualification in a good cavalry officer. The regular brigade of cavalry charged seven times, and lost heavily in officers. I understand Noyes is wounded, but cannot learn how badly; so they go.

---

[3] Benjamin Franklin Davis (1831–June 9, 1863), known as "Grimes," was a Mississippian who fought for the Union. Killed at Beverly Ford near Brandy Station (National Park Service website, 2019).

Poor Cross is the fourth one in the crowd that met in Marsh's tent the Sunday before the battle of Chancellorsville. We are all under orders to move at very short notice; to go wherever Hooker orders. I found, when I arrived in camp, that General Patrick had appointed me as inspector-general of his entire command; I reported to Colonel Schriver,[4] inspector-general of this army, and he said that he was very glad that he had me in his department. Lieutenant-Colonel Davis (his assistant) and myself have always been very good friends, and were at Bull Run together.

I am not relieved from my regimental duties, and do not wish to be. I intend to make it all pay at some future time. I have no increased rank, but Colonel Schriver says I ought to be a lieutenant-colonel. I saw General Patrick this evening for the first time since my return, and he shook hands with me very cordially, saying that he 'was glad to see me back again.' The Fifth Corps is up at the fords. I expect we will go somewhere very shortly.

On the 12th, the entire 3d Corps passed us and as the writer was on picket on the road about a mile from camp, toward Morrisville, a good opportunity was had for watching this command pass in review. In it we had many friends. On foot and marching with the One Hundred and Fourteenth Pennsylvania (Collis' Zouaves) we saw "French Mary."[5]

The 1st Corps passed us on the 13th, and on the same day at dark we broke camp for good, leaving our beautiful camp at Grove Church, and moving to Morrisville, two miles, bivouacked for the night. We had started at last on our long and weary pilgrimage.

On June 14 the battalion of the 8th Infantry, with General Hooker at Headquarters, Army of the Potomac, left camp on the Gettysburg campaign. It marched to Dumfries, twenty-one miles, very hot and dusty; reveille was at 3 a.m.; started at 4 o'clock.

---

[4] Edmund Schriver (1812–1899), West Point 1833, railroad executive, reentered service in May, 1861, retired 1881 as a brevet major general.—2019

[5] Marie Tepe Leonard (1834–1901), was awarded the Kearny Cross for services at Chancellorsville. She also apparently ran a thriving business in contraband whiskey in the camps.—2019

While waiting for a pontoon bridge to be thrown across the Occoquan, they watched a thousand cattle swim that river; they then crossed the bridge and camped on high ground, June 16; they marched to Fairfax Station, eight miles, before 8 o'clock, and on the 17th, headquarters was at that place.

Our brother of the regulars now writes:

Camp at Fairfax Station,

June 17, 1863.

I have just time to say that I am well; I have not seen the boys since my return; we will probably move this evening, or early tomorrow morning; I suppose our destination is Harper's Ferry. *** My duties as inspector-general and quartermaster keep me on the jump.

It had now been discovered for the first time that the enemy no longer confronted us along the river fords. Hooker did not then know that Longstreet was already on his march northward. [Alfred] Pleasanton had superseded Stoneman in command of the cavalry and was making strenuous efforts to discover the whereabouts of the enemy. The battle at Beverly Ford had stiffened up the troopers wonderfully, increasing their morale and confidence. A new era began to dawn upon our hitherto somewhat disorganized cavalry force, for it was seen that the Confederate cavalry, with its easily accumulated prestige, was now slightly on the wane, more especially because they could no longer rely upon blooded remounts. Pleasanton claims to have fully disclosed and thwarted Tee's plans, uncovered his movement, and compelled him to take the indirect route of the valley, instead of along the eastern side of the Blue Ridge, with Stuart's Cavalry as a protecting flank.

On the 14th we moved early, and made a long and exhausting march of twenty miles through Bristersberg. We bivouacked near Catlett's Station on Deep Run, passing through several little hamlets en route. We found but little water, and the weather being now hot and dry, the column suffered severely. We halted one hour to make coffee. Orders were to move on to Bristow Station, but these were countermanded, and the men received with cheers the order to remain at Catlett's Station. On the 15th we marched at 5.30 A M. through Catlett's to near Bristow Station about five miles—over a cleanly swept tract of the Bull Run country, which bore all the unmistakable evidences of war's destructive hand. It was terribly hot and dusty. Little or no water was to be had and there was the usual suffering. The regiment was paid off here, and we remained in camp during the 16th in a miserable, unattractive field, low and flat. Here the gamblers of the command indulged in poker or bluff, sweat boards and every species of gambling.

On the 17th, we passed through Manassas with its wreckage of locomotives, cars and debris of all kinds; crossed the Bull Run stream below the Stone Bridge (Mitchell's Ford) and striking the crossroad to Gum Spring, with Centerville in full view to the right, we gradually veered to the left and encamped that night near Gum Spring, after one of the hottest, most wearisome marches along the old Manassas route which the regiment had ever made. At this season of the year the streams and springs having dried up, indescribable suffering was the result. Where we forded Bull Run, the water was about the color of milk and molasses, warm and nauseous. After leaving it, there was nothing but slimy mud holes to drink out of, and the suffering increased. At every semblance of a spring, crowds of men swarmed, and woe to the sentinel stationed there by some considerate (?) officer to secure pure water for his own use—who tried to beat back the raging, thirsty, suffering crowd. He was quietly lifted to one side and the scooping and filtering of mud and grit went on. Men, horses, mules all rushed pell-mell into the warm, disgusting pools and puddles and drank the filthy fluid to quench their thirst, regardless of results, and sifting sand enough, as an old veteran said, to "build a fortification."

Several men were sunstruck in the column during the day. Towards afternoon, however, we gained the shelter and shade of a partially wooded road, and striking a slower gait, gathering up the wretched stragglers, we staggered into camp. Colonel Gleason of the Twenty-fifth New York, a two-year regiment of our brigade, died of exhaustion and sunstroke, and it was said that seventeen men died in the division on this day's march. Many men of that regiment deserted while passing Centerville. Their time was practically out, however, for the entire regiment left us while we were lying at Gum Spring.

On this march all sutlers' teams were ordered out of the wagon trains and sent to Washington. Having been paid off at Bristow Station, many of the officers and men intrusted their money to our sutler, Ephraim Hackett. He started for Washington, carrying a large amount to be expressed. On the way he was warned that the country was then swarming with guerillas between the army and Washington, and the chances were that he might be "gobbled." He pressed on, keeping a sharp lookout, and towards night went into camp.

Soon after, camping, the sorriest looking "cracker outfit" was seen approaching. Two old, broken-down mules hitched to an old, dilapidated go-cart, no two wheels alike, and containing five or six men, who proved to be sutlers of different regiments who had "seen" Mosby, and been "cleaned out" of everything—horses, wagons, goods, money, and, in some cases, the coats from their backs. They had started back on foot, and on their way had picked up this "outfit," and pressed it into service.

They camped with Hackett, who fed them well out of his own supplies, and in the morning they went on their way rejoicing, while Hackett, on his way, thought his turn might come next.

But fortune favored him, and he got through safely, delivered the money, got receipts and started back. In the meantime, news had reached the regiment that "Hackett is captured, and of course our money;" and when he rode into camp one afternoon, a shout went up that he did not quite understand until the crowd gathered, saying they never expected to see him again.

We remained at Gum Spring on the 18th, in a very good camp, with good Water. Had a very heavy thunderstorm in the afternoon. Frequently on this march, the exhausted men, after a few hours' rest, would start to regain the column. If along the route a house offered the tempting inducement for a bite, any addition to the meagre larder in the haversack, its capacity was amply tested before reaching camp. On one occasion the writer, by force of circumstances, was compelled to fall out. After a rest of an hour or more, he again resumed the march. Seeing a collection of Negro huts in the distance, he wended his way toward them. The orders on this march were very stringent against straggling, and the Provost Guard following in the rear seemed omnipresent. Their drag-net succeeded in securing many a victim, who, after a severe reprimand or some light form of punishment, was released at night or the following morning and sent to his regiment.

The innocent and guilty or chronic straggler suffered alike. Scarcely had the writer got the words out of his mouth—"Got any pies, Auntie?" to the good-natured looking wench that appeared at the door, before he saw the Provost coming from the road across the lane to the ranch. "Yas, sah! I'se got some blackberry pies right in de oben just now." "Quick, then, give us one!" was the anxious request, one eye cast over our shoulders at the rapidly approaching guard.

A hot, juicy blackberry pie was slipped into the outspread hands opened to receive it, and a twenty-five cent scrip was transferred to the delighted "dark"—and we scurried around the corner of the old "ramshackle" house, just as the Provost came in on the front. But now came the agony.

The pie was full of boiling juice; the crust was hot and moist. The juice commenced to leak through the thin .material. Our speedy exit over rough ground, and desperate efforts to carry a gun in one hand, and a hot pie in two, had broken it apart, and now the hot liquid was pouring up the arm sleeves of our thin blouse, blistering at every step. But after such a compromise to our dignity and efforts to escape arrest, we held on and saved the pie, which was enjoyed later on by our famished stomach, even while ruefully regarding our burned hands and wrists.

On another day's march, the writer's rations had given out. Hot, dry, dusty, dirty and completely worn out, he had thrown himself down after the long day s march, weary and faint, to chew the cud of bitter reflection. It had called for every element of grit and pluck, or as the western men express it, "sand in our craw." We felt as though if we could have some milk to wash down the gritty dust, and cool the parched throats, or some little delicacy that would satisfy the craving of the stomach, how much better satisfied we should feel to make our bivouac for the night in the rank grass.

Surely the slave of Aladdin must have heard this wish, though unexpressed, for presto! at that very moment our brother appeared with a canteen of new milk and nearly a whole chicken, which he had, by aid of industry and greenbacks, accumulated.

After eating hardtack and milk till we could hardly see, and finished off with that spring chicken till we were full to repletion, or, in other words, had a good square meal, and washed and cleaned ourselves at the creek nearby, the prophecy was fulfilled, and we did bivouac and sleep soundly, the sleep of satisfied, yet tired soldiers, with the ground for a bed, and the star-spangled canopy of Heaven for a roof. There were many anxious glances and really envious looks given during these little episodes, and earnest wishes, which often broke forth, sometimes in bitter, but more often in humorous expressions—"What will you take for a look at that milk?" or a "Smell of that chicken?" "What will you sell the whole lot for? I'll give you a dollar!" "Oh! don't be mean now!" "Where's the sutler, partner?" etc., etc.

War with its hardships and privations brought out all that was good or bad in men, and especially during the first years of the war, before stern discipline with relentless hand had governed and softened the hitherto unrestrained activities and passion of thousands who had never known what it was to want or be deprived of their individual liberties of thought and deed.

If a man was selfish, it broke out into positive piggishness among his comrades. If he was lying and deceitful, crafty or cunning, he was now magnified into a mountain of deceit and treachery. If he was a thief, the cravings of a hungry stomach led him to attempt the practice of his vocation, with a renewed vigor; but thieving was not tolerated, and a professional soon came to grief, for the outraged company generally had many satisfactory ways of disposing of him.

If a man was sour, ill-natured, cross-grained, peevish, or irritable, he found plenty of time and opportunity to vent it now, if not upon the company, with one or two boon companions. If he was a constitutional grumbler, now he was, during his spare moments from duty, always with that select circle at the cook house, grumbling and growling at everything and everybody from the cook down., The beans were not done, or the soup was burned, or the hardtack was too full of "fresh meat," or the government, the administration, "Old Hooker" were frauds, and the war for the liberation of the d—d niggers a failure.

The jealous man grew green with the bile of his fancied imaginations, the envious spiteful in his greedy covetousness.

Gambling, drinking and chewing propensities increased, and but for the iron hand of order and discipline, might have effected the absolute ruin of the army in a short time. Vice and crime of all degrees and shades might also have triumphed, but for the same reason. In fact the army was for the pure-minded a hot-bed of temptation, and an iron school of self-denial and personal discipline, from which many of the best, the truest, and most honorable men in this land today emerged as from a fiery furnace, not unscathed, but purified and regenerated, a living example of what self-sacrifice, denial, hardships, privations, and the elements, together with the storm of bloody battle, will accomplish for true nobility.

And what of the wrecks who fell by the wayside, or came forth scorched?

To the critical we would say—"First pluck the beam from thine own eye," and remember that you did not wade through the storm of battle, of suffering, distress, nor the temptations of camp and field; and to the well and strong, recollect that the true test of goodness, amiability, unselfishness, etc., is trial, temptation, hardships, and all that tested our brave boys. Without this, it is an easy matter to set up a standard for morality, good nature and true manhood.

During our halt here at Gum Spring, a curious and amusing incident occurred, in which much patience and forbearance were exercised, and chagrin and mortification resulted. The officers at regimental headquarters had engaged meals at a certain house. As soon as they had eaten, the lady of the house, who had previously engaged to do so, prepared something nice for a few of our company, among them, our brother.

The officers were in another room, playing upon a seraphim, and singing. When all was ready, our boys advanced to the attack, having a pass to go to the house. Presently a commotion was heard in the kitchen, and the voice of the lady, saying: "I have not engaged for you. Those gentlemen must eat first, for I promised them." It seems that some other officers had come, and called for supper, giving her no previous notification. Feeling that they were slighted, they became angry, went to the officer commanding the patrol, and just as our boys were about to jump at a big mouthful of hot biscuit and butter, having paid for their supper in advance, in stalked an officer. "What are you all doing here? Leave this house! Soldiers are not allowed here in the same house with officers!"

Our brother, who was spokesman, hesitated a moment before rising, saying "We have a pass from our Colonel, who gave us permission to leave camp, also permission from this lady to eat supper, for which we have paid."

"Can't help that, you must go out of this!" and seeing him hang back a little, put his hands upon his shoulders and pushed him slightly towards the door. Our big brother's hand nervously itched to strike and demolish him in righteous indignation, but he quelled and stifled his rage, and quietly went through the open door, vainly expecting our own officers would explain matters, but they did not.

370

His pride was sorely humbled. All were tried in the furnace, and felt that they had acted the better part, although our brother's letters say: "I felt like a whipped cur when I left the house, although I was strong enough in body to have demolished that officer's equilibrium several times, I think. I felt as though I had dishonored myself by permitting a man to do as he did for no cause, except petty spite, because she had refused a party of officers supper, and we had anticipated them a little in their wants."

Such was the effect of discipline.

Our cavalry in force had been moving ahead for some days, watching the enemy's movements and striving to check Stewart's [*sic;* Stuart] demonstration on Washington. From the 17th to the 21st of June, there had been more or less severe fighting about Gum Spring and Aldie, indecisive, resulting in no gain. Although our losses were severe, the enemy had been compelled to fall back towards Ashby's Gap. At General Pleasanton's request, our division (Griffin's) was then detached from the Fifth Corps, and on the 19th at 3 P. M. proceeding beyond Aldie (to which we had marched from Gum Spring on the 18th) towards Middleburg, took position for the support of the cavalry in any engagement it might have. Here we found the entire Cavalry Corps, and visited their camps. They had had a rough-and-tumble time of it, and our friends of the First Massachusetts were loud in their denunciations of the Johnnies' method of fighting them with mounted infantry dismounted and firing from behind stone walls with rifles. The First Rhode Island Cavalry, in camp in a small grove nearby, was fearfully cut up, as was the First Maine.

On the 21st, a beautiful day, preparations were made at early dawn for a desperate cavalry light, and all was bustle in our little brigade. We moved out bright and early at 3 A. M., in support of the cavalry—out through and just beyond Middleburg—and from a slight wood-crowned hill or knoll to the right of the road could see way off to Ashby's Gap in the Blue Ridge Mountains, a distance of nearly fifteen miles. The scene was grand; the open, rolling country was lovely and picturesque. The mountains rose in their mighty grandeur and, sharply defined against the blue sky, seemed to look down upon this varied, undulating battleground like a gigantic empire chosen by the Great Unknown for the occasion. On this ridge, prolonged, our entire cavalry corps was drawn up in a long battle line by regiments in close column by squadrons, their guidons and battle-flags straightening out in the breeze that slightly stirred.

Our brigade moved up in line of battle on the right of the road, under cover of the ridge just behind Kilpatrick's[6] division, and the First Massachusetts happened to be directly in front of our regiment, so that we could talk to the mounted troopers in the waiting squadron, some of whom we knew. The 3d Brigade (Vincent's) was on the left of the road; the 2d, in column in reserve. Soon the shells began to come over from the enemy's guns. Without waiting for them to fully develop their position, our cavalry threw out a cloud of dismounted skirmishers (relieving our infantry, which had first been sent out under a protest by General Griffin) and, moving rapidly, the battle was at once opened.

The mounted squadrons immediately followed up this movement, first at a trot, and well together, but soon it was a gallop and a run, and then what appeared to be, from our position on the knoll, to which we had now been moved, a country full of charging troopers—all eager to get in first. The cracking of carbines and pistols for a few minutes was sharp and lively, then this gradually dying away, we could see the puffs of smoke, and through it the fall of some unfortunate man in going over a fence, or through a gap previously torn down by the advanced skirmishers. Men were reeling in their saddles when shot; riderless horses were dashing by us here and there into the town; dismounted men were trying to catch them, or were striving to gain cover of tree or wall.

---

[6] Hugh Judson Kilpatrick (1836–1881) was so aggressive, fearless, and ambitious, his men gave him the nickname "Kil-cavalry due to their rate of losses. See *Kilpatrick and Our Cavalry*, Moore, 2014.

The rebels scattered and sought shelter of barn or haystacks, but were soon dislodged by our men, and being pressed hard, the dim distance soon shut pursued and pursuers from sight. All was like some vast changing panoramic view, which, moving hither and thither over hill, dale and plain, gradually faded away into the shadows of the Blue Ridge at Ashby's Gap. Our reveries and appreciation of this novel and beautiful battlefield picture were soon rudely disturbed by the command—"Fall in! forward!!" and we soon filed out on the road, moving rapidly towards the Gap in the distance, scarcely knowing whether we would be in battle fighting Lee's infantry supports before night or not.

It was a hot day, but the road was hard and in excellent condition. We had had a good rest at Aldie and excitement kept us up. We passed Rector-town Cross Roads and Upperville, and arrived within a mile or two of Ashby's Gap late in the afternoon, catching occasional glimpses of our cavalry on the way and were assured of their complete victory by meeting on the road, dismounted and under guard, many prisoners who had been captured. They were dressed for the most part in new grey cavalry jackets, probably brought in by some blockade runner. The turning point of the day's fight was at the bridge over Goose Creek near Upperville, where a rebel mounted battery had been posted to command it. It was a single-span stone bridge, quite narrow. The approaches were marshy. Here our cavalry received a brief but decided check. The 4th New York Cavalry (di Cesnola's[7]) met with a repulse but Randol's mounted battery of the First Artillery by a lucky shot burst a rebel caisson, while another dismounted a piece; the 5th U.S. Cavalry made a successful charge and the enemy's battery then fled. The hill on the other side was carried and the enemy made no other stand. Dead and dying horses were thickly strewn about on the banks of the stream and in the marsh. As we plodded along the turnpike some "bummer" discovered an amputated arm, with a hand and fingers outstretched, lying on the road and partially covered with dust,

---

[7] Luigi Palma di Cesnola (1832–1904), Italian-American soldier, diplomat, and amateur archaeologist. He was awarded the Medal of Honor for his actions at Aldie.—2019

near a house, where some surgeon had carelessly thrown it. The temptation proved too much. He gave it a slight kick with his toe, probably to see what it was, but that was enough. It became a football for everyone, and had to run the gauntlet, from the head of the brigade to the rear along the road to Upperville.

Such was the blunting, hardening influence of grim, diabolical war. We bivouacked with the cavalry on that lovely moonlight night near the Gap, and around our flickering fires the bold troopers gave vent to many a Munchausen yarn, camp jest and story, expressing their complete satisfaction at the complete defeat of "Jeb" Stuart's Confederate riders hitherto considered invincible by the South. Orders were still stringent against foraging.

While returning this day, a chicken came out upon the road in the most tempting manner. There was no resisting it; a man in our regiment threw his little hatchet, and, strange to say, it severed the head from its body, which, flopping about over the ground, jumped into the hands held to receive it. The hatchet was picked up, and the chicken was coolly carried to camp to be converted into rations.

The next morning, at 3 A. M., we started to withdraw from our position. The cavalry had been ordered to withdraw to Middleburg. Hastily leaving our bivouac, our fires left burning to deceive the enemy, we retraced the roads and fields of the day before. A slight shelling of our retiring columns, shortly after our withdrawal, was the only incident. We moved through the silent streets of Middleberg (all the blinds being closed and the curtains drawn) about 6.30 A. M., and remaining until [?] P. M., marched beyond to Aldie into camp. Here we experienced a fearful storm which flooded our camp and drenched us though and through.

As this side movement to Aldie was a part of the operations of the Fifth Corps during the Gettysburg Campaign, and had such a vital bearing upon the decisive results of the battle in compelling Stuart to retire through Ashby's Gap and to give up any further attempt to move upon the east side of the Blue Ridge, it has been introduced here. Our entire loss in the division was only three or

374

four men wounded. Stuart's absence later from the flank of the Confederate army is not a part of this story, but it has been shown by many Confederate writers to have been fatal to General Lee's plan of campaign—if he had any well-defined plan, which is extremely doubtful in the light of many letters and papers. Perhaps had Lee lived longer, or Stuart not been killed in 1864, we would now have known more of the real historical truth of this matter (all this is problematical) and also whether Stuart's being forced through Ashby's Gap by the cavalry supported by the first division of the Fifth Corps changed General Lee's plans as to passing to the east side, or any contemplated attack or feint by him upon Washington by the old Bull Run route as has sometimes been rumored might have been done, had a favorable opportunity offered.

On the 24th we had quite a novelty in the shape of a brigade drill.

On the 25th we (the 22d Massachusetts) were detached from the brigade and ordered, with the corps train, to Fairfax Station to load and then to rejoin the army. Taking the Little River Turnpike, we passed through Chantilly and Fairfax Court House, and after loading the train with forage and rations, destroyed the remainder, and that night moved very quietly but rapidly away, the rearguard having a slight skirmish with a small body of the enemy. We passed through Germantown and bivouacked near Frying Pan. On this day we saw the 25th Maine near Chantilly and met many of our old Portland, Me., schoolboy friends. The force of rebels coming in directly after we left Fairfax Station shelled it vigorously, and captured a few stragglers not on hand when the command moved.

On the 19th the 8th Infantry had marched from Fairfax Station, and on the 25th was in camp near Fairfax Court House. Learning of this, we started on the night of the 25th to find our brother, but darkness coming on, and ascertaining that it was several miles, and the roads uncertain, as it necessarily meant an all-night trip we gave it up.

On the night of the 26th, still escorting the corps train, the regiment bivouacked near Dranesville, Va. On the 27th, we moved at 4.30 A. M., and after a short march, followed by a very long halt until one P. M., and the Sixth Corps train had passed (during which the writer sat on one end of a large fallen tree, while General Sedgwick, commanding the 6th Corps, and his staff sat on the other end) we crossed the Potomac River at Edwards Ferry, at 10 A. M., and bivouacked at Bennett's Creek. The country through which we had passed was lined with heavily loaded cherry trees; the branches from which we gathered the ripe fruit defined the trail of our column as it still guarded the 5th Corps wagon-trains across the pontoon bridges, and on to Frederick, Md.

On June 25th reveille in the camp of the 8th Infantry was at 1.20 A. M. It marched at 4 o'clock and passed through Hunter's Mills and Dranesville, where it struck the Leesburg pike. It arrived at Edwards Ferry at 6 P. M., crossed the river, and camped at Poolesville, Md., at 10 P. M., a march of thirty-one miles.

While I lay here (Bennett's Creek), a laughable incident occurred. The cherry trees were filled with men, who were breaking off boughs loaded with fruit, and throwing them to the men below. Gen. Robert O. Tyler of the Artillery Reserve was seated on a horse block beneath one of these trees, in the shade. Seeing a branch fall near him, he stooped, reached for and got it just as a private of the Twentieth Indiana, named Meacham, was about to pick it up. The latter, unaware of the rank of his successful rival, gave him a kick that sent him sprawling in the mud, and sent his spectacles flying in the other direction. The mirth of the bystanders, who were now laughing at this little episode, seemed to enrage the general more than the kick, and he ordered an officer attached to the Provost Guard to place the man under guard until evening. During that day's march, however, he mysteriously disappeared, and nothing further was heard of it.

On the 28th the 8th Infantry moved through Barnesville and Urbanna to Frederick, taking nearly the same route as on the

Antietam campaign. On June 29 it, with Headquarters Army of the Potomac, moved through Ladiesburg and Woodbury to Middleburg, twenty miles.

On June 30 it moved to Taneytown, but on July 1 headquarters were changed to Westminster, fourteen miles, where the 8th Infantry with our brother remained until July 4. From here they forwarded many thousands of prisoners, captured during the campaign.

On June 30 there were at general headquarters, Army of the Potomac, under Gen. M. M. Patrick, organized as a brigade, 50 officers; Provost Guard composed of eight companies of the Eighth U. S. Infantry, Capt. EW. H. Read commanding; Ninety-third New York, Col. John S. Crocker commanding; Second Pennsylvania Cavalry, Col. R. Butler Price commanding; companies E and I, Sixth U. S. Cavalry, Captains L. H. Carpenter and James Starr (Commanding Personal Escort); Engineer brigade, 40 officers and 906 men; Signal Corps, 6 officers and about 30 men; guards and orderlies, 2 officers, and 47 Oneida (New York) Cavalry, Capt. Daniel P. Mann commanding; aggregating about 3,050 officers and men. The First Massachusetts Cavalry was also temporarily detached for duty at headquarters during the battle of Gettysburg.

John Morrison[8] was a farmer's boy. He had worked for a man by the name of Day at the Upper End of Bradford (now Haverhill), Mass. He had light, sandy hair, florid complexion, steel blue eyes, sharp features and chin, and was spare built and wiry. He was a comical character. According to his own story, one day he was mowing in the field. An impulse seized him; he thrust his scythe under the swath, and that he might not do a rash act, he went to the spring, took a drink of cool water, and then going to his employer, told him he rather thought he should enlist for the war. His employer reasoned with him, but he said if his mind was made up he should not try to hold him back. In some way this

---

[8] John H. Morrison (1841–July 3, 1863) enlisted on August 22, 1862 (enlistment records, 2019).

story had leaked out and on the long, hot march from Virginia, many a chaff and joke were given at John's expense.

"How would you like to be swinging that scythe today, John?" would come the question. As quick as a flash would come the reply—"Rather be here—let the old scythe rust—I like this." He was the life of the company, and kept many a depressed spirit on that dreadful march in good humor. But on the night march from Hanover, when all the courage that was in our craw was put to its severest test, the question was once more put to John Morrison— "John, that scythe will surely rust; wouldn't you like to be swinging her now?" The answer came back, the face streaked with sweat and dust—"I wouldn't mind swinging her once more." All saw that John Morrison's spirits had undergone a change and for once he was like many others—quiet, depressed, nervous, anxious and apprehensive. A wonderful gloom had come over quaint John Morrison's dreams, his small steel blue eyes no longer twinkled, nor did he seem inclined to joke. All noticed the sudden change in his whole manner.

Through the jealousy, obstinacy and incapacity of General Halleck, who was trying to fight all the battles in front of Washington by wire, and a more or less panicky feeling on the part of the administration, who seemed to turn for professional knowledge, advice and military counsel to General Halleck, Hooker was refused the garrison at Harper's Ferry which he rightly considered would be of more use in reinforcing his own army than to be left behind with a chance of again being captured as was done in September, 1862. This he represented in his usual forcible manner to General Halleck, but still being refused, and feeling that he was sure to be tied down and hampered by a Chief of Staff who lacked everything that a soldier needs except technical knowledge, he (Hooker) resigned, and General Meade[9] was appointed to the command.

---

[9] George Gordon Meade (1815–1872) was a career officer, civil engineer, and Mexican War veteran. See the superb *Meade's Headquarters*, Lyman, 2014.

Again was the patriotism, intense loyalty, superb discipline and morale of the gallant old army to be put to its greatest test, for no severer strain can be put upon a huge marching column, and that in the face of a bold and aggressive enemy, already on an offensive campaign, than to relieve its head and commander. But the Army of the Potomac was getting used to this sort of thing, and there was scarcely a ripple upon the smooth wave of such an *esprit de corps*.

While General Meade was known to be a good corps and division commander, and of undoubted courage and bravery, he was regarded as conservative and cautious to the last degree, good qualities in a defensive battle, but liable to degenerate into timidity when an aggressive or bold offensive becomes imperative. It was a critical period, and one of grave responsibility. There wasn't a grumbler who aspired to or desired such a promotion at that moment. All the corps were put in motion, but strange to say neither Meade nor Bee knew the whereabouts of each other until about the 28th, and the former's line of march, although due northward, still covered the approaches to Baltimore and Washington, while the latter, after [Confederate General Richard] Ewell's advance to Carlisle, York, and even to the Susquehanna River, as a menace to Pennsylvania's capital, did not commence concentrating upon Gettysburg until he ascertained that the Army of the Potomac was at Frederick and Boonesboro directly upon his line of communications.

Had Meade known this he might have saved himself much unnecessary anxiety, and perhaps the loss of many good men, for he now commenced to lay out the line of battle on Little Pipe Creek, some fifteen miles from Gettysburg, where he could fight a purely defensive battle.

What Meade's instructions were to General [John] Reynolds, commanding the First Corps, will never be known. It is possible and more than probable that the commanding general intended that both he (Reynolds) and [John] Buford, commanding the leading cavalry division, should make a bold reconnaissance, and

379

upon meeting the enemy should fall back to the strong defensive line thus selected. But it is also possible, and still more probable that Reynolds himself, than whom there was no better nor more able soldier in the whole army, determined, upon arriving at Gettysburg and seeing the natural advantages of the position, and Buford already engaged, decided to hold Lee in check until word could be sent to Meade and the remainder of the army could be hurried to his assistance.

It is certain that up to the moment of Buford's accidental meeting with Lee's advance, neither Meade nor Lee had any personal knowledge of the importance which the meeting of ten roads and one railroad gave to the little town of Gettysburg, or the strong positions which nature had created there. Both Early and Ewell had passed through a few days previous, but do not appear to have sent any special report to Lee concerning its strategic importance. There is, however, another general who has never historically figured in this most historic battle, but who, upon arriving in advance of the First Corps early on the evening of June 30, with a keen military instinct and a sweeping glance of the terrain, took in all the possibilities and decided advantages of the position and determined at whatever odds and at whatever cost to place himself across the lines of Lee's converging columns.

To the sagacity, therefore, and foresight of that brave *sabreur*, the great cavalry leader—John Buford[10]—may be attributed the virtual selection of Gettysburg as the "high-water mark" of the Rebellion, to be handed down to future generations as the greatest battle on record with its far-reaching results and possibilities.

It was Buford who, arriving at Gettysburg with his small division of 4,000 men on June 30, 1863, unbeknown to the enemy, moved out on the Chambersburg or Cashtown road and met the advance of A. P. Hill's Corps (Confederate) marching

---

[10] Sadly, the next December, Buford lay dying of illness. In his final hours he was attended by his aide, Irish immigrant Captain Myles Keogh, who died with Custer at the Little Bighorn on June 25, 1876.—2019

down that road to occupy the town. Buford was in Gettysburg on the morning of July 1, surrounded by his staff, having sent his scouts and pickets well out to the west, when a quartermaster of Reynolds' (First) Corps rode in ahead of his command to get some shoes for Wadsworth's division. Buford turned to him and said:

"What are you doing here, sir?" The reply was that he had come in to get some shoes. "You had better return immediately to your command," said Buford. "Why, what is the matter, General?" At that moment the far-off boom of a single gun was heard, and Buford replied, as he mounted his horse and galloped off, "That's the matter!" It was 9 A. M. Buford had three guns fired for a signal for his dismounted skirmish line to open on the enemy. The guns were from Calef's Horse Battery (Second Artillery) and the Battle of Gettysburg had begun.

With his small force Buford boldly attacked Heth's Division of Hill's Corps, and for nearly four hours he disputed possession of the Fairfield and Chambersburg roads leading into the town and resisted his advance, until the First arid Eleventh Corps were able to hurry to the field and render assistance.

To the intrepidity, energy, push and fidelity of this most modest cavalry general, to gallant John Buford and his fighting division, the country owes the battlefield of Gettysburg.

While Buford anxiously scanned the line from the cupola of the Lutheran Seminary, and this terrible and unequal fight of the first day was raging, thus commenced by Buford in the morning and continued by Generals Reynolds and Howard in the afternoon and evening, General Meade was at Taneytown—miles away— leisurely planning on an obscure creek called Little Pipe Creek, a defensive line of battle, when a dispatch from Buford aroused him stating that Reynolds was killed, the two corps were hardly holding their own, and if he expected to save the pieces the army must be moved up at once.

Unfortunately Buford had not before communicated his knowledge and plans to Meade nor to anyone except Reynolds, now dead, and accident alone furnished strange ground and a position upon which to fight the greatest battle of the war.

The line of Pipe Creek, previously referred to, would undoubtedly have been the best strategically, covering as it did both Washington and Baltimore, had Lee consented to have advanced in that direction and to have fought on ground of Meade's own selection instead of flanking it, and provided also that Meade had not been forced by Buford to fight at Gettysburg, and so the battle took place in a good tactical, but a bad strategical position for the Union forces, because it could be easily flanked on the south and its evacuation compelled.

For the same reason it was a good strategical position for Lee and a bad tactical one, unless he could force Meade to attack him or he adopted General Longstreet's plan of maneuvering Meade out of position. But he also was afraid of placing himself between Meade and either Baltimore or Washington, and endangering his line of communications through the mountains.

At Frederick, on the 28th, we again joined the brigade from our train escort duty—after passing through Poolsville, Barnesville and Buckeystown. Marching on a fine turnpike road, and crossing the Monocary,[11] we bivouacked about a mile from the town, near the cemetery and Ballinger's Creek. Again the spires of Frederick, in the beautiful Monocary valley, greeted our eyes, and in the bright sunlight of the beautiful June morning succeeding, how cheering and refreshing it appeared, surrounded by smiling grain fields, green trees, mountain background, intervening meadows and valleys which so strikingly mark this lovely region.

Here General Hooker was relieved from command of the Army of the Potomac at his own request, and General Meade, who had been commanding the Fifth Corps, was assigned to its command. General Orders Nos. 65 and 66 were published and we escaped a grand review which General Butterfield, Chief of Staff, on the ground of General Lee's daily depredations and movements, urged there was no time for. On the 29th we again started

---

[11] *Sic*; Monocacy Creek.

marching through Frederick, Harmony Grove, Mt. Pleasant, and passing through Liberty, Md., we bivouacked two miles beyond, a distance of twenty-two miles. From here our route lay rapidly through Johnsville, Frizzleburg and Unionville to Hanover, Pa. The long tramp was unbroken in its monotony, except by the daily incidents which in a column on the march break out, either in gleams of sunshine or the darkest clouds of depression.

Men became ragged, footsore and chafed. Many were marching in their drawers, and, with handkerchiefs of many colors tied about their heads or necks, certainly presented anything but a martial appearance. Some were marching in their stocking feet, while others were barefooted, the rough pikes having long since torn their flimsy paper-soled contract brogans from their feet. Sunstrokes were numerous and during the long-drawn-out afternoons, when every step seemed accompanied by a wail of anguish, or a groan of exhaustion, involuntary straggling grew to be serious.

We generally moved from our bivouacs in the long grass in the fields by the roadside before daybreak, without fires or coffee, munching our hard bread, as we clinked, clanked along. In a few hours the laugh and jest, the chaffing of the uncontrollable wag had died out, and each boy and man in that hurrying column was a busy thinker, a machine which, once set in motion, goes to the utmost of its endurance. Such was the intelligent private soldier of the Army of the Potomac.

It commenced to shower almost daily, and as we moved early and went into camp late, there was little chance for drying our clothes.

On the 30th we moved at 4 A. M. and, passing through Johnsville, Md., on a good road, made a rapid and terribly exhausting march of twenty-five miles. Here the writer, by an extraordinary streak of good luck, secured a very large, bright, yellow silk bandanna handkerchief for the price of one dollar, which, for many weeks thereafter, fulfilled the triple purpose of a coffee and sugar bag, to mop the streams of perspiration ever flowing down his face, besides serving its own legitimate function.

Passing through Union Bridge and Union, we reached Union Mills at 6.30 P. M., and bivouacked in the meadow near the town, on Pipe Creek, at the crossing of the road from Littlestown to Westminster. The brigade went on picket during the night, Generals J. E. B. Stuart, Fitzhugh Lee and Wade Hampton had spent the previous night at the house of Mr. Schriver, who owned the mill. The rebel cavalry had left about four hours before our arrival.

At early dawn, July 1, without coffee we left our beds in the long grass, while it was so dark that the head of the column was indistinct, and munching our hard bread as we moved, washing it down with coffee and sugar which had been allowed to swash in our canteens, we struck out for another day's solid work. The flesh had got hardened and we were down to marching trim. We marched through Frizzleburg about noon, the men straggling more than usual. It was said that there was a barrel of whiskey on tap here, in a carriage shed under a barn. During the day whole companies, and even regiments *with* their colors, had fallen out. In the afternoon, somewhere beyond Frizzleburg, we struck the border of Pennsylvania, the line being marked by a substantial stone bound. As the head of the column reached this point, it dawned upon our boys that we were entering a free state, and cheers arose from the dusty throats that had seemed incapable of uttering other than sounds of grumbling and growling. The sight of this monument had an electrical effect. Cheer after cheer passed along the line, those in the rear wondering what was up; as they also passed the reviewing point, the cheers grew louder by reason of our being prepared for something to cheer for.

In the afternoon, when the strain had proved almost too much for our powers of endurance, long, hot, dusty and depressing, when hundreds were falling exhausted by the roadside and every face looked like a piece of leather, bestreaked with sweat, and besprinkled with dust, afar off on a parallel road was heard the sound of bugles, and then of the drum corps sounding off as upon parade.

It was caught up by our own drummers and buglers, and then by the bands of the Sykes Division of regulars, until the sweet strains prolonged could be heard far and near. Every weary and footsore soldier, the halt, lame and chafed patriot, played out, exhausted and about to deposit his weary bones by the wayside, gathered inspiration from the sound, took the step, and with renewed courage plodded into camp. Every corps, division and brigade went into bivouac that night with increased numbers. For a moment keenly observant, we thought of the "Pied Piper of Hamelin," whose magic flute drew the children dancing to the river's bank. Such was the power of music upon the drooping spirits of the rough, bronzed veterans of the gallant old Army of the Potomac. It was the order of General Meade, the commanding general. We had never heard music before on the march, and but once before, at the battle of Chancellorsville.

We passed on and hurried into Hanover this bright afternoon, passing among the dead horses and debris of the cavalry fight of the previous day between Kilpatrick and Stuart; the dead having been buried and the wounded cared for in schoolhouses, markets and residences, and about 4 P. M. sank down for rest after our most exhausting march of over twenty miles.[12]

The bivouac fires of the Fifth Corps were gleaming in the meadows west of Hanover, and our worn and wearied men, having made coffee and eaten some freshly killed beef—yet warm—were just ready to catch a few hours' sleep, when suddenly a mounted courier rode into our lines. At once the long drawn-out harsh strains of the infantry "pack-up" call, or "general," sounded drearily in our ears and a few moments later the half-dazed men were again rapidly filing out in the road—this time to battle. We had not heard during that long day the sound of a gun or the

---

[12] This bivouac was on very low ground just to the west of Frederick Street at the entrance to which was on one side a brick yard, on the other an old tannery; both had been removed in 1892. The little stream nearby is Plum Run. The small clump of houses, near where the Westminster Pike comes in from Union Mills to the south (the road we marched on), was called "Mudville" during the war; it now enjoys the much more dignified name of "Pennville."—note in original

noise of battle in which the First and Eleventh Corps had been engaged.

So sudden was this call that we were moving before we were hardly conscious of the fact. It was nearly dusk, or about 7 P. M. It was an all-night pull. It meant another fifteen or eighteen miles. As we passed through MacSherrystown and Prussia, and other small hamlets, the people were all astir, and tried to encourage us by stolid cheers and "God speeds," to which some of our chronic grumblers made anything but courteous and polite rejoinders, gruffly telling the honest burghers to "Fall in, take a rifle, and defend your own fireside!" The rapid gait, with the terrible march of the day, soon began to tell upon our men, and falling out again began. Every effort was made to urge the column on, but no halts were made. It was midnight, and still the weary tramp went on— on though the little villages and hamlets of Pennsylvania. Men, almost fainting, could be seen stealing off by the roadside into the fields and woods, too exhausted to proceed farther. With them the limit had been passed.

But the First Corps had met with a bloody repulse. General Reynolds had been killed, and the vital position of Cemetery Hill might be lost. We must push on! Soon, by the clear light of the moon, we could distinctly see the form of a courier or staff officer making his way, with difficulty, along the column; could hear a very faint cheering as he announced, and it was passed along, that General McClellan had arrived with 60,000 troops and was again in command of the old army. I never knew who that faker was. But the hitherto inspiring name of "Little Mac," had lost its magical charm. No longer could it be juggled with, especially with men who had marched over thirty miles on a hot July day, over the turnpike roads of Maryland and Pennsylvania. It fell dead on our ears. What a year before might have been most joyful intelligence to many (but not all) of the rank and file, now called forth little or no enthusiasm in the thoroughly seasoned, much marched, but badly handled and worse fought body of veterans in the Army of the Potomac; a few feeble sounds from some of the commands greeted this lying fakir, and the column stalked on in moody silence.

They were strangely undemonstrative; a singular hush reigned over all. About one o'clock on the morning of July 2 the corps bivouacked near Bonneauville on the Hanover Road, east of Rock Creek, to make coffee, until our positon could be assigned, but at 4.30 A. M. it again marched toward the point of battle.[13]

We were temporarily in support of the Twelfth Corps, where we could be moved to the support of either wing. The Fifth Corps was soon moved, however, by the left flank, along the meadows which skirt Rock Creek over to the Baltimore pike, then changing position to the front, moved in columns across Rock Creek Bridge, and was massed on the left of the road, partly in an orchard, about three-fourths of a mile north of or above the bridge, the balance of the corps on a hill, just across from McAllister Hill on one side and Powers Hill on the other.

At Frederick, the writer had drawn [from stores] sometime in the night a pair of government brogans (having worn out one pair on the march from Fredericksburg, Va.) which were number 8. There was just one pair. His size was number 9. He was nearly barefooted. It was "Hobson's choice." A march of nearly seventy miles, with these shoes a size too small, had got his feet in a most pitiable condition. The toes were doubled up, and although the points of the shoes were cut to loosen them, the bottoms of the feet were covered with large water blisters, the torture from which was almost unendurable. On this night march from

---

[13] After leaving its bivouac near Bonneauville on the morning of July 2, the corps proceeded along the Bonneauville or Hanover Road, until it reached a point about one and a half or two miles southeast of Gettysburg, near Brinkerhoff's and Deodorff's house and barn, just north of Cress Run. The First Division was formed in line of masses to the right of the road and about one-half mile from, and parallel to it, the brigades occupying positions in order of their numbers from right to left. The Second (Sykes') was on the right of the First. Shortly after this, the First Division changed front to the left, at nearly right angles to its former position, and formed line of battle by battalions, in close column by divisions.—note in original

Hanover, already described, these blisters broke, the sand worked in and every movement was like stepping on hot coals. Contrary to his pride and oft-expressed determination never to be a straggler, under this pressure involuntarily he was forced to become one. At midnight on July 1, leaving the column with sudden impulse, he climbed a fence into the woods, threw himself upon the ground, and was soon in an exhausted sleep, oblivious to pain and the terror of approaching battle.

The sunlight of early morning streaming into his face warned him that daylight and the time for action had arrived. A good Samaritan at a house nearby furnished some milk, hard bread soaked it up, and the hungry stomach soon absorbed it. A brook cooled the aching feet, and we were just congratulating ourselves upon such providential favors, when boom! boom!! boom!!! rang out upon the morning air.

Hastily tying shoe strings together, and slinging the now useless shoes upon his rifle, the writer sprang forward barefooted upon the hard, cool pike, still moist with night dew, and most grateful to the feverish feet. The little village of Bonneauville was reached after a march of a mile or two. Scores of stragglers were passed. Gamble's Brigade of Buford's Division of Cavalry was met on its way to Hanover, and we were informed for the first time of the position of the Fifth Corps. As we were hurrying through the village of Bonneauville, a lady came out of a house, with a pie in her hand, and offered each of us (myself and two schoolmates) a piece. The writer's two comrades wanted to stop and eat theirs, but the sound of the cannonading urged me on, and taking mine in my hand I ate it, as I hurried on. It was a fresh cherry pie. I had just drank a quart of fresh milk, and had early been impressed with the fact that such a mixture was sure death to anybody eating it, but considering the fact that we were hastening towards the same risk at the front—death— after first refusing it, I did not hesitate but bolted it down without further protest. The fruit proved to be golden. Youth, a good digestion, and the excitement of approaching battle made us oblivious to any danger in that direction.[14]

We crossed Rock Creek Bridge. Soon the red badge of the Maltese Cross was visible in the distance. Each boom of the guns inspired us to move faster, and as we saw in turn upon the ridge the division and brigade flags, with their appropriate symbols, our joy knew no bounds. It was about high noon. Regardless of results, the writer jumped over a rail fence into a wheat stubble-field, with his bare, blistered feet, the pain from which he scarcely felt, as he sought the regimental colors and white flag of the Old Bay State. As the stubbles caught in the lacerated blisters, blood flowed from every pore, but he was soon among his comrades, and cared little for pain then, for he was no longer a straggler. We were massed in reserve, nearly in rear of the center, and within easy supporting distance of either wing. Our battle flags hardly stirred in the light morning breeze. The dark line, which a few moments before had been outlined against the blue sky, had sunk as if by magic to the ground, and nothing now marked it but the stand of colors and an occasional group of irrepressible individuals that never sleep or rest when any excitement or danger is near. Our ranks had, however, been much thinned by the straggling of the exhausted men for several days.

---

[14] Upon visiting the battlefield in October, 1886, we rode out to Bonneauville and found without much difficulty the brick house with high steps, where this good woman had unconsciously tried, twenty-three years before, to deprive us of the privilege of participating in the great battle of Gettysburg. She was dead.—note in original

No more glorious sun ever shone than that which ushered in that morn of July 2, 1863, and revealed to our eyes that beautiful valley, with its wealth of yellow grain, the meadows tinted with buttercups, and the wood-covered slope of the battlefield of Gettysburg; the Blue Ridge Mountains in the far distance, lent a charming background to the picture. Fifty years have not banished the remembrance of such a scene from our memory. During most of that perfect July morning, the bronzed, dusty, ragged—many shoeless and hatless— almost exhausted men of the Fifth Corps were lost in deepest slumber among the rocks that crown the ridge, the prolongation of Power's Hill, even in the midst of approaching battle. Their long, weary journey from the Rappahannock and their all day and night pull of over thirty miles from Union Mills, to reach the scene of battle, had well earned them this brief rest. It was a hard bed; their heads rested on rocky pillows. Neither the constant roar of cannon nor the sharper crackling and rolling of musketry disturbed the weary men, or even created a ripple of excitement.

Hour after hour went by; the Third Corps had now become engaged;[1] the guns still belched and boomed; the shells cracked here and there; the fragments shrieked, buzzed, whizzed and grated—these sounds which had now grown so familiar to our ears—whose peculiar howl a soldier alone knows; musketry rolled and rattled incessantly, and yet our motionless line was lost to the world without and to thoughts of fear and anxiety within. As has been shown by our notes, it was purely a defensive battle General Meade was fighting, and on ground accidentally chosen, the direct result of Gen. John Buford's rapid movements with his division of cavalry on June 29 and 30, and his prompt action on the morning of July 1. Meade had already made choice of, and had his engineer layoff, a defensive line of battle on the line of Big Pipe Creek, which we had crossed on June 30 at Union Mills. He would now, in case his flank was turned, and the dominant

---

[1] This was Sickles' nearly disastrous move out in front of the Union line which left his flanks hanging.

ground or key-point seized, be compelled to change his hastily and imperfectly conceived program, perhaps retire to the line already referred to as first selected. What was the key-point? We shall see; and also it would be well to consider whether the claim which has been pressed since the battle has been well established, that a point on the line of fighting during Pickett's charge on July 3, or what is known as the "Umbrella Copse of Trees," or "Bloody Angle," was really the "High-water Mark of Rebellion."

It was shortly after 4 o'clock when the summons came for the Fifth Corps to move out to the support of the Third, now hard pressed. We were rudely awakened from our deep slumber and transitory journey to dreamland by a sharp "Fall in!"

Every man sprang to his feet. We knew full well the ominous sound of that call, and, hardly recovered from the stupor which such sound sleep produces, a moment later the long, blue column was moving due west across the open fields and byroads or lanes, almost mechanically into battle. It was a magnificent sight. A century could never efface it. As our division (Griffin's, now commanded by Barnes) swept down the gradual slope of over a mile, passing along the northerly slope of Little Round Top, and across the lane that leads over from the Taneytown Road to the Emmittsburg Pike, through what is now variously known as The Valley of Death, The Wheat Field, The Whirlpool and The Loop, we immediately came under a heavy fire from the rebel batteries, and shot and shell bounded, ricocheted and tore through our marching column. Glancing down from the rear, over the heads of the men, along the line of flashing bayonets, one could readily detect the tremulous wavering movement as the bodies ducked down when a shell or shrapnel burst accurately over the moving column, and then rose again immediately after.

We entered the point of woods south of Trostle's farm, and just west of and bordering on "The Wheat Field," and immediately throwing out our skirmishers and forming a line of battle, halted on the edge' of a little ravine that lower down enters Plum Run. It is now (1913) known as The Loop. We were 500 yards east of the Rose House[2] (afterwards owned by Wible), in the tower of which we heard the melancholy ring of the field bell, when later the bullets clipped and struck it as they tore, buzzed and shrieked across the open glade.

There was a gap in the line. When we reached this gap there were none of our troops visible, and although John B. Bachelder's map of Gettysburg shows the Twenty-second Massachusetts at this point, being, in support and in rear of De Trobriand's[3] Brigade of the Third Corps, which had previously occupied this position, it is absolutely certain that it (De Trobriand's Brigade) had been sent to our left just before or immediately upon our arrival.

To the right of our little brigade, the right of the Fifth Corps, there was a big gap—which had been vacated by the Third Corps—in which, facing nearly south, were the Fifth (Phillips') and the Ninth (Bigelow's) Massachusetts Batteries. The latter was a new battery and had never been in action. They had no supports and were at least from 500 to 800 yards from our position.

"Sergeant-major, recall the line of skirmishers!" This as we saw the Confederate battle-flags trying to come obliquely across the space southwest of Rose's house. The writer's brother sprang to the front, crossed the ravine and disappeared. A death-like silence reigned—such as precedes a storm. The skirmishers came running in—our brother's tall form, with sword drawn, among them.

"Fix bayonets!" rang through the woods—no other command. A shot, one, two, three, and then with a perfectly startling rattle and roar, the line blazed forth, followed by an incessant cheer that seemed to thrill to one's very marrow. The battle was on—the battle of the Fifth Corps, to save the position from which the Third Corps had been driven. Many, placing a heap of cartridges

---

[2] The house of George and Dorothy Rose still stands about two miles south of the town of Gettysburg on the eastern side of Emmitsburg Road.—2019

[3] Philippe Régis de Trobriand (1816–1897) was a French aristocrat, lawyer, and writer. He also served in Dakota after the Civil War. See his *Army Life in Dakota*, de Trobriand, 2016.

and caps on the ground in front of them, were soon busily engaged loading and firing as rapidly as possible. The discordant screeches and exultant yells of the grey-coated "Johnnies" rose high above the din and noise about us, instantly followed by our hearty, steady, solid cheers.

Across the run, the indistinct form of masses of men, presenting the usual, dirty, greyish, irregular line, were dimly visible and moving up with defiant yells, while here and there the cross-barred Confederate battle flags were plainly to be seen. Nearer and nearer came the charging masses. There seemed to be nothing on our minds but a strong, resolute desire to check the living torrents and a slight tendency to doubt oneself, when the bullets buzzed so closely by without touching some part of the body.

There was mingled with this thought, however, an occasional flash of sadness, as the pain-stamped face of some dying man was presented to view, when carried hurriedly to the rear. So much din, yelling, and cheering, however, kept the leading ideas uppermost, and if any man had sensations of fear before or while going in, he had no time or opportunity for such thoughts now, and the loading and firing, the cheering and yelling, wholly engrossed every animated, human machine.

We had marched too far and borne too much to be pushed over the ridge. Now came the groans of the bullet-stricken wounded. Nothing was seen but the heavy clouds of smoke which the still air hardly stirred. The green leaves and twigs overhead fell in a constant shower, as they were clipped by the singing bullets.

The first man struck in the regiment was in our company, Charles Phillips,[4] a Bradford boy; he was next on the writer's left in the front rank; a thud, a sickening, dull cracking sound and his head—his face streaming blood which filled his eyes and nose and gurgled in his mouth—fell upon the writer's left shoe (the same No. 8 drawn at Frederick City, which had caused so much pain

---

[4] Phillips (1839–1919) survived his wound and mustered out in October, 1864 (military and census records, 2019).

and suffering, and which is still preserved as a souvenir). The writer ceased firing for a brief moment to seize our comrade and lay him quietly on his back—the days had gone by when two men could leave the ranks to carry one wounded man to the rear—and then went on with his duty.

These are hasty reflections. We were not there long. Hood's Division, Longstreet's Corps (McLaw now commanding, Hood having been wounded early in the charge), had charged, and swinging into this gap left between the two corps (Third and Fifth), soon doubled back the right and left, and with exultant yells had pressed around and overlapped us. We were flanked. The command "Change front to the rear by the right flank!" was passed along the line, for no orders by voice or bugle could now be heard above the roar and din of battle. We knew what it meant. It was not executed tactically, nor can such an order be under conditions of battle, for the tactical units being continually destroyed, the file closers and guides being killed or wounded, it is impossible to restore such units under such a fire. The command "About face!" was given, and our veterans without further orders proceeded to execute this most difficult tactical maneuver in the face of a most terrific fire. While passing out of the Rose woods into the Wheat Field, we moved through a division of the Second Corps (Caldwell's) which had been sent to fill a gap to our left, and were moving by their left flank. We were soon almost inextricably mixed up with them, and subjected to a terrible cross fire. (See the way the movements and markers of the Second and Fifth Corps are mixed up in the Loop and woods where the Irish Brigade was absolved by their chaplain at the big rock a few yards in rear of our position.) Here we lost a great many men, and for a few moments the uproar and confusion were most appalling even to older men and stouter hearts.

No military reader can fail to see what the effect must have been on a brigade changing front to the rear by the right flank, in the midst of a fierce charge by many lines of battle massed, and meeting a division, closed en masse, marching by the left flank. And yet the Twenty-second coolly picked up their cartridges and percussion caps, carried all their wounded out on blankets, and even the latter's guns to the rear.

As we emerged from Rose's woods into the open swale or pasture, then the Wheat Field, studded here and there with large boulders and stone walls which time has not changed, we shook ourselves clear of our Second Corps brothers and still moved in ordinary quick time. At this point, the northwest angle of the former wheat field, the lane connecting the Taneytown and Emmittsburg roads, divides this wood from Trostle's farm, and the land rises rather abruptly to the northwest, terminating in a plateau, or open, roomy ridge. On the north of the lane, at this point, there is also a piece of thin woods, leaving an open space a little over 150 yards in width. Here the rebels were pouring through—Kershaw's and Wofford's Brigades.

When coming out of the woods I saw two of our sergeants (Abbott and Hazeltine, for we had no ambulance men or stretcher carriers on that line) carrying a writhing form in a blanket, their rifles acting as carriers or bars. It proved to be quaint John Morrison. I could hear his pleading: "Oh, let me down to rest! Oh! I can stand it no longer! Let me die!" He was shot through the bowels. As they rested him on the ground for a moment and he heard the yells of the oncoming enemy, he would feebly say: "Oh, take me up, Charlie (Hazeltine) don't let them get me!" and so he passed out of our sight to the rear to a strange Division Field Hospital (Eleventh Corps, near George Spangler's house), and there died. John Morrison's presentiment made on our day and night march through Hanover to Gettysburg, that he "would like to swing that scythe once more," the look we all noticed on his face as he said it, a feeling that death would overtake him the next day had come true. It was many years after the battle that the writer, alone, found out where he died, and where he is buried in Section "G," North, Lot No. 29, among "the dead of unknown regiments" in the National Cemetery. And may the ashes of that brave boy ever rest in peace, and may his spirit hover over Rose's woods where he met his fate, as our children and grandchildren go there to Gettysburg to see what we did to preserve the Union,

395

so that "a government of the people, by the people, and for the people" should not perish from the earth.

We had fallen back a few hundred yards, faced about and were now fronting this gap or elbow between the two corps (Third and Fifth) toward the peach orchard, and were soon firing northwest. We had been firing southwest. Although our line was somewhat broken or irregular, every man kept his eyes on the colors and each company organization, although depleted, was complete. Pandemonium now reigned. There was a horrible din, and for a few moments the uproar and confusion were appalling. The scene beggars description. The hand palsies, the tongue grows silent, as we attempt to portray the awful tragedy of this hour. All was confusion, noise, flashes, smoke, and deafening explosions. Cheers, yells, shrieks and groans, one incessant flash and roar of artillery (two batteries were within fifty yards of us), one ceaseless rolling and crackling of musketry. The solid, ringing cheers of the men in blue, the peculiar, high-pitched and unpleasant yells of the men in grey, rose above the din.

Generals, colonels, aids and orderlies galloped about through the smoke. The hoarse and indistinguishable order of commanding officers, the screaming and bursting of shells, canister and shrapnel with their swishing sound as they tore through the struggling masses of humanity, the death screams of wounded animals, the groans of their human companions, wounded and dying and trampled underfoot by hurrying batteries, riderless horses and the moving lines of battle, all combined an indescribable roar of discordant elements—in fact, a perfect hell on earth, never, perhaps, to be equaled, certainly not to be surpassed, nor ever to be forgotten in a man's lifetime. It has never been effaced from my memory, day or night, for fifty years. It was grim-visaged war, with all its unalterable horror, implacable, unyielding, full of sorrow, heart breaks, untold sufferings, wretched longings, doubts and fears.

As already stated, to our left as we faced when changing front in the elbow between the two corps and in the direction of the Peach Orchard, directly in the gap, were Phillip's and Bigelow's

396

Massachusetts Batteries. General Barnes and staff and Colonel W. S. Tilton, commanding our First Brigade, were here also. The fire of shot and shell through this breach and across our line had become, if possible, more terrific. Here General Barnes was wounded, Colonel Tilton of our own regiment had his horse shot, and Lieut. Walter Davis of the Twenty-Second, who was on General Barnes' staff, had the rim of his hat carried away.

Nothing could live before such a fire. The horses and many of the men of the batteries were shot away while bravely struggling to check the onward rush of the rebel masses. The rapid flashes and incessant peals from the guns of those two batteries told truthfully that the awful work allotted to them was being well performed, and the desperate bravery of these gallant cannoneers in that fearful breach can never receive too much praise. Bigelow was fighting, retiring with prolonge ropes attached. Lieut.-Col. F. McGilvery, Chief of Artillery of the First Volunteer Brigade of the Artillery Reserve, had ordered him to hold that point at all hazards. In the midst of the smoke, we could plainly see the cannoneers using their pistols, handspikes and sponge-staffs. He lost three officers, twenty-eight men and over eighty horses. The Eighth South Carolina, forming the left of Kershaw's Brigade, was the regiment that went directly in among Bigelow's guns, followed by some of Wofford's Georgia Brigade. The battery was practically captured at one time—four guns being abandoned to the enemy, all of which were subsequently brought off that night by Capt. Ed Dow, commanding the Sixth Maine Battery, who used his gun teams for that purpose. This is taken from Captain Bigelow and Captain Dow's own statement to the writer. He (Bigelow) was taken off the field supposed to be in a dying condition, but subsequently recovered. The battery expended three tons of shot and shell, including ninety-two rounds of canister, firing in all five hundred and twenty-eight rounds. Two other officers were killed, six out of seven sergeants were killed and wounded (two killed), seven corporals and twelve privates were killed and wounded and two taken prisoners. The enemy were standing in among and on the limber chests of Lieutenant Melton's section. Private Ligal brained with a rammer head a Confederate who tried to capture him. The statistics of the War Department show that, with the single exception of a battery captured by a sudden charge at Iuka, Miss., it sustained the heaviest losses of any light battery in any single engagement of the whole war. We fell back through the Wheat Field, Colonel Jeffords, of the Fourth Michigan, Second Brigade, being bayonetted while trying to save his colors just to our left. Standing waist deep in the beautiful yellow grain, the blue strongly contrasting, was the Regular Division, Gen. Romeyn B. Ayres[5] commanding, dealing sledge-hammer blows. It was moving through the wheat field in column of battalions, close en masse, but marching as steadily as upon parade. They were delivering volleys from the front line, and the contrast of the tall yellow grain, so soon to be trampled by the succeeding columns, was very striking, and a scene never to be forgotten. Ayres had struck the enemy in flank as they were closely following our change of front through Rose's woods, had doubled them up and driven them back, but was in turn outflanked from the direction of the Devil's Den to the south.

A large body of the enemy had gained his left rear, and facing about as we passed, he fought his way through and into our lines before dark, with a loss of more than half his force. As we were slowly falling back, firing as we went, "Here," said an officer of another company, a little panicky, and somewhat separated from his own men, to the writer, "Where is your company?" "Let that boy alone!" said our captain (J. H. Baxter), but a few feet distant, "he knows what he is about!" So did we all! for every man was intent upon preserving the regimental organization, and doing his entire duty. This officer proved to be the one whom our brother had driven back to the lines on the night of May 4 at Chancellorsville, when the pickets flushed, and he was sprinting for the rifle pits in the moonlight.

Col. Thomas Sherwin,[6] commanding our regiment, was seen to fall on his knees, just after crossing the low stone wall (standing

[5] Romeyn Beck Ayres (1825–1888), West Point 1847, Mexican War veteran, and career officer.—2019
[6] Thomas Sherwin (1839–1914), later breveted a brigadier general for

near the group of houses on the lane just north, built since the war but now (1913) removed) as though shot through the body. Several sprang forward to assist him, but he immediately rose to his feet. A bullet had passed through his clothing and grazed his breast, without wounding him, but with sufficient force to knock him down. We halted at the foot, and on the northwest slope of Little Round Top. Eustis's Brigade of the Sixth Corps was coming up and forming line of battle, about three to five hundred yards to our right. The uproar and confusion lulled. The Confederates came charging into our lines, and we captured many of Wofford's Brigade at this period. One "Johnny" had got in advance of their line, the charge having already spent itself like a huge wave upon the ocean beach, and they were much scattered. He was unattended and directly in front of the Eighteenth Massachusetts. The situation was ludicrous. "Hello, Johnny!" came from our boys, "you aren't going to capture us all alone, are you?" He came in. Many incidents could be related which have never been told of this afternoon's battle.

The shades of night gathered; only a few scattered shots could be heard, which, with the groans of the wounded, the cries for water, and the hum of thousands now lying on their arms as each related his experiences of the day, made a contrast to the fury of an hour before that was almost painful, and the reaction and the relaxation of the tense nerves almost prostrating. A tall Georgia sergeant, bare-headed—his coal black hair and fine features just visible in the gathering dusk— stepped over our prostrate bodies, and a voice cried out to the prisoner, "Going to the rear, Johnny?" "Yes, and I'm right glad to go to the *rare!*" We threw ourselves upon the ground, well wrapped up in a half blanket as a protection from the cold dew, and with a canteen for a pillow, we soon lost in peaceful slumber all remembrance of the perilous movements and the exciting details of the struggle which has been so imperfectly described.

Night glided by and another perfect day dawned. Shortly after daybreak, passing along the westerly face of Little Round Top, we

---

his actions at Gettysburg.—2019

moved to a position in front of the ravine or gorge that separates the two Round Tops.

It was wild, rocky, and savage. Lying down among the large boulders that everywhere abounded, piling up the loose rocks and making ourselves as thin as possible, we awaited a development of the day's events. It proved to be full of thrilling hair-breadth escapes. We were to the east of or directly in front of the Devil's Den. So intent had we been in watching the massing of the rebel columns in the center, for the final grand charge of Pickett's Division, that we had scarcely noticed the sharpshooters gathering among the gigantic boulders which make up the surroundings of this impregnable position.

The artillery opened. Shells, shrapnel and canister tore through the cedars and scrub oak; shrieked, buzzed and grated among the rocks and bounded over our prostrate line, now flat on the ground, spread out thin, and covering every inch of person possible. Battery "D," Fifth United States Artillery, previously mentioned, was just over us, firing over our heads. The sharpshooters also began their deadly work, and the sharp zip— p-i-n-g-g-g—of the spiteful rifle ball, more dangerous than its larger brother, added to our perils. Under almost perfect cover they became so persistently annoying and dangerous that we could not show a finger without a warning in the shape of a bullet. Our dead and wounded were lying in full view, the latter by the hundreds, all intermingled with the Confederates, and within hailing distance. Their cries and entreaties for water and assistance would have melted hearts of stone. Many of the wounded were hit again; many died from fright and nervous exhaustion, from loss of blood, etc., that could have been saved. In vain did we try to succor them. Some crawled out on their hands and knees and held water to their dying lips; others crept out and threw canteens of water. We hailed the sharpshooters, explaining our object and telling them that they were wounding their own men. It was of no avail, the merciless fire went out, every man was shot at, and after a sergeant and others had been wounded in the attempt, it was given up.

Lookouts were stationed among the large rocks to warn us when the rebels were going to fire. At this moment all would rise up and pour in a lively fire across the swale (here about 500 yards in width) upon their position, which was concealed, determined to surprise and kill them off if possible. But they proved vigilant, were not to be caught napping, and finally played the old Yankee trick of displaying caps upon their rammers. Both regiments of Berdan's sharpshooters were sent out crawling over our prostrate forms as far as possible, to the left and front, and securing cover, they tried to dislodge these imperturbable Confederates. The cannoneers of Hazlett's Battery (formerly Weed's[7]) D, Fifth United States Artillery, on Little Round Top, were picked off and the guns almost silenced by their skill.

Pickett's Division moved up in three lines, formed in close column by division, with strong supports on the flanks. About one o'clock was the hour, and 155 guns covered the movement. General [Henry Jackson] Hunt, our chief of artillery, used but 80 guns in reply to the cannonade preceding the charge, which he soon ordered to slacken their fire, for canister range, and to economize ammunition.[8]

Much lead was wasted all along the line in an effort to move or silence these murderous fellows, and it was not until near sunset that a portion of Crawford's Division of the Fifth Corps, advancing from our right and making a left wheel to envelop the Devil's Den, succeeded in dislodging and capturing them. They came through our lines, and proved to be of the Third Arkansas, Hood's Division, Robertson's Brigade, and were as ragged, unkempt and tough looking a body of men as it had ever been our fortune to see in the army of northern Virginia. They were all dead shots, armed mostly with the old-fashioned muzzle-loading Mississippi, or squirrel rifle, carrying a small pea ball that

---

[7] Stephen Hinsdale Weed (1831–July 2, 1863) was a career officer. He was attended in his final hours by young Tillie Pierce. See *At Gettysburg; or What a Girl Saw*, Alleman, 2016.

[8] The author's regiment, according to a note by him, was positioned within a few feet of where the monument to Strong Vincent is placed today.—2019

sounded spitefully murderous, as they sharply sang among the cedars and flattened with a dull, ominous thud against the moss-covered boulders that composed our fortifications.

Of the charge on that afternoon of July 3, we saw but little from our position, the smoke in the valley hiding much of the movement from view. We saw the limbers blowing up. Rittenhouse,[9] who had succeeded Hazlett[10] in command of Battery D, Fifth United States Artillery, just over our heads, (I had occasion to go through this battery several times during the day, down the easterly slope of Little Round Top for water), had a plunging fire across the valley. Rittenhouse had advanced his guns, except one or two, and turned them so as to have a plunging fire across the valley into the flanks of Pickett's massed battalions, and with shell and shrapnel was dropping them with fearful accuracy in their midst. It is said that one shell killed and wounded thirty-nine men in one regiment.[11]

---

[9] 1st Lieutenant Benjamin Franklin Rittenhouse (1839–1915).

[10] 1st Lieutenant Charles Edward Hazlett (1838–July 2, 1863) was killed by a sharpshooter while bending over the mortally-wounded General Weed.

[11] September 24, 1904. Lieutenant-Colonel Fuger, who was the First Sergeant of Cushing's Battery C, 4th United States, at Gettysburg, stated to me today that the battery lost forty-five men out of ninety-three, that all the horses were killed except four or five, that nine ammunition chests blew up during the action, and that there was not a wheel or any woodwork of the battery that was not raked or scarred. It was directly in the storm center of Lee's artillery fire. Lieutenants Cushing and Milne were killed, and he (Fuger) was left in command; all ammunition was expended (solid shot, shell and shrapnel) except canister, of which they had plenty.
Cushing's last order to Fuger was to have all of this taken out of the chests and piled up between the guns, leaving just room enough for Nos. 1 and 2 to work their pieces which were three-inch ordnance guns. They were run up to the wall, and fired one, two and three cases, the last as Armistead came over the wall. Alonzo Cushing, commanding this battery, was a classmate of our brother at West Point, as was Woodruff who commanded a battery on his right, also killed about this hour.
The two stones, marked "Armistead" and "Cushing," mark the spots where both fell, Armistead with his hand on No. 3 gun. Fuger fired at him with his pistol when less than forty feet away. Cushing was not shot in the bowels, nor did he say to General Webb, "Webb, I'll give them one

General Lee's plan on this day was really a forlorn hope, as was our movement upon Marye's Heights at Fredericksburg, Va., December 13, 1862, and it was directly opposed to the judgment of his trusted (but now much calumniated) Lieutenant-General Longstreet—the best corps commander and the hardest fighter, with the most level head, that he ever had. It was to form a column of assault under cover of a heavy artillery fire, and moving with a rush through the Union center, thus separating our two wings, then attack either or both wings, especially the left. Ewell was to follow up his advantage gained on the

2d, while Stuart was to watch for an opportunity to co-operate by penetrating our lines from the rear near Cress Run and Rummell's farm. There was not a ghost of a chance for this poorly conceived and badly executed plan. For once, Lee had

---

more shot!" or pull any lanyard while his bowels were protruding, but he was shot three times; first in the shoulder, second in the privates, and third in the mouth, which last shot killed him, and he dropped dead in Fuger's arms. Fuger has tried to correct those lies for years. The battery, after the battle ceased, went to the rear about one and a half miles into camp by order of General Hancock, near the Baltimore Pike. Fuger could not find his horse, and he was not among the dead horses. He had been left with the drivers who were ordered to be down with the reins over their arms. Fuger and all were exhausted. Somebody gave him a piece of bacon and hardtack. He fell asleep with these in his hands, too exhausted to eat, beside Cushing's body, which he had brought off the field and which was covered with a piece of tarpaulin or shelter tent. A man awakened him and said, "Sergeant, your horse is here at the picket line." He went there and found that his horse had found the battery in some mysterious way, but he was mortally wounded, having had one hip knocked off by a projectile. He had to order him to be killed to put him out of his misery.

Where the 72d Pennsylvania monument now stands (Baxter Zouaves), a Zouave with clubbed rifle, the position was in dispute, and was finally settled in the courts. Fuger was one of the principal witnesses. He testified that the color bearer and others were on that spot, and that he saw them. This determined the position of the present monument. He wrote John B. Batchelder several times about the mythical story regarding Cushing's remark to General Webb. General Hancock sent for Fuger on the field, and told him he had sent in his name for a commission for gallantry on the field. He received a Medal of Honor.— note in original [Alonzo Cushing was awarded the Medal of Honor on December 19, 2014.]

overstepped himself. It was a miserable, wretched failure. A column of from fifteen to eighteen thousand men moving upon troops in a selected position— behind natural and artificial barricades—with plenty of supporting lines of battle in the rear (the entire Sixth Corps, only one brigade of which had been engaged), simply invited the same disaster that befell our own movement at Fredericksburg, although it was not nearly so strong a position to carry by assault as the latter. The fighting was short, desperate and decisive. Those that were not killed, wounded or captured, fled in a rout out of range. No human being could stand up in the face of forty or fifty guns massed and firing double canister into massed columns at from thirty to three hundred yards range. It was simply a physical impossibility, and all the drivel about the Union Center being pierced is too absurd for any veteran of Gettysburg who was either engaged or looking on and seeing such a pitiable spectacle, to entertain for a moment. We will say right here, then, that any historian who may, in the future, claim even a partial success for this charge of Pickett's, will only subject himself to ridicule so long as a soldier is alive who was in the battle and saw this gallant charge but wretched disaster to Lee's Confederate veterans.

Only about two hundred men with Armistead dribbled over the stone wall in the face of Cushing's Battery, and whether he or any one man laid his hand on gun No. 3 of that battery, it does not matter; they were all killed or made prisoners in a few moments. This is what some buncombe writers who were not there—some newspaper correspondents—said, who wanted to hand down and perpetuate a few more historical lies. (The Lord knows we have had enough of them ever since our colonial days.) This is what they call "piercing the center," "gaining the works," etc., etc. Behind this center and but a short distance away lay en masse the entire Sixth Corps which had been doubled-quicked to this position, when the charge was seen coming for that point. They numbered over fifteen thousand men, most of whom had not pressed trigger. Besides this, there was Stannard's Vermont Brigade[12] which swept the flanks of Pickett. They had never been in action before.

This practically ended the battle of Gettysburg. Volumes have been and could be written of the events of this one incident of the great conflict. The Twelfth Corps had recovered by stubborn fighting at daybreak on the 3d their own position on Culp's Hill.

From our position at the foot of Little Round Top the roar of nearly 300 guns was terrific. It is said the roar, jar and concussion were heard at Philadelphia, over eighty miles away. Each successive discharge seemed to lift us from our rocky beds; the whole ground trembled and jarred under the tremendous impact. The fiends of the unknown region seemed to have turned loose. But the indistinct lines of struggling men were soon lost to view. The battle was over, the victory of Gettysburg won. It was the soldier's battle, for never was a contest so fiercely fought by the desperate energy, indomitable courage, marvelous staying powers and intelligence of the rank and file of the Army of the Potomac as at Gettysburg. There was little or no plan of battle, no strategy, tactical maneuvers, nor audible commands from superior officers. Such seems now to be the opinion among those who participated in the great battle after all these years of serious, sober reflection. At all events it is my own.

No pen can paint the awful picture of desolation, devastation and death that was presented here to the shuddering beholders who traversed these localities, July 5 and 6, 1863. Death in its ghastliest and most abhorrent forms everywhere. Festering corpses at every step, some still unburied, some hastily and rudely buried, with so little earth upon them that the appearance presented was almost as repulsive as where no attempt at burial had been made. It was a hideous and revolting sight.

In charging across the piles of rocks at Plum Run, many dead and wounded fell in the chasms between. The heavy rains that followed the battle washed down and lodged in these places other corpses from positions higher up the flat. These bodies were never recovered, but gradually decomposed, whilst the bones were washed away and covered with rubbish.

---

[12] See *Vermont at Gettysburg*, Cheney, 2014.

This stream was clogged with the dead bodies of Confederates, and in this valley so much was the course of the stream obstructed that great ponds formed where the waters were dammed up by the bodies of the southern soldiers. The dead were everywhere. In some cases nothing but a few mutilated remnants and pieces of flesh were left of what had been so late a human being, following his flag to victory or death.

More than a month after the battle, in one of these chasms was presented the hideous spectacle of the remains of five rebels piled upon each other, just as they had fallen, in a place from which it would have been impossible to extricate the bodies. For weeks after, an Alabama soldier in the Third Corps Hospital, partly delirious and moaning with pain from his wounds, would exclaim, 'Awful rocks, awful rocks!!'

There is a field of forty acres surrounding the Devil's Den with the edge of the woods, formerly belonging to the Rose Farm. On this farm lay, July 2 and 3, 1863, more dead and wounded men than on any other one farm of the field of the battle of Gettysburg—perhaps more than on any one farm during the entire war. On this farm alone were buried one thousand, five hundred of the men in grey, according to the statement of Mr. Rose, when he advertised his farm for sale shortly after the battle. In the garden of the Rose house in full view, nearly one hundred rebels were buried. All around the barn, even within the house yards within a few feet of the doors, were in numbers the scantily buried followers of the Confederate cause; two hundred and seventy-five were buried behind the bam. A rebel colonel was buried within a yard of the kitchen door.

All the fields and road from the Emmetsburg Road to the base of Round Top were one vast, hideous charnel house—the dead were everywhere. All was one trodden, miry waste with corpses at every step, and the thick, littered debris of battle, broken muskets, shattered caissons and black, defiled clothing, trodden cartridge boxes and splintered swords, rifled knapsacks, and battered canteens.

On the night of July 3, the writer was sent out on picket, and posted from three to five hundred yards, in front of the motionless and sleeping forms of the thoroughly worn-out men. The night was warm and muggy; the moon, partially obscured by

406

a haze, shed a dim and sickly light over the ground. Advancing carefully through the oaks and cedars, avoiding the large boulders everywhere about, almost indistinct in the soft, yellow light that enveloped them, we gained our position and sat down upon a large flat wall with our backs against a tree.

There was ample opportunity for reflecting upon that wild, strange scene about us, so rare in a boy's life. The midnight hour approached; the writer could reach out his rifle in any direction and touch a dead body, could distinctly see them scattered thickly about, many with their ghastly faces showing here and there, by twos, threes and fours or in clumps, just where they had gone down in the death struggle. Stillness now reigned, painful by contrast, only broken by the distressed and rattling breathing of a dying man, or the piteous appeals of the wounded scattered about everywhere.

Behind a boulder, lying upon his back, one poor fellow was vainly endeavoring, with fast-waning strength, to check the flow of blood. His foot was braced against a rock; a sword or bayonet was thrust through a handkerchief tightly bound about his leg. He was an officer, a captain of the 5th Texas, a Georgian by birth, with a handsome, intelligent face, full of courage and cheerfulness, even while his life was apparently fast ebbing. The death sweat stood out in great beads upon his pallid forehead. The writer talked to him and gave him water in which he had soaked coffee and sugar. It was palatable; a good imitation of cold coffee, he said, of which he had had none for many a day. He expressed his gratitude and gave us a partial history of this attack, saying that they expected to meet nothing but organized militia.

While advancing through this wild, rough gorge to the attack, his heart misgave him. He felt disaster would be their fate, and when our men rose from behind their rock breastworks, at the foot of Round Top, and poured in the volleys that withered their lines, and he saw the red maltese crosses of the Fifth Corps on our caps, he quickly turned to his company and said, "No militia there, it is the Fifth Corps. The Army of the Potomac is up; get behind the rocks, quick!"

He fell a few moments later. Of the entire brigade but few went back, I never learned the name of this officer, but remembering that he had told me he was from Athens, Ga., in the spring of 1905, while in Birmingham, Ala., being advised by an old soldier to place a query in the Confederate Veteran briefly reciting these facts, I soon received a reply, and at last learned whom I had relieved from distress over forty years before, that July night on the battlefield. His name was Captain Turner. He was taken off the field in the early morning, sent to one of our field hospitals, paroled, spent some time in the Chimborazo Hill hospital at Richmond, Va., was then furloughed home (Athens) where my informant went with him, and he could not then say at that date whether he was still living or not. He was in his company and lay nearby him, also wounded.

The writer met an old Confederate soldier of the Fifth Texas in the winter of 1876 on the far western frontier of Texas. He had lost his leg in front of the Round Tops in the charge of the Texas Brigade (Robertson) and he also lay in this very spot I have described. He stated that the hand-to-hand fighting in that place, among the rocks, with a part of the First Division of the Fifth Corps, was the most desperate and savagely contested that he had ever experienced during his service in the Army of Northern Virginia.

The picket duty having been performed, we were relieved and going still further to the front, in the early morning of July 4, we made a tour of this blood-soaked field, the enemy's pickets having been withdrawn to or beyond the Emmittsburg Road preparatory to their retreat back to Virginia.

In every direction among the bodies was the debris of battle—haversacks, canteens, hats, caps, sombreros, blankets of every shade and hue, bayonets, cartridge boxes—every conceivable part of the equipment of a soldier of the blue or grey mingled with the bodies of Yankee and rebel, friends' and foes, perchance father and son. They were in every possible position, with arm uplifted, with clenched fist and menacing attitude, some with the smile of peace as though death had come gradually and without pain.

Others, and the majority, had a settled and determined expression as though filled with revengeful thoughts. Some were in the act of tearing a cartridge, others just loading or reaching for the rammer—all called forth in a moment, in the twinkling of an eye—to the mysterious hereafter. As day approached, it could be seen that the wounded were being carried to the rear as rapidly as possible, though hundreds still remained uncared for.

Our tour extended well to the front, across the swale, inside our picket fines, now held by the Pennsylvania Reserves (Crawford's Division), which had been swept by the Fifth and Ninth Massachusetts Batteries. The scenes of that spot, as the fast-quickening day revealed its dreaded horrors to our astounded gaze, still finger on our memories. We have seen it partially described in Wert's Guide Book, which we have referred to. Masses of Kershaw's and Wofford's Brigade advancing up to the muzzles of these guns, which had been loaded either with double shotted canister or spherical case, with fuzes cut to one second—to explode near the muzzles—had been literally blown to atoms—and in a moment's brief space into eternity. Corpses strewed the ground at every step. Arms, legs, heads, and parts of dismembered bodies were scattered all about, and sticking among the rocks, and against the trunks of trees, hair, brains, entrails and shreds of human flesh still hung, a disgusting, sickening, heartrending spectacle to our young minds. It was indeed a charnel house—a butcher's pen—with man as the victim. One man had as many as twenty canister or case shots through different parts of his body, though none through a vital organ, and he was still gasping and twitching with a slight motion of the muscles and vibrations of the pulse, although utterly unconscious of approaching death. This ground was along the lane at the northwesterly edge of the Wheat Field leading over to the Emmittsburg Road already described, over which we had fought on July 2.

We retraced our steps. When nearly within our lines we witnessed a sight— or rather a vision, for often even now it rises before us like a phantom. The moon, though slightly overcast, still threw its pale sickly yellow light through the rocks, bodies and wild, weird surroundings of that bloodstained place. As we turned to go around a large rock, we suddenly came face to face with a young man, who seemed from his position to be partially reclining against a cedar tree. His cap was off, his hair thrown back, the moonlight showed a remarkably, fine cut, youthful face, which seemed turned upward to Heaven, as though in the act of prayer. It was an imploring and yet a calm and resigned expression; his hands were clasped. We started back as though from an apparition and for a full moment could scarcely believe that the figure was not alive, or else a marble statue shaded by the trees. He was dressed in the rebel grey, and it proved to be the body of a young boy firmly fixed in the forked branch of a small tree. He had caught as he fell and, growing suddenly rigid in death, had retained a life-like attitude. We were so startled that for a few moments we walked on in silence. The dead had now to be buried. The writer was detailed on the burial party, but just as we had commenced the horrible task, some of our would-be and involuntary sore-footed stragglers coming up at that moment, our captain, Joseph E. Baxter (afterwards mortally wounded at Cold Harbor), said to the first sergeant, "Relieve that detail, and put the stragglers to work at that duty."

They were so far decomposed that we had to run rails under the bodies, which, as they slid into the trenches, broke apart, to the horror and disgust of the whole party, and the stench still lingers in our nostrils. As many as ninety bodies were thus disposed of in one trench. When it was possible, blankets were rolled about them, but most of them were tumbled in just as they fell, with not a prayer, eulogy or tear to distinguish them from so many animals.

Our brother at headquarters now writes:

Camp of the Eighth United States

Infantry, at Westminster, Md.,

July 4, 1863.

We whipped Bee's army yesterday, and they are in full retreat. Major-General Hancock is wounded, and sent to Baltimore; General Gibbon, commanding a division of the Second Corps, is also wounded. General Weed is killed. I have not heard of many low ranked officers. Cushing of my class was killed while defending his battery; he saved his pieces, but almost every man and horse were killed. The carnage has been truly frightful. We have taken six or seven thousand prisoners so far, and they are still coming in.

Why don't General Dix take Richmond now? The regular division is wiped out. Meade will pursue the rebel army as fast as possible. They will probably stop our advance by fortifying the mountain passes through which they retreat.

The Pennsylvania Militia are heavy dogs; I wish Lee had got a little further into the state. Longstreet is a prisoner, and wounded at General Meade's Headquarters at Gettysburg. I cannot hear anything of the boys.

On the 4th of July, in the afternoon, we moved out to the left and front of the Round Tops, southwest (a detail of two hundred men under Maj. Mason W. Burt of the Twenty-Second Massachusetts) on a reconnaissance. We developed but slight resistance, merely skirmishing with the enemy's rear guard, and orders having been given to feel them carefully, and not to press them, we returned, a severe and drenching thunderstorm breaking upon us in full force. The detachment of the Fifth Corps thus had the honor of firing the last shot at Lee's rear guard of the Army of Northern Virginia at Gettysburg, for the enemy was now in full retreat from northern soil. Meade did not seem to manifest the slightest desire to renew the contest. The well-known military axiom that to a flying enemy must be given a wall of steel or a bridge of gold, was here unmistakably instanced by presenting the latter. It was hard to convince him that the enemy had gone—word went forth, "On no account bring on a battle." We saw upon our return through the woods, along our line of march, many of the Confederate dead, where they had crawled behind rocks, stumps, trees and hidden nooks to die, too painfully wounded or exhausted to keep up with their retreating columns.

Within the gates of the old Evergreen Cemetery, at the time of the great battle, was a sign bearing the following inscription: "All persons using firearms in these grounds will be prosecuted with the utmost vigor of the law." With what a grim smile must that insatiable demon, war, have greeted this injunction of the simple residents, while glutting his appetite during the carnage among the tombstones that marked the dead villagers of Gettysburg.

About 5 P. M. on the evening of the 5th, the Fifth Corps passing to the rear of the Round Tops, and striking the Taneytown Road, moved on it a short distance, then leaving it before it crosses Rock Creek, marched over to the Emmittsburg Road, and taking it, started in pursuit, plodding, slipping and wallowing along the wretched roads until amid darkness that could be well compared to Erebus, and rain that descended in torrents, in almost inextricable confusion, not being able to distinguish the road we were marching on, we floundered out of it into an orchard near Marsh Run, and bivouacked for the night in wretched misery. The fatigue, excitement, and almost total loss of sleep, for almost an entire week, the appalling sights we had witnessed, the loss of our comrades, lying among the dead and wounded, the stench from which had nauseated us almost to the limit, had all proved too much for us, and finding some high clover under an apple-tree, the writer sank like a log and at once became oblivious to campaigns, battles, the dead and dying and the many thrilling details of the battle of Gettysburg.

AFTER GETTYSBURG

The Provost Guard, Army of the Potomac, left Westminster July 5, and marched to Gettysburg; camped near the cemetery. Here our brother wrote again:

Camp at Gettysburg, Pa.,

July 6, 1863.

I have only time to say that I heard from Walt and Bob yesterday morning on my way to headquarters; they are both all right. I trembled when I asked for them, for I could not believe that they

412

would both escape. I rode over the battlefield last night; it is awful! We are following them rapidly. O'Rorke, Cushing and Woodruff of my class are killed.

July 6, at 4 A. M., the rain descending in torrents, we marched slowly along the muddy and blocked-up roads a few miles farther, and waded the swollen creeks to near Moritz Cross roads. The mud rested upon a mass of flinty stones that tore through our solid (?) government brogans as though they were paper, and many a man tore the flimsy things from his feet, and plodded along in his bare feet, unable longer to stand the grinding wear and tear upon feet blistered by the long march from Fredericksburg.

On the morning of the 7th, we marched through Emmittsburg, a drizzling rain falling continually; the wretched roads, cut up by artillery and cavalry, being one immense hog-wallow the entire distance. Darkness again overtook us, and in the pouring rain nothing could be distinguished.

Men in vain sought to keep the road, and follow the column. They fell out by scores; the commands melted away, and sought shelter wherever they could find it in the fields beside the route— a confused, huddled-up, completely lost body of men. Our bivouac was near Utica.

On the 8th, we passed over the Catoctin Mountains, at High Knob, and marching through Creagerstown and Utica, commenced the descent into the valley. The sun for the first time now broke through the dark clouds with unusual brightness, and sent a flood of light over hill and dale, that gave to the stretches of rich, yellow grain, and stripes of dark green, alternating with the belts of woods scattered here and there, a richer beauty than when we had approached it before.

We bivouacked at Middletown, near the spot where the September previous we moved out for the battlefield of Antietam. On the day following, as we moved almost mechanically from our bivouacs in the grass, the writer, afflicted with that Scourge of the army—chronic diarrhea—was compelled to fall out soon after we started.

A few moments later, seeing a large bend in the road, and the brigade flag ahead, he attempted by the usual cut off, to save time and distance in regaining the regiment. Unfortunately just at this time General Meade was taking this same short cut with his staff. "What command do you belong to, sir?" sternly inquired the Commander of the Army of the Potomac. "First brigade, first division, Fifth Corps," was the reply. "Rejoin it immediately, sir!" "I am doing so, sir!" "No, sir! you are straggling," said the General, now angry. "I 'fell out' because it was necessary—I had—" "Never mind, sir! You are away from your regiment without a pass. That is straggling. You know the penalty. No more words, sir, or I'll have you arrested!" said the now thoroughly aroused commanding general. Seeing that the argument was about to become a little one-sided, the writer humbly strode along across the bend, in rear of the brilliant mounted staff, industriously chewing the cud of reflection, yet conscious of having committed no sin. Appearances were certainly against me.

It was thus that the sick, the halt, lame and chafed patriot had to suffer for the inveterate grumblers, "coffee coolers" and stragglers. It was hard to discriminate, or draw the line of distinction.

We marched through the gap (Turner's) in South Mountain, chaffing most unmercifully a part of Schenck's or French's Corps, which had just come from Baltimore and, lining the road as we passed, were cheering for this and for that corps of the Army of the Potomac. Their uniforms were new, their buttons bright, their knapsacks varnished, and paper collars predominated. We were ragged, dirty, shoeless, hatless and blackened by a month's steady marching. Envious of their newness our bummers vigorously shelled them with pork and, hardbread.

Our brother Walter now writes:

Camp near Boonesboro,

July to, 1863.

Left Middletown yesterday, and passed over South Mountain, and after marching a few miles, bivouacked in our present location. We move this forenoon toward Sharpsburg, Hagerstown and Williamsport, only three or ten miles distant, where I anticipate a fierce battle.

We will win a final victory, I am most positive. You do not know with what confidence this jaded-out army goes forth to the harvest of death; we will fight bravely, and I hope to come out unscathed. Be sure, however, that I am where the bullets are as thick as anywhere, and that your sons Walt and Bob are doing their whole duty.

I heard from Gene through the Quartermaster this morning; he is trying to get the shirts, etc., to us. We drew fresh meat this morning, but have got to leave it. They generally issue it to us while yet warm, and then we have to move, and can't carry it for fear of its getting fly-blown. *** The Bucktail rifles are passing and the band is playing 'Marching Along.'

We crossed the Antietam Creek on the 10th, and bivouacked near Delaware Mills, and slowly moved in line of battle on the 11th, along the Hagerstown turnpike, to near Williamsport. The enemy were constantly on our front, and skirmishing was going on continually. We constructed barricades, and every preparation was made for a great battle. It was a lovely season of the year. The entire Army of the Potomac was in line of battle. Occupying the extreme left, we could glance along the whole line, which was stretched out for several miles. The batteries were unlimbering, ready for action. The cavalry was moving here and there, their many guidons fluttering in the breeze. Aids and orderlies continually galloped in rear of the line. We had never seen the entire army in line of battle before.

We were in an immense grain field up to our waists. In front, as far as the eye could see, was a line of skirmishers moving slowly to the front, from which frequent puffs of smoke, followed by the crack! crack!, told that they were feeling the strength and developing the position of the enemy. The sun was yet an hour high, and the contrast of the long blue line, closed in masses in the yellow grain fields, striped off with alternate green, and the

415

fringe of the woods in front, all softened by the lights and shadows of the declining sun, and, resting peacefully in the far off meadows, the farm houses; altogether there was presented one of the most spirited scenes, if not the grandest spectacles our eyes had ever rested upon, and rarely observed in a man's lifetime.

While advancing on the 12th near St. James College, and as the popping of the skirmishers grew more and more brisk, our brother rode up. He had searched for us about Gettysburg, had gone over the battlefield, got trace of us, and having a small package from home, had come upon the line. We had barely time to take the little bundle, open it, and extract a new shirt, get under the lee of a fence, and exchange our old one, which had clung so long and closely to us, grasp his hand and say good-bye, before we were pushed out on the line. On this occasion also, Senator Wilson again visited us. Always solicitous for the welfare of the regiment, he had never neglected an opportunity to be near and cheer us up. As the skirmishers opened fire and the bullets were spitting about, some officer said to him, "Look out, General, this is no place for you," and he was quietly hurried to the rear, out of danger. His hands were full of letters, which he had offered to mail for the boys. His face was wet with tears. His voice choked with emotion as he said, "God bless you!" and even while several of us hastily ran up and thrust a pencil scrap—the first since Gettysburg, in his hands, he was quickly led away. It was a stirring scene.

Our brother of the regulars had left Gettysburg on the 7th, and passing through Taneytown had camped at Woodborough, twenty-six miles. On the 8th, they moved to Frederick in a drenching rain and passing through, camped at Middletown, nineteen miles.

One of the first sights which greeted the Provost Guard, as they were pitching camp, was the body of Richardson,[13] the spy,

---

[13] William Richardson was a Confederate spy from Baltimore who was hanged July 5, 1863, near Hagan's Tavern on Old National Pike (*Frederick News Post* website).

416

hanging from a limb of a tree close by. Pinned to his breast was a placard with this inscription:

Tried, convicted and hung as a spy.
Any one cutting down this body without orders will take his place.
By order of
Major-General John Buford,
Commanding Cavalry

On the 9th they marched to "Mountain House" on South Mountain, where they remained until the 15th.

He rode from the camp in search of us, and thus describes his finding us in the following letter:

Camp op the Eighth U. S. Infantry,

July 13, 1863.

I mailed a letter to mother yesterday, and told her I was unwell, but I was all right the next morning, so I armed myself with soft bread and butter, some tongue, and the bundle mother gave me for Walt and Bob when I was last home, and started in search of the Fifth Corps.

I rode about eight miles, and found the First Division advancing in line of battle. I followed, and as soon as they rested, Walt saw me; he cried out to Bob, and they both started to meet me. They were very glad to see me, and Bob was particularly glad to see a clean shirt. He immediately divested himself of a *fifteen day older*, and came out in a clean one; Walt had a pretty clean one on.

They were both very hungry, and the little bread and tongue that I had was soon gone. The bugle sounded the advance and they had to run. I watched them until they gradually got out of sight, and then turned my horse's head toward home, wondering if I had seen them for the last time alive and well.

Father, you have no idea how much anxiety those boys cause me. I was opposed to their enlisting from the first, for I thought that two from one family was enough. I can never join in the general jubilee caused by a victory to our arms, for the reason that I am always afraid that one or both have spilled their blood to help gain it. *** Walt took a musket at the last battle. *** I saw four companies of the Fourteenth Massachusetts (First Mass. Heavy Artillery) on their way to join the army yesterday. John's company was left behind with the others; I am glad of it. ***

I think Lee's army will get terribly thrashed before he gets back to Richmond. We occupy Hagerstown, and if Lee does get across the river, we will worry him into a battle before long. Our pontoons are here, and we threw twenty thousand men across the river yesterday. We have been reinforced some, and the eight thousand at Harper's Ferry will join us if they have not already. Everything seems to be bright now; we are moving at the same time all over the country.

Grant is after [Confederate General Joe E.] Johnston; we are making an attack upon Charleston to keep Beauregard there, and Dix is keeping the garrison at Richmond busy. Lee's army has to draw their supplies from Culpeper, and his cavalry are nowhere in comparison to ours, although ours are pretty nearly worn out.

We expect to have a fight tomorrow. I think two Bradford boys were wounded, one in the temple, and one in the side; both were doing well when last heard from; I do not remember their names. General Prince is with the Army of the Potomac; he hailed me on the road the other day, and appeared very glad to see me. He was riding in a carriage with General Ingalls, Chief Quartermaster, Army of the Potomac, and Colonel Clark, Chief Commissary. I knew them all.

Our brother Walter writes on the same day:

Near Funks town,

July 13, 1863

In line of battle between Hagerstown, Funkstown and Williamstown.

We are now building barricades along our line. The Sixth Corps join us on our right, and last night Generals Griffin, Ayres and Major-General Sedgwick were in consultation. Most of our brigade is on picket. Bob is at the front, and was perfectly happy when he started out last night, with the words: 'You always detail me, Walt!' I wrote day before yesterday * * * gave it to Henry Wilson, who, happening to be here, kindly offered to take all letters; he came to see our little regiment, and was cordial enough to all our officers; he promised that we should soon be filled up.

418

We gave him three ringing cheers. When I handed him the letter, and was about to depart, he said in a trembling voice, 'good-bye,' as if he had an interest in every soldier; he is a kind-hearted man.

Gene came ten miles to see us yesterday, all the way from South Mountain Gap. I caught sight of him coming long before he had any idea we were near. I cried out to Bob, and if we did not leave the ranks in a hurry! He brought mother's package, and it was a perfect godsend—shirts, odd buttons and all. *** Bob donned his shirt double quick, when he opened the bundle and found it there, but late in the afternoon, a violent thunderstorm wet him all through, shirts, pants, blouse and shoes. *** Our poor barefooted chaps were provided with shoes yesterday, and now if we get new pants, blouses, etc., we shall be complete.

My pants will hardly stay on, they are so full of holes, tears and rips. I feel anything but pleasant as I present myself to the view of guards, details, etc.

I hardly comprehend the situation at the present time; I only know that we are taking things cool and easy on our side, and should judge by the aspect that General Meade was confident of success in his intentions. He probably has the rebs just where he wants them, or else he would advance to the attack. They certainly haven't crossed [back into Virginia]; whether they can or not, I am unable to say. *** We shall soon have a great battle; our lines are all established, and the Army of the Potomac will yet be the pride of the people. Every one of its members has some claim to the name of Washington, inasmuch as they are the saviours of their country at this trying hour.

God speed the right; give us victory, and cause us to rejoice in peace, and that we may again see you in health and strength, tried and found not wanting, with our armor brighter than ever before, still the objects of your continued inquiry and love, is my cherished hope.

Our brother Bob now writes:

Near Williamsport,

July 14, 1863.

I wrote on the road from Morrisville to Aldie, and sent it at Aldie, enclosing ten dollars; I see by your letters that you have not received it. *** Walt has written you several, but actually, I have not had time.

We have been on the march day and night for over a month, and you have probably read of how much we have suffered. Whole regiments would fall out and catch up again before morning, only to fall out again. I fell out just twice, and not till my feet were raw and bloody, sticking to my stockings. *** We suffer everything on such marches. It was the hardest time the army ever saw, but I went through it all, and am safe and sound. We went into the bloody battle of Gettysburg feeling that we had suffered too much for the wretches, not to give them a licking, and we fought like devils. I almost prayed on the road that they would not 'skedaddle,' so that we might get at them; every step that I took with my raw feet made me savage and ugly.

We, our division (Jack Griffin's), whipped their crack division (Hood's, Longstreet's Corps), the Texas Rangers; we slaughtered, literally piled them up. I went down in the moonlight and talked with the wounded. They were surprised to find the Army of the Potomac fighting them; said that we had whipped their best division. All the horrors of war were again renewed; the awful stench of the blackened corpses; the bloody, groaning forms borne to the rear; the awful din of the bursting shells; the crack of the musketry; the stifling, sulphurous smoke; the exciting cheers of our boys, and the demoniac yells of the charging rebs. Oh, what a scene is war! I am alive yet, and father, I am proud to say that I have marched hundreds of miles, gone barefooted and ragged, fought one of the most terrible battles on record, and whipped— Glory!!! and chased them by thunder!!! We are in line of battle, expecting a battle every moment; they are skirmishing now in front. God bless you all! Good-bye! *** We have seen Gene; got the bundle, shirts, etc.; God bless you for them![14]

The 13th was foggy and misty, and that night it rained. We picketed our front, and captured some prisoners, and some deserters came in; both stated that the rebel army even then was huddled up on the banks of the river, having left a double line of pickets to keep up a noisy, spluttering fire to deceive us; that they

---

[14] This letter was finished under fire, and sent by the hand of Senator Henry Wilson (afterwards Vice-President of the United States), and bears his frank.—note in original

had, for a pontoon bridge, rafts chained together and constructed from old houses and barns which had been torn down in the vicinity for this purpose and they were submerged. Their stories only confirmed our suspicions. We knew they were crossing. We sent them in with a report to this effect to headquarters. But a Council of War had met; that was enough, and as councils never fight battles, the enemy folded his tent and stole away, to give the badly marched, badly handled, poorly fought, and much abused, but invincible Army of the Potomac another two years of toil, danger, hardships and suffering. It is said that Griffin, upon receiving the report of the pickets, sent word to General Meade and begged to be allowed to lead his division forward. It is also said that General Meade intended to attack the next day, but by 8 A. M., Lee with his army was once more on Virginia soil.

Had Griffin, then in his prime, and a bold, fearless, fighting commander, but had the authority at daybreak to have given the word for that 125,000 men to advance simultaneously all along the lines, with no reserves, clear to the river, and lent his magnetic presence to the troops, Lee's already defeated and dispirited army could not have held the slight rifle pits we went over in the morning for a moment. It is idle for apologies to be made for our brave and wise, but too cautious commander of the army, now dead. Thus escaped Lee and the Army of Northern Virginia, and with it the best opportunity that we ever had until Appomattox's fateful day, to destroy, perhaps capture, their main army, and shorten up the Rebellion. The Army of the Potomac could and should have finished up the business right then and there.

The men were full of fight—we had the prestige of a great victory—we had been reinforced beyond our losses. It was scarcely, if ever, that the commanders of the Army of the Potomac understood the temper of the young volunteers under them, or fully appreciated their intelligence and thorough comprehension of events as they rapidly occurred. The men in the ranks had, at all times, risen superior to the petty jealousies, internal dissensions, inefficiencies, drunkenness and moral worthlessness of many of the men who had held brief sway and iron authority over them. The man with subtle genius, magnetic force, directness of purpose and military far-sightedness, had yet to be found who could make his presence felt on the field of battle, could grasp opportunities at the right time, or who could fight the Army of the Potomac through to a decisive finish.

It was a sad morning on the 15th, when we went over the slight knoll, and through the weak rifle pits—which the enemy had hastily dug—and realized that they had gone—vanished— and our faces were again directed toward Virginia.

A deep murmured sigh of profound disappointment and regret went up from the ranks. It was a hot, sultry day—the march led us again through Sharpsburg. Many of the boys visited the battlefield of Antietam, to revive again the memories of the scene, to see the blood-stained bridge, the bullet-scarred trees; perhaps to mark the grave of some friend. In one short year many changes had taken place, trees had been cut down, fences built, land ploughed, and where once it was strewn with the bodies of the dead and dying, was now transformed into ripening grain field.

We marched the steep roads leading over South Mountain. They were lined with exhausted men—many were sunstruck—the artillery horses died by the score. The ambulances were crowded, and the new troops, sent to reinforce us, were scattered to the four winds of Heaven. We bivouacked at Burkettsville, near Crampston's Gap, after a march of over twenty-five miles—a dreadful day—a mere baker's dozen only arrived in camp. Those of us who had made strong efforts to refrain from straggling were rewarded (?), as we had been on many a similar occasion on this campaign, by being placed on picket.

On this march our brother got lost and thus describes it in two letters:

Knoxville, July 16, 1863.

I am just now at this moment in this place with Mose Noyes. I have lost the corps, and come many miles out of the way to find it, but have at last got track of it at Berlin; we marched yesterday from

422

Williamsport to Harper's Ferry, twenty-five miles, and it was an awful jaunt; I saw Fred Bosworth, Will Munroe and Colonel Bill Coggswell[15] on the road, and passed over the Antietam battleground, the bridge, and the very place we lay in reserve almost a year ago; also passed through Sharpsburg. Colonel Coggswell was glad to see me, and asked after Gene, Bob, etc.; invited me to call and see him whenever I could. I had quite a long talk with him and Will M.; the latter is temporarily detailed for duty as assistant surgeon. I was only ashamed to be seen in such a wretched plight as regards clothing; I am suffering with piles dreadfully; I can but hardly walk.

Good-bye, I am again on the road. What do you think of General Meade? Couldn't we have fought and whipped them at Williamsport? But the rebs are gone, and we arc after them. I must be off.

Camp near Berlin,

July 16, 1863, 5 P. M.

I have reached camp after marching ten miles from Knoxville; we had a hard march, however, it was so warm; the regiment had a very hard time also, but did not march as far as we did. The way I got lost was after this wise: I had a severe colic, and was troubled with piles; got a pass to fall out; let the Corps get ahead too far, and following directions, landed at Harper's Ferry. Since I have got in camp, I have bought a second-hand pair of pants of the Quartermaster, and after a good wash, a change of shirts, socks, etc., I am feeling extremely well; it is the first time that I have been wholly clean for over two months *** I never saw the troops so used up, and in so destitute a condition as they are now.

Yesterday there were scores who fell out, officers and men; the roads were lined with them; artillery horses died by twos, and many horses gave out and had to be replaced. Whole regiments caved in, and the 9-months reinforcements were scattered to the four winds. *** There is a prospect of my getting another pair of pants tomorrow; if so, I shall rejoice Bob by letting him have the pair I have on; his are torn from top to bottom, as were mine, lice

---

[15] Bradford, Massachusetts native William Cogswell (1838–1895) was a lawyer and politician.—2019

predominating. I saw a battalion of the Fourteenth Massachusetts, four companies, on the road today, as infantry.

They are being detached to fill up batteries temporarily. I also learned at General Meade's Headquarters that Gene had gone to New York with the Eighth Infantry; they carry with them the heartfelt good wishes of the Army of the Potomac for a triumphant success. If they but carry out our sentiments, every traitor in New York City will be shot.

The Fifth United States Artillery (Battery D), Griffin's old thunder roarers, has also gone to help them out.

I see that there is trouble in Boston;[16] how disgraceful it is, and if you only knew the feeling it has created in the Army of the Potomac. We are mad with rage to think they should give our enemies encouragement in this, their day of defeat, and of our triumph. Bob is full of fun tonight, joking over his misfortunes, 'and, for why did he come for a soldier.' ***

We have not heard from Morrison or Phillips yet. The Blanchards have returned to their regiment; they were captured by the rebs, but escaped in the mountains.

The battalion of the Eighth Infantry left their camp at Mountain House, Turners Gap, South Mountain, July 15, and marching through Burkettsville and Petersville, camped at Berlin, Md., the same day, fourteen miles, on the same spot which it had occupied October 28, 1862. On the 16th, Companies E and G, under the command of Captain Read, went to New York by rail and steamer, arriving on the 17th, for the purpose of assisting in quelling the draft riots. Companies H and K, Ninety-third New York, relieved the two companies of the Eighth on Provost Guard.

On the 16th, we marched through Petersville to Berlin on the Potomac, crossed the pontoons to Lovettsville the next day, and while here a guard was placed around our division, because some of the "bummers" had torn down an old barn for firewood.

We learned here for the first time of the disgraceful riots in New York and Boston, and we could hardly repress our outraged and

---

[16] A reference to the Boston draft riots and the much worse New York draft riots.—2019

incensed feelings that "these malcontents and copperheads in the rear, together with the dough-faced office-holders and politicians, should give encouragement to our enemies in the field." The noble old Army of the Potomac felt, more than we could describe, the keen disgrace of the monstrous act.

We learned also that our brother with the Eighth Infantry had been ordered to New York to assist in suppressing the riots and restoring order. On the 18th we moved to Purcellville. We had now fairly inaugurated a new campaign, which seemed to foreshadow a long and tedious, stern chase down the mountain range, to prevent the enemy from moving through the gaps.

Our route lay along the Blue Ridge. On the 19th we were in a valley opening out of the mountains on the west, near Philemont, and the blackberry season being at its height, the entire corps, after halting for the night, filled up with the finest and most luscious of fruit. Never in our lives had we seen so many, or such a sight as thousands of men blackening the landscape picking berries.

Reveille sounded at 2 o'clock on the morning of the 20th and we moved at 5 A. M. on the Philemont road, and passing through Union bivouacked shortly after noon near Panther Skin Creek between Middleburg and Upperville, where we spent the day in much needed rest, cleaning up, washing and picking berries, everywhere abundant. Here we remained the following day.

About noon on the 22d we moved again, and after a march of about fourteen miles, passing through Uniontown, we bivouacked very near where we had been just one month before, after following up and supporting the cavalry in their battle at Aldie and Middleburg; this was near Rector's Cross Roads, or Rectortown, near Goose Creek.

On the 23d, a clear, fresh morning, we moved out at 7 A. M., and marching via Markham's Station, Farrowsville and Linden to the near vicinity of Manassas Gap, we were here ordered to follow in support of the Third Corps which had struck the enemy at Wapping Heights.

We reached the vicinity of the action about 4.30 P. M. Forming line of masses with battalions doubled on the center, we here experienced the rare opportunity of witnessing an engagement at long range without participating. General French's Division of the Third Corps became engaged, and Spinola's Excelsior Brigade, after a spirited engagement or encounter, drove the enemy. Both columns had struck, rebounded, and then caromed off.

It has been said that General Meade intended to give battle with the whole army, and was much disappointed that French did not attack with more vigor and bring on a general engagement. There seemed to be plenty of opportunity for a fight, but neither seemed to have any stomach for it, and again Lee slipped off.

On the 24th the division was ordered to take a certain hill, the First Brigade to support the Second and Third. At 7 o'clock we moved up the rugged hillside by the "right of divisions to the front," the other two brigades being in line in advance. The hill was nearly perpendicular. Overhanging crags, huge boulders, a thick growth of stunted trees, dense underbrush and tangled thickets covered the slope to its summit. Reaching the top after one of the hardest climbs of the war, without finding any enemy to oppose us, we halted for a rest.

To those of us whose love of nature proved greater than our exhaustion from this toilsome ascent, there was some compensation in the richness and grandeur of the view.

From the summit the picturesque Shenandoah Valley, its war scars hardly visible, the splendid farms still rich in verdure, its granaries filled with the newly harvested wheat; its broad, shining river at our feet, and the rich, undulating lands and woods as a background—all would have been attractive and beautiful to the senses had not our craving appetites just then demanded something more substantial. But the men were hungry, and the magnificent scenery, although it is still vivid in our memory, was neglected.

The top of the hill proved to be covered with ripe blackberries, and soon all thoughts of battle and hardships were forgotten in our eagerness to fill a long-felt want.

At noon the division returned down the mountainous sides of our elevation, and went into bivouac about a mile from its base. Reveille was sounded at 4 o'clock on the 25th, and the march began at 7.30, with our brigade as rear guard. We move via Farrowsville and Barber's Cross Roads to Orleans, which we reached at 5.20 P. M. It was a clear, warm day, but it rained hard during the night,

On Sunday, the 26th, it was clear and hot. We moved about 5.30 A. M., with the Third Brigade leading, and bivouacked, after a few hours' march near Warrenton, the men exhausted by heat and lack of shade.

On the 27th, moving at 5 o'clock, the regiment marched until about 9.15, when it halted and bivouacked beyond Warrenton, in the direction of Fayetteville. Here the thoroughly worn-out, ragged men got a few days of rest, and a chance to clean off the dust and dirt of the past week's marching. Clothing and shoes were issued, and glad indeed were all to shed the vermin-infested rags, and perforated foot-gear, which had stood by us with almost a pathetic, human friendship through Virginia, Maryland, Pennsylvania, back to Virginia again.

Our letters say:

Camp near Ashby's Gap,

July 21st, 1863.

Your letter and mother's of July 12th, with enclosures, came duly to hand, and today, yours of the 17th, with all back papers. It makes us feel so happy when we hear from you, for if there is anything gratifying to a son who loves his home, it is to have tokens of affection from those who dwell there, and stand in the nearest ties of relationship to him, and when you close your letter with expressions of pride for us, surely it is all we can ask for. It is more than we could expect, perchance deserve; at any rate it is very cheering, and it will be a stimulus toward our striving to ever

427

remain sources of joy and pride to our father and mother, *** It is the height of humble ambition almost, for surely a kind father's opinion, high appreciation of a son's endeavors, when it is given in praise of him, always leads to a good end, and to have you say you are proud of us makes us believe that we must be on the right path, on a sure road to respectability and position in the future.

Oh, that it may be so for your sake, as it shall be so if our exertions can obtain it! Then mutual satisfaction and increased affection, all bound together from the past to the future, will be the grand result.

I am sorry that Bob's letter never reached you; he is a little unfortunate in losing, both in sending and here in camp. He has just been deprived of a glorious opportunity of recreation and enjoyment, which would have been so acceptable and pleasant; no less a chance than a trip to Springfield, Mass., and back. Three officers and six enlisted men were detailed to go to the above mentioned place, and names sent up to corps headquarters for approval; the order has just now been countermanded, Governor Andrew sending word that he has enough to escort the conscripts out here, so that is gone up.

There was only one private selected in the whole regiment, and Bob was the man. Soon we shall have the regiment filled up. * * * Lieutenant Knowles is dead; he died from wounds received at Gettysburg, in an old barn back of that place, in awful agony, perfectly unconscious to everything but pain. We all feel deeply pained, and are going to send a word or two to the *Tri-Weekly*.

We are near the place where we were in the late cavalry fight; it almost seems impossible. Today the whole army has had a holiday, and it has been spent in bathing, picking berries (plenty of them), and having a good, gay time generally. Tomorrow we go to Warrenton; so we move, and may soon see the "rebs," when old Halleck decrees. I am afraid he is binding Meade down.

Camp near Warrenton,

Sunday, July 26, 1863.

Have just got here, and am dreadfully fatigued. * * * We have been at Manassas Gap for two days, and was a reserve to the Third Corps when they were fighting; we went in day before yesterday expecting to fight, but the "rebs" had gone.

428

We got into an awful place, and am afraid we should have been whipped if the "Johnnies" had fought. Fred Bosworth was dangerously wounded in the thigh; I am so sorry.

July 27, 1863.

We moved from our camp six miles back this morning, and are now pleasantly situated for a transient stay of two or three days, 'they say.' I hope so, for we need rest; in fact we cannot stand our present state more than two days more at the longest. We have been living on hard bread, pork, coffee and sugar for over three weeks now, and our systems are completely run out. We have not the substance within that can bear up any longer; to be sure we have fresh beef once in two days, but they issue late at night, after a march, and the men must eat it when it is warm and jumping, or else carry it along to spoil, for we are off at 5 in the morning, reveille at 3.

I cannot drink the coffee; it hurts me, and consequently I live on raw salt pork, (lean), hard bread and sugar. I cannot sustain a working life on that 'fod.' What would a farmer think of such living, while in the hot, noonday sun? What do they do more than we?

A weary, dragging existence is ours—'marching along,' and oh, it is only thoughts of the encouraging love of you at home that keep our bodies from sinking, and our hearts from failing. If you could only see the roads strewn with dead mules and horses (and in two instances, dead men in our division), with the sickening sight of broken down, sore-backed animals in camp, not mentioning the emaciated, worn-out men, you would say that the cause of humanity demands imperatively that we should halt here for rest, nourishment and supplies of every kind.

We deserve not to succeed as a nation, if they do not favor us now. We have fought well, and are now used up after this fearful campaign. We did not stop long enough at Berlin to half clothe us, and three of our regiment are without blouses and pants. They march in dirty shirts and drawers; it is dreadful to think of. If we do not stay here for at least four days, I am gone up. *** In answer to your inquiry 'How did you lose your corps?' I will just say that I fell out sick, got a pass from the surgeon, with instructions to get along as fast as possible and went to the rear; met Fred Bosworth of the Third Corps, and kept along with his regiment—Seventeenth Maine—on the same road as the Fifth Corps. Soon we came to cross roads, and supposing that I was still on the same roads that the Twenty-second had taken, I continued on until the Third Corps had camped.

By inquiry I learned that I was on the wrong road, and started for the right. Mose Noyes and myself got lost, and as an only alternative, marched to Harper's Ferry that night. We reached there at 8 o'clock, having marched thirty miles, and over-exertion, excitement over my strange position, brought on my trouble. This is the history up to Harper's Ferry; my letters give the sequel, written from Knoxville and Berlin. It came out all right, much to my gratification.

The Regular band has just been playing 'Schubert's Serenade' on a neighboring hill, and it sounded splendidly in the clear, night air.

What glorious news we are reading now! Tonight we have papers, the first time in a week and a half. I am sorry that we sustained a repulse at Battery Wagner, Charleston,[17] but have ultimate confidence in the success at that place.

Notwithstanding all this halo of victory, which surrounds our flag now, with the brilliant light of a dawning future day of peace, yet it seems to me only an imaginative play, only a mirage; I cannot believe this war near at an end. I have settled down to the sober belief that my time is not to be completed until my term of enlistment has expired; admitting that the fighting is to be over. What then?

Why, the stock jobbers of the two contending parties get together, and try to arrange terms; they can never come to an understanding. It will be continual fighting; we poor fellows will have to remain. The radicals will be the bone of contention on one side, and they will have their individual weight of influence. They were the cause of the war, and they will try to close it up, or at least to have a hand in it. Slavery was the mainstay, the prime cause, the hydraheaded monster, but the miserable agitators (few but mighty) armed it with poisoned fangs, full to overflowing, until it shot forth of its

---

[17] The Second Battle of Fort Wagner, July 18, 1863. The battle was significant to the world as a demonstration of the valor of African American troopers. The all-black 54th Massachusetts under Colonel Robert Gould Shaw made a desperate frontal attack on the fort, depicted in the 1989 film, *Glory*.—2019

abundance, and pierced its iron barbs into the heart of the Union, aimed a blow at our liberties, and commenced this 'cruel war,' with the first gun at Sumter, fearful usherer in of a nation's woes and trials.

We have got to stay until this is over, and possibly the regiment's time may be over during the confab. *** What a stir the draft is causing; I only hope that all the shirkers will have to come. I do not like the $300 provision of the Conscript Act; it is said by some that it places the $300 man on an equality with the rich men who boast of their thousands. I admit that it does, but does it give the poor man, who just earns his daily bread, a fair chance with the $300 man? He is the one who suffers. I am in favor of all going who are drafted unless exempted by medical authority. *** I have worn out two pairs of shoes since I started from Grove Church; I drew another pair today *** the material is poor, prices low and wear terrible; pants get holey, infested with vermin, etc., and then they are thrown away. *** I know that Charlie Knowles is dead as I have written before. I have worn his sword and belt since he died. I have written to his sister, Mrs. James Bradley, East Parish, Haverhill.

July 30, 1863.

Did I ever mention an incident that took place at Gum Spring? If not, I will do so now, and I think it will assure you of one change in your quick-tempered, impetuous Walter; viz., self-government. * * * While in camp there, Emerson, the cook, engaged meals for the headquarters officers at a certain house, and after they were done, the lady of the house got up something nice for Emerson and myself. One night, when our officers had finished their suppers, they stayed longer than usual, in the same room, playing upon a seraphim, singing and having a good time generally; we thought they were in another room by the sound outside, and after waiting a long time, were assured that everything was ready; as soon as we got to the door, and saw our officers up in a corner, we were inclined to remain behind. * * * I had a pass to leave camp from the colonel, who was then back in his tent, and everything was perfectly straight, but still I felt delicate; but in we went. Bill (Emerson) was understood to eat there, the two boys of the lieutenant-colonel and the adjutant being there, also the major's and young Rock.

The officers nodded to us, as we said good evening very respectfully, and the lady showed us our scats. We commenced eating; presently there was a commotion in the kitchen; I had previously noticed some officers apparently waiting, and had heard the lady say to them, 'I have not engaged for you, these gentlemen must eat first, for I promised them.' They had presumed to call there for supper, without giving the lady time for preparation; she had her hands full and refused them, saying she could not accommodate them; they, feeling they were slighted, got mad; here's the result.

They go to the officer of the patrol, guarding the house, and complain that we had superseded them. We were informed of this afterwards, for we hardly knew anything about their requests before we went in, merely obeying the lady's instructions, considering her as mistress of her own house, and ourselves, as long as we had a pass, as equals of any officer within that threshold. It seemed, however, that every person ought to have had a written pass to that particular house, although if the people were willing, there was no need of it in our particular case, the guard said, and the old gentleman of the house acquiesced.

We knew nothing of it before that night. Well, just as I was about to jump at a big mouthful of biscuit and butter, in comes a regular officer, and coming up to me, says: 'What are you all doing here? What right have you here? Reave this house! I don't want a non-commissioned officer or private in this house where officers are!' I hesitated before rising, the rest vacating immediately. Said he: 'Leave!' I looked at him and said:

'I have a pass from my colonel; he gave me permission to leave camp, and I also have permission from the lady of the house to eat my supper here, which I have paid for.' He said: 'Can't help that, you must go out of this!' And seeing me hang back, put his hands upon my shoulders and pushed me slightly toward the door.

I was then enraged, and about to strike him, when I bethought myself of interference by our lieutenant-colonel and company, which I had expected all along, but it didn't come, and I for once quelled my anger, and left the house, going straight to camp, and from that day to this nothing has ever been said about it, only the major said we were treated shamefully, and yet not one of them interfered for outraged men of their own regiment.

You can imagine my feelings, my chagrin, and the queer position in which I was placed; my pride was sorely humbled; I was tried in the furnace, and hope I acted the better part. I felt like a whipped cur when I left the house, although I was strong enough in body to have demolished that officer's equilibrium several times, I think. I felt as though I had dishonored myself by permitting a man to do as he did, with no cause, for I was civil and gentlemanly.

We remained in camp near Warrenton until August 3; on that day, about 9 P. M., "pack up" again sounded dismally in our ears, and taking up the march on the Warrenton turnpike at 6 P. M., we bivouacked near Bealton Station. Here arbors were put up to break the intense heat, but they were not needed, for at 6 A. M. we moved our camp to a hill a short distance away, where we remained until the 8th. Another short march on this day brought us to the near vicinity of the Rappahannock where we went into a nice camp in a shady piece of woods.

On the 9th of August our camp was at Beverly Ford on the Rappahannock River, near Bealton, Va. Our father having expressed a desire to visit the regiment at this time, our letters say:

> Camp at Beverly Ford,
>
> Rappahannock River,
>
> Aug. 9, 1863.

It is an extremely warm day, and at this time (3 o'clock P. M.) all is quiet in camp; it is really a Sabbath afternoon of rest, and our boys are enjoying it in the cool shade of the forest where we are located. *** I am glad of the opportunity of bathing and general cleanliness; I have improved the benefits offered, even during the short hours of this afternoon. *** I wish I was able to give you information about the facilities provided for a citizen's visit to the Army of the Potomac. I can only say that after you get to Washington, General Martindale is the one to go to for information. Lieutenant-Colonel Conrad in Washington signs all passes at present. You take the cars from Alexandria on the Alexandria and Orange R.R., and stop at either Bealton's Station or Rappahannock; from there (B. I think the best), go to Headquarters, Army of the Potomac, near B., and find out where the Fifth Corps is; then foot it by directions to the Twenty-second Massachusetts, and I will promise you as hearty a reception as this country affords.

How glad we Bradford boys will be to see you again. Ed Holt was over from brigade headquarters (where his Provost Guard is stationed) today, and he said: 'If your father will only come, I do not know a man in B. I would rather see.' *** LeRoy is back in the regiment. I hope you can come before many days. *** George Lovejoy has been relieved from Division Provost, a new guard having been detailed, Perry, Co. D, Edes, Co. C, and a sharpshooter from our regiment.

August 14, 1863.

We are under orders to move at a moment's notice; where we are bound of course no one knows. The regulars of the corps, Sykes' old division, have all gone to Alexandria, leaving only two small divisions in our corps. We are in hopes, from the general appearance of things, and the hinted reorganization of the Army of the Potomac, that we are possibly to go in the same direction; if so, we shall be well contented. Do you hear any intentions at home that Governor Andrew and Senator Wilson are trying to get this regiment and the Second Massachusetts, Colonel Coggswell's, back to Massachusetts, for a short time, to help enforce the draft? It is rumored so here from reliable sources.

I have been very much interested in the accounts sent me of the attack on Fort Wagner; it is such a refutation of those foul-mouthed maligners of the Negro race, who added to their general denunciation of the African the stigma of cowardice, and tried in every way to establish their declaration, that the Negro will not fight. What heroic bravery they showed in the face of grape and canister. Verily they have shown they are men, and as such are entitled to the indefeasible rights and privileges of freemen. They can never be reduced to 'hereditary bond-men,' says Parson Brownlow, 'without committing a crime against God and humanity,' man slavers to the contrary notwithstanding.

The visit of our father was made; it was a red letter day in the history of our service in the army during those days when a red letter was conspicuous by its absence.

Our letters thus refer to it

August 24, 1863

434

Emerson had a letter from his wife, saying that father had called upon her in Boston, so that I know he is now at home, and ere this has given a full, detailed account of his visit *** his welcome arrival was a surprise, and all the more pleasant from the fact of its being at the close of my first year in Virginia and vicinity, and in every possible manner was an event desired above all things. While here, I did but very little talking, preferring to hear his voice at all times; I wanted to hear him speak continually. *** Since he has been gone I have thought of many inquiries I wish I had made, but I was so taken up in listening while he was present that I forgot home, friends and everything else. *** I never sent a message to anyone; no, not when I left him at Bealton Station. It is easily explained, however; I was completely overcome. * * * I delighted, too, in the idea of father's making such a good impression upon my comrades, and making himself such a general favorite *** not a few compliments have I had about my 'old man.'

The colonel was so polite to him, doing so much more for his comfort than I could possibly have done, and his finding us after so comparatively little trouble, and in such excellent quarters, improved in looks, health, and in general condition; all in all it was so glorious, so beneficial to all, such a perfect time for enjoyment. Any written sketch of mine were inadequate to express what fills my mind in regard to father's visit.

I did not conceive of the pleasure before, and the effects have been beyond my expectations. I am a good soldier now; I am fat, jolly and happy; I can do more and eat more than ever it has been in my power to do before. I only weigh 182 pounds (yesterday's weight), and am perfectly contented at present, all of which are the fruits of the citizen conscript's visit. *** It is food for me to live upon in thought for a long time, and I hope at the close of my second year, I can reciprocate it all by presenting my own personal body at the front door of the 'Straw cottage,' and there be subject to a united welcome, and express my joy at the meeting, and thanks for the close of this wicked rebellion.

Oh, that I could grasp time by the forelock, and cause him to speed his chariot of peace swiftly to the looked-for bound!

Since father went home, I have learned that Fred Bosworth is dead; died of his wounds at a Washington hospital, with his father only at his side. You don't know how sad it is to me; my old friend

435

Fred, my Portland schoolmate, my Boston chum, to think lies a sacrifice to his country; one more gone to his death; a brave-souled, noble fellow. * * * I have been expecting to hear from Mr. Bosworth for some time, as I had written him about Fred's wound. I am now almost inclined to write again begging a photograph of poor Fred. *** I want it as an ever-present reminder of the days that will never be again; those ties must be thrust back, but they can never be severed. *** Let the soldier rest; he now walks the banks of the crystal river, beside its still waters, a loss to earth, a gain to heaven.

Ed Walton is in a hospital in Washington; all the rest of our boys are well, tell their friends. When the dark angel of war moulds again the peace he has undone, then I will be with you in the flesh, as I am now in the spirit.

A nice camp had been laid out, from which we did picket duty principally. The usual drills, inspections and parades were again inaugurated. We drilled two hours in the morning and two in the afternoon, and our letters say: "We go in swimming every night, the Rappahannock River only being a third of a mile distant."

We announced that, "Our first regular debating meeting came off last night and was a decided success. Our regiment being out on picket a new subject was discussed: 'Is it advisable for the government to employ Negro soldiers?' It was decided in the negative, although I think we sustained our side best. Too many hunkers present, who voted what they believed rather than what the merits of the debate established. We meet again Tuesday. The influence exerted by the club is very beneficial so far."

On the 29th, the execution of five deserters from the division took place, and it was a dreadful spectacle. Its impressions will last forever. Every arrangement for the event was perfect, and the minutest detail was carried out with the utmost dispatch and precision. These men all belonged to the 118th Pennsylvania. Their names were as follows: Charles Walter, Gion Reanese, Emil Lai, Gion Folaney and George Kuhn. Two were Roman Catholics; another was a Jew, and the others, if they had any faith, were Protestants.

436

The court which tried them was presided over by Col. Joseph Hayes, 18th Massachusetts Volunteers, convened under G. O. No. 35, August 15, 1863, Headquarters First Division, Second Brigade, Fifth Corps. The order fixing the time for execution as Wednesday, August 26, between the hours of 12 M. and 4 P. M., was published to the prisoners on the 24th by Major C. P. Herring of the 118th Pennsylvania, in the presence of the chaplain of the 118th, through an interpreter.

The difficulty in securing the services of a priest and Jewish rabbi induced a respite until Saturday the 29th, between the same hours. An appeal for mercy in the handwriting of one of the prisoners, and signed by all, was addressed to General Meade. Captain Crocker was placed in charge of the guard over them, assisted by Lieutenants Lewis, Bayne and Thomas, all of the 118th Pennsylvania. Four men inside and four outside the place of confinement were continually on duty.

Lieutenant Lewis searched the prisoners. Inside a pocketbook found on the Hebrew was discovered a sharp lancet. This was a sad blow to the hopes of the condemned men. The officiating clergymen were Father S. L. Eagan, a Catholic priest from Baltimore; Chaplain O'Neill of the 118th Pennsylvania; and Dr. Zould, a Jewish rabbi. Twenty men under Sergt. H. T. Peck of the 118th were detailed to bear the coffins, and ten pioneers with spades and hatchets under Sergeant Moselander of the 118th were charged with filling the graves and closing the coffins.

Captain Crocker, to whom was assigned Lieutenant Wilson, both of the 118th Pennsylvania, commanded the guard of thirty men. At about 3 P. M., Captain Orne of the 118th, the division provost marshal with fifty men of his guard, ten to each prisoner, as executioners, preceded by the band, led the funeral column into the square formed by the Fifth Corps; then there were two coffins, borne by four men each, and in their rear the condemned Hebrew with his rabbi. At Major Herring's suggestion, the man representing the most ancient of religious creeds was assigned the right.

437

The other coffins, each borne by four men and followed by the condemned with their priest and chaplain, brought up the column. Captain Crocker with his escort brought up the rear. The prisoners were all manacled.

Four of them moved steadily, and stepped firmly; one, with weak and tottering gait, dragged himself along with great difficulty, requiring support. The procession moved slowly, the guard with reversed arms, keeping step to the mournful notes of the "Dead March." The silence was broken only by the low, mournful music, the whispered words of consolation of the man of God, and the deliberate, martial tread of the soldiers.

The column, in this manner, moved around the three fronts of the immovable square, and halting at the first, or open front, faced outward. The five coffins were placed opposite the foot of five newly made graves, and a prisoner was seated on each. The provost guard, subdivided into detachments of ten, with loaded pieces, one blank, faced the prisoners at thirty paces. The attending clergymen engaged in low, but earnest, fervent prayer. The President had been appealed to, but had refused to reprieve or pardon them.

Fifteen minutes only of the time remained. General Griffin now became restless under the awful suspense, and suddenly breaking the dreadful silence, shouted in his shrillest voice to Captain Orne, "Shoot those men! or after ten minutes it will be murder! Shoot them at once!"

Lieutenant Wilson quickly bandaged the eyes of the condemned men. Full of the vigor of life and health, they were literally upon the very brink of the grave. The terrible pause was but for a moment. "Attention guard!" resounded the clear, ringing voice of the provost marshal, "Shoulder arms! forward, guide right, march!" Every tread of the guard fell upon the stilled hearts of the motionless corps. Twenty-five paces were quickly covered. At six paces there was a slight pause, then came the stern, deliberate command, "Halt! ready! aim! fire!" Simultaneously fifty muskets flashed. Military justice was satisfied and the law avenged. Four bodies fell back heavily with a solid thud; the fifth remained erect.

438

"Inspection arms!" hurriedly ordered Captain Orne, and every rammer sprang in ringing tones from the breech. Every musket had been discharged; no soldier had failed in his duty. Pistol in hand, the provost marshal quickly moved to the figure which still sat erect upon the coffin. It was his duty to shoot the prisoner had the musketry failed, but Sergeant Thomas had pronounced life extinct and the body was laid upon the ground with the others.

The masses changed direction by the left flank, and amid the stirring notes of "The Girl I Left Behind Me," broke into column of companies, at full distance, and marching by the bodies to see that the work had been effectually done, the troops were soon back to their camps again.[18]

Our letter of August 30 says:

It was the most dreadful spectacle I ever witnessed and I pray that I may never be permitted to see such a sight again. The doomed men marched to the dirge of the 'Dead March in Saul,' preceded by their own coffins, borne by four men each, the whole led by the Provost Marshal of the Division, band and Provost Guard. The men were dressed in blue pants, white shirts and new caps. They walked with mournful steps, and two had to be supported to their very graves.

Arriving at the place of execution, they were seated beside their graves upon the head of their coffins. After prayer, they bade each other good-bye, kissed in a most affecting manner, and were then blind-folded. The firing party was drawn up, the word of command given, and they fell, riddled with balls. Death was instantaneous in every case. Not a groan or sigh. They only ceased to breathe, and entered an unknown world. It was awful. How impossible it was for us to fathom the agony of their souls, as they marched to their own funerals, saw their own coffins, and their very graves before their eyes. Oh, it was terrible! Poor privates must suffer for their crimes, but officers for the same offense are dismissed, or imprisoned for a few months.

On September 1 our letters say:

---

[18] See *Desertion During the Civil* War, Lonn, 2016.

439

We have been under orders to move during the last two days; it will probably amount to nothing. Our camp is somewhat improved since you were here. Our tent has been repitched, and large pine trees set all around; also the guard house has been shaded, and a new tent added to the headquarters.

September 3d.

In this camp, beyond all others, we have had novelty. Why, only think! we have a debating club; meet every Tuesday eve, and every Saturday night; the exercises are varied; declamation, reading, singing, and a paper, all under the control of an association in the regiment called 'The Gove Lyceum.' Mixter is president, and I am secretary and treasurer; officers and privates, all have joined, and signed their names to the constitution; it is grand, and flourishes beyond mere success. We also have preaching every Sunday, and our prayer meetings are regularly and fully attended. The officers have a class in tactics, and Mixter and myself have formed a class for drill and exercise in 'Casey.' We meet every day at one o'clock, and continue an hour and a half; drills are in the morning and evening; squad A. M., company P. M., then occasionally a battalion drill, and every night a dress parade, and very often, besides our 'Sunday morning dose,' we have a line inspection.

Occasionally the colonel invites Webster, Wood, Ware and Newton into his tent, and they have a glorious sing. Colonel Tilton is at home; Benson is back. Charlie Day is now leader again of the Twenty-second band, and the drummers having new drums, the full brass and string instruments swell on the morning air hugely.

The Michigan First is up to new things too; they have new games, and new, original ideas, but on a different ground from ours. They have erected a large swing, wholly of wood, an ingenious contrivance, and perfect in its workings, and they have also constructed a curious arrangement after this pattern, viz., a tree is cut down, and upon the stump is hewn a pivot; upon this is placed a large beam, the pivot passing through at the center, that part being well greased; contrivances are fixed at either end, and a stake is driven into the beam for the person to hold on to. Two persons being seated, another stands at the post and pushes the concern around, and away they go like shot, describing two revolutions a minute; if they keep on they are smart; few dare to try. Then there is another new and laughable game, 'tossed up in a blanket;' twenty or thirty get hold of two blankets doubled, and a man being placed in the center, he is thrown up ten or fifteen feet, and comes down all afloat in the blanket; it is most amusing. Such is camp life now, the pleasantest I have ever experienced.

Camp near the Ford,

September 5, 1863.

John Dodge and myself are going to build a house together; I have slept in that mess tent long enough; we are to have bunks, and everything is to be in perfect taste with army fashions, a few elegancies added, perhaps.

Emerson is to go back to the company in a week or so; he has cooked long enough he says, and now that the Adjutant (B.) has come back, he can't agree with all as well as formerly. E. is strictly temperate, *** and the liquor arrangements conflict with Bill's plans very often, so he is going to leave very soon. I hear that Gene has been home. We had a third meeting of the Lyceum last evening; declamation, singing and the paper, 'Lyceum Casket,' composed the programe; it was largely attended by the whole brigade, officers and privates, and was a decided success. Colonel Sherwin says it is the best thing ever gotten up in the regiment; we have a fine place to meet, two large hospital tents having been erected near the battery.

September 6, 1863.

Ed Walton came back from Washington hospital three days ago, but has now gone into our regimental hospital, sick again; he returned too soon altogether. I wrote to the editor of the *Tri-Weekly* Publisher (Haverhill) yesterday, and you may possibly see it in Saturday's paper, if they conclude to publish any part of it.

I only intended to wake up the Haverhill people to the fact that Company H is still alive, and must not be forgotten. We are expecting conscripts daily, and have even drawn ponchos for them. Major Burt has started with them. *** I must go at the book of Tactics; it's all the rage here now.

On the 9th of September our recruits arrived, and our letters thus describe their coming.

September 10, 1863.

Our conscripts, two hundred in number, have arrived, and we are having great times in this region; our class of men is very good on the whole; a few scatterings, however, betoken a rough element. It is very amusing to see how some of them enter upon their new duties. Last night, for the first time since the recruits joined at Hall's Hill, our quiet camp was changed into a perfect bedlam— shouting, music, talking, gambling and sick were the amusements, and such a clashing I never heard; it made us old' soldiers stare. Major Burt and Captain Field came with them.

Company H has a good squad; one is named John Morrison, and one or two are old soldiers; we have one grand drummer, an old French drum major. Sam has now his drum, and we are to have a good drum corps now. There are any quantity of old salts, and many discharged regulars (Ninth U. S.). Several sailors told me that they got tight when they left their craft, a man-of-war, went cruising around, sharpers got hold of them, and before they knew it they were on Long Island as three-year substitutes; that accounts for desertions; one of our number left for parts unknown last night; it is a pretty dangerous risk to run though.

My loud voice has come to an end at guard mounting; we had brigade guard mounting this morning, to be continued hereafter; adjutant-general mounts it, and our adjutants in the brigade act as sergeant-majors; we have only to verify the detail of our guard before it marches to the brigade parade ground. Yesterday, we had a brigade drill by Colonel Hayes, Eighteenth Massachusetts. We are having high times in camp; never was happier since I was in the army; your coming had greatly to do with it. I am a 'better soldier,' in your words to the Washington officer.

September 13, 1863.

I am in the office now; Mixter has received permission from the War Department to go to Washington, to appear before a Board, of which Silas Casey is president, to be examined for the office of an adjutancy in one of the Negro regiments that Adjutant-General Thomas is forming, a sort of regular arrangement. He is going in a week, and will probably never come back, and I am now in his place until someone is found competent to relieve me. We are sorry to lose M. for he knows his business thoroughly, and it will be a long time before things go on so systematically as in times past. It is going to insure the occupation of my whole time now; I have been dreading it to come, but now that it is before me I shall do my best *** We are under marching orders today, and in case we are called for, to support the reconnaissance in force that has gone out toward Culpeper, we shall have to vacate these premises for a day or two, perhaps longer.

The sound of guns can be heard plainly eight miles distant, and the conjectures are that our own troops have 'run against a snag' already.

I expect every moment to hear the 'General [alarm],' and be hustled into an engagement. The thought of this doesn't disconcert me in the least; I have learned not to fear the scene of conflict. I do not court it, but am always ready for it, and can always retain my self-command in the fiercest struggle.

September 18.

Is it well to accept a commission, if I am qualified, as the matter now stands, 'three years from date of my commission,' and not as formerly, 'for the unexpired term of service?' Every applicant for a commission has to be named by the colonel, and must be examined by a board of five officers, and only two from this regiment are allowed, as the number of men only admit it. We must be recruited up to a full standard before a full complement of officers will be maintained by the government; this is a late order.

Two sergeants have been named by Colonel S. and have had their examination. Roby passed, but Kinsley did not. The latter is to try again. *** Formerly all got a commission who were recommended by the colonel to Governor Andrew; in consequence many who are now officers never could pass the present Board of Examiners. *** I do not want to bind myself down for three years from date. Some say, 'Oh! you can get out of it easy enough if you are an officer.' I say no, not honorably, and I will never go out dishonorably. * ** If there is a chance in the regiment offered (none at present), I can pass the board, I believe, but then I have got to stay in Uncle Sam's service three years, which is a little tough. I can hardly see it; military service does not suit me well enough; besides, a term of service extended to that time would unfit me for any particular profession or business at home. Ask Gene what he thinks of it. Such is a plain statement of facts, showing the difficulties under which I labor for a commission. Write me about it.[19]

At last our rest was broken, and on September 16 the dread "pack up" sounded, and again we started for we knew not where. The day was hot. We crossed the Rappahannock River, and wended our way toward Culpeper. Our newly arrived conscripts lined the road, but "took the pill" good-naturedly, contenting themselves with munching hard bread, and exclaiming, "You can't kill us the first hitch." We camped near Culpeper at 4 P. M. The next morning we moved early, and marched about three miles beyond the town, nearly five miles from the Rapidan River.

We passed through the principal street, and it was the usual specimen of tumble-down Virginia. Its outbuildings were poor, and one could plainly detect the ravages of war within its deserted confines. Verily the old Commonwealth is culminating, and soon the "Old Dominion" will live only in story. Pope's historic "skedaddle ground" was around about us, and Cedar Mountain, with its memorable record of bloody deeds and the skilful generalship of Massachusetts' "Iron Man," was not far off.

Our letters say:

Camp near Culpeper Court House,

September 17, 1863.

We started from Beverly Ford yesterday morn, crossed the Rappahannock, and marched to Culpeper, twelve miles; it was a pretty hard march, the day being warm. Our conscripts gave out in large numbers; this morn we started again, and are now three miles beyond Culpeper Court House, and within five miles of the Rapidan. The Eighteenth Massachusetts and First Michigan are in Culpeper doing provost duty. We are to do guard duty on the railroad, they say, that is, our regiment and the 118th Pennsylvania. Today heavy guns have been heard toward the Rapidan; we are on the very ground of the Pope skedaddle, and Cedar Mountain is in the foreground, and the battleground is nearby where Banks fought so fiercely.[20]

---

[19] Our brother was, against his wishes or desire, commissioned a first lieutenant, Twenty-second Massachusetts Volunteers, February 20, 1864, but declined to muster, and continued as sergeant-major of the regiment until he was mustered out at the expiration of his term of service, October 17, 1864.—note in original

Culpeper is as hasty a hole as I ever beheld. I am in great haste with these few words. We shall have a fight soon. I am all ready for that as usual.

The following are brief extracts from a long letter written to the *Tri-Weekly* publisher of Haverhill, Mass.:

Beyond Culpeper Court House,

September 23, 1863.

We are on the eve of a great movement, and a veritable 'Hooker caravan,' with five days' rations on our backs, and three in our haversacks, is being formed once more against the rebels; we are expecting orders to move hourly, and as extensive preparations have been made, they will soon be coming. *** I trust that this expedition may result in a great victory, that the bonds of war may be loosened and our country go free, its wailings to be heard no more. This is the fond hope of every true American patriot; let the nation's heart not faint, nor its hand grow weary. The time is soon coming when peace shall be ours, and of our abundance of costliest treasures we must give to insure the wished-for end. Since my last we have changed base; we moved from Beverly Ford last Wednesday morning, 16th instant, crossing the Rappahannock in the morning *** the troops suffered much, it being the first march of the season. *** If, as it is rumored, our cavalry occupy Gordonsville, its passage (the Rapidan) will be more easy than if we had attempted it three days ago, when rebel cannon swarmed on the opposite heights. I ought to have mentioned before a scene we all participated in before we left Beverly Ford; our regiment was on picket when the order came to move; as soon as it was relieved, it came directly to camp, and there on the eve of march, a comrade who had died in the regimental hospital was given a decent burial. To the praise of our colonel, be it said, a minister was present, and a Christian's service was the poor fellow's winding sheet at the very beginning of the march.

All these plans and arrangements were perfected and carried out and the fact is worthy of special note *** it is illustrative of the intentions of a good commander; it has been spoken of many times

---

[20] The Battle of Cedar Mountain took place on August 9, 1862; Union General Nathaniel P. Banks vs. Stonewall Jackson.—2019

by the new members of the regiment, and the effect of it was plainly seen.

We are looking anxiously for southwest news. Rosecrans is no doubt hard pushed, but we trust that all will be well with him. Burnside is moving forward, and it is good for the prosperity of the country that his army was not checked by an acceptance of his resignation; he is too efficient an officer to lose just now. He does not submit to whims and fancies, and his suppression of that kind of speech which gives comfort to the enemy is the same kind of straightforward work we wish to see commenced everywhere.

People cannot make much capital out of his dabbling in politics; he is a patriot soldier and a good general; what more can be required of a man in the field just now?

General McClellan is again before the Army of the Potomac just now (a candidate, perhaps, for their suffrages, informally); this tests the army's regard for him, and in a most tender locality the hook is baited. When you touch the pocket you try a man's friendship exceedingly. But I think the affair will succeed, for the boys have unbounded confidence in 'Little Mac,' and still show their former regard for him.

They pulled out the 'scrip' generously, and McClellan will soon be presented with a magnificent offering of an army's affection and esteem.

We passed over the scene of the late cavalry advance (13th), when we came to our present location. Trees showed the marks of severe shelling, and several dead horses bore testimony to the effect of rifled carbines; our brave Yankees made the southern champions flee like sheep before them; it was impossible to resist such determined onsets. *** Our camp is alive with pleasant scenes, and it is impossible to delineate our life at present with any dark outlines. If our friends will only continue to write to us often, we shall be perfectly happy where we are; if they could only look in upon us when we receive their messages, and see our faces light up with hopes of a future union, they would never fail to keep us supplied with letters and wholesome reading. Our camp fires now glow right cheerfully, and the groups that gather about them these autumn evenings are larger than those a year ago.

It is worth one's while to visit these scenes of army gaiety every night, and there see and hear what passes.

But soon 'hard times will come knocking at the door,' saying in our own language, 'get up and git!' and as we march along we shall be accompanied with all that is to be dreaded in war; on the march we experience all our troubles. When we do go we will trust to ultimate victory, knowing that energetic action, with a will, is the sure way of success. Ask all to remember us as we plod along over the weary road of our expected movement.

Our letters home continue:

October 3, 1863.

It is terribly cold tonight; no more balmy, summer evenings for us. The air is keen and bracing. Flies drop dead from the wall of my tent, and mosquitoes are numbered now either with the slain or missing. Everything proclaims the wintry season, and heaven alone knows what is before us ere it arrives. I enclose Dodge's photograph.

I was well-nigh drowned out when it (letter) was handed me; our tent was wet through, clothes damp, and the wind threatening to break up our houses every moment. The rainy season had in reality commenced, and great drops were beating down upon our thin shelter; fires could not be kept, and it was bitter cold. All but officers suffered. The wet of whiskey within their bodies kept out the wet without. One side of our shanty came down at the height of the tempest, and I being the only one present at the catastrophe, was obliged to repair damages in the rain. It was then that our clothes got damp, the canvas being loose and not shedding water properly *** the storm continued all night, and I was as wet as you please during the long hours.

This morn the sun is out in all its splendor, smiling beautifully, as if nothing had happened. Indeed, no one could tell what we had passed through were it not for the Virginia mud everywhere present. I have on dry clothes (except pants and blouse) and look decent, with the exception of the aforesaid mud in copious quantities upon my brogans, red clay softened and almost impossible to clean off, and then it is so much like brick that a hammer and wedge have to be used to pry it off.

I pity the poor pickets on duty last night; what a contrast between many a sumptuous home parlor and the gloomy outposts, where, in darkness and silence, chilled by the night dews, or pelted as they were last night by the storm, they keep watch and ward; it was a rough night for the Army of the Potomac.

Major Burt has arrived, back for good, also Colonel Tilton; the latter is to be presented with a magnificent sword tonight by the officers of the Twenty-second. He is in command of the brigade still, and may be brigadier. *** I drew a pair of pants a week ago, and the same day I wore them, the whole seat ripped and tore out; I had them mended, and then returned them. As for any more shoddy, I do not want, nor will I have it. *** We expected to move ere this, but the order has been countermanded, 'eight days rations and all.' In consequence of the disaster to Rosecrans, we had to send him aid.[21]

Here we remained until October 9. At 11 o'clock we were ordered to get our rations, and at 5 A. M. on (Saturday) the 10th, started from our pleasant camp. We marched to the Rapidan at Raccoon Ford, stayed all day, observing the enemy, and returned to camp at 7 o'clock.

On Sunday the 11th, we moved again and through Culpeper. The Fifth Corps was rear guard, and our provost guard, deploying as skirmishers outside the town, advanced in line and, sweeping through the streets, brought all stragglers along. Before noon we passed the plantation of John Minor Botts,[22] a noted Union man in that section of Virginia; the enemy followed closely, and the rear guard was engaged several times during the day.

Mr. Bott's house was burned soon after we passed it, for which he was liberally paid after the war, as well as for hundreds of cords of wood, rail fences, supplies, etc. Continuing our march to the Rappahannock, which we reached at 7 P. M., we crossed it and bivouacked for the night near Beverly Ford at our old camp at

---

[21] The Union loss at the Battle of Chickamauga, fought September 18–20, 1863.—2019

[22] Politician and Unionist, John Minor Botts (1802–1869), nevertheless, was a slaveowner.—2019

9 o'clock. It was very dark. The Third and Fifth Corps had covered the withdrawal of the army.

The latter covered the approach from Rapidan Station. On Monday the 12th, we recrossed the river and, advancing in line of battle with the Second and Sixth Corps over the plains of Brandy Station, supported the cavalry while they slowly pushed the enemy back. For over three miles, with only slight skirmishing, we moved through level fields, blackberry bushes predominating, which stripped our clothes, tore out our flimsy shoes, and soon penetrating the stockings, made our feet sore and bloody. The spectacle, however, was magnificent.

The men became lame and chafed, and when we camped for the night near Brandy Station all were much worn and wearied. We had again recommenced the game of "shuttle-cock"—Meade was trying to find Lee. The latter thought he was trying to give battle, and moved out to meet him. Meade supposed Lee was trying to outflank him, and "disturb the peace" at Washington, and on Tuesday, October 13, at 1 o'clock A. M., we started back again for Beverly Ford, camped at the "old camp" just long enough to eat breakfast, and then at three A. M. on the 14th went on.

We were to move along the north side of the railroad, crossing Broad Run at Milford, and from Manassas Junction move to Blackford's Ford on Bull Run, forming on the left of the Third Corps on Centerville Heights. It was a race between both armies, Washington the gigantic stake. On—on we went, and about 5.30 P. M. we landed at Stone's farm on Walnut Branch, about two miles from Catlett's Station, having been "on the go" and marched over twenty miles since early morning.

The next morning, Wednesday, we continued our march to Manassas Junction and to Broad Run, which we reached at 1 P. M. We had scarcely left a small hill near Broad Run near noon, where we had halted to rest a few minutes, when a battery dashed up to the spot, and pitched a dozen or more shells in quick succession into our rear. We did not stop to investigate their object, but left the place in good order, the shells flying about us in every direction, killing several men in the rear (Second and Third) brigades.

At Bristoe there was a gap between the Second and Fifth Corps, and Heth of A. P. Hill's Corps was ordered to throw himself between the two corps. We were ordered to go back to the support of the Second Corps, General Warren, who was now engaged with Heth. We reached the east side of Broad Run about 4 P. M., and went into position. We arrived too late to join in the engagement. We remained in line of battle until dark, when we returned to Manassas Junction, and moved toward Bull Run, crossing at Blackford's Ford about midnight, and arrived in the vicinity of Centerville at 3 A. M. on the 15th, where we made a very hasty bivouac.

We had marched nearly thirty miles. Men fell out by scores. The road was lined with stragglers, mostly the newly joined substitutes, many of whom were captured by the closely following enemy. Most of the time, the guns were constantly booming in our rear, and keeping us waked up to a keen appreciation of a further necessity for renewed efforts. We all slept that night, or rather morning, at a place within two miles of Centerville. I suffered terribly from my feet, and was obliged to beg a pair of stockings for the expected early tramp."

About 5 o'clock it poured down in torrents, and leaving our bivouacs about 8 A. M., sore, stiff, and lame, we hobbled over the heights of Centerville, and marched to a point near Fairfax Court House, on the Chantilly, or Little River Road, where we announced ourselves as "a shoeless, sore-footed personage all the way from Culpeper." We were ordered to hold all the roads coming in at Germantown.

It continued to rain all day, soaking everything and everybody, and as we were still in blissful ignorance as to all this fuss for nothing, we were indeed an uncomfortable lot, and the whole movement was voted a veritable *"Hooker Caravan."*

Our letters thus describe this movement:

Camp near Fairfax Court House,

on the Chantilly Road,

October 16, 1863.

I am twenty-one years old today, and I feel as if I must write
home to you all; I am, father, poorly situated I confess, for a free
man, for, upon this my birthday, I am a perfectly used-up man and
individual bodily, which of course always affects a person mentally;
but if the few scattered ideas that I have can be collected by the
feeble strength that I possess, you shall be welcome to the
unwelcome intelligence they convey to you. I know you wish to hear
from me at all times, and I never let the slightest opportunity pass,
when I can write to you, especially on the march, and now that the
first chance has presented itself for a period of seven days, I avail
myself of it *** it is unpleasant for you to know that I suffer, but I
must tell you just how things are, and as I shall be patched up in the
weak spots, I beg you not to worry on my account *** my shoes gave
out (good when I started) the second day, while advancing in line of
battle (supporting cavalry) for over three miles, through fields
where the blackberry vines predominated, this side of Culpeper. I
had to wade streams with these shoes, and the gravel getting in, and
holes being in my stockings where they protruded through the
apertures in the leather, my feet became sore and very much
blistered; as we marched more and more, they grew worse, until the
blood came, and from that time I was in agony continually. I was
chafed badly, and as I carried a heavy load (no mules or teams for
baggage that we carry for comfort on the march at this time), my
shoulders became lame, and when I arrived here last night, I was
almost gone up.

I carried eight days' rations in two haversacks, and that hung
down terribly. Our officers had to carry all their rations and
blankets, for the teams went ahead and didn't come to the regiment
nights.

We have seen no papers or letters, and are all worn out. Rumors
in regard to Lee, Bragg and Rosecrans are rife, and we hardly know
what is before us. It is a most complicated movement to all, but
Meade has our confidence. Everyone says he has shown himself a
general, even in this last move, although he has almost killed his
men; perhaps it was necessary; we cannot tell.

Most of us Bradford boys are up and well, considering LeRoy
suffered from his feet, and Sam Appleton was pretty well played

451

out. Ed Holt stood it pretty well; we all hung to the regiment throughout the entire march. Sam lost his haversack, tell M., and in consequence is out of provisions; I have just given him some hardtack; I had enough grub on this toot, I assure you. I was only out once, and then we drew rations, and I filled up for eight days; have got plenty now.

Our crackers are poor, being filled with fresh meat. Ed Holt's brother is released from arrest, and is in the company; Ed worked hard for him, and Colonel Sherwin showed him favor, and as much as intimated that he knew all of us boys had done well, and was inclined to be lenient toward Holt for the reason that it was a peculiar case, and Ed was one of our number, F. being his brother. I am glad it turned out so well.

They consider all men deserters at this accursed place if they go without leave, preferring to keep them and make money out of the government. It is a contract throughout and the more men they keep there (these officials), the more money they make. Someone has got to ventilate that camp (Convalescent Camp at Alexandria, Va.) one of these days, and show up all of the wrong deeds committed there. Lovejoy, Webster and Emerson are in camp, and feel pretty well; I just went in to see Emerson a few moments ago; he was sitting on a small tin box, his tent floor covered with water, knapsack and duds upon a log in the center. We had a good laugh over it. No mail goes tonight, and I will close. There is a prospect of our moving back tonight; I hope not, for it will surely rain all the time. When I get through this campaign safe and well, I will write about many things I wish to bring before you. I write this in haste and under many difficulties. Please send stamps in your next; I am out and can't buy.

On the 16th the regiment returned from Fairfax Court House to Centerville; remained there during the 17th, and on the 18th marched back again to Fairfax Court House, and from thence on the same day to Fox's Mill. On the 19th it passed Centerville on the right, crossed Bull Run at Island Ford, and halted in the afternoon on the old battlefield, passing through Newmarket and Groveton. Here we bivouacked for the night on Benjamin Chinn's farm. The ground was low and soaked, The rains had washed the bodies from their shallow graves, and reaching our bivouacs after dark, more than one individual was horrified to find, in the grey of the early morning, that he had slept in a snug little hollow between two skeletons, and amidst the putrid flesh of our dead comrades, the stench from which was horrible.

Skulls, legs, feet and arms protruded here and there all about the field. It was a cold, raw, penetrating night with a heavy fog, and our brother caught a violent cold and fever from the exposure, which necessitated his transportation in an ambulance to Auburn Mills, and through New Baltimore to near Thoroughfare Gap, toward which we slowly marched. The journey he thus describes: "We had to freeze two nights in an ambulance, with no one near to aid us, and riding in there upon our backs, was literally murdering us at every revolution of its wheels."

At this halt the exposed remains of an officer of the First Michigan, belonging to our brigade, who fell there, recognized by his teeth, were given a second burial, and the grave was properly marked for future identification. Near it the rain had uncovered the body of an unknown cavalryman. He had been buried booted and spurred with belt and saber; his uniform and equipments were found to be well preserved, but the flesh had slipped from the bones, and in attempting to lift the body by the belt, the skeleton fell in a confused mass of bones and clothing.

He was reburied, but there was nothing to distinguish the remains from hundreds of the forever unknown dead. Many unburied Confederates, of the Eleventh North Carolina and Eighteenth Georgia, as recognized by their uniforms and insignia, were seen and reburied.

Capt. J. P. Bankson, our brigade-inspector, while on the march to Gettysburg, had lost a pocket album, containing a few mementos and photographs. With no thought of its recovery, he rode over the ground, and much to his surprise and joy found it. The contents were much injured by the sun and rain, but were still recognizable.

Near Buckland on this day's march, an officer of the 118th Pennsylvania, the "Corn Exchange," our old friends (?), asked an old, lean, unkempt native, "Where does this road go to, my good man?" "It stays right here where it is, and don't go anywhere!" came the quick, crisp reply; and then it is related that there came a stern chorus from the men in the ranks of that regiment in unison. "Beware! old man, beware! there are Massachusetts men behind us; an answer like that to them will bring down upon your hoary head *** the dire vengeance of all New England."

On the early morning of the 20th, we moved by the Warrenton turnpike to Gainesville, and on the 21st through Groveton, Buckland and Broad Run to the vicinity of New Baltimore, where we remained several days. Our camp was on a hill off the main road. On the 24th we again took up the march, after waiting for Lee to get back, for the railroads to be repaired, etc., and on that day we moved to Auburn, changing camp the next day to about one mile beyond, and on the 30th to Three Mile Station, near Warrenton Junction, on the Orange and Alexandria Railroad, a section of the country with which we had now become familiar. Here we remained until November 6. The railroad ran by the camp, and supplies were obtained from Warrenton Junction.

A comrade, in a letter to our father, thus describes the condition of our brother:

Camp near New Baltimore,

October 23, 1863.

You will, no doubt, be greatly surprised at receiving this note from me, but as the friendship which has always existed between Walter and myself has not changed since we became soldiers, I as a matter of course feel in duty bound to do all that I can to promote his comfort and happiness in this, the difficult path in which we are traveling.

This morning I went to see him and found him in his quarters, completely unable to inform you of his condition, and knowing you would feel quite anxious at not receiving any of his often written letters, I determined to write to you. During the march toward Fairfax Court-House, he was troubled with his feet, owing to wearing a new pair of government's, but by the time we got back to Bull Run they were much better.

454

We camped on the horrid battlefield one night, and as the ground was quite damp, and being surrounded by the unburied remains of those who fell at the last great battle, it was very unhealthy and I wonder that it did not make us all sick.

The next morning we were routed out; it was dreadful cold, and we suffered much, and in addition to his previous troubles, he caught a violent cold, and being obliged to march to this place, it completely used him up. He complains of a great deal of pain in his head and back, but does not appear to be very feverish this morning, and as he thinks he feels much better than he did yesterday, I hope soon to see him about.

I am guarding a plantation about two miles from camp, and shall be able to get some soft bread and milk from the planter to send him, so you see he is in good hands. A sick man in the army gets little sympathy. He will write to you as soon as able. I hope we shall remain at this camp for some time, for we are very well situated; but I cannot tell anything about it, for perhaps tomorrow's sun will find us once more upon the dusty or muddy road.

Our brother now writes:

Camp near Auburn Miles,

October 28, 1863.

I have been in division hospital, but am now in Mose Noyes' tent, ambulance train, convalescent. I have had a severe time of it, and am only glad to know that I gain strength every hour. I am perfectly disgusted with the medical department in this army; we had to freeze two nights in an open ambulance, with no one near to aid us, and riding in them on our backs, was literally murdering us at every revolution of its wheels. The 'pack up' sounded terribly to me as I lay so comfortably in my tent; I shall rejoin the regiment for duty in a day or two; it is very kind to me. *** I have spent some pretty lonely days latterly, and long to be well and on duty. I received a short note from Gene yesterday.

In Camp near Warrenton,

October 31, 1863.

By my general way and manner you may judge I am improved in health. I am very much better, and felt so well yesterday that I rejoined the regiment. I am not doing duty yet, and shall not until I am perfectly strong. I came very near having typhoid fever; I should have been a gone chicken if I had, for there was no shelter or care for a sick man. Oh! it is terrible to be sick on the march; I have had all the experience I wish in that line, during my short illness. As soon as I have a good chance for writing I will write a good letter home, and one to the *Tri-Weekly*.

The letter to the *Tri-Weekly* follows:

November 5, 1863.

The expected Hooker movement mentioned in my last letter was, it seems, countermanded, and another one quite as brilliant toward the rear substituted. Our retreat in good order from the vicinity of Culpeper was commenced rather suddenly, and for days and nights we kept up a vigorous march.

Our regiment advanced once as skirmishers over the plains of Brandy Station, when we recrossed the Rappahannock for the purpose of attracting General Lee's attention, and saving some of our trains. Was under fire once; just as we arose from our quiet noon rest, a rebel battery having been placed in position upon a neighboring hill previously occupied by our division on the line of march, and we participated in one of the longest marches at one time, that has ever been our lot since the 'recruits' joined; of course the veterans of the Peninsula campaign endured longer tramps, and saw bigger sights. We started in the morning from W. Junction, October 14, and reached Manassas in the afternoon soon after we had received the rebel compliments of shot and shell. Firing in the direction of Bealton Station gave us notice of the attack upon the Second Corps, and we were marched back to their support, but arriving too late to join in the engagements, we remained in line at Kettle Run until after dark, when we returned to Manassas. From there we marched to Bull Run, and were on the move all the long night, fording the stream at midnight, and continuing toward Centerville until 3 o'clock in the morning, bivouacked, cold, famished and wet.

It was a most tedious march, not that we got over so much ground, but such a continuous strain upon the faculties, that it exhausted every power of endurance, and left us wearied and almost unfit for immediate duty. Still we went on, passed Centerville Heights, and reached Fairfax, where we remained until

456

our forward movement, being constantly on the move, however, to protect our flanks from attack.

Then we commenced our advance, and after long delays and short marches during which time the subscriber was *non est* (a used-up person in division hospital ambulance), we reached our present camp October 30.

On our way hither we passed over Bull Run battlefield, and slept one night on that blood-stained ground; you would scarcely credit what I might relate about this fearful place, where for twelve long months the bones of the dead have been waiting a proper burial.

Many a brave man's remains were carefully deposited in the dust to which they were rapidly returning; in the still hours of the night many a dear one was recognized by his cross belt, or time-worn cartridge box.

There were many revolting sights and we were glad enough to leave the sickening testimonies of that hard-fought field. I have reference particularly to the second Bull Run. The dampness of the atmosphere was almost unendurable, it being prevalent over the entire field; then our close proximity to the graves and trenches was anything but agreeable; we were quite willing to vacate this temporary camping ground, I assure you.

As we increased the distance between us and it, we could not help contemplating what a terrible conflict this is in which we are engaged; here once were the fields of husbandmen, flourishing in the sunlight of peace, changed now to bleak, barren wastes, a receptacle to the noble dead, and still the turbid waves of the ocean of war sport in awful mockery over these once flourishing places, and everything seems surrounded by a desolating curse. Deserters come into our camp occasionally, and as usual, have their long yams to tell; much reliance cannot be placed upon them, nor the stories they give utterance to; they look upon a flattering tale as a kind of recommendation. They cannot possibly know the force at a general's disposal, yet they presume to sum up the total number of guns in the rebel army, and by such subterfuges gain a place in the rear.

General Meade still controls the running machine, oftentimes called Army of the Potomac. He came near being shelved if newspapers are correct; probably the War Department and the commander-in-chief considered him too tender to keep well even in cool weather and concluded not to lay him by in the cupboard at this time, so we shall have many more long marches and little fighting in future.

Wherever the sad trail of war is seen, its divine footsteps follow (Sanitary Commission), and wherever the scourging hand is uplifted to wound, its quiet presence is there to heal; its privileges conferred are sometimes abused, and the sick of a regiment on the march rarely receives its benefits on account of its contributions being absorbed by those who have no right to them.

We are all wishing for winter quarters; something definite must be settled upon soon, as the rainy season is approaching. We look for exciting news from the south and southwest daily.

Our camp at Three Mile Station was in an oak grove, but it was far from healthy. On November 6, orders came to move at 6 o'clock on the following morning. The move was supposed to be merely a change of camp to the vicinity of the river, where wood and water were more plentiful and available.

The morning of the 7th broke sharp and clear, and at the hour named we were off. The brigade led the corps, and the 118th Pennsylvania led the brigade. The mud had dried, the road, which ran for a part of the way beside the railroad, was very dusty, and the march toward the river disagreeable.

Gen. J. J. Bartlet,[23] a former brigade and division commander in the Sixth Corps, commanded the division during the temporary absence of General Griffin.

The Sixth Corps was on a road well to the right and in advance of us. The route of march was well known now to all. Upon reaching Bealton Station, it was found to have entirely disappeared; its buildings burned, railroad track, ties and telegraph poles destroyed, it was a wreck of its former self.

About noon the head of the column ascended a wooded ridge which rose abruptly from and terminated the level plain over which we had marched all the morning. On the left of the railroad

---

[23] Joseph Jackson Bartlett (1834–1893).

458

the ridge descended again to another plain which extended to the river. Here the column halted in position for the advance, with the right of the 118th Pennsylvania resting on the railroad, and the Eighteenth Massachusetts and the First Michigan, with the Twenty-second Massachusetts on the left.

We were about one mile and a half from Rappahannock Station. The brigade was formed in line of battle by battalions closed en masse. The other divisions of the Fifth Corps, as they arrived, extended the line still further to the left. Fires which had been made, while we were awaiting the order to advance, by which to make coffee, were ordered to be put out.

About 3 o'clock our line promptly advanced through the woods on our front for about 500 yards, debouching into the open plain.

The enemy immediately opened with artillery.[24] The command was halted, and the 118th Pennsylvania and our regiment on the left were thrown forward 200 yards, deployed, and the line again moved forward. The guns in the enemy's works that crowned the crest to the right could be distinctly seen, as well as their skirmishers, which were but 300 yards from our lines. The sun, slowly sinking, glistened on both lines as they lay watching each other without exchanging shots, anxiously watching for the Sixth Corps, which had been selected to make its charge, its left brigade joining our brigade on the right of the railroad. The skirmishers sprang forward, beginning their advance with a sharp volley. "Forward, guide center, march!" was the command we heard all along our line, and we pressed forward for about half a mile under a severe and constantly increasing fire from the batteries on our front. General Sykes had given orders that under no circumstances were we to cross the railroad, as that ground had been specially reserved for the Sixth Corps, charged with the attack on that side. But despite these orders, our right got across and in the final charge of the Sixth Corps, our skirmish line, taken from the Eighty-third Pennsylvania, Sixteenth Michigan, Forty-fourth New York and Twentieth Maine, entered the works.

---

[24] The Second Battle of Rappahannock Station, a Union victory.

A battery of our artillery (D, Fifth U. S., and C, Third Massachusetts) coming up at this moment, and opening fire, drove the enemy's gunners from their works. When they resumed the fire was diverted from us to the offending batteries. The line of battle of the Fifth Corps halted, and the attention of the enemy was wholly directed in an effort to repel the charge of the Third Brigade of the first Division of the Sixth Corps, composed of the Fifth Wisconsin and Sixth Maine, which, as a double skirmish line, supported by the Forty-ninth and 119th Pennsylvania, the other two regiments of this brigade, made one of the most brilliant, sweeping, spirited and successful charges of the war.

The fight was transferred to that part of the line, in fact it was apparent before the fight had ceased that our line of battle, so prominently displayed upon the open plain, extending nearly a mile, was intended to first attract the attention of the enemy while the heavy charging columns were passing out of sight, concealed by the hillside. It was rough handling for a parade occasion, but the honor achieved by the splendid victory of the Sixth Corps comrades was full compensation for our inconvenience and exposure to fire.

Soon, the fort with all its garrison, besides many others prisoners, fell into our hands, the result being 1,500 prisoners, four guns and seven battle flags for the Sixth Corps, while the Fifth Corps skirmishers captured besides eight officers, seventy-eight men and one battle flag, and lost twenty-nine killed and wounded, four missing.

Our loss in the Twenty-second 'was one officer and seven men wounded. A young, beardless officer of a Louisiana battery had remained in the enemy's works after the others had fled. An officer of the Sixth Maine, who had mounted the parapet of the fort, saw him in the act of pulling the lanyard of a shotted gun in his face. "Drop that lanyard!" he shouted. The young rebel refused, and he fell a moment later, shot dead at his post. Many lives were saved by this act.

The Twenty-second was moved into the woods on the left while the other two regiments were ordered to take shelter under the

460

railroad bank; later they joined us, where we all bivouacked for the night.

After the fight General Sykes took to task the officer in command of our right flank regiment for permitting himself to be forced across the railroad in violation of his orders. The officer replied, "General, if the devil himself had been in command, he could not have prevented the men yielding to the overwhelming pressure coming from the left that forced them from their position." "Well!" said the general, smiling, "if that powerful personage could have done no better, you are certainly exonerated from censure or reproof."

The prisoners did not seem to be seriously cast down, and some of them shouted, "Boys, we are all going to Washington to live on soft bread and fresh beef!"

A horse ridden by the adjutant of one of our regiments was shot through the bowels in this fight. The rider heard the thud, but, as the animal did not stagger or fall, he thought perhaps he had not been hit, and rode him through the rest of the engagement and until dark. As he was dismounting, just in the rear of a company of Pennsylvania Dutchmen, all of them farmers and well acquainted with horses, the animal dropped, rolled over, and kicked as though he had the colic. The adjutant called one of the men to him for assistance, and told him to bleed the horse for colic. The Dutchman thought before doing so he would examine him. He soon felt the wound, and inserting his finger shouted, "Odjutant, dot horse no colic got, vot ails him he is dead; dere was a ball gone clean through."

On the morning of the 8th we moved at 4 A. M. to a point near Kelly's Ford, about 8.30, marching by the road running by Payne's house and the toll-gate, and halted for two hours. We then crossed the river, marching two miles beyond, bivouacked between Paoli Mills and Stevensburg where a road to Brandy Station branches.

All of the regiments in the division had to drill in the afternoon because some of the boys called out "hardtack" to a certain staff

461

officer, who proved to be General Bartlett.[25] Before we got through drilling, the bugle sounded the "pack up," and at six o'clock we were on the move. We crossed Kelly's Ford, and bivouacked1 for the night about five miles beyond. A driving snowstorm about midnight caused much suffering in our shelterless condition, as few had pitched their tents. On the afternoon of the 9th we returned to the vicinity of Kelly's Ford; recrossed the river during the evening, and bivouacked in the vicinity of the wagon train, about two miles from the ford. On the 10th we again shifted camp to a more favorable site in a neighboring belt of timber. This camp was not far distant from that spot described in "The Campaign of Gettysburg" of pleasant memory, at Grove Church, near Wykoff's Gold Mine, where we had spent such a delightful week just preceding the great campaign. Cold, bitter winds followed the storm. A general order was published the next day, highly complementary to the corps for the work accomplished at Rappahannock Station.

Our rations had of late been poor, consisting mainly of maggotty hard-bread, and the boys gave vent in loud and prolonged grumbling. On the 11th, we were detailed to guard Kelly's Mills and property at Kelly's Ford, although the owner was of questionable loyalty.

The order came at noon, just as we were finishing chimneys, bunks, etc., to make us comfortable. We left them with wistful eyes, and hurried on to parts unknown. This was a special detail. All soldiers longed for a change, but when it came we soon tired of it.

Duties were now more exacting and numerous than ever. Details for river guard were constant, for camp guard, and fatigue parties frequent, and we still had to furnish our regular quota to the brigade picket, five miles away. We voted that we did not like this kind of a special detail. Stone was abundant, and we

---

[25] William Francis Bartlett (1840–1876) lost a leg at Yorktown, was seriously wounded again at Port Hudson, was captured while fighting in the crater at Petersburg, and nearly died of disease in Libby Prison. See *A Harvard Hero in the Civil War*, Palfrey, 2016.

commenced again to erect chimneys, huts, etc., and here we remained until the 19th, when the entire regiment went on picket, three miles beyond the river. This was in the vicinity of Paoli's Mills on Mountain Run, which empties into the Rappahannock just below Kelly's Ford, the mill being but a few miles from its mouth. Near us was an old Confederate camp, evidently intended for permanent winter quarters, and their huts had not for some reason, upon being abandoned, been destroyed. In some instances shingles covered the roofs; hinged doors and window sashes with glass were in evidence, all of which were eagerly utilized by those regiments not compelled to go on picket.

Our letters describe these events as follows:

In Camp near Beverley Ford,

November 11, 1863

No goods are allowed to come into camp at present, and there is a dearth of almost every article really needed. We are on the Washington side of the Rappahannock guarding this ford. We recrossed Monday night and bivouacked on the banks of the river; we had a hard, driving snowstorm at night, and being without shelter, suffered from the cold a good deal. Our camp is now in the woods, some distance from the river, and we do picket duty constantly. Winter prospects are probable, and we are all wondering what a day may bring forth.

Strange events have happened, and all our ideas of last Sunday are now changed from the course we have pursued since that time. Soon I hope to be able to send my address for the box.

I am glad that father is again elected to the Senate, that is if he desires the honor. How I would have admired to have been at home at the reception. I am glad mother did not know of my lacking an overcoat during my illness.

Camp near Kelly's Ford,

November 15, 1863

We are now close beside the rushing river, guarding Kelly's Ford and Mills. It is called thus for the reason that a man by the name of Kelly lives opposite us, and upon his estate is the ford and mills.

We guard his property and all his household, although he is of questionable loyalty. Our regiment received its detail yesterday at noon, just as we were finishing a chimney, bunks and everything of that kind, designed to make us comfortable; we left them with wistful eyes I assure you, and hurried on to parts unknown. Soon the truth became known, and we are in a poor camp, all alone, specially detailed. The regiment has long been waiting for something of this kind, but I notice there has been more cursing and swearing about our present situation and duties than ever before. Details for river guard are constant, camp guard large, and fatigue parties frequent, and we still have to furnish our regular quota to the brigade picket, though their camp is five miles off; the fact is, a soldier is never satisfied; he longs for change, but when it comes he soon tires of it.

It is truly a terrible life for a young man to lead, that is, one of any aspirations. There is a large amount of stone about us, and chimneys are rapidly being built; I have been handling heavy stone all day, and am quite a mason in laying them, and plastering up with mud and mortar; shall never let a job of that kind out when I get home, hoping to be an adept in that business myself by time, especially if I stay three years, and by the way, father, if I thought the government would keep us I would re-enlist again and then my time would commence from date of re-enlistment, and I should only have to stay one year longer.

I congratulate you upon your re-election to the Senate, and the increased majority of your vote, showing your popularity among the loyal men of the old Bay State.

Have you read General Meade's congratulatory order on our late victory? He speaks of the Fifth Corps. He is in great favor with the Army of the Potomac now.

On picket beyond Rappahannock river,

Saturday night, November 1863

Your letter with K's, was handed me last night after I had gone to bed; *** I arose, lit a candle, and soon was buried in your choice letters. To think of me as you partake of some delicacy on the home table is almost too much; if it causes you to choke at the table when you eat your meals, I shall not tell you, mother, what I have to eat on the march. Don't imagine me so great a sufferer, especially when

464

in camp. I pray you not to worry so much on my account. Remember that I am now perfectly well, and am living pretty well; even this morning out here on picket, I had toasted soft bread, butter, cheese, coffee and apple sauce; it was the result of a strike I made at a neighboring house, in our last camp. I lived in a small, wall tent, had a stone fireplace with cheerful evening fire in it, and had good things to eat; rations of hard bread, fried meat, boiled potatoes and dried apple sauce.

My position is far preferable to a poor private's; my meals cooked, more to eat, and better quality, for we noncommissioned staff have the first pick, and all the surplus. I am thankful for it all. On the march, however, 'we meet on the level,' and sometimes by circumstance I suffer more than those in the ranks. Do not then, my dear mother, constantly keep alive your anxiety about your 'poor boy.' Rather be cheerful now, for the summer is over, the harvest of death just at present is ended, and winter quarters are nigh; yet your Walter still lives and is among the favored ones, happy and full of hope.

We moved camp Thursday morning, and now lay three miles this side of the river; our whole regiment is at this time on picket, and the adjutant and myself are out for the first time since I have been his sergeant-major; we are to remain three days. I am quite comfortable, having a poncho tent up, and a hospital attendant for a mate. I shall have very little to do, and intend to answer some of the letters received when I was sick.

Our regiment was paid off yesterday; they are paying the rest of the brigade today; the boys are gambling high tonight. You can scarcely imagine what a rage there is for playing cards as soon as greenbacks arrive; some play all night, and before morning their greenbacks may be all gone, or they may be 'ahead' $100.

Many families suffer on account of this; it is a terrible evil. I can say with pride that I never played for money, and never will. Our B. boys are about the only ones who do not gamble in the regiment. As I write tonight (by candle light this time), the moon is clear, and about a quarter of a mile distant the woods are on fire, or rather the deep layer of leaves, throwing a rich, red glare high up into the air; the flames dart up hissing and crackling as the leaves are licked away by the devouring element; it seems like a prairie on fire, and is magnificent. I have just sent a large detail of men to put it out; they will have exciting sport.

Colonel Sherwin is commander of the picket, and Major Burt is in command of the regiment. Headquarters is in front of me, and the left wing of our regiment is in reserve. I am a sort of an attaché to the staff; I guess I can pull through all that is required of me though.

I expect we shall move on the enemy soon; if we are to act in conjunction with General Butler we must move soon; by report he is at Bottom's Bridge, Peninsula; a big fight in prospect *** my fingers are getting numb, and I propose to quit. When will I be a happy mortal in your presence? I have just been reading an account of the spirited debate in the Senate over father's amendment to Senator Davis' Bounty Bill. I am very sorry that father got defeated, for I like his plan, as does every other soldier of Massachusetts in the field.

Our brother of the artillery now writes:

Fort Whipple, Virginia.

I should think you and mother would feel almost deserted to have us all away, but then I suppose you will soon get accustomed to it. In regard to my re-enlistment; I have thought it all over; nothing in the world would tempt me to lead this life another three years. *** But I will not talk of it, for I cannot pass the doctor; I went yesterday before I received your letter to be examined, and *** he refused me. I am not much sorry after all, for I think three years are long enough to be a soldier and live as we do. About half of the old soldiers will re-enlist. I haven't heard from Gene for a long time. * * * My face has all broken out with salt rheum and I wish you would ask mother what I shall do for it. Everything here goes on in the same manner, the colonel being as popular as ever.

Thursday is Thanksgiving, but we shall not all meet this time as in years gone by. I can imagine you all at the table on that day.

On the evening of the 23d, we returned from our tour of picket duty to our camp near Kelly's Ford, having been relieved by the Ninth Massachusetts. From this camp we emerged upon the Mine Run Campaign.

Upon our return from picket on the night of the 23d, it was announced that we would move, and on the morning of the 24th the entire army marched early in a rainstorm.

The Fifth Corps was ordered to move at daylight, enter the main ridge road at Madden's, keeping on the left hand side, and proceed via Richardsville to Culpeper Ford, where it was to cross the Rapidan River and move by the shortest route to the Orange and Fredericksburg plank road at Parker's store, and, if practicable, advance upon that road to where the cross road comes in from Robertson's Tavern.

Starting at 5.30 A. M, we splashed along for about two miles, "*a la Burnside.*" The mud became deeper and deeper, artillery commenced to mire. One battery forge got stuck. Two horses went down. In fact things began to look seriously discouraging, when the whole column, artillery, cavalry and infantry, were ordered to "About face!" and return to camp.

The order suspending the movement found the head of the Fifth Corps where the roads divide or fork, going to Germania and Fly's fords, while our division was with the pontoon bridge in the vicinity of Richardsville. The wheels of the leading batteries were halfway up to the axles.

Again we reckoned, "General Meade was a man of sense," and before he became "Meade stuck in the mud" around the plains of Brandy Station, and in the waxy soil about Culpeper, had concluded to countermarch the army. It only rained two hours, yet the hollows and ditches soon became pools and ponds, and the roads impassable.

We returned drenched through and covered with mud. We hugged the huge log fires these cold, bitter nights, and drew from them pretty much all our comfort, and a great deal of cheerfulness.

Officers were sent out on the 25th to examine the roads, and Captain A. P. Martin of the Third Massachusetts Battery reported on that day that the road taken on the 24th was very bad until the Stevensburg road was reached, after which the road was very good to within two miles of Richardsville and was reported by the cavalry to be in passable condition to the river. The distance from our camp to the main road was about three miles:

Our letters thus describe this campaign:

Camp beyond Kelly's Ford, near

Brandy Station,

November 24, 1863.

We returned from three days' picket last night, having had a very easy time on post. This morning the whole army moved early in a rainstorm. *** upon our return the opinion was expressed by many that General Meade probably saw how things would turn out, if we pursued our way to Culpeper, and wisely countermanded the order. Had it been a good day, favorable for operations, and succeeded by fair weather, I have no doubt but what it would have been the biggest move yet of the Army of the Potomac.

In three days I should have been either a dead or wounded man, or else a live member of a victorious army; I think we shall move yet, just as soon as the mud dries up. *** It does not take long for baggage and artillery trains to spoil these new roads in the woods.

I got wet to the skin, but am very comfortable tonight. *** We shall move soon and stop for good, for soon the season will not permit of great doings in Virginia, unless it be magnificent splurges in the mud. *** When this reaches you, Thanksgiving will have gone by; how I have longed to be with you at the festive board; it is the second, and I trust the last absence from home on that day of all days to a New Englander.

Next year I hope and pray I may sit beside you, and the family circle preserved and unbroken still, with peace all over the land, as our blood-purchased heritage for all future time. Oh! what a happy meeting will it be for a loyal family of true-born Americans. If Gene and John could be with us *** with sisters dearly loved, and honored father and mother, all having done our part in the glorious struggle, each feeling 'well done!' in their own heart, how rejoiced we will all be in the contentment that comes of well-performed duty. We then shall have passed through the great trial, and come

468

out safe from severest afflictions. God speed the day of our 'Family Thanksgiving!'

On the 26th, we again started, marching directly for Ely's Ford, about twelve miles distant, where we crossed on the march to Chancellorsville, which we reached just at noon; but hearing heavy firing at Culpeper Ford (the next above), we were ordered there, where we arrived about one o'clock.

Upon our way there, it was ascertained that the firing was upon our own men; by order of General Sykes, the Third Massachusetts Battery had been directed to fire upon any body of troops seen upon the opposite side of the Rapidan, before we crossed. The battery took a position, and soon opened upon a regiment of rebel cavalry, as they supposed, but which proved to be a regiment of General Gregg's division, which had crossed above, and was on picket near the ford. Only a few men were wounded. They got out of range "double quick." We rested before crossing for an hour or more, and here had our Thanksgiving dinner, little thinking of what was in store for us, and only drawing strong comparisons with the Thanksgiving of a year before, when we fished up our luxurious dinner: from the mud about "Stoneman's Switch." Some had been preparing largely, and baked beans, mutton, puddings, etc., had been counted in by many a *common dogan,* but the move upset such a *Delmonico menu.*

We crossed about 2 P. M., and then halted until the second and third corps had crossed. At 3 P. M. we resumed the march, and after marching several miles along the Wilderness road, bivouacked for the night near the intersection of the Germania with the Orange and Fredericksburg plank road. It was intensely cold, the weather having changed directly after the rainstorm.

It is said that on this day two regiments of the enemy's cavalry passed across the front of the Fifth Corps, coming from the direction of Ely's Ford, where Gregg's division of cavalry had crossed. The marching had been slow and spasmodic, our movements having been delayed by the dragging motions of the Third and Sixth Corps.

469

On the 27th we moved out at 6 o'clock, our objective being New Verdiersville, near where the cross road coming from Robertson's intersects the plank road referred to. We struck the plank road at Parker's store about 10 o'clock, having to wait for the cavalry (Gregg's) which soon commenced skirmishing, and our progress was very slow.

We were in rear of the corps, and were proceeding quietly along the forest road when a shot rang out, followed in quick succession by several. The teams came rushing by, and suddenly an officer dashed to the head of the division to inform the general of the cause of the firing. It appeared that a small squad of the enemy had concealed themselves in the woods until after the corps had passed along, then made a dash on the wagon train. They ran a number of our teams down the plank road toward Fredericksburg. It was a daring act to undertake in the face of an army corps.

It proved to be a detachment of the Sixth Virginia Cavalry, Rosser's command, of the enemy which had succeeded in capturing, by this sudden dash, the general's headquarter team and fifteen ammunition wagons. General Bartlett and Colonel Sweitzer of our division had lost everything. The ammunition was set fire to, making things decidedly lively. During this little scrimmage, Colonel Sherwin of our regiment borrowed a gun from one of the sharpshooters, and shot one of the rebel raiders, who was seen to fall, and the balance got away.

Companies B and E and the sharpshooters were now detailed as special wagon guard. General Bartlett ordered the Twenty-second to act as flankers for the train the rest of the way. General Meade was very angry because no proper guard had been sent with the train, and said to General Bartlett, "I wish they had got away with all your personal baggage!" to which the latter replied, "They did so, general!"

After this little affair, we passed Parker's store, and early in the afternoon reached New Hope church, and after forming line of battle and supporting the cavalry, which was soon withdrawn, the division skirmished a little and bivouacked for the night, as we supposed. The country was heavily wooded and very difficult to advance over. At 7 P. M. on the 27th, General Sykes, commanding the Fifth Corps, reported that the left of the corps was at the intersection of the road taken by Gregg from Ely's Ford with the Germania plank road, at the point where he (Sykes) turns to the right to get on the Orange and Fredericksburg plank road, the country here, literally a wilderness, the woods admitting of no formation whatever, and no connection either with the First or Second Corps.

Two companies were sent to guard the train, which parked in the Wilderness. It commenced to rain, and toward morning an order came for us to move by a cross road over to the Orange Court House pike, and be at Robertson's Tavern at daylight. No fires were allowed, and without coffee, shivering in the bitter, cold air, we spent the livelong cheerless night. The enemy occasionally opened with artillery, and the pickets kept up a spluttering fire.

Before daylight, we moved over, a march of several miles, and swept slowly forward in line of battle along the turnpike, supporting the other corps, except the Third, which we were waiting for, while it was inextricably mixed up between Jacob's Ford and Robertson's Tavern. A heavy rain set in. We reached Robertson's Tavern by 2 P. M., and the entire corps was massed behind breastworks. Here we made coffee. Some skirmishing occurred during the day with slight loss, and we bivouacked in line of battle. Our position was across the turnpike in front of Mine Run.

Sunday morning, the 29th, about daybreak, we moved to the front, on the Orange Court House turnpike, about four miles, and took up a position about two thousand yards from the enemy, east of Mine Run, where he was strongly entrenched upon a crest. The first and second divisions extended from the left of the Sixth Corps to the road we had marched over, and the third division joined the First Corps. The field between us and the enemy was almost entirely open, besides being crossed by Mine Run, at this time more than waist deep. We relieved the third division of the Sixth Corps, at the front, and formed line of battle in the woods.

The enemy was distinctly visible on the opposite side of the Run, and were busily engaged in fortifying. At first the pickets on both sides popped away at every head that was shown, but soon there was a mutual understanding, and all was quiet along the lines.

In the afternoon orders came to leave our knapsacks and blankets should we get into the fight before night. We bivouacked in line, ready to move at a moment's warning, and as night came on it grew intensely cold. In consequence of French's failure to connect, Lee had been able to put his corps in motion and choose his own position behind Mine Run, one very strong, both naturally and artificially. Twenty-four hours had enabled him to make his line almost impregnable. The ravine of the Run was difficult of passage; the ground west of it had been cleared for more than a thousand yards, rising gradually over one hundred feet, with a space well up the ascent flanked by heavy belts of timber on both sides. The summit was crowned with intrenchments for infantry and artillery strengthened by abattis.

The stream had precipitous banks with boggy approaches throughout the entire length of the valley. Between our position and the enemy's works an advancing line would soon become broken and disordered, while floundering through the bog, and the men quickly chilled in the icy waters of the stream. General Meade, however, decided, after conferring with the commanders, to attack at three points, the Fifth and Sixth Corps to assault on the extreme left of the enemy, and the Second, with two divisions of the Third under General Warren, to attack the enemy's right; the other division of the Third Corps to make a demonstration against the center.

We remained concealed in the woods all day Sunday. There was no picket firing, and wood and water was got, and occasionally a chat indulged in, by both parties. The night was freezing cold, and we suffered severely while waiting for the word. Having received an order to prepare ourselves for a charge, we had stripped off all knapsacks, rolls, etc., everything that we did not need, and in order to go light, piled them, and waited silently for the word. But it did not come. We bivouacked on our arms with orders to be

472

ready to move at daybreak. On November 30 about 2 o'clock, all were roused up in the keen, bitter air, and ordered to again "pile knapsacks."

We moved to our right and were again massed in thick pine woods.

No fires were allowed, and in our concealed position, momentarily expecting the order which we all felt would send us to our doom, we shivered the long day out.

During the forenoon, at times it was pitiful and yet a comical sight to see the various methods employed to keep warm. Our letters say: "Some were stamping feet, others walking, running and jumping. One party would form a ring and run around a tree, another would march double quick, single file. The woods were filled with armed men, puffing and blowing in their endeavors to 'keep up steam,' and avoid freezing. Rations had given out and the men foraged for corn, left from the horses' feed upon the hard ground."

The column of attack which had been formed was later deployed in line. The First Michigan was detailed as skirmishers, and the Twenty-second with the other regiments of the brigade formed the first line. At daylight the carelessness of some of the men revealed our position to the enemy, although no fires had been allowed. General Warren had orders to attack at 8 A.M., and at the special request of General Sedgwick the artillery of the center was to open at the same hour and continue the fire until nine, when he was to assault with the Fifth and Sixth Corps. The "ball opened" promptly at 8 A. M. The cannonading from the position we had left was enlivening, but it was decided not to assault the works, and under cover of darkness we fell back to our old position, which had been held by the First Corps across the turnpike.

General Warren had reported that the enemy had been reinforced with artillery and infantry on his front, that his works had been strengthened, that it would take eight minutes for our troops to gain the works, exposed to a terrible fire, and that there was, in his opinion, no clear chance for success. In fact, as it had been left to his judgment, he felt it his duty to suspend the assault. General Sykes reported practically the same thing in front of the Fifth Corps.

We had worn out the dreadful night. The thermometer was below zero. Water was frozen solid in our canteens. The bitter, chilling wind had congealed every vital current in our bodies. To us, this preparation for attack seemed worse than Fredericksburg, and all feeling that certain death was to be their fate, prepared themselves accordingly, some pinning their names, written on paper, to their bodies, as a means of identification for those who should survive. All felt that it would be madness to assault. The agonizing suspense while that order of suspension was impending nearly blanched years of youth out of our hearts, and the Army of the Potomac grew years older that one long night by reason of it. As morning broke it was a strange sight to see the many methods employed along the line by the men to divert their minds from what seemed to be their impending doom.

We were ordered the day following to make our rations hold out for the time they were issued, i. e., until December 4. We were already out, December 1.

At dark we again took up the line of march.

We had been ordered to withdraw at 6 P. M., take the turnpike and then to pass over to the Germania plank road, by a wood road which a guide was to point out, and move to Germania Ford, and after crossing the Rapidan River we were to mass near the ford until the Sixth Corps had crossed.

We halted every few minutes during the first of the night, which made the march very tedious and wearing. Several hundred stragglers, mostly substitutes and new recruits, were picked up by the enemy who closely followed up the movement.

Taking the Germania plank road, we reached and crossed the river at Germania Ford about 4 A. M., December 2, and proceeding three miles beyond the river, halted near Coney Mountain and rested for nearly four hours, many getting a good sleep, which we were much in need of. About 8 A. M. we again started and marched to within a few miles of Culpeper, and bivouacked for the night. While here the First Corps passed us. Our orders were to follow the Sixth Corps, taking the plank road to its termination, then turn into the Stevensburg road at Halley's and take position at Stevensburg; we were not to leave Germania Ford until at least a part of the First Corps had crossed.

While halted, one dollar was freely offered for two hardtacks, and we thought of our generous Thanksgiving dinner at Culpeper Ford. Our brother visited a mill nearby and finding a lot of old, hard, dry crumbs of bread, scraped up a handful, and after blowing out the dirt and dust, ate them with a keen relish.

One of our buglers, hearing that a battery was nearby to which an uncle belonged, proceeded to find him, and was rewarded by his going to a caisson chest, and extracting hard bread, coffee, sugar, etc., which he considered at this critical period a decided "raise." At 8 A. M. on the 3d, we moved out and, after passing Brandy and Rappahannock stations, we crossed the Rappahannock River at 2 P. M., and at 4 o'clock were back at Beverly Ford and camped in the woods, a march of about ten miles. Rations were issued and we were happy again. Here the corps separated. Notwithstanding the croakers' and war correspondents' statements that "all were anxious for a decisive charge at those impregnable works," we felt that "to have attacked during that long, cold December day, while the impending command of advance was hanging over us, would have been madness."

We blessed the day when General Meade displayed his wisdom by ordering the army to fall back, and its "voice rang clear and high in praise" of him upon its return. We changed camp about one mile on the 4th and prepared for our winter quarters at Beverly Ford. But for the restrictions on General Meade from Washington, instead of falling back on this line, he would have taken up a position in front, of Fredericksburg. In that case the battle of the Wilderness might never have been fought, but the campaign of May, 1864, would have been fought in more open country.

The Fifth Corps was now ordered to relieve the First in guarding the railroad. One brigade was to be stationed at Rappahannock Station, one (ours) at Beverly Ford, one at Elk Run Bridge and Germantown, one at Warrenton Junction; one at Bristoe, and one division distributed at Catlett's, Cedar Run, Nokesville, Kettle Run Bridge and Manassas Junction.

We were ordered to "log up" 10 by 6 on the inside of houses, and in one line in rear of stacks of arms. We were now on ground formerly occupied by the Ninth Massachusetts, near our old camp in September, less than a mile from Rappahannock Station, where we could almost see where a part of the Sixth Corps had stormed the enemy's works in November.

The brigade did picket duty along the Orange and Alexandria railroad, on a line between the river and Bealton Station, protecting the flanks from guerillas, cavalry raids, etc.

Our camp was called Camp Barnes. Colonel Tilton occupied a room in the house on "Merry Hill," owned by a Mr. Jennings, the farm including six hundred acres. On December 6, 1863, the regiment went on picket to relieve the Eighteenth Massachusetts, one of whom was fired upon and wounded the night before. Orders were given to patrol the ground constantly between pickets, and to keep away from fires, except at the reserves.

Our letters say:

Saturday Eve.,

December 5, 1863

Now for my Thanksgiving. *** Preparatory to crossing at Culpeper Ford, we had a rest of an hour's duration, between 1 and 2 o'clock. Then it was that Stone (commissary sergeant), Watson and myself had a feast. It was such a striking contrast to my last year's dinner at 'Smoky camp,' when we were actually starving, not even having the privilege of buying hard bread.

Then we made our meal of pickings of mouldy crumbs, in a pile found in the mud, but this year good hard bread, butter, coffee, with sugar and condensed milk in it, cold fried meat and cheese, were temptingly spread out before me; I really enjoyed it, sitting there upon the red, clay bank of the roadside, the sunlight falling smilingly upon us, and so many round about us, feasting upon the same luxuries; some were laughing, others talking, and the whole road resounded with gleeful animation.

We had heard of victory, and were, as we fondly hoped, on the eve of another triumph to be won by ourselves; we were indeed merry. All were thinking of home, and those sitting at the festive board at about the same hour. The jokes cracked; the wishes expressed, the hopes and longings spoken would fill pages.

It was a jovial, jolly, soldier's Thanksgiving. If we had stayed in camp we should have done better, and some were preparing largely *** but the move upset our plans; as it was, however, we did as well as possible in our time, place and circumstances. After we had completely annihilated our dinner, Watson and myself went to the First Corps behind us, and I saw Brainard Blanchard and his brother; they had calculated on a big feast, their sutler having come up for the 25th with a load of goods, but the march disappointed them.

General Meade's object in going toward Orange Court House and his object in falling back I cannot blame any, for the enemy's works could never have been taken where we were; it was worse than Fredericksburg. I felt death in my very bones all day, while the impending command of advance was hanging over us, during that long, cold day of December, when no fires were allowed, no warm drink to be had save by chance, like mine; when water froze in canteens; when men froze on picket, some even unto death; when bitter chilling winds congealed every vital current in our bodies *** what would have become of the wounded? They would have died in twenty minutes, if they had remained still, their life blood oozing out, or stagnant in their veins. If the order had been given, Sir Walter would have gone to the very death, but I bless the day that General Meade ordered his army to fall back to its present position.

Croakers may talk, but curses be upon them for their murderous desire. *** I am for a fight always, when there is some chance, but when forces are equal, and the rebs are entrenched at Orange Court

House, I am for a safe return to familiar places, rather than the murder of two-thirds of the gallant army; it would have been butchery, and I have seen enough of that.

Thank heaven that we are back to our old camping ground, and that I still live. In the fight at Germania Ford, when the Third Corps was engaged, I fear I lost some friends in the Seventeenth Maine, Birney's division. Herman Mason, now lieutenant, I believe was wounded, and a number more; any quantity of my old Portland friends have been promoted in that regiment; they came out as privates, and are now lieutenants and captains. The three-years regiments offered good opportunities, but the new recruits in old regiments are jumped always; old men first, then new ones.

They gave me my position because I earned it at the battle of Fredericksburg *** they always jump me in every promotion. They did when I might have had a lieutenancy for the unexpired term, and now they have again (in accordance with my best pleasure, however, this time). I do not care now, but I did once when I was working for a promotion. I did want a lieutenancy once, but do not now, with a three years' tail of honor attached.

I mean now to retain my position, do my duty, as I have ever tried to do, give myself no uneasiness in regard to any ghosts or bugbears appertaining to the future *** and the Ford permitting, return to you all next year with a strong determination to excel in something *** and be a respectable member of society.

How I wish I had time to describe to you all the incidents of the late campaign *** it was a severe time for us all. The nights were chilly, cold and frosty; we had all we could do to keep warm. *** I shall never forget it, nor shall I cease to remember those eight winter nights in the open air, nor the midnight march and crossing of the Rapidan at 3 o'clock A. M.

It forms another page in my army history. I am finishing this Sunday afternoon. Our regiment is on picket, the line through our old camp, where father was. The order to be in readiness to move was countermanded last night; it is still cold, but I am comfortable.

Duties were severe, details coming in for building this bridge or that, fatigue, guard, picket, etc. No sooner had we got our huts made, than the re-enlistment fever commenced. Then boxes began to arrive, and the regiment settled down to an active winter life.

December 17 our hill proved to be a "Merry Hill" without the —i, as Mr. Jennings, the owner, broke out into a crazy fit, and smashed things generally.

Our habitations were much more comfortable than the previous winter at "Stoneman's Switch." They were all above ground and although exposed to wintry blasts, being on a small, bald knoll, yet we were well satisfied. The re-enlistment was discussed pro and con. Angry debates took place, only to be followed by genuine good feeling. Many who had heaped abuse upon those who had joined them from purely patriotic motives, and been strongest in their expressions, when we joined, of "You d—d two hundred dollar recruits," were now loudest in their desires for a large bounty, a veteran re-enlistment furlough, etc.

Our letters say:

How I have been importuned to reenlist; over thirty of the old men have signed the papers, and expect to go home on their thirty-five days' furlough at once. It is going to be the cause of stopping all our furloughs. *** I will not re-enlist for three years, just to get a furlough home. I shall go through my remaining service with a willing heart, always at the front in every fight, at my post in danger, and will do my duty always in the field and in camp, so that when I come home next autumn I shall be a free man, with conscience void of offense regarding my country, and a record untarnished by any cowardly act in the army; all the more glad to see you, and perhaps more welcome at home. What may happen before then, we cannot tell; we can only claim the present ever, by snatching an hour from the contemplated future.

Captain Baxter and Lieutenant Steele will go home in a day or two; you will see them both probably. We expect LeRoy back tonight.

We calmly thought there were enough young men in the North, who, if they had patriotically volunteered to help crush out the rebellion, there would have been little need for conscripting, or the old veterans to have pledged themselves for another term of service, and we so expressed ourselves in the following letter to the *Tri-Weekly* publisher.

479

We rejoice that quite a number of regiments in our corps among the First Michigan have gone, and are now going, on furloughs, on account of their enlisting in bodies, and that the work goes bravely on, and hope that the good people at home, the patriotic sons of worthy sires, will emulate the example furnished by the 'Old Guard.' "You can hardly imagine how the old soldiers in the field wish for the personal presence and co-operation of the brethren at home in their endeavors to bring the war to a speedy close. By all means we say to you, enlist! and help us put down this wicked rebellion, so that we may see the dawning light of a new day.

We would earnestly urge the 'Yeomanry of the North' 'to go in out of the draft' ere it be too late, and it comes with good grace from us, for we have borne our part in the great salvation that awaits the nation on the future, and desire that you shall share some of the glory and honor with us. The time has gone by for excuses. All who can, ought to enlist now.

A wife, sister or sweetheart should not prevail against the dictates of one's conscience. Their cries and entreaties should be of no avail. Let them listen to the mourning of the afflicted ones at home, who have given up their all to the good of our suffering country, and then blush for shame, that they are such unworthy, recreant daughters of the republic. It is easy for women to cry, 'I will not let them go,' but there are sons, brothers and husbands in the ranks, and some in the 'valley of the shadow of death,' that are as dear at home as the precious ones you would keep from duty.

Now is the time to make the sacrifice, greater than ever before. Is not the cause worthy of the noblest crosses which, if borne cheerfully, will be a source of joy, when 'all is well,' all over the land? It is easy for men to fold their arms, and not help us in this struggle; many of such are 'copperheads,'[1] others of the 'milk and water' order. Some will not lend their aid because of a thing called the administration, some quote one thing, some another, but the brave boys in the Union army will take good heed to it, that all such are remembered and will be duly dealt with in coming time.

They will have their reward most assuredly. Oh! for one more grand uprising of the people, that would result in the overthrow of the enemy, and carry dismay into the rebel ranks'. Then might we

---

[1] Copperheads were anti-war northerners.—2019

hope to regain once more our rank among nations, and our flag be the emblem of the rising star in the 'New World.'

Our leader, General Meade, is fast becoming a favorite among all grades in the army; his conduct in the last campaign has fastened his name firm in the hearts of those who compose his army. His declaration that 'when he fought men, he wished to gain a victory commensurate with the loss of life,' and his utterances like these to his personal friends 'that he did not wish to charge his conscience with the burden of a needless exposure of his men to death, for the sake of our advance, and great battle' (or words to that effect), have entitled him to a high place in the affections of the army, and when we remember the sufferings experienced during those winter days and nights across the Rapidan, we say, with one accord, 'all honor to General Meade!'

We never ascertained whether this youthful but fervent appeal for recruits among our backward brethren had its desired effect or not. Certain it is that drafting went on, and the reenlistment craze in the regiment did not abate. The rainy season set in. Mud predominated. It stuck closer than a brother, and its stain was hardly less erasive than a grease spot, as many of our letters still testify after over fifty years of seclusion from the light of day.

It froze and thawed alternately, and tenaciously adhered to all our clothing, making life at times a muddy burden. Ladies commenced to come (among them Mrs. W. S. Tilton, wife of Colonel Tilton, and Mrs. Field, wife of Captain Field), and it was a hard task at first to restrain from gratifying our curiosity by a full glance at a real live lady. Their presence lent a cheerful aspect to our rude habitations and surroundings which we had not experienced before, and we felt to see one was "something a little different from the continual separation from all that was good at home, and most gratifying to one accustomed to better things. It does seem so good to catch a view of the ladies occasionally. It is a variety that softens the harsh, coarse, everyday life in the army, so full of everything hostile to society, and evils that blunt the finer sensibilities and feelings.

Our letters say:

481

January 2, 1864.

We are having fine times here at present, mud is plenty, and we have plenty to eat, a soldier's chief solace. I can't complain much of my fare this winter; rations have not troubled my mind much. * * * I am in perfect health, strong as a moose, and am almost able to fight for the champion belt of England. * * * If the mud continues, it is very certain that the Army of the Potomac will not move at present; when it does, may success crown its every movement, and victory crown its endeavors for a lasting peace.

Our brother of the artillery had written from Fort Whipple, November 29, 1863, notwithstanding his rejection for re-enlistment at the first examination, "Well, mother, I am a veteran! I have had a second examination and passed. I shall in all probability be with you next month," and in this letter of January 2, we say, "I am glad John is at home; how I would like to see him."

January 4, a snowstorm commenced, and lasted all day, and orders were received to move across the river to a new camp. The prospects of leaving our comfortable huts made us pretty blue. It was said we were to occupy the ground then held by the Sixth Corps. Our visions of solid comfort were in danger of being disturbed.

Our letters say:

January 5, 1864.

It is a bitter cold night, and I sit down to write you, long after the camp has sunk into repose, and my tent-mate is sleeping for dear life, and it seems as though I was the only one up in the regiment. The only thing to keep me company is the howling of the wind without.

We are upon a hill, surrounded by no trees whatever, and every breeze sweeps over us a perfect hurricane; the bleak, bare hills of the Blue Ridge frown down upon us beyond, and now that their peaks are capped with the snowy garb of winter, every breath of air from that quarter is chilled, and its icy breath creeps through every crevice of our rude dwellings, and makes us think of other days, when houses were air-tight and water-proof.

482

I am comfortable, however; a large fireplace, with a blazing fire within, throws out its cheerfulness and with a 'plain table,' candles, writing materials, etc., I guess I can make out a respectable letter.

It is considered by all a sure thing that we leave these desirable quarters tomorrow morning for a new camp across the river, to occupy a vacant place of a division in the Sixth Corps. You can perhaps imagine our feelings, by placing yourselves in a similar position at home, only on a more extensive scale. Suppose you were to move your whole household arrangements on your backs to a piece of woods on the Haverhill side of the Merrimac River, and then look out for yourselves, build your own shanty, and make up your own nest for the winter nights that are now upon us; this, too, when the snow is on the ground, as it is here at present (a snowstorm commencing yesterday morning, and lasting all day); isn't it maddening to leave this place of solid comfort, and begin anew for winter, make new plans, etc.? We knew, of course, the risks we ran of relying on 'a sure thing;' yet we hoped for the best.

It is a great disappointment, 'but hopes caressed, will always be blasted,' and here in the army we are doomed to something of the kind all the time. If we do enjoy the harvest season for a short period, it is with the knife over our necks, liable at any moment to drop and sever all our joys, not counting in the loss of our heads, etc.

If we do go, so be it, is all that I can say; it is surely an aggravation and hard to bear.

Our letters of January 10, however, say:

We have not moved across the river, as much as we received notice for. Colonel Tilton sent a remonstrance by a number of officers, and the move was countermanded. I am glad enough for that special Providence. I borrowed much trouble on account of it.

Our chaplain came about January 16, and immediately a new log chapel was put up by the pioneer corps, and covered with canvas through the generosity of the sanitary commission. Prayer meetings were held, and quite a religious interest developed. This chapel was occupied and used as a Masonic lodge, being designated Warren Army Lodge, No. 1. It was also improved during the week for purposes of intellectual and moral advancement.

A photographic gallery was established within the limits of camp, all of which gave an air of civilization to all our surroundings, and added to our general happiness.

Furloughs were only granted to reenlisted men, but for the purpose of a surgical operation for the removal of fungous flesh in his mouth, our brother finally obtained a short one, about January 20, 1864, and upon returning, February 6, settled down once more to the routine of camp.

Washington House, Washington, D.C.,

February 5, 1864.

I arrived here too late for the 9.45 train to Rappahannock Station, and shall have to go tomorrow. *** I have got a pass for the first train in the morning. I have seen Henry Wilson and his son tonight; they stop here." "In camp, February 6, 1864.

They have been having fine weather out here while I have been gone; the mud has disappeared to a great extent, and the frost is out of the ground. Since I have been away they have built a new chapel, a photograph establishment is in operation, and a sutler's bakery is issuing hot biscuits for twenty-five cents per sheet, and gingerbread at fifteen cents a cake.

One of our company, William Downing, died while I was away; he went to bed at night, and was dead before morning. My dream is over; I awake to find myself in camp, in the land of Sodom.

On the evening of February 9, the "Gove Lyceum" started with a new boom, the first time since the previous October. General Tilton, Colonel Sherwin, and all the staff and line officers were present. Doctor Stearns delivered a lecture or travesty on phrenology,[2] taking one of the corporals (E. M. Walton) of Company H, as a subject, who good-naturedly consented to contribute to the fun of the audience. Our good surgeon's witty examination convulsed the audience with laughter. The famous dagger scene from Macbeth was recited by one of the captains

---

[2] Phrenology was a popular pseudoscience.

484

(Tucker); declamations were given by our brother and others, songs by "Our club," and the entertainment finished with the grand finale, "America," sung by all.

When the thermometer ran low, as it frequently did to zero, and the wind blew furiously, we tried to make ourselves comfortable in our seven by ten log coops. But with the parlor, dining room, sitting room, wash or bath room, and chambers all upon one floor, and no connecting doors between, we were sometimes cramped for room, and we sought for every reasonable means of pleasure and recreation to drive dull care away and kill what leisure time we had.

At the second meeting of the Lyceum Chaplain C. M. Tyler told the following anecdote of an old debating society to which he belonged when a boy. The subject before the meeting was, "Which is the more beautiful, Art or Nature?" One member arose, and expressed himself thus, "Mr. President and gentlemen. There is some things in art that are purty slick, but there is things in "nature considerable slicker."

On the night of February 10 a grand ball took place in the chapel. A music stand was erected, and as there was room to form "four sets," a grand time was anticipated. All the officers in the corps above and including the rank of captain, with their ladies, were invited. General and Mrs. Geo. Sykes, Gen. J. J. Bartlett, and other distinguished guests were present. It was a dedicatory ball, the chapel being the only one of the kind in the corps. One of our captains was in arrest. He had a previous engagement, so during the ball, it having become monotonous for the non-invited, he and all the lieutenants in camp had a "house warming" by themselves, instituting a competitive ball on their own hook. It proved to be a "Lanergan's ball," and while there was revelry by night at one end of the camp, there was a most lively dedication at the other. Rats began to swarm.

Our letters say:

February 14, 1864.

485

We have any quantity of rats in camp; every night they parade upon my bed, and their regimental bands, in an embryotic state, keep up discordant music. It is most repulsive to one's nerves to sleep with these rats. I wonder if mother has a portable receipt for their destruction. All the "nigs" about yer had a prayer meeting this afternoon on their own hook; it was very interesting and laughable, their performances. Dodge went home on a fifteen days' furlough yesterday.

Our letters of February 16, 1864, to the Haverhill *Tri-Weekly* publisher say:

Some thirty-five men have reenlisted from 'Wilson's pet lambs,' but I doubt if even the honorable, senator from Massachusetts, our old colonel, could induce, with all his eloquence, another man to join at present for three years' more service. The 'Vets,' as they return one by one, are objects of interest to all in camp. The men eagerly gather around him to hear words of home spoken, and the earnest inquiry of many a rough, storm-beaten man receives a welcome reply, such a one as warms his heart and cheers his spirit.

Camp life with all its ennui is, nevertheless, agreeable to us this winter. It is such a change from our laborious duties of last summer and fall, extending even into December.

With all the varied pleasures, however, of a gay camp life, a continued round of drilling, eating, sleeping, gossip and tame amusement, there are many who will rejoice when the bugle sounds, and the drums beat a forward movement; there is something exhilarating in the scene, when camps are broken and troops are marshaled in all the pomp and grandeur of military array.

The dullness of camp gives way to the life and stir of busy preparation; the pleasant excitement causes everyone to be filled with hopeful expectations, and the laugh and jest are upon every lip.

Many there are who hail the coming march, a constant round of the same duties, with no variation, makes life dull and insipid. The thought of comfortable firesides comes up and makes men homesick, and this preys directly on their spirits, and consequently oftentimes their health; a good military band in each regiment would go far to correct this; in the minds of many it was a great mistake abolishing them from the service; surely good music would be more elevating and inspiring than card playing and whiskey drinking. We were under orders to move at various times, but aside from one or two companies starting out hastily to intercept some raiders, or on ordinary picket, we dragged out the long winter.

During March the rains came and the floods descended. The river overflowed and the swamp back of camp was a vast pond, which then became frozen into a vast, sheet of glare ice, with not a skate within hundreds of miles. Everywhere there was a wilderness of mud, alternately thawing and freezing.

Our letters say:

February 19, 1864.

I have just been down to the Rappahannock River, and saw a long, narrow, winding field of ice there, the finest skating I ever beheld, and yet not a skate nearer than Washington; isn't that a provocation almost beyond endurance, especially to one who enjoys the pastime as well as myself?

February 21, 1864.

Since yesterday, the re-enlistment fever has broken out in the regiment very unexpectedly; all seem to be talking about it. George Lovejoy, Emerson, Walton and two more from Company H have re-enlisted and several men are talking about it. They all urge me strongly to join in; if I go five more will do likewise; if not, they will decline. I shall not re-enlist! East night the adjutant asked me if I would consent to be mustered in for a three years' term as a first lieutenant. I replied, 'No, sir!'

February 28, 1864.

We are under orders to move; there seem to be so many speculations as to our whereabouts, and they are all so vague, that I have come to the conclusion that no one in our camp has the least shadow of a thought concerning our real destination; we possibly may not go, but everything indicates it at headquarters.

I dislike the idea of leaving camp just at present, for we are certainly enjoying peace and quiet. I am not one of those who are so anxious to hear the bugles sound a forward or a backward movement; I desire rather to remain where we are, until regular moving time comes, about next April.

We must, however, submit to the decrees of the powers that be. One of the private's wives arrived yesterday; she staid in the quarters last night. It affords much merriment to all; the idea of a soldier's wife coming to live in camp *** it is bad enough for officers' wives to be here, and see and hear what they do. It is a pleasure for us to see ladies, and the results are good in camp to have women present, but the effect upon the ladies must be bad *** the impressions they form, and the every-day familiarity acquired of such things as they never heard or saw before are not at all improving to their feminine ideas and graces.

March 9 General Grant had been promoted to lieutenant-general and was assigned to command the armies. March 10 he visited our camps, but could not review us, much less move us against the enemy. We much feared that the reputation of "Unconditional surrender,"[3] would suffer with Virginia mud and Washington atmosphere as a test.

He announced his intentions of staying with us for a while, his reasons for doing so being "the transcendent importance of the issues in Virginia, upon which the fate of both the national and the rebel capitals depended," and the fact that "the army of northern Virginia was the strongest, the best led, and the best appointed army in the Confederate service," also on account of "the political and personal influences of various sorts and of various individuals which centered at Washington, having thwarted and interfered with all who had commanded the Army of the Potomac during the war."

We thought all this was a good enough reason why he should come, among us, and we welcomed him with true Virginia hospitality, i. e., mud by the square mile, and rain by the flood, and there were weeks when "he could not have reviewed us if he would, and we don't know that he would if he could," so we felt

---

[3] When asked for terms for the abandonment of Fort Donelson, Grant had replied "unconditional and immediate surrender." Playing off his initials, U.S. Grant became nationally prominent for the first time as "Unconditional Surrender Grant." When Lincoln heard complaints about Grant's drinking, he stated, "I can't spare this man. He fights."—2019

safe on that point, and continued on in our monotonous routine of life in the winter cantonment at Beverly Ford.

Our letters say:

> Mud predominates; the army has been turned and twisted over again and now we will see how quick the Army of the Potomac will kill the reputation of 'Unconditional surrender.' *** I am very certain events will determine his success or failure, and I hope and trust the former will crown his efforts.

A commission of first lieutenant was now formally offered to our brother by Gov. John A. Andrew, which he declined March 15 after three days' deliberation, and having weighed the matter well. His choice was made: if he ran safely the chance of war, he would then continue the study of law, perhaps stenography.

About March 18 to 20, anticipating a cavalry raid, arms were stacked in the company streets. We slept with one eye open, and one foot out of our blanket beds, ready at a moment's notice to "harness up." On the 22d of March nearly all the ladies had gone, and we were under orders to move. Three companies of the regiment (heavy artillery and sharpshooters) were off on a scout, and a heavy snowstorm was raging.

Our letters say:

> The rebels are supposed to be near on a raid; we expect to go soon; now that Grant has got us by the legs, we will either ruin him, or he will us, and the Confederacy. We have had a pretty gay time this winter, and no mistake, it is bitter cold; I pity all poor devils on post; indeed I do.

April opened stormy and the whole country was in a terrible condition.

We trusted that "U. S." might stand for "Unvarying success," as well as "Unconditional surrender." Shortly after this, and prior to the campaign about to be inaugurated, our entire division was reorganized. It was still commanded by Gen. Chas. Griffin, but our brigade, the oldest in the corps, which had always been the First, under Gen. James Barnes, was now commanded by Col. Jacob B. Sweitzer of the Sixty-second Pennsylvania, Gen. Barnes having been relieved. It now consisted of the Ninth, Twenty-second and Thirty-second Massachusetts, Sixty-second Pennsylvania and Fourth Michigan. The new First Brigade was commanded by Gen. Romeyn B. Ayres, and was composed principally of General Sykes' old brigade of regular troops, while the new Third Brigade was commanded by Brig. Gen. Joseph J. Bartlett and was composed of the Twentieth Maine, Eighteenth Massachusetts, Forty-fourth New York, Eighty-third and One Hundred and Eighteenth Pennsylvania, and the First and Sixteenth Michigan.

On the 23d no passes were allowed officers escorting wives to their homes, and the camps were now practically clear of females and non-combatants, and the army was reorganized.

The old First Corps was consolidated with the Fifth, making four divisions. The first and third divisions, being the old Fifth, were now commanded by General Griffin and General Crawford; and the second and fourth, the old First Corps, commanded by Generals Robinson and Wadsworth.

General Sykes was relieved, and Gen. G. K. Warren placed in command of the Fifth Corps. The reorganization at first created much dissatisfaction and growling, on account of the differences in the histories and associations of the corps and, now that their identity was lost, their pride and esprit de corps were wounded. Our First Corps brethren, however, after much grumbling and considerable chaffing, gracefully yielded, but for some time wore the Maltese Cross and round lozenge ingeniously combined on the seats of their pants.

Our letters say:

March 27, 1864.

We have had a terrible snowstorm here; last Wednesday there were eight inches of snow on the ground; now it is all gone. The Blue Ridge alone shows its presence. The night of the storm, the snow blew through my tent, and before morning my bed was white with the feathery material; it was a bitter cold night, and all suffered more or less, particularly the pickets. Our corps is now very large, the First having been merged into it, the whole commanded by General Warren.

We are to have heavy fighting this next campaign beyond a doubt. You will see in the papers about the reorganization of the army. We like it well enough, for our corps still remains in status quo. I imagine the First and Third are vexed.

March 30, 1864.

We have been under orders to move for three or four days and nights; two days' extra rations are on hand, and we are anticipating great times. Last night at the base of one of the mountains in the Blue Ridge, some forty miles distant, we could see many camp fires, indicating the presence of the enemy. Let them come, say we! The ladies are all going home tomorrow. and then the fact that General Grant is soon to make this army his headquarters argues well for an early decisive spring campaign; we are expecting it.

April 13, 1864.

The enclosed photo of my good friend, departed Charlie (Knowles) ** * I am so thankful for, to you, his sister, and all connected with its being sent to me; I shall prize it highly.

His principal features of character were firmness, noble faithfulness, and unswerving friendship *** He had a generous nature, was frank, outspoken, and a friend to all the boys; we miss him dreadfully. *** Well do I recollect that day when he was carried off to die; I can see the agonizing look of pain upon his face now, as he was carried back to the rear; shall I ever forget the same night when I roamed about the field among the dead and dying, the pale moon reflecting from the fallen ones their piteous look of suffering; each face was a story in itself.

How weary I was that night; tired nature needed repose. Two nights after, I was at the foot of Round Top, mingling at midnight with the shadowy forms of our enemies; what fearful times those were! I learned many lessons then and there. *** I shall soon be on the march, and in battle. I stand in awe of danger, but shall meet it like a man, with a spirit of high resolve, though I may wish I were far away when engaged fiercely for the defeat of our foe; still, I shall do my whole duty regardless of consequences. Pride will conceal the inward fear of death by bullet or shell; a quivering lip, or shaky limb, will be stilled to a firm calmness, and with no vaunting of courage. I assure you that in the fight I shall be at my post. *** Grant is doing big things, but the mud will not allow him to review the troops; Virginia soil asks no odds of him.

April 24, 1864.

Our sermon this forenoon was a capital exhortation to 'be grateful to God for all he has done for us,' and is continually doing in our behalf. *** Our Father is just as directly personal in these everyday kindnesses, which we ascribe to natural laws *** as in the greater manifestations of His love and goodness. *** We must be grateful for the commonplace blessings, as well as those extra, and publicly acknowledged. *** The discourse was full of choice illustrations and abounded in incidents connected with the closing battles of last summer's campaigns, Gettysburg, Vicksburg, and Port Hudson.

One allusion to the Fifth Corps, with regard to its march by midnight from Hanover, and its appearance upon the field before the afternoon of that famous Thursday, when the war-worn veterans, weary and well-nigh exhausted, lay sleeping among the rocks of Little Round Top, almost brought tears to my eyes, it was so feelingly spoken, and so touching in its relation to the wide-awake millions at the North, fearing, trembling, and watching for the strife that commenced four hours after.

It brought to my mind my own experience at that time, when I was sleeping upon my arms, with scattered groups of dirty, lousy, worn-out heroes round about me, endeavoring to snatch a few hours of the same repose I was enjoying.

Poor Rob was five miles to the rear, almost shoeless, trying to learn the whereabouts of the regiment, and earnestly striving to catch up, with hobbling steps of lameness.

I can imagine how his heart beat with anxious feeling, lest he should not be with us in the fray, and be called a 'skedaddler.' I was worrying for him every time I heard the skirmishers firing at the front, or a whistling admonition of the coming struggle in the shape of a rebel shell.

I can remember well how glad I was to see him when he came limping up, a brave smile of satisfaction on his face, despite the care-worn, suffering expression beneath.

Oh! those are the proudest days of my life, in memory. I would not sell the honor of being a poor humble member of that brave band of men who fought the bloody battle, for all the gold that gilds the treasury.

Did you ever pause and think what we saved you from, those three days of carnage? If it had not been for that line of immovable patriots at Gettysburg, resolved upon beating the tide of rebellion back, there would have been consternation and dismay in every northern village and city. There would have been 'hurryings to and fro;' no longer would there have been peace at home; in every street would war have waged rampant. For all this, Mr. Tyler said, 'be grateful to God!' And I hope we are.

He closed with a violent denunciation of swearing and cursing, and drew comparisons between our treatment of earthly heroes, who died for our country, and the heavenly hero, who died for all and that all might be saved. We laud the former, and sing hosannas of praise to their memory; we curse the latter, and obey not His precepts. If we were only susceptible to gratefulness how noble our minds would be, and how much less of feverish passion there would be in our desires.

April 25 the sanitary commission covering was removed from our chapel, indicating a move. No more lyceum meetings, religious gatherings, or Negro prayer meetings.

This last feature in our camp life at Beverly Ford had been most amusing. We attended them often. One colored *gemmen* would get up, pose the subject, which he said was somewhere *in de Bible.* "Hunt for it, as I did for Jesus!" he exclaimed. "I will not weary your patience, nor tarry your minds any furder. I will soon leab yer in de hands of the Great Redeemer, Jehoby. Will sing de song in long meter. Say turnbacks, will yer meet us? All sing togedder, and follow one-right after de. odder."[4]

Our brother in the Eighth Infantry, after the riots in New York had somewhat subsided, was ordered to Fort Columbus, New York harbor, where he remained on arduous and important

---

[4] This is a frequent and typical example in Union letters and diaries to write the southern dialect of African Americans, with whom they had seldom if ever interacted.—2019

duties connected with the draft, general recruiting service, and the preservation of peace in the city, until February 1864, when he was ordered to Springfield, Illinois, on mustering and disbursing duty, where he remained until the end of the war, disbursing many hundreds of thousands of dollars, not one cent of which stuck to his fingers. No safes, and not always a guard, were allowed him, and in making trips to Cairo and other parts of the state he carried sometimes from forty to fifty thousand dollars[5] loose in a satchel, put it under his head with his pistols at night, and slept with one eye open.

Brig.-Gen. James Oakes, U.S. Army, commanded the station, and many duties here and elsewhere faithfully performed were lost sight of in the hurry, anxiety and intense excitement preceding the last go down of the Confederacy at Appomattox. A volume alone could be filled with the adventures, incidents, and daily perplexities of those responsible posts of duty, where the little band of regular officers, while detached to perform this necessary work, got neither laurel wreaths, glory nor brevets.

In January, 1865, he was again transferred to New York as aide decamp on the staff of Gen. Philip St. George Cooke,[6] in charge of general recruiting service, forwarding thousands of recruits to the army, etc., where he remained until May, when he was assigned to duty at West Point, as instructor in ethics and later in infantry tactics, but was relieved at his own and General Cooke's request, and he returned to duty in New York, and afterwards to years of honorable service in the south and extreme southwest, where he was engaged in many and responsible duties in our little regular army as a captain in the Twenty-ninth and Eleventh U. S. Infantry.

---

[5] Equivalent to $635,000–794,000 in 2019.
[6] Philip St. George Cooke (1809–1895) had written the primary training manual for army cavalry. See *American Civil War Cavalry Tactics*, 2014, BIG BYTE BOOKS.

THE WILDERNESS CAMPAIGN

The great campaign from the Rapidan to Petersburg and Appomattox was about to commence.

Our letters of April 27 say:

At any moment the dreaded 'pack up' call may be sounded, and we have to create our own circumstances at present. We have only two wagons to our regiment, and I believe my coat will have to go up, for I cannot wear it during the warm weather, and when the order to send extras to the rear was promulgated there was every reason to believe that our transportation would not be cut down to the extent it has been; besides, it is a sure loss to send any clothing to be stored in government warehouses; over two-thirds of the surplus we sent away from Potomac Creek was lost in Washington, and the men received no payment for it. Our mails have not been stopped yet in the Fifth Corps; there was an order out to that effect, but it has not been put in force; yet I shall trust this letter to the post-office at all events.

The 'Sunny South' is once more applicable to 'sacred Virginia.' The warm rays of the sun have been acceptable alike to man, nation and beast. The air is redolent with the perfume of peach and apple blossoms, and the charm of spring is quite perceptible.

The wintry pall has lifted its dark shadows from the earth, to gladden our eyes with the hitherto concealed beauties of early spring. The peeping grass and innocent flowers were just visible on 'Fast Day.' The time of bursting leaf and singing birds is already come, as if nature would be herself again, rich with melody.

The summer days are almost here, when we shall be wearily plodding over the roads once more in search of victory or death. Many a poor fellow will find the latter, and may it be a solace to him. I dread the approaching campaign. I can see horrors insurmountable throughout the summer months.

The calm quiet of camp seemed like home this afternoon, in our imagination, and I almost forgot myself amid the singing of birds and sonorous voices of the frogs. The river rolled along in gentle murmur, and the whole scene from my camp reminded me of New England. I have not forgotten her beauties in my months of immolation on the country's altar.

One more united effort, one full, strong move of banded, loyal patriots, rolled downward against the front of treason, and its hosts lie at our mercy. Then the wise and the good shall array themselves against slavery. We will wheel into line in the new position and grant freedom to all men, no longer ignoring the fact that we are all fellow brethren, and children of a common father.

The hour has come, and God grant success to liberty! Good-bye!!

Such were the views partly retrospective, and future of a loyal heart in the Army of the Potomac, just about to plunge into battle, from the Wilderness to Petersburg. It has been introduced simply to show what feelings animated the men who wore the blue in the ranks, the unquenchable spirit and undying courage that won the battles, and endured everything but death, during those storm laden weeks, when life wasn't worth the "flip of a copper," in order that the nation might live.

April 30

We have just received orders to be in readiness to move at short notice. All the corps have received the same orders. The regiments composing the division, which have lined the railroad during the winter from Beverly Ford to Alexandria, have all joined their respective brigades; last night, the low fires of the marching columns were to be seen all around us. I imagine it will be hard to sleep upon the ground in a poncho tent, even in May. Burnside's Corps is along the route, ordered to the Army of the Potomac. What distribution is to be made of them is more than our feeble minds can tell. The brigades of colored troops are relieving us upon the railroad, and I presume will remain to guard it. The Fifth Corps does not like it much, but I think there must be a good reason for it.

I am determined to believe 'everything is for the best this summer.' Retaliation has a place in my thoughts, and I hope the first battle will be a hand-to-hand fight. I believe I could do my share in the line of vengeance for the foul cruelties lately indulged in by a savage foe, and I am going in for some 'tall' fighting. When this reaches you, we may be on the march for a fiercer conflict than that of Gettysburg. I know not what awaits me in the path of duty, but I have faith that all will be well! *** Be assured that no opportunity on my part will be lost to inform you of my whereabouts and wellbeing.

One can hardly imagine the scene of a camp breaking, especially after having been so long settled in a winter camp. It was most exciting as well as amusing. We left an unusual amount of public as well as personal property. Transportation was cut down to the lowest possible limit. The darkies about our premises realized a rich harvest. We never saw so much destroyed. Twenty families could have set themselves up in housekeeping from the remnants of our regiment alone.

Crockery, clothes, furniture, bedding, ham (boiled and raw), potatoes, pork, bread, etc., were thrown away without thought, and thus it is always when an army moves, and we wished it could have been distributed to poor families at home. What a "May party" there would have been, even on Sunday. We took what we could; the remainder was what had accumulated from boxes, etc., during the entire winter.

We dreaded to leave our comfortable quarters, but at 8 A. M., May 1, the 'pack up' sounded, and night found us across and five miles from our winter camp beyond the Rappahannock River, near Brandy Station."

Our letters say:

The die is cast, and I am in for the little two by four tents so near the ground. We are about one-quarter of a mile to the left of and below Ingall's Station, about as far from General Meade's headquarters, and to the right of it. We shall move in a day or two, the whole army; we may be reviewed as a corps before we go. Every soldier is in high spirits, and I never saw such confidence in success manifested. General Grant's operations produce no partisan feeling, and that fills all hearts with hope. All are in good spirits, and confident of success. We had a prayer meeting this evening just after all our tents were up— the last one in the regiment. Mr. Tyler spoke beautifully. May 2 we remained in camp. During dress parade at night a heavy gale sprung up, filling the air with dust. We were obliged to 'make a break' for our old shelter tents 'double quick,' and hold on to prevent their blowing away.

The following day, May 3, at midnight, we broke camp and marched to within about two miles of Culpeper, where we halted.

497

Our route was across Mountain Run at the double pontoon bridge, then to Stevensburg, then toward "Doggett's," and from there about one mile to a place marked "ruins," then by a road marked by men placed along the route to the plank road to Germania Ford, the head of the column reaching there at 6 A. M.; commenced crossing about 7; our regiment crossed about 8. There was but little resistance; although the enemy had strong earthworks, they evacuated them. We advanced on the Germania plank road, passing the ruins on the left side near the ford, then about two miles further on to Orange Grove near Spottswood. Here the roads fork. About a mile beyond we passed the "Tannery," and immediately after we reached the intersection of the plank road with the Orange Court House pike. Turning here squarely to the tight, we moved down the pike about a mile, passing the Lacy House, and halting, went into bivouac about 4 P.M., near Old Wilderness Tavern, and threw out pickets. Our division held the road leading to Robertson's Tavern.

In the early morning, line of battle was formed, barricades were commenced by our pioneers, but the picket line having advanced as skirmishers, before they were fully aware of it, we found ourselves in contact with the enemy. Our brigade was at an oblique angle to the left, with Bartlett's, whose right rested on the road. At 12.15 PM. skirmishing began with the enemy on Bartlett's front. *** Soon the Twenty-Second was changed to the other (right) side of the road, with the Thirty-second Massachusetts on its right, both regiments under Colonel Tilton. We moved toward the enemy in this line to relieve Bartlett's Brigade, partially concealed by bushes. The Twenty-second was posted nearly parallel to the road, and the Thirty-second on the right, refused. The enemy came out of a wood on the opposite side of a clearing on our front. Here we remained under a severe fire until 3 P. M., when we were relieved and returned to the first position occupied by us in the morning. The fight of the Wilderness was opened by Griffin's Division of the Fifth Corps. At about one o'clock we had encountered the whole of Ewell's Corps. Our attack failed because Wright's Division of the Sixth Corps failed to make connection with our division on account of the density of the woods. We lost heavily in this attack, and owing to the dense underbrush there was much confusion in our lines. Our division was engaged at different times with Jones' Brigade of Johnson's Division, and Battle's and Dole's Brigades of Rhodes' Division.

The battle raged back and forth all day, and the dense forest rang with the roll of musketry. The thickets were so close that it was impossible to use artillery, neither could lines of battle be maintained. Men became separated from their commands, and it was hours before they could rejoin. Some wandered into the enemy's lines and at last, when darkness overtook us, we sought water at the same streams or springs with the Confederates, neither knowing the presence of the other, or friend from foe, until accidentally discovered, when desperate efforts were made to secure prisoners.

By night the line had surged back to about where we had built our breastworks, and the wearied line dropped in its tracks on its arms to sleep. One of our company officers during the day, while lying behind a log, expressed the wish that he might get a slight wound, a "hospital," or "thirty days' scratch." Scarcely had the words escaped his lips, before a glancing ball tore through his shoulder, passing out through the shoulder blade. He started quickly for the rear. A new regiment was stationed behind us. They opened on him in their excitement, and it was only by shouting and partly lying down and creeping, that he succeeded at length in reaching our field hospital. He got his leave, but while at home gangrene got into the wound and confined him to his bed.

His condition got so low that upon consultation of the physicians he was given up. He overheard the conversation, arose from the bed during the absence of his mother, dressed, walked down town, entered a billiard room, took up the cue, made one shot and fell in a dead swoon to the floor. He was picked up and carried home, was replaced in bed, but from that moment commenced to recover, and when near Petersburg he rejoined the company. It illustrates the strength of man's will power or mind over matter, for he was certainly at death's door. A man who had joined us but a short time before from an indefinite leave of absence, and was a constitutional coward, when the uproar began, started for the rear, running like a deer. It was the last ever seen of him. He died in Andersonville prison.

It is supposed that he kept on to the river, took shelter there with other skulkers and stragglers, and was captured by the enemy's cavalry, after our advance to Spottsylvania.[1]

The 6th was but a repetition of the previous day's fighting along our portion of the line. We returned at 2.30A. M. to the scene of our fighting on the 5th, the brigade forming on the left of the road *** there was some skirmishing when we took up this position. The day passed without any direct attack in our front, but it was made uncomfortable by a constant fire between the sharpshooters of our regiment (Second Company, Massachusetts Sharpshooters), and those of the enemy. We held on all day, gaining no appreciable ground. Some batteries were dragged into the open and shelled us severely. We lost a few men. The principal fighting was on the left in front of the Second Corps, supported by the Sixth in part, the Fifth and Burnside's Corps. Just at night the enemy broke through the line of the Sixth Corps, and we were ordered to retire toward the line of breastworks made by us on the 5th, but we were afterwards ordered to return to the position held by us during the day. The enemy had not discovered our absence. We threw out pickets and lay down. Our loss in the regiment was 15 killed and died of wounds, 24 wounded, 3 missing.

A little after midnight we commenced falling back to again occupy the line of barricades that had been built by the pioneers on the 5th, and the enemy came out of the dense thicket to follow it up; thinking we were retreating, about 5.30 A.M., they attempted a charge, which we met and repulsed with great slaughter. Some of our guns opened with double shotted canister at close range and cut them down like grass. They fled back under

---

[1] Today spelled "Spotsylvania."—2019

cover of the timber. We found the Sixth New York Heavy Artillery occupying our barricades, and, after we had repulsed the charge of the enemy, we took position in the rear of the Sixty-second Pennsylvania, which had gone in on the right of the "Heavies." A heavy cannonading was opened upon us about 12.30 P. M., and we lost several from the company. One man was hit in both hips, both legs were amputated, and he was left in the division hospital, where all were made prisoners, but were subsequently recaptured by our cavalry, which being sent back, barely rescued them from being burnt up, as the woods had been set afire by our shells.

He was brought up to our position at Spottsylvania, and was taken from there to Washington, where he died. A drummer boy (Appleton) went to him while lying in the ambulance, and gave him a drink of brandy. "Tell the boys," said Nickerson, "that I did not lose my legs trying to get to the rear." We lay in the breastworks until nearly 11 o'clock at night, when we were suddenly but quietly withdrawn, and marching along the narrow forest roads, over to the Brock road, passed by the Second Corps in line of battle, and from thence toward Todd's Tavern. Our route was by the Orange Court House turnpike, back to the intersection of the Germania plank road; then marching on this road about one mile and a quarter, we struck the Brock road. About one mile farther, we crossed the Orange plank road, and three miles beyond the unfinished railroad near where "Stonewall" Jackson passed out by the Trigg and Stevens houses the year before, in his famous march to attack the right flank of the Eleventh Corps at Chancellorsville.

The night was very dark, the road a narrow defile through the forest, making the march painfully slow and wearisome. Robinson's Division led the corps, and the Second Corps followed ours. About 1 o'clock the road became blocked by the mounted provost guard following headquarters of the army, and besides, Fitzhugh Lee, divining Grant's intentions in his efforts to seize Spottsylvania Court House, had barricaded the road at Todd's Tavern by felling trees, and had brought Merritt's[2] Cavalry to a temporary standstill.

501

It was hot and we were choked with dust. There were many stragglers, and it was difficult to move the column along. When we arrived near the tavern about 7 o'clock on the morning of the 8th, we found the cavalry skirmishing heavily with the enemy, and we halted some time for the rear to close up, and the advance to clear the road. But once started, the enemy kept moving, and about 8 o'clock we started down the Brock road, by Todd's tavern, around which was Merritt's Division of cavalry, until we struck from the woods into the clearing at Alsop's farm, where the road forked. We took the right hand road past Alsop's, and after advancing a short distance, came within sight of the Third Brigade skirmishing, and at once came under a shell fire. The enemy had just arrived, and repulsed Robinson. We swung into line of battle on the "double quick," our batteries on the left. Our skirmishers were driven in and we opened. The enemy charged. We scattered their center in all directions, but upon our left, a line came in obliquely upon our batteries and left flank, and having protected them until they could limber up and take a new position, we coolly fell back to their support.

All day long we fought fiercely, contesting every inch of ground, and at night our pickets occupied a rail fence near a peach orchard belonging to Spindler's farm, and our line slept on their arms upon the wooded ridge, which we called "Laurel Hill," where we threw up breastworks.

The Twenty-second now numbered 180 men.

It was the first day's fighting about Spottsylvania Court House. Our column had been intended for the advance and occupation of the Court House, but the enemy (Field's Division of Longstreet's Corps) had anticipated our movement by shorter routes. But for the presence of Fitzhugh Lee on the Brock road, across our line of

---

[2] Wesley Merritt (1834–1910) served in the Civil War, Indian Wars, Spanish American War, the Philippine–American War, and was the first Military Governor of the Philippines. He also sat on the board of inquiry investigating charges of cowardice against Major Marcus Reno after Custer's death at the Little Bighorn. See *Reno Court of Inquiry*, 2015, BIG BYTE BOOKS.

march, the Fifth Corps should have been at the Court House at daylight. Our path was blockaded and both lines strengthened their positions. When we left the Wilderness, details from the regiment (about 100 men) had been made for picket, and left on post; this left us but eighty guns.

They were not withdrawn until 3 A. M. on the 8th, and upon being relieved, had followed on after us. When they got to the clearing at Alsop's, a halt was made for a rest, as they had marched rapidly. General Crawford rode up to the officer commanding, and directed him, by General Warren's order, to join his (Crawford's) division, which was on our left. At about dusk the Sixth Corps moved out through dense woods upon the enemy. General Crawford, with his division and this miscellaneous command, followed in the rear. The Fifth Corps picket details supported Crawford as a second line. The Sixth became engaged, but, after a short struggle, fell back.

Crawford with the second line was ordered to lie down. On came the enemy with loud yells. Crawford's line broke, and went through our line, disappearing through the darkness. Our men fired a volley or two, rose up, faced about, and moved back a few rods, to avoid being flanked.

Again facing about, the enemy came pell-mell into our lines. It was dark; they were much broken up. Our line was solid. Our men ordered them to surrender, and in the gloom of the forest, and neither hardly able to distinguish the other, there ensued a desperate hand-to-hand fight. There was no time to reload, men threw down their arms, and went in rough-and-tumble where fists were freely used. Our little detachment alone succeeded in taking over sixty prisoners, including one captain.

Sergeant Andrew Wilson ordered a man to surrender, a rebel officer. He refused to surrender to an enlisted man—and a "C" Company man shot him dead. The sergeant took his sword as a trophy. A little later he captured the battle flag of the Sixth Alabama Regiment.

A rebel captain, after being relieved of his sword, took a survey in the darkness, then inquired "which way it was to the rare" (rear). Had they known that this line was made up of detachments, with no connection either on the right or left, and, after Crawford's disappearance, unsupported as we were, they could have escaped. In this fight our old friend "Daddy" (Wm. Mulhearn, previously referred to) distinguished himself, and is said to have killed six or more of the enemy with his own hand. After delivering his fire, he is reported to have gone in with his bayonet and butt of his rifle. It was said that he had lost a brother in some other regiment who had been bayonetted while lying on the field wounded, and after he had begged for mercy. After "Daddy" got his fighting blood up on this eventful night, he showed an almost ferocious spirit, and it was with the greatest difficulty that he was restrained from wreaking his vengeance upon the rebels already gathered in as prisoners, but who had not yet thrown down their arms.

The detachment lay in line all night.

Toward morning they were fired upon by a picket line which had been thrown out between them and the main line during the night. The mistake, however, was soon made known. They rejoined the command in the morning (9th) in front of Alsop's. Sergeant Wilson cut a pole upon which he displayed the colors of the Sixth Alabama captured the night before, but before the detachment rejoined the regiment, one of General Crawford's staff officers compelled him to turn it in as one of Crawford's trophies (?).

Toward evening our pioneers dug rifle pits for our pickets, which we were to occupy as soon as finished. A strong skirmish line drove in the enemy's pickets about dark, and occupied these pits. The enemy made a night attack, our men came flying in, and the "Johnnies" took possession of them, keeping up a constant fire and annoying us, as they were but a short distance from our line and much larger than our own force. On the 10th, our regiment with the Fourth Michigan about 11.30 A. M. were ordered in a single deployed line of battle, to charge the enemy with fixed bayonets and retake the pits at all hazards. We did so, but at a great sacrifice. Our line swept forward at a run, and with a wild hurrah, drove them out pell-mell. Our loss was about eighty men in a brief moment of time.

After driving out the enemy, we advanced still further, until we found ourselves within fifty yards of their breastworks, which were just inside the woods. A murderous flank fire was kept up on our left, and a sweeping fire of canister and shrapnel down the road, which cut our line. Our company and some men from others, finding the pits full, had crossed the road, and without shelter were lying flat on the edge of the woods, exposed to the terrible fire.

Johnny Kimball was behind a small pine tree watching for a shot at their cannoneers. "I see him," said he, and raising his rifle for a shot, exposing his head at the same time, fell, with a ball crashing through his lungs. A sharpshooter had got ahead. "Tell them good-bye! Give it to them!" said he. He was buried at Belle Plain.

Another was shot in the ankle. He crawled into a pit and lay there until about ten o'clock at night. Our brother offered to carry him in on his back, the stretcher carriers being in the rear, but his dread of being hit again was so great that he refused. Late in the afternoon, the companies in the rifle pits were relieved, but no relief could reach those who had crossed the road. About noon our brother was sent to cross the road (Brock Road) to the right, and communicate the dangerous position of these men, and get some relief. Crouching for a supreme effort, he darted forward at full speed. The entire rebel line opened. The balls flew all about him; one sung by his face, seared and burnt the eyelid, and closed his eye for several days.

Several pierced his rubber roll, and his escape was miraculous. (He was mentioned in Colonel Tilton's report of this battle for bravery.) Sergeant Eastwood, in attempting to do the same thing later, was instantly killed, and it was not until about 10 o'clock at night that one after another crept in from this spot of death. Sergeant Wilson, who had captured the colors on the night of the

8th, was killed in the charge on the pits. Capt. Ben Davis, who had captured the "Johnny" and sent him to the rear, sauntered up to the rifle pits on the morning of the 9th, near where they crossed the road, to take a look at the enemy's position, was picked off by a sharpshooter, shot through the breast, and died on the 11th in a house nearby. General Sedgwick was killed also on the 9th,[3] near the same spot and in precisely the same way. His body was taken back to Alsop's House. Our losses thus far since leaving the Rapidan had been 2 officers and 118 men out of a total of 254.

All night our brother moved up and down the line of rifle pits in the peach orchard of Spindler's, shaking and keeping the men waked up, that they might be prepared for any charge of the enemy to recapture them, but beyond the usual spluttering of the pickets, all was quiet. Wednesday, May 11, we held on; there was not much fighting on our front, but on our left it was desperate and incessant. A work was thrown up to cover the men from a shell fire. On the 12th, our line advanced in the center. We occupied the pits and supported the movement, and the battle raged fiercely on our left, where the Second Corps had affected a lodgement in their work sat McCool's. It commenced raining.

A charge was made from our lines by the Ninth and Thirty-second Massachusetts, and Sixty-second Pennsylvania, but it was unsuccessful, and they came back in disorder, having suffered a severe loss.

At night we were again ordered on picket to reinforce the line and prevent the enemy from following up their advantage. There had been no opportunity to bury the dead, and as we lay in the pits on Friday the 13th, under a constant fire, expecting death

---

[3] "Uncle John" Sedgwick (1813–May 9, 1864), West Point 1837, a Mexican War veteran. He was heard to say immediately before he was killed by a sharpshooter, "What? Men dodging this way for single bullets? What will you do when they open fire along the whole line? Why are you dodging like this? They couldn't hit an elephant at this distance." Meade wept when informed of Sedgwick's death. Grant, upon hearing the news, repeatedly asked, "Is he really dead?" He apparently considered Sedgwick's death worse than the loss of a division.—2019

momentarily, the putrid corpses, black and festering, lay all about us, repulsive and sickening, but from which we could not escape. The enemy fortunately made no attack on the night of the 12th, as it was stormy. The pits were half filled with water.

At night we were relieved by the Ninth Massachusetts, and were marched back about two miles in a drenching rain, to near headquarters. A few of the men pitched tents for shelter, among them our brother. He fried some meat, made some coffee, and was about to enjoy his comfort when orders came to move at once. We started in less than five minutes, leaving our supper untasted.

The Fifth Corps was ordered to * march this night, as a part of the projected plan for a move by the left flank, by cross and wood roads, via Shelton's and Landron's, and thence to Landron's ford on the Ny River, about half a mile distant; then crossing it, to move over the fields and across the country to the Fredericksburg road, near the Harris house, and after advancing along that road, recross the Ny, form on the left of the Ninth Corps, and attack on the Fredericksburg road at 4 A. M. on the 14th.

All night we trudged, knee deep in soft mud, through dark forests and swamps, over stumps, across creeks, fording the Ny where it was nearly three feet deep. Every precaution had been taken to mark the route by posting mounted men, and building small fires, but it proved impracticable; the fires were put out by the rain and mist, leaving us to flounder about in the inky blackness of that dreadful night. In spite of all efforts, men lost their way, and after lighting matches to regain the road, many threw themselves on the ground exhausted. Not an object could be seen even at arm's length, and after stumbling and wading about all night, but 1,000 men were up at the appointed hour, and the attack was given up. We lay in line all day, while log breastworks were being put up. Toward evening we expected to advance. There was some shelling. It rained all night.

The following, short note written by a friend, was the first news, of our brother's safety after the battles from May 5th to the 13th.

Near Spottsylvania Court House,

May 11, 1854.

At the request of Walt, I write these few lines; have just seen him and regiment; he says tell (them) I am all right so far; the regiment has been in every day of the seven, since the fight began, and is covered with glory. We have lost 121 men, and now number but 130 present. I would write more particulars, but he only wished to send news of his welfare. *** Hopeful for the success and triumph of our cause, and that Walt may be spared to the embraces of his friends.— Geo. F. Stone.

Our letters now describe the events of those days:

Near Spottsylvania Court House,

Friday, May 13, 1864.

I hardly dare to write you of my safety, lest I am a dead man before the vain assurance reaches you; many wrote yesterday, and today they lie a few hundred yards from here, stiff, blackened corpses. I just live, father, and that is about all; I have been lying in a rifle pit for 24 hours, during a continued rain, and with the severe cold, enemy's bullets, and the deep mud and water, not mentioning the cramped position of my poor body, you may imagine my present position.

Our corps is holding this advanced position as a ruse, while all the rest of the army (save a small reserve back in the breastworks) have departed on a grand movement.

This is the 9th day of uninterrupted fighting, the most fearful and protracted that has ever taken place on this continent, no doubt. We have lost hosts of men, and so have the rebels, I trust. Over half of our regiment have been shot away, and the rest are perfectly used up.

Company H went into the first day's fight near Jacksonville (where "Stonewall" died) with 12 men; today it numbers 6; Leroy has lost his right foot; John S. Kimball will die; Lieut. Steele has a bad wound in his right shoulder. These are all the casualties which you have special interest in. I had a rubber blanket (a new one) shot through and through, and my blouse pierced once. In a grand charge upon the enemy's rifle pits last Tuesday by our regiment and the Fourth Michigan, my cheek bone was badly burned by a passing bullet; it came near finishing me. We took the pits, and following up to the woods, were met with grape and canister, and discharges of rifles and fell back to the pits.

It was a gallant charge, and our Twenty-second covered itself with glory, but at the sacrifice of 84 men, a terrible loss, considering that we advanced as skirmishers. I never expected to see the light of another morning, yet alive I am. In falling back, I happened to step into the very pit where poor LeRoy lay, with a bullet through his ankle; he was hit while advancing, and had presence of mind enough to crawl into the pit for safety; I did everything I could for him, even at the risk of my own life.

I offered to carry him to our breastworks on my back, but he dared not risk it; besides, the strain of his ankle hanging down would cause such pain. At last when our regiment was relieved, three of us offered to carry him in on a blanket, but fear of being shot again caused him to doubt, and at last when he concluded he would risk it, I looked for the men and they had fled.

I then left him, promising him the earliest attention, and the first thing I did when I got within our works was to get two stretcher men to go after him, and soon had the pleasure of seeing him safe. I met him with a drink of water in my hand; we gave him Whiskey, and fixed him up generally, and he seemed quite comfortable when he was started to the rear; his foot was taken off the next day, and he is now at Fredericksburg.

I cannot write the particulars now of these terrific times I am in; I shall write you all about it sometime. Are not our veterans fortunate? They have not yet arrived. Good-bye! I shall fight tomorrow with a stout heart, bent on success.

On May 13, 1864, the First Massachusetts Heavy Artillery, in which were our eldest brother and a cousin, was under orders to move and join the Army of the Potomac under General Grant. Our cousin in a letter dated says:

Fort Craig, Va.,

May 14, 1864, 3.25 P. M.

We received orders last night to join Grant's Army of the Potomac as soon as possible. We shall probably start tonight. 'Bully for us,' I say! Perhaps we may sing another song before long; but just give us a sight, and I think we are all right. I have packed my trunk, and shall send it to your care. We are all aware of the fortunes of war. I have made some remarks on things in trunk, providing for the worst; but take no notice of them for the present.

You may think me foolish in regard to the disposal of things, but I go in for being forehanded.

P. S., Noon, Sunday.

All 'falling in'; go to Alexandria; take transports for Fortress Monroe; so reported; expect to join Butler.

May 15,

4 o'clock P. M., Sunday.

My dear Aunt: We are off!

The regiment marched to Alexandria, 5 miles, and embarked on transports for Belle Plain, where it arrived on the 16th and bivouacked on the ridge near the landing.

It was assigned to the Second Brigade, Gen. R. O. Tyler's Division of provisional troops, made up of every command that had arrived or was arriving at this point as reinforcements for the troops at the front. Colonel Tannatt of the First Massachusetts Heavy Artillery was assigned to command this brigade. It was composed of the Second, Seventh and Eighth New York, and First Maine and First Massachusetts Heavy Artillery. General Grant wrote General Tyler on the 16th saying: "I must have the whole of your command here by tomorrow night at farthest," and urged him to "forward what troops he had at once."

The organization of the division was incomplete, but on the 17th the regiment started, and marching through Fredericksburg, arrived at 2 A. M., on the 18th, and bivouacked about one mile to the left of the Fredericksburg road near General Grant's headquarters, but at 6 o'clock moved one mile and took up a position in support of a battery (McKnight's [?]), on the right of the road. It had marched about twenty-three miles. It was a muggy, muddy morning, and as this fine looking body of new (?) troops, with their clean uniforms and equipments, marched by the "Brown House," the inquiry was frequently made at the head of the column by the groups of old soldiers, "What regiment is that?" "First Massachusetts Heavy Artillery," was the reply. After the column had marched by awhile, someone would again ask what regiment it was, only to find it still the First Massachusetts Heavy Artillery. The strength of these heavy artillery regiments, of from 1,800 to 2,000 men, struck the Army of the Potomac with surprise. A single regiment was larger than one of their own brigades. The regiment was jeered at and called "Abe's Pets," "Paper Collars," "Band-box Soldiers," etc. After the fight at the Harris house an old soldier came over and said "Well, you can fight if you did come out of the forts." It was frequently shelled during the forenoon. At 4 P. M. it marched up the road about two miles, and bivouacked in the woods for the night.

At 2 P. M. on the 19th it marched two miles to the Harris farm, and massed in front of the house in support of a battery. At 4 P. M. the enemy was reported in the woods in its front and advancing. Companies F and D were deployed, as skirmishers, and soon became engaged. The First Battalion, Major Rolfe, was ordered to the support of the line. It was soon followed by the Second Battalion, Major Shatswell, on the right of the First. Both became heavily engaged. Ewell's Corps, in making a reconnaissance in force through the woods toward Fredericksburg, for the purpose of ascertaining whether our army was still moving to their right, and perhaps with a view of striking the immense supply trains parked along this road, had run into this division.

There was a great stampede of trains, camp followers, etc., and the enemy was close to headquarters of the Army of the Potomac. The regiment stood up to its work like veterans, and for a time it was alone opposed to Rhodes' entire division. It had punished him severely, and had nearly succeeded in repulsing him, when about 6.15 P. M. Birney's Division of the Second Corps came to their assistance, followed later by the other two divisions of that corps and a portion of the Fifth Corps. The enemy was soon driven across Ny River with heavy loss.

The engagement lasted until about 10 P. M. The regiment went into this action with 1,617 officers and men. Its loss was 2 officers killed, 15 wounded, 53 enlisted men killed, 297 wounded, and 27 missing. Unfortunately, at the beginning of the battle, there was lack of room for proper deployment, and amidst the confusion and excitement of this, their first battle, and the dense smoke in the woods, one wing of the regiment overlapped the other, and a few men were killed and wounded by their own line.

This battle was called the Battle of the Pines by some, by others Harris' Farm and the Battle of the Ny, as it was fought but a short distance from the Ny River. The regiment remained on the field all night, returning to the bivouac of the previous day at 10 A. M. on the 20th.

On May 14 we (Twenty-second Massachusetts) were ordered to get our coffee and sleep. At 7 P. M. the regiment was ordered with the Fourth Michigan and Sixty-second Pennsylvania to support Battery D, Fifth U. S. Artillery. The enemy shelled us as we went into position, but fortunately with but little effect, as we were under cover of several ravines.

On the 15th we were joined by about twenty returned re-enlisted veterans, who were received with many manifestations of joy. It was unusually quiet all along the lines. At 6.30 P. M. we were ordered with the other two regiments of the brigade to move in rear of Ayres' Brigade as a second line. We remained here until 8 P. M., when we moved back a short distance and bivouacked.

Our letters continue (scraps of paper in dim pencil):

Sunday in the Field,

May 15, 1864.

We are enjoying a day of rest, according to the commandments, which sometimes are overlooked in this warfare; I write in good spirits today. I feel confident of victory, and although I am weary in body and mind, and have endured everything terrible, night and day, I am still quite cheerful, and of good courage. I believe you would hardly know me at this minute; my face is very thin, and covered with a heavy growth of light whiskers, the skin underneath tinged with dirt, well baked on; my cheek bones and nose are pealing, and my countenance is well browned by the sun; my clothes are torn and muddy, my elbows are out, and my knees are visible, and my general appearance not at all prepossessing.

Yet I possess a treasure within, the requisite of a soldier, viz.: a sense of right, and an ability. I believe I was never tried so before. I know I never fought so hard before and with such a determination, and if I should be killed, father, in the next struggle (perhaps tomorrow), you will have the satisfaction of knowing from all in the regiment that I have been at my post continually. I know the Colonel and Major will have a good report of me.

As I said in my last, I cannot now write particulars of the nine days' fight; I have not the mind, time or opportunity. Friday night we left our last position (near the rifle pits, where we lost so heavily), on the road to Spottsylvania Court House, where General Warren failed to obtain a position to support our occupation of the Court House by stupid mismanagement.

He marched our division from the Wilderness (where we had fought three days), all Saturday night (a week ago), and in the morning, instead of halting us and pushing forward fresher troops, kept us tramping and rested a whole .division four hours. Many of our men were sunstruck when we reached the contemplated position to be held, and without any preparation, two of our brigades were sent in, and we were to support them; they were driven back with slaughter (the enemy having reached there first), and our own brigade was flanked while trying to retrieve the fortune, and save the few batteries that were in position.

All the rest of our corps were too far back to do any good, and we lost what we fought for. It was only after the most desperate battling that we gained the ground lost again, dug our pits, and held them during Sunday afternoon, Monday, Tuesday, Thursday and Friday; every day was a battle, and we suffered heavily. Friday night our brigade was relieved (having been at the front every day), and we were marched back two miles in a drenching rain to corps headquarters.

Sergeants Haseltine and Abbot of [Company] H and myself pitched a tent for the first time, fried some meat, and made coffee and were about to enjoy our comfort, when orders came to move, and we started in less than five minutes, leaving our supper untasted; all night long we trudged, knee deep in soft mud, through dark forests, over stubs, stumps, across creeks and one river three and a half feet deep (the Ny), and arrived here at 4 o'clock A. M.

Here we are awaiting developments; on a neighboring hill the rebs can be seen distinctly near the Court House. The position we lost and failed to obtain afterwards by severe fighting the rebs took advantage of, and they recovered Spottsylvania from that very base.

We shall be at it again soon. I want you to save me every one of the papers with accounts of the battles, so that I may see them some time. Please inform Mrs. Haseltine that Charlie is safe. The veterans have not arrived; only 6 men left in Company H. Nickerson lost both legs, and had to be left at old hospital, it being dangerous to put him into an ambulance. He was probably taken prisoner; he cannot live. Johnny Kimball is dead; he was a noble fellow. *On to the fight says Carter Walter, and Heaven give us success!* hove to dear mother; tell her not to worry for me *** if I should fall, I desire to lie in Virginia, in the very grave my comrades dig for me (if I should be so fortunate after death), it will signify at least amidst the haunts of treason, that there are men who stand by their country, and they may take warning.

It is always well to speak of these things, for we know not what may happen, and you know my life is in danger. Good-bye! and do not be overanxious; have faith, and trust well that I may be saved.

On the 16th we drew rations and rested, and the next day we threw up some rifle pits, went on picket duty at night, and were close up to the enemy's line.

May 17, at 8.30 P. M., the lines were moved 500 yards to the front and intrenched.

Our letters say:

In the Field,

May 17, 1864.

We have not moved since I last wrote on Sunday; we are having quite a rest, and if reports be true, the rebels will be compelled to break through our lines, they are so completely environed and cut off. I have heard the same 'Hooker Proclamations' before, and give no credit to such favorable stories.

Sunday evening our corps was drawn up in three lines of battle, and there was every indication of an advance upon the enemy's lines in front; it was occasioned by a threatened attack upon our right, Burnside's Corps, and in that case we were to advance and flank the rebs.

All was quiet, however, at 7 o'clock, and we slept upon our arms; it rained all night. Yesterday we drew rations, and rested finely. Last night Burnside was to attack, and we were to shell on the left, but all things were quiet along the lines at sunset, and another night was passed in peace. Today is very warm, and the men are employed in cleaning their guns, and preparing for anything that may happen.

Our bodily strength is much recruited and when the army moves again, it will be with renewed strength and vigor. It is reported from Army Headquarters that we have sustained a loss of 45,000 men; isn't it frightful? I saw in a paper yesterday that the Fifth Corps was attacked the night of the 6th in the Wilderness, and forced back; it is untrue. The Sixth Corps was turned at our right, and we fell back to avoid being flanked, but advanced again toward night.

At midnight we all marched into our breastworks for a feint (to draw on the enemy the next day), and early in the morning we were eyewitnesses of the success of Jack Griffin's ruse. On came the rebs, and our skirmishers were driven in; the enemy came out of the woods in line of battle, and then Griffin was in his element. This greatest of artillery officers opened some 25 pieces, double shotted with grape and canister, and spherical case, and the rebels were literally slaughtered; the balance went back lively.

The next night we left for Spottsylvania, where we have been having our fiercest fighting. Our chaplain came up last night. He said that LeRoy was quite cheerful when he went to Fredericksburg; he bore up nobly, and had as much firmness as is possible for one to have. A terrible accident occurred a few moments ago; a man in a regiment nearby carelessly discharged his gun, and killed one man, and wounded two severely in another regiment. Such occurrences are frequent.

Will Blanchard was killed and Brainard badly wounded in the late battle. I am losing all of my old army friends; how fortunate I am in still being spared; we have no mails as yet; how I long for a letter.

We were on picket on the 18th, and from 7.30 to 8.00 A. M. there was a heavy artillery duel between our batteries which caused us all to hug mother earth closely for our lives; again from 9 to 10 A. M. We were relieved at night, and were now in the second line about 1,000 yards from the enemy, the court house plainly visible. We spent a good portion of the 19th cleaning ourselves, for we were a rough, dirty looking set. Toward evening, about 5 P. M., there was an attack on our right. We* formed line to receive them, and moved half a mile to the front in support of our two batteries, D, Fifth United States, and Ninth Massachusetts, but did not get engaged.

In the Field, 1,200 Yards from the Enemy,

May 19, 1864.

If you will buy the *New York Herald* of the 11th and 12th, and read the account of Sunday's fight, the 8th of May (by the Fifth Corps), you will gain quite an insight into that part of our battle, aided by the corrections I make, and the rough plan I send (pencil sketch). I observe that the newspapers report very erroneously, and the reports are deficient as a general thing, in the true facts of this campaign; they are full of the most exaggerated blunders, and many absurd stories are circulated; I wonder at it.

Even 'Hendricks,' our Fifth Corps correspondent, has been strangely misled; the matter is here: they dare not come to the front for reliable information, but derive their knowledge from those at the rear.

I will not particularly mention the battle of the Wilderness, only so far as to say that the attack upon the Fifth Corps, Friday night, is a mistake; nothing of that kind occurred.

Saturday night, we marched all night long, and passed the cavalry at Todd's tavern; a mile further on we came in sight of our Third Brigade skirmishers. Soon we were shelled slightly, for the rebs had scarcely any artillery in position (having, as I believe, only just arrived there in any force), and upon the double quick we went into line of battle, where I have indicated the artillery upon our left. The skirmishers were driven in. We commenced firing; the rebs charged and we scattered their center in all directions, but upon our left, in a diagonal line from the road (dotted line), they came down upon our battery and left flank, and we left very coolly, having protected our artillery until it limbered up and went to the rear. Our little regiment saved Martin's Battery, Third Massachusetts.

All day long we fought backwards and forwards, fiercely contesting every inch of ground; at night our pickets occupied a rail fence this side of the peach orchard, and we slept on our arms on the wooded ridge.

We threw up breastworks, and the next day, Monday, we were fighting off and on all day, neither side gaining in front of our division.

In my opinion, if we had not been ordered into the fight Sunday morn, we might have held the hill at first, and driven the rebs; we did not have force enough at hand; Warren kept too many back resting, while he shoved the First Division through.

When we left the Wilderness that Saturday night, we left six of our companies out on picket; they were withdrawn early Sunday morning, and started in command of Lieut.-Col. Herring of the 118th Pennsylvania (Corn exchange), to join us; they failed to do so, and in the attack on Sunday night, on our left, by the Pennsylvania Reserves (who have acted miserably throughout the fight), they formed, with other battalions and regiments, the second line of attack.

The reserves broke and came back through them, with the exception of those they stopped with the bayonet, and the rebs came on exultant; our boys hugged the ground near the top of a knoll in the woods, and the bullets passed over harmless. When the 'Johnnies' got within ten feet, up rose our Yanks, and there in the dark they slaughtered and captured about three or four thousand of our enemies.

Our boys literally hauled them in, and a B. Company man went to the rear with 37 alone. Captain Davis (?) captured a rebel flag, Sixth Alabama, and not the Thirty-second Massachusetts as reported. He was not killed, however, until Monday, after he had rejoined the regiment; he sauntered up to our works to look at the position, and a sharpshooter picked him off, shooting him through the right breast; he was unconscious until he died during the forenoon.

While fighting that Sunday night, he went up to a reb, and, said he, 'who are you?' 'In my place, where I have been all day,' was the

517

reply. 'Well,' said Davis, presenting his six-shooter, you had better change places now, and go to the rear!' pointing to our lines. 'Johnny' dropped gun, and vamosed under guard.

Sergeant Wilson ordered a man to surrender—a rebel officer; he refused, and a C Company man shot him dead; Wilson took his sword as a trophy; our boys covered themselves with glory and honor. Tuesday, Wilson was shot in the charge upon the pits, and lost his life. Monday night we dug pits in front of the peach orchard, and the picket line of our division was to occupy them as soon as the pioneers completed them; the Thirty-second and Ninth Massachusetts were out. The rebs made a night attack, and our men came in 'fluking.' Tuesday, the Fourth Michigan and the Twenty-second Massachusetts were ordered to take the pits at all hazards, and hold the edge of the woods if possible; we did it at a great sacrifice, and upon the left of the road our left flank, Company D, rested, the pits being already full; I was with them.

The Sixth Corps failed to connect with us; we had no shelter, were within fifty yards of the rebel breastworks, a rebel flank fire upon our left (where an officer was waving a white flag, the villainous devil) and a sweeping fire down the road preventing our recrossing it, together with a front fire of canister, grape and musketry; 1 never was in so hot a place.

How I escaped I know not; more than half of us there were killed and wounded; we could not do anything but lie close and await our doom. Our regiment was relieved in the afternoon, and this company never got in until 10 o'clock at night, and Sergeant Eastwood of D was shot dead by our own men while crossing the road; it was a fearful place.

I ran the gauntlet about noon, to communicate the situation to Major Burt, our brigade officer of the picket; I should think I had a haversack of bullets thrown at me. I escaped, however, and found Captain Cunningham (Thirty-second Massachusetts) used up in the second rifle pit, first line; he could do nothing.

In the fourth rifle pit I found LeRoy, and after we were relieved I had him brought off under fire; we held our own rifle pits, drove the enemy from their own in the edge of the woods and this ended the day.

Wednesday, there was no fighting in our front, but upon our right and left it was desperate. Thursday, the Thirty second Massachusetts and Sixty-second Pennsylvania charged in our front, and all along the center the line advanced; we lost scores of men, but gained nothing in the center.

Our regiment supported and occupied the pits all night Thursday; all day Friday and at night we stayed there in mud and water. Saturday, we were relieved, got some rations, had a bite to eat and drink, and at night started for this place. You know our operations here up to Tuesday; on that night we advanced, and before moving, we had a magnificent line of works constructed, and we are now back of the second line.

Yesterday morning there was an artillery duel; we had to hug mother earth well. Today all is quiet so far as I know. Our pickets are quite friendly; they exchange papers and shake hands; both sides are plainly visible to each other, and walk about on rifle pit and breastwork apparently unconcerned and with perfect safety.

The Thirty-fifth Massachusetts is nearby; Ed Morrill is in a hospital sick.

The First Heavy Artillery is a mile back; many of our boys have seen John. I dare not go for fear we may move; if it is possible I shall see him soon. They have thrown away everything on their march. George Steele, who has just got back from Washington, where he has been nursing Bill, saw all of them, and gave us some ludicrous accounts of these 'heavies.' He made all manner of sport of the New York regiments. *** Colonel Sherwin was kicked by a horse near Brandy Station while on the march, and is in Washington; he feels dreadfully not to be with us, so all those who have seen him say.

We are directly in front of Spottsylvania Court House now, and the enemy has an impregnable position there; what's up, no one knows! Grant is moving troops to the left today. Go in and win, 'U.S.,' say I! We will back him up as well as we can. Emerson and Lovejoy are at Belle Plain guarding prisoners; they sent me mail yesterday. I had lots of papers come in the afternoon. Wasn't I happy, reading and talking of home.

I never saw a pleasanter, more good-natured set of boys than we were. Home is our constant theme. *** Tell Mary A. I have just seen

519

Sam Appleton for the first time in two weeks. All musicians have been ordered away from the hospitals in the rear to join, or to be near the troops; he is looking hale and hearty; not much like the poor chaps at the front.

On the 20th all was quiet along our line. We rested during the day, and at night the bands of both armies favored us with music. The following day, Saturday, the 21st, about noon, we suddenly left our breastworks, which we had held as a blind while the Second Corps was swinging out for a fight with anything it might meet—and in full view of the enemy and marching to the Fredericksburg and Richmond railroad—followed it for a few miles, then taking the road, and marching some fourteen miles farther, bivouacked for the night at 5.30 P. M., near Catlett's, having passed Guiney's Station and crossed the Po River at Guiney's Bridge, near Guiney's, where "Stonewall" Jackson had been carried to die just one year before. The advance crossed the Ta River at Madison's Ordinary [variety store].

We were on picket, and on the day following took the advance along the telegraph road about 10 A. M. There was some skirmishing all day; we were halted several times and we took some fifty prisoners; about 4.30 P. M. we halted near Dr. Littleton Flippo's and bivouacked. Our pickets and scouts reported the enemy as passing all night on another road, and it is now known that Longstreet's Corps was but a mile or so from us, hurrying to outstrip us in the race to Hanover Junction, which he supposed was our objective. Our advance skirmished with the cavalry all day, and at 1 P. M. they were met in some force at the crossing of the Mat River, near Dr. Flippo's.

On the 23d, after marching some miles, starting at 6 A. M. we turned to the west at Mount Carmel Church about 11 A. M.; after marching about a mile we took a different road from the rest of the column, turning to the left through plantations, the Ninth Massachusetts in advance as skirmishers, and after scouting up and down the North Anna River for some time, about 3 P. M. we arrived at Jericho's Ford.

We were in the lead and, without waiting for the pontoons to be laid, we at once forded it and scrambled up the steep, rugged banks. The stream here was about 150 feet wide, with bluff banks from 50 to 75 feet high. Our little regiment—now much reduced in numbers, having scarcely one hundred men—was deployed as skirmishers. General Warren was at the ford hurrying us across, and General Griffin upon the bluff diligently posting artillery to cover our crossing. We advanced rapidly through the woods, then through an open field, and into a belt .of woods again, our line of battle directly in our rear. We had not proceeded far into the last woods before we ran into the enemy's skirmishers.

The corps had now crossed on the bridge, and formed a line in our rear. The skirmishers of the other brigades connected with ours. We threw up a light breastwork near Fontaine's house, the line of battle doing the same, and awaited further developments. We hadn't long to wait. About 5 o'clock we saw in the distance, back of the road, the rebel flankers coming from the south (Hanover Junction) parallel to our line, and back of them could see the dust of a heavy column advancing with them. In the woods to their, rear was a train of wagons going in the opposite direction "double quick." Soon the flankers halted, faced toward us, and advanced. Then came their line of battle. We exchanged a few shots and fell back to the line, and the battle became general. Our artillery, now in an excellent position, threw solid shot, shrapnel and canister over our heads into the rebel line, doing fearful execution. The fight roared and raged for two hours. It was a gallant fight— this battle of the North Anna River—and as General Lee afterwards stated that he sent the corps (Hill's) to pitch upon the Fifth and whip us, we felt pretty proud after driving them off. We went on picket at night, and many amusing as well as thrilling incidents took place.

Our lines were so close that men in wandering about got into the enemy's lines and were captured. A rebel colonel came into our regiment and was sent a prisoner to the rear. Our colonel was walking but a few yards from our line, when a "Johnny" seized and was about to shoot him, the colonel in the meantime struggling and grasping the rebel's rifle, when a man from our company, Private George Brown, sprang out and grappled with him, and, several following, the contest was soon decided.

We remained in our breastworks during the 24th, and toward evening, about 6 o'clock, marched to Noel's Station on the railroad, where we again built breastworks. All night long the boys were running trains up and down the road "on their own hook," having captured many hand cars. On the following day, at 5 A. M., as much of the road was destroyed as possible, and we started off on a scout in a southeasterly direction to find and watch the enemy. We found them across Little River. At 6 A. M. we halted on Anderson's plantation and skirmished with them during the day. Later we were sent on a reconnaissance, and at 3 P. M., having been relieved by the Seventh Massachusetts, joined the brigade, which we found in line of battle, the enemy being in position on the south side of the river.

Our letters say:

South of North Anna River,

May 25, 1864.

Our regiment is out on a scout, while the division is endeavoring to advance. Our reserve is in a large field, and as George Stone is with me, and will try to get this letter to the rear if we have an engagement, I will try to write you a few words concerning myself and doings for the past four days. George does not have to go to the front, being adjutant's clerk and unarmed. Skirmishing is going on all about us, and there is a small river directly in our front, emptying into the North Anna; our cavalry is trying to effect us a crossing; I can scarcely credit the report that they are across; however, we may all be before noon, then for Hanover Junction and the South Anna River.

Last night we heard that Hancock had possession of the junction; there was heavy firing in that direction all day yesterday.

We camped last night on the Virginia Central R. R., and all night the boys were running trains on their own hook; we captured any number of hand cars. But let me tell you of our advance from Spottsylvania, and how Grant compelled Lee to fall back without attacking him and how we have been marching toward Richmond parallel to the rebel forces, until now we are within thirty miles of the rebel capital.

We started Saturday afternoon last (the 21st), leaving our breastworks (the rebels looking at us) by the left flank; we marched to the Fredericksburg and Richmond R. R., followed it for two miles, then went west, and afterward south; we rested for the night at a point within seven miles of the North Anna River, stopping at 10 o'clock P. M., having marched some fourteen miles.

I went to bed tired; the next day, Sunday, we marched a few miles further. Monday we scouted about everywhere, up and down the river, and at 4 P. M., we forded it a mile above Noell's Station; our brigade was ahead, and the Twenty-second in advance. General Warren was there to hurry us across, and he appeared very nervous and excited.

General Griffin was upon the bluff, posting artillery to cover our crossing; as soon as our brigade was fairly across the Twenty-second was deployed as skirmishers, and we moved forward through the woods, then through a field, and into woods again, our lines of battle directly in our rear. We had not gone a great distance into the last named woods before we encountered the enemy's skirmishers, and after a short fight, drove them, losing two of our men and killing one of them, and wounding several. We advanced to a rail fence, and halted in full view of the Virginia Central R. R.

Our corps, some wading and others crossing the pontoon bridge, ran across, formed a line in our rear, and skirmishers joined our line on the right and left; our brigade built breastworks. About 5 o'clock we discerned in the distance, back of the road, the rebel flankers coming from the south, parallel to our line, and back of them could see the dust of a heavy column advancing with them; in the woods to their rear was a train of wagons going in an opposite direction, double quick.

Soon the flankers halted, faced toward us, and advanced; then came their lines of battle, and in a short time the whole of A. P. Hill's Corps was upon us.

Our regiment, after exchanging shots, fell back to our lines, and the battle became general; our artillery was in position, and threw solid shot, shell, grape and canister over our heads into the advancing rebels. The battle raged for two hours. Our whole right flank was turned once (composed of the old First Division, First Corps, now our Fourth Division) and a panic taking place, defeat seemed certain, but we kept the center, new troops were put in on the right, and at 8 o'clock the rebel line was totally repulsed. It was a gallant fight; I never was scratched even; our regiment lost one killed, nine wounded, and three missing; we have had some hard marches, and I am about played out. Have not changed clothes since I started; will write again soon. I have seen John and Lewis; they were in a hard fight on our right at Spottsylvania and did splendidly. John is looking finely, with the exception of a burnt nose. Severe thunder shower at night, with thunder and incessant lightning.

The First Massachusetts Heavy Artillery remained on the field near the Harris house all night, and at 10 A. M. on the 20th returned to its bivouac of the previous day. At 1 A. M. on the 21st, it moved on the road to Milford, passing through Bowling Green at 11 A.M.

It arrived at Milford Station; crossed the Mattapony River and bivouacked about one mile beyond at 2 P. M., having marched about thirty miles.

On the 22d were ordered to throw up breastworks about two miles from Milford. At about 6 A. M. on the 23d marched to the North Anna River, sixteen miles, and bivouacked at 3 P. M.; lay on their arms all night in reserve. On the 24th lay in the rifle pits near Taylor's Bridge, while the Ninth Corps crossed the North Anna, under a heavy shell fire, 1 man killed, 11 wounded. At 4 P. M. left the pits for the purpose of crossing the bridge, but were ordered back, and resumed its position in the pits.

On the morning of the 25th crossed the river on pontoons, having moved at dark the previous night, and marching about one mile beyond, went into camp and commenced throwing up rifle pits. At 8 P. M. moved and recrossed to the north side of the river, and marched toward the Pamunkey River.

On the 27th moved at 3.30 A. M. and massed in a large field about one mile in rear of first line. Pioneers sent out to destroy bridge above enemy's position, 2 men wounded. At 12 M. marched down north bank of the river, and continued the remainder of that day and night until 2 A. M. of the 28th and bivouacked, having marched twenty-two miles; at 9 marched again, and crossing the Pamunkey on pontoons at Nelson's Ferry, below Hanover Court House, bivouacked, and were engaged in throwing up breastworks the remainder of that day and night. Its position was about three miles from the river, at the extreme left of the line.

It rained hard during the 26th, a very heavy storm striking us during the afternoon, and after destroying a portion of the railroad, by twisting the rails, we (Twenty-second) crossed it and about 8P.M. started to recross the North Anna. It was dark, muddy and rainy. After recrossing at Quarle's Ford, about two miles below Jericho's Ford, we drew rations and halted several hours for the Sixth Corps to pass; about 3 o'clock on the 27th resumed our march. Taking a road more remote from the river than the other corps by Moncure's plantation, we plodded along all night, passing through Saint Paul's Church, where we halted at 6.40 A. M. to make coffee, having made but ten miles. We went through some large plantations, one said to be a part of the estate of John B. Floyd, ex-Secretary of War of the Confederacy. Our route was now through a most luxuriant country, never before trodden by either army. We crossed several small creeks, among which was Dorrill's.

Droves of hogs, flocks of sheep, and plenty of poultry offered tempting inducements to the multitude, which could not be resisted. The severity of the march had caused unprecedented straggling, and at no time had we ever seen such unstinted foraging.

Everything disappeared before the knife and gun, until the whole immediate country was swept clean. After making coffee we kept on until about 5 P. M. The regiment came in with 44 guns after a dreadful march of twenty-one and a half hours, having covered over thirty miles.

Our bivouac was about one mile from Mongohick Church, which was about ten miles from Hanovertown on the Pamunkey River.

As we marched from our bivouac in the early morning (28th) the sun was in its glory. Peach and apple blossoms filled the air with their perfumes, a thousand sweet birds warbled their glad notes of welcome, the green grass and tree-covered hills surrounded us; battle flags, equipments and rifles, reflecting in the light, spoke of the martial array of war.

Bands played their sweetest airs, and although we had left many of our comrades back in the peach orchards, near Alsop's and Spottsylvania Court House, and on the sloping banks of the North Anna, yet refreshed by a good night's sleep, everyone seemed in good spirits, and with buoyant step we started at 5.30A. M.; passed through Mongohick Church at 8.30, then Brandywine, and at 11.30, Plaindealing and estate of Enfield, lately belonging to Colonel Dabney, deceased, and about noon we crossed the pontoon bridge at Dabney Ford, Hanovertown on the Pamunkey, seventeen miles from Richmond, eight miles from Hanover Court House, and seventeen miles from "White House."[4] We formed in two lines, one mile from the river and made barricades. This was in front of Dr. Brockenborough's house, and our line extended from the Totopotomy to Mrs. Newton's. Orders were issued that all stragglers would be fired at by the marching column, and all foraging must be discontinued, upon penalty of death. Here we had two extremes on two different days. We thought they would have met anyway, for we were now in a country entirely destitute of subsistence, the old Peninsula route being on our left. Just a year before a bummer belonging to the old Irish Brigade was met near this spot by an officer. He had a hen and a goose dangling from the end of his rifle. "What have you there, sir!" angrily exclaimed the officer to the culprit "Oh! Bedad, S-r-r-r," said Pat, "this goose came out as I was wending my way along pacably, and hissed at the American flag, and bejabez I shot him on the spot." "But the hen, sir!" said the angry officer. "The hin is it, So-r-r-r?

---

[4] Plantation of Martha Custis Washington.

Well, begorra, I found this hin laying eggs for the Ribil Army, and I hit her a whack that stopped that act of treason on the spot, too."

Our letters thus describe our movements (scraps of paper in pencil):

Across the Pamunkey River,

May 28, 1864.

After I wrote you a few days since, we moved further to the front, and were in position a day and a half, losing one man, killed by sharpshooters. At 7 o'clock Thursday night (the 26th), we left secretly, and marched rapidly to the river, where we recrossed two miles below our first crossing; all night long we kept on our way, resting at 6 o'clock for coffee. On we went, through a most luxurious country, never before trodden by an army; such foraging I never witnessed; we plundered without stint, and completed our inroad only when everything had disappeared before the gun and knife. No special orders were out, and as the severity of the march caused unprecedented straggling, the whole immediate country was swept clean of living animals; rich and poor alike suffered.

We went through John B. Floyd's estate; his widow seemed a fine lady, but that was no barrier; the women are the fiercest devils of them all, and we just told them so yesterday.

I kept up with the regiment, and came in with it (44 guns); at 6 P. M. I supped on fried pork and chicken, coffee and hard bread.

For a long time our marching seemed unendurable, but I bore up and astonished my own expectations by exceeding them. As we came within sight of the river, first our course seemed in the direction of Hanover Court House, by way of Little Page's Bridge (you will see it on the map, I think), but we soon struck off in a southeasterly way, and crossed here, eight miles south of Hanover Court House, and within eighteen miles of Richmond.

I am on the Peninsula now, and I hope to be nearer the rebel capital on the morrow. Heavy cavalry firing is in our immediate front; the Fifth and a part of the Sixth Corps are over, but where Hancock and Burnside are, no one can tell among us. Our marching is about over, I hope; the ten miles this morning is about the last hard one, and now for the grandest opportunity of the war, which I have the proud honor of figuring in to a certain humble degree.

There is an individuality in this crisis that belongs to everyone here, notwithstanding the gigantic vastness of the plan and general purpose.

The poor Negroes were delighted to see us, and would have followed us gladly, had they been allowed. They had been taught lately that when we came along, we would mutilate and basely treat them, and 'dey is so mistaken,' they said. One poor woman told me that after she had refused to go to Richmond for safety's sake (according to General Lee's orders), that she might remain with, and help her mother; her master beat her for it; he also struck her across the back with a hoe handle, almost breaking her back because he ran the point of his plow and struck against something she had failed to remove when clearing the ground the day before.

The brute found one of her children upon the floor, sick, and gave it such a kick that it died soon after, and we found it unburied in his barn, after the body had been laid there four weeks since, by his own hands; it smelt foul and cried to Heaven.

And yet the wretch would neither bury nor cause it to be buried. I believe he was insane with fiendish ugliness, and yet this man came from his house when we were acting as a corps of observation, and claimed protection as a Union man, because two or three of his hens had been killed, and some of his garden vegetables 'confiscated.'

We soon found out that he was a rebel commissary, a by-way convenience for the rebels, and his barn had one hundred and fifty bushels of corn in it, and his cellar was piled with smoked sides of bacon, such as the 'Johnnies' have issued to them. Oh! my, didn't we 'go through' him with a vengeance. Took all his butter, milk, meal and everything eatable, burned all his outhouses, and left him a wiser, poorer, perhaps a better man.

Today on the march an order was read that all foraging must be discontinued, and all stragglers would be fired from the marching column.

There we have two extremes in two separate days; the old Peninsula route on the left, I hope it will not prove a McClellan, Gaines' Mill affair.

As we marched out from our bivouac in the early morning, the scene was particularly suggestive; the sun was in its glory, and banners, equipments, and all the martial array of war shown with resplendent reflection; hills surrounded us, and the bands were playing their sweetest airs; all seemed to speak a triumphant journey.

Emotions I never had before rose within me; it seemed as though I never appreciated such a sight before. We arose so refreshed and rejuvenated by the night's rest, and everyone seemed so happy, and in such good spirits, I was elated, and started with an excitement I never experienced before; it was a stimulant throughout the march.

I fear, however, if it had continued until tonight, I should have lost its main strength. While marching yesterday, I was many times completely prostrated, and it was with difficulty that I came to time after a halt. While marching and suffering, I imagine the contortions upon my face, forced by the binding strap tightly drawn, and my sore feet, were indications of my feelings and thoughts within; I wondered often, as I stooped over to gain strength of limb in climbing a hill, if my body was always to be so deformed, and my step so devoid of grace and elasticity.

I wondered if some time I should not be unfettered by the burdens now so wearisome and injurious to mind and body. If I can only escape the deadly bullet, I can yet regain proportionate form and an easy carriage which I have now certainly lost by long marches, and heavy loads, fatigue and toilings; I have a good substance to live upon, and I trust I may be permitted to live through these times.

I would rather die than lose two legs and two arms; yes, than lose a leg and arm; I will die before I am taken prisoner, and death will come to one or two Johnnies at about the same time, in case of such an extremity. I wish that I might get a slight wound, that I might be otherwise safe. In case it were my lot to live, I would not lose the chance of going through the battles yet to come, before my time is out. Marching I hate; I would rather fight.

Walton, Lovejoy, and Emerson are still away, and Willey and Allen are back. Carlton's account of the Wilderness is very good as a general account; the Fifth Corps commenced that, but his account of the Spottsylvania battle is most ridiculous and absurd and not in the least authentic.

He places the Fifth Corps on Sunday, on the Todd's Tavern (Brock) road, in the wrong position; we occupied a line on the right of it, and the left of our corps rested on the right side of the road, the Second on our right, the Sixth upon the left; he has us on the left of the road altogether.

He omits to state that our division opened the fight, with Martin's Battery, our Third Brigade as skirmishers, Second Brigade as lines of battle, First in the rear hurrying up, Second, Third and Fourth Divisions way back.

It was not until we had gone through a fierce fight, and had been driven back, that our First Brigade and these divisions came up, and we reformed line with them, and fought successfully with the enemy until night, all the corps now engaged.

He says Crawford's, Robinson's and Cutler's Division, forgetting to mention Griffin's Division; such things cut. I wonder if he will find out that the Twenty-second Massachusetts first crossed the North Anna, and that 'Jack' Griffin's Division opened that fight, and bore the brunt in the center, when the two flanks were forced back, and rebs were in our rear; so much for 'Carlton.'

Tonight our bugles are blowing 'tattoo,' the first time since we started. Our cavalry are steadily driving the enemy. I know one thing terrible in this campaign, which I mention; wounded privates ride in army wagons to the rear, while officers take the ambulances, and many (ambulances) are doing nothing. I wrote Wednesday the 11th of May, after the fight in which LeRoy was wounded. I hope LeRoy can get home very soon.

We went on picket at night. At 7 A. M. on the 29th we moved about three miles to the front and then took a crossroad to the left and formed a new line. There was some skirmishing, and the cavalry ahead were having a sharp fight near Hawes Shop, and in the direction of Mechanicsville. At 1 P. M. we started again and ran into the rebel pickets at 3 P. M.; at 4 P. M. we formed line of battle, faced to the south on Mr. Via's plantation, where we bivouacked for the night' near or on Teally's plantation and made a successful raid for bacon and potatoes, and had the pleasure of eating a few ripe strawberries. We were now across the Totopotomoy.

A little incident occurred here, which seemed to show how, in the midst of want and the exigencies of war—a brisk skirmishing, liable to cut us off at any moment—little things elevated and inflated our spirits and how it was emphasized in our letters. The hospital steward gave our brother a lemon.

Our letters say (continuous with the last in pencil):

May 29, 1864.

We have moved this morning about one mile and a half, and are now about three miles from the river (Pamunkey), in the direction of Mechanicsville and Gaines' Mill Farm; the whole army is now here, and we are resting for the Sabbath apparently.

Our cavalry drove the rebs yesterday a long distance; everything is quiet, and we await movements. They say that Gaines' Mill place has been destroyed by our men. I hope so, and am glad of it if it be true; he is an old reprobate *** you will observe I use all sorts of paper; what I do get I either beg, borrow or steal; my stamps are all gone too; I am bound to write as long as I can borrow.

'Ezra' of the sharpshooters was shot the other day while scouting for General Griffin. He exposed himself to get a shot, and a bullet pierced his brain *** my health is excellent, and I can now eat hardbread, pork, and drink coffee with a keen relish; I depend a good deal upon sugar, and manage to have a good supply with me generally. I have had enough of the kind to eat on this march. Grant feeds well; I have smuggled some blankets and ponchos; 1 only need a rubber now, and am on the lookout for one.

I secured one yesterday, but found an owner in Captain Rock, who claimed it. I hear that Sweitzer and Hayes have secured brigadiers' commissions. *** I had a luxury today; our hospital steward came up yesterday from the ambulances, and gave me a lemon; one of the drummers got some ice, and we had a dipper of lemonade. 'Depart trouble!!'

Tell Kate I have thought much of her exhortations, but I am not afraid to die, even suddenly upon the battlefield; I haven't much fear of anything or anybody, I believe.

The thought, I know, is frightful to some; to live, to see; to be in full possession of vigorous activity; to have health, joy; to feel that you have lungs to breathe, a heart that beats, and a strong will that

531

reasons; to speak, to think, to love, to hope; to know that you have a dear home, a father, mother, brothers, sisters, and then as you press on to the glittering glory of victory before you, to be suddenly pierced with death's messenger, and feel yourself sinking into oblivion, even before there is time to cry out; it is certainly terrible to be launched out into such an abyss of unconsciousness, and be ushered into a new existence; but tell K. that with all my faults and nonprofessions I fear not; why it is I cannot explain. It is my nature. Send me the best and most reliable map you can find. I want one for reference very much.

On May 29, Tyler's Division was broken up and distributed among the other commands. The First Massachusetts Heavy Artillery was assigned to the Second Brigade (Col. T. R. Tannatt), Third Division (Gen. D. B. Birney), Second Corps (Gen. W. S. Hancock), marched at 12 M. and joined its new brigade, and went into position near and immediately in front of Salem Church, on the left of the Richmond road, where it helped them to build works. At 6 P. M. it left this position, and advanced along the road to a point near Totopotomoy Creek, where it formed line and built works just to the right of the Richmond road. Not being able to procure shovels or picks, bayonets and tin plates were used.

The brigade was now composed of the following regiments: Fourth and Seventeenth Maine, Third and Fifth Michigan, Ninety-third New York, Fifty-seventh, Sixty-third and One Hundred and Fifth Pennsylvania, First United States Sharpshooters and First Massachusetts Heavy Artillery. The latter numbered 67 officers and 1,585 men.

Our letters (small scraps of paper in pencil) say:

Across the Pamunkey River,

Sunday, May 29, 1864

I saw John this morning. I ascertained he was near by, as I marched along, and sought him out. I found him sleeping after a long search for Company E. It seemed like finding a regiment in a division bivouac. He was looking quite well. I left a paper and R's. letter with him.

It was most amusing to go through the 'First Heavy' after their fight of Thursday, the 19th; they were very much excited, and were pleased beyond measure; they talked like wild men. They get no news whatever in that regiment, no mail, no papers, no anything1 John says 'we are not broken in yet!' I have not seen him since Sunday.

The wagons failed to get up, and they were out of rations. They worked all night, and held these works all day of the 30th.

On the 31st the "First Heavy" was held in reserve until 9 A. M., when it moved to the front and, advancing a heavy skirmish line, crossed Totopotomoy Creek and formed in line, closed up on the First Brigade, and there lay all day under a heavy artillery fire from the enemy; loss 5 men wounded and 3 men missing from the picket line at night. During the night, preparations were made to withdraw, and at daylight on June 1 the regiment moved back to the position it had left on the previous morning, on the north side of the creek, now become the front line, where it lay until 9 P. M., when it again changed to the left of the road, a little to the south; it remained here until nearly daylight when it marched toward Cold Harbor.

After marching the remainder of the night and until 2 P. M. on the 2d, it reached Gaines' Mills, and bivouacked about half a mile from Cross Roads. On this march the old homestead of Stephen Hopkins of Revolutionary fame was passed; a neat white cottage occupied by descendants of the "Signer," and standing near the site of the Hopkins' mansion. The house where the old patriot lived was in ruins, only a pile of brick and stone remaining to indicate the spot where it stood.

The weather was very hot and the roads dusty. The regiment lay massed in the woods until about dark, when it was moved to the left of the army and formed in rear of the First Division.

The night was dark and stormy; the rain fell in torrents; the thunder echoed, and reverberated louder than artillery; bright flashes lit up the scene; the wind swept in fierce gusts, and the trees bent and snapped in the faces of the men, while all the streams rose and swelled into raging torrents.

The contemplated attack was postponed. On the 3d, which was dark and gloomy, we moved one mile to the right under a terrific fire of shot and shell, were posted on the right of the Eighteenth Corps, and lay in reserve all night and until the afternoon of the 4th, when the division joined the corps and the regiment occupied its position of the previous night.

It remained there until the afternoon of the 4th, when it moved after dark about two miles to the left, and into the woods it had left on the 3d, and massed in support of the Ninth Corps. This was on the Shady Grove Church road, near Barker's Mill.

At dark on the 5th, it moved a short distance still further to the left toward the Chickahominy, connecting with the First Division.

The brothers were now pretty close together, and very near to where our brother of the regulars had been when with the headquarters of General McClellan just one year previous, at Dr. Curtis' house.

A new line was established, running toward the Chickahominy, which was fortified immediately upon the arrival of the Second Corps. On the morning of the 6th all were busy strengthening the works they had constructed. Pickets were within talking distance, but by mutual agreement they ceased firing altogether. Here the regiment remained until the 12th, doing fatigue and picket duty, and more or less digging and strengthening of the works in their front, being under fire at times. Loss 2 killed, 13 wounded and 16 missing.

Our cousin, Lieut. Lewis Powell Caldwell,[1] writes from this point as follows:

Headquarters First Battalion, First Massachusetts Artillery, Tannatt's (2d Brig.) Birney's (3d Div.), Hancock's (2d) Corps, on the Old Gaines' Mill Battlefield

June 8, 1864.

I find another opportunity to write to you, and for fear that John cannot for want of an opportunity, I will do so. For the last four days we have been under fire most of the time; more quiet today; we changed our position last night and threw up a rifle pit directly under the nose of the rebel pickets, which we occupy today without molestation. Have found an opportunity to wash face and hands today. I have had many narrow escapes since writing you last;

---

[1] Cousin Louis Caldwell of the 1st Heavy Artillery died on June 17, 1864 of wounds received before Petersburg the previous day. He'd only shortly before made lieutenant rank (military records, 2019).

almost think the bullet is not made that goes into this chick. It may come along, yet I do not know it.

I saw some Maine troops today (17th Maine), got into conversation with a lieutenant and found him to be a brother of Miss Sparrow visiting at your house when I was at your home. *** I have received no letters since I left the forts. *** Love to all, and accept this from your nephew with love. *** John is looking and feeling well.

On the 30th the Twenty-second Massachusetts moved out early, in advance of the brigade as skirmishers, the Fourth Michigan in support.

We were on the Shady Grove Church road. We drove the enemy steadily before us for some hours. It was hard and constant work. The enemy at first retired slowly. After falling back about two miles, they came to a standstill, having some buildings and rail fences to shelter them.

We were ordered to charge, and fixing bayonets, we went bounding out of the woods with a yell and soon drove them out in every direction, captured a number of prisoners, and late in the afternoon we had driven them several miles through the woods and open toward Mechanicsville. Our loss was 4 killed, 15 wounded, including 1 officer wounded. About 10 o'clock at night we came back a mile or so, were relieved by the Ninth Corps, and drew rations. The following day (May 31), we lay in a beautiful, shady grove, enjoying complete rest. The charm of summer was all about us, and nature never looked so green and smiling. General Grant passed by us; many did not know he was near until the cheering commenced, then all joined in the tremendous hurrahs for the "Old man."

At 12 M. on June 1 we moved to the front, in rear of Ayres and Bartlett, facing southwest. There was continued firing along the line, and at 6.15 P. M. there was smart skirmishing, and later there was a heavy fight. We were ordered up to the support of our First and Third Brigades, where we lay in line of battle all night. On the morning of June 2 we moved up the road, further to the left, and were now resting, apparently in reserve for emergencies, near Bethesda Church on the old church road to Mechanicsville.

As we were upon the drive this morning, we met some of, our re-enlisted veterans returning from their furloughs. There was not much time for greeting, but as soon as we halted we met indeed, and hearty was the greeting between our boys and the "veterans." Alas! how brief. A box of cake and a package of candy was our remembrance from home, and was safely deposited in our brother's haversack for quiet enjoyment that night.

A heavy rain drenched us through late in the afternoon, and at night, Burnside, in attempting to leave his breastworks on our right and moving further to the left toward Cold Harbor, betrayed the movement by his pickets coming in too soon, and Rhodes' Division was ordered by General Lee to sweep down their entire line (Confederate). There was a fearful engagement, the enemy seeming to attack at all points.

Our brigade was moved at double quick to all unprotected parts of the line, and we were kept busy.

The enemy gained all the ground left by the Ninth Corps, but we checked their further advance. At 6 o'clock in the morning of June 3, we moved out as skirmishers from near Bethesda Church, with the brigade in line of battle in the rear. We had not proceeded far before we found the enemy strongly intrenched with artillery. We charged their rifle pits, carrying everything before us, and halted only when we had lost over one-fourth of our men, captured their rifle pits, the pickets, and got within one hundred and fifty yards of their main line of works.

We held our own in the edge of the woods, while our line of battle advanced obliquely to the right, where we lay all day exposed to a terrific cross fire from their batteries. Our line being somewhat in the form of a bow, their shells frequently came in our rear. One of our veterans whom we had so cordially greeted upon his return, Corporal Walton, was ahead while advancing. He was firing at the rebel cannoneers. Immediately he was struck by a ball in the chin. It passed completely through. He never said a word, but casting upward a most imploring look, passed into eternity.

Another veteran was shot through the heart, and fell a corpse. Our Captain (Baxter) was shot through the bowels, and died in a few hours in the hospital in the rear of the line. Our loss was 1 officer and 22 men. We buried our comrades, put up neat head-boards, and placed ourselves behind a small breastwork of logs and dirt. The bullets were flying thickly and from our shelter we could see the graves in plain sight. On the night of the 2d, while raining, our brother went to a small fire to make coffee. He covered up his haversack with a rubber blanket. When he returned it was gone and with it sugar, coffee, pork and the wedding cake and candy, which had made our mouths water in anticipation. There were always some with whom hunger knew no law, and they would pilfer. There was no clue. We were obliged to fall back upon the haversacks of the dead.

Among our number was a tall, straight, clean built, soldierly looking corporal, with light curly hair, fair, rosy complexion and blue eyes. He was the model of a neat, trim soldier, but he was unfortunately a great coward.

He had been promoted, reduced, "made" and "broken," until at last he had been given up as incorrigible. He never neglected an opportunity to skulk out of a fight.

He was a fearful stammerer, and when he became excited, this grew to be painful. In the advance across the open from Bethesda Church on the 3d, our movement was so rapid that he had no chance to "skedaddle." Our gallant little major was watching him with a keen eye. The corporal came to a small tree and sidling up to it, compressed himself to the flattest, thinnest bulk possible. The balls seemed to spit in from front, rear, and flanks, and the now thoroughly terrified man was going around the tree to avoid them. The imperturbable little major walked up to him with his six-shooter and dropping it upon him said: "Now, Corporal W— this is the first time that I've seen you at the front for many a day. Go right straight up, or I'll shoot you!" "M-m-raa-j-o-r-r," stammered the unhappy man, "I've b-b-bee-n round this t-t-tree s-s-seventeen t-t-times and I'll be d—d if there's any f-f-front to it!"

At 8 o'clock on the morning of the 4th, we advanced as skirmishers on a reconnaissance on the old road to Shady Grove Church. The enemy had retired during the night. We counted 22 battery horses which testified to the skill of our battery near Bethesda Church. At 12.15 we fell back to our old line again, and rested for the night, the order for an advance having been suspended.

Our brother in the Second Corps had been in the slaughter of Cold Harbor, a few miles to our left, where his regiment suffered severely, but he escaped unharmed. While we prevented the enemy from turning the right flank, the most obstinate and bloody fighting had taken place there.

On the afternoon of the 5th we again started out on another reconnaisance, deployed as skirmishers, and supported by the Sixty-second Pennsylvania. We had no sooner passed the picket line than we came in contact with the enemy's skirmishers. We at once charged and drove them for half a mile, where they made a stand behind earthworks and piles of brush. Here they were supported by artillery and a strong reserve. Orders came to charge again, but they were countermanded, and we fell back to the line of woods, where we made a stand and skirmished until dark. We then fell back inside our picket line. The enemy made two assaults upon our line during the night, but we repulsed them easily with slight loss.

At midnight we were routed out and spent the remainder of the night, and until 8 A. M. of the 6th, in moving about five or six miles to a position further to the left and rear, near Allen's Mills. General Griffin, as we passed by his headquarters, said: "Poor fellows, they ought to have four days' rest, but I can only give them one." We improved the day washing our clothes, and attending generally to personal cleanliness, where in the army, as elsewhere, it proved "next to godliness." We also contrived to have three square meals, and with plenty of rations, new, complete kits to replace the ones stolen, there was wrought a marvelous change in the morale and spirits of our hard-fought, hard-marched, dust and dirt-begrimed soldiers.

The night before we were plodding along, stepping every moment into human excrement, with bloody feet, sore toes, lame shoulders, shoes worn out, and with faces dirty and sticky, and bodies covered with "gray backs," we were indeed used up individuals. Once we stopped to drink, but the water was covered with the slime and filth of the drainings of the Fifth Corps.

How changed now! Although our shirts and stockings were washed in water that would nauseate a wash woman, and give a Troy laundress a nervous chill, yet we concluded that because of the exigencies of the service it would do for soldiers. On the 7th we moved about daylight, four miles in rear of the army, to near the Chickahominy, and held from the left of the Second Corps to Despatch Station, near Sumner's (lower) bridge, and here we remained in two lines of battle behind formidable breastworks until the movement to the James commenced.

The change of base having been effected to White House on the Pamunkey, and Tree from deadly strife and day and night battling, we enjoyed complete rest, reading over the battles and skirmishes which the newspaper correspondents at the rear had caused us to figure in, much to our amusement, sometimes to our indignation.

Were the true history of the War of the Rebellion to be compiled from such a mass of hospital records, and bird's-eye views of newspaper correspondents and straggling bummers ten miles to the rear, some of our veterans would feel like turning over in their graves and demanding a "new deal."

Our letters thus describe these events (scraps of paper, in pencil):

4 o'clock P. M., May 30, 1864

We have been skirmishing for seven hours; briskly drove the enemy three miles. We have lost 3 men killed, and 14 wounded, about 20 per cent of what we took in with us; we are diminishing our numbers rapidly; our lines have all advanced, our division in front. I know it is so, and 'Jack' Griffin would back me up in the statement if he knew I was writing; we drove them so fast that we were ordered to halt until the Ninth Corps joined us upon our right, and the Third Brigade upon our left. While resting, I write these few words *** Jim Abbott was wounded in the leg, a flesh wound.

Not a scratch yet, father; do I not bear a charmed life? I am thinking of you all tonight; I have finished my frugal meal of hardtack, soaked in coffee. It tasted good, but I am afraid that I shall not have that tomorrow. I am now getting short; we are supposed to have two days' rations from tomorrow, but the men have nothing.

We lost two days' 'grub' in that rainstorm at Spottsylvania; everything got wet and spoiled. Moreover, the men threw away their knapsacks in that charge, and have only their haversacks, which hold three days' rations. I hope to get food tomorrow; I have done well thus far. Much love, my dear father, to all; tell them as you read this that I am full of that spirit that leads to ultimate victory; I trust all feel as I do. John is somewhere on our right; I am constantly anxious about him; I hope he will be as fortunate as I have been *** no one in the regiment writes but myself, I believe.

Same night, or in the morning of May 31:

I am desirous to keep you fully informed, and at every halt I scratch off a word or two. Came back last night two miles to rest and ration up. Got your letter; my very first letter you have not yet received, from what you say. I wrote in it an account of LeRoy's being wounded, and my being in the pit with him, and getting him off; have you received that one? Your letter gave me intense satisfaction; I am in the best of health and spirits. Have got grub enough now, and am full of fight; depend upon it, I shall weather the storm. We are within thirteen miles of Richmond, and are steadily but slowly pushing forward with the utmost caution. I sit down by the roadside to say this much.

In pencil, May 31, 1864, within four miles of Gaines' Mill:

Your letter last night, it seems to me, is a model of a letter to a soldier, so encouraging, and so full of sympathy, subdued to a degree that occasions none of that blue feeling which is so often the result of home letters in time of battle.

I rejoice in such a letter; I wish all were so fortunate in having a father who writes the kind of letter that you do; I do actually rejoice in the one received.

It adds to my excellent morale and *esprit de corps*, and makes me a solid, substantial man, upon a firm footing. My first letter in this campaign gave you an account of our charge on Tuesday, May 10; of my narrow escape and the position I occupied; how I went back for the relief of Company D; saw LeRoy in the pit wounded, stayed with him, and helped him, and after we were relieved, saw that he was brought in, etc. Have you received that letter?

Baxter was out in an advance pit (rebel), and came near being killed; he had to play dead for a long time, so as to avoid being fired at; finally, just after noon, he, with those with him, ran the gauntlet, and joined Company D, as I have since told you in a letter, accompanied by a plan of Alsop's (?) (Spindler's) farm.

He is all right, and yesterday had command of the left wing in skirmishing, and did splendidly. When Haseltine, Baxter and Abbott joined Company D, they found Johnny Kimball there, he having been separated from the rest of H in the charge, and been in a pit to the right of the road. He had only gone over to Company D, because of a concentration of fire on him where he was; I fear he found it warmer still in his new place, and made a poor exchange.

He went to Company D just after I left, and before Haseltine and Baxter arrived there from the prison house of fire they had occupied.

You observe the big pine tree I indicated on the plan, at the corner of the road; Haseltine, Kimball and a sergeant (Campsey), of Company F, (in the pit with H. and B.), were on the watch there for a reb up the road, whom they had seen firing. Johnny K. cried out, "I see him!" and prepared to fire; Campsey saw the reb, and blazed away, but not quick enough, for the reb shot first, and the bullet pierced Johnny's right arm, near the shoulder, entered the right side, went through his lung, and came out on the left side of his back bone.

He fell like a log; the boys carried him to the edge of the woods in the shade, did all that they could for him, and waited for night; at dark (long after the regiment was relieved) they brought him within the front line of pits, and after they got within the breastworks they

542

sent stretcher men for him, and we soon had him on the way to the hospital.

As he was starting, I shook him by the hand; he recognized me and said, "Good-bye, boys, give it to them!' He was moved to Belle Plain, died, and was buried there; a noble fellow, a much loved comrade; words cannot express how much we miss him; all winter long, in camp, he has been a favorite with us, and as caterer for Company H was a special benefit to everyone. He could cook splendidly, and always delighted to get up something good for us. All his letters were burned; our orderly (sergeant), took his money and watch, but afterwards he sent for them, and they were returned; it is supposed by us that they are safe. Maybe LeRoy took his effects; this is all I know about poor Johnny, and I write this for the family's benefit; please read it to them all.

Haseltine has got the ambrotype of Ves Kimball, the one he sent to John lately; isn't it sad that these two likely young men, such fine specimens of farmer boys, such glorious sons for work, John and Gam, should now be lying in soldier's graves? Heroes they are, and lasting be the chaplets of memory that we all do weave so gladly o'er the places of their burial; we shall always remember them.

We are lying still yet; cannot tell when we shall be called to go to the front. This is the first time we have been to the rear since the campaign commenced. Our advance yesterday was only to obtain a position. Our division was massed and only a brigade line wide, our regiment in front skirmishing, and flankers joining our left. The Pennsylvania Reserves were to keep up with us, but they kept behind, were flanked, and ran like a flock of sheep; we were way out in front, with no connection on our left, and only flankers to prevent a surprise, and we came near being cut off.

If it had not been for fresh troops, who changed front and formed a line at right angles with us, we should have been overwhelmed. We were ignorant, however, of this state of affairs, and pushed on. Several times when we halted at open spaces, we could see in the distance heavy rebel columns moving to our left, and we sent word back to have our supports hurry up, and General Griffin sent word to General Crawford to push forward his lines, and connect with us; he failed to do so, and the rebs came down to the rear, of us, upon his flank, and drove him back.

543

At first our left connected with Sheridan and his cavalry, but the orders were changed, and the reserves were to join us, the Ninth Corps upon our right.

We got ahead of them all, and when someone asked General Griffin (in the hearing of Stone) if we were not moving faster than usual. 'Yes,' said he, 'there's a good regiment ahead.' At one time when we were advancing yesterday, the Thirty-second (Mass.), just back of us in line of battle, got excited and charged; the right went over us, yelling like fiends, and driving the reb skirmishers with a vengeance; the line was then halted, we were relieved, our ammunition being out, and the Thirty-second sent on picket.

Day, of Bradford, was shot in the groin while on post; I am sorry for him; he is a fine fellow. I have seen him often in this campaign; he is very cool and brave. I hope it is not a mortal wound. Today there is a great battle on our right; Grant evidently wants to get north of Richmond, and cross the James; he don't like the way of Chickahominy River and swamps, I guess.

Oh! the sorrowful families at home, who mourn the slain in battle, and the anxious ones awaiting the confirmation or denial of their fears; what sights of maimed limbs and scarred features will meet our eyes in the future, after the war is over; isn't it terrible?

The gallant Thirty-fifth Massachusetts, with its Company G (the only Haverhill company in the field (?)), is now a band of pioneers. They are so few in numbers (we number 106 guns), that they were detached on this duty. I wonder if the roll of Company G was called in H. if over two-thirds of its old members wouldn't answer to their names?

Scraps of paper, in pencil:

June 1, 1864.

Summer is with us, and there is a sense of beauty dwelling in the shady woods where we are; I wish we might remain just where we are all summer. I have read the New York Herald up to the 24th, and the Boston Journal of the 23d; I am perfectly disgusted with the newspaper reports and the editorials and column articles in regard to this fighting campaign; it is the Second Corps everywhere.

Even the commencement of the flank movement last Friday is awarded to Hancock, and yet it is a well-known fact that the Fifth

544

Corps moved from the breastworks at 1 o'clock P. M., and marched until 9 o'clock, crossing the Ta River, and we reached the North Anna, and crossed it first Monday, and fought a great battle there, in which, it is said, General Fee was wounded; I wish the truth might always be published.

Generals Grant and Meade just passed by; three cheers were proposed for Meade, no one knowing that Grant was there; I did not notice him; he must have been plainly dressed, and very humble this time in appearance. * * * There seems to be firing all along the line; nothing serious I guess. I'll write when I can.

Near 12 A. M.; on the march; where we are going, do not know; perhaps to battle.

June 2, 1864

There was a heavy fight last night, and we were moved up to the support of our First and Third Brigades. We lay in line of battle all night, and this morning moved up the road further, and have been resting most of the day, a reserve for emergencies.

There is evidently a movement on foot; perhaps a swinging to the left, by the corps. Indications are of such a character as to almost warrant the belief that such will be the fact before morning.

Ed Walton, George Lovejoy and Emerson joined us on the road this morning, while on our way to this place; we were on the drive when we met them, and could scarcely stop and welcome them; after we had halted, we met them indeed, and glad was the greeting between soldiers and veterans. The box of cakes and drops are in my haversack, untasted as yet. I contemplate enjoying its contents with the boys tonight. We are now on the stage road to Mechanicsville; yesterday, we were upon a more northerly road, to the same place, called the 'Dry Road.' Everything is perfectly quiet, and something is probably brewing.

Continuous, June 3, 1864

Just as I supposed it would be; last night was big with events. Burnside left his breastworks, to swing to the left, but his pickets coming in too soon betrayed the movement, and the enemy perceiving this, followed up, and swinging to their left, made a general flank movement in force; a terrible engagement was the result, the enemy attacking at all points; they moved our brigade at double quick to all unprotected parts of the line, and we were kept busy.

We lost one man, Richardson of the sharpshooters. The enemy gained all the ground that Burnside left, but we checked their further advance; the line is now very favorable to the rebels, being a right angle, they having the outside, with the advantage of an enfilade fire; I hope it will not result unfavorably for us.

Afternoon, 3 o'clock, Skirmish Line.

We have had a terrible time, losing 22 men, among them Ed Walton and George Steele killed, and Captain (Baxter) mortally wounded. Benner and Frothingham of H wounded; Haseltine and myself are safe; how, why or wherefore, I know not; amid such an iron hail of grape, canister and bullets, I cannot conceive how anyone escaped.

Only think, dear mother (I speak to assure her perhaps failing courage), your son was never touched. We advanced at 8 o'clock this morning; soon after I had finished my first paragraph of this day; our regiment and the Fourth Michigan, deployed as skirmishers, and the Thirty-second and Ninth Massachusetts, and the Sixty-second and Twenty-third Pennsylvania (the latter a new regiment, dismounted cavalry), armed with Spencer rifles, 1,200 strong, forming a line in our rear.

We carried everything before us, and halted only when we had lost one-fourth of our men, and got within 150 yards of their breastworks. We held our own in the edge of the woods, and silenced all their batteries, while the line of battle obliqued to the right, and drove the enemy.

We lay in our places all day, subjected to cross fires, and their shells in our rear; we were in the edge of the woods, and our line like a bow in shape (pencil sketch); we suffered heavily on that account. Walton was ahead with Haseltine; he was firing at the rebel battery men, and said he: 'We keep them down, Charlie!' Immediately he was struck by a bullet through his chin, passing completely through; he never said a word, but casting up a most imploring look, passed away.

Steele was shot dead through the heart, Baxter through the bowels. I have Ed Walton's watch and money; his diary was lost, but we know that money was due him, and I will try to collect it if I can, and live. Ed was a great favorite, the most amiable young fellow I ever knew, so modest and unassuming, and so even and pleasant in disposition. Could you have seen us shed tears as we buried him, your heart would have melted.

I will send his effects to his mother as soon as I can. Emerson and Lovejoy were in the hottest of the fight, and escaped unharmed. East night someone relieved me of haversack with valuable contents, sugar, coffee, salt, bread, meat and pork. I had just been to a fire to make some coffee, and as it was raining I covered my things over with a rubber blanket (which I had found in the morning); when I got back, my haversack was gone.

I lost everything, even the drops and wedding cake; was it not abominable? The boys were short, and were about pilfering; I have tried to find a clue to its whereabouts, but to no purpose. It is like a poor nigger woman I heard of a few days since. Some of our men took her bedspread, and she asked some of them very innocently: 'Gemmen, can you tell me whar my bedspread am dat yo people borrowed yesterday?' My prospects of finding the strayed or stolen property are about as good as hers. I haven't had a mouthful since last night, and haven't anything to hold my rations when they are issued.

I am now behind a small breastwork of logs and dirt which a few of us have constructed; the bullets are flying thick, but I manage to keep under cover. Ed's body is in plain sight, or rather his grave; we have put up neat headboards to each one of their graves.

Continuous, June 4.

I am finishing this June 4. The rebs left in the night, and our brigade went on a reconnaisance this morn, discovering nothing. We counted twenty-two of their artillery horses killed; they must have lost heavily; we did, I know, being the attacking party. The reserves have gone home; we have a new division in their place, also a new regiment in our brigade, Twenty-third Pennsylvania. Will write again soon. 'Captain Baxter is dead, so we learn from Colonel Sherwin just arrived. We shall probably move tonight to the left, a secret movement. The Ninth Corps has gone; I hope we will do better than they did. I have just got me a haversack, and have drawn rations; I am now in good trim. I went 'skiving' among the dead; oh! wasn't I hungry?

547

In pencil, near Cold Harbor:

Your last letter just received, and I am as happy as usual after the receipt of a home message. We left our position on the right last night, and were all night marching five miles. We camped this morn, and 'Jack' Griffin said, as we passed his headquarters, 'poor fellows! they ought to have four days' rest, but I can only give them one.'

I have improved the day, washing, changing clothes, and attending generally to my personal cleanliness. The teams have been up for the first time, and I have had a square meal this noon; there have been great improvements in son Walter this day; his face is cleanly shaved, and he is feeling exceedingly well. I believe only a bullet can possibly kill me. I have a complete kit now throughout; blankets, haversack, canteen, plenty of rations, new shoes, etc., etc.

I am in perfect condition. One day has wrought a complete change in me; last night I was plodding along, stepping into human excrement without number, tired, my shoulders lame, toes underneath bloody and sore, boots all out, body lice upon me, my face dirty and sticky, and in fact, a used-up man.

I stopped once to get a drink, but the water was covered with the slime and filth of the drainage of the Fifth Corps, and I was not much refreshed.

How changed now! I am a new man. I washed a shirt and a pair of stockings, and have them dry for my next change. They were washed in water that would make you sick to look at, but they will do nevertheless for soldiers. All your letters are received, also papers. The *Army and Navy Journal* accounts of the battle are very good; the writer confounds the Third Brigade of Griffin's division with another. The First is commanded by General Ayres; the regulars, and New York and Pennsylvania Zouaves are in it. The Second (ours) is commanded by Sweitzer; the Third by General Bartlett, formerly our division commander. I hear now that a reorganization is to be effected immediately. Carleton's letter from Fredericksburg is a very truthful and beautiful one, I think.

Continuous, Tuesday.

We skirmished again up the dry road to Mechanicsville, meeting with the enemy in a short time; we drove him a mile to his very breastworks; we lost 1 man killed, and 4 wounded, 1 from H. I escaped as usual; it was warm work; I was very much exhausted when I got back to camp. We marched soon after, accomplishing our swing better than the Ninth Corps. Will write again in a day or two.

In Camp Near Gaines' Mills,

June 8, 1864.

I am enjoying a complete rest today; nothing troubles me, no calls upon me from headquarters, no details, no outside pressure of business in any line of military duty; sweet repose to all in body and mind.

We are within two miles of the Chickahominy, Woodbury's Bridge, our left resting there, fronting Gaines' Mills, within nine miles of Richmond. We are formed in two lines of battle, behind most formidable breastworks; what is in the wind we cannot anticipate. Two days here and one at Cold Harbor have been the means of building me up wonderfully; I am in the best of health and spirits; I never was so well, although I am on the borders of the famous swamp, so charged with malaria.

I have plenty of rations, and clean clothes upon me, all the bodily comforts possible under the existing circumstances. The common inconveniences and repulsives features of the life are as nothing in my mind when I am possessed of these necessities, food and raiment; the mind too, is providentially provided for.

I have plenty of papers; I have been reading the *New York Herald* most of the day, up to June 3, and have laughed heartily over some of 'Hendrick's'[2] accounts of the Fifth Corps; especially his praises of the Pennsylvania Reserves, when flanked May 30, in trying to keep their connection with Griffin's division.

'They did splendidly,' he said; perhaps they did, but troops just going home have not done well yet, in this campaign, as a general thing; the First Massachusetts is the only exception I know of.

---

[2] It's unclear why the author puts correspondent Leonard A. Hendricks' name in quotes.—2019

At the first onset the reserves broke and ran; the rebs, like a huge wedge, pressed into the gap, and soon we were almost cut off; we won the fight, however. Please send me *Army and Navy Journal* containing the third week's accounts, also Carleton's, and the Boston *Journal* containing our chaplain's (Charles M. Tyler) account, or rather, two brief letters in reference to the Twenty-second; we have done well, and have gained a splendid name.

If I were a correspondent, and could write, situated as I am, accounts of this struggle in the Fifth Corps, I would throw Hendrick into the shade; I wish it was policy for papers to employ their correspondents from the ranks; they would, at least, be furnished with correct accounts.

As it is now, even if we should write voluntarily, the manuscript would be an old story by the time it reached its destination, for our letters even are detained now a long time on the way.

I have been thinking today of our comrades fallen; it seems as if all had gone; as I look over the regiment, I can only count twenty familiar, friendly faces (those with whom I associate) with us now, among the many score who marched away from our winter camp, May Day. It is so sad.

I have been presented with a lemon today; our hospital steward brought it to me from the hospital. Watson came from the trains and brought milk (condensed), butter and cheese; I have some farina also, and Stone and myself are luxuriating upon these niceties with the utmost satisfaction; you cannot imagine what a treat we are having; it will only last until tomorrow.

What do you think of the nomination of Fremont?[3] Will it result disastrously to Abraham if Grant should be nominated at Chicago? Will it be a hard task to defeat these two elements embodied in Fremont and Grant? My vote is for Abe if I live. Emerson is in my tent and Haseltine, Lovejoy and Appleton are nearby; all well except Sammy, who says his head aches; nothing serious I guess; he says it is because he is near the swamp; it is all imagination.

---

[3] John Charles Frémont (1813–1890) "The Pathfinder," explorer, soldier, and politician, had been the first Republican presidential candidate in 1856. In 1864, he ran for the Radical Democracy Party. Lincoln received nearly 76% of the Union soldier vote.—2019

Our corps is again reorganized; First Division commanded by 'Jack' (Griffin), a new First Brigade from Fourth Division, formerly First Division, First Corps, commanded by Colonel [Joshua Lawrence] Chamberlin, Twentieth Maine (in our Third Brigade). This appointment cuts out Tilton, the ranking colonel in the division. Generals Griffin and Sweitzer are much provoked at Warren's doings in the matter. Second and Third Brigades same as before; Second Division commanded by General Ayres who has his (our old First Brigade, after the very first, ourselves, was broken up) brigade with him, commanded by one of the colonels of the regiments composing it; the Third Division commanded by Crawford; the Fourth by Cutler. I like the corps and division commanders very much, also old Grant, although he is almost too much of a butcher, and has too little regard for human life.[4]

When I read of accidents by land and sea, north and south, and think of the lives lost by them, and remember the dead of the battlefield, I am truly appalled; what a gathering of human-souls before God.

Near Gaines' Mills,

June 10, 1864

We are now lying behind breastworks; the orders this morning were; 'Clean muskets, draw rations, get all the sleep possible, and be ready to move at a moment's notice.' If you ever heard of a more ridiculous farce, let me know, when and where. Akerman woke up his cook, and told him the orders were to 'get all the sleep he could.'

How Zeph Dean, Company C, did swear; so did Haseltine. ***

I send you a list of the killed and wounded of the regiment; you will see many familiar names. Poor Baxter, Walton and Steele fell in our last fight; it was a sad day for Company H. It has taken me so long to write the list that I have no time today to write a letter; I will write perhaps tomorrow.

The Ninth Massachusetts went home this morning; they were the happiest lot of men you ever saw; how I wish I were among the

---

[4] This charge against Grant was common at the time and for more than a century after the war. Historian Edward H. Bonekemper III has convincingly argued that Grant's casualty rates actually compared favorably with those of other Civil War generals, including Lee.—2019

number. In making up the list of wounded, 181, many are counted in twice upon field reports, having been wounded at two separate times; you will notice mine foots up less; many of the wounded have since died. Frank Holt and Anson Durgin are prisoners.

Mose Noyes skedaddled, and is in Alexandria, Acting Commissary Sergeant. Thomas Hoar has just got back to Company H; you will remember he was the man who had the shakes near Fairfax Seminary. I had to rule my list with a piece of cracker box; I could not stop to classify; I put the names down just as I remembered them.

About 35 men are missing. I will not put their names down; you only know one, Joseph Young, Company K; he was probably left dead at Alsop's Farm. I have put the names down more in order according to the date of their death or wound, than rank. Carleton's account of the North Anna fight isn't at all true; our division led. May 30, in the attack upon our flank, the reserves ran; yet correspondents say 'they did splendidly.'

John was over from the Second Corps this morning. He is just to our right; we are the left flank of the Army of the Potomac, and rest on the Chickahominy River. John is looking rough, but is feeling quite well. We had a cup of coffee, milk in it (condensed), some hard bread and raw pork together; quite a jovial time. I am so glad to be near him. John said the First 'Heavy' got a large mail night before last, but nary a letter for him. *** I sent Ed Walton's (killed) watch and pocket-book to his father by John. Please inform his mother so that she may know *** I concluded not to send them to her when I found Mr. Walton so near.

June 11

Nothing has transpired to disturb our continued quiet, except a few shells from the enemy having been lodged in our midst, causing some alarm, and doing some execution; one exploded yesterday in the Fifth Massachusetts Battery, killing three men and wounding five; when I hear them coming, I dodge them. I have actually learned how; at least I think I have. East night I received the papers that mother sent me. *** Carleton's[5] account of the North Anna battle was miserable.

---

[5] John Carleton Coffin of the Boston *Journal.*—2019

I guess he was at Taylor's Bridge with the Second Corps, and took the story of a Fourth Division straggler as authentic. Our brigade crossed first; our regiment advanced as skirmishers, drove the rebs, and we were the first ones who discovered the advance of the new lines of the rebs. The Fourth Division was upon our right; when they broke, we were in danger of being' flanked; the Ninth Massachusetts and Fourth Michigan ran. The Sixty-second Pennsylvania, Thirty-second Massachusetts and Twenty-second Massachusetts (rye had just been driven in as skirmishers, and rallied at the Second Brigade breastworks, the only ones then constructed) held their ground until the Third Brigade regiments came to our help; it was a gallant mill!

The New York Times correspondent wrote the best account I have yet seen. The accounts of the Pennsylvania Reserves in the battle of May 30 are most laughable; 'they behaved splendidly,' and yet I saw the woods full of their stragglers at night. The Fourth Division and Brigade of Heavy Artillery saved the day for the left.

I wrote a list of Company H, killed and wounded, and sent it to the *Triweekly Publisher* for publication.

An entire, complete list has been sent to the Boston *Journal*, but the editor does not see fit to publish it. All the boys are well, and ready to go where Grant says.

At the North Anna, the First Brigade, General Ayres, was upon our left, the Third, General Bartlett, in reserve. Did you see the yarn of the First Massachusetts man who fired his musket 250 times the last day of his service? His gun must have been a new pattern, cartridges plenty, and his regiment a long time at the front before being relieved. Such enormous stories, so contrary to common sense, must be discredited by an intelligent reader.

While waiting at the Chickahominy behind the breastworks, we visited our brother in the Second Corps to our right. We learned that the regiment had suffered fearfully at Cold Harbor. Four companies were temporarily detached to the Third Brigade, Second Corps, Second Division, but all were engaged in the charge on the enemy's works in the morning, and the repulse of the enemy in this night charge. It now appeared with frightfully diminished numbers, but the First "Heavy" had covered itself with glory, and could now be classed among the veteran regiments of the gallant old Second Corps.

From June 4 it had occupied the position where we found it on the Shady Grove road, near Barker's Mills, under fire nearly all the time.

Our cousin was battalion adjutant. We went to his quarters and took dinner with him, and from thence to the Seventeenth Maine, where we saw some of our old Portland acquaintances. But it was sad to look over these decimated regiments, and feel that among them, as well as in our own, containing so many of our friends, many were now dead upon the bloody battlefields from the Rapidan to the Chickahominy.

Upon our return, we found some kind friends from the rear had collected and brought up some commissary stores. Ham, potatoes, beans, pickles, .etc. It was a delightful surprise.

Dead horses, mules, and offal had been scattered all over our immediate vicinity, and between the lines were many dead bodies of both armies, unburied and festering in the burning sun. The country was low and marshy—sickness had increased in consequence. To correct this all were set to work policing, and efforts had been made to bring up large quantities of vegetables. Hence our good fortune when returning from our trip to the Second Corps. Good effects were at once manifest.

We had scarcely time to record this flying visit, and stow away our newly acquired rations, before we were ordered to move.

Sunday, June 12, 1864.

I have just returned from a trip to the First 'Heavy' where I saw John and Lewis. I found John on picket within 200 yards of the enemy; we could see them plainly. One of the boys had just exchanged a religious paper for a Richmond Examiner-, he 'played it' upon the 'Johnny.' The editorial in the paper was a perfect bombast, deriding Grant's 'feather-bed raid.' It will change its tone shortly. John said that the rebs in front were North Carolinians, and had agreed not to fire on our pickets. Just on the right of the First 'Heavy' a Virginia (Union) regiment 'was confronted by a 'reb'—

554

Virginia, and they were blazing away constantly. John was suffering some from pain in his bowels, and said he was troubled with diarrhea. I told him to eat cheese (if he could get it) and plenty of apples—green or otherwise. He will outlive it, I guess. I am never troubled that way at all and I eat quantities of fresh beef, and fried hard tack (all bosh about its being hurtful), Gene, to the contrary, notwithstanding. Lewis is battalion adjutant. I went up to his quarters and took dinner with him; had coffee, hard bread, tongue, and pickled cabbage. We went over to the Seventeenth Maine together. I saw several of my Portland acquaintances. Most of my friends in the regiment are either killed or wounded now; Fred Bosworth, Lute Bartel, and many others.

When I came back I found Watson and Stone had collected some commissary stores; ham, potatoes, beans and pickles. It was an agreeable surprise to us. If John comes tomorrow, I will astonish him with a good dinner; he said he should try to come. Lewis said he would answer M.'s letter today.

I saw Mr. Walton while up in the First Heavy, and told him all about poor Ed; he feels the blow keenly.

I think he (Ed) and LeRoy Kimball were our pets in the company; they were so good-natured, and withal so brave. Now we have lost them both, and we are sad over it. *** I have been reading the accounts of the Wednesday, Thursday and Friday battles in the New York Herald; Thursday, we were in reserve, but the 'heaps of rebels killed and wounded' I did not see; neither did the Fifth Corps regain the line that Burnside left.

Friday, we charged the reb line running parallel with the Pole Green Church road; we approached it from the Bethesda Church; we did not drive them from their entrenchments; we only compelled them to withdraw to them. Then it was that we lost Baxter, Walton, and Steele, and your humble servant came near 'going up' (pardon the expression). Next morning, the rebs had gone, and Sunday we skirmished up the same road (we had fought there the Monday before), and found the rebs thick, losing six men in driving them half a mile.

We move tonight, perhaps, across the river; you will hear from me soon.

It was the last seen of our noble cousin. About 10 o'clock on that same night, the twelfth, moving noiselessly, the First Heavy Artillery withdrew from their breastworks, near Barker's Mills, and marched to the left. It was bright moonlight, and the utmost caution was observed that the enemy should not discover their intentions. It marched via Barker's Mills, halting there until n o'clock, when the march was resumed, and with few halts or rests until daybreak on the 13th.

At 7 o'clock crossed the York River Railroad at Despatch station, and at noon massed near Long Bridge on the Chickahominy preparatory to crossing. The bridge had been destroyed, but at 3 P. M. the command crossed on a pontoon bridge, and marched all day via St. Mary's Church and Charles City Court House, bivouacking near the latter place at 5 P. M.

About 10 P. M. the command was moved to the vicinity of Wilcox landing where it was massed in a large field, and at 11 o'clock was moved a short distance; formed line of battle, and orders were received to throw up works, but they were countermanded and the command bivouacked for the remainder of the night.

At 9 A. M. on the 14th moved a short distance to Wilcox landing, and at 10 commenced crossing the James River to Windmill Point on transports and by 4 o'clock the Second Corps and 4 batteries of artillery were on the south bank. The command encamped for the day and night about two miles from Windmill Point down the river in an immense clover field on the Wilcox plantation, which is situated on the heights above the river.

About noon on the 15th marched some ten or twelve miles in the direction of Petersburg, arriving in the immediate vicinity of the Dunn House, near Petersburg, shortly after dark, just after the charge and capture of the same by the colored troops, and after much marching about and maneuvering during the night, finally took a position at daylight on the 16th on the left of the Suffolk turnpike, at the line of works captured the previous day (15th) by the Eighteenth Corps.

The right of the First Massachusetts Heavy Artillery rested on the Suffolk pike, with the One-Hundred and Fifth Pennsylvania on its left. The enemy s line was some 400 yards in their front, across a small stream which traversed a deep ravine.

Threw up works. Before sunset, about 6.30 P. M. a charge was ordered, and advancing across an open field, and through some woods, under a terrific fire of artillery, soon came upon the abandoned winter huts of the enemy; here the regiment met with such a fearful fire that it was impossible to advance further. Here it remained still under a most galling fire until about 9 P. M., in the meantime throwing up a temporary breastwork.

The regiment was then withdrawn to the position it had occupied before the charge. It had met with a terrible loss, 2 officers killed, 6 wounded, 23 enlisted men killed, 126 wounded, and 5 missing. Colonel Tannatt, commanding the brigade, was wounded, and Colonel R. McAllister, Eleventh New Jersey, assumed temporary command. Among the mortally wounded was our gallant cousin, First Lieutenant Lewis Powell Caldwell. Held position until morning of the 17th, when by a flank movement to the right and left, the enemy was compelled to fall back. Our lines were somewhat advanced on the right of the plank road leading into Petersburg, and two lines were now formed, the first near a piece of woods, close to the enemy, the second in rear behind the crest of a hill.

On the morning of the 17th the regiment was in a large field on the north side of the Petersburg pike, about halfway between the old farmhouse on the heights and the heavy strip of woods in front, where it had been ordered for the purpose of getting itself together after its terrible loss in the assault of the 16th.

During the afternoon a battery of 20-pounder guns (Parrot's) went into position on the heights, a short distance to the south of the turnpike, in a large field just below the orchard lying a little to the right of the old farmhouse, and near the breastworks thrown up on the morning previous by the First Heavy Artillery.

The topography of the heights afforded an excellent position for the battery. Petersburg lay to the left about three miles, its spires clearly outlined against the clear, blue sky. Just as the battery went into position, Gen. D. B. Birney, commanding the division, with his staff, rode up, and ordered the gunner of the left piece to give it an elevation of twenty degrees, and train it on one of the spires of Petersburg. As soon as the elevating screw was adjusted and the gun sighted the lanyard was pulled.

Every eye of the party was strained to witness the progress of the shell. It exploded at the base of the spire, just where the gunner had sighted it— shattered it badly, and scattered pieces in every direction. "Capital shot!" exclaimed General Birney as he rode away with his staff. So it was, and the verdict of the Heavy Artillery pronounced it one of the best shots ever fired from any battery on the height during the siege of Petersburg.

At nightfall, in less than twenty minutes after our letter was written on the 12th, the Twenty-second Massachusetts was in motion. We marched until 2 o'clock A. M. on the 13th, and halting near Tong Bridge, on the Chickahominy River, in a wheat field, for about two hours, we continued on, crossing the river on pontoons about 4 A. M., and moving immediately in the direction of White Oak Swamp, secured the White Oak Bridge and all the flank approaches about Riddel's Shop. At 6 A. M. we halted.

We lay in position all day, a part of the corps skirmishing heavily with the enemy, while the remainder of the army moved on rapidly toward James River. About 9 P. M. we again moved, marching all night until 3 o'clock on the 14th, then halted for about two hours near Saint Mary's Church. The Twenty-second was rear guard.

About 5.30 A. M. we again started, and continued on to Charles City Court House, which we reached about 10.30 A. M., and rested several hours. At 2 P. M. we moved again, and camped at night about a mile from the James River at Wilcox landing. On the 15th we awaited transportation across the river. We crossed at 8 A. M on the transport Star, landing near Windmill Point, and halted in a large bend of the river upon a large plantation, rich with waving grain, and green with the emerald tints of its smooth velvety lawns.

We remained here four hours, and meanwhile we had orders to go in bathing, of which delightful privilege we at once availed ourselves without urging. After washing our shirts, stockings, handkerchiefs, towels, etc., our brother swam about one-quarter of a mile out in the stream. We were anticipating a good rest when we were ordered to resume our march. We started about 3 P. M., marched all the afternoon and night, and after a severe pull of over twenty miles, halting at 9 P. M. at Prince George Court House for coffee, went on and reached Petersburg at 1 A. M. It was excessively hot. The road was filled with thick clouds of blinding dust.

We remained all day on the 16th, massed, and supporting the Ninth Corps which fought a bloody battle, lost heavily, and gained nothing. By obliquing, the enemy was enabled to pour in an enfilading fire and they broke and fled in great disorder. When this disaster occurred, many parts of the rebel line could be seen falling back. Batteries were limbering up, caissons exploding, etc. Later in the afternoon Birney's division charged and carried the outer works, losing many men, but were repulsed.

Our letters thus refer to the movements of the Second Corps, our cousin's death, etc. (in pencil):

Near Wilcox landing, five miles below Harrison's Landing, James River, Va., June 15, 1864.

I had scarcely time to finish my last letter to you, written last Sunday (12th), soon after a flying visit to John and Lewis. I had to close very abruptly; I was speaking of John's contemplated call on the morrow, when orders came to move at nightfall, and in twenty minutes after I subscribed my name, we were on the move.

We marched until 2 o'clock A. M., and rested two hours in a wheat field, and then moved on, crossing the Chickahominy at Long Bridge about 8 o'clock in the morning, and moving immediately in the direction of White Oak Swamp, secured White Oak Bridge and all the flank approaches; we lay in position all day, our entire corps, while the rest of the army moved on toward James River.

Tuesday night we again moved, marched all night, resting from 2 to 4, the same as the night before; and then marched the entire forenoon on the Charles City road, reaching Charles City Court House about 3 o'clock P. M., where we stayed an hour or two. Toward night we moved again and camped in our present place, within two miles of the river; we are now awaiting transportation across the river.

I imagine we are now to operate south of Richmond, and the first thing we have to do is to retrieve Butler's fallen fortune[6] by taking Petersburg. I am sorry we lost so many men in front of Richmond; I believe it was a senseless waste of human life. We might have tried this first. Grant's battle[7] a week ago Friday (June 3) was a defeat; we lost heavily; I believe it was a slaughter for naught.

It's no use for the *New York Herald* correspondent to exaggerate facts and claim a victory. I know better. I was in the fight, and saw blood flow like water; I know what I see with my own eyes, and I tell you, father, we gained nothing, and lost thousands of brave men. Poor Captain Baxter, Steele and Eddie Walton, besides four more in H, and twenty besides in the Twenty-second Massachusetts, were vain sacrifices on that terrible day; it was a fearful time. I shall never forget such scenes, never!

It is a most delightful part of Virginia that we are now in; the most fertile and luxuriant I have yet been in. Every kind of vegetation is thriving finely, and in this most beautiful month the fields of grain are looking beautifully. Nature is green here in all her loveliness.

Mixter was here today to see the regiment; he rode ten miles from Wilson's wharf, where General Hinks and General Wildes, with their Negroes, are entrenching for the protection of the James River line of transportation; he is adjutant of the Thirty-seventh U. S. colored troops.

---

[6] Butler's expedition at Bermuda Hundred, where he was bottled up, unable to move. This was a series of actions from May 6 to May 20, 1864.—2019
[7] Cold Harbor was fought from May 31 to June 12. The heaviest fighting was on June 3rd and included a second assault that Grant forever after regretted. The campaign was a Confederate victory.—2019

We enjoyed his visit much, he always being a favorite with us. Write me soon; send me the map, some stamps, and when you can, by mail, a light hat for army wear; my cap isn't shady enough this warm weather; my face is burned dreadfully, the sun is so blistering in its effects.

Night marching plays out more men than any other part of campaigning. I can stand it, however, after a fashion. Sam, Haseltine, Lovejoy and Emerson are quite well.

In pencil:

Before Petersburg, Va.,

June 17, 1864.

We crossed the James River yesterday morning early, in the U. S. Transport *Star*, and rested four hours on a plantation near a bend of the river; the corps had orders to go in bathing, and employ the time in avocations of cleanliness; we availed ourselves of the delightful privilege, I assure you.

I swam about a quarter way across the river, washed myself thoroughly, and enjoyed the time exceedingly. I washed two shirts, a pair of stockings, handkerchief and towel, so you may suppose I am prepared for a two weeks' march. We started for Petersburg at 2 o'clock P. M., and after a most severe march of twenty miles, reached here at 1 o'clock this morning.

It was excessively warm, the roads dusty, and there was a scarcity of water hardly equaled in our Manassas–Centerville march, a year ago at this time. I suffered much from thirst, and at one time my tongue actually hung out and was covered with dust; I could spit cotton without any exaggeration.

It was a very tiresome march and stragglers were very numerous; I had a mind to fall out several times myself, but pride, and some extra pluck, kept me up in my place. I have been deprived so much of sleep that it is with the utmost difficulty that I march at all nights; the whole campaign has been a series of night marches and bloody fights.

I suppose the cover of darkness is more favorable to Grant's flank movements; we are in possession of the outer works of the city, and the indications are that most herculean efforts will be made to enter the gates at the earliest day possible; the whole army is now drawn up before this place, and operations will probably be commenced immediately.

I have no doubt of its fall; what do you think of the movement? The Gettysburg campaign does not even compare to this in point of hardships and fighting. I am in good health, capital spirits, and am in as good trim every way as could be wished for, or at least expected. I have plenty of rations, blankets enough, my clothes are very dirty, and all full of holes and slits, but that is of no account; I cannot be too thankful when I think how fortunate I have been, and the favorable condition I am in now.

All the houses on the road have been deserted, and all such establishments that savor of wealth of Virginia F. F. V's. we burn and destroy; we are raising Cain with this 'Sacred Soil.' Love to all; will write again soon.

I had just seated myself against an old hut in the shade, and was writing, when a fellow on the top spit over the roof and you see the consequences below (a large tobacco stain). I said nothing, of course.

On the 18th a desperate effort was made to force the lines, but the enemy had had sufficient time to mark out another strong line in rear of the first which was as strong as logs, earth, etc., could make it. At 5 A. M. we broke camp and marched to the front, stacking arms in rear of the Second Corps, where we made coffee. As we passed over the ground at 8 A. M., advancing to the front and left, where the charge of the previous day had been made, dead bodies strewed the field. Heads were knocked off and completely scooped out, and the sights we beheld were sickening, almost disheartening.

We passed over the enemy's abandoned lines of works, some of them almost impregnable, with flanking forts and salients. When within half a mile of the new works, in front of the Norfolk Railroad, our regiment deployed in an open field near Colonel Avery's house in front of the brigade.

Our letters thus describe our movements:

Before Petersburg,

June 19, 1863.

My last letter I wrote the 17th, just after our arrival before this place. We remained all day in mass, supporting the Ninth Corps. They fought a bloody battle in the afternoon, and lost heavily, gaining nothing. By a strange misunderstanding, the line obliqued according to an order said to have been given, and the rebs poured in an enfilading fire from their works in the edge of the woods; the line broke, and fled in great disorder; the loss was very severe when the boys fell back.

If they had kept straight forward, the works would have been carried, for when the disaster occurred, many parts of the rebel lines were falling back, their batteries limbering up, their caissons exploding, etc. All this in front of where our boys made a steady pull directly for the center, when other parts of the line broke. When the men obliqued, the rest caught the impetus rearward, and away they went.

Later in the afternoon Birney charged again, and carried the entire works, losing many men, and slaughtering many Johnnies. When they 'got up to git' out of their stronghold, a whole single line of dead marked the discharge of our rifles. Our own men strewed the field in front of their batteries, and such a sight I never beheld as we passed over the ground the next morning.

Heads knocked off, and completely scooped out, leaving only the shell of the skull in some cases. We passed over three or four lines of heavy breastworks that we have wrested from the enemy since we came in sight of Petersburg, some of them most impregnable, with flanking forts and salients; those that the Negroes captured were very strong in position.

Yesterday morning the Fifth Corps moved, and when within half a mile of the rebels' new line of entrenchments, in front of the Weldon and Petersburg Railroad, the Twenty-second deployed as skirmishers in front of the Second Brigade.

Our orders were to move forward, double quick, and occupy a ravine directly in front of the Petersburg and Norfolk Railroad.

I know nothing in regard to the movements of the rest of our division, or the other, therefore, will only relate our own operations in the engagement of yesterday; we moved rapidly in the face of grape and canister, and the fire of the rebel skirmishers, who were just upon the brow of the steep overlooking the ravine.

563

Emerson got separated from Company H in running backward, and joined the right; he was struck within twenty-five yards of the ravine; Sergeant Allen says he was struck in the side of the head; I think from the swelling in his left eye that he was struck in that region.

I keep constantly thinking of him, for I always liked him. I tented with him while he was cooking for the colonel in the Gettysburg campaign, and how much to his credit it is that he gave up his chance for his old place in ranks because he thought it was his duty to serve his country there.

A letter was received from his wife tonight, and Lovejoy opened it. Little did she dream in all her anxiety, that he to whom she was writing would be in his quiet, plain soldier's grave at the time of its arrival; what a halo of glory rests upon that mound of fresh dug earth. I can scarcely believe that he is gone. Lovejoy mourns his loss dreadfully.

All of us see the frail threads that our lives hang upon more vividly day by day, as our little band dwindles away; a bullet may cut it at any moment. All day today the bullets have been buzzing through our ranks. Only a few moments ago 'Shag' Board-man of Haverhill, in Company PI, was struck by a spent ball, hurting his leg slightly.

A swift ball may strike any of us at any time, and yet some of the boys are sleeping as if everything was safe. We have been relieved too, and are at a respectable distance to the rear. Shattuck died today—another H man gone; but I am digressing; I have lost the thread of my story. Let me continue where I left off.

The left of our line reached and held the ravine. The right got into it, but the rebs raked them with a most destructive fire, and they were obliged to come back. They ran up a second ravine nearly at right angles, and here the shells from the rebel batteries began to make fearful havoc, raking the whole place.

Orders came for the right to move forward again, and hold the ravine. It did so with a yell, pushing the enemy back. The whole regiment then, with a part of the Sixty-second Pennsylvania, moved forward as skirmishers, the rest of the Sixty-second acting as a skirmish reserve, the whole being under command of Colonel Tilton. Away we went, taking the Petersburg and Norfolk Railroad,

564

driving the rebs into their breastworks, and occupying a position within a hundred yards of their intrenchments, a glorious success certainly. Our lines of battle were soon up, and at 6 o'clock P. M. a charge was ordered.

The One Hundred and Fifty-fifth Pennsylvania, Thirty-second Massachusetts, and Twenty-first Pennsylvania formed our brigade line, the Sixty-second Pennsylvania and Twenty-second Massachusetts and Fourth Michigan remaining behind (the latter's time being out). The First Brigade, under Colonel Chamberlain, was to move upon our left.

Our regiment, which had been sent out all day as skirmishers, was ordered to remain behind. A part of the regiment, however, failed to obey the order and 'went in.' Forward went our brigade. The enemy opened a withering and terribly deadly fire, and shell, shrapnel, canister and bullets flew like hail. The First Brigade failed to move forward; Colonel Chamberlin was wounded,[8] Colonel Prescott, 32d, mortally wounded. Our brigade received all the fire upon its flanks that should have been taken by the First Brigade. Our killed and wounded were dropping fast. We reached a point within twenty yards of the breastworks, leaving our dead nearer than any other line had done. Some of the 'Johnnies' seized their colors, and prepared to vacate. Still the fire remained unslackened from other parts of the works. It was beyond human endurance to stand such an iron hail without stronger supports. Our men broke, and came back, a bleeding, routed body of men. It was simply indescribable. We lost some 400 men killed and wounded, and all for the misconduct of another brigade; there seemed to be no concerted movement at all, and it is one great fault in this campaign; we always move by brigades or skirmish line; no heavy charges by massed columns; you see the result.

I never expected to live through the fire that we withstood; I would have sold myself cheap, yet I escaped, while our hitherto

---

[8] Chamberlain was shot through the right hip and groin, the bullet exiting his left hip, yet he drew his sword and stuck it into the ground to stay upright and continue to rally his troops. After several minutes he collapsed and lay unconscious from loss of blood. He was reported dead but returned to command by November. Chamberlain received the Medal of Honor in 1893 for his actions at Gettysburg. He was president of Bowdoin College and Governor of Maine.—2019

invulnerable orderly, Haseltine, received a flesh wound in the leg during the first charge. I would like to buy his wound for fifty dollars; instead of that I must still run the bloody gauntlet, my life not worth a 'fip.' Darkness came on. We carried off what dead and wounded we could.

The line went back and reformed, while our regiment was left to dig rifle pits, and hold the picket line. We dug some pretty good holes, and held on for dear life all night, exposed every moment to the blaze of an unceasing and deadly fire. As I lay in those pits, under fire every moment, how often did I think of you all at home sleeping so securely. I went to the rear under cover of darkness, made coffee, came back to the rifle pit, ate a supper of 'hard tack' and pork, sewed a button on my pants, lay down toward morning, took a snooze, and we were relieved under a brisk cannonade.

Here I am safe and well, ready for just what U. S. Grant says. I have some grit left yet, although the greater part of my boldness was frightened out of me yesterday afternoon. We are to draw rations tonight, then I am all right. I can conceal quantities of government forage about my person without any trouble.

The Ninth, Fifth and Second Corps are here under Meade; Grant has the Tenth, Eighteenth and Sixth operating elsewhere, so we think, and Ben Butler is with him.

I wrote Billy Steele today; in addition to what I told him, please say to him that I know where George's grave is, and that a head board, neatly cut, marks the spot. Holt received a letter from his father today, he seems to be anxious; he need not be, for Ed is in a safe department. Tell — Tom Warren was killed yesterday; he was mounted orderly for Sweitzer. Papers received tonight; the correspondent of the *New York Times* gives a perfect description of the battle of the 3d June (Friday), and he tells the truth.

Carleton's accounts have lost their charm for me since his North Anna letter. Love to all at home. Oh! how continually you are thought of. If I can only see you in September *** can it be a vain thought? ***

Pressey of H still lives; he is in the ranks, tell his father.

All day on the 17th of June the First Massachusetts Heavy Artillery lay under a heavy fire and lost 9 men wounded. On the

18th at sunrise it was found that the enemy had left their old line and fallen back to a new one. The regiment made an assault about 4 A. M. near the Flare house, driving the enemy through the woods toward Petersburg, across the Petersburg turnpike to a line near the Hare house, where it halted and reformed.

At 12 M. another charge was ordered, the enemy's works being about 400 yards distant. It failed for want of proper support, and the perfectly murderous fire of musketry, canister and spherical case which swept the open field in front. The losses were very heavy, but 100 yards had been gained on the right and left of the line, where rifle pits were immediately thrown up, which subsequently enabled the corps to construct strong earthworks in that position. The right of the brigade moved forward to a line of pine trees, and the left advanced the same distance to the right of the Hare house. This advanced position was held until 5 P. M. when the regiment was relieved and moved to the left of the Hare house where it threw up works during the night, and remained until the night of the 20th. Its losses from June 17 to the 20th were 6 officers wounded, 4 enlisted men killed, 45 wounded.

Our brother of the artillery in a letter dated "In front of Petersburg, June 19, 1864," says:

> You have no doubt all worried very much concerning my safety for the past two weeks, but thank God, I am still in the 'land of the living,' but ere I have finished these few lines my time may have come, for I am behind a rifle pit which we threw up last night, and rebel bullets are continually passing over our heads, and striking the bank.

> Since we started we have been continually marching and fighting, and I am nearly worn out. Yesterday I was struck by a spent ball in the side, and I am quite lame today; but I am thankful it was no worse. Our regiment has lost nearly half its number since it started; it is horrid. I have seen such sights within the past few weeks as you at home can hardly realize.

> Poor Lewis fell day before yesterday (16th) mortally wounded, and died in a few hours. I could not get a chance to see him, as our battalion was a long distance from his. As soon as I can, if I myself live, I shall find out what was done with his body and personal

effects. Walter I have not seen since we left 'Kidd's Mills' the other side of the James River, but I trust he is not hurt. Grant may take Richmond, but I doubt it; if done at all, it will be at a fearful sacrifice. Lee may be forced to evacuate by the capture of Petersburg; we have captured two lines of their fortifications, the strongest of which was surprised and taken by Negroes under General Wilde. We made two charges yesterday, but were repulsed and lost heavily. I do not know how they are making out in the other part of the lines. Please send me an envelope all directed, as I have no ink. With much love dear father and mother, I will bid you good-bye. I am in the Second Brigade, Third Division, Second Corps. Tannatt was slightly wounded yesterday, and it has affected his brain.

On the night of the 20th, the regiment was ordered to the rear about two miles, and on the 21st at 5 P. M. marched to the left and took a position in front of the Jones house. Our letters say:

June 21.

John was over to see me this morn before we left the bivouac; he has been in two fights in front of Petersburg, and is unharmed.

Shortly after this meeting of the brothers, the First Massachusetts Heavy Artillery left their position in rear at 9 o'clock, and crossing the Norfolk and Petersburg Railroad near the "Deserted House," and taking a course through the woods, struck the Jerusalem plank road near the Williams house. Finding the enemy's cavalry in front, near and covering the Weldon Railroad, it halted within two or three miles of it, and lay in position during the night on the left of the Fifth Corps.

About 3 P. M. on the 2 2d, advanced into the edge of the woods near the enemy's line, and were ordered to throw up breastworks near their position, a general advance having been ordered to connect with the right of the Sixth Corps. The regiment had just commenced to throw down rails and build the works when suddenly a perfect storm of bullets came from the rear and flanks. The enemy had broken through a gap between Birney's (3d) and Barlow's (1st) divisions, while the latter was getting into position on the left of the former, in the woods, and had penetrated to the rear.

568

In a few moments, the First Division came running down through the regiment, and in a line parallel to the works. The whole line was thrown into confusion, so sudden was the attack, and driven some distance, with considerable loss of prisoners, and McKnight's (12th N. Y.) Battery. But it was soon rallied, and about sunset made a gallant charge across a cornfield to the woods beyond; drove the enemy back, and recaptured many of the prisoners.

The loss in the regiment was 1 captain (J. W. Kimball) killed, 1 wounded, 6 captured (2 of whom were wounded), 8 enlisted men killed, 45 wounded, 175 captured.

During this violent and partially successful attack, the enemy was, at one time, very close to Corps Headquarters, which was just in front of the Jones' house, near the Jerusalem plank road, their bullets and shot striking in among headquarters' tents.

General Meade was present during the attack.

Colonel R. McAllister, of the Eleventh New Jersey, commanding the brigade, is reported to have shouted when he saw his command break: "Stand fast, men! Rally round the flag, men!" But when he saw that to remain longer in that position meant certain capture or annihilation, he sang out at the top of his voice: "Run boys, run! Run like the devil!"

THE SIEGE OF PETERSBURG

The assaults were abandoned—the attack failed. On the night of the 20th, while in the rear lines, we received a large mail, but no light being obtainable, we had to forego the pleasure of reading precious letters. We had but just gone to sleep when we were saluted with the pleasing (?) orders to move immediately. We packed up, left the railroad, and went into bivouac a mile in rear, and on the morning of the 21st we moved again to our left flank, into a piece of woods, where, while most of the regiment were sleeping, letters were read, and we sat down in the cool shade to write the offerings of a thankful heart for them, and for a wonderful escape from death, wounds, and sickness. That we remained safe so far, and comparatively unscathed through all this storm of battle, was certainly little short of a miracle. Our reflections partook somewhat of a character pertaining to a belief in destiny. While exclaiming that perhaps we were invulnerable, we added—"Thus they go; only a fragment is left; shall we be spared?" Sometimes in those letters we gave way to despondency, and remembering the poor comrades who had gone, thought our chance small, but hope reappeared and showed us a more pleasant path for our thoughts to stray in.

Our letters say:

Before Petersburg, Va.,

June 21, 1864.

Last night I received your letter, *** a map from father, etc., etc.

You can imagine, or form a slight idea of, my feelings, when I tell you that I could not read them until morning, no light being obtainable; there I was in possession of these priceless treasures for twelve hours, and no chance to look at their inside.

After we had gone to sleep we were saluted late at night with the pleasing order to move immediately; we packed up, left the railroad, and went into bivouac a mile in the rear. This morning we moved again to our left flank, and we are now lying in the woods. While most of the Twenty-second are sleeping, I sit myself down in the shade, and try to write you the offerings of a thankful heart for the choice favors of yesterday, and to express myself in view of my wonderful escape, from death, wounds and sickness.

To think that I am still unscathed through all this storm of battle and have weathered this frightful tempest, is certainly a miracle in my mind. My reflections are of a character incident to a faithful believer in destiny almost.

Tom Willey is a straggler in the rear; he failed to come to time Saturday on our first charge; ditto L.; they both hugged a ditch, and L. joined the regiment the next morning after we were relieved, while W. stayed behind; we have seen nothing of him since poor Emerson was shot a few moments before L. halted on the charge. I wrote Mrs. Walton yesterday afternoon; I intend writing to poor Mrs. Emerson.

John was over to see me this morn before we left the bivouac; he has been in two battles before Petersburg, and is unharmed.

Lewis is dead; he was badly wounded in the hip, and died Thursday, June 16; my favorite cousin is gone; I was with him only a week ago; God help us who may be left.

Couillard of Bradford is killed, and a Mr. Lamb, who was a blacksmith with C. in the Peabody shop, Salem Street, killed; thus they go; only a fragment left. *** Charlie Haseltine is quite comfortable; I believe he was sent away yesterday.

The map I like; I am sorry it does not include Petersburg and surroundings of our present scene of operations. Ask father if he cannot procure the *New York Herald* with such a map on the front page. I believe I saw it today, and as it is cheap and good, I would like it. In these little matters of interesting information, you can not only help, but make my way easier in a certain degree. *** I still live in the hope of seeing you some time; I give way to despondency often, and remembering my poor comrades who have gone, think my chances small; but hope reappears, and shows me a more pleasant path for my thoughts to stray in, and joyfully I walk therein, knowing if I reach the end, it leads to the dear ones at home, ready to greet me with warm hearts and loving hands. Good-bye, with love for the country and all at home. Sam A., George L. and Ed H. are well; we miss our fallen ones so much; it is lonely enough for the company now that they are gone. I miss Charlie Haseltine very much.

June 22, 1864.

All quiet in front today, and as I have devoured all the reading matter in camp, I will occupy a short time in writing. *** I sent Emerson's watch by Lieutenant Look today; he has been discharged and goes to Boston *** I am obliged for the map; I wish it covered more territory, now that we are operating in front of Petersburg; I never dreamed we should come here when I sent for it.

I should not be surprised if we struck for the Rocky Mountains any day; the Army of the Potomac is a shuttlecock for anybody's use you know *** my flesh is breaking out with humor, and it irritates me very much; I want a change of diet *** send me an *Army and Navy Journal* again; I want to see the third, fourth and fifth weeks, and so on.

The Second Corps is on our left now; I have not seen John since yesterday morning; I presume he is well. Heavy skirmishing is now going on in front of us; I do not anticipate any trouble from it. We are remaining very quiet indeed; we are having a nice rest; I wish it might be continued for three months.

On the morning of the 22d we again returned to our old camp, and at night marched to the extreme left of the army to prevent a flank and rear attack upon the Sixth Corps, which had been trying to occupy the Weldon Railroad.

Our letters say (in pencil):

Extreme left of the Army of the Potomac,

June 24, 1864.

The heat is so oppressive that it is with extreme difficulty that I do anything that draws in the least upon mind or body. * * * Since I last wrote you, I have had a hard pull.

Tuesday night, the Second Corps was attacked and flanked and we were routed out suddenly for their support * * * we had a hard time all night *** lost 4 men wounded, including Mark Hanson of Company I, the 12th New York Battery was taken, and at the same time the First 'Heavy' was much cut up.

Our march was a terribly severe one. Not a breath of air was stirring, the heat was scorching, and the dust shoe deep and ground to a fine flour. We could not see a person in the ranks ahead of us, and no water was obtainable. The suffering which we endured from our dry, dusty, parched throats was inconceivable agony.

Drenched with perspiration, covered with thick dust, and burdened with heavy loads, I wish that I might have rushed into the house about then, and falling upon the floor, shown you a poor, panting, suffering soldier, just about 'gone up.' *** Men fell out by scores, many were sunstruck, and there had been few occasions when all had endured any more.

It was dreadful hard to write now, and good spirits are on the ebb. These times are getting almost too hard. They draw upon the body tremendously. I shall try to weather it.

I never witnessed such suffering on the march; no water then, nor now; we need rain dreadfully. We are still here; a part of the Sixth Corps is moving, also the Second. Heavy fighting took place on the right this morning, and we were called up three times during last night; we slept on our arms.

Our letters of the 25th say:

While gone, Holt says the shells flew among the tents of the Provost Guard, and one solid shot killed two men instantly on the turnpike (of a New York regiment, one of them just from home), and passed through a tent of the guard; it was so sudden to those young men.

I saw Lieutenant Worth for the first time since I used to visit Eugene at Falmouth; he was very glad to see me, and was very cordial in his invitations, inquiries, etc. He desired to be remembered to 'Carter' (Eugene). He is a very fine fellow. Ed Morrill is at home; I am so glad for him; I saw his regiment yesterday a few days since, the Thirty-fifth; it isn't so small as ours, yet it is in the Engineer Corps, in consequence of its reduction in numbers; we number seventy-nine guns. I can't tell when I shall write again.

On the 24th we marched back again to our old camp; it was dreadful, and the dust so thick; one could almost cut it. The army was suffering greatly for want of water.

On the morning of the 25th we walked over to the Twelfth Massachusetts, whose time of service was out, and who were crying out, "Now for Massachusetts!"

Our letter of that date says:

Upon our way we saw a horrid sight, four men stretched out, mortally wounded by a shell. Two had their hips shattered to pieces, one his bowels protruding, and the fourth a leg shot off. They were begging to be carried off, and their lives went out while they were imploring help. From all this I have been delivered; can we be too thankful?

While walking over to the Twelfth with Ed this morning, we could not help remarking upon our own viability. We run the same risks daily, and when I go in, the chances of death increase treble.

John is safe, though many of his regiment were captured Tuesday evening. They number 400, so an officer told me today.

William Blanchard is not dead so much as he was; he was over to see me today; he has just been detailed on Provost Guard, Third Division, General Crawford.

He spoke of poor Brainard and his wound. We had soft bread and potatoes issued yesterday; Grant feeds his army well. Chaplain Tyler sent me two cans of beef from the hospital this morning; wasn't it kind in him? Did you see my short note in the Tri-Weekly? I intended only the list for publication.

See that they publish W. L. Emerson's death, June 18, and First Sergeant Haseltine, Company H, wounded the same day. *** Heavy firing to be heard on the right; a battle is going on there, I think; Grant does not gain much just now. Gilmore lost the day for us here at Petersburg. Lovejoy, Holt and myself are well; Sam Appleton is not so well; heat affects him; it is terribly warm, almost suffocating. The letter in the *Journal* of Chaplain Tyler (C. M. T.), dated June 14, is very interesting; what do you think of it?

On June 23d, the First Massachusetts Heavy Artillery remained on the same line, moving back a short distance through the woods, but on the 24th moved a short distance to the rear, and was ordered to build works in the open field near the Jones house, but it was countermanded. Here the men suffered from the sweltering heat and a scarcity of water. Colonel B. R. Pierce here assumed command again on the 26th. Remained in this position until June 27, when it moved again to the front and assisted in building works to the left of the Jerusalem plank road, and between it and the Williams house.

We were now in reserve and resting. The thermometer ran above one hundred degrees in the shade. We washed clothes and cleaned up. Wells were dug; the teams came up. Sutlers arrived at City Point, and we commenced to draw rations of soft bread, potatoes and other vegetables, and regale ourselves on canned peaches, condensed milk, etc.

Our letters say (in pencil):

On Reserve, near Petersburg, Va.,

June 26, 1864.

Today I have devoted to avocations of cleanliness. The teams have been up, and I have washed a shirt, blouse, pair of socks, handkerchief and towel, and all this labor performed under a boiling sun, one hundred degrees in the shade (beats all our Sharpsburg experience in the effects of warm weather on the poor bodies).

The chaplain has been up, and preached to us splendidly; only an audience of forty brave men. The last time he preached to us was at Brandy Station, and nearly the whole regiment turned out to hear his good words, as we were about to enter the mystery of the dreadful future. What a contrast it was as we stood about him today, one and all of us worn down by exposure and hardship.

He is a fine man. * * * His style is perfectly beautiful. ***

The sutlers have begun to bring up goods to City Point, and today I regaled myself upon (or with) canned peaches, sardines, condensed milk, etc.; Dodge came up with chickens and cheese, and Stone, Watson and myself have lived high all day.

It is the old story, however, 'feast today, and starve tomorrow.' I have 'skived' pretty well for grub on this campaign, and though not having such a field of operations as the states of Maryland and Pennsylvania afford, still I have succeeded well; if I had been possessed with half the energy and enterprise that I have now, then I should have been a gay soldier on the Gettysburg campaign.

I know how to live better now; I cook and eat, drink my common coffee, eat my pork, tack and meat, without any grumbling and wastings, and with the little *etcs.* thrown in, I manage to just live. *** A week ago Saturday we had a big fight; we advanced in the face of the enemy about two miles, only halting after a gallant but unavailing charge upon his last line of entrenchments. We lost Emerson and Shattuck (the latter a Vermonter), Saturday, and poor Charlie Haseltine was wounded, Al Emerson of B, Kenfield of E, wounded, Tom Warren of D, killed *** we lost 5 men killed, and 21 wounded. *** When the Second Corps was flanked, and the Twelfth New York Artillery so much used up, our division, with Crawford's, were ordered up to support. We lost 4 wounded, among them Mark Hanson of Company I; since then we have been resting. It is terrible to endure this heat, dust and scarcity of water. * * * My dreams of B, night and day, and the memories, the thoughts of our poor boys gone, and my loneliness with Charlie gone, you can well imagine. Oh! the thronging thoughts, I cannot tell them to you on paper.

June 30, 1864.

Father's closing sentence (in his letter) impressed me deeply with thoughts I never seemed to have before *** what assurance it gave me of the joy in store for me when I come marching home; the happiest time for us all will it be, if war does not invade the whole land and we escape its dangers and risks. Can we hope sufficiently strong? Oh! that plans and expectations may not be suddenly shifted by the wonderful mysteries that are abroad daily in this part of our distracted land.

We can only hope and pray while the boys fight on. Our teams have been up; we have been making out rolls, reports, returns, etc., all day. Our regiment has been laying out company streets, clearing up the brush and accumulated rubbish.

We have been mustered for the last two months' pay, and seem to be preparing for a sit down before the walls of Petersburg; there seems to be little prospect of taking it, however, for if we failed on the 18th inst. we must certainly fail again, so far as gaining the works by charging is concerned.

What Generals Grant and Meade contemplate, we are hardly supposed to know; they are very uncommunicative, both of them. There are numerous rumors and reports concerning our cavalry operations in circulation today not at all encouraging to the army or the people at home; I hope they may prove false.

Just think of the loss of fifteen guns by Kautz and Wilson's[1] cavalry division, artillery and all surrounded in an attempt to destroy parts of the Weldon R. R. One thing I do know, and that is, the Second and Sixth Corps have gone that way today, leaving only their skirmish line in front of their breastworks; what's up will be determined before the sun sets tonight.

Lieutenant-Colonel Sherwin is now on General Griffin's staff as division inspector. Major Burt is now in command of us, and the regiment is consolidated into a battalion of four companies, A, B, C and Sharpshooters, commanded respectively by Captains Rock, Meands, Field and Smith. There is some talk of organizing us into a band of sharpshooters for the division. I hope it is not so.

Day of the Thirty-second, Bradford boy, died of wounds received, and the Moulton fellow was formerly of Company D, got wounded at Gaines' Mill, and was either discharged or detailed on government railroads; that is all I am able to learn about him at present.

I went over to the First Massachusetts Artillery yesterday with Ed I found only one person in Company E that I knew; George S., and he looked as if one of his feet was in the grave, and the other soon to follow; he is perfectly played out; thin, troubled with diarrhea, affected by the climate, and the hardships of this first month of service, and just ready to give up.

He was without soap or towel, longing for sutler's goods, gingerbread and lemons; had sent for money, and was intending to commence living very soon. He is a subject for fever; we couldn't help laughing at him, he had changed so much. We met him in the first place over a mile from camp, buying cakes for his chum, for which he received compensation in said cookies to the tune of two.

---

[1] James Harrison Wilson (1837–1925) was a career officer, and later a railroad engineer and executive. He was a prolific writer on topics of the Civil War, including the only biography to date of Grant's aide, John Rawlins, whom Wilson considered the most extraordinary man he met in the war. For more on Wilson's raid on the Weldon R.R., see his memoir, *Under the Old Flag*, Wilson, 2018, BIG BYTE BOOKS.

You ought to see his sunken sockets and great saucer eyes. We left him with assurances of our distinguished consideration.

John was half a mile in front, on picket; I always find him away, and this time I did not see him. I left my love, and an invitation to come and see me today, and take dinner with me. I have not seen him as yet; I know he is well, and that he has been very fortunate so far you all know. They only number 375 men; I imagine they all have seen more reality than poetry in their first campaign. *** yes! father, people do grow older nowadays than formerly. I am older in life and thought this minute than I should have been had I stayed at home and the war had never been.

Every hour now wears as steadily as little drops of water do the rocks. It is almost perceptible, this wear upon the patience and upon the mind itself, yet I discountenance by influence and example the grumbling complaints of many about me, who suffer and are weary of this long age of existence they have lived in Virginia. Why not be a man, and bravely bear it, knowing the great reward? You both can bear me witness that I have been of cheerful heart, and imbued with a right spirit during the campaign, looking at the magnitude of this greatest of struggles.

I know I have done my duty to all; I never tried to do so well before. I know the effect upon others, and have tried to set a good example. I threw away my old clothes a few days since; when I parted with them I wished several times that I might send them to you; I think they would look well besides Rob's of Gettysburg fame. They were worse in point of dilapidation, and every rent and hole spoke words that I never shall forget; I wish you could have seen them. I am covered with the 'ground itch,' or 'Carter' itch (the battery men term it, on account of a person by that name suffering from it severely). I cannot seem to do anything for it; I must bear it. It is very troublesome night times, and irritates my flesh almost beyond endurance; the extreme heat is not at all favorable for it; I have to stand over a fire a great deal, and that does not help it any.

I hope to soon rid myself of it. Carleton's accounts have been few and far between lately I notice, and this afternoon I see by the journal the reason for it; it seems that the wear and tear of this campaign have been too much for his constitution (has a horse to ride, plenty to eat and drink, and nothing, so to speak, to do), and he has been rusticating and recuperating; poor fellow, how I pity him! I don't think much of him as a correspondent. He is very versatile, and gifted with great powers of diction, but his reliability in regard to facts, I doubt; he depends too much upon reports and stories of men to the rear. His letters do not possess for me the interest that they did.

July 1.

John is here with me, and we have been having a 'feast of letters, and a flow of conversation.' He is in fine spirits; seemed really like our Portland John. I have prevailed upon him to write today and he 'felt better,' he said, after he had finished.

We had a nice wash, and now we are gay fellows *** my spirits are revived; my *esprit de corps* is most excellent, if you will apply the phrase to a solitary individual.

Lewis was shot on the 16th, taken back to the hospital, and died on the forenoon of the 17th; he went to sleep before he died, and never awoke; he spoke no parting words, and left no last wishes or will; if anyone knows about him it is John, and he assures me of this much. He had no personal effects with him of any account *** his body was buried just as he died, and his clothes were searched; no writings were found, and you know now all that is known concerning the poor fellow.

He was the 'bravest of the brave;' his last company, F, idolized him before he was made adjutant. The captain of it is dangerously wounded; the captains of E and F are killed. * * * I saw Lieutenant Beardsley of Company F, and he said that Major Shatswell had Lewis' sword and belt in safe keeping. He confirmed what has already been said and written concerning Lewis' death, his effects, last wishes, etc.

We have enjoyed a glorious breakfast and dinner; John is much pleased with my mode of living; he said he had not eaten so much before for a month; we had meat, potatoes, farina, apple sauce, molasses, cheese and lemonade. Sutlers are numerous, and we must recruit upon their goods for a short time. * * * Bill Kent's flask (with the whiskey in it of course) was a fortunate preservative; I am sorry for poor Bill Steele; he is our favorite officer; I do hope he will live. Remember me to him, and tell him how anxious we are for him. I am perspiring at a great rate; only 105 in the shade. I cannot write any longer; I shall melt if I try *** live in the joy of the present, and the thankfulness therefor; be as happy, cheerful and contented as I am, my darling mother, and remember that we shall meet again.

Our brother of the artillery writes on this same day, July 1:

I am now sitting under Walter's 'shelter,' and I think I will write you a few lines while he is engaged in cooking 'dinner.' 'Tell them we are going to have a gay one, he says. We are now having a little rest, but I do not know how long it will last; still, we ought to be thankful for the smallest favors. We have had one fight since I wrote you, and for the first time the 'Johnnies' had it all their own way; they whipped us beautifully. There was no connection between our corps and the Fifth, excepting a light line of skirmishers, which the 'rebs' soon found out and took advantage of, coming in on our left flank, causing us to 'skedaddle' in the most approved style.

They captured about 1,000 men, and killed and wounded about as many more. In our company we had 1 man killed, 3 wounded and 33 taken prisoners, our very best men. The Johnnies got so near us before we were aware of it that it was a hard sight for a man's line for him to run, and that is why our boys stopped in the pits, preferring to be taken prisoners rather than run the risk of running; but I did not 'see it in that light' (cooped up in a Georgia prison on reduced rations this hot weather is not pleasant), and having considerable confidence in my legs, I made a bold push, and they failed me not, although many dropped at my feet.

Our family has been very fortunate so far in this horrid war; I don't understand it, for I am quite sure that we have never skulked, or hung to the rear. I have often wondered how I have escaped, for I have been in many places where it seemed impossible for a man to live an instant, and yet have come out all right. But I expect the 'Johnnies' are getting one ready for me for a future occasion. Well, father, if I am killed or injured by the enemy, you will have the satisfaction of knowing that I met my fate with my face toward them.

Our army could whip them in five minutes out of their fortifications; they are a set of mean, cowardly devils when we are on an equality with them, but when they get a good advantage over us, then is the time for you to see 'southern chivalry.'

After our last fight, when we retook the rifle pits which they drove us from, we found our dead all stripped, perfectly nude, and one in our company who was killed, was bayoneted to death after being shot. We found his naked body with the bayonet wound in it.

Walter, who will write, will tell you all I know about Lewis; it will be impossible to get his body, as he was buried without any coffin.

July 3, 1864

A year ago today, I was lying at the foot of 'Round Top,' expecting every moment to have my limbs mangled by the pieces of shells then flying through the air; it was Friday, and all day long we lay there while Hancock in the center fought his fierce but victorious battle.

Yesterday, a year ago, we fought our Thursday (July 2) fight, repulsing the rebels in every direction toward nightfall, and then the calm, clear moon came sailing out, looking down upon a field I ever shall remember. Poor Rob was sleeping, while I stepped lightly among the dead and wounded lying among the tall clover-and green grass.

That night and the next day, and the night among the rocks and the poor rebel wounded, are occasions that live as fresh in my memory today as upon their very birth. Today is the Sabbath and we are still resting, though I have made out three monthly returns of deserters for my day's work, without troubling my conscience in the least; we must do here while there is opportunity, not knowing what a day may bring forth.

We have no preaching; Mr. Tyler has got a leave of absence to recruit his health; he intends to get his discharge in Washington; he is a fair weather man. Six months, with a horse to ride, plenty to eat, and a place in the rear, have used him up, and he caves.

Yesterday morn I had a large mail. *** I donned my sombrero, and devoured all the contents of the letters, lay back in the shade, read papers, and enjoyed myself hugely. John came over, and we had a feast of matters and things; he lost his rations by staying so long with me the day before, and he came over principally to fill up his haversack; I did that for him in a jiffy. Tell father to thank Mr. Davis for his gift; the hat is a *banger; a peeler*. I live under its shadow in perfect comfort, though the boys make fun of my appearance with it on, shouting 'how's corn and potatoes this morning,' etc., etc. *** I heard from Newman today; he has found out that he is going home when the regiment does, and wants to find out when that is. I wrote to him and told him September 17; only seventy-six days more and then—

He is in Company C, Twelfth Reserve Corps of veterans, played out invalids. *** Lieutenant Bourne is our brigade inspector now, and Captain Bennet is Brigade A. A. A. G. The Sixty-second Pennsylvania has gone home and Colonel Sweitzer has left us. Colonel Gregory of the 155th Pennsylvania Zouaves is in temporary command of the Second Brigade.

I wrote all about Lewis in my last letter to father. * * * He suffered none at all while dying, and his body cannot be sent home yet; there are orders against it. I know nothing further, nor can I find out.

I knew that Charlie Carter was wounded, but when or where, I am ignorant of; please let me know. 'Deacon' Morse of B is all right in the hospital.

July 4

Independence Day, and John is here; we have just partaken of a plain, unassuming repast, and he is about to leave me; he says he wishes to see the boys of his regiment go on their homeward journey. Their time is up tomorrow, and they start for City Point this afternoon. He feels sad enough over their departure; how he wishes he were going. He says 'it's rough on the veteran volunteers' (re-enlisted men).

Fourth of July Evening

It has been a very still day; no celebration at all in the army. No salutes have been fired, or even heard, and there are to be no fireworks tonight, I believe; it has been a day of no unusual occurrence. Perhaps there has been more picket firing on account of its being our day of national salvation.

July 6 the First Heavy Artillery went to the rear for the purpose of making out muster rolls and mustering out the men whose terms of service had expired. This included all original members and recruits who had not re-enlisted.

As soon as completed the regiment went into camp, remained there until July 11, when orders came to level these works in the vicinity of the Williams' house, and mass near the same.

July 9.

I have just been over to see John. I found him just returned from picket, and we had a real pleasant, social time together; he kept me on the broad grin continually by his funny allusions and apt sayings; he spoke several times of the regiment going home, etc., but seemed to be cheerful over the prospects. The boys were falling into line for their departure when I left; they were discharged and mustered out of service two days ago, but owing to incapability of officers have been delayed in the field so long. They have been impatient and anxious the whole time they say, and were happy enough when the order came to fall in.

I learned while there that Mr. Walton (Ed's father), was taken prisoner on the 21st ult. Mrs. W. may naturally suppose that the watch, chain, ring and wallet belonging to Ned, which I transferred to Mr. W., are now in the hands of 'Johnny Reb,' but assure her that they are safe, and on their way to her. Mr. Barker of Andover, the chaplain of the regiment, has them.

Mr. W. entrusted them to him for safe keeping some time since, and very fortunately too, now that Mr. W. is in the hands of the rebels. Poor George S. looks miserably; he is feverish, has a headache, backache, and is weak every way. He is very poor and out of his mind at times; still he keeps up, and tries to be a soldier, while his constitution is running down like a clock, and no appliances by which to wind it up.

The doctor knows nothing, and if he did has no medicine; they don't know enough to send him to the hospital. The 'First Heavy' is played out at best; had it been decently officered it would not have met with the losses it has sustained this campaign. Poor S. is a wreck of his former self; you wouldn't know him.

Tell Mary A. that Sammy has left division hospital, and gone to City Point; he may go to W.; she need have no fear for him. He is doing finely. *** We are building a large fort; details go every day. What do you think of the 'raid,' naval victory and abandonment of Marietta? It's time for Ulysses to move. If Pennsylvania and the North can't take care of the few 'Johnnies' in Maryland, let the state suffer; we can't help them; we have all we can attend to here. What do you think of Pitt Fessenden's[2] nomination and acceptance of the Secretary of the Treasury? It is capital, I think.

---

[2] William Pitt Fessenden (1806–1869) was a Maine politician.—2019

I am persuaded every moment that I shall see you in September. It seems as though I couldn't wait. What a glorious meeting it will be for us. Then for whatever is before me; I shall be equal to anything. I shall create circumstances for myself, if they do not appear before me. I enclose a sample of clay dug from the ground; isn't it a curiosity?

Every one of the officers of the regiment who has been promoted, and mustered in for three years (my own case had I accepted the commission), have got to remain. Yet some say: 'Oh! Carter, what a fool; you could have got out of it when the regiment starts for home,' etc.

Ah! but I know Uncle Sam too well. The First Heavy officers are illustrations of my forethought *** be hopeful, and never fear. We are taking care of ourselves finely now, and the Lord will look out for us in the day of battle, if it is for the best. You must not secure so much unrest and disquiet on our account.

You see by the papers the accounts of the distributions of canned meats, porter, tobacco, lemons, etc., by the Sanitary Commission, to the soldiers; also vegetables by the commissaries; it is all a humbug, and I wish to let you know it so you can refute it.

The commission sent these articles for distribution to the troops; headquarters take a share, and send it as a lot to the division for a second pick; then it goes to brigade, and after they deduct two dozen milk, a barrel of beer, canned stuff, etc., it is sent to regimental headquarters, who divide it up into company shares, and yesterday, such a distribution footed up four cans of meat for each of our companies, of an average of twenty-two men each.

After such a transfer, through the regular channels, who can expect anything different? This is the way the 'Sanitary' gets taken in, and the manner in which your large Northern sums of money, the result of patriotic fairs, goes to the soldiers.

The stars, eagles and bars [i.e. officers] get all the cream of that part, sent to the privates proper of the army. The hospital arrangements are carried on better, though the surgeons and outside attendants draw largely upon the materials intended for the sick and wounded. Today our regiment drew two gallons of pickles for one hundred men present; that is a sanitary issue; about a mouthful for a man. The issue of vegetables has been just one small slice of cabbage this day to a man; these are the great things done for the soldiers you read about in flaming paragraphs, having such 'a salutary effect upon their health,' etc.

Your will is as good as the deed you perform; we know and see the one, but the result of the other is only on paper. Wait until some of the boys, who see and observe these things, come home, and then for a shaking up in high places.

I have been reading of the funeral of General Prescott;[3] isn't it sad? Friday, June 3, I was sent to him by Colonel Tilton to make inquiries concerning the picket line; that was after I had seen to the burial of poor Ed Walton; he was way down to the right of the open field, which I marked out on the diagram I sent to father. After some difficulty (under fire most of the way) I succeeded in reaching him, and as I proceeded to deliver my message, standing all the time in an attitude of attention, he said, 'Down, my man, or you'll be shot!' No sooner had the words escaped his lips, than a score of bullets came whizzing by, hastening my compliance with his warning.

He was a brave, good man, * * * he was a perfect glutton in a fight, and dealt in blood alone; he cared not for himself; I honor such a man.

Give me bravery in the field; a coward I do hate; I do not believe I am one. I try not to be; I would take a twelve pound shot through my breast before I would turn, when orders were 'forward.'

In connection with the little drawing I enclose (pencil sketch of position June 18), please read to Mrs. E. the following additional particulars concerning the death of her husband.

I accidentally learned them last night from Captain Rock, who had command of the left wing of the skirmish line the 18th ult. He has never uttered a word before; he saw Will fall, and this is his story.

"Our first halt was upon the brow of the hill; here a severe fire greeted us; Will, to escape it, came away from the left' and got mixed up with the right wing. The order was to advance rapidly,

3 George Lincoln Prescott (1829–June 19, 1864), veteran of Bull Run, Gettysburg, The Overland Campaign; wounded June 18, Second Battle of Petersburg.—2019

and gain, ravine number 2, upon the top of which, concealed, were the rebel skirmishers. Forward they went, gained it, drove the rebs, who rushed over toward the fence, where they poured an enfilading fire through the ravine, causing us to evacuate; we ran into ravine number 1, and here the shells, grape and canister of the rebel batteries began to make fearful havoc, raking the whole place, as you'll perceive they could easily do. 'To the road!' shouted Rock, and our men started in a diagonal line; then it was time for the rebels to pour in their fire.

"Will reached the road, where there was shelter behind its bank, turned to look toward the rebels, and received his death wound in front of the head somewhere, the ball passing clean through, coming out at the back of his neck.

"He fell face down, a little upon his side, head toward the road, inclined in the direction we had come in the morning; he never uttered a word; no groan even escaped him. His shoulder move perceptibly, a brave heart ceased to beat.

"These are the particulars, and with what I have already written, constitute all the details of his death and burial.

"I was at a hospital a few days ago. I never saw such horrible sights at a place of that kind before. Whole rows of dead men lay there in their blankets, who had died the previous night, with no kind hand near to soothe their last moments. Limbs were lying under the table, and everything had an air of butchery about it. Oh! the sorrowing at home, mourning those lost, who can never-be replaced.

"Though unpretending head boards mark the places where the private soldier lies, yet the dawn of the great hereafter will behold those slaughtered heroes, resurrected and beautified, the recipients of a well-earned crown. They may be unknown now, and will sleep in their humble places, but they are destined to be exalted far above the lauded heroes that poets sing about and the world praise."

July 12, the First Massachusetts Heavy Artillery joined the brigade, and was moved to the left of the Williams house, to cover the shortening of the lines.

From the 12th the regiment lay in line of battle about forty-eight hours; no enemy appearing, and troops and trains having been withdrawn, crossed the Norfolk and Petersburg Railroad to the Norfolk and Petersburg turnpike, where it went into camp to the right and left of it, and near the "Deserted House." July 15 was the first time the regiment had pitched a regularly laid out camp since it left the forts about Washington.

On the night of the 12th we were very unexpectedly ordered to the front, and upon arriving there found the troops gone, their breastworks destroyed and the lines shortened.

Our letters say (in pencil):

At the Front,

July 13, 1864

Fast night, very unexpectedly, we were ordered to the front, and were very much surprised to find so few troops here; the Second and Sixth Corps have gone somewhere, perhaps to Maryland, and upon our left the line curves, and finally ends in a series of forts just constructed.

The rebels are only 100 yards from us, and their pickets only fifty from our own. We are on most peaceable terms, walk behind our breastworks in perfect safety, and live as we would in our own camp.

Our pickets lounge upon the grass; some of them play cards with the 'Johnnies,' and the whole duty is a perfect farce. Once in awhile the rebel batteries will open upon our men, who are engaged in working on a fort nearby; and then it is amusing to see the pickets drop their cards, and seek a place of safety; the firing commences, and the men who were engaged in friendly games (seemingly) only a few moments before, are seeking each other's lives.

It is a strange fact, but it lacks any significance in view of this strangest rebellion. John has gone; where I know not. He was over to see me day before yesterday, and said then that his regiment was under orders to move, we shall hear of his whereabouts soon.

It was most provoking to be compelled to move last night; I had made a move in the morning. Stone had his office tent put up, and a bunk made; Watson and myself put up a tent, summer style, and

587

made us a nice bedstead of cracker boxes. The pioneers and fatigue part put up a bough covering and arbors. We made tables, seats, cleaned up and prepared generally for solid comfort; we worked all day, and had just completed everything, when this order to march, and 'fall in' at once came, and away we went from all this contemplated pleasure.

It is no small matter to move one's house and cooking arrangements in the army, and it takes a long time, after a conclusion so to do, to put your plans into execution; but after it is done, and you are well satisfied after your toils, and anticipate compensation in enjoying the benefits of your creative genius, how discouraging to have to leave it all untasted.

Some of the boys say 'I'll be satisfied to stay a single night in the shanty,' but even this was denied us. You would laugh to see us move our places of residence here in the army from one part of the camp to another. *** We have no women to help us, and you know that they alone know the details of moving aright.

But we moved, and gained nothing; wasn't it a disappointment? I had to go without washing or even eating any supper, and last night I slept in the trenches, and for the first time in Virginia was troubled with mosquitoes.

We are in hopes to go back to camp again and to do picket duty out here. I hope so truly. We are very much excited by the news from Washington and Baltimore, and all wish we were there.

I had a letter from Eugene yesterday; very short (busy mustering). *** He said he had been ordered to New York as aide-de-camp on Gen. P. St. George Cooke's staff, and he and M. would start about the 13th. *** Lyman Goodell came over to see me (us boys) four days ago *** he is a second class private in Reserve Signal camp, near General Butler's headquarters, Bermuda Hundreds [*sic*]. He is pleased with his kind of service, and well he may be *** no one has more sympathy for the rank and file than myself; I have been there, and to a certain extent am with them now, but on the average I am vastly in advance of them in comfort and privileges, my surroundings are so much more favorable. I am indeed thankful for my position, and I shall never regret that I came into one of the best Massachusetts regiments, the gallant Twenty-second.

It rained a little night before last, and it looked a little like it last night, but all signs of a wished-for rain, a regular fall of water, failed, *** When our boys left last night, they were obliged to throw a great deal of their grub away; it always happens so.

Our team went away this morning after another load, and returned this noon with plenty of dried apples, pickles, turnips, crackers, and one or two boxes of peaches and milk. The commissary issued beets, cabbages and onions. One of our teamsters gave me a quarter of a cheese, so you see I am all right; a soldier is happy as long as his food is good and sure.

I am in perfect trim, and by September shall be as fat as I was when you found me at Beverly Ford. They are beginning to shell us, and I close abruptly. *** The Third Division of the Sixth Corps (division of the Monocacy) is the poorest in the Army of the Potomac. *** I received a note from Sammy A. today dated from City Point; he is improving every day.

The siege of Petersburg and our life in the trenches had now fairly begun. A guard was left in our old camp, to which we went for supplies, clothes, etc. News now reached us of the raid upon Washington by Early,[4] and we wished we were there, and we wrote:

Shame to any young man, now at home, and able to do duty in the field, if he does not rush 'to arms,' and help drive the invaders from northern soil.

If my time was out and I had only been at home a day, and this crisis was at hand, I would go to Washington in a minute. Why do they not go forward in legions now, when all depends upon them? If the people at home -will only take care of these "raiders" with the little help we can give them, Grant will destroy and occupy Petersburg, in a very short time. I do hope and pray that all is well with the republic. Heaven prosper the right at this 'critical moment.'

Our letters say:

We have now adopted a new system of procuring sanitary goods. Our Surgeon, Doctor S—, took a team, and went direct to City Point

---

[4] Jubal Anderson Early (1816–1894), the cantankerous and unpopular Confederate general, made moves on Washington and Pennsylvania hoping to draw Union forces away from Richmond.—2019

and loaded it full of supplies for our regiment alone. In consequence, we received new potatoes, dried apples, pickled onions and cucumbers, tea, mustard, and a few cans of fruit, while the officers got wine, milk, chocolate, preserved peaches, tomatoes, etc.

Doctor Stearns[5] gave the non-commissioned staff (me, myself and the rest), a can of apple sauce, strawberries, chocolate, a bottle of port wine, and a can of milk. The issue was a very liberal one, and all got a bountiful supply. The commissary issued onions, cabbage, pickles and soft bread at the same time, so you see we are just living high.

At the Front,

Sunday, July 17, 1864

Still we lie here, in the trenches, doing nothing all day long; the burning rays of the sun, the dry, parched ground, ready to be blown away in clouds of dust by the slightest breath of air, and the lack of letters during the foolhardy raid of the invaders, have been bur only blessings.

The long, weary hours pass so tediously too. Oh, dear! how can a mortal being endure this southern climate and live happy and contented?

I abhor the air of Virginia. I hope the whole sacred soil of the ancient dominion will be blasted beyond the power of rejuvenation. May it be buried never to rise again, even from the dead. As I write, I am in plain sight of the rebels; our boys are exchanging soap for tobacco with them. *** I have not heard from John since the Second Corps went to the rear.

Under the new system we continued to receive many an additional morsel to our army ration. We had now settled down to the routine of siege work. There would be enough incidents in the trenches to fill one entire volume. Night alarms were frequent, and on one or two occasions we were up all night.

There was much exchanging or bartering going on. A rebel starts from a rifle pit and comes about midway to a stump between the

---

[5] Isaac H. Stearns (1825–1927) served as surgeon in the 22nd Massachusetts for two years, mustering out in October, 1864. He lived to be 102.—2019

lines, a sort of neutral middle ground. After depositing his treasure, which is generally tobacco, in the hollow of said stump, he returns from whence he came. 'Yank' advances with stores, generally soap, coffee or salt, picks up Johnny's bundle, leaves his own and returns.

Groups gather about the chief actors, and naturally signify their satisfaction by shouts and cheers. These scenes with the digging, occasional shelling and many *etceteras* of camp life in the rear (where we go occasionally, having a guard there now, preserving our tents and effects until we are relieved) at our old camp, constitute our daily life, full of monotony and quietude.

We have actually commenced the siege of Petersburg; the Fifth and Ninth Corps are to conduct the operations, under the supervision and watchfulness of the acting chief engineer of the army (Duane[6] by name), and chief of artillery (General Hunt), Burnside and Warren to be lookers on, Meade to be chief cook, amenable to Grant.

The other corps are to help, when we need their services, in case of sorties by the enemy, or when special duties are to be performed.

I rather like the plan. I guess I can stand two months of siege work; no more charging to be required of your humble sergeant-major, and I am a sure pin on the map of September's doings. I haven't been well for three days past, but am improving now; I had a slight touch of fever, and was troubled with diarrhea. I am almost over both now, and my appetite is gaining again.

No letters from home for a week and a half; no Sunday letter; nothing about the 4th. I don't know what to think of it; to be sure the mails were stopped, but none were captured coming to the army, and communication by steamer with Baltimore has given us last Tuesday's mail from home.

Eugene is by this time in New York City, I suppose.

I have heard where Charlie H. is, and have written a long letter to him; he is in Judiciary Square hospital, and doing well; has every comfort and want supplied; a lady, as good and kind as she is beautiful, anticipates his every wish, brings him flowers, sits beside him, talks to him, and in fact waits upon him with all the charm and delicacy that woman is alone capable of; she is indeed the angel of

---

[6] James Chatham Duane (1824–1897), West Point 1848.

the ward *** he has a severe wound and has to be careful. I wrote several letters *** perhaps one of them has been captured by the rebels. What a perfect failure the rebel invasion has turned out to be, save in the capture of food, forage and animals. Franklin's escape, with that of Sumner's and Tyler's, must be sore losses for them; they must swallow them however, and prepare for worse pills before Petersburg and Richmond.

I believe in the success of Grant. I am confident that we shall enter [Petersburg and Richmond] both before next January.

July 18, 1864

The insurmountable difficulties of writing at this season of the year, particularly in this part of Virginia, are certainly as the Peninsula boys said, for such a place for torrid heat I never was in before, and the flies are perfect nuisances, lighting upon our hands and faces, and sticking closer than brothers *** darkies brushing away flies at a table I imagined to be only a silly custom of chivalry and royalty, indeed a perfect piece of nonsense *** it is a positive necessity, and I would myself pay a darkey or any other man for his services this afternoon. If I can only stand it two months longer, it will be sufficient for the evil thereof endured. *** L. is acting orderly sergeant of Company H, though it is consolidated for convenience sake (in everything except making out returns, reports, muster rolls, etc., which latter duties L. attends to and thereby escapes details), with Company C, Captain Meands, and Charlie Jones is therefore orderly sergeant of both companies.

Haseltine was, before he was wounded, he being the ranking sergeant. Brown, Pressey, Tom Hoar and Joe Welch are the only ones left besides L. Tom W. left us during the battle of the 18th ult., before Petersburg, and hasn't been seen since. Reports are that he is in the hospital sick; he joined us after we crossed the Pamunkey River, and was in several battles. Johnson and Day are at Portsmouth Grove hospital; they have never returned from furlough. *** Our loss in the regiment now is 224 killed and wounded, and 14 missing.

Over ninety have been killed; many of those wounded have since died. Slight wounds have terminated fatally in this campaign.

We are now at the front, and siege operations have been commenced by the Fifth and Ninth Corps; we are to do all such, according to army orders; I am glad of it; it makes my chances better for two months longer. As I write, I am in plain sight of the rebel pickets; no firing goes on between the opposing forces on the line of our brigade and the Third Division upon our left.

We exchange merchandise daily; night alarms are frequent; we were up all night last night. Deserters come in every night in squads; over fifty men ran away from Confederate service. A whole North Carolina brigade will come in if they get a chance, so a deserter said to General Griffin.

Lieutenant Bourne is at brigade headquarters, as Acting Inspector General. Captain Bennett is Assistant Adjutant General. Colonel Gregory, 155th Pennsylvania, commands us.

Mose N. is at City Point bumming on the hospitals; so is Ike M. *** Henry W. and H. (drummer). Royce has been on Warren's Staff as topographical engineer; he drew a map on this campaign. He is now Ass't Q. M., detached (Fifth Corps); Dodge is acting Quartermaster. Royce takes the place of Capt. Oscar Morse, Charlie H's. cousin, who has gone home with the Thirteenth Massachusetts. Dr. Perkins is at present Acting Brigade Surgeon. Chaplain T. is discharged. *** Brown is going with all the battalions forming in the division as sharpshooters.

Sanitary comes down nowadays to enlisted men, when not issued through division, brigade or regimental headquarters. We get a can of peaches and milk today for our mess. We cook for ourselves at present. Dodge has old Jordan at the teams.

In camp, July 19, 1864

I am back to our old reserve place for a few hours. *** It rains; commenced last night at 10 o'clock and soaked Sir Walter through and through in the trenches. That's why I am back at camp, to get dry clothes. It appears to be a genuine storm, and we hope it will continue for a week; the last time we had a storm to speak of was June 2.

In the trenches, July 24, 1864

I had four letters night before last, and the Army and Navy Journal; last night two more, and papers. *** I have been reading the article copied from the *Georgia Constitutionalist* in the *Herald* you sent me. It does indeed afford satisfaction to loyal men, and gives grounds for strong hope in the successful termination of this unhappy strife. It is very indicative, and shows the feeling of a certain class in the South, who are not very weak in influence, or in point of numbers.

Such an article is a representative expression of the people who are behind the scenes. I have no doubt that there are thousands who think the same in the Confederacy, and yet dare not, through fear of a supposed evil, say as much.

It is owing to the despotic rule of the powers that be in rebeldom that the war hangs on.

Were it not for despots in Richmond, and their sway of tyranny over the poor whites, where would be all this seeming persistency and obstinacy of the soldiers? They fight worthy of a better cause; yet they are pushed into battle; they accept the best horn of the dilemma they are placed in.

A hundred deserters come in daily to the lines of the Army of the Potomac; they utter the same meaning words of the Constitutionalist. They dared not say them, or even whisper a thought of them while in the rebel lines, and they would have fought us as valiantly a few hours before the desertion as the deepest dyed Confederate traitor.

Their officers are the higher rank, in an aristocratic point of view, and they rule their men with an iron rod; the soldiers fear them and the least sign of Unionism shown to them would result the same as though Jeff Davis were present. It is quite certain that the 'Stars and Bars' are sinking beneath the waters. The whole system of government, raised upon that accursed corner-stone of slavery, is rotten; the old timbers are cracking. A few more railroads, factories, and the city of Atlanta, Petersburg and Richmond, the only firm joists (getting a little, shaky these days), in poorly built structures, and then down comes the hovel, and up goes the 'flag of freedom;' 'long may it wave!' *** every word of your letter about the constitutional clause and its repeal is truth itself, and you can scarcely know how favorable an aspect it bears to the soldiers in the field; they hailed the event with enthusiasm. 'Now for a draft,' say they!

Such a cut-up country as this about Petersburg never was seen before. It is far ahead of Yorktown digging, so say the Peninsula 'vets.'

You should hear the officers of the First Heavy talk, those who were mustered in 1864, higher grade for a new term, and have been kept. They feel pretty sore over it and even the patriotic ones denounce the 'acts of the Administration' as unwise. Those in our regiment, who have been laughing over my folly of late, now call me wise.

All the Eighteenth Massachusetts officers have got to stay. Since I wrote my last, I have moved out of the trenches and am just a few rods back, near headquarters. The trenches were filthy, and we had not cleaned up, expecting to be relieved every day; now the whole thing has been remedied; everything is clean there, tents are up, new shades line the works, and the boys have settled down here for the remainder of their service.

I have built me a triangular redoubt, and have set a poncho tent within. I have made me a bunk, and with a bed of leaves for a couch, I manage to rest more easy than secure nights, for shell can reach me. I go to camp to draw my rations, and that is about all the exercise I take. They have all the cooking utensils there, but I manage, by the use of several old tin cans, to get some wholesome dishes. Even Watson and Stone do their own cooking. It is too near the front for Dodge, and the cook stays with the trains where D. is, so he gets all the benefit.

My humor still annoys me; I awoke this morning to find my limbs running with blood; I scratched myself while asleep. I can stand anything that Gov't or nature can heap upon me, if the former will permit me to stay right here until my time is out. Wonder if I am being tried in view of that assertion; I will not be found wanting certainly; they may send Job's trials and the seven plagues, and I'll weather them all. *** I am in the best of trim; my generalship is without question in the campaign. I am a perfect soldier now, and can take my gruel three times a day regularly.

Lieutenant Look, to whom I entrusted Emerson's watch and chain, is delayed in Washington on business.

At dusk on the 28th we were move to the right and were again near the scene of our charge of June 18, near the Hare House, where Fort Stedman or "[Fort] Hell" was afterwards built.

The scene at night, as we wound in and out the subterranean dugouts, would have reminded one of the old-time concert or basement saloon in New York or Boston, with their cellars ablaze, and the whole ground, thrown up in heaps, resembled an immense prairie dog village.

The covered ways were six feet deep, twelve feet wide, the barricades of logs, were four feet high and four feet through. A wagon train could pass rapidly within one-quarter of a mile of the rebel earthworks. Our bomb proofs consisted of an excavation about six feet square by six deep, covered with earth, under which were logs, and a little back cellar way was left on the side away from the enemy. Our shelter tents we pitched on top the bomb proof. Some lived in the upper story, but were always ready to drop down into the cellar whenever firing commenced. We had become so used and hardened to danger that we sometimes became careless.

Our letters say:

One night, while washing in a tub, three shells exploded near us; one piece struck within a few feet of the major's tent, where he and the adjutant were sleeping.

They immediately *vacated their abode.*' I wiped myself, got into bed, and hugged my log fortress for safety.

From our position, we could plainly see the dirt thrown up, where Colonel Davis' (39th Massachusetts) tent stood, who was killed only a day or two before, while apparently secure in his bomb-proof castle built about him. On the night of the 28th, a ball buried itself near our brother, and later a mortar shell exploded close by. It was a strange sensation to be awakened at night by the picket firing, or the booming of cannon, when one, perchance, was dreaming of hearing the clock ticking on the mantel at home.

Our letters say:

In front of Petersburg,

on right of Fifth Corps line,

July 29, 1864

We have moved again; last night at dusk we moved out of our trenches on the left, and came to this place. We relieved the Third Brigade, Second Division; the Fourth Division is still upon our right. We are quite near to the scene of our charge on the 18th ult. The 'Petersburg Express' (now called 'The Seven Sisters,' 30 pdr. Rodmans) is close to us, and the iron messengers are being sent into the city at regular intervals. Last night there were fires burning there, and we could hear bells ringing the alarms distinctly.

This morning I can see the spires plainly from our breastworks and bomb proofs. When we came in last night, all the regiments of the brigade were put into the front line except ours; there was not room for ours apparently, and we were put into the roadways (covered ways), which are cut all through the Federal lines.

We have received no orders yet, and where we shall eventually be placed is uncertain just at present. Probably we shall have to build our own proofs. The rest of the brigade was fortunate enough to step into them already constructed. It did seem so strange to us when we came here last night to see the ground all heaped about us like a prairie dog village, and then the subterranean residences all lighted up, and the occupants so seemingly at home; it did look like home streets, with the cellar in a blaze.

I was forcibly reminded of the underground saloons in New York City where the waiting maids handed over the drinks, and amused the patronizers by their songs and dances; not that I ever strolled into such places, but I have often read of them in the *New York Clipper*, that paragon of morality.

These siege operations are something new to me. It is very interesting, also these bomb proofs, dug deep in the ground, logged up, covered over with timber, and the whole coop covered with earth and banked up. It is a beautiful sight to see the mortar shells wing their way through the air, tumbling over and over until they explode. A mortar when fired has a sort of hollow, empty sound, but the shell is big with solid noise; it is different from a rifle cannon shell. As soon as I look about I shall have an abundance of material for a long, descriptive letter.

It is said that we have abandoned the whole of that line where our brigade was last night, before moving here. You know I said it was only temporary. The line now crosses from left of First Brigade to a fort where the Third Division is on the flank; it cuts across diagonally, leaving the line left by us on the outside of no further use; we may go up there if there isn't room for us here.

The Second Division, General Ayres, is to act as a reserve to the Fifth Corps.

I have no fault to find; we have been treated well since the 18th of, June. *** A mortar shell just exploded uncomfortably near; last night, while sleeping, a minie buried itself near me; it came from the picket line. The Maryland Brigade of the Fourth Division, Fifth Corps, is the only body of troops on the left of Burnside who fire on picket. It is a strange sensation one has, when he awakens at night, with only the air above him, and hears the picket shot instead of the familiar clock tick in the kitchen below. *** Charlie Carter's death is still a mystery inasmuch as I do not know how, when or why he was at the front near New Orleans; the last I heard of him he was at Alexandria as Brigade Quartermaster.

Our brother of the artillery now writes:

Near Petersburg, Va.,

July 17, 1864

Everything is quiet here now, but the storm is coming, and before many days you will be called upon to peruse another account of blood and carnage. I have not seen Walter for about a week as we have moved back about a mile or two to the rear, and are now enjoying a comparative rest.

I wish you would please inform Mr. Silsby that his son is quite sick, and is now in the division hospital; I took him over there day before yesterday; I have not heard from him; he is all broken down.

On the 21st of July the First Massachusetts Heavy Artillery moved to Fort Bross and remained there until the 26th.

Our letters say:

In the Trenches,

July 24, 1864.

John was over here day before yesterday; he was one of a working party nearby, detailed from the 3d Division, 2d Corps, to build a road for siege trains, etc. They are to build it under the superintendence of army engineers. They dig 6 feet deep and 12 feet wide; then the barricade is 4 feet high and 4 feet through. Any amount of munitions of war can be passed along in perfect safety, even within a quarter of a mile of the rebel fortifications. I went over to where he was working, after he had been with me a short time. *** John and I went to camp, and I cooked a good dinner; we enjoyed ourselves over it; he said he had not eaten so good a meal since he left the breastworks, and thereby ceased to visit me.

When he left me, he said he would come to see me again soon. I could see him almost all day from the trenches where I was.

At 5 P. M. on the 26th the regiment (First Heavy Artillery) moved out from its position near Fort Bross, and taking the road toward City Point, but diverging to the left near Commissary Station, marched to Point of Rocks on the Appomattox River, and crossing it on pontoons about 10 P. M. marched all night to Jones Banding on the James River, arriving at 4 A. M. on the 27th.

Crossed the James River at 5 A. M. distance marched twenty-four miles. Halted one hour for breakfast. At 7 o'clock formed line of battle in the woods to the left of the Burnt Chimneys, and facing Strawberry Plains. Here the regiment was subjected to a severe artillery fire from the enemy.

On reaching the City Point road on the 26th, the column marched by a double gallows, on which the night before two teamsters of the Seventy-second New York had been hanged. Their term of service had expired, and the next day they were to have left for home. But they were accused of an outrageous assault upon a poor woman, who was living alone in a house nearby. At daylight she made a complaint to the Provost Marshal; search was made; she identified the men; they were speedily tried and convicted, and hanged in full view of the enemy's lines. Thus was prompt justice meted out in the Army of the Potomac.

Our skirmishers being engaged with the enemy in the edge of the woods, half a mile distant, the Fifty-seventh Pennsylvania and the First Massachusetts Heavy Artillery were ordered as a support. They advanced across open fields and through a ravine under a heavy artillery fire and halted within a few rods of the skirmish line' of the Second Division, where they remained until about 2 P. M. and then rejoined the brigade. Lay in the woods all night. One man wounded.

At 11 A. M. on the 28th, moved to the right and formed line of battle with the brigade; at 2 P. M. moved to the left and built breastworks facing the New Market road. Soon after this, it was ordered to a position on the extreme right of the Second Corps, connecting our right with the cavalry. From this position, marched by the left flank and formed a new line through a piece of woods, the left connecting with the right of the First Division, while the right rested near the New Market Road.

Colonel Chaplin of the First Maine Heavy Artillery had been in command of the brigade from the 26th owing to the illness of Gen. B. R. Pierce, but on the 28th, the One Hundred and Forty-first Pennsylvania having been transferred to the brigade, Col. H. J. Madill of that regiment assumed command.

At 8 P. M., or shortly after dark, the regiment was withdrawn and commenced its march back to Petersburg. Recrossed the James at Deep Bottom, and the Appomattox at Point of Rocks at midnight. At daybreak on the 29th halted on the right and in rear of the Eighteenth Corps line. Bivouacked all day in the woods just east of the City Point railroad until dark, when it moved up into the front line of works and relieved a portion of the Eighteenth Corps. This was about half a mile from where the mine was exploded. Distance marched, twenty-two miles.

Soon after daylight, while all were watching for the spectacular display which they had been promised for the 30th, two heavy rumbling sounds were heard as though coming from the bowels of the earth, and the whole sky seemed blackened with dirt, fragments of timber, debris, and what appeared to be dark objects that looked like human bodies.

The regiment remained in the trenches, and were ordered to keep up a continuous fire on the enemy, who was about 200 yards distant. It expended on an average, about 150 rounds per man. Its loss while in this position was one man wounded.

Our letters of July 29 say:

In front of Petersburg,

On right of Fifth Corps

John is off on a 'toot' with the Second Corps. I have not seen him for two or three days now. We are anxiously awaiting tidings from the gallant Hancock, also from Sheridan's cavalry, now eighteen days on a raid.

On the 30th at 10 P. M. the First Massachusetts Heavy Artillery was relieved by a portion of the Eighteenth Corps, which returned to its old position, and the regiment moved to the place it had occupied on the 26th, which it reached about 3 A. M. on the 31st.

Our brother of the First Heavy visited us in the bomb proofs. He had had a hard time with the Second Corps at Deep Bottom, across the James, but had been withdrawn in time to reach the lines in expectation of a charge on the 30th of July.

August 1, moved out of the breastworks and back toward the center and rear of the front line, and went into camp, where it remained until August 12. On the 5th, an alarm, said to have been caused by an explosion of a mine on the line of the Eighteenth Corps, brought out the entire Third Division, and it marched toward that point, but soon returned, and resumed its position. It was intolerably hot and dry, causing much suffering.

Yankee wit was too much for them. Everything had been removed from the fort, and our troops were massed to receive them. They charged four lines of battle deep. Our lines opened with shrapnel, canister and musketry, and they went back to their works in the greatest confusion. The ground was strewn with their dead. 'Tit for tat,' was the cry along the lines.

We were all kept busily at work digging on the night of the 29th. One of our company was taken with cramp colic while thus engaged, and our brother, by diligent chafing and rubbing, undoubtedly saved his life. All night long we were up and anxiously awaiting, yet with a sort of nervous dread, the coming of the morrow. The mine, which had for so long been in process of construction, was now completed, and was to be sprung at 3.30 o'clock. We were held in readiness for a charge on the left of the Ninth Corps. The mine was run at a point of the works known as Elliot's Salient, and almost precisely where we had charged on the 18th of June. With almost breathless suspense, trembling with alternate hope and anxious fear, we awaited the result. When we saw the earth shoot up like a volcano at 4.25 A. M., we shouted for joy, and immediately upon the artillery opening with its terrific roar, we looked for the charge from the covered ways, which run along in rear of our advanced works. We were so intent upon the success of this movement that we forgot our caution, as did every other soldier in the vicinity, and mounting the parapets, swarmed our breastworks in plain sight of the enemy.

Then tardily came the feeble charge. All was apparently successful for a time, and a counter charge made by the rebels about 11 A. M. was repulsed, but soon we saw our discomfited men come streaming back, and there was nothing after but newer and fresher stories of disaster, blood and carnage. It made our hearts sick. By night we had lost, for a third time, our chances of entering the "Cockade" city of Petersburg.

To the rear, the railroad was lined with troops in reserve. Our works were crowded with men. Yet, through imbecility, cowardice and incompetency, thousands of brave men had been wantonly sacrificed for naught. Late in the afternoon, when we saw the Ninth Corps leave the crater, our chagrin and anger knew no bounds.

Our letters say (in dim lead pencil):

Near Petersburg, Va.,

July 31, 1864

Your letter came when danger was round me, and during a time most momentous in our country's history. July 30th, it thundered all along the Union lines; the air was thick with hissing shell, buzzing bullet, and the death cry of many a brave man. I'll tell you about it on the very sheet of paper you sent me; if you had not enclosed it I couldn't have written, for all my things were in camp, and had been ordered to be packed up with the rest of the baggage. *** I do not know as it is safe now, as a great deal of material was left behind for want of transportation.

Night before last we were ordered to the rear of the 'roadway' (covered way), and we commenced to build bomb proofs for ourselves. About 6 o'clock in the morning Major Burt came to us and said, 'You must finish these proofs tonight, men. At 3.30 o'clock in the morning, the mine under the rebel works where you charged will be sprung; three divisions of Burnside's Corps will charge supported by the Second Corps, and the Second Division of the Fifth. You are to be in readiness to move at 4 A. M.'

You can imagine our feelings perhaps, the excitement and anxiety produced among us; the whole night long I helped dig and build. It was a very warm evening, and as the long hours wore away into the morning I must confess I felt nervous regarding the impending struggle. I hoped for our success. I worried lest I, in my course of duty, might be taken from you just two months from the time you are all hoping to see me in Bradford. Let me tell you one event of the night. Welch, a private of Company H, was shoveling dirt upon the logs covering the pit, when he fell flat upon his face saying, 'Oh, my God! something in my stomach has given away!' He groaned and writhed in agony; instinct told me at once what ailed him, and in a moment I had him stripped and was rubbing him with both hands; he had the colic like that of poor Rob's when he was at 'Smoky Camp.'

Soon a cramp set in, and it took the united efforts of four men, one on each arm, one holding his legs, and one straightening the cords of his neck, to keep his body from tying itself into a knot. For over two hours we had this suffering man under our care; every time a cramp would seize him he would give us warning, and we would try to keep his limbs straight, but sometimes his strength far exceeded ours, and then it was terrible to see poor suffering humanity writhe and twist in an inconceivable agony and torment. Why! he would twist his limbs about me, and snap my two arms like a whipcord; he is a weak man in his usual condition, but he certainly was a giant when in pain.

We finally eased him, so that I had him carried to the rear on a stretcher; he said before he left: 'Carter, you have saved my life; I never would have been alive but for you.' I believe him, and how happy I am to know that I am an instrument in saving a soldier from a death more horrible than that of the bullet.

In the grey of the morn the fort blew up, earth, guns, men, and all; it was a signal for the opening chorus of Grant's Minstrels, and from the James to the left of the Fifth Corps, every gun and mortar battery attuned its voice to the grandest music of the war; never was heard such a cannonade.

The Rebs could not reply. The charge was made; the fort was carried; our lines advanced, were repulsed, held the fort again, were attacked by the enemy who were driven back in disorder, and then for the last time fled from the enemy, who attacked again at 3.30 P. M.

The ruins of the fort were theirs; we had gained nothing. We lost plenty of Negroes and white men. Today in our front the pickets are friendly, and walk the lines unconcerned, and where all was still and quiet in the rebel works yesterday, is life and activity today. They are repairing damages. My paper is out, and I cannot write particulars as I intended to; as soon as I get settled again I will describe the battle to some of you; I saw it all, after the shelling had subsided somewhat. It was a magnificent spectacle, the grandest I ever witnessed; I would not have been absent, now that it is over, for the world.

I can see the rebel fort now; a flag of truce has been denied us; our dead still lie in plain sight, and our wounded are suffering in the hot sun. *** We shall move, think; I hope so, and if we make a charge, we will gain our point and hold it; I am right on my fight.

I hate to be defeated, and to have my part of the army driven. I always want it retrieved.

Our letters say:

Before Petersburg,

August 3, 1864

I have not written home for a few days because it has been an impossibility; first, it has been too hot for mortal man to sit down with such an intention; second, I have been too angry to contain my big self, in view of the late, most stupendous blunder of the war.[7]

The swarms of flies that make a man's life miserable here have also withheld me from doing what I would; my short letter to M. was unworthy the name, but it was all I could do, on the ever to be remembered day of July 30.

All night of the 29th I was on my taps, and eagerly did I wait for morning, yet with a sort of dread, for with victory comes the slaughter of men, and the First Division (Fifth Corps) I knew had orders to be in readiness at an early hour.

When I saw the rebel fort go up at 4.15 o'clock, I shouted for joy, and during that awful thunder of artillery, I was looking for the charge from the embankment of the dug road, which runs along in rear of our advance works, and parallel to them.

I forgot myself, as did most every other soldier in the army. We were intent upon success, and every entrenchment in front, in plain sight of the rebel works and the rebels (if they only dared to look), was lined with our troops looking at the fort.

The charge was made, and all was apparently successful during the forenoon; one charge made by the "Johnnies" a little past 11 o'clock, was repulsed, but everything gained was lost at a later part of the day, and at night we lost for the third time what we ought to have gained, the 'Cockade City of Petersburg.'

Only the rebel fort was blown up, and a few rebels killed and wounded, while we lost four or five thousand men, and have the effects upon us of a defeat, the result of mismanagement of minor officials, and not after a gallant fight with no possibility of success.

Only three rebel divisions were in our front, and they were withdrawn for the charge upon the fort in the afternoon, leaving only a single weak line for appearances. Even this small number kept close, so as to give the appearance of a ruse. To our rear, the railroad was lined with our troops in reserve. Our works swarmed with men, yet this fort was relinquished. I would have had that fort and kept it, if it had taken the whole Second, Fifth and Eighteenth Corps to accomplish the result. I see by the *New York Herald* and

---

[7] Grant considered the crater assault "the saddest affair I have witnessed in this war."—2019

Washington Chronicle that the Second and Fifth Corps were engaged; it is not so, but oh, how we longed to be. When I saw the Ninth Corps leave the fort, late in the afternoon, I was beside myself. I would have given my four months' pay to have been in a charge by 'Jack' Griffin's division, at that time.

General Warren sent to General Meade, and said that he 'had a division that could retake and hold the fort,' but Meade declined the offer, saying he 'did not want to sacrifice the men.' That is a fact, father, and the First Division was the one alluded to. We would have been glad to try it; I never wanted to fight so in my life.

I wouldn't have cared if I had been wounded or killed, if we had won the victory. The whole thing was against us; a most damnable disgrace, and the blame rests somewhere. We could have taken Petersburg that day, I am certain. Directly in our front was a rebel fort, completely silenced by a mortar battery of eleven nine-inch mortars (no lb. shell). We could have charged and gone through their line on its left. If you see the *Herald*, you will see that the fort is placed near the Appomattox River; it is a mistake; it is just to our right, and we are almost at the extreme left of the front line.

If I could get a *Herald*, I would send you one with the fort properly designated upon the map on the first sheet (or rather page).

Sherman lost colors and guns on the 22d; Grant lost enough on the 30th, and now the rebs are in Pennsylvania. It is time to do something desperate now; let us adopt General Hood's policy and go in for close quarters. We excel them, I know we do. I want the last ten days wiped out speedily; I am ready for anything devoted to that purpose. Mortar shells are constantly bursting over our heads. We eat our meals, and watch for them while swallowing our food, as cool as you please; sometimes it provokes a smile to think of the dire consequences that would happen to a dinner should a bomb descend upon it (not saying a word about ourselves). Surely all is not for the best that comes from above.

Our batteries have been leaving; also the ten-inch mortar batteries; something up. Good-bye!

Our letters of August 6, 1864, say:

Billy Steele has been ordered to report at Annapolis, where a board of officers is convened, to inquire into the absence of officers over their legitimate time.

Two years ago this day I was mustered into the U. S. service at Lynnfield, and as I review the time gone by, I must say they are the hardest years I ever lived; no one knows what we have suffered and endured; the worst is now almost over, and then for home. What a change it will be for me. I have not changed much, I think. *** Last night Major Burt received word from Massachusetts that our time was out September 5, and our regiment's notice has been sent to the corps as going home in less than six weeks.

John has been here all day; he has been having a pretty hard time of late on the other side of the James. His division (Mott's) expected to charge on the 30th; he is looking well. Poor fellow! I wish he didn't have three years to stay.

August 6

I received a letter from Eugene last night for John. John had only left me a few hours before, near his camp, where I had walked with him; he spent the day with me.

While writing yesterday, a whirlwind came roaring through my tent and carried a letter half written to — and a half quire of thin note paper up into the air. The last I saw of it was toward the rebel lines; I imagine they will be edified in perusing it.

Wait patiently, and never dream of evil to either of us. I feel as well as I ever did, and am still confident in the success of U. S. Grant. People at home ought never to despair of the republic, when the soldiers are so hopeful and so long suffering. The fates seem to be against the Potomac Army, and yet 'how the boys hang together and fight.' We bless the people at home for their sympathy bestowed upon our poor unfortunate soldiers, wounded in the late engagements, and for the moral and social appreciation given to us in the field, which is dearer than life to a hero's heart.

THE SUNNY SIDE OF ARMY LIFE

Now came a decided change in our life and service at the front. Word came to the division to send a regiment whose term of service was nearest out, and which numbered the least, to City Point to guard the government machine and repair shops. Notwithstanding the thousand and one rumors at different periods that we were going to do duty in Alexandria or Washington; were to assist in preserving order in New York and Boston during the riots of 1863, or were to be ordered home to recruit the regiment, this was indeed our first "soft job." We would not believe it was true, until word came on the 7th that the order was then at division headquarters, and we would leave the breastworks in the morning. General Griffin designated the Twenty-second for this duty.

August 7, 1864:

We go to City Point tomorrow to do guard duty at the government machine and repair shops; the order is at division headquarters, and we expect it tonight. Colonel Sherwin and Major Burt say we will be on the road in the morning; is it not a glorious thing for us? Only a little time there, and we shall be in good trim for a journey homeward.

Rebel shells and bullets do not reach this point, I believe. If I live through this night, I shall, in all human probability, see you at home in September; I shall take the best possible care of myself, and try to avoid all fevers and ailments. ***

John has been here all day, and he was delighted with the (mother's) letter. Night before last his division was double quicked to the Eighteenth Corps, at the time of the attack there.

I was intending to go to City Point tomorrow with J. Watson. *** It is just as well as it is, only we shall walk instead of riding.

*** A large fort has just been completed on our left. The 'Seven Sisters' is to be remounted there, and the bombardment is to commence again next Tuesday; let them shoot! It is all right if I am at City Point.

I am right in my element tonight, happy as you please, and almost too sanguine of the future.

On Monday morning, the 8th, "sure enough" we started for our "soft job" of guard duty at City Point, and after an easy march of nine miles, arrived about noon. We pitched our camp on the left bank of the City Point Railroad, facing the front, near General Grant's Headquarters, and were directly under the orders of General Rufus Ingalls, Chief Quartermaster of the Army of the Potomac. The Appomattox River was nearby, affording us ample facilities for bathing, also the Army Corps Hospitals, that immense canvas city for the sick and wounded. We drew our rations from a Post Commissary and from the Sanitary Commission, and got our water from a curbed well about fifty feet in depth. It was by far the best camp and the best duty the regiment had ever seen.

There were over five hundred citizens employed about us, and we guarded their shops and all the war material about the immense war depot. On the day following our arrival the terrible explosion of the ammunition boxes took place at the landing, and it was frightful, even to us, who had just come from the bloody carnage from the Rapidan to the James, and when every moment had well-nigh seemed our last, to see the mutilated, dead bodies, the wounded and fragments gathered up.

We saw fifteen dead bodies and twenty-eight bags of blackened, charred pieces of humanity (black and white men) in one wagon load, gathered or shoveled up, to be placed in the trenches. How fearful the thought of passing from life to death in a moment of time. The brief span that separated one from the other.

This was believed to be the act of somebody in the employ of the enemy. There were 250 employees and soldiers killed and wounded; 600 feet of warehouses were thrown down, besides 160 linear feet of wharf torn out. Immense quantities of shot and shell were thrown into the air, and much of it, with debris, fell into General Grant's headquarter camp, one piece wounding Col. O. B. Babcock of the Engineer Corps, who was on Grant's staff.

Our letters now say:

U. S. Sanitary Commission,

City Point, Va.,

August 11, 1864

Now for regimental news and then I will tell you about our experience here, and this City Point affair generally. Whittaker is in the Invalid Corps, and Welch is here at the Point, in Division Hospital, sick. *** Billy Steele is at Annapolis *** he overstayed his time and the Government finds fault with the brave, wounded officer.

Captain Bennett is brigade inspector, Bourne, A. D. C., and Akerman, ambulance officer, the latter in place of Lieutenant Wood, now absent sick. Lieutenant Clapp has been sick a long time; he joined tonight, and goes home tomorrow morning on a 15 days' leave; good for 30 I reckon. Bourne and Davis have been promoted to captains; N. and W. are back with the regiment; both have been tried by general court-martial. N.'s sentence is fourteen dollars per month during the remainder of service, and to wear a placard marked 'Skulker' two hours each day, for ten days.

It will go hard with Tom W., I guess. All our non-commissioned staff are here, and I am eating Jordan's cooked messes the first time in three months and a half.

I have learned to cook in style during that time, I assure you.

I am now living with Soden,[1] Hospital Steward (Newmarch discharged), in a nice wall tent made of ponchos; we have nice bunks, covered with fly netting and filled with straw; we have a tin pail, wash basin, and everything comfortable, from the 'Sanitary' canned stuff, wines, etc. Dodge and Watson are on our left in a small wall tent, and Stone to their right, in the rear.

Sunday, August 7, we were ordered to City Point for guard duty, and early Monday morning we started, and arrived here toward noon. *** We shall have the best camp that the regiment ever had as soon as we can have time to fix up. *** We guard the shops belonging to the Government, both machine and repair. Ike Mattoon and Sam Appleton are over at Division Hospital in the dispensary; I go over to get my soda water, ice cream, porter, and a

---

[1] Arthur H. Soden (1843–1925) was later a Major League Baseball executive and president/owner of the Boston Base Ball Club.—2019

little blackberry and sherry wine at times; Sam helps me to canned stuff, crackers, etc.

We bathe in the Appomattox every night, and listen to the music in that camp city (where everything is as perfectly arranged as in Boston), and enjoy a communion with the muses. Haze Goodrich is in charge of the Ninth Corps dispensary. I took dinner with him yesterday; he lives magnificently, he gave me a large box of goodies and a can of milk, not mentioning a glass of ale. Had bread and butter, apple sauce, and a boiled dish for dinner, bread pudding for dessert. Isn't this life an unexpected, great and sudden change?

Isn't it a big thing for the regiment? Ditto for us in particular.

John was over to see me last Sunday, before I knew we were going; I had a good dinner for him; I enjoy his calls so much. I wrote to him yesterday, telling him to come down on the railroad.

I was over to Emerson's grave when the order came for us to move; Lovejoy and I fixed up around it nicely. Holt, Day, Eaton, Orell and Sprague are still up at brigade headquarters; they wish to come down; perhaps they may. I hear from Gene now. I saw the whole fight on the 30th ult., the grandest spectacle I ever witnessed, and when we were repulsed, you can imagine my feelings, for no order came for the Fifth Corps to charge; my feelings were honest; I ached to retrieve that disaster so needless.

We now heard that the Second Corps was again (August 14) on the north side of the James, and that Mott's Division had been severely engaged with the enemy near Bailey's Creek, but it was several days before we could ascertain the safety of our brother. Also that our own corps, the Fifth, was on a raid, August 17, to the Weldon Railroad. We were busy cleaning up our camp, and making ourselves comfortable for the few weeks of our stay, and could well afford now to be more patriotic than ever. We keenly watched the effect of the nomination of Abraham Lincoln, and General McClellan and the blatant *peace cry* from the *tired out* non-combatants at the North, and we thus expressed our minds.

I am hoping for great success now. All faintheartedness and childish whining are unbecoming a great people at this time. Emulate the spirit and courage of the soldiers, even amidst reverses. I would say to the people! We must *work* for the war, *talk* for the war, and *fight* in the war, with fixed convictions that it is Heaven's own war, and that we are all commanded from on high, to curb this rebellion speedily.

No peace with treason or Copperheads. How ridiculous the *soi-disant* Peace Commissioners in Canada! I liked Abraham's summary manner of disposition. He shall have my vote in November. What tact he displayed in his proclamation—To whom it may concern:

"No peace until the South yields obedience to the laws of the land. The treason of the master has freed the slave, and the South must join the Union without slavery. What loyal mind deems it necessary to leave nothing unattempted which offers the slightest hope of permanent peace, just for policy's sake? Not one! No sentiment of liberality or justice should yield to anything but the safest of policies, the bayonet and an honorable peace as the result. Let us 'go in' on this basis, and January, 1865, sees this war at an end!"

At 3 P. M. on August 12, the First Massachusetts Heavy Artillery, Col. C.A. Craig, 105th Pennsylvania, commanding brigade, moved out, and again took the road for City Point; very hot, roads dusty; several sunstrokes; marching until 9 P. M. it reached the banks of the James River at City Point where it bivouacked for the night. Remained here during the 13th until 7 P. M. when it embarked on transports and proceeded down the river until Windmill Point was reached, when the boats came to anchor until 10 P. M. Anchor was then weighed, and they proceeded up the river until Jones Neck or Deep Bottom was reached; arrived at 1 A. M.; remained here for the rest of the night; suffocatingly hot on the boats, and mosquitoes infernally tormenting. Commenced disembarking early in the morning; by 7.30 all of the division were on shore. Marched at once over Strawberry Plains to the woods, where the regiment remained bivouacked all day and night, waiting for orders to fight or return to the boat. This position was near what was called the tavern and "Pottery" on the New Market and Malvern Hill road. On the 15th it was ordered to report to Gen. D. B. Birney, now commanding the Tenth Corps, and to make a reconnaissance to the extreme right of the position toward the Charles City road with instructions to push on and reach that road if possible.

Forming line of battle, with the First U. S. Sharpshooters as skirmishers, the brigade advanced; the Eighty-fourth Pennsylvania on the right, the First Massachusetts Heavy Artillery on its left and the One Hundred and Fifth Pennsylvania on the left. This line was supported on either flank by the One Hundred and Forty-first Pennsylvania and Fifth Michigan, while the Ninety-third New York was massed in column of divisions behind the line of battle. The right flank was protected by cavalry, and the Fifty-seventh Pennsylvania was deployed as flankers to protect the left.

In this order the line advanced through the woods for nearly five miles. About one mile out the enemy was met, and skirmishing continued nearly all day, the enemy falling back continually before the line. When the Charles City road was reached, he made a stand. His position was charged and he was driven out. Took position on both sides of the road, and held it until relieved at dark. Loss, 1 man killed, 7 wounded. The day was very hot.

On the 16th the brigade acted as a support to General Turner's Second Division, Tenth Corps. The First Massachusetts Heavy Artillery and Fifty-seventh Pennsylvania were massed in column of divisions in rear of the line to extend the skirmish line to the right, or to support the line of battle as the case might be.

The skirmish line was the First U. S. Sharpshooters and Fifth Michigan, supported by a line of battle which was made up of the Ninety-third New York, One Hundred and Fifth and One Hundred and Forty-first Pennsylvania.

Soon after the advance commenced, the First Massachusetts Heavy Artillery deployed on the right of the Fifth Michigan as flankers. Brisk skirmishing ensued and continued from 10 A. M. to 10 P. M. when a charge was made which went over and beyond three lines of works, but our line withdrew to the front line of their captured works, and it was held all night. Loss in the regiment, 1 killed. Colonel Craig, commanding brigade, and Col. D. Chaplin, First Maine Heavy Artillery, were both mortally wounded. On this day (16th) Gen. J. R. Chambliss of the rebel cavalry was killed at Deep Creek near the Charles City road, and was buried by the Third Brigade at the "Potteries," where the New Market road crosses Bailey's Creek, in front of the road.

August 17, the regiment was relieved from duty with the Tenth Corps, and reported back to the Third Division, Second Corps, and held left of line, extreme left resting on Bailey's Creek on left of the "Potteries."

At 8 P. M. on the 18th the regiment marched back across Bermuda Hundred to the James River; recrossed it at midnight, and arrived at Ninth Corps headquarters at 8 A. M. on the 19th, relieving General White's division. Distance marched, 25 miles.

On picket duty until August 25, the line extending from Fort Tilton to Strong's house.

September 1, the regiment was ordered to garrison Fort Alexander Hays, where it remained doing garrison duty until September 25, when it was relieved by a regiment of the Ninth Corps, and joined the brigade in rear of the Jones house on the line of the military railroad. Here Gen. B. R. Pierce took command.

City Point, Va.,

August 19, 1864

(Soldier's letter, franked, Dr. Stearn, Surgeon, Twenty-second Mass.)

I have been keeled up; my left thigh in front has been swelled to twice its natural size, from the effects of ivy poison; I have been abed all the time and in perfect misery; the doctor seems to regard my case with much interest [?], and the hospital department was lacking in remedies, so that I became enraged and took the matter into my own hands; I obtained some sugar of lead, made a wash and put it on twice a day; washed the parts affected, each time with castile soap suds.

This morning I am up for the first time; my leg is almost healed, but my old humor, prickly heat, rash or itch troubles me yet a little; I am perfectly well otherwise, and gain in flesh every day; September will find me in good trim, I hope.

The Fifth Corps moved night before last (we were not there, thank fortune), and we hear that they have gone in the direction of the Weldon Railroad. Our batteries opened again yesterday morning in front of Petersburg, probably for the purpose of covering the movements in process; these operations of the Second and Fifth Corps are evidently to aid General Grant in some project of his; I trust that all will be well as he wishes.

The operations of Hancock have been thus far successful. I am somewhat anxious concerning John, for I hear that his division has been engaged; I hope he is safe.

We are very comfortable where we are now; not a particle of lead or iron is thrown at us, which renders our stay here particularly agreeable. We appreciate our detachment very much, coming as it does when the boys most desire a place at the rear; I think there is no doubt but we shall stay here until our time expires.

We are cleaning up for our home journey, and yesterday we were inspected by the brigade inspector for the last time. I have drawn a new pair of new government brogans for my trip to Boston; I started away from the 'Hub' clean and in good condition and it is my intention to enter its portals again, as well provided for in raiment and as clean and healthy every way! All hail the day! *** Lieutenant Steele arrived tonight, August 20. I have the red pepper and 'Sulphia Quinia.' He is not discharged from the service as a letter of George Lovejoy's states.

(U. S. Sanitary Commission paper):

City Point,

August 29, 1864

I am doomed to suffer; no sooner had my humor begun to leave me than I was sorely afflicted with poison, and now as that has left me three boils have broken out upon my poor body, and I am stiff and sore under their painful influences.

Excepting these trials, I was never better in my life. Tell mother not to worry for me; I am all patience and endurance. If I only get

615

home, I shall look back upon all this experience as a trifle compared to the joy at the end. *** Colonel Sherwin came from the front yesterday morning, and brought us news from division headquarters. He says that the paper sent by Major Burt to the War Department *** has been returned with this endorsement *** that our time is out October 8; you can imagine our indignation.

Martin's Massachusetts Battery came out with the Twenty-second, was mustered in at the same time and after the same manner, and the whole command goes to Massachusetts, September 5.

Our headquarter officers, line officers and the men wonder at it, and are all much enraged; our detail at City Point alone kept the cork in the bottle. Perhaps I am not mad. Edgar has rejoined the regiment.

September 1, the enemy's cavalry made a dash against our cavalry picket lines, driving it in on the left of the Gurley house. The Second Corps was ordered under arms. On the 4th a national salute was ordered to be fired along the lines, the guns to be shotted, and directed into the enemy's lines. Every fort and battery took it up, and it made a deafening roar.

There was much angry discussion over our time of muster out, and when the Third Massachusetts Battery, which was attached to, and came out with the regiment, came down to City Point on the 4th of September, it made many of our grumblers curse the administration, and wish for the success of the Chicago nominee—General McClellan.

Our letters of September 5, 1864, say:

The Third Massachusetts Battery is bivouacked in the rear of our regiment; it embarks this morning for Washington. Captain Martin and his officers remained at our headquarters last night; Ves Farnsworth goes home too, just one month before his old company does; he was in the First New York Battery until a few days ago, and getting transferred into the Third Massachusetts gives him a chance to strike for home; I wish we were going too, and it is Captain Martin's opinion that we ought to accompany them; however, we shall be soon coming.

616

The regiment will escort them to the boat at 8 o'clock this A. M.; we are waiting so patiently to be paid off. I see by the papers that General Woodbury, Key West, is dead;[2] was he not a classmate of yours at West Point?

What glorious news! Fort Morgan and Atlanta ours. Why, father, we shall whip the South into submission before 'Little Mac' can propose peace, should he be elected (and I doubt such a result). Now if Grant could take Petersburg we could organize one grand advance on Richmond, a victorious one, and close up the Rebellion by an immense triumph. I have not heard of or seen John yet; he promised to write me. Adjutant Davis went up to the First Massachusetts Heavy Artillery last Wednesday, and took a letter and some paper to him, but forgot to see him.

I would like to be there to see, but as for participating even now in the capture of Petersburg and Richmond, I am willing to forego it; I am very well satisfied with my fighting career. Gene says he shall not vote, and does not know who his presidential favorite is; I pitched into him good about it. I cannot swallow McClellan; his platform is too shallow and there are too many subterfuges in it. I think Abraham's supporters have pretty plain sailing, and will achieve signal triumphs on the stump. What do you think of Fremont's letter? It is a straightforward, manly document, and right to the point; I agree with it, but cannot look upon his course in opposition to the administration as right. He is right upon the goose but not upon the gander. *** Tell Mary A. that Sam was sitting up last night; he still continues to have turns of sickness; the poor fellow's lungs are affected; we blistered him the other day.

Steele and myself dined with Haze Goodrich last Thursday; I went to meeting yesterday at Sanitary Chapel; saw ex-May or Fay of Chelsea there. On my way back, saw Henry M. of B.; he is ward master in Third Division, Second Corps hospital; he is looking quite well; says he has his bitters regularly. Colonel T. is back to the regiment for good. *** We have graduated two able generals from the line of the Twenty-second, viz: General Charles J. Paine (Tenth Corps), and General Nelson Miles.[3]

---

[2] Daniel Phineas Woodbury (1812–August 15, 1864) died of yellow fever.—2019

[3] Nelson Appleton Miles (1839–1925) played a prominent role in many Civil War battles and later in the Indian Wars. He was named

It is quite cool here *** We feel better every way.

Upon passing the Christian Commission tent one day we saw, standing in the doorway, an old, familiar countenance, and pushing toward it, recognized J—, who had been our teacher for a short time before the war. He was in charge of an issuing branch of this benign institution. He said he liked his place so well that he "should stay and see the thing out;" and thereby escape the draft (we mentally added).

He generously gave us brown bread, canned peaches, etc., and told us not to want for shirts, stockings, towels, comfort-bags, blankets, etc., while he was there. He promised to come up and see us in a day or two, and we inwardly resolved to 'renew the acquaintance,' and continue it while tarrying here on probation, for the material as well as social advantages it offered. We could not help thinking, however, how generous and kind this class of young men were with all this liberal contribution of goods, which cost them nothing, and which they were so unwilling to march, fight, bleed, or sacrifice comfort for. There were swarms of these strong-minded, well-educated, Christian young men, who were out with the army simply as clerks and attaches of the different commissions and their departments, who, while spoken of as making the best of soldiers, were rarely in the ranks as actual combatants on the field of battle.

Statistics, will, I believe, bear me out in this statement. Perhaps, as the Duke of Wellington once said, 'Christian sensibilities unfit a man for the avocation of war.' Certain it was that there have been but few noble exceptions, the Havelocks, Vicars and Howards, and in our own army, clergymen with fighting propensities were few and far between.

The letters written home at this time were numerous. Politics now ran high, and we thus discussed the Chicago Platform.

I wonder how any army officer can vote for 'Little Mac,' on such a shallow, rotten platform as he must stand upon, unless he comes out and defines himself differently, and even then his words would

---

Commanding General of the United States Army in 1895, a post he held during the Spanish–American War. He was married in 1868 to a niece of William Tecumseh Sherman.—2019

be received with distrust, as mere subterfuges, whereby to evade the question and blind his followers, who may now be doubting.

These factions, containing every stripe of humanity in the political school, are all bound together by one common tie, 'hatred to administration.' For its overthrow, this conglomeration of politicians will sacrifice all principle and love of country for the desired end. I rejoice now in the auguries of a conquered peace. Atlanta is ours, and Mobile and Richmond soon will be. We ought all to have courage and good cheer now, for a crown of victory falling through the air has alighted upon our banner everywhere. Success of the Administration both now and in November.

Our friend J—, from the Christian Commission, came to see us. One of our officers was a decided wag, and knowing his want of knowledge concerning military life, was inclined to tease and poke fun at him. "Will you stay and see guard-mounting?" said our wag to J—. "Yes; thank you. Do they mount on horses?" "Why yes; certainly," said our nonchalant wag. A few moments later, this attach of the "C. C." picked up a corkscrew, and asked its use. Our wag, without cracking a smile, answered, "That is to bore auger holes with," and J— bowed assent. Among the institutions at City Point was the "bull ring," in which were confined deserters and the worst characters being continually sifted from the army. Nearly every day, when the mail boat arrived from Washington, several deserters were apprehended at the landing.

City Point, Va.,

September 8, 1864

I paid 50 cents a quire for this note paper this morning at the landing. The sutlers charge such enormous prices that it takes our entire pay to keep our stock of necessary articles full *** we pay half as much again for things here as you do in Massachusetts. *** I am quite well now; my humor has left me and my poison has disappeared. It is cool daytimes, and blankets are in great demand nights. I have not got one now, although I can get one to bring home with me.

We shall leave here probably the 7th, the last moment. Good for Rich, and glory to the Star of the East, Maine! Down with 'Mac,' and up with 'Abe and Andy!' I shall try to see John.

619

I look at the extended length of our service in the same light that you do, and am inclined to be very reasonable, in view of our good fortune in the main. I am content to abide my time, and submit gracefully to the decision of the War Dep't, *** I am sorry to learn of poor LeRoy's condition as not improved; has he not suffered dreadfully? He is too noble and brave to endure so much; I do hope he will be spared a second amputation.

Charlie Haseltine is improving again; gangrene got into his wound (he was not taken care of properly), and he was obliged to have it burned out, a very painful operation; I trust we can take him with us when the regiment passes through Washington.

Welch has been to see you. *** I never so completely prostrated myself as I did on that night trying to overcome that attack of cramp colic *** this violent exertion with the watchfulness and anxiety of the morrow's conflict, marked out plainer than ever before, the places where the wrinkles are to be.

Hard times those; I am glad I lived through them. *** Everything is lovely here at City Point, and nothing here to molest us.

It seems fallish even here in Virginia; the hues of gold and red are beginning already to deck the leaves in gayest colors. I dread the season so melancholy in its aspect. *** Shall you accept if you are nominated for senator this campaign? Lovejoy has got a detail as brigade forage master; good thing for a veteran. Holt is to be made a corporal.

September 10, three regiments from the First Brigade, Second Corps, were ordered to attack the enemy's picket line at 1. A. M. in front of and to the left of Fort Steadman (Fort Hell). This was done, the balance of the division being in readiness to support the movement. Our brother of the First Massachusetts Heavy Artillery was in this movement.

About one and a half miles of entrenched picket line were captured, with some prisoners, besides inflicting some loss in killed and wounded.

Sharp firing on the picket lines all the next day and night, and from the redan on the left of Fort Hell; also heavy artillery firing, which continued during the nth and 12th.

September 14, the enemy shelled the railroad train near Fort Crawford, our batteries replying; severe picket firing during this day and the 15th.

Our letters say:

September 14, 1864

Will Whittier called to see me; he is in the Fifty-ninth (Mass.) and has charge of a most magnificent horse formerly owned by Lieutenant-Colonel Hodgkins. Will got a transfer from the First Massachusetts Cavalry. *** We shall start for Massachusetts with about 175 men all told, present and absent, who are entitled to go at that time. It was rough to have the Third Massachusetts Battery go off without us. We are gaining men every day, and pick up lots of deserters at the landing every time the boat comes in from Washington. We detected two yesterday, who came out with the 'Subs' a year ago, and deserted when we marched over the Bull Run battlefield; one of them had jumped a bounty home, and was a sergeant of cavalry in charge of recruits.

He is feeling pretty blue now in our guard house, and charges of desertion and bounty jumping preferred against him. *** Martis is corps forage-master, and Corporal Munroe is on division provost guard; all the old details have been returned to the regiment. *** Frothingham is on division provost guard. All the 'vets' are getting soft jobs before we go home, and the Major (Burt) is helping them all he can.

Captain Field is discharged; he resigned. 'Chub' Fletcher of Company F is dead; he was sent away sick some time since. I tent with Soden, our hospital steward; he is a conscript and a gay boy; he enlisted in the Nineteenth and Thirty-third Mass. Regiments at the time we came out, but his family would not allow him to come. He then made them agree that he should be allowed to Stand the draft, without the payment of commutation. When drafted, he was bound to go, and here he is, for the war.

September 22, 1864

621

A letter from Charlie Haseltine says that he does not perceive that his wound has healed a particle, and thinks that he will not be able to go home before Christmas; thus it has been during this campaign; those who have had slight wounds have suffered the most and many a poor fellow who wished for 'a nice hospital wound' received it and afterwards languished upon a death bed until the dark angel released them.

I received a letter from Eugene three nights ago; he wriggled and quibbled on politics, and talked as many of 'Mac's' would-be followers would, if they dared to do. He seems to favor Lincoln at this time, but prefers McClellan if the war were over; he thinks 'Mac' would straighten out matters and things in favor of the regular army; he shall not vote. 'It is against the rules',' besides, he 'does not wish to meddle in politics, and excite feuds among citizens and soldiers.' He has 'to support all administrations, and desires to be in a neutral position,' etc., etc. *** Every American citizen should vote, and thereby show an interest in the affairs of the state, and take part in the administration of the Government.

He need not become a blustering politician, haranguing the multitude in embittered words *** he does not declare his intention to resist the party he opposes, should they join in the ascendency, in this simple act of a free man. I think it is his duty as a military man to vote at the coming election (and for Abraham Lincoln too), *** I am thinking of your thoughts expressed upon my getting out a book. I wish with you that I could have kept a diary during the two years of my service. I might have done so during the last twelve months, but I omitted it, because I failed to keep a record of the first part of my experience.

McClellan's policy has gained him a few friends among the bolters, but he is so mixed up, and is so willing to have his 'better half' (Pendleton) coupled with his policy (a feint), that his chances in the eyes of the people appear to be hopeless, and today he is below a medium in the minds of the Army of the Potomac and Sherman's host. *** I cannot believe or realize that I am so soon to bid adieu to scenes that have been such a contrast to civilized life. The anticipation of a reunion with you at home and the enjoyment that will naturally follow are too much for a soldier.

The same letter says, after a visit to our brother of the artillery:

My visit was a most agreeable one; he is a corporal and if he does well he will soon be a sergeant.

A few days before that happy event of the expiration of term service, our letters say:

What glorious victories we are having. The last won by Sheridan, in the [Shenandoah] valley, is a glorious triumph in the cause. Grant's turn comes next, and I hope it will result grandly to our armies before November. Then we will elect Abraham Lincoln, repudiate McClellan and ignore the Chicago platform, and peace and quiet will soon come apace,

Our land will be free indeed, and the antipathy of foreign nations will be changed to friendliness and a desire to emulate the deeds of the greatest nation upon the earth. Heaven speed the day! 'As go the armies, so go the states,' and I am willing to let this be the case. Maine has spoken in a loud voice. Westward ho! the stirring cry of liberty goes, kindling a fire in all hearts, and the mighty verdict will be given in November.

I now rejoice that I entered the Twenty-second Regiment in accordance with your advice. I am associated with its achievements in all pride, and I would not give up the honor of one of its well-fought fights for all the accumulated wealth of those ignoble sons who have remained at the rear and reaped the home harvest during these years of war.

I am rich indeed in experience, and would not sell it for untold gold. I would rather be as poor as Lazarus was, and die as he did, than have remained at home during these historical times. I glory in the word soldier, as applicable to myself even, and I'll never regret my army life.

We started for the front, September 30, to see our brother, but learning that his brigade had advanced to the support of the Fifth Corps at Peeble's farm, and along the line of the Weldon Railroad, where severe fighting took place, we returned, and at once wrote:

There will be some terrible fighting the coming week. Grant knows it is his turn now, and that a good opportunity is open. He will pound at the Rebellion with all his strength, and mighty will be the Confederacy if it stands in these days.

Nothing can stop the immutable principles of our cause, on their way through the universe to destiny. We shall be victorious and the sky will be irradiated with the glory of our triumphs. All we want is peace, but upon the terms of the Union—"Obedience to the Constitution and Laws, and slavery to be considered obsolete."

Our letters say:

In camp,

October 1, 1864

We are to turn in our guns and equipments, camp and garrison equipage at City Point, and I hardly care now what kind of an appearance I make from a soldier's standpoint, for we shall go home an unarmed mob any way, if we are deprived of our equipments.

General Tilton is trying to have that extract of the order rescinded, so that we can go to Massachusetts armed. *** The order for our relief has come, and we start next Wednesday morning at 10 o'clock; if we go direct, and meet with good success, we shall be in Boston Saturday (8th). Possibly, if we are received by the 'Corn Exchange' (118th Pa.), of Philadelphia, we may not be at home before Tuesday of the week following. *** I started for the front yesterday, to see John once more, but learning that his corps had moved, I came back.

There is fighting along the entire line tonight, even during this cold rainstorm. Our corps and the Ninth are after the South Side Railroad, and Generals Ord and Birney are on their way to Richmond. The wounded have been coming in all day long; poor fellows! How I pity all in the fore front tonight. I know their every circumstance, and as I sit and write, I am not unmindful of them.

I shall see John before I go if it is a possibility.

October 3 and 4 the First Massachusetts Heavy Artillery was engaged in building Forts Cummings, Emory, Siebert and Clarke near the Clements find Smith houses and Poplar Grove Church, to cover the left and rear of our position at Peebles House.

October 3, our letters say:

624

I have just returned from a last call on John at the extreme fore front. I found him twenty miles from here, after a long tramp and some trouble. I took up a few things to him for which he was so thankful. They are having a hard time, having been on the move since last Saturday. They were engaged last night, and the First Massachusetts Heavy Artillery lost thirty men wounded. John was looking rough, but still in good health; spirits rather low. I hated to part with him tonight, and long was the wistful look he gave me as I turned away; indeed I felt sad at leaving the front, and as I passed by familiar scenes of camp life and localities of fierce battles, in which I was engaged last June and July, I almost hated to look upon them for the last time. I passed through both lines of intrenchments taken by the Fifth Corps; they had a hard fight up there.

I must be brief, for it is late at night, and I am tired. *** He (Ed. Holt), was made a sergeant today while absent with me. We start Wednesday morning; everything is lovely, and we are happy.

Johnson started this morning.

Those days were part of our life, of our youth and experience, long, hard and hitter though they were, yet inseparable from all that is good, noble and unselfish in our natures.

The following letter from Gen. Charles Griffin, our old and beloved division commander, afterwards commanding Fifth Army Corps, shows how the regiment was regarded in the Army of the Potomac:

Headquarters, First Division, Fifth Army Corps.

Before Petersburg, Va.,

October 3, 1864

General:

As your regiment leaves the army on the 5th inst., by reason of expiration of term of service, I desire to express to you, your officers and men, my satisfaction at the manner you have conducted yourselves since I have commanded the division in every circumstance of trial and danger. The valuable and efficient service you have rendered your country during the past three years of its eventful history is deserving of its gratitude and praise. You leave the army with an enviable record, and with the regrets of your comrades at parting with you.

Sincerely yours,

(Signed) Charles Griffin,

Brigadier General, Commanding Division

Brigadier General W. S. Tilton, Commanding Twenty-second
Massachusetts Volunteers

The regiment was in twenty-two engagements, and marched about two thousand miles. It lost 141 killed in action and 143 died of wounds or disease, and 244 were discharged for disease or wounds contracted in the service.

History records that only 45 regiments of Union infantry lost each 200 men and upwards in killed during the War of the Rebellion. The Twenty-second stands number 27 on this list with a loss of 216. In a list of all Union infantry regiments that lost over ten per cent in killed on the field, the Twenty-second stands number 13, with a per cent of 15.5. The Eighty-third Pennsylvania has the same per cent. It served in the same division (First Division, Griffin's).

It is worthy of note that it was the only regiment commanded by a man who afterwards became Vice-President of the United States. It was the only regiment that embraced a company of sharpshooters throughout its term of service. It was the first regiment to draw the fire of the rebel batteries at Yorktown, and the first to plant a flag on the works after its evacuation. It was the last regiment to leave its position at Gaines' Mills, and but one other regiment lost more men in that terrible battle.

As a skirmishing regiment it had no superior in the Fifth Corps, if it did in the Army of the Potomac. It lost 59 per cent of its men at Gettysburg, and had the honor of firing the last shot at the retreating enemy.

It furnished five general officers, Tilton, Sherwin, Wardwell, Miles (N. A.), and Paine (Charles J.).

The request sent in to General Meade to retain our arms having been refused, we were busily engaged, October 4, turning them in. Fifteen officers were in camp to go home with the regiment, and many men on detached service had now joined, so that the regiment numbered about 125 guns.

On Wednesday, October 5, we took the transport steamer *Kennebeck*, a crazy, dilapidated old hulk, and after many trials and tribulations and a tedious and uneventful stop at Hampton Roads we arrived in Washington, gladly transferring our bodies once more to terra firma on the afternoon of the 6th. On the 7th we resumed our journey, and arrived in Boston on the 10th at 1.30 A. M., and were marched to the Beach Street barracks, welcomed all along the route with cheering and such honor as only the "Hub" could give her returning veterans. Our little band formed a strange contrast to the full regiment, eleven hundred strong, which marched forth so proudly three years before.

We had left one hundred and eighty-one of our comrades, who had reenlisted, and were now with the Thirty-second Massachusetts at the front.

These figures show what the regiment had been called to do during its three years of arduous service, and how well it had done its duty.

At the barracks we had time to remove the dust and stains of travel, and prepare to meet our friends. At eight o'clock, by invitation of a committee, of which Capt. C. O. Conant was chairman, we marched to the United States Hotel, where a fine breakfast was served. Here we began to meet our fathers, mothers, and all the expectant friends who had been eagerly waiting for our arrival, together with many old comrades whom wounds and disease had marked for an earlier discharge from the service, but who now thronged the hotel, having heard that "Johnny comes marching home again;" all anxious to do something "to fill with joy the warrior's heart."

They almost outnumbered us, and, thus reinforced, we were able to make quite a respectable line.

The First Company of the Independent Corps of Cadets tendered us an escort, and the city of Boston a banquet at Faneuil Hall, both of which were accepted.

Line was formed with the Cadets, Twenty-second and discharged veterans, and the route lay through Beach, Washington, Boylston, Arlington, Beacon, Park, Tremont, Winter, Washington, State, Merchant's Row to Faneuil Hall. As we passed the Common, a national salute was fired. The writer was left guide of Company H on this march. All along the route the people gave us the most enthusiastic reception, and our last march was a triumphal one indeed.

From Faneuil Hall the regiment was dispersed to reassemble on the 17th for muster out, and on that day the Twenty-second Regiment, Massachusetts Volunteers, passed into history as an organization.

Our welcome home to the little town of Bradford and its more bustling and manufacturing neighbor, the city of Haverhill, was even more enthusiastic and cordial than in Boston, for we were now among our own, our dear father and our fond, loving, patient mother, our neighbors and friends, who greeted us with every demonstration of such joy and affection, for which we had been looking forward to with hungry anticipation so long that, once filled with a full realization of such priceless gifts, we at once left all remembrances of the horrors of the past to be merely treasured up for the memory of future years, while we fairly reveled in the sweet pleasures of the joyous present.

There now remains for us to add the simple narrative of our brother in the gallant "Heavies" of the Second Corps, who alone remained in the splendid old army to the end, to push his way with our other storm and battle-stained comrades onward to Appomattox's fateful day.

THE CAPTURE OF PETERSBURG

On the night of September 30, the division massed in the woods and near the trestle bridge in rear of the Avery House. October 1, at 12.30 P. M., the First Massachusetts Heavy Artillery left camp, and taking cars, the column was embarked at two points, Hancock's Station and the Trestle bridge. There were three trains, and they made three trips. The command was unloaded at Warren's Station, near the Yellow Tavern. Marched from there past Poplar Grove church to near the headquarters of the Ninth Corps, reporting to General John G. Parke, commanding that corps at 2.40 P. M., and bivouacked for the night in the rear of Peebles house, about two and a half miles from the Weldon Railroad. The rear was up by 5 P. M. At 7 A. M. on the 2d (Sunday), marched with the brigade on a reconnaissance to the left of the Peebles house, moving in front of our line of intrenchments, and then on the Squirrel Revel Road. The First U.S. Sharpshooters were deployed as skirmishers; the First Massachusetts Heavy Artillery were ordered to support them. Formed line of battle at 8 A. M.; advanced and found no enemy; reached the first line of works, found them abandoned.

By some misunderstanding the regiments on the left halted at the first line of works, leaving the left flank of the regiment exposed. At 12 P. M. the balance of the brigade came up and formed line of battle; the regiment connected with the Ninth Corps (Wilcox's Div.) on its right; advanced to an open field near the enemy's second line of works.

At 2 P. M., formed line to charge the works. About 3 P. M. the enemy's second line was developed and the regiment charged the enemy's works with three other regiments and was repulsed. At dark fell back to the position occupied in the morning. The assaulting column was formed in a ravine about 300 yards from the works, First Massachusetts Heavy Artillery in the front line. Enemy opened a battery masked in an angle of the work with a raking fire of canister and spherical case. Gained a position about 50 yards from the works, but supports not coming up had to

629

retire. Loss, 2 officers wounded, 2 enlisted men killed, 9 wounded, and 8 wounded and captured.

General Meade did not wish a second assault to be made, and at 5.15 the column returned to the line of works near the Clements house.

October 5, broke camp and the regiment went on picket; relieved from picket at 11 P. M., and marched back to position in line to rear of Fort Hays and bivouacked for the night.

On October 6 the regiment returned to Fort Hays, where it remained until 10 P. M. of the 25th. During this period the regiment assisted in building Forts Cummings, Emory, Seibert and Clarke, covering the left and rear of position at Peebles farm, when it was relieved and joined the brigade in rear of the Jones House, and at 2 P. M. on the 26th it marched via Widow Smith's, the Williams and Gurley houses, passing through the breastworks of the latter, thence to the Yellow Tavern, or Vaughn House on the Weldon Railroad, near General Warren's Headquarters, where it bivouacked at 5 P. M. for the night, near the Lewis house. On Thursday, October 27, at 3.30 A. M., the march was resumed, following the Second Division down the Halifax to the Church road, thence by the way of the Wyatt house and Mrs. Davis' house to the Vaughn road, down this road to near the Cummings house, and continued the march for about two miles until Hatchers Run was reached. Found the ford obstructed.

Ordered to mass until the ford was cleared. Crossed the run at 8 A. M. which was about waist deep. Some skirmishing took place; advance delayed here for some time. The column then advanced by a narrow cart or lumber road through to Dabney's sawmill, where the road intersected another on which the Second Division was lying, reaching the Boydton plank road about one mile below Hatcher's Run, about noon. The Boydton plank road is a highway extending from Petersburg, Virginia, in a general southwesterly direction, to Dinwiddie Court House and beyond.

It was entirely within the rebel lines, and distant about two miles and a half to the west, from the extreme left of the Union lines. Eight miles out from Petersburg, this road is crossed by the upper part of Hatcher's Run, which flows in a southeasterly direction. At this point the road runs nearly north and south. Less than a fourth of a mile further south, and beyond the run, the White Oak road enters it from the west, and in the northern angle stood Burgess' Tavern, and in and about the farm there were several strong works, one of them being in the back yard, and the others in front of the house.

General Wade Hampton's cavalry formed a line through a portion of this farm, and it is said that Hampton's son was killed near the fence in front of the house.

Vedettes had been thrown out on all roads; flankers were out on both flanks, and the rear was kept well closed up! The ground was rough and heavily wooded.

A halt of about an hour was made. The regiment was massed with the brigade (Pierce's) in an open field on the right and near the junction of the roads (Boydton and Dabney's Mills), but at 2 P. M. it advanced and formed line of battle in a corn field on. the right of the Boydton plank road, and was placed in support of a section (Metcalfe's) of Battery C, Fifth U. S. Artillery (Beck's), connecting with the One Hundred and Forty-first Pennsylvania on the left. Metcalfe had advanced to a secondary ridge some distance to the right, or east side of the Boydton road, and about midway between the Dabney road and Burgess' Tavern. These two guns and Pierce's Brigade looked north. Crawford's division of the Fifth Corps were supposed to be on the right of the Second Corps. Lay in line about one hour under a heavy artillery fire. About 3 P. M. the line became heavily engaged with a large force of the enemy and the regiment was ordered to move up by the right flank and form line of battle near the edge of the woods. The right of the regiment had just reached the woods when a heavy fire was opened on them and the regiments in the woods fell back, making it impossible to form line. Fell back in some disorder to the plank road, and the woods on the left of the road.

It is said that the enemy wore our uniform and carried our colors, and were enabled to advance without suspicion. About 4 o'clock P. M. a heavy volley of musketry on our right, followed by a continuous fire and air-piercing yells, indicated that the enemy was advancing. This was but the prelude to an attack by the enemy on our flank and rear, and soon they came pouring from the edge of a thick wood into the gap between the Fifth and Second Corps, overpowering the gunners at Metcalfe's section of battery, and nearly surrounding, for a few moments, the First Massachusetts Heavy Artillery regiment.

At once there was a scene of confusion and excitement, rarely witnessed upon a battlefield. A regiment on the right came into our ranks and forced back our right, stampeding all the non-combatants, including many pack mules, which ran past us double quick.

A volley was given, and the enemy charged with continued yells. An attempt was made to change front, but the enemy came in such numbers that it was found to be useless.

This stampede was communicated to those in the rear, including a section of Battery K, Fourth U. S. Artillery. General Pierce was captured, as was almost all of the First Massachusetts Heavy Artillery. Our forces had been completely cut in two, and the rebels (Mahone's Division), extending their right to the plank road, were now firing, faced to the south. Finding the enemy could not be checked, the brigade was ordered to fall back on the road and reform, which was done.

As soon, however, as the temporary panic caused by this flank and rear attack had somewhat subsided, Battery K, Fourth U. S. Artillery (Roder's), and Beck's Battery opened, the former's guns unlimbering just as they stood, with closed intervals, and pouring a destructive fire into the enemy at close range, drove them with confusion into the woods. A sudden movement of Egan's Brigade (coming from the direction of Burgess Tavern) which was formed across the Boydton road, just in front of the Dabney mill road, in turn caught them in rear, recaptured the disconsolate "Heavies," who, rallying with the Fifth Michigan, made a counter charge, assisted by many volunteers from the brigade and division.

It was a quick dash across the fields, and resulted in the recapture of Metcalf's section referred to, which was temporarily in the enemy's hands, and the guns were drawn by hand from the field.

The brigade was then formed on the right of the First Brigade, which had formed at right angles to the plank road. Remained in this position until 11 P. M. when the command was withdrawn and marched back by the road it had come up in a heavy rainstorm. Having crossed Hatcher's Run it massed near Widow Smith's house until daylight, when the regiment marched and bivouacked near the Wyatt house until 12 M. on the 28th. Fires were kept up along the line to deceive the enemy and to guide the stragglers in. This was called officially the "Battle of Boydton's Plank Road," but by the men "The Bull Pen," since at one time the regiment was nearly surrounded. Its loss was 1 killed, 6 wounded, besides many captured who were afterward brought in. About thirty men were now missing, but succeeded in escaping and reaching our lines after dark, leaving but twelve unaccounted for. The night was dark, and a heavy cold rain set in which continued all day.

At 12 M. on the 28th the march was resumed, and at 7 P. M. the regiment went into bivouac on the ground it had left on the 25th at the Jones house.

This house was owned and occupied by its owner, William Jones; it was now used by General Mott as headquarters of the Third Division, Second Corps.

There were about 750 acres of land about it, and before the war Jones had been considered a wealthy man; he had owned many slaves, and then had four houses in Petersburg. But now everything had gone to ruin; his slaves had all gone; his wheat, oats, corn and other crops had been trampled underfoot; his horses, cattle, sheep, hogs and fowls had all been carried off, and he found himself without money, servants, provisions or anything. Everything was swallowed up before his eyes.

His son, an officer in the Confederate army, had been captured, and was then a prisoner of war at Point Lookout, Md. and his wife and two daughters had remained at the Jones house with the grandfather. The division commissary and the officers' mess literally supplied them with food or they would have starved.

In the midst of these cruel hardships, the youngest granddaughter had typhoid fever and died. A mahogany coffin was procured from City Point; the younger officers bore her body to the grave, and she was buried at the foot of the garden, in the little family cemetery, a chaplain conducting the services.

The distance marched to Hatcher's Run and return was forty-three miles. On the evening of October 29, under cover of darkness, the regiment moved to the front and again occupied Fort Hays, the brigade occupying the line between this fort and Fort Davis and as far as Battery No. 24. While lying here several executions took place, two deserters in the corps being shot, and several substitutes[1] hung for various crimes; all of which were witnessed by the troops in line. It remained in this position, doing the usual amount of picket and fatigue duty, until November 28, when it was again relieved by a regiment of the Ninth Corps, and withdrawn and massed to the rear about one mile near the Southall house. At 6 P. M. on the 30th it moved to the rear line of works, and then to the extreme left and rear of the line at the Peebles house, the brigade occupying the line between Forts Siebert and Emory. It went into camp outside of the works and near the Vaughn road, taking the position of the Ninth Corps. Here for the third time orders were given the men to make themselves as comfortable as possible. Supposing the campaign was ended, and that the regiment would go into winter quarters, the men set to work with a will to build log huts, and in four days had good winter quarters finished, with comfortable fireplaces.

The remark was made: "If Uncle Sam cannot pay rent, it ought to discharge us. I do not believe in moving so often, for it damages our furniture, and our housekeeper is getting tired of it."

----

[1] A man could pay to have a substitute serve for him if he were drafted.

December 1 received orders to hold itself in readiness to move at a moment's notice. December 2, advanced the line one mile and camped.

On Tuesday, December 8, received orders to move at 6 A. M. on the 7th with six days rations and 100 rounds of ammunition per man, and to report to General Warren. At that hour moved out and marched to a point just south of the Yellow Tavern, at the Gurley house, following Ayres' Division of the Fifth Corps, and being joined by Battery B, Fourth Artillery, the march was continued on the Jerusalem plank road. Arrived at Hawkins' Tavern at 4.30 P. M., and the Nottoway River about dark; being delayed by a wagon having run off the bridge breaking a boat, crossed it at 7.30 on a pontoon bridge, and the command bivouacked near the forks of the roads leading to Stony Creek and Sussex Court House. Distance marched, twenty miles. On the morning of the 8th the pontoons were taken in, and the march was resumed at 6.30, the brigade as a rear guard to the general trains. Passed through Sussex Court House and Conan's Wells, arriving about 3 P. M. at the Chambliss farm, the owner being a relative of General Chambliss who was killed August 16 at Deep Bottom. General Warren, however, ordered the command to move forward to within one and a half miles of the Weldon Railroad and bivouac, which it did at 4.30 for the night, bivouacking about three miles from Jarratt's Station.

At daylight on Friday, the 9th, moved and struck the Weldon Railroad a little south of Jarratt's at 7.30 A. M., and immediately commenced the destruction of the road. The division was drawn up in line facing the railroad, and stacked arms on its banks. The rails were so bolted together at the ends as to make a continuous rail, rendering the destruction of the track very difficult. Each brigade, under the immediate supervision of the brigade commander, took hold of the rails and ties on one side, and the entire track—a whole brigade front at once, was turned up on the ends of the ties on the side opposite, as if by magic.

While held in this position, the ties were knocked off, and piled up on the bed of the road, making a narrow top, the rails broken apart and laid across the stack of ties, the center of the rail resting on the apex of the pile. The pile was then set on fire. A fence of dry rails on each side of the track greatly facilitated the burning.

The heat of the burning ties, with the weight of the ends of the rails, caused them to bend into nearly the shape of a semicircle, and rendered them unfit for further use. The brigade commanders called the portion of the road for them to destroy "their contract."

The sight presented by the burning road, bridges, piles of wood, and fences, was sad and grand in the extreme, a terrible comment on the waste and ravages of war.

The command continued marching and effectually destroying the road until 4.30 P. M., from Jarrat's toward Three Creek, when the command was ordered to bivouac, which it did on the Bailey farm in the midst of a furious storm of rain, hail, sleet and snow, during which the men suffered severely. At 7 P. M., however, when the men had made things as comfortable for the night as the circumstances would permit, the brigade was ordered to proceed still further down the road and destroy from Three Creek to within one mile of Bellfield, a length lying between Ayres' division of the Fifth Corps and the cavalry, which had advanced as far as the Meherrin River on the borders of North Carolina. At the crossing of the Meherrin they had had a brush with the enemy's cavalry.

The work of destruction was resumed, the brigade moving further south than any other infantry, and the last piece of road they destroyed was where they met the cavalry in the work of destruction on their return.

Returned to the Rev. Mr. Bailey's, and bivouacked again on his farm. He was a Baptist minister. He estimated his losses in cotton destroyed, with the building in which it was stored, etc., at from $75,000 to $100,000.

The object of the expedition having been accomplished, having destroyed about twenty-five miles of railroad so that it could not soon be used, orders were given to withdraw at 7 A. M. the next morning. At 8 A. M. on the 10th started, and marched steadily all day on a road parallel to the one which the regiment had come, until 6 P. M., when darkness having set in, the command bivouacked about four miles south of Sussex Court House, a march of eighteen miles. Rain had fallen most of the night, and frozen as it fell. Every tree, twig, and shrub was heavily loaded with ice. The ground was slippery and the mud as deep and plentiful as that in which Napoleon fought the battle of Waterloo. It soon turned to freezing, and a cold northwest wind set in.

December 11, resumed the march at daylight and arrived at old camp about 2 P. M.; halted and made coffee. Many Negroes had joined the column the day before, including women and children, whole families, old and young.

Small parties of the enemy's cavalry had been seen on the flanks, watching to pick up stragglers; to guard against this, two regiments of infantry and a section of Stewart's Battery (B, Fourth U. S.) were left across the river. The latter fired a parting salute of six shots, and by dark the last man was across.

On December 12 the ground was so frozen that it bore up the artillery and wagons. At 6 A. M. the march was resumed, and at 2 P. M. reached the vicinity of its former camp between the Vaughn and Halifax roads. Distance marched, ninety-six miles.

Thus ended one of the most extensive, important, and successful infantry raids in the history of the war; one of the most damaging to the enemy. Officially it was known as the "Weldon Raid," but among the men it was more often referred to as the "Apple Jack Raid."

The men suffered severely upon this raid, as the weather was very cold and stormy. Many of the men came back over the ground barefooted, the rough, hard clay having torn the shoes from their feet. The regiment had no engagement on this raid. Four men straggled from the command, and fell into the enemy's hands. The country through which the regiment passed had not been overrun, and the foragers, who would leave the column in spite of all precautions, found many good things; among other novelties they secured a supply of apple jack, which induced among some a very hilarious condition. On the second day the regiment passed through Sussex Court House and Cronan's Well. Bushwhackers began to follow up the rear, and it is presumed the stragglers fell into their hands. Just before the column reached Sussex Court House, about two miles south, on the return, the road goes through a cut, and standing against the nearly vertical banks were the dead bodies of two of our own men, perfectly naked and filled with stabs.

They had straggled, been killed by bushwhackers, and set up where our column should see them. This inhuman barbarity becoming known to General Warren, he ordered all buildings within five miles to be laid in ashes. This was done, and nearly every building, including Sussex Court House, for miles was given to the flames, among them the house of a rebel colonel near which three men were found, and the large tavern near the Nottoway, where guerillas were concealed in the cellar. The women and children were taken out and placed in ambulances, and given the opportunity, if they desired it, to go with the column. Many did so. The incident had a good effect upon the chronic stragglers, who kept up after this with remarkable pertinacity.

On the morning of the fourth day, the column turned toward Petersburg. The night before, snow had fallen to the depth of several inches. This now melted, and the roads were in wretched condition. A comrade picked up a yam this day, and after getting into camp, concluded to boil it for supper. It nearly filled the dipper, and the water boiled away about as fast as it was possible to supply it. At last it became a question which should be cooked, the soldier or the yam, and it was 2 o'clock in the morning before the yam surrendered. It wasn't good for much after it was cooked, but he thought it would not do to let a Virginia sweet potato conquer a Yankee soldier. Sunday noon, on the fifth day, Nottoway River was reached and crossed, and soon the little army of 35,000 men was across the pontoon bridge. The rebels followed up the movement, but there was no engagement. The cavalry, which accompanied the expedition, had light skirmishing the second or third day out, near Bellfield, for about an hour. After crossing the Nottoway the regiment went into bivouac about two miles from Hawkin's Tavern, on the Jerusalem plank road toward Petersburg. It was severely cold. Much amusement was created after crossing the pontoon by the orderly of the colonel of another regiment going to a house, finding a horse and buggy, hitching the colonel's horse in, and driving him about the field. After marching through mud all day Sunday, the weather changed, and at night the roads were like stone, and the following day the men limped and straggled into camp. The damage done on this raid was considerable, for it broke an important line of supplies, which came over the Weldon railroad to Stoney Creek Station, thence by wagons to their Confederate army. The rails were torn up from Stoney Creek to the Oconee River.

On the 13th the regiment changed camp a short distance to the right, and here it remained, a short distance to the right and in front of the works at the Yellow Tavern, until February 4, 1865.

On the 31st of December the regiment was encamped between the Halifax and Vaughn roads, the Third Division holding the extreme left flank of the army. It was about three miles from the "Yellow Tavern." Our brother writes, January 17, 1865, as follows:

Dear Brother Bob:

I received your letter yesterday, also the box, which was in very good condition, taking into consideration the time it has been on the way. The pork and turkey were a little mouldy on the outside, but not to hurt. The cavendish was very acceptable, as was everything else, and from your own experience, my dear brother, you must know how highly I prized it, for after a soldier has dieted on 'marching rations' four or five months, he, if anybody, can appreciate something good to eat.

The little bag was just what I needed (to hold sugar and coffee). Our division now holds the left flank of the army, about three miles from the Yellow Tavern. Walt knows the position. I have to go on picket once in five days; it is rather hard with our other duty, yet it is not as dangerous as doing picket duty where we were before—in front of Fort Hays.

Last week, there were four 'Johnny' ragamuffins came in on my post; they told the old story, that the Confederacy was played out, etc.; I don't have much sympathy with the devils anyhow, and as I had charge of the post I used them just about as mean as I knew how, while I had them in charge.

I can't help thinking how cruelly they use our prisoners; as soon as they fall into their hands they commence to rob them of everything. When we were in the fight on the Boydton plank road, our regiment was nearly all taken prisoners at once, including our general, but were recaptured by the Third Brigade; while in their hands, they went through them all. One little fellow in our company had on a good hat when a strapping 'Johnny' caught him by the throat, took his hat in exchange for an old canteen covering, which he used for covering his ugly head.

I have made up my mind that when I get a chance I will just retaliate a little. We have now got comfortable quarters, and I trust we are settled for the winter; my 'shebang' is 12 feet long and 8 feet wide, with the door and fireplace in one end, and is quite comfortable.

I shall probably be made a sergeant in a few weeks for 'gallant and meritorious conduct, I suppose. Well, Rob, I have stuck pretty well this summer; I haven't been to the hospital once, and I have done duty all the time; at one time the company was reduced to three men for duty, and your humble servant was one of the number.

I wish I could get a furlough this winter, but they will not grant them except in cases of sickness, but as I believe my relatives are in a pretty good state of health, I think there is a small sight for me. I don't blame Walter for not enlisting (re-enlisting); if he was sure of a commission in the regular army, it might do.

On February 4, 1865, the regiment received orders to be ready to move at daylight on the 5th. Promptly on that day the command moved to the crossing of the Vaughn road over Hatcher's Run, following the First Brigade to near the point where the picket line crossed the road. Gen. Geo. W. West, Colonel of the Seventeenth Maine, commanded the brigade.

Orders were then received to follow the ambulances of the Second Division to the Cummings house. Arriving near Hatcher's Run, which was found to be obstructed by felled trees, and deep holes dug in the bed of the stream, the brigade was placed in line of battle across the Vaughn road, on the north side of the run.

At 2 P. M. the brigade crossed the creek and formed line of battle to the left of the road, the right resting on the road, and the left refused, resting 'on the creek. A strong skirmish line was then advanced, and breastworks were thrown up in the shape of an arc of a circle.

About 4.30 P. M., heavy firing being heard on the right, the First Massachusetts Heavy Artillery was sent to report to General McAllister. It was followed later by the entire brigade. General McAllister was found heavily engaged, and the regiment arrived just in time to assist in repulsing a heavy attack. The balance of the brigade supported the line. They were engaged about one hour, with, however, but little loss. The enemy charged this line three times and was repulsed. Darkness coming on he withdrew, leaving his dead on the field. This line was near the Tucker house. Strong works were thrown up. At 3 A. M. on the 6th the brigade was relieved by troops of the First Division, Fifth Corps. Lay in line all day until 5 P. M., when the Fifth Corps, being heavily engaged, the brigade was ordered to follow De Trobriand's brigade down the Vaughn road to the crossing of Hatcher's Run in support. But before they could reach there the emergency had passed.

At 4 o'clock Fort Stedman had been taken by the enemy by a sudden dash; at 8 A. M. it was recaptured, and the movement of the regiment was in support of the attack to retake it. It was soon returned again to the line, and having massed in rear of McAllister's Brigade, bivouacked for the night. It was a rapid movement. A strong picket line was thrown out. During the night of the 5th, 16 prisoners were brought in on the brigade front. On the 7th and 8th remained bivouacked in position. Large details were made for constructing a new line extending from the left of the former line at Hatcher's Run, and making abatis and slashing the timber in front of it. On the 9th moved to near Humphrey's Station, about 1,500 yards in rear of the line and near the Vaughn road and went into camp. This line stretched from Fort Cummings to Hatcher's Run at the Vaughn crossing. Here the regiment remained doing picket, fatigue and camp duties until 6 A. M., March 25, when it received orders to be ready to move at a moment's notice. Broke camp and remained under arms until 2 P. M., when it was moved through the main line of works to the front and placed in line to the rear of the First Brigade, just in advance of the old picket line. A line of rifle pits had been captured from the enemy in the morning, and orders had been given to connect these pits. While these details were at work a brigade of the enemy charged and drove our working parties in on the line of battle. This charge extending to the front of the left wing of the brigade, it gave way and came near carrying the second line with it, but the First Massachusetts Heavy Artillery was at once rallied and with the Fifth Michigan advanced to the first line, and a counter charge being made, the pits were retaken, and the enemy driven from their position on the crest of the hill near Duncan's Run, with the loss of many prisoners.

The line was now held by the regiment until relieved by the posting of the pickets at 1 A. M. on the 26th, when it was marched back to its old camp, and joined the brigade. Loss, 2 killed, 7 wounded. The regiment now numbered 424 men. The regiment was highly commended for this affair, both by General Mott, commanding division, and General Pierce, commanding brigade.

On March 29, at 6 A. M., the regiment marched out on the Vaughn road again. It was a clear, cold, crisp morning, and the white frost lay thickly on the ground. Crossed Hatcher's Run, and moved about one mile beyond; crossed another small run [Gravelly (?)], and brigade formed line of battle on the north side of the road, connecting with the Second Division, and threw up a line of works. A reconnaissance having discovered an entrenched line held by the enemy's pickets, about three-fourths of a mile ahead, at 4 P. M. the line advanced through the woods and occupied them, the pickets having been driven out.

Lay in line all night in a drenching rainstorm. At daylight on the 30th advanced in line of battle toward the Dabney's Mill road, crossed it and a small branch of Hatcher's Run, and moving forward found the enemy's second line abandoned. After moving about 500 yards beyond, halted and again threw up works under a heavy shell fire from a battery in front. Here it remained all day; the position was near the mill. The line now extended from J. Crow's house toward the Boydton plank road. The march this day was through dense woods, deep ravines, swamps and wading through water, in many places two feet deep, until about 10 A. M. At 3 A. M. on the 31st, still raining; advanced, moving to the left, and threw up works on the right of the Boydton plank road, taking the same position that the regiment had occupied October 27, 1864. The regiment was temporarily commanded by Captain Davis. At 10 A. M. the rain had ceased. At 12 M. the regiment with the Fifth Michigan was ordered to charge a battery on its front near the Crow house, as it was believed to be held by a few men; charged under a heavy fire of artillery and infantry, but found the abatis, and slashing in front of the enemy's position so thick that it was impossible to get through, which being reported to General Pierce, the two regiments were ordered back to the brigade line. The loss of the regiment was 1 killed and 10 wounded. April 1, skirmishing and picket bring during the day and night. Remained in line until daylight April 2, when a combined attack of the whole line was ordered. The regiment advanced, and found the works in front nearly deserted, the enemy having moved most of their artillery during the night; occupied the works to the left of fort in front of the Crow house.

The entire line of the Second, Sixth and Twenty-fourth Corps was now pressing forward. The white flag was shown over the enemy's works, and our troops occupied them. About 8 A. M. the brigade moved over the works by the flank up the plank road to the Whitworth house, near Petersburg, where it arrived about 2 P. M. near the South Side Railroad.

At 4 P. M. formed in line with the Sixth Corps, and moving to the left about one-half mile, skirmishing, and under a heavy artillery fire, which continued until dark. Losses in the regiment since starting were 2 killed, 12 wounded. Remained for the night in line around the house formerly occupied by General Mahone as headquarters, the right of the line resting about 200 yards from it, and the left upon the Appomattox about one mile in rear of Petersburg.

At daybreak on the 3d it was ascertained that Petersburg had been evacuated during the night. The corps at once marched in pursuit at 6 A. M., taking the South Side road toward Burke's Station—what was known as the river road—toward Lynchburg; bivouacked beyond Maimborough about 9.30 P. M., after a hard march of eighteen miles; many prisoners picked up.

April 4 marched at sunrise; day cloudy and roads muddy, it having rained heavily during the night. At 8 A. M. the regiment was detailed to repair the roads, corduroying, etc., and assist the artillery and trains to pass; worked until dark, then joined the brigade. Distance marched, eight miles. April 5, the roads being in better condition, moved out at 4 A. M. and marched rapidly. At 9, halted, and two days' rations were issued. Reached the Danville Railroad at 7 P. M. after marching sixteen miles; crossed it near Jetersville and took position on the left of the Fifth Corps. At 6 A. M. on the 6th moved out, and at 8 A. M. formed line of battle, right of Second Brigade resting on the road, and moved slowly in line all day down the Jetersville and Deatonsville road in the direction of Amelia Court House; soon came upon the enemy's trains arid rear, and ascertained that he had been moving past our right all night.

Skirmishing now commenced, and the command moved with a rapid step. While pushing them in fine style General Mott, commanding the division, was wounded. Crossed Flat Creek near Amelia Sulphur Springs, all the time keeping up a running fight and a brisk skirmishing, until the crest of a hill was reached. Neither the skirmishers nor the line could be held back; the artillery moved with the former, the first instance known during the war. Pushed on to about three miles west of Deatonsville, at J. Holt's house, where the road from Deatonsville forks, one branch turning to the right, and running down Sailor's Creek, the other to Rice's Station. This was reached at 4.30 P. M. Perceiving that Ewell's Corps of the enemy was posted op. the north side of Sailor's Creek and knowing that the Sixth Corps and Sheridan's Cavalry were near at hand, the Second Corps was continued in pursuit of Gordon's Corps some' three miles further.

The road was strewn with tents, camp equipage, battery forges, limbers, wagons, etc., etc.

At 6 P. M., the enemy's entire line having been developed, a charge was made up the road by the First and Third Divisions in the midst of a cannonading and intense excitement. Everywhere the enemy's line gave way, and scores of prisoners, flags and guns were gathered in. It was a race with the First Division, which was moving in line abreast of the Third on the road, in the fields. Twenty-eight wagons and five guns had already been taken. The line no longer halted even to load. When the obstacle presented itself, behind which the enemy made a pretence of standing, the skirmishers ran upon them with cheers; the regiments nearest dashed forward, and the position was carried before even the rest of the line knew what was going on.

The Second Brigade was now leading . The line had just passed a large farmhouse at the highest point of the crest, when, at the bottom of a narrow valley, through which flowed Sailor's Creek, more than two hundred wagons could be seen hurrying pell mell to cross the stream on a bridge half destroyed.

In a few moments the brigade was among them, and the entire outfit was captured. The corps had now captured, besides, about 300 wagons, 1,700 prisoners, six guns, an artillery guidon, and eight flags. It was a beautiful day, and it had been full of intense excitement and glorious results.

At dark the regiment went on picket for the night. Distance marched, ten miles.

At 6 A. M. on April 7, having found that the enemy had left their position during the night, moved out in pursuit, and soon came upon High Bridge across the Appomattox River just as the enemy had blown up a redoubt that had formed the bridge head, and had set fire to the bridge. This was a fine viaduct of twenty-one arches. A strong detachment, armed with axes borrowed from the different regiments, hurried to the fire; by the sacrifice of a third span, the upper part of the bridge, on which was the track, was saved while the lower, or foot bridge, was but slightly damaged, and after some repairs was available for the trains; but a pontoon bridge was quickly laid for the troops, and the Second Division crossed at once in hot pursuit.

Wreckage everywhere strewed the road, and prisoners were picked up continually. Cannons that had been abandoned and concealed were pointed out by the faithful Negroes, who had located them, but without stopping the column hurried on. The column moved on a road that ran northwest, intersecting the old stage road at Lynchburg. Arrived near the latter about 1 P. M. Here the enemy was found entrenched in some force. A heavy skirmish line was pressed up against him, and skirmishing was continued until after dark.

At daybreak on the 8th it was found that the enemy had again abandoned his position during the night; pressed on in pursuit; halted near Sydney Church about 1 P. M. Struck the Lynchburg road at 3 P. M. Passed through the town of New Store at 7 P. M., and halted about two miles beyond, but resumed the march at 10 and, after marching until midnight, bivouacked for the night. Distance marched twenty-two miles. It had been a very exciting day; many prisoners had been picked up; the debris of the enemy's rapid retreat cumbered the road, and signs of his speedy disintegration existed everywhere. Longstreet's Corps was but three miles in advance of the Second Corps.

At 3.30 A. M. on the 9th moved out rapidly, the enthusiasm of the men now knowing no bounds. About 10.30 began to overtake Longstreet's rear. General Lee had sent two requests to General Humphreys, now commanding the Second Corps, not to press forward upon him while negotiations were pending for a surrender of Lee's army, but General Humphreys had been notified by General Grant that while certain communications between himself and General Lee had passed, looking to the surrender of the Confederate Army, they must in no way interfere with a vigorous and continuous pursuit and General Humphreys so replied to General Lee.

The staff officer of General Lee, at the last interview, was so very urgent that General Humphreys had to send him word that he must withdraw from the ground at once.

At this moment the head of the Second Corps was not more than 100 yards distant, in full sight of the enemy, and dispositions were being made for an immediate attack. The columns, however, continued moving. At 11 A. M., about half a mile beyond this, it came upon Longstreet intrenched in the near vicinity of Appomattox Court House. The Second Corps formed at once for the attack. At the moment when the order for the charge was about to be made, it was suddenly suspended by an order from General Meade, who had granted General Lee an hour for a truce, pending negotiations for surrender. Had marched twelve miles.

The place of the halt is called Clover Hill, although there are few living today who were in that expectant column formed for the charge, who thought they were in clover at that moment.

About 5 P. M. while anxiously awaiting future developments, the whole command was startled by the cry, "Lee has surrendered his whole army!" and a moment later General Meade rode along the lines,[2] shouting the glad news and waving his hat. The scene that followed beggars all description. The war was over!![3] Cheer after cheer burst among the lines: it grew louder and louder, and came rolling along the front of the Second Corps in a continuous roar.

---

[2] Meade had been sick and riding in an ambulance for days. On hearing news of the surrender, "Meade rode back along the line, stopping at each regiment to announce the news...." *Meade: Victor of Gettysburg*, Sauers, 2004.

[3] With Lee's surrender of the Army of Northern Virginia, the war was effectively over. But Joe Johnston had yet to surrender his army to Sherman.

The columns in rear, hastening forward to the supposed scene of battle, heard it, and for a moment knew not its meaning, but taking up the cheer, the electric sound sped on its way, until the forests and valleys rang out with outburst.

The war was over! The great rebellion was ended!! Great strong, bronzed men embraced each other and cried for joy; they danced all over the ground; threw up their caps, canteens, haversacks or whatever there was about their persons, and for hours pandemonium seemed to be turned loose. The long agony of blood and diabolical war, of cheers and shouts of joy, of tears and prayers in which the country had been purified and regenerated, seemed to be lost in this one hour of returning peace.

The scene of the surrender was sublime. Our brother, he alone of the four, witnessed this solemnly impressive spectacle. The silent forests —the silent ranks—without bugle note or drum beat; the stacking of arms, and deposit of the ragged, old cross-barred battle flags; the unconcealed tear; the courteous and magnanimous salute of the victors; and then that quiet filing away of the men in gray, was a never-to-be-forgotten scene; the mental impression of a lifetime, which we have many times since wished we could have beheld and participated in.

Bivouacked at Patterson's farm near Clover Hill until the morning of the 11th, most of the time short of rations. Ours had been transferred to the famished "Johnnies," and, besides, the movements for the past few days had been so rapid as to make it almost impossible to get the supply trains up. On the nth the regiment marched back to New Store, passing near Buckingham Court House and High Bridge. At 6.30 A. M. on the 12th. marched one and a half miles; struck the plank road, thence through Curdsville; crossed Little Wells River, passing through Farmville, and camped near Bush River.

Early in the evening it commenced to rain, and continued all night. Moved at 8 A. M. on the 13th; still raining; at 10 A. M. the rain had ceased. Crossed the Appomattox River, water waist deep. Bivouacked near Burkesville, 48 miles from Clover Hill.

Received orders to go into camp; tents and baggage were sent up. Here the regiment received news on the 16th of the assassination of the President [on the 14th] which cast a gloom over the entire command in striking contrast to the lightheartedness and cheerfulness of but a few hours before. Heard also of the death of J. Wilkes Booth, his assassin, and capture of Herold, his accomplice. Remained here until May 2. On that day, at 2 P. M., the regiment marched on the Jetersville and Amelia Court House road, passing through Burkesville Junction, and crossing the South Side Railroad a little to the east of the junction; went into bivouac at Jenning's Ordinary at about 5 P. M., near the same ground occupied by the regiment on the night of April 5. Distance marched, 10 miles.

May 3, moved at 6 A. M.to Goode's Bridge, via Amelia Court House, and crossing the Appomattox went into bivouac. Distance marched, 19 miles. May 4, moved at 6 A. M.; again crossed the Appomattox, and went into bivouac. Distance, 18 miles.

At 5 A. M. on the 5th, resumed the march, 4 days' rations having been issued the night before; at 8 o'clock it began to rain; at 11 A. M. reached Manchester, on the south bank of the James River, opposite Richmond, and went into bivouac. Preparations were made during the forenoon of May 6 for the march through the Confederate Capital, and crossing the James at 12 M., and entering Richmond, the corps marched through the city which it had taken four long years to capture, in column of companies. Thus our brother, after all our toil, hardship, agony and "bloody sweat," alone of the four, had the honor as well as pleasure, of seeing the conquered stronghold of rebellion, and of traversing its streets.

Passed out on the Brook Pike and bivouacked about 5 miles north of Richmond on Brook Creek. The day was very hot and there were many sunstrokes. Distance, 9 miles. Moved at 6 A. M. on the 7th on the Brook Pike, turning to the right about four miles beyond New Yellow Tavern, crossing the Chickahominy at Winston's Bridge, thence through Hanover Court House to

Littlepage's Bridge on the Pamunkey, which was crossed, and the command bivouacked on the north bank. Distance, 18 miles.

On the 8th, moved at 7 A. M.; day very hot; men suffering terribly from heat and thirst; passed through Renly's Swamp, by Concord Church, Chesterfield Depot, Old Chesterfield, Mount Carmel Church; thence north by the Telegraph Road to near head branches of Pole Cat Creek, where the regiment bivouacked on Wahoo Creek near Golinsville.

Moved at 8 A. M. on the 9th, and crossing Pole Cat Creek, and taking the Telegraph Road, passed through Athens village and Thornburg; crossed the Mat and Ta rivers and went into bivouac on the south bank of the Po. This was another very hot day, but with frequent showers. Distance, 16 miles. Halts were ordered of 15 minutes every one and a half hours, and at the end of 8 miles a halt of an hour was made.

Starting at 6 A. M. on the 10th, crossing the Po and Ny rivers, and passing Massaponax Church, the command moved on the Telegraph Road to Marye's Heights, where it halted an hour for dinner. Its route this day had been over the old familiar battlefields, among new made graves, and over bodies still unburied and the horrible wreckage of just one year before, but a sense of security was felt in those unpicketed bivouacs, wholly different from when they rang with the boom of cannon, and the deadly lead whistled across the swales and through the dense woods and forests of the Wilderness and Spottsylvania.

At 1 P. M. marched into Fredericksburg, across the town via Hanover street, up Water or Caroline streets, and down to the pontoon bridge opposite the Lacy house, thence through Falmouth and by the Stafford Court House road to a point about five miles beyond, camping near Claiborne Run, near Washington's house.

On May 11, owing to the almost impassable condition of the Stafford Court House and Dumfries road, the regiment moved at 6 A. M.; the left hand road was taken, passing Washington's, Musselman's and Oder's. At Oder's the right-hand road was taken to Cockley's store on Potomac Creek, thence past Old Tavern, Hickerson's, Tusculum, and from thence to Bland's Ford on Wolf Run Shoals on the Occoquan.

The regiment halted for dinner about 2 P. M.; resumed the march at 3; at 6 P. M., a terrific thunderstorm set in, accompanied by lightning, hail and a terrific wind, in the midst of which it went into bivouac. The tornado lasted about two hours, and then settled into a steady rain which continued all night. May 13, moved at 7 A. M.; crossed Wolf Run Shoals at 10; halted for dinner at 1 P. M.; moved again at 2, and at 4 P. M. crossed the Orange & Alexandria Railroad at Burke's Station, and at 7 P. M. bivouacked at Annandale. -Distance, 16 miles.

Remained at Annandale on the 14th, and at 8 A. M. on the 15th moved to Bailey's Cross Roads, on the Leesburg Turnpike, about 5 miles from Washington, where the regiment went into camp. It was just one year from the day that the First Massachusetts Heavy Artillery had so proudly left the fortifications it had helped build and garrison, with full ranks, now decimated and reduced to the proportions of one of its former companies.

Camp guards were established, but there was no more picket duty; no front, no enemy, and there was a perfect sense of peace and security that had not been felt for four long years. At Last the Cruel War Was Over!

On May 20, orders were given for the Grand Review to take place before the President, the Secretary of War, Generals Grant and Sherman, and all the foreign diplomats. On the 23d, taking the Columbia Pike from Bailey's cross roads, the regiment moved at 7 A. M. to Long Bridge; crossed it and the bridge over the canal on Maryland Avenue, and moved south of the Capitol. About 1.30 P. M. it formed line on Second Street, east, the right of the division resting near Pennsylvania Avenue, the left extending toward the river.

The corps followed the Fifth Corps in column of companies at half distance, 20 files front, with shortened distances between regiments, brigades and divisions. The wild enthusiasm, the inspiring cheers, seemed sufficient recompense for all those years of blood, of toil, of heartrending suffering, of hardships and privations beyond the power of tongue or pen to ever faithfully portray.

The proud bearing, the elastic step, the moistened eye, the quivering lip of those brave, strong veterans in blue, the best soldiers the world ever saw, as they marched past the grand stand on that perfect May day, told the story and it has passed into history for all time; it and the noble Army of the Potomac of which it was an integral part.

At the completion, of the review the Second Corps turned off at Washington Circle into K Street, thence over the K Street bridge across Rock Creek in column of fours, and crossing the pontoon bridge at the foot of High Street, into Virginia, returned to Bailey's cross roads, via the lower road past Arlington, and the Columbia Turnpike.

Thus our oldest brother, alone of the four, after being three years in the forts, was present at the surrender, had marched through Richmond, and had participated in the Grand Review.

The regiment remained in camp until June 15, in the meantime taking part in the review of the corps on May 30 for the major-general commanding, when orders were received to report to General Hancock upon his application, for duty again in the fortifications, and was assigned to Fort Ethan Allen near Chain Bridge. On the 27th of June, however, it was moved to Forts C. F. Smith and Strong, both north of the Falls Church road, and west of the Aqueduct Bridge.

July 19, orders were received from the adjutant general's office for the command to be consolidated into four companies, it being so reduced in numbers, and with the Third Massachusetts Heavy Artillery, retaining the name of First Massachusetts Heavy Artillery.

July 20, moved to Fort Bunker Hill, south of the Bladensburg Road, and between Forts Slemmer and Saratoga. Owing to the absence of one of the companies of the Third Massachusetts

Heavy Artillery, the consolidation ordered for the 19th did not take place until July 31. All supernumeraries and non-commissioned officers were mustered out. August 11, orders were received from the adjutant general's office for the command to be at once mustered out of the United States Service, and to report to the Mustering Officer of Massachusetts for final payment.

Left Washington on the evening of August 17; arrived in Boston Sunday, August 20; was then ordered to Galloupe's Island. Received final discharge, August 25, 1865, having been in the United States Service four years, one month and twenty-one days.

Our brother, who had re-enlisted November 28, 1863, was retained until the final expiration of the term of service of the re-enlisted men, recruits, etc., which dates August 16, 1865, and returned to Boston with the regiment, receiving final payment at Galloupe's Island.

Thus passed into the great aggregate of civil life three of the "Four Brothers in Blue." This narrative has been compiled almost entirely from the mass of letters written by this quartette of boys, as stated in the introductory, the official records only being consulted to make up the itinerary of the marches, verify dates, positions, etc.

In reviewing these letters, and noting carefully their contents, there seems, throughout their entire length and breadth, a wonderful sense of duty, which seems to govern every thought and action. When we carefully consider that all of the sentiments herein expressed were written under the most trying circumstances in which it is possible for mortal man to be placed, in the camp, on the march, on picket, on the battlefield, in the trenches, now here, now there, moving under fire, in the rain, mud, snow and sleet, amidst sickness and death—all manner of suffering, hardships and privations, it is wonderful, that in all, and under all, there shines forth this largest of Christian words next to Charity—Duty.

There was a self-consciousness of duty done in the most useful sphere that we could well perform it at our youthful ages. We learned our first duties of camp, guard, picket, fighting and military economy, and rapidly progressed until in our humble opinion we became obedient, self-reliant soldiers; that type of a soldier which, when actuated by patriotic motives, and high intelligent resolve, with zeal and good health to support it, will go through hardships and privations innumerable, even death itself, cheerfully and willingly, to accomplish the desired end.

To have served in any capacity in the old Army of the Potomac as a soldier of the Union, upholding the flag of our country, is honor enough for a lifetime; a priceless heritage, a proud legacy to our children. Money, untold wealth, cannot purchase it. It can sometimes buy position; but honor, duty, devotion, patriotism, battle service—never! These spring alone from the heart's best impulses and loftiest purposes. Such principles inculcate self-respect and mould the life to a nobler cause of action.

When men who lost the opportunity of showing their love of country, or periling their lives in its defence, shall have died, are buried and long forgotten, history shall still record what our brave boys dared to suffer and endure for duty's sake on many a weary march and on many a bloody battlefield of our country, and their names will live forever and immortal on its brightest pages.

Without our four years of work, of toil, of exposure, of suffering, of bloody sweat, those years of sacrifice and devotion to our country and its star-spangled flag, I think no doubt now exists in the minds of either the old Union or Confederate soldiers (so far as the writer was able to obtain their unbiased judgment during his visit to Gettysburg, Pa., from June 29 to July 6, 1913) but that this country would, under the pressure of a few more years of such a war between brother and brother and son and father, have become disintegrated and soon degenerated into a lot of wrangling, quarreling states—states seceding from the Confederacy, county seceding from state. In other words, we would have become Mexicanized, revolutions continually arising, and military dictators springing up at every fresh outbreak. All this instead of the strong, virile, wealthy, self-reliant, united nation that we all see and are so proud of today, the asylum and refuge of the oppressed and downtrodden of all other waning, dissatisfied countries. We trust that these services of our Union soldiers more than fifty years ago will never be overlooked or forgotten in this get-rich-quick period of commercialism, greed, grasping for wealth and influx of foreign population who, having little in common with us or our institutions, are so hard to readily assimilate. When that day comes, if come it ever shall, it means the downfall of this republic and a revolution compared to which the fall of the Roman Empire and the French Revolution will be as a mere zephyr.

If, now, we educate our children to be true, loyal, patriotic men and women of this great country; to love the flag, and to fight for it if necessary, as we did; then we shall have fulfilled the better part of our mission here on earth, i. e., our duty to our country and mankind. For what is life after all, if it is not a measure of duty, and devotion to right? Now if, in addition, we fulfil our duty to God, there can well be inscribed upon our tablets the modest epitaph, "Well done, good and faithful servant!"

THE END